## 18 MILLION AMERICANS USE
## THIS BESTSELLER . . .

Homemakers of America have clearly shown their overwhelming preference for the BETTER HOMES AND GARDENS® NEW COOK BOOK, making it the bestselling cook book of all time. Why? Because it has over 1500 delicious triple-tested recipes (professional home economists duplicate the working conditions and time limitations you face every day), meal planning guides and menus, hundreds of kitchen-tested cooking tips, recipes for appliances, easy meals, and exciting new entertaining ideas.

Whether you are an experienced cook or a newcomer to the world of preparing three meals a day, BETTER HOMES AND GARDENS® NEW COOK BOOK will be your best friend . . .

# Better Homes and Gardens®

# NEW COOK BOOK

**EVERY RECIPE PERFECTED FOR YOU
IN OUR TEST KITCHENS**

BANTAM BOOKS
TORONTO · NEW YORK · LONDON

*This low-priced Bantam Book
has been completely reset in a type face
designed for easy reading, and was printed
from new plates. It contains the complete
text of the original hard-cover edition.*
NOT ONE WORD HAS BEEN OMITTED.

BETTER HOMES AND GARDENS® NEW COOKBOOK

*A Bantam Book / published by arrangement with
Meredith Corporation*

PRINTING HISTORY

*Meredith edition originally published November 1930
Better Homes and Gardens® Family Book Service
edition October 1963
Latest revised edition published March 1976*

*Bantam edition / October 1979*
2nd printing .... February 1980    3rd printing ..... February 1980
4th printing ....... January 1981

ISBN 0-553-14866-4

*Published simultaneously in the United States and Canada*

---

---

PRINTED IN THE UNITED STATES OF AMERICA

13  12  11  10

## EVERY RECIPE TESTED IN
## OUR KITCHENS FOR
## PERFECT RESULTS IN YOURS

The Better Homes and Gardens Test Kitchen provides you with the best in creative food preparation. In this Test Kitchen, professional home economists duplicate the working conditions and time limitations you face every day. Using modern home appliances and food products, they prepare each recipe again and again until it meets Better Homes and Gardens' high standard of quality—and only then does it go into our book.

Each recipe is carefully and critically evaluated by a taste panel of experienced home economists which keeps in mind the problems of planning meals that are appealing and nutritious. Several factors are considered: *ease of preparation, texture, color,* and *flavor appeal,* as is the *cost* of each recipe, keeping in mind how it will be used. A successful result is a must for each recipe.

Until it earns the Test Kitchen Seal of Approval, every recipe is tested and re-tested . . . assuring that every recipe will produce perfect results in your kitchen—*every time!*

# CONTENTS

# HOW TO ACHIEVE PERFECT RESULTS

There's more to cooking than throwing something into a pot and turning on the range. We call it PRP—planning, reading, and preparation.

First, plan menus for at least several days at a time. This enables you to make a well-organized shopping list and take advantage of good food buys.

Next, read through the entire recipe. By doing this you accomplish two things: you can set out all ingredients and utensils and at the same time synchronize preparation time with your schedule.

Measuring ingredients carefully and following the recipe directions exactly are equally important.

Refer frequently to Chapters 16, 17, and 18 for tips, menu ideas, and guides to help you handle any cooking situation.

Good meals don't just happen—they are the result of careful planning. Organizing an area for cook books and other references makes food planning fast and easy.

*Left:* Save time and dishwashing by measuring, then mixing in the measuring cup.

When making a pie, use a rolling pin to transfer the top crust from the counter; simply unroll onto the filled pie.

Instead of soaking fresh vegetables and fruits in water, use a colander to wash and drain them easily.

To preserve flavor, texture, and appearance of prepared foods, wrap them with moisture-vaporproof materials before freezing or refrigerating. Label and date all foods.

Make crumbs by crushing dry bread, crackers, or cookies in two plastic bags (one placed inside the other).

Kitchen tongs are handy for holding and dipping many foods. They're especially good for turning broiled meats.

Create an orange chrysanthemum to garnish a serving platter of fresh fruit by combining two or three orange peels that have been sectioned and cut into small "petals."

You can shape ground meat mixtures into loaves, muffins, or rings. Just remember to handle the meat carefully.

Use cucumber baskets as containers for salad dressings or snack dips. Hollow out cucumber, then pare strips of peel.

To sieve fruits, place a strainer over a bowl. Use a metal spoon to press fruit against the mesh. For smaller amounts, use a small strainer placed over a measuring cup.

# Dear Reader,

From cover to cover, this Better Homes and Gardens *New Cook Book* was written with you in mind. Whether you're an experienced cook or a newcomer to the world of cooking three meals a day, we want it to be your best friend in the kitchen.

Choosing recipes for this edition was a great challenge because we tested so many good ones. As we made our selections, we tried to reflect the growing number of new food products as well as up-to-date appliances. Of course, we just had to keep some of the time-tested favorites. So, along with modern short-cut recipes, you'll find many of the old-fashioned favorites from our earlier cook books.

You'll find helpful ideas from planning and buying on through meal preparation and serving. Color pictures and test kitchen tips are packed with ideas for preparing and arranging foods. We want your meals not only to taste delicious, but to look appealing, too. You can be assured that every recipe has been tested to give you the quality meals you and your family expect.

These are busy days for all of us, so we've placed emphasis on ease in cooking. Electric cooking appliances are versatile, as well as convenient. That's why we've included a superb collection of recipes for your microwave oven, crockery cooker, pressure pan, and electric skillet. And, there's a special chapter called Barbecues and Easy Meals. Easy-meal recipes can be fixed in a jiffy or well ahead of serving time. Barbecuing has become an American way of life. This method of cooking presents a world of new flavor, so we've included a number of outdoor cooking recipes and grilling tips. Our discussions with homemakers tell us you're much more interested in flavor than you've ever been. So you'll find flavor, in just the right portions, throughout our new edition. These are just a few of the many important particulars we've built into the *New Cook Book*.

We hope these recipes will bring joy and good eating to you and your family. If there are special problems with which you think we can help, do write us. We'll try to be of service.

Cordially,

BETTER HOMES AND GARDENS

*The Editors*

1716 Locust Street
Des Moines, Iowa 50336

# NEW
# COOK
# BOOK

# 1

# APPLIANCE
# COOKING

1

# ELECTRIC SKILLET COOKING

## GLAZED PORK CHOPS

6 pork loin chops, cut
½ inch thick
1 1-pound 4-ounce can
pineapple chunks
(juice pack)
½ cup plum jam

1 tablespoon vinegar
1 tablespoon soy sauce
¼ teaspoon ground
ginger
4 green onions, sliced

Trim fat from chops; cook trimmings in electric skillet (350°) till 1 tablespoon fat accumulates. Discard trimmings. Brown chops well on both sides in drippings. Reduce heat to 220°. Season with salt and pepper. Drain pineapple, reserving juice. Combine ½ cup juice, jam, vinegar, soy sauce, and ginger; pour over chops. Cover and simmer 25 minutes, adding ¼ cup more juice, if needed. Add pineapple and onions. Spoon pan juices over. Cover; cook till hot. Serves 6.

## SWEDISH POT ROAST

1 3- to 4-pound boneless
beef chuck eye roast
4 whole cloves
2 medium onions,
quartered
1 cup chopped carrots

½ cup chopped celery
1 tablespoon corn syrup
3 anchovy fillets
2 tablespoons all-
purpose flour

Trim fat from roast. Sprinkle electric skillet (350°) with 1 teaspoon salt. Brown meat slowly on both sides. Cover; reduce heat to 220°. Stick cloves in onions; add to meat. Add next 4 ingredients and ⅓ cup water. Cover; simmer 2½ hours, or till meat is tender. Remove meat; keep warm. Skim off fat. Blend ¼ cup cold water into flour; stir into pan juices; mash carrot and onion, if desired. Cook and stir till bubbly. Season. Serve with meat. Serves 6 to 8.

## POACHED SALMON

4 fresh or frozen salmon
    steaks, cut 1 inch thick
1¼ cups dry white wine
2 tablespoons thinly
    sliced green onion
    with tops
2 or 3 sprigs parsley

1 bay leaf
¼ cup whipping cream
2 well-beaten egg yolks
½ teaspoon lemon juice
2 tablespoons snipped
    parsley

Thaw frozen salmon. In electric skillet (350°), combine wine, onion, parsley sprigs, bay leaf, 1 teaspoon salt, and dash pepper. Heat to boiling. Add salmon. Cover; reduce heat to 220°. Simmer about 10 minutes, or till fish flakes easily. Remove fish, parsley, and bay leaf. Keep fish warm.

Boil wine mixture down to ¾ cup. Mix cream, egg yolks, and lemon juice; slowly add *part* of wine mixture. Return to mixture in skillet. Cook and stir on low heat till thickened and bubbly. Spoon over fish. Garnish with snipped parsley. Serves 4.

## CHILI BEEF SKILLET

1 pound lean ground
    beef
¾ cup chopped onion
1 1-pound can tomatoes,
    cut up
1 15-ounce can red
    kidney beans
¾ cup uncooked
    packaged precooked
    rice

3 tablespoons chopped
    green pepper
1½ teaspoons chili powder
½ teaspoon garlic salt
3 ounces sharp process
    American cheese,
    shredded (¾ cup)

Brown meat and onion in electric skillet (350°). Stir in next 6 ingredients, ¾ cup water, and ½ teaspoon salt. Cover; reduce heat to 220°. Simmer 20 minutes; stir often. Add cheese. Cover; melt cheese. Serves 6.

## VEAL PAPRIKA

1½ pounds boneless veal
   shoulder, cut in 1-inch
   cubes
2 tablespoons butter
1½ cups chopped onion
1 1-pound can tomatoes,
   cut up
1¾ cups water
2 tablespoons paprika

1½ teaspoons salt
1 teaspoon sugar
½ teaspoon dried
   marjoram, crushed
8 ounces (6 cups)
   medium noodles
1½ tablespoons all-
   purpose flour
1 cup dairy sour cream

In electric skillet (350°), brown veal in butter. Add chopped onion; cook and stir till onion is tender but not brown. Add tomatoes, water, paprika, salt, sugar, and marjoram. Cover; simmer for 30 to 35 minutes, stirring occasionally. Cook noodles according to package directions; drain and keep warm. Stir flour into sour cream. Stir a small amount veal mixture into sour cream. Slowly blend sour cream into veal mixture in skillet. Serve over the cooked noodles. Makes 4 servings.

## GARDEN SKILLET SALAD

½ medium head
   cauliflower
2 tablespoons salad oil
1 tablespoon sugar
2 teaspoons cornstarch
2 teaspoons instant
   minced onion
1 teaspoon prepared
   mustard

½ teaspoon garlic salt
¼ teaspoon salt
⅓ cup vinegar
2 cups fully cooked ham
   cut in 1½-inch strips
6 cups torn lettuce
1 cup halved cherry
   tomatoes
½ cup sliced celery

Separate cauliflower into flowerets; cook in boiling water till crisp-tender. Drain and slice lengthwise. In electric skillet (300°), combine oil, sugar, cornstarch, onion, mustard, garlic salt, salt, and dash pepper. Blend in vinegar and ⅔ cup water. Cook and stir till mixture thickens and bubbles. Add cauliflower and ham; heat through. Toss with lettuce, tomatoes, and celery. Cook 30 seconds longer. Serve at once. Makes 8 servings.

## CANADIAN SMOKED LIMAS

1 10-ounce package
  frozen lima beans
1/2 cup dairy sour cream
3 teaspoons brown sugar
2 teaspoons all-purpose
  flour
1 teaspoon chicken-
  flavored gravy base

3/4 teaspoon grated
  orange peel
3 tablespoons orange
  juice
1 tablespoon butter
6 slices Canadian-style
  bacon, cut in thin
  strips

Cook limas according to package directions. Drain well, reserving 1/4 cup cooking liquid. Combine reserved liquid, sour cream, 1 teaspoon brown sugar, flour, gravy base, orange peel, and orange juice.

Melt butter in electric skillet (350°). Add meat strips; brown lightly. Remove meat from skillet and toss with remaining brown sugar; keep meat warm. In same skillet, combine limas and sour cream mixture. Heat and stir just to boiling. Turn out onto serving platter. Arrange meat strips over top. Makes 3 or 4 servings.

## SCALLOPED POTATOES AND HAM

Cook 6 medium potatoes, pared and sliced, in boiling, salted water for 10 to 15 minutes, or till tender. Drain, reserving 1 cup cooking liquid. Place potatoes in 8x8x2-inch baking dish. Melt 3 tablespoons butter or margarine in electric skillet (300°). Remove 1 tablespoon butter; toss with 3/4 cup soft bread crumbs, 1/2 teaspoon paprika, and 1/8 teaspoon dried thyme, crushed. Set crumbs aside.

Into remaining butter in skillet, blend 2 tablespoons all-purpose flour, 1 teaspoon dry mustard, 1 teaspoon salt, and 1/8 teaspoon pepper. Add reserved liquid and 1 cup milk or light cream. Cook and stir till thickened and bubbly.

Stir in 2 cups cubed fully cooked ham and 4 slices process American cheese, cut up. Cook till cheese is melted. Pour sauce over potatoes. Sprinkle with crumbs. Place on low rack in electric skillet. Cover and bake with vent open at 350° for 1 hour. Makes 6 to 8 servings.

## CHICKEN IN GOLDEN SAUCE

3 chicken breasts
  (2 pounds)
1 tablespoon lemon
  juice
1/4 cup all-purpose flour
1 teaspoon paprika

Dash freshly ground
  pepper
3 tablespoons butter
1 clove garlic, halved
1/2 cup dry white wine
Golden Sauce

Skin and split chicken; rub with lemon juice. Mix flour, paprika, pepper, and 1 teaspoon salt in paper or plastic bag. Add 2 or 3 pieces chicken at a time; shake to coat well. Heat butter and garlic in electric skillet (300°). Discard garlic. Cook chicken till golden on both sides; add wine. Cover; reduce heat to 220°. Simmer 20 minutes, or till tender. Uncover; cook 10 minutes, or till liquid is reduced to 1/4 cup. Remove chicken; keep hot. Prepare Golden Sauce. Serve over chicken. Serves 4.

*Golden Sauce:* In saucepan, combine pan liquid, 4 beaten egg yolks, 1 cup whipping cream, 1 tablespoon *each* snipped parsley and chives, and 1/8 teaspoon ground nutmeg. Season with salt and white pepper. Cook and stir on low heat till slightly thickened. Add 1/2 teaspoon lemon juice.

## APPLE FRITTERS

1 cup sifted all-purpose
  flour
2 tablespoons sugar
2 teaspoons baking
  powder
1/4 teaspoon salt
1 beaten egg

2/3 cup milk
2 tablespoons butter,
  melted
3 or 4 apples, pared and
  cored, *or* 18 thin
  pineapple slices
Salad oil

Sift together dry ingredients. Combine egg, milk, and butter. Stir into dry ingredients till smooth; do not overbeat. Slice apples crosswise into rings; dip fruit in batter one at a time. (Add more milk or flour, if needed, so batter coats.) In electric skillet, heat 1 inch oil to 375°. Fry fritters 3 minutes, or till brown; turn once. Drain. Serve hot. Sprinkle with confectioners' sugar, if desired. Makes 18.

## SUKIYAKI

2 tablespoons salad oil
1 pound boneless beef tenderloin, very thinly sliced across the grain
2 tablespoons sugar
1/2 cup beef stock or canned condensed beef broth
1/3 cup soy sauce
2 cups bias-sliced green onions
1 cup bias-sliced celery

5 cups small spinach leaves
1 1-pound can bean sprouts, drained
1 cup thinly sliced fresh mushrooms
1 5-ounce can water chestnuts, drained and thinly sliced
1 5-ounce can bamboo shoots, drained
Hot cooked rice

Preheat electric skillet or wok; add oil. Add beef; cook quickly, turning meat over and over, 1 to 2 minutes, or just till browned. Sprinkle with sugar. Combine beef stock and soy; pour over meat. Push meat to one side. Let soy mixture bubble. Keeping in separate groups, add onions and celery. Continue cooking and toss-stirring *each group* on high heat about 1 minute; push to one side. Again keeping in separate groups, add remaining ingredients *except* rice. Cook and stir *each food* just till hot. Serve with rice. Serves 4.

## SCALLOPS AMANDINE

3/4 pound fresh or frozen scallops
1/3 cup all-purpose flour
1/4 cup butter or margarine

3 tablespoons slivered almonds
1 tablespoon lemon juice
1 tablespoon snipped parsley

Thaw frozen scallops; cut large scallops in thick slices. Coat with a mixture of flour and 1/4 teaspoon salt. In electric skillet (350°) cook in *half* the butter till golden. Remove to warm platter. Melt remaining butter; add almonds and toast till golden. Stir in lemon juice and parsley; pour over scallops. Serves 4.

## SASSY ZUCCHINI

1 pound ground beef
1 cup chopped onion
1 1-pound can tomatoes,
   cut up
1 1-ounce envelope
   spaghetti sauce mix

1 cup uncooked
   packaged precooked
   rice
1½ pounds zucchini, cut in
   1-inch strips (4 cups)

In electric skillet (350°) cook beef and onion till meat is browned. Stir in undrained tomatoes, sauce mix, ¾ cup water, and 1 teaspoon salt. Bring to boiling. Stir in rice and zucchini. Cover tightly; reduce heat (220°). Simmer, stirring occasionally, 15 to 20 minutes or till zucchini is tender. Makes 6 servings.

## ORIENTAL PORK

1 pound boneless pork,
   cut in 1-inch cubes
1 beaten egg
¼ cup cornstarch
¼ cup all-purpose flour
1¼ cups chicken broth
   Salad oil
1 large green pepper,
   diced

½ cup chopped carrot
1 clove garlic, minced
2 tablespoons salad oil
½ cup sugar
⅓ cup red wine vinegar
2 teaspoons soy sauce
2 tablespoons cornstarch
   Hot cooked rice

Trim excess fat from pork. Combine egg, ¼ cup cornstarch, flour, ¼ cup chicken broth, and ½ teaspoon salt; beat smooth. Pour salad oil into electric skillet to depth of 1 inch; heat to 375°. Dip pork in batter; fry in hot oil for 5 to 6 minutes, or till golden. Drain and keep warm.

In a skillet, cook green pepper, carrot, and garlic in 2 tablespoons oil till tender. Stir in 1 cup broth, sugar, vinegar, and soy sauce. Bring to boiling; boil rapidly 1 minute. Blend ¼ cup cold water into cornstarch; stir into skillet. Cook and stir till thickened and bubbly. Stir in pork. Serve with rice. Serves 4 to 6.

# PRESSURE PAN COOKING

## PORK CHOP SUPPER

2 teaspoons shortening
4 pork chops, ½ inch thick
½ cup chicken broth
4 small potatoes, pared and halved or quartered

4 medium carrots, pared and cut up
1 small onion, chopped
2 tablespoons all-purpose flour

Heat shortening in 4-quart pressure pan. Season chops with 1 teaspoon salt and dash pepper; brown on both sides in hot shortening. Add broth. Place vegetables atop chops. Sprinkle with additional salt and pepper. Close cover securely. Cook 10 minutes at 15 pounds pressure. Cool quickly under cold running water.

Remove chops and vegetables to serving platter. Blend flour and ¼ cup cold water. Add to juices in pan. Cook and stir till thick and bubbly. Pass gravy. Serves 4.

## SPEEDY CHOP SUEY

1 pound beef, pork, or veal, cut in ½-inch cubes
2 tablespoons shortening
1 cup sliced celery
1 cup sliced onion

1 6-ounce can broiled sliced mushrooms, undrained
¼ cup soy sauce
3 tablespoons cornstarch
1 1-pound can bean sprouts
4 cups hot cooked rice

Brown meat in shortening in 4-quart pressure pan. Add 1 cup water, ½ teaspoon salt, and dash pepper. Close cover securely. Cook 10 minutes at 10 pounds pressure. Reduce pressure under cold running water. Add celery and onion. Close cover. Cook 2 minutes at 10 pounds pressure. Reduce pressure under cold running water. Add mushrooms. Mix soy and cornstarch; stir into mixture. Cook and stir till bubbly. Drain sprouts; add to mixture. Serve over rice. Serves 6.

## JIFFY SPAGHETTI SAUCE

1 pound ground beef
2 large onions, sliced
2 8-ounce cans (2 cups) tomato sauce
1 6-ounce can (2/3 cup) tomato paste
2 tablespoons salad oil
1 to 1½ teaspoons chili powder

1 teaspoon sugar
½ teaspoon salt
½ teaspoon garlic salt
Dash cayenne
8 ounces long spaghetti, cooked
Grated Parmesan cheese

Combine all ingredients except spaghetti and cheese in 4-quart pressure pan. Cook 12 minutes at 15 pounds pressure. Reduce pressure quickly under cold running water. Serve over cooked spaghetti. Top with Parmesan cheese. Makes 6 servings.

## NEW ENGLAND DINNER

1 small clove garlic
1 bay leaf
2½ pounds corned beef brisket
6 small potatoes, pared and halved

6 medium carrots, pared and halved
1 small head cabbage, quartered
1 small rutabaga or turnip, cut in chunks
4 peppercorns

Place garlic, bay leaf, and 1 cup water in 6-quart pressure pan with rack. Place meat on rack. Close cover securely. Cook 45 minutes at 15 pounds pressure. Let pressure drop of its own accord. Open pan and add potatoes, rutabaga, carrots, cabbage, and peppercorns. Close cover securely and return pan to heat. Cook 6 to 7 minutes at 15 pounds pressure. Reduce pressure quickly by placing under cold running water. Makes 6 servings.

# MICROWAVE COOKING

## BARBECUED SPARERIBS

3 to 3¹/₂ pounds pork spareribs
¹/₄ cup molasses
¹/₄ cup prepared mustard
¹/₄ cup lemon juice
1 tablespoon Worcestershire sauce
¹/₂ teaspoon bottled hot pepper sauce
¹/₄ teaspoon salt
Lemon slices

Cut ribs in serving-size pieces. Arrange in 12x7¹/₂x2-inch glass baking dish. Cover with waxed paper and cook in countertop microwave oven for 20 minutes, rearranging ribs every 5 minutes. Drain off juices and rearrange ribs in baking dish. Combine molasses, mustard, lemon juice, Worcestershire, hot pepper sauce, and salt. Pour mixture over ribs. Micro-cook, uncovered, about 10 minutes*, or till ribs are done. Occasionally baste and rearrange ribs in dish. Garnish ribs with lemon slices. Makes 3 or 4 servings.

## PIZZA CUBED STEAKS

1 8-ounce can pizza sauce
¹/₄ cup chopped onion
¹/₄ cup chopped green pepper
1 teaspoon cornstarch
¹/₂ teaspoon sugar
¹/₄ teaspoon dried oregano, crushed
¹/₄ teaspoon dried basil, crushed
4 beef cubed steaks
1 slice mozzarella cheese

In 12x7¹/₂x2-inch glass baking dish, combine first 7 ingredients. Cover with waxed paper. Cook in countertop microwave oven 3 minutes; stir. Add meat in single layer; sprinkle with ³/₄ teaspoon salt and ¹/₈ teaspoon pepper. Cover; micro-cook 5 minutes. Turn meat over; micro-cook, covered, 3 minutes* more, or till done. Remove from oven. Cut cheese in 4 triangles; place one triangle

atop each steak. Let stand 1 minute to melt cheese.
Serves 4.

## CREOLE JAMBALAYA

2 tablespoons butter
2 cups cubed fully
  cooked ham
1/2 cup chopped onion
1/2 medium green pepper,
  cut in 1/2-inch squares
  (1/2 cup)
1 clove garlic, minced

1 1-pound can tomatoes,
  cut up
1 bay leaf, crushed

1 teaspoon instant beef
  bouillon granules
1 teaspoon sugar
1/2 teaspoon dried thyme,
  crushed
1/2 teaspoon chili powder
1/8 teaspoon bottled hot
  pepper sauce

1 4 1/2-ounce can small
  shrimp
2 cups cooked rice

In 12x7 1/2x2-inch glass baking dish, melt butter in countertop microwave oven, about 30 seconds. Add ham,
onion, green pepper, and garlic. Cover with waxed paper.
Micro-cook 5 minutes*, or till vegetables are tender; stir
once. Stir in next 7 ingredients, 1/2 cup water, and dash
pepper. Micro-cook, covered, 4 minutes. Drain shrimp;
stir in shrimp and rice. Micro-cook, covered, 3 minutes;
stir. Micro-cook, covered, 3 minutes*, or till bubbly. Pass
additional hot pepper sauce. Makes 6 servings.

## CRANBERRY MEAT SAUCE

In large glass measuring cup, mix one 8-ounce can whole
cranberry sauce, 3/4 cup bottled barbecue sauce, and 3/4
cup apple juice. Cook, uncovered, in countertop microwave oven 4 minutes*, or till bubbly; stir twice. Blend 2
tablespoons cold water into 1 tablespoon cornstarch; add
to hot mixture. Micro-cook, uncovered, 1 minute*, or till
thick and bubbly; stir once. Serve with pork or ham.
Makes 2 2/3 cups.

---

* The timings are approximate, as countertop microwave ovens
vary by manufacturer. But after trying a few recipes, you will be
able to adjust recipe timings to your microwave oven.

## FRANK-BURGERS

1/4 cup catsup
1 tablespoon butter or
   margarine
1 tablespoon molasses
2 teaspoons vinegar
         * * *
1 beaten egg
1 teaspoon instant
   minced onion

1/2 cup soft bread crumbs
1/8 teaspoon salt
   Dash pepper
1/2 pound ground beef
4 frankfurters
4 frankfurter buns, split
   and toasted

In 1-cup glass measure, combine catsup, butter, molasses, and vinegar. Cook, uncovered, in countertop microwave oven about 1 1/2 minutes*, or till bubbly, stirring once. In a bowl, combine the egg and onion; let stand several minutes. Add bread crumbs, salt, and pepper; mix well. Add ground beef and mix thoroughly. Divide meat mixture into 4 portions. Shape meat around frankfurters. Place in shallow glass baking dish. Micro-cook, uncovered, for 4 minutes, rearranging and turning meat over after 2 minutes. Brush with catsup mixture. Micro-cook, uncovered, about 4 minutes*, or till meat is done, turning meat once and brushing with sauce. Brush again with sauce and serve in toasted frankfurter buns. Makes 4 servings.


## GLAZED SQUASH RINGS

2 acorn squash
1/2 cup maple-flavored
   syrup

1/4 cup butter or
   margarine

Prick skin of whole squash. Place squash in 12x7 1/2x2-inch glass baking dish. Cook in countertop microwave oven, uncovered, for 8 to 10 minutes*, or till soft. Let stand 5 minutes. Cut in 1-inch slices; discard seeds and ends. Return squash to dish. Season with salt and pepper. In glass measuring cup, combine syrup and butter. Micro-cook for 15 seconds. Pour mixture over squash. Cover with waxed paper. Micro-cook for 3 to 5 minutes*, or till heated through, basting once. Serves 6.

## SPARERIBS CANTONESE

4 pounds pork spareribs
1 12-ounce jar orange
  marmalade
½ cup soy sauce

½ teaspoon garlic
  powder
½ teaspoon ground
  ginger
Dash pepper

Cut ribs in serving-size pieces. Arrange in 12x7½x2-inch glass baking dish. Cover with waxed paper. Cook in countertop microwave oven 10 minutes. Drain off juices; rearrange ribs. Combine marmalade, soy, garlic, ginger, pepper, and ¾ cup water. Pour over ribs. Micro-cook, uncovered, 30 minutes*, or till done. Occasionally baste and rearrange ribs. Garnish with orange slices, if desired. Serves 4 to 6.

## MULLED NECTAR

1 12-ounce can apricot
  nectar
1 cup pineapple *or*
  orange juice

4 whole cloves
4 whole allspice

In large glass measuring cup, combine nectar, pineapple or orange juice, and spices. Heat, uncovered, in countertop microwave oven for 5 to 6 minutes*, stirring after 2 minutes. Pour through strainer into heat-proof glasses. Makes 4 servings.

## BUTTERSCOTCH FUDGE

In a 1-quart glass casserole, place one 3-ounce package cream cheese, cut up; ½ cup butterscotch pieces; and 1 tablespoon milk. Cook, covered, in countertop microwave oven for 1 minute*, or till butterscotch melts, stirring once. (Tiny cheese lumps will remain.) Stir in 2 cups sifted confectioners' sugar, ¼ teaspoon vanilla, and dash salt. Fold in 1 cup miniature marshmallows. Immediately turn into waxed paper-lined 8½x4½x2½-inch loaf pan.

---

*The timings are approximate, as countertop microwave ovens vary by manufacturer. But after trying a few recipes, you will be able to adjust recipe timings to your microwave oven.*

Chill till set. Turn out; cut in pieces. Store in refrigerator. Makes 1 pound.

## BEEF AND PORK RING

| | |
|---|---|
| 1 beaten egg | 1 pound ground beef |
| 1/2 cup milk | 1/4 pound ground pork |
| 1 1/2 cups soft bread crumbs | 2 tablespoons catsup |
| 2 tablespoons finely chopped onion | 1 tablespoon brown sugar |
| 2 tablespoons finely chopped green pepper | 1/4 teaspoon dry mustard |

Mix egg, milk, crumbs, onion, green pepper, 1 teaspoon salt, and dash pepper. Add meats; mix well. In 9-inch glass pie plate, shape meat into ring, 1 inch high, around small juice glass. Cover with waxed paper. Cook in countertop microwave oven 8 minutes; give dish quarter turn every 2 minutes. Spoon off fat. Mix remaining ingredients; spread over meat. Micro-cook, uncovered, about 2 minutes*, or till done. Let stand 5 minutes. Serves 4 or 5.

## PEPPY ITALIAN CHICKEN

| | |
|---|---|
| 1/2 cup chopped onion | 1/4 cup dry white wine |
| 1/4 cup chopped celery | 1/2 teaspoon dried basil, crushed |
| 1/4 cup chopped green pepper | 1/2 teaspoon dried rosemary, crushed |
| 2 cloves garlic, minced | Dash bottled hot pepper sauce |
| 1 8-ounce can tomatoes, cut up | |
| 1 8-ounce can tomato sauce | 4 medium chicken legs |
| 1 3-ounce can sliced mushrooms, drained | 4 medium chicken thighs |

In 12x7 1/2x2-inch glass baking dish, combine first 4 ingredients and 2 tablespoons water. Cover with waxed paper. Cook in countertop microwave oven 3 minutes. Stir in next 7 ingredients, 3/4 teaspoon salt, and dash pepper. Add chicken; coat with sauce. Micro-cook, covered, about 40 minutes*, or till done; turn dish every 10 minutes. Serves 4.

## ORIENTAL CHICKEN

1½ cups uncooked
   packaged precooked
   rice
1 green pepper, cut in
   strips
1 cup bias-cut celery
1 tablespoon cornstarch

1 10½-ounce can
   condensed cream of
   chicken soup
2 tablespoons soy sauce
2 cups cubed cooked
   chicken
1 1-pound can chop suey
   vegetables, drained

In 1-quart glass casserole, heat 1½ cups water, covered, in countertop microwave oven till boiling, about 2½ minutes. Stir in rice. Cover; let stand at least 5 minutes. Fluff up with fork before serving.

In 1½-quart glass casserole, mix green pepper, celery, and 1 tablespoon water. Micro-cook, covered, for 3 minutes; stir once. Blend ¼ cup cold water into cornstarch; stir into vegetables. Stir in soup and soy. Add chicken and chop suey vegetables. Cover; micro-cook for 2 minutes; stir. Micro-cook, covered, about 4 minutes*, or till hot. Serve with rice. Serves 6.

## APPLE-HAM OPEN-FACERS

2 tablespoons sugar
2 tablespoons cornstarch
1⅔ cups apple cider or
   juice
1 teaspoon
   Worcestershire sauce
¼ cup chopped onion
2 tablespoons sweet
   pickle relish

1 12-ounce can
   luncheon meat
2 tart cooking apples,
   pared and thinly sliced
   (2 cups)
12 slices French bread,
   toasted

Combine sugar and cornstarch in 1½-quart glass casserole. Blend in cider and Worcestershire. Add onion and relish. Cook, uncovered, in countertop microwave oven for 6 minutes; stir once. Cut meat in 18 slices. Add meat and apples to sauce; stir till coated. Micro-cook, uncovered, for 3 minutes; stir. Micro-cook, uncovered, about 3 minutes*, or till hot through. For each sandwich, place 3 slices meat atop 2 slices bread. Spoon sauce over. Serves 6.

## TARRAGON FISH FILLETS

| | |
|---|---|
| 1½ pounds fresh or frozen fish fillets (4 fillets) | 1 tablespoon bottled steak sauce |
| ¼ cup sliced green onion | 2 teaspoons vinegar |
| 2 tablespoons butter or margarine | 2 teaspoons honey |
| | ½ teaspoon dried tarragon, crushed |

If fillets are frozen, place in 12x7½x2-inch glass baking dish. Thaw in countertop microwave oven as follows**: Allowing a 2-minute rest period between each thawing time and turning fish over one time, micro-cook for 2 minutes; 1 minute; 1 minute; then 30 seconds. Separate fillets; set aside. In glass measuring cup, mix onion, butter, steak sauce, vinegar, honey, tarragon, ½ teaspoon salt, and ⅛ teaspoon pepper. Micro-cook, uncovered, 1½ minutes*, or till bubbly; stir. Arrange fillets in 12x 7½x2-inch glass baking dish; tuck under thin edges. Pour sauce atop. Cover with waxed paper. Micro-cook 6 minutes*, or till fish flakes easily; baste fish and turn dish every 2 minutes. Let stand, covered, a few minutes before serving. Serve sauce with fish. Serves 4 to 6.
** If microwave oven has defrost feature, follow manufacturer's directions.

## CRANBERRY PORK CHOPS

| | |
|---|---|
| 4 pork rib chops, ½ inch thick | ½ cup whole cranberry sauce |
| Salt | 2 tablespoons bottled barbecue sauce |
| Pepper | 2 tablespoons water |

Arrange pork chops in single layer in an 8x8x2-inch glass baking dish. Season with salt and pepper. Combine cranberry sauce, barbecue sauce, and water; pour over pork chops. Cover with waxed paper. Cook in countertop microwave oven about 12 minutes*, or till done. Spoon sauce mixture over chops and give dish a quarter turn every 3 minutes. Makes 4 servings.

## ZUCCHINI CASSEROLE

2 pounds zucchini,
sliced ³/₈ inch thick
(7 cups)
¹/₄ cup chopped onion
1 10¹/₂-ounce can
condensed cream of
chicken soup
1 cup dairy sour cream

1 cup shredded carrot
¹/₄ cup butter or
margarine
2 cups herb-seasoned
stuffing mix (about
¹/₂ of an 8-ounce
package)

Combine zucchini and onion in 12x7¹/₂x2-inch glass baking dish; add ¹/₄ cup water. Cover; cook in countertop microwave oven about 15 minutes*, or till zucchini is tender; stir every 3 minutes. Drain. Combine soup and sour cream; stir in carrot. Fold in zucchini and onion. In glass bowl, melt butter in microwave oven, about 30 seconds. Stir in stuffing mix. Spread *half* the stuffing mixture in bottom of same baking dish. Spoon zucchini mixture atop. Sprinkle with remaining stuffing mixture. Microcook, uncovered, about 7 minutes*, or till hot; give dish a half turn after 4 minutes. Serves 6.

## CORN AND CABBAGE COMBO

In a 1-quart glass casserole, combine one 10-ounce package frozen whole kernel corn, 2 cups chopped cabbage, 2 tablespoons chopped onion, and 2 tablespoons water. Cover; cook in countertop microwave oven for 3 minutes; stir. Micro-cook, covered, about 3 minutes* longer, or till vegetables are tender. Drain in collander. In the same casserole, combine 1 cup cream-style cottage cheese, 2 tablespoons grated Parmesan cheese, ¹/₄ teaspoon salt, and ¹/₈ teaspoon pepper. Stir in drained vegetables. Micro-cook, uncovered, for 2 minutes; stir. Micro-cook, uncovered, for 2 minutes; stir. Micro-cook, uncovered, about 2 minutes* longer, or till heated through. Stir. Serves 5 or 6.

*The timings are approximate, as countertop microwave ovens vary by manufacturer. But after trying a few recipes, you will be able to adjust recipe timings to your microwave oven.*

## CHERRY-BANANA COBBLER

| | |
|---|---|
| 3 firm medium bananas | 3 soft macaroon cookies, |
| 2 teaspoons lemon juice | broken into coarse |
| 1 1-pound 5-ounce can | crumbs (1/2 cup) |
| (2 cups) cherry pie | Vanilla ice cream |
| filling | |

Peel bananas and cut into thirds. Place in 10x6x2-inch glass baking dish. Stir lemon juice into pie filling; spoon over bananas. Cook, uncovered, in countertop microwave oven for 2 minutes. Stir to coat bananas; sprinkle crumbs atop. Micro-cook, uncovered, about 2 minutes*, or till heated through. Serve with ice cream. Serves 6.


## DATE PUDDING CAKE

| | |
|---|---|
| 1/2 cup snipped pitted dates | 2 teaspoons baking powder |
| 2 tablespoons butter | 1/2 teaspoon salt |
| 1/2 cup granulated sugar | 1/4 cup chopped walnuts |
| 1/4 cup brown sugar | 3/4 cup brown sugar |
| 1 slightly beaten egg | 1 tablespoon butter |
| 1 cup sifted all-purpose flour | Vanilla ice cream |

In large glass measuring cup, heat 3/4 cup water in countertop microwave oven till boiling, about 2 minutes. Add dates; cool. In large glass mixing bowl, melt 2 tablespoons butter in microwave oven, about 30 seconds. Blend in granulated sugar and 1/4 cup brown sugar. Add egg; mix well. Sift together flour, baking powder, and salt; stir into sugar mixture till smooth. Stir in nuts and date mixture. Pour into 8x8x2-inch glass baking dish; spread evenly.

In 4-cup glass measuring cup, heat 1 3/4 cups water in microwave oven till boiling, about 3 1/2 minutes. Add 3/4 cup brown sugar and 1 tablespoon butter to boiling water; stir till dissolved. Carefully pour evenly over date mixture. Micro-cook, uncovered, about 8 minutes*, or till wooden pick inserted in cake portion comes out clean. Give dish a quarter turn every 2 minutes. Serve warm with ice cream. Serves 6.

## MIXED FRUIT COMPOTE

1 1-pound can peach
   slices
1 1-pound can pitted
   dark sweet cherries
$1/2$ cup brown sugar
$1/3$ cup orange juice

$1/2$ teaspoon grated lemon
   peel
2 tablespoons lemon
   juice
1 cup (5 ounces) dried
   apricots

Drain peaches and cherries, reserving the syrups. In 2-quart glass casserole, combine reserved syrups, brown sugar, orange juice, lemon peel, and lemon juice. Stir in dried apricots. Cover and cook in countertop microwave oven about 10 minutes*, or till mixture boils. Let stand, covered, 30 minutes. Stir in peaches and cherries. Micro-cook, uncovered, about 3 minutes*, or till heated through. Serves 6 to 8.

## HONEY BAKED APPLES

Remove core from 4 large baking apples and enlarge hole slightly to allow for filling. Pare a strip from top of each. Place each in 6-ounce custard cup. Combine 1 small banana, chopped; $1/3$ cup cranberries, chopped; 3 table-spoons honey; and $3/4$ teaspoon ground cinnamon. Fill centers of apples. Pour 1 tablespoon water over each apple. Cook, uncovered, in countertop microwave oven for 5 to 7 minutes*, or till nearly tender; rearrange once. Let stand till cooled slightly. Serves 4.

## DEVILED NUT SNACK

In $12x7^1/2x2$-inch glass baking dish, melt $1/4$ cup butter in countertop microwave oven, about 30 seconds. Stir in $1^1/2$ teaspoons chili powder, 1 teaspoon Worcestershire sauce, $1/2$ teaspoon garlic salt, and $1/8$ teaspoon cayenne. Add 3 cups bite-size shredded corn squares cereal, 1 cup cashews, and 1 cup walnuts; toss to coat. Micro-cook, uncovered, 5 to 6 minutes*; stir often. Makes 5 cups.

\* The timings are approximate, as countertop microwave ovens vary by manufacturer. But after trying a few recipes, you will be able to adjust recipe timings to your microwave oven.

# SLOW CROCKERY COOKING

## INDIVIDUAL POT ROASTS

2 medium carrots, thinly sliced (1 cup)
1 medium turnip, coarsely chopped (1/2 cup)
1/2 cup chopped green pepper
1/2 cup chopped onion
1/2 cup sliced celery
1 3-pound boneless beef pot roast
1 clove garlic, halved
2 tablespoons snipped parsley
1/4 cup all-purpose flour

Place first 5 ingredients in slow electric crockery cooker. Trim excess fat from meat; cut meat in 6 portions. Rub meat with cut surface of garlic; season with 1 teaspoon salt and 1/8 teaspoon pepper. Place atop vegetables in cooker. Add 1/4 cup water; sprinkle with parsley. Cover; cook on low-heat setting for 8 to 10 hours.

For gravy, remove meat and vegetables to serving dish; cover to keep warm. Measure meat juices; add water, if necessary, to make 1 1/2 cups. Slowly blend 1/2 cup cold water into flour; turn into medium saucepan along with meat juices. Cook and stir over medium heat till thickened and bubbly; cook 1 minute more. Spoon some gravy over meat; pass remainder. Serves 6.

## MAPLE BAKED LIMAS

Rinse 1 pound (2 1/2 cups) dry lima beans. In large saucepan or Dutch oven, combine beans and 2 quarts water; bring to boiling. Cover and simmer 1 1/2 hours. Transfer to bowl. Cover and refrigerate overnight.

Drain beans; reserve 1 cup liquid. Combine beans; reserved bean liquid; 1 cup chopped onion; 4 slices bacon, cut in small pieces; 1/2 cup maple-flavored syrup; 1/2 cup catsup; 1 tablespoon Worcestershire sauce; 1 teaspoon salt; 1/8 teaspoon pepper; and 1 bay leaf. Mix well. Pour into slow electric crockery cooker. Cover; cook on low-heat setting for 7 to 10 hours. Or, cover and cook on high-heat setting for 3½ to 5 hours. Remove bay leaf. Serves 6.

## CHICKEN CASSOULET

- ½ pound (1 cup) dry navy beans
- ¾ pound Polish sausage links
- 1 cup tomato juice
- 1 tablespoon Worcestershire sauce
- 2 teaspoons instant beef bouillon granules
- ½ teaspoon dried basil, crushed
- ½ teaspoon dried oregano, crushed
- ½ teaspoon paprika
- ½ cup finely chopped carrot
- ½ cup chopped celery
- ½ cup chopped onion
- 1 2½- to 3-pound ready-to-cook broiler-fryer chicken, cut up

Rinse beans; place in saucepan with 1 quart water. Bring to boiling. Cover; simmer 1½ hours. Transfer to bowl; cover and chill overnight. Drain beans. Halve sausage. Mix beans, sausage, tomato juice, Worcestershire, bouillon granules, basil, oregano, paprika, and 1 teaspoon salt. Set aside. Place carrot, celery, and onion in slow electric crockery cooker. Sprinkle chicken with salt and pepper; place in cooker. Pour bean mixture atop; press beans down into liquid. Cover; cook on low-heat setting for 7 hours, or till done. Remove meat. Mash bean mixture slightly; serve in soup bowls with meat. Serves 6.

## RIBS AND KRAUT

Cut 3 pounds pork spareribs in pieces to fit slow electric crockery cooker. Season with 1½ teaspoons salt and ¼ teaspoon pepper. Brown ribs in large skillet. Place ribs in bottom of cooker. Combine one 8-ounce can tomatoes, cut up; 2 tablespoons brown sugar; and 1½ teaspoons caraway seed. Stir in one 1 pound 11-ounce can sauerkraut, rinsed and drained; 1 large unpared tart apple, thinly sliced; and 1 onion, cut in wedges. Place mixture on top of meat in cooker. Cover and cook on low-heat setting for 6½ to 8 hours. Serves 6.

## OLIVE SPAGHETTI SAUCE

1 pound lean ground beef
1/2 pound bulk Italian sausage
1 1-pound 12-ounce can tomatoes, cut up
2 6-ounce cans tomato paste
1 6-ounce can sliced mushrooms, drained
1/2 cup Burgundy
1 large onion, chopped
1 large green pepper, chopped

1/2 cup sliced pimiento-stuffed green olives
3 bay leaves
2 cloves garlic, minced
1 1/2 teaspoons Worcestershire sauce
1 teaspoon sugar
1/2 teaspoon chili powder
2 tablespoons cornstarch
Hot cooked spaghetti
Grated Parmesan cheese

In skillet, brown ground beef and sausage; drain off fat. Transfer meat to slow electric crockery cooker. Add undrained tomatoes, tomato paste, mushrooms, Burgundy, and 1/2 cup water. Stir in onion, green pepper, olives, bay leaves, garlic, Worcestershire, sugar, chili powder, 1 teaspoon salt, and 1/8 teaspoon pepper. Cover and cook on low-heat setting for 10 to 12 hours. To serve, turn to high-heat setting. Heat till bubbly. Blend 2 tablespoons cold water into cornstarch; stir into meat mixture. Cover; cook 10 minutes longer. Serve over spaghetti. Pass cheese. Serves 8 to 10.

## SPICED APPLESAUCE

4 pounds tart cooking apples, pared, cored, and thinly sliced (12 cups)
1/2 cup sugar

1/2 teaspoon ground cinnamon
1 cup water
1 tablespoon lemon juice

Place apples in a slow electric crockery cooker. Combine sugar and cinnamon; mix with apples. Blend in water and lemon juice. Cover and cook on low-heat setting for 5 to 7 hours *or* on high-heat setting for 2 1/2 to 3 1/2 hours. Makes about 6 cups.

# BARBECUE SANDWICHES

1 2-pound beef pot roast
1 15-ounce can tomato sauce
3/4 cup chopped onion
1/4 cup chopped green pepper
2 tablespoons brown sugar
2 tablespoons Worcestershire sauce

1 tablespoon dry mustard
1 teaspoon salt
Dash bottled hot pepper sauce
1 tablespoon mixed pickling spice
2 tablespoons all-purpose flour
Individual hard rolls

Trim excess fat from pot roast. Cut meat in half and fit into bottom of slow electric crockery cooker. Combine tomato sauce, onion, green pepper, brown sugar, Worcestershire sauce, dry mustard, salt, and hot pepper sauce. Pour tomato mixture over meat. Tie pickling spice in cheesecloth bag; add to tomato mixture. Cover and cook on low-heat setting for 10 to 12 hours, or till meat is very tender.

To serve, turn to high-heat setting. Lift pot roast and spice bag from sauce. Skim off excess fat. Remove meat from bone; discard bone and spice bag. Cool meat slightly; cut across grain into thin slices. When mixture in cooker bubbles, put 1/4 cup cold water and 2 tablespoons flour in a shaker; shake well. Blend into sauce mixture. Return sliced meat to cooker. Cover and heat for 10 minutes. Fill hard rolls with meat mixture. Makes 15 to 20.

# GOLDEN FRUIT COMPOTE

1 1-pound 13-ounce can peach or pear slices
3/4 cup orange juice
1/2 cup dried apricots
1/4 cup light raisins

1/8 teaspoon ground cinnamon
1/8 teaspoon ground nutmeg

In a slow electric crockery cooker, combine undrained peach or pear slices, orange juice, apricots, raisins, cinnamon, and nutmeg. Completely immerse fruit in liquid. Cover and cook on low-heat setting for 6 to 8 hours. Makes 6 servings.

## MEAT LOAF FLORENTINE

2 slightly beaten eggs
1/2 cup milk
1 1/2 cups soft bread crumbs
1 10-ounce package
frozen chopped
spinach, thawed and
drained

2 tablespoons soy sauce
1 1/4 teaspoons salt
1/4 teaspoon bottled hot
pepper sauce
2 pounds ground beef
Mushroom Sauce

Combine eggs, milk, bread crumbs, spinach, soy sauce, salt, and hot pepper sauce. Add ground beef; mix well. Lightly grease bottom and sides of slow electric crockery cooker. Shape meat mixture in round loaf to fit bottom of cooker; place inside cooker. Cover and cook on high-heat setting for 4 hours. Using two spatulas, remove meat loaf; drain off excess fat. Serve with Mushroom Sauce. Makes 8 servings.

*Mushroom Sauce:* In saucepan, blend one 3-ounce can sliced mushrooms, undrained, into 2 tablespoons all-purpose flour. Add 1 cup dairy sour cream and 2 table-spoons snipped chives. Cook, stirring constantly, over low heat just till mushroom mixture thickens. *Do not boil.*

## APPLESAUCE BREAD PUDDING

In a large mixing bowl, combine 3 beaten eggs, 2 cups milk, one 1-pound can applesauce, 3/4 cup sugar, 2 table-spoons melted butter or margarine, 2 teaspoons vanilla, 3/4 teaspoon ground cinnamon, and 1/2 teaspoon salt. Trim crusts from 9 slices slightly dry bread, if desired. Cut bread in 1/2-inch cubes; gently stir bread cubes into applesauce mixture.

Turn into a lightly greased 2-pound coffee can or a 3-pound shortening can. Cover with foil; place can in slow electric crockery cooker. Add 1/2 cup hot water to cooker. Cover cooker and cook on high-heat setting about 3 hours, or till done. Remove the can from cooker. Spoon pudding into serving dishes. Top with frozen whipped dessert topping, thawed. Makes 8 servings.

## PORK STROGANOFF

1¹/₂ pounds boneless pork
   shoulder, cut in ³/₄-inch
   cubes
1 tablespoon salad oil
¹/₂ cup chopped onion
1 clove garlic, minced
1 3-ounce can chopped
   mushrooms, drained
1 tablespoon instant
   beef bouillon granules

1 teaspoon dried
   dillweed
¹/₈ teaspoon pepper
¹/₂ cup dairy sour cream
¹/₄ cup dry white wine
3 tablespoons all-
   purpose flour
Hot cooked noodles

In skillet, brown pork in oil; drain fat. Add onion and garlic; cook till onion is tender. Transfer to slow electric crockery cooker. Combine mushrooms, bouillon granules, dillweed, pepper, and 1 cup water; pour over meat. Cover and cook on low-heat setting for 8 to 10 hours. To serve, turn to high-heat setting. Heat 15 to 20 minutes, or till bubbly. Blend sour cream, wine, and flour; stir into hot mixture. Heat through, about 15 minutes; stir often. *Do not boil.* Serve over noodles. Garnish with snipped parsley, if desired. Serves 6.

## HAM-LENTIL SOUP

1 pound (2¹/₃ cups) dry
   lentils
1¹/₂ cups chopped carrots
1 cup chopped onion
1 cup chopped celery
¹/₄ cup snipped parsley
1 bay leaf

1 teaspoon salt
¹/₄ teaspoon dried
   marjoram, crushed
¹/₈ teaspoon pepper
1 1¹/₂-pound meaty ham
   bone

Rinse lentils; place in slow electric crockery cooker. Add vegetables, parsley, and bay leaf. Stir in salt, marjoram, and pepper; place ham bone atop. Add 7 cups water. Cover and cook on low-heat setting for 9 to 11 hours. Lift ham bone from soup. Remove meat from bone; discard bone. Return meat to cooker; season to taste. Remove bay leaf. Serves 10.

## SAUSAGE CHILI

*If you wish, freeze a portion of this unusual crockery chili for another meal—*

1 pound ground beef
1 pound bulk pork sausage
1 large onion, chopped (1 cup)
1 cup chopped green pepper
1 cup sliced celery

2 15½-ounce cans red kidney beans
1 1-pound 12-ounce can tomatoes, cut up
1 6-ounce can tomato paste
2 cloves garlic, minced
2 teaspoons chili powder
2 teaspoons salt

In skillet, cook ground beef and bulk pork sausage till browned; drain off excess fat. Transfer meat mixture to a slow electric crockery cooker. Add onion, green pepper, and celery. Stir in undrained kidney beans, undrained tomatoes, tomato paste, garlic, chili powder, and salt. Cover and cook on low-heat setting for 8 to 10 hours. Makes 10 to 12 servings.

## HAM-POTATO SALAD

8 medium potatoes, cooked, peeled, and cubed (5 cups) or 3 1-pound cans sliced white potatoes, drained
1 cup chopped fully cooked ham
1 10½-ounce can condensed cream of celery soup

½ cup finely chopped onion
¼ cup vinegar
2 tablespoons sweet pickle relish
2 tablespoons chopped canned pimiento
1 tablespoon sugar
¾ teaspoon celery seed
½ teaspoon salt

Place potatoes and ham in bottom of a slow electric crockery cooker. In small bowl, combine celery soup, onion, vinegar, pickle relish, pimiento, sugar, celery seed, and salt. Mix thoroughly. Stir into potato-ham mixture. Cover and cook on low-heat setting for 4 to 6 hours. Serves 6.

## CORNED BEEF IN BEER

6 potatoes, pared and
quartered
3 medium onions,
quartered

1 cup thinly sliced
carrots
1 3- to 4-pound corned
beef brisket
1 cup beer

Place vegetables in bottom of slow electric crockery cooker. Trim fat from corned beef; place meat atop vegetables. Pour beer over all. Cover and cook on low-heat setting for 9 to 11 hours, or till done. Serve meat with vegetables. Reserve broth for a vegetable soup. Makes 6 servings.

## FRUIT FILLED SQUASH

2 small or medium
acorn squash
1 cup chopped apple
1 medium orange,
peeled and diced
($\frac{1}{2}$ cup)

$\frac{1}{2}$ cup brown sugar
$\frac{1}{2}$ teaspoon grated
orange peel
4 teaspoons butter or
margarine

Cut squash in half crosswise; remove seeds. Sprinkle cavities with salt. Combine apple, orange, brown sugar, orange peel, and $\frac{1}{2}$ teaspoon salt. Spoon into squash cavities; dot each with 1 teaspoon of the butter. Wrap each half securely in foil. Stack, cut side up, in slow electric crockery cooker. Add $\frac{1}{4}$ cup water. Cover and cook on low-heat setting for 6 hours. Unwrap squash and lift to serving plate. Drain any syrup remaining in foil into small pitcher; serve with squash. Makes 4 servings.

## HOT BUTTERED LEMONADE

9 cups hot water
1$\frac{3}{4}$ cups sugar
1 tablespoon shredded
lemon peel

1$\frac{1}{2}$ cups lemon juice
(8 lemons)
Butter or margarine

In slow electric crockery cooker, thoroughly combine water, sugar, lemon peel, and lemon juice. Cover and heat on low-heat setting for 4 to 6 hours. Serve in mugs; dot each with butter. Serve with stick cinnamon stirrers, if desired. Makes 12 servings.

# BARBECUES
# AND
# EASY MEALS

## 32 • BETTER HOMES AND GARDENS COOKBOOK

# BARBECUES

**Choosing a grill:** The size and style of gas, electric, or portable grill or hibachi you need depends on your outdoor cooking needs. How large is your family? How often do you plan to use the grill for family and company meals? Will you use the grill away from home? What types of foods will you prepare most often? The portable grills range upward from tabletop size and may or may not have covers. Gas and electric grills are easier to regulate and also are available in a number of different models.

**Before cooking:** Line firebox (and hood of a smoker) with heavy-duty aluminum foil. Doing this not only speeds cooking, it catches drippings for easier cleaning. Add a 1-inch-deep bed of gravel to help prevent the firebox from burning out and to provide a better draft so heat is more evenly distributed. The gravel catches fat drippings, so after a number of cookings wash in hot water, let it dry, then replace.

To help prevent flare-ups, trim all excess fat from steaks and chops. Rub trimmings on grill to help keep meats from sticking.

**To build the fire:** Charcoal briquets are easier to use and burner longer with more uniform heat than lump charcoal. The number needed depends on the type of food to be cooked and the size of the grill. In the firebox, scatter briquets in a single layer to cover a slightly larger area than the food surface; gather into a pyramid in the center and soak with liquid lighter. (NEVER use gasoline or kerosene.) Let stand a few minutes before lighting. Allow about 30 to 45 minutes for coals to burn down. Or, use an electric fire starter; coals will be ready in about 15 minutes. To start an electric or gas grill, follow manufacturer's recommendations.

Cooking coals appear ash gray during the day and have a red glow at night with no flame. If the fire is too hot, meat will dry out and lose good juices.

To make a reserve of hot coals when grilling roasts,

add briquets around the cooking coals after the fire is ready.

**To estimate heat:** Hold palm of hand over coals at height the food will be cooking. Begin counting "one thousand one, one thousand two," and so on. The number of seconds you can comfortably hold your hand over the fire indicates the temperature. One or two seconds is a hot fire (good for steaks, burgers, and kabobs); three or four seconds is a medium fire (good for roasts); and five or six seconds is a slow fire (good for pork chops and spareribs).

For direct cooking (burgers and steaks), spread out the hot coals and place the meat on grill directly above the coals. For indirect cooking (roasts), place the coals on both sides of a drip pan set in the center under the food to be cooked.

**To adjust heat:** To increase heat, tap ashes off burning coals. Open drafts to let more air through. Add warm coals from reserve around the fire's edge. Lower the grill if adjustable. Narrow the ring of fire.

To reduce heat, do the reverse.

**For hickory flavor:** Use hickory chunks, chips, or sawdust. Avoid soft or resinous woods, which give an unpleasant odor.

Open grill: Wrap fistful of dry hickory chips in foil. Puncture top of package with a fork; place on hot coals. Smoke will last about 30 minutes.

Closed grill: Soak hickory chunks and bark in water for 1 hour. Or, dampen hickory sawdust flakes or chips. Sprinkle dampened hickory over cooking coals and close the hood.

**Cooking tips:** A wire broiler basket is great for small pieces of food, such as appetizers. It's easy to turn and food won't slip through the grill. Or, use foilware pans or a piece of heavy-duty foil. Puncture the pan or foil first with a fork.

**After cooking:** For easier cleaning, remove hot grill and place on wet newspapers or wrap in wet paper towels. Extinguish the fire by closing dampers and covering with hood. Or, transfer hot coals to metal bucket and smother by covering tightly.

**For safety's sake:** Invest in long-handled forks, tongs, and turners plus durable hot pads. Keep a water sprinkler handy to put out any flare-ups. Remember that barbecuing is an *outdoor* activity.

## OUTDOOR STEAKS

Choose tender steaks, about 1 inch thick. Slash fat edge at intervals to keep steaks flat. When coals are *hot,* tap off gray ash with fire tongs. Let grill top heat, then grease it and put on the steaks (orders for "rare" go on last). When you see little bubbles on top side of steaks, they are ready to turn (heat forces the juices to the uncooked surface). Flip steaks with tongs and pancake turner—piercing with a fork wastes good meat juices. Broil second side less than first—turn only once. For 1-inch steaks cooked medium, allow 13 to 15 minutes *total* time.

Salt and pepper each browned side of steak right after turning, or season steaks as they come from the grill. Serve sputtering hot, with a pat of butter atop.

If you like steak with a deep-brown, crusty coat, sear first side by lowering grill top close to coals for 2 to 3 minutes. Then raise grill to finish cooking first side. Turn steak, and sear second side; raise grill and complete cooking.

## LEMON CHUCK STEAK

| | |
|---|---|
| 1 beef chuck steak, cut 1½ inches thick (about 4 pounds) | 1½ teaspoons salt |
| | ⅛ teaspoon pepper |
| | 1 teaspoon Worcestershire sauce |
| * * * | 1 teaspoon prepared mustard |
| 1 teaspoon grated lemon peel | |
| ⅔ cup lemon juice | 2 green onion tops, sliced |
| ⅓ cup salad oil | |

Score fat edges of meat. Place in shallow dish. Combine remaining ingredients; pour over steak. Let stand 3 hours at room temperature or 6 hours in refrigerator, turning steak several times.

Remove steak from marinade; with paper toweling, remove excess moisture. Cook over *hot* coals about 12 minutes on each side for rare, or 15 minutes on each side for medium. Brush occasionally with the marinade. Carve meat across grain in thin slices. Makes 6 to 8 servings.

## SWANK PORTERHOUSE

Slash fat edge of one 2½- to 3-pound porterhouse or sirloin steak (about 2 inches thick). Slitting from fat side, cut pocket in each side of lean, cutting *almost* to bone. Combine ¾ cup finely chopped Bermuda onion, 2 cloves garlic, minced, dash salt, dash pepper, and dash celery salt; stuff into steak pockets.

Mix 3 tablespoons claret and 2 tablespoons soy sauce; brush on steak. Broil over *hot* coals a total of about 25 minutes for rare, or till done to your liking, turning once. Brush occasionally with soy mixture. Heat ¼ cup butter and one 3-ounce can sliced mushrooms, drained; pour over steak. Slice across grain. Serves 4.

## GRILLED RIB EYE ROAST

Have a 5- to 6-pound beef rib eye roast tied with string at 1½-inch intervals. Center meat on spit; fasten with holding forks. Attach spit; turn on motor. Have *hot* coals at back of firebox and drip pan under roast. Roast 2 to 2½ hours for medium-rare or to your liking. Meat thermometer will register 140° for rare, 160° for medium, and 170° for well-done. Let stand 15 minutes to firm up before carving. Serve with Herb Butter, dabbing a little on each serving of meat—it's potent.

*Herb Butter:* Blend ½ cup butter with 2 teaspoons seasoned salt, 1 teaspoon *fines herbes,* ¼ teaspoon freshly ground pepper, and few drops bottled hot pepper sauce.

Score fat edges of steaks, chops, or ham slices to prevent curling while cooking. Cut to *but not into meat.* Remove excess fat to keep flare-ups at a minimum.

## BUTTERFLY LEG OF LAMB

1 5- to 6-pound leg of
lamb
1 or 2 cloves garlic,
minced
1 teaspoon salt
1 teaspoon *fines herbes*

$\frac{1}{2}$ teaspoon pepper
$\frac{1}{2}$ teaspoon dried thyme,
crushed
$\frac{1}{4}$ cup grated onion
$\frac{1}{2}$ cup salad oil
$\frac{1}{2}$ cup lemon juice

Have meatman bone leg of lamb and slit lengthwise to spread flat like a thick steak. In large glass dish or baking pan, thoroughly blend remaining ingredients. Place meat in marinade. Leave at least one hour at room temperature, *or* overnight in the refrigerator, turning occasionally. Remove meat and reserve marinade. Insert 2 long skewers through meat at right angles making an X *or* place meat in a wire basket. This will make for easy turning of the meat and keep meat from "curling" during cooking. Roast over *medium* coals $1\frac{1}{2}$ to 2 hours turning every 15 minutes till medium done. Baste frequently with reserved marinade. Remove skewers and cut across grain into thin slices. Serves 8.

## ROAST PORK CHOPS

1 cup chopped onion
1 clove garlic, minced
$\frac{1}{4}$ cup salad oil
1 cup water
$\frac{3}{4}$ cup catsup
$\frac{1}{3}$ cup lemon juice
3 tablespoons sugar
2 tablespoons
Worcestershire sauce

1 tablespoon prepared
mustard
2 teaspoons salt
$\frac{1}{4}$ teaspoon bottled hot
pepper sauce
6 rib or loin chops, 1 to
$1\frac{1}{4}$ inches thick

Cook onion and garlic in hot oil till tender but not brown. Add remaining ingredients except chops; simmer uncovered 15 minutes. Set aside. Lock chops in a spit basket. Rotate over *slow* coals 45 minutes to 1 hour, or till done. Baste with sauce during last 20 minutes of cooking.

## PEANUT BUTTERED PORK

5- to 6-pounds boned
pork loins
1/2 cup orange juice

1/4 cup creamy peanut
butter

Tie pork loins together at 1 1/2-inch intervals with fat sides out. Balance roast on spit and secure with holding forks; insert meat thermometer. Season with salt and pepper. Arrange *medium* coals at rear of firebox, knock off ash. Place a foil drip pan in front of coals and under roast. Attach spit, turn on motor, and lower hood. Roast to 170° (about 3 hours).

Combine orange juice and peanut butter. When thermometer reads 170° brush the sauce on roast and continue cooking and basting 15 to 20 minutes. Serves 15.

## ROSY HAM SLICE

1/2 cup extra-hot catsup
1/3 cup orange marmalade
2 tablespoons finely
chopped onion
2 tablespoons salad oil
1 tablespoon lemon
juice

1 to 1 1/2 teaspoons dry
mustard
1 1-inch slice fully
cooked ham (about
1 1/2 pounds)

Combine all ingredients except ham slice. Slash fat edge of ham and broil over *slow* coals 15 minutes, turning once. Brush with sauce and broil 15 minutes more, turning and basting once. Heat remaining sauce on edge of grill; serve with ham. Makes 5 or 6 servings.

## SPINNING HAM

Buy round, boneless, fully cooked ham. With sharp knife slit casing lengthwise; remove. Score ham if desired. Tie with cord if necessary. Center lengthwise on spit; adjust on rotisserie. Let rotate over coals till hot through, about 10 minutes per pound. Last 20 minutes, brush with Pineapple Glaze.

*Pineapple Glaze:* Drain one 8 3/4-ounce can crushed pineapple, reserving 2 tablespoons syrup. Mix pineapple, syrup, 1 cup brown sugar, and 2 tablespoons *each* lemon juice and prepared mustard.

## BARBECUED RIBS

4 pounds loin back ribs*

* * *

1 cup chopped onion
1/4 cup salad oil
1 8-ounce can tomato sauce
1/2 cup water
1/4 cup brown sugar

1/4 cup lemon juice
3 tablespoons Worcestershire sauce
2 tablespoons prepared mustard
2 teaspoons salt
1/4 teaspoon pepper

Lace ribs on spit accordion style, and secure with holding forks. Adjust on rotisserie above drip pan. Let ribs rotate over *slow* coals. In a saucepan, cook onion in hot oil till tender. Add remaining ingredients; simmer uncovered 15 minutes. After ribs cook 40 minutes, baste well with sauce; add damp hickory to coals. Cook 20 minutes longer or till well done.

*Or use spareribs. Have meatman saw them lengthwise in two strips. Beginning with narrow end of ribs, lace on spit accordion style. Start second strip at wide end, third at narrow end. Use a holding fork for each slab of ribs.

## LUAU RIBS

2 4 1/2-ounce jars or cans strained peaches (baby food)
1/3 cup catsup
1/3 cup vinegar
2 tablespoons soy sauce
1/2 cup brown sugar

1 clove garlic, minced
2 teaspoons ground ginger
1 teaspoon salt
Dash pepper
4 pounds meaty spareribs

Mix all ingredients except ribs. Rub ribs with salt and pepper. Place bone side down on grill over *slow* coals. Broil about 20 minutes; turn meat side down and broil till browned, about 10 minutes.

Again turn meat side up, brush with sauce and broil without turning, about 30 minutes or till meat is well done. Brush frequently with sauce. Serves 4 to 6.

Easy way to barbecue long strips of ribs is to lace them accordion style on a spit. Then secure with holding forks so they'll stay in position while rotating over coals.

## BARBECUED SHORT RIBS

   3 pounds beef short
      ribs
   1 teaspoon salt
   ¹/₂ cup water

   1 cup chili sauce
   1 12-ounce jar (1 cup)
      pineapple preserves
   ¹/₃ cup vinegar

Trim excess fat from ribs. Sprinkle meat with salt and pepper to taste. Place ribs in Dutch oven. Add ¹/₂ cup water; cover and simmer till tender, about 2 hours (add more water during cooking if needed). Drain. Combine remaining ingredients; coat ribs. Grill over *slow* coals 15 to 20 minutes, brushing with sauce and turning frequently. Heat remaining glaze and serve with ribs. Makes 3 or 4 servings.

## SMOKY RIBS

Salt 4 pounds loin back ribs and place bone-side down on grill of barbecue smoker, away from the coals. Add dampened hickory to *slow* coals and close smoker hood. Hickory-barbecue about 3¹/₂ hours, basting with Gaucho Sauce last half hour. Makes 4 servings.

*Gaucho Sauce:* Combine 1 cup catsup, 1 tablespoon Worcestershire sauce, 2 or 3 dashes bottled hot pepper sauce, ¹/₂ cup water, ¹/₄ cup vinegar, 1 tablespoon sugar, and 1 teaspoon *each* salt and celery seed. Simmer 20 minutes; stir occasionally.

## PIZZA IN A BURGER

1½ pounds ground beef
⅓ cup grated Parmesan
cheese
¼ cup finely chopped
onion
¼ cup chopped pitted
ripe olives
1 teaspoon salt
1 teaspoon dried
oregano, crushed

1 6-ounce can tomato
paste
4 slices mozzarella
cheese, cut in strips
8 cherry tomatoes,
halved
8 slices French bread,
toasted

Combine first 7 ingredients and dash pepper; shape into 8 oval patties. Broil over *medium* coals 5 to 6 minutes. Turn; top each with cheese and tomatoes. Broil 5 minutes or to desired doneness. Serve on toasted French bread slices.

## DILLY HAMBURGERS

Combine 1 cup dairy sour cream, 1 teaspoon prepared mustard, and 3 tablespoons snipped fresh dillweed. Form 1 to 1½ pounds ground beef into 4 to 6 patties, ½ inch thick. Broil over *hot* coals 5 to 6 minutes; turn and sprinkle with salt and pepper. Broil 5 minutes longer or to desired doneness. Season again. Serve on hot toasted buns. Top with dill sauce. Makes 4 to 6 servings.

## 1-2-3 SAUCE

Combine one 12-ounce bottle extra-hot catsup, 2 tea-spoons celery seed, 3 tablespoons vinegar, and 1 clove garlic, halved. Chill several hours; remove garlic before serving. Grill hamburgers a few minutes on each side, then baste with sauce. Makes about 1¼ cups barbecue sauce.

## BLUE CHEESE BURGERS

2 pounds ground beef
1/3 cup chopped onion
1/3 cup crumbled blue cheese
2 teaspoons salt

1 tablespoon Worcestershire sauce

\* \* \*

1 loaf French bread
1/2 cup butter, softened
1/4 cup prepared mustard

Combine first 5 ingredients. Shape mixture into 10 oval patties slightly larger than diameter of French loaf. Cut French loaf in twenty 1/2-inch slices (freeze any extra bread). Blend butter and mustard; spread generously on one side of each bread slice. Reassemble loaf, buttered sides together. Wrap in heavy foil; place on grill over *medium* coals 15 minutes. Broil burgers 5 to 6 minutes; turn and broil about 5 minutes. Serve between bread. Makes 10.

## OUTDOOR BURGERS

1 pound ground beef
1/4 cup chopped onion
2 tablespoons finely chopped green pepper (optional)
3 tablespoons catsup

1 tablespoon prepared horseradish
1 teaspoon salt
2 teaspoons prepared mustard
Dash pepper

Combine all ingredients; mix lightly. Shape in 4 patties about 1/2 inch thick. Broil over *hot* coals 5 to 6 minutes, turn and broil 5 minutes or to desired doneness.

## POCKETBURGERS

Mix 1 pound ground beef, 1/2 teaspoon salt, and dash pepper. Between sheets of waxed paper, roll out patties 1/4 inch thick. Center half of patties with small amount of shredded process American cheese, chopped onion, and dash barbecue sauce. Top with meat lids. Press around edges to seal. Broil over *hot* coals for 10 to 12 minutes or to desired doneness, turning once. Makes 3 large burgers.

## HILO FRANKS

1 cup apricot preserves
1/2 of an 8-ounce can
　(1/2 cup) tomato sauce
1/3 cup vinegar
1/4 cup dry white wine
2 tablespoons soy sauce
2 tablespoons honey

1 tablespoon salad oil
1 teaspoon salt
1/4 teaspoon ground
　ginger

2 pounds (16 to 20)
　frankfurters

Combine first 9 ingredients. Score franks on the bias. Broil over *hot* coals turning and basting often with sauce. Heat remaining sauce to pass. Serves 8 to 10.

## NUTTY PUPS

Broil frankfurters over *hot* coals. Serve in hot toasted buns spread with chunk-style peanut butter. Pass pickle relish.

## BEST HAMDOGS

1 cup finely chopped
　cooked ham *or*
　luncheon meat
3 tablespoons pickle
　relish
2 tablespoons finely
　chopped onion

2 tablespoons prepared
　mustard
2 tablespoons
　mayonnaise

1 pound (8 to 10)
　frankfurters
8 to 10 slices bacon
　Bottled barbecue sauce

Mix first 5 ingredients. Slit franks, cutting almost to ends and only 3/4 the way through. Stuff with ham mixture; wrap with bacon and secure with wooden picks. Broil over *hot* coals, brushing with sauce, till filling is hot and bacon crisp. Serve in toasted buns. Serves 8 to 10.

## FROSTED LUNCHEON MEAT

Anchor canned luncheon meat on a spit. Blend 2 parts pasteurized process cheese spread and 1 part Dijon-style prepared mustard; spread on all sides of meat. Broil over *hot* coals till golden brown. Slice and serve on toasted buns. Pass sauce.

## BAR-B-Q MEAT LOAVES

| | |
|---|---|
| 2 pounds ground beef | 1 1/2 teaspoons salt |
| 2 slightly beaten eggs | 1/2 teaspoon dry mustard |
| 2 cups soft bread crumbs | 1/4 cup milk |
| 1/4 cup finely chopped onion | * * * |
| 1 tablespoon prepared horseradish | 1/2 cup butter or margarine |
| | 1/2 cup catsup |

Combine first 8 ingredients and mix well. Shape in 6 miniature meat loaves about 4 1/2 x 2 1/2-inches. Heat butter with catsup just till butter melts. Brush over all sides of loaves. Cook meat loaves over *medium* coals; turn and brush all sides frequently with sauce. Cook 40 minutes or till done. Pass remaining sauce. Serves 6.

## GOLDEN GRILLED CHICKEN

Split ready-to-cook broiler-fryer chickens in half lengthwise. Break joints of drumstick, hip, and wing, so birds will stay flat. Brush with melted butter or salad oil. Season with salt and pepper. Broil over *slow* coals, bone side down, 20 to 30 minutes. Turn and cook 20 to 30 minutes longer, brushing with butter occasionally during cooking.

*Doneness test:* Leg should move easily. Thickest parts should feel very soft.

## MARINATED DRUMSTICKS

| | |
|---|---|
| 1/4 cup catsup | 1/4 cup salad oil |
| 2 to 3 tablespoons lemon juice | * * * |
| 2 tablespoons soy sauce | 12 chicken drumsticks |

Combine first 4 ingredients, mixing well. Add chicken legs and turn to coat. Refrigerate overnight, spooning marinade over occasionally. Place drumsticks in wire broiler basket. Broil over *medium* coals for about 1 hour or till tender, turning occasionally. Baste with marinade now and then. Makes 6 servings.

## CHICKEN WHIRLIBIRDS

Salt cavities of broiler-fryer chickens (about 2 to 2½ pounds each). Fasten neck skin to back with shewers. Tie with cord to hold. To mount each bird: Place holding fork on spit, tines toward point; insert spit through chicken, pressing tines of holding fork firmly into breast meat. Slip 24-inch piece of cord under back of chicken; bring ends of cord to front, looping around each wing tip. (Make slip knots so wings can't straighten.) Tie in center of breast, leaving equal cord ends. Slip 18-inch piece of cord under tail. Loop around tail, then around crossed legs. Tie very tightly, again leaving cord ends. Pull cords attached to wings and legs together; tie tightly. Adjust holding forks and tighten screws. Test balance.

Attach spit to rotisserie and turn on motor. Use *medium* coals at back of firebox with a drip pan under birds. Baste chickens frequently with a mixture of ½ cup salad oil and ¼ cup lemon juice. During the last 30 minutes, brush frequently with Basting Sauce. (Allow about 2 hours roasting time without barbecue hood—1¾ hours with hood down.)

*Basting Sauce:* Combine ¼ cup salad oil, ¼ cup dry white wine, ¼ cup chicken broth, 2 tablespoons lemon juice, 2 tablespoons apple jelly, 1 teaspoon salt, 1 teaspoon snipped parsley, ½ teaspoon prepared mustard, ½ teaspoon Worcestershire sauce, and dash each celery seed, rosemary, and pepper. Beat the sauce well to remove lumps.

## CORNISH GAME HENS

Rinse four 1-pound Cornish game hens; pat dry with paper towels. Lightly salt cavities. Stuff with one 1-pound 4½-ounce can pineapple chunks, drained. Truss birds and tie cavity closed. Mount crosswise on spit, alternating front-back, front-back. Do not have birds touching. Secure with extra long holding forks. Combine 1 teaspoon salt, ½ cup butter, melted, and 2 tablespoons lemon juice; brush birds with mixture. Place on rotisserie over *medium* coals. Broil 1 to 1¼ hours or till done, brushing with lemon butter every 15 minutes. Makes 4 servings.

## HICKORY SMOKED TURKEY

Rub inside of one 14- to 16-pound turkey with 1 tablespoon salt. Skewer neck skin to back. Insert spit; anchor turkey with holding forks. Check balance. Tie wings flat against body. With another piece of cord, tie legs to tail. Attach to rotisserie. Arrange *medium-slow* coals at back and sides of firebox and a foil drip pan under bird. Brush bird with melted butter. Lower hood and start rotisserie. Sprinkle hickory chips over coals every 20 or 30 minutes; brush bird with butter occasionally. Roast 5 to 5½ hours.

## GRILLED TURKEY PIECES

| | |
|---|---|
| 1  6- to 7-pound ready-to-cook turkey | 1 tablespoon honey |
| * * * | 1 teaspoon ground ginger |
| ¼ cup salad oil | 1 teaspoon dry mustard |
| ¼ cup soy sauce | 1 clove garlic, minced |

Cut turkey in pieces as follows: 2 wings, 2 drumsticks, 2 thighs, 4 breast pieces, and 2 back pieces. Combine remaining ingredients for marinade. Place turkey pieces in marinade about 2 hours at room temperature or overnight in the refrigerator. Place pieces on grill 6 to 8 inches above *medium-hot coals*. (Add wings and back ½ hour later.) Broil, turning occasionally, 1 hour. Baste with marinade; broil 30 minutes. To test doneness, cut into drumstick—no pink near bone. Serves 10 to 12.

## GRILLED HALIBUT

Thaw one 1-pound package frozen halibut fillets until they come apart. Brush with mixture of 2 tablespoons soy sauce and 1 teaspoon lemon juice. Season with salt and pepper. Using ½ cup dairy sour cream, coat both sides of fillets. Combine ½ cup fine cornflake crumbs and 2 tablespoons toasted sesame seed. Roll fillets in crumb mixture. Place fish in an oiled wire broiler basket. Broil over *medium* coals 10 minutes, turning once. Serves 4.

## FISH IN A BASKET

1/4 cup butter or
    margarine, melted
2 tablespoons lemon
    juice

1 8-ounce package
    frozen breaded
    fish sticks
5 toasted frankfurter
    buns
    Sandwich spread

Combine butter and lemon juice; quickly dip *frozen* fish sticks in mixture, coating all sides. Broil in wire broiler basket over *hot* coals 5 to 7 minutes, brushing with lemon butter and turning once. Meanwhile, split and toast frankfurter buns. Spread hot buns generously with sandwich spread; tuck 2 fish sticks in each. Serves 5.

## HICKORY FISH BAKE

2 pounds fish fillets
1 lemon, thinly sliced

1/4 cup butter, melted
1 clove garlic, minced

Sprinkle fish generously with salt and pepper. Arrange *half* the lemon slices in bottom of a shallow baking pan; add fish in single layer. Place remaining lemon atop. Combine butter and garlic; pour over fish. Add hickory to *slow* coals. Place baking pan atop grill. Close hood and cook 25 to 30 minutes, basting frequently. Serve with the lemon slices and butter mixture. Serves 6.

## BARBECUED SHRIMP

1/3 cup butter or
    margarine
1/2 teaspoon curry powder
1 clove garlic, minced
1/2 teaspoon salt
    Freshly ground pepper

1/2 cup snipped parsley
    * * *
2 pounds large raw
    shrimp, peeled and
    deveined

Cream butter with remaining ingredients except shrimp. Divide shrimp equally on 6 pieces of heavy-duty aluminum foil. Top with butter mixture. Bring foil up around shrimp; seal tightly. Place shrimp directly on *hot* coals. Cook 5 to 7 minutes. Serve in foil packages. Serves 6.

## KABOBS

Select quick-cooking foods such as lamb, tender steak, fully cooked ham, green pepper, mushrooms, canned potatoes, canned onions, fresh or canned pineapple. Peppers and fresh mushrooms won't split if first dipped in very hot water a minute. Cut in cubes or pieces approximately the same size. Tiny tomatoes, summer squash, and spiced crab apples may be left whole. For cuts of meat that aren't tender use marinades or meat tenderizer.

When different kinds of food share the same skewer, choose only those that cook in the same length of time. Leave a little space between pieces so heat can reach all surfaces. *Exception:* For meat kabobs cooked rare, push foods close together.

Brush vegetables with melted butter before and during cooking. Baste meats often with marinades. Sauces go on near end of cooking. Cook over *hot* coals so food stays moist, yet browns well.

## FIESTA BEEF KABOBS

| | |
|---|---|
| 1/2 envelope (1/4 cup) *dry* onion soup mix | Dash bottled hot pepper sauce |
| 2 tablespoons sugar | 1 1/2 pounds beef chuck, cut in 1-inch cubes |
| 1/2 cup catsup | Instant unseasoned |
| 1/4 cup vinegar | meat tenderizer |
| 1/4 cup salad oil | |
| 1 tablespoon prepared mustard | 1 green pepper, cut in pieces |
| 1/4 teaspoon salt | 1 sweet red pepper, cut in pieces |

In saucepan, combine first 8 ingredients and 1/2 cup water; bring to boiling. Reduce heat and simmer 20 minutes. Cool. Add meat; toss to coat. Refrigerate overnight; drain meat, reserving the marinade. Use tenderizer on meat according to label directions. Thread meat and pepper alternately on skewers. Broil over *medium* coals 20 to 25 minutes, turning once and brushing with marinade 2 or 3 times. Heat remaining marinade to pass. Serves 4.

## TERIYAKI

*If desired, weave canned pineapple chunks with the meat. Use the marinade on steaks, too—*

1/2 cup soy sauce
1/4 cup salad oil
2 tablespoons molasses
2 teaspoons ground ginger
2 teaspoons dry mustard
6 cloves garlic, minced
1 1/2 pounds beef chuck *or* round steak, cut 1 inch thick
Instant unseasoned meat tenderizer

For marinade, combine soy sauce, salad oil, molasses, ginger, dry mustard, and minced garlic cloves; mix well. Cut steak in strips 1/4 inch thick. Use meat tenderizer on steak according to label directions. Add meat to marinade, stirring to coat, and let stand 15 minutes at room temperature. Lace meat strips accordion fashion on skewers. Broil over *hot* coals 5 to 7 minutes or to desired doneness. Turn frequently and baste with marinade. Serves 6.

## ARMENIAN SHISH KABOBS

1/2 cup salad oil
1/4 cup lemon juice
1 teaspoon salt
1 teaspoon dried marjoram, crushed
1 teaspoon dried thyme, crushed
1/2 teaspoon pepper
1 clove garlic, minced
1/2 cup chopped onion
1/4 cup snipped parsley
2 pounds boneless lamb, cut in 1 1/2-inch cubes
Green peppers, quartered
Sweet red peppers, quartered
Onion wedges, precooked

Combine salad oil, lemon juice, salt, marjoram, thyme, pepper, garlic, onion, and parsley; add meat and stir to coat. Refrigerate several hours or overnight, turning meat occasionally. Fill skewers with meat cubes, chunks of green and red pepper, and onion wedges. Broil over *hot* coals, 10 to 12 minutes, turning and brushing often with marinade. Serves 6.

## HAM AND FRUIT KABOBS

2 to 2¹/₂ pounds fully
cooked boneless ham,
cut in 1¹/₂-inch cubes
Spiced crab apples
Pineapple slices,
quartered
Orange wedges (with
peel)
¹/₂ cup extra-hot catsup

¹/₃ cup orange marmalade
2 tablespoons finely
chopped onion
2 tablespoons salad oil
1 tablespoon lemon
juice
1 to 1¹/₂ teaspoons dry
mustard

Thread ham and fruits alternately on skewers. For sauce, combine remaining ingredients. Broil ham and fruit over *slow* coals 12 to 15 minutes; brush often with sauce. Use a rotating skewer, or turn skewers frequently during broiling. Serves 6.

## GRILLED SAUSAGE TREATS

Spread large slices of Bologna or salami with prepared mustard. Center each with ¹/₂-inch cube sharp process American cheese *or* slice of candied dill pickle. Overlap two opposite sides of meat; repeat with 2 remaining sides. Insert skewer to hold meat together. Thread several on skewer; add an olive to each skewer.

Broil over *hot* coals about 10 minutes or till meat is lightly browned, brushing frequently with bottled Italian salad dressing.

## SAUSAGE KABOBS

Alternate brown-and-serve sausages, canned peach halves with a maraschino cherry in center, and mushroom caps on skewers. Brush generously with melted butter. Broil 4 to 5 inches from *slow* coals about 5 minutes on each side till hot.

## BARBECUE BREADS

**Grilled Garlic Slices:** Melt a little butter in shallow pan over grill; add garlic powder *or* minced garlic to taste. Toast thick slices of French bread on grill. Dip into garlic butter. Serve hot.

**Rolls on a Spit:** Thread brown-and-serve rolls on spit. Brush with melted butter; rotate over coals 10 to 15 minutes.

**Onion-cheese Loaf:** Cut French bread loaf in 1-inch slices cutting *to but not through* bottom of loaf. Combine ⅓ cup butter, softened, and 3 tablespoons prepared mustard; spread over cut surfaces of bread. Insert slices of sharp process American cheese and *thin* slices of onion in slashes. Wrap loaf in foil; heat over *medium* coals about 15 minutes or till hot.

## ROASTED CORN

Remove husks from fresh corn. Remove silk with a stiff brush. Place each ear on a piece of aluminum foil. Spread corn liberally with soft butter and sprinkle with salt and pepper. Wrap in foil (don't seal seam, but fold or twist foil around ends). Roast over *hot* coals 15 to 20 minutes or till corn is tender, turning ears frequently. Pass extra butter and salt.

## GRILLED TOMATOES

Cut tomatoes in half. Brush cut surfaces with bottled Italian salad dressing; sprinkle with salt, pepper, and dried basil, crushed. Heat, cut side up, on aluminum foil or greased grill over *hot* coals about 10 minutes or till hot through (don't turn).

## CHEESED SPUDS

Scrub medium baking potatoes; pare if desired. Cut into ¼-inch lengthwise sticks. Place individual servings on pieces of foil. Sprinkle each with onion salt, celery salt, pepper, and 2 tablespoons grated Parmesan cheese, making sure all surfaces are seasoned. Dot each with 2 tablespoons butter. Bring edges of foil together and seal, leaving room for expansion of steam. Cook potatoes on grill over coals about 30 minutes or till tender, turning packages several times. Serve in foil.

## FOILED POTATOES

Scrub medium baking potatoes or sweet potatoes. Brush with salad oil. Wrap each in foil. Bake 45 to 60 minutes on grill or right on top of coals. Turn occasionally. Pinch to tell when done. Cut crisscross in top of package; push on ends to fluff. Top with butter; season to taste.

## FOILED VEGETABLES

Place one block of frozen vegetables on a large square of foil. Season; top with pat of butter. Wrap, leaving room for expansion of steam. Cook over *hot* coals 10 to 15 minutes; turn occasionally.

## PINEAPPLE ON A SPIT

Pare 1 medium pineapple, leaving crown attached. Remove eyes and replace with 15 to 20 whole cloves. Center pineapple on spit (pull out center crown leaves and pierce with a small skewer first); secure with holding fork. Wrap crown in foil. Rotate over *hot* coals 45 minutes to 1 hour, basting often with mixture of $1/2$ cup maple-flavored syrup and $1/2$ teaspoon cinnamon. Slice; serve hot.

## S'MORES

Toast marshmallows. Sandwich 2 hot marshmallows and a square of milk chocolate bar between graham crackers.

## CAKE KABOBS

Cut pound or angel cake in $1^{1}/_{2}$-inch cubes. Spear each on fork; dip in melted currant jelly or in sweetened condensed milk. Then roll in flaked coconut to cover. String cubes on skewers and toast over *very hot* coals turning often till golden.

## DONUT HOLES

Cut refrigerated biscuits in thirds; roll each piece into a ball. String on skewers, leaving about $1/2$ inch between each. Brown over *hot* coals, *turning constantly,* till done through, about 7 minutes. Push off skewers into melted butter; roll in cinnamon-sugar mixture. Serve at once.

# EASY MEALS

## QUICK MEAL BEGINNINGS

- Pour a little ginger ale or lemon-lime carbonated beverage over melon balls.
- Broil grapefruit halves till bubbly. Sprinkle with ground cinnamon or ginger.
- Serve apple wedges or rings spread with blue cheese.
- Fold sliced strawberries (fresh or frozen) into strawberry-flavored yogurt.
- Freeze tomato juice to a "slush"; serve with a sprig of watercress or fresh mint. Or, serve tomato juice warm with a dab of butter or margarine.
- Pass herring and onion rings marinated in dairy sour cream.
- Stir crab meat into mayonnaise or salad dressing; serve atop avocado slices.
- Add sauteed fresh onion to onion soup from a mix. Sprinkle with Parmesan cheese.
- Serve beef broth "on the rocks" sparked with a dash of bottled hot pepper sauce or Worcestershire sauce.

## QUICK BEEF STROGANOFF

1 pound beef sirloin
1 tablespoon shortening
1 medium onion, sliced
1 clove garlic, minced
1 10½-ounce can condensed cream of mushroom soup
1 cup dairy sour cream

1 3-ounce can broiled sliced mushrooms, undrained
2 tablespoons catsup
2 teaspoons Worcestershire sauce
Poppy Seed Noodles

Cut meat in ¼-inch strips. Brown in hot shortening. Add onion and garlic; cook till onion is crisp-tender. Combine remaining ingredients except noodles. Add to meat. Heat through, but do not boil. Serve over noodles. Makes 4 servings.

*Poppy Seed Noodles:* Cook 4 ounces noodles in large amount boiling salted water according to package directions; drain. Add 1 tablespoon butter and 1 teaspoon poppy seed; toss together.

## STUFFED BURGER BUNDLES

1 cup packaged herb-
  seasoned stuffing mix
1/3 cup evaporated milk
1 pound ground beef

1 10½-ounce can
  condensed cream of
  mushroom soup
2 teaspoons
  Worcestershire sauce
1 tablespoon catsup

OVEN 350°

Prepare stuffing according to package directions. Combine evaporated milk and meat; divide in 5 patties. On waxed paper, pat each to 6-inch circle. Put ¼ cup stuffing in center of each; draw meat over stuffing; seal. Place in 1½-quart casserole. Combine remaining ingredients; pour over meat. Bake, uncovered, at 350° for 45 minutes. Makes 5 servings.

## SANDWICHES STROGANOFF

In large skillet cook 1 tablespoon chopped onion in 1 tablespoon butter or margarine till tender but not brown. Blend in one 10½-ounce can mushroom gravy or one 10¾-ounce can beef gravy, ½ cup dairy sour cream, 1 tablespoon dry white wine, and dash dried basil, crushed. Add 6 slices leftover roast beef. Heat through, stirring occasionally, about 5 to 7 minutes. Serve roast beef mixture over 6 slices hot toast. Makes 6 servings.

## SWEET-SOUR MEATBALLS

Drain one 8¾-ounce can pineapple tidbits, reserving syrup. In medium saucepan, combine ¼ cup brown sugar and 2 tablespoons cornstarch. Blend in reserved syrup, ½ cup water, ¼ cup cider vinegar, and 1 teaspoon soy sauce. Cook and stir over low heat till thickened and bubbly.

Carefully stir in one 1-pound can meatballs in gravy, one 5-ounce can water chestnuts, drained and thinly sliced, 1 green pepper, cut in strips, and pineapple. Heat to boiling. Serve over hot cooked rice. Trim with tomatoes. Serves 4.

## PORCUPINE MEATBALLS

| | |
|---|---|
| 1 pound ground beef | $^1/_2$ teaspoon salt |
| $^1/_4$ cup uncooked long-grain rice | $^1/_8$ teaspoon pepper |
| 1 slightly beaten egg | 1 $10^3/_4$-ounce can condensed tomato soup |
| 1 tablespoon snipped parsley | |
| 2 tablespoons finely chopped onion | $^1/_2$ cup water |
| | 1 teaspoon Worcestershire sauce |

Combine meat, rice, egg, parsley, onion, salt, pepper, and $^1/_4$ cup condensed tomato soup. Mix thoroughly; shape in about 20 small balls and place in skillet. Mix remaining soup, water, and Worcestershire sauce; pour over meatballs. Bring to boil; reduce heat; cover and simmer 35 to 40 minutes, stirring often. Makes 4 or 5 servings.

## SKILLET SPAGHETTI

*An easy all-in-one spaghetti supper—*

| | |
|---|---|
| 1 pound ground beef | 1 1-pint 2-ounce can tomato juice ($2^1/_4$ cups) |
| 2 teaspoons chili powder | |
| $1^1/_2$ teaspoons dried oregano, crushed | 2 tablespoons instant minced onion |
| 1 teaspoon sugar | 1 7-ounce package uncooked spaghetti |
| 1 teaspoon salt | |
| 1 teaspoon garlic salt | Grated Parmesan cheese |
| 1 6-ounce can tomato paste | |

In 12-inch skillet, brown ground beef; drain off excess fat. Stir in chili powder, oregano, sugar, salt, and garlic salt. Blend in tomato paste. Stir in tomato juice, onion, and $3^1/_2$ cups water. Bring to boiling. Carefully add spaghetti; stir to separate strands. Cover and simmer, stirring frequently, for 30 minutes. Serve with grated Parmesan cheese. Makes 4 to 6 servings.

## LAZY DAY LASAGNE

6 ounces lasagne
noodles
¼ teaspoon dried
oregano, crushed
1 15½-ounce can
spaghetti sauce
with meat

1 cup cream-style
cottage cheese
1 6-ounce package
sliced mozzarella
cheese

OVEN 375°

Cook noodles in boiling salted water following package directions; drain. Add oregano to spaghetti sauce.

In greased 10x6x1½-inch baking dish, make layers in order *half each* noodles, cottage cheese, mozzarella cheese slices, and spaghetti sauce. Repeat. Bake in moderate oven (375°) about 30 minutes. Let stand 10 minutes before serving. Serves 4.

## BEEF MUSHROOM LOAF

*An easy oven meal with Crisscross Potatoes—*

1 3-ounce can broiled
chopped mushrooms
Milk
1 slightly beaten egg
1½ teaspoons
Worcestershire sauce
1 teaspoon salt
½ teaspoon dry mustard
Dash pepper

1½ cups soft bread crumbs
1½ pounds lean ground
beef
2 tablespoons catsup
1 tablespoon light corn
syrup
Broiled mushroom
crowns
Pimiento strips

OVEN 350°

Drain the chopped mushrooms, reserving liquid. Add enough milk to mushroom liquid to make ½ cup. In mixing bowl, combine liquid, egg, Worcestershire sauce, seasonings, and bread crumbs. Let stand about 5 minutes. Stir in beef and chopped mushrooms; mix lightly but thoroughly.

Shape into loaf in 13x9x2-inch baking dish. Bake in moderate oven (350°) 1 hour.

Combine catsup and corn syrup; brush on meat loaf.

Bake 15 minutes more. Garnish with mushroom crowns topped with pimiento spirals. Makes 6 servings.

## OVEN POT ROAST

OVEN 400°

Place a 3- to 4-pound beef pot roast in center of double thickness of heavy-duty aluminum foil. Sprinkle all sides of meat with 1 envelope *dry* onion soup mix. Spoon one 10½-ounce can condensed cream of mushroom soup atop. Seal meat in foil. Place in 13x9x2-inch baking pan. Bake at 350° for 2½ to 3 hours. Remove meat to platter. Skim off excess fat from meat juices. Serve juices with meat or thicken for gravy. Makes 6 to 8 servings.

*Note:* For a more onion-flavored pot roast, omit the mushroom soup.

## PORK AND LIMA SKILLET

| | |
|---|---|
| 2 10-ounce packages frozen baby limas | 1 tablespoon all-purpose flour |
| 5 or 6 smoked pork loin chops | ½ teaspoon dried basil, crushed |
| 1 teaspoon chicken-flavored gravy base | ¾ cup water |

Cook limas according to package directions, omitting salt in cooking water; drain. In skillet, brown chops over medium heat. Remove chops from skillet. Pour off all but 1 tablespoon drippings.

Add gravy base to skillet. Blend in flour and basil. Add ¾ cup water; cook and stir over medium heat till thickened and bubbly. Add limas to skillet, stirring to coat with sauce. Arrange chops over limas. Cover and cook over low heat about 5 minutes, or till heated through. Serves 5 or 6.

## PORK CHOPS CACCIATORE

OVEN 350°

In skillet, brown 6 pork chops, about ¾-inch thick, on both sides. Season with ½ teaspoon salt and dash pepper. Place in 11x7x1½-inch baking pan. Top each chop with a thin onion slice.

Combine 1 envelope spaghetti sauce mix, one 1-pound can tomatoes, and 1 tablespoon brown sugar. Pour over chops. Cover. Bake at 350° for 1 hour. Uncover; top each chop with green pepper ring. Bake 15 minutes. Serves 6.

## PORK CHOPS ON RICE

6 pork chops, ³/₄-inch thick
1¹/₃ cups uncooked packaged precooked rice

1 cup orange juice
1 10¹/₂-ounce can condensed chicken with rice soup

OVEN 350°

In skillet, brown pork chops on both sides; season with salt and pepper. Place rice in 12x7¹/₂x2-inch baking dish; pour orange juice over rice. Arrange pork chops on rice. Pour chicken soup over all. Cover and bake at 350° for 45 minutes. Uncover; bake 10 minutes. Serves 6.

## PORK AND BEAN BAKE

2 1-pound cans pork and beans in tomato sauce
5 or 6 lean pork rib chops
Prepared mustard

¹/₂ cup brown sugar
¹/₂ cup catsup
5 or 6 onion slices
5 or 6 thin lemon slices

OVEN 325°

Turn beans into a 13x9x2-inch baking dish. Arrange chops over beans. Dash chops with salt and pepper, then spread tops lightly with mustard; sprinkle brown sugar atop and spread with catsup. Bake at 325° for 1¹/₄ hours. Place onion and lemon slice atop each chop. Bake 15 minutes. Trim with parsley. Serves 5 or 6.

## SAUCY PORK CHOPS

6 pork chops, ³/₄-inch thick
1 medium onion, thinly sliced

1 10¹/₂-ounce can condensed cream of chicken soup
¹/₄ cup catsup
2 to 3 teaspoons Worcestershire sauce

In skillet, brown chops on both sides in small amount hot fat; season with salt and pepper. Top chops with onion slices.

Combine remaining ingredients; pour over chops. Cover; simmer 45 to 60 minutes, or till done. Remove chops to platter. Spoon sauce over. Serves 6.

## BROILED HAM DINNER

| | |
|---|---|
| $^1/_2$ cup apricot preserves | 1 $^3/_4$-inch slice cooked |
| $^1/_2$ teaspoon dry mustard | ham |
| $^1/_4$ teaspoon ground | 1 8-ounce package |
| ginger | frozen potato patties |
| $^1/_4$ teaspoon salt | 3 tablespoons butter, |
| 1 tablespoon water | melted |

Mix first 5 ingredients. Slash fat edge of ham. Place ham and potato patties on rack in broiler pan. Spread *half* the apricot glaze on ham; brush potatoes with *half* the butter. Broil 3 inches from heat 6 minutes. Turn ham and patties. Spread ham with glaze. Butter patties; season with salt and pepper. Broil 6 minutes. Serves 4.

## HAM AND POTATOES

OVEN 400°

Cut one 12-ounce can luncheon meat into 8 slices; place in 11x7x1$^1/_2$-inch baking pan. Top with potatoes from 1 package dry au gratin potato mix, one 3-ounce can chopped mushrooms, drained, and cheese sauce mix from potato mix. Continue as directed on package, adding 1 teaspoon Worcestershire sauce to butter and boiling water called for. Cover; bake at 400° for 40 minutes. Serves 4.

## LUNCHEON MEAT DINNER

| | |
|---|---|
| 2 12-ounce cans | 1 8$^1/_2$-ounce can |
| luncheon meat | sliced pineapple, |
| $^1/_2$ cup orange marmalade | halved |
| 1 1-pound 2-ounce can | $^1/_4$ cup butter, melted |
| sweet potatoes, | |
| drained | |

OVEN 375°

Slice each piece of meat crosswise 3 times, slicing ¾ of the way through; spread with orange marmalade. Place in 12x7½x2-inch baking dish. Arrange potatoes around meat. Brush pineapple slices with butter. Insert in cuts in meat. Add remaining 2 half slices to dish with potatoes. Drizzle remaining butter over potatoes. Heat at 375° about 30 minutes, or till browned. Baste often. Serves 6 to 8.

## HAM WITH CHERRY SAUCE

1 5-pound canned ham
1 10-ounce jar apple jelly *or* guava jelly
1 tablespoon prepared mustard
⅓ cup pineapple juice

2 tablespoons dry white wine

*   *   *

1 1-pound 5-ounce can cherry pie filling
½ cup light raisins

OVEN 325°

Place ham fat side up on rack in shallow pan. Heat in slow oven (325°) for time indicated on label (about 1½ hours for a 5-pound ham). Half an hour before end of heating time, remove ham from oven and score top in diamonds.

In medium saucepan, combine jelly and mustard; stir in pineapple juice and wine. Cook and stir to boiling; simmer 2 to 3 minutes. Pour ⅓ of glaze over ham and return to oven. Spoon on remaining glaze at two 10-minute intervals.

In saucepan, heat cherry pie filling and raisins to boiling, stirring occasionally. Remove ham to serving platter. Add glaze from baking pan to cherry sauce. Bring again to boiling. Spoon some over ham on platter; pass remainder. Makes 3 cups.

## FRANK AND POTATO SALAD

1/2 pound (4 or 5)
   frankfurters, cut in
   1/2-inch pieces
1 tablespoon butter
1/2 envelope (1/4 cup) *dry*
   onion soup mix
1 tablespoon all-purpose
   flour

1 tablespoon sugar
   Dash pepper
1/2 cup water
2 tablespoons vinegar
2 1-pound cans (4 cups)
   sliced white potatoes,
   drained
1/2 cup dairy sour cream

Brown franks in butter; remove from heat. Stir in soup mix, flour, sugar, and pepper; add water and vinegar. Return to heat; cook and stir till boiling. Reduce heat and simmer gently, covered, for 10 minutes. Add the potatoes and sour cream; heat through. Makes 6 servings.

## WIENER-BEAN BAKE

1 10-ounce package
   frozen limas, cooked
   and drained
1 1-pound can pork and
   beans in tomato sauce
1 1-pound can kidney
   beans, drained
1/2 cup chili sauce
1/4 cup molasses

1/2 to 1 teaspoon dry
   mustard
1/2 teaspoon
   Worcestershire sauce
1/2 envelope (1/4 cup) *dry*
   onion soup mix
1 pound (8 to 10)
   frankfurters, cut in
   1-inch pieces

OVEN 350°

Combine first 3 ingredients. Stir in remaining ingredients. Turn into 2-quart casserole or bean pot. Bake, covered, at 350° for 1 hour. Uncover; stir; bake 30 minutes longer. Makes 6 servings.

## HOT DOGS DELICIOUS

Cook 1/2 cup chopped onion in 1 tablespoon hot shortening till tender, but not brown. Stir in one 14-ounce bottle (1 1/4 cups) extra-hot catsup, 2 tablespoons pickle relish, 1 tablespoon sugar, 1 tablespoon vinegar, 1/4 teaspoon salt, and dash pepper. Score 1 pound (8 to 10) frankfurters; add to sauce.

Simmer till franks are heated, about 10 minutes. Serve in hot toasted frankfurter buns. Makes 8 to 10 servings.

## QUICK WESTERN RAREBIT

1 10-ounce package
corn bread mix
1 11-ounce can
condensed Cheddar
cheese soup

2 tablespoons milk
Dash bottled hot
pepper sauce
1/4 cup sliced ripe olives

Bake corn bread mix according to package directions. Combine soup, milk, and pepper sauce. Heat slowly, stirring often, until hot. Add olives; heat just to boiling.

Cut hot corn bread in squares; split in half and spoon sauce over. Pass extra corn bread with butter. Makes 3 servings.

## HURRY SEAFOOD CURRY

Cook 1/4 cup chopped onion with 1 to 1 1/2 teaspoons curry powder in 1 tablespoon butter till onion is tender, but not brown. Add one 10 1/2-ounce can condensed cream of chicken soup, 1/3 cup milk, and 1 cup canned crab meat *or* lobster, flaked or cubed, *or* 1 cup canned or cooked cleaned shrimp, split lengthwise.

Heat, stirring frequently, till soup mixture is hot. Serve over fluffy hot cooked rice. Pass curry condiments— raisins, shredded coconut, peanuts, and chutney. Makes 4 servings.

## SHRIMP AND RICE DELUXE

1/2 cup milk
1 10 1/2-ounce can
condensed cream of
celery soup
1 7-ounce package
frozen rice and peas
with mushrooms

1 4 1/2- or 5-ounce can
shrimp, drained, *or*
1 1/2 cups frozen
cooked shrimp
2 tablespoons snipped
parsley
1/2 teaspoon curry powder
Toasted slivered
almonds

In 2-quart saucepan, gradually blend the milk and 1 cup water into soup. Add frozen rice and peas with mushrooms, shrimp, parsley, and curry powder. Cover and simmer gently for 30 minutes. Stir occasionally. Garnish with nuts. Serves 4 to 6.

## FILLETS ELEGANTE

| | |
|---|---|
| 1 pound frozen fish fillets | 1 4½- or 5-ounce can shrimp, drained |
| 2 tablespoons butter | ¼ cup grated Parmesan cheese |
| 1 envelope cheese sauce mix | Paprika |

OVEN 400°

Thaw fillets (sole, haddock, or halibut) enough to separate. Arrange in buttered 9-inch pie plate. Dash with pepper; dot with butter. Prepare sauce mix following package directions; stir in shrimp. Spread sauce over fish; sprinkle with cheese and paprika. Bake at 400° for 25 minutes. Serve with lemon wedges. Serves 4.

## SPEEDY TUNA SKILLET

Cook 1 medium onion, sliced, in 1 tablespoon butter till almost tender. Add one 10¾-ounce can condensed cream of shrimp soup, ½ cup milk, and 1 cup drained canned peas. Cover and heat just to boiling, stirring occasionally. Add one 6½- or 7-ounce can tuna, drained and broken in chunks, and dash pepper. Heat thoroughly. Serve over warm chow mein noodles or hot cooked rice. Serves 4.

## TUNA RICE CASSEROLE

1 6½- or 7-ounce can tuna

1 10½-ounce can condensed cream of celery soup

¾ cup uncooked packaged precooked rice

¼ cup milk

2 slightly beaten egg yolks

1 tablespoon lemon juice

2 tablespoons chopped canned pimiento

2 teaspoons instant minced onion

2 stiffly beaten egg whites

½ cup milk

1 tablespoon snipped parsley

OVEN 350°

Drain tuna and break in chunks; combine with *half* the soup and next 6 ingredients. Fold in egg whites. Turn into greased 10x6x1½-inch baking dish. Bake at 350° for 20 to 25 minutes or till set. Heat remaining soup with ½ cup milk and parsley. Spoon over servings of tuna. Serves 6.

## TUNA JACKSTRAW BAKE

OVEN 375°

Reserve 1 cup shoestring potatoes from one 4-ounce can for topper. Combine remaining potatoes with one 10½-ounce can condensed cream of mushroom soup, one 6½- or 7-ounce can tuna, drained, and one 6-ounce can (⅔ cup) evaporated milk.

Add one 3-ounce can sliced mushrooms, drained (½ cup), and ¼ cup chopped canned pimiento. Turn into 1½-quart casserole. Top with reserved potatoes. Bake at 375° for 25 minutes or till hot. Makes 4 to 6 servings.

## CHICKEN-BROCCOLI BAKE

OVEN 350°

In saucepan, bring 2 cups chicken broth and ⅔ cup long-grain rice to boiling. Simmer, covered, 15 minutes. Remove from heat; let stand, covered, 10 minutes.

Melt 3 tablespoons butter; stir in 3 tablespoons all-purpose flour, 1½ teaspoons salt, and dash pepper. Add

2 cups milk. Cook and stir till bubbly. Stir in 2 cups cubed cooked chicken; cooked rice; one 10-ounce package frozen chopped broccoli, cooked and drained; and one 4-ounce can sliced mushrooms, drained. Bake, covered, in 2-quart casserole at 350° for 30 to 35 minutes. Top with ¼ cup toasted slivered almonds. Serves 6.

## QUICK TURKEY CURRY

Cook ¼ cup chopped onion in 1 tablespoon butter or margarine. Add one 10½-ounce can condensed cream of mushroom soup and ¼ cup milk; heat and stir till smooth. Stir in 1 cup dairy sour cream and ½ teaspoon curry powder. Add 1 cup cubed cooked turkey or chicken; heat. Garnish with snipped parsley. Serve over fluffy hot cooked rice.

Offer curry condiments of chutney, raisins, toasted slivered almonds, sliced green onion, and mixed pickles. Serves 4.

## BUTTERMILK CHICKEN

| | |
|---|---|
| 1  2½- to 3-pound ready-to-cook broiler-fryer chicken, cut up | ¼ cup butter or margarine |
| 1½ cups buttermilk | 1  10½-ounce can condensed cream of chicken soup |
| ¾ cup all-purpose flour | |
| 1½ teaspoons salt | |

OVEN 375°

Dip chicken into ½ cup buttermilk. Then roll in flour seasoned with salt and ¼ teaspoon pepper. Melt butter in a 13x9x2-inch pan. Put chicken in pan, skin side down, and bake, uncovered, in a moderate oven (375°) for 30 minutes. Turn chicken and bake 15 minutes. Blend remaining 1 cup buttermilk and soup; pour around chicken. Bake 15 minutes more. Serves 6.

# CHICKEN AND BISCUIT PIE

1 15¼-ounce can
chicken stew
1 10½-ounce can
condensed cream of
chicken soup
1 tablespoon instant
minced onion
½ teaspoon dried
rosemary, crushed

1 8-ounce can peas,
drained
1 4-ounce can
mushroom stems and
pieces, drained
1 5-ounce can boned
chicken, diced
1 tube refrigerated
biscuits, halved
(10 biscuits)

OVEN 450°

In 2-quart saucepan combine stew, chicken soup, onion, and rosemary. Stir in peas and mushrooms; carefully stir in chicken. Heat slowly, stirring occasionally, till mixture boils. Turn into a 2-quart casserole. Arrange biscuits atop *hot* chicken mixture. Bake at 450° for 12 minutes. Serves 4 or 5.

# CHICKEN DINNER OMELET

1 10½-ounce can
chicken a la king
2 tablespoons chopped
canned pimiento
¼ cup chopped onion

¼ cup chopped celery
3 tablespoons butter
½ cup garlic croutons
5 slightly beaten eggs
½ cup milk

Combine chicken and pimiento; heat through. Meanwhile, in 10-inch skillet cook onion and celery in butter till tender. Add croutons; toss lightly. Remove mixture from skillet. Combine eggs, milk, and ½ teaspoon salt; pour into hot skillet. Cook slowly, lifting eggs to allow uncooked portion to flow under. Place vegetable mixture on half the omelet; fold over. Tilt pan and roll omelet onto hot plate. Pour chicken mixture over. Serves 2 or 3.

## BLUEBERRY CREAM SALAD

1 3-ounce package
  lemon-flavored gelatin
1 cup boiling water
1 1-pound 5-ounce can
  blueberry pie filling

2 tablespoons lemon
  juice
  * * *
1/2 cup dairy sour cream
1 tablespoon sugar

Dissolve gelatin in boiling water. Set aside to cool. Stir in pie filling and lemon juice. Chill till partially set. Spoon *half* the gelatin mixture into 8 1/2x4 1/2x2 1/2 -inch loaf dish. Chill till set. (Keep remaining gelatin at room temperature.)

Combine dairy sour cream and sugar. Spread evenly over gelatin in loaf dish. Top with layer of remaining gelatin. Chill 4 to 5 hours or overnight till firm. Cut in squares and serve on crisp salad greens. Makes 6 to 8 servings.

## CRANBERRY RELISH

1 3-ounce package
  strawberry-flavored
  gelatin
1 cup boiling water
1 8 3/4-ounce can
  pineapple tidbits
    * * *

1 10-ounce package
  frozen cranberry-
  orange relish,
  thawed
1/3 cup finely chopped
  celery

Dissolve gelatin in boiling water. Drain pineapple, reserving syrup. If necessary, add water to syrup to make 1/2 cup; add to gelatin along with relish. Chill till partially set. Stir in pineapple and celery. Chill in 1-quart mold till firm. Serves 6.

## ONION-DRESSED SALAD

OVEN 350°

Heat one 3 1/2-ounce can (2 cups) French-fried onions in moderate oven (350°) a few minutes to crisp. Break 1/2 head lettuce (about 5 cups torn) and 5 cups romaine in bite-size pieces. Add 1/3 cup Italian salad dressing; toss lightly. Scatter warm onions atop. Toss gently. Garnish with tomato wedges. Serve at once. Serves 6.

## FAST SALAD IDEAS

- **Apple-orange Toss:** Dice 1 tart apple into bowl. Add ½ teaspoon shredded orange peel, 1 orange, peeled and diced, 2 tablespoons broken walnuts, and ¼ cup mayonnaise or salad dressing. Toss together. Serve on lettuce. Serves 2 or 3.
- **Avocado-cranberry Salad:** Arrange avocado halves or quarters on lettuce. Top with mixture of cubed canned cranberry sauce and diced celery. Serve with bottled French salad dressing.
- **Cheese-peach "Sandwiches":** To softened cream cheese, add chopped walnuts and cut up dates; blend. "Sandwich" two chilled canned peach halves together with mixture. Serve on salad greens.
- **Golden Peach Plate:** Crown chilled canned peach half with cottage cheese. Top with chopped walnuts or bits of candied ginger. Trim plate with curly endive and maraschino cherries.
- **Pear-cheese Salad:** Arrange pear halves on lettuce leaves. Top with mayonnaise, then a sprinkle of shredded sharp process American cheese.
- **Cheese-topped Lettuce:** Thoroughly chill blue cheese in freezer for 20 to 30 minutes (allow about 1 ounce per serving). Cut lettuce in crosswise slices and place on salad plates. Spoon oil and vinegar salad dressing over each slice. Shred a generous fluff of blue cheese over each lettuce slice. Serve immediately.
- **Festive Lettuce Salad:** Cut lettuce in 1-inch slices. Place each slice on salad plate. Top with tomato slices, green pepper and onion rings. Pass favorite Italian or French salad dressing.
- **Beet-topped Lettuce:** Thoroughly drain one 8-ounce can diced beets, reserving liquid. Mash beets slightly with fork. Stir in ½ cup mayonnaise or salad dressing, 1½ teaspoons prepared horseradish, and dash salt. Add beet juice if needed to make mixture of desired consistency. Spoon over 6 lettuce wedges. Serves 6.
- **Corn-aspic Salad:** Cut canned tomato aspic into cubes and toss with drained whole kernel corn and creamy French salad dressing. Serve in lettuce-lined bowl.
- **Creamy Bean Salad:** Chill cooked green beans and lima

beans. Toss with chopped pimiento and creamy onion salad dressing.

## CREOLE GREEN BEANS

Cook ¼ cup chopped onion in 1 tablespoon butter till tender, but not brown. Add ¼ cup chili sauce, ⅛ teaspoon salt, and one 1-pound can green beans, drained. Heat through; stir often. Serves 4.

## BROCCOLI PARMESAN

Cook two 10-ounce packages frozen broccoli spears in *unsalted* water till tender. Drain. Cook ¼ cup chopped onion in 2 tablespoons butter. Blend in one 10½-ounce can condensed cream of chicken soup, ⅔ cup milk, and ⅓ cup grated Parmesan cheese. Heat. Serve atop broccoli. Serves 6.

## CARROTS PIQUANT

Drain two 1-pound cans small whole carrots, reserving ¼ cup liquid. In saucepan, blend 1 tablespoon cornstarch with ¼ teaspoon salt and several dashes ground nutmeg. Stir in the carrot liquid and ⅔ cup orange juice. Cook, stirring constantly, till mixture thickens and bubbles. Boil 2 minutes, stirring constantly.

Add 2 tablespoons butter and carrots; heat through. Sprinkle with snipped parsley before serving. Serves 6 to 8.

## FRIED CORN AND ONIONS

Melt 2 tablespoons butter in skillet. Add ½ cup chopped onion; season with salt and pepper. Cover; cook over low heat 4 minutes, shaking skillet often. Add one 12-ounce can Mexican-style whole kernel corn, drained, and dash dried basil, crushed; mix. Heat uncovered about 4 minutes, or till hot. Makes 4 servings.

## OVEN PEAS

OVEN 350°

In a 1½-quart casserole, combine two 10-ounce packages frozen peas, thawed enough to separate, one 3-ounce can sliced mushrooms, drained (½ cup), ¼ cup chopped onion, ¼ teaspoon salt, ¼ teaspoon dried savory, crushed, dash pepper, 2 tablespoons butter, and 1 tablespoon water. Cover; bake at 350° for 1 hour, or till tender. Stir once or twice. Serves 8.

## HOT DEVILED POTATOES

Packaged instant
mashed potatoes
(enough for 4 servings)
½ cup dairy sour cream

2 teaspoons prepared
mustard
½ teaspoon sugar
2 tablespoons chopped
green onion

OVEN 350°

Prepare potatoes according to package directions. Heat sour cream (do not boil). Add mustard, ½ teaspoon salt, and sugar; stir to blend. Mix into hot potatoes with onion. Immediately turn into 1-quart casserole. Sprinkle with paprika, if desired. Bake at 350° about 10 minutes. Makes about 5 servings.

## CRISSCROSS POTATOES

OVEN 350°

Scrub 3 medium baking potatoes; halve lengthwise. Make diagonal slashes, about ⅛ inch deep, in cut surfaces of potatoes, forming a crisscross pattern. Brush cut surfaces with 2 tablespoons butter, melted; season with salt and pepper. Arrange in baking dish. Bake at 350° for 1 hour. Sprinkle potatoes with paprika; continue baking 15 minutes more. Makes 6 servings.

## DOUBLE POTATO BAKE

Packaged instant hash
brown potatoes
(enough for 4 servings)
1 10½-ounce can
condensed cream of
potato soup
1 soup can milk

1 tablespoon instant
minced onion
1 tablespoon snipped
parsley
⅓ cup shredded
Parmesan cheese

OVEN 350°

Prepare potatoes according to basic recipe on package, *reducing cooking time 4 minutes;* drain. Combine soup, milk, onion, parsley, and dash pepper. Heat soup through; add to potatoes, mixing lightly. Turn into 10x6x1½-inch baking dish. Sprinkle with cheese. Bake at 350° about 35 minutes. Makes 6 servings.

## QUICK COFFEE BREADS

• **Quicky Crullers:** Unroll one tube refrigerated crescent rolls (8 rolls). Pinch together diagonal perforations of each 2 crescents, making 4 rectangles. Cut each rectangle in thirds lengthwise. Tie each strip in knot. Fry crullers in deep hot fat (375°) till browned. Drain on paper towels. While warm, brush lightly with confectioners' sugar glaze.

• **Jiffy Doughnuts:** Stretch and flatten slightly each biscuit from 1 tube refrigerated biscuits (10 biscuits). With finger, punch hole in center and shape in doughnut. Fry in deep hot fat (375°) about 2 minutes; turn once. Drain well on paper towels. Roll each doughnut in a mixture of ground cinnamon and sugar. Serve warm. Makes 10 doughnuts.

• **Caramel Coffee Ring:** Combine ⅓ cup vanilla caramel sundae sauce and ¼ cup light corn syrup. Pour mixture into bottom of a well-greased 5-cup ring mold. Sprinkle ¼ cup chopped pecans evenly over caramel mixture in the mold.

Separate rolls from one tube refrigerated butterflake dinner rolls (12 rolls). Dip each roll on all sides in 2 tablespoons butter, melted. Arrange rolls, side by side, in mold. Bake in a hot oven (400°) for 20 minutes. Let cool 1 to 2 minutes. Loosen sides; invert on serving plate.

• **Jam Brown and Serves:** Brush 1 teaspoon butter, melted, over tops of 6 brown-and-serve dinner rolls. Make lengthwise cut in top of each. Spread 1 teaspoon apricot preserves in each cut. Bake rolls in greased 11x7x1½-inch baking pan in hot oven (400°) for 10 to 15 minutes or till rolls are lightly browned.

• **Honey Crunch Loaf:** Slice 1 round loaf unsliced white bread *almost* to the bottom, 4 or 5 times in each direction. Place loaf on foil on baking sheet; turn up edges of foil to catch excess topping.

Combine ½ cup butter or margarine, melted, and ¼ cup honey; spoon over top of loaf letting excess drizzle between sections. Combine ½ cup sugar-coated cereal, ½ cup flaked coconut, and ½ cup brown sugar; sprinkle atop loaf and between sections. Drizzle with ¼ cup honey. Heat in moderate oven (350°) for 20 minutes or till lightly browned.

## PEAR COFFEE CAKE

| | |
|---|---|
| 1 1-pound can sliced pears, drained | ¼ teaspoon ground cinnamon |
| 1 teaspoon lemon juice | ¼ cup butter or margarine |
| ½ cup sugar | 1 14-ounce package orange muffin mix |
| ½ cup all-purpose flour | |

OVEN 400°

Sprinkle pears with lemon juice. Mix sugar, flour, and cinnamon; cut in butter till crumbly; set aside. Prepare muffin mix using package directions. Turn into greased 9x9x2-inch pan. Top with pear slices; sprinkle with crumbly mixture. Bake in hot oven (400°) for 30 to 35 minutes.

## EASY BREADSTICKS

OVEN 450°

Prepare 1 package hot-roll mix using package directions *except use 1 cup warm water and omit the egg.*

When dough has risen, turn out and toss lightly on floured surface. Divide into 3 parts; divide each third into

10 pieces. Roll each piece with hands on lightly floured surface to make an 8 to 10 inch stick. Place on greased baking sheet.

Brush with mixture of 1 slightly beaten egg white and 1 tablespoon water. Let rise uncovered about 20 minutes. Brush again with egg white mixture. Sprinkle with sesame or poppy seed. Bake at 450° for 10 to 12 minutes. Makes 2½ dozen.

## ONION SUPPER BREAD

½ cup chopped onion
2 tablespoons butter
1 14-ounce package corn muffin mix

½ cup dairy sour cream
½ cup shredded sharp process American cheese

OVEN 400°

Cook onion in butter till tender. Prepare mix using package directions. Pour into greased 8x8x2-inch pan. Sprinkle with onion. Mix sour cream and cheese; spoon atop. Bake at 400° for 25 minutes. Let stand a few minutes; cut in 9 squares.

## CHEESE TOPPED BISCUITS

2 tubes refrigerated biscuits (20 biscuits)
4 ounces sharp natural Cheddar cheese, shredded (1 cup)

2 tablespoons light cream
½ teaspoon poppy seed
Dash dry mustard

OVEN 425°

Overlap 15 biscuits around edge and rest of biscuits in center of well-greased 9x1½-inch round pan. Mix remaining ingredients; crumble atop. Bake at 425° for 15 minutes. Remove from pan at once.

**Parmesan Biscuits:** Mix ¼ cup butter, melted, 2 tablespoons snipped parsley, and 1 clove garlic, minced. Dip 2 tubes refrigerated biscuits (20 biscuits) in butter mixture. Arrange in pan as above. Top with remaining butter and ¼ cup grated Parmesan cheese. Bake as above.

## CRUNCH STICKS

1 tube refrigerated
   biscuits (10 biscuits)
Milk

1 cup crisp rice cereal,
   coarsely crushed
1 tablespoon caraway,
   celery, or dillseed

OVEN 450°

Cut biscuits in half. Roll each half into 4-inch pencil-like stick. Brush with milk. Mix cereal crumbs, seed, and 1 teaspoon salt in shallow pan (be sure salt is well distributed). Roll sticks in mixture. Bake on greased baking sheet at 450° for 8 to 10 minutes or till lightly browned. Makes 20.

## TOASTED CHEESE LOAF

OVEN 400°

Cut crusts from top and sides of unsliced sandwich loaf. Make 8 slices crosswise *almost* to bottom crust; make one vertical cut lengthwise down center *almost* to bottom.

Place on baking sheet. Blend 1/4 cup butter, softened, one 5-ounce jar sharp cheese spread, and 2 tablespoons snipped chives. Spread between slices, over top and sides. Tie string around loaf. Bake at 400° for 10 to 12 minutes or till bread is crusty. Serve as pan rolls. Makes 16.

## FRENCH BREAD FIX-UPS

• **Parsleyed Bread Slices:** Slice 1 loaf French bread on the diagonal. Spread slices with 1/2 cup butter, softened. Sprinkle with paprika and 1/2 cup finely snipped parsley. Arrange slices on baking sheet. Bake at 350° for 15 to 20 minutes, or till toasty. Serve warm.

• **Herb-buttered Bread:** Combine 1 1/2-teaspoons *each* snipped chives and snipped parsley, 1/4 teaspoon dried tarragon, crushed, 1/4 teaspoon dried chervil, crushed, and 1/4 cup butter, softened; mix well. Spread on 8 slices French bread. Arrange slices on baking sheet; toast at 350° about 20 minutes.

• **Poppy Seed-cheese Bread:** Combine 1/4 cup butter, melted, and 1/2 cup grated Parmesan cheese. Spread mixture on both sides of six 1-inch slices French bread. Sprinkle the bread on both sides with 1 tablespoon poppy seed.

Arrange slices on baking sheet and toast at 350° about 12 minutes, turning once.

• **Toasty Garlic Bread:** Melt $1/3$ cup butter in 11x7x$1^1/2$-inch baking pan. Add 1 or 2 cloves garlic, minced. Add six 1-inch slices French bread, turning quickly to butter both sides. Let stand 10 minutes. Heat at 350° for 20 minutes or till toasty.

## CARAWAY FINGERS

| | |
|---|---|
| 6 frankfurter rolls | $1/4$ cup grated Parmesan cheese |
| $1/4$ cup garlic spread | |
| $1/4$ cup butter or margarine | 2 teaspoons caraway seed |

OVEN 450°

Quarter rolls lengthwise. Melt spread and butter; brush on cut sides of rolls. Sprinkle with cheese then caraway. Bake on baking sheet at 450° for 5 to 8 minutes.

## ONION-BUTTER ROLLS

OVEN 350°

Blend $1/2$ cup butter, softened, 1 tablespoon *each* finely chopped green onion and parsley, and $1/4$ to $1/2$ teaspoon dried rosemary, crushed. Halve 6 hard rolls. Spread with butter mixture. Wrap in foil. Heat at 350° about 15 minutes or till hot.

## CARAMEL CAKEWICHES

*For an extra quick dessert, heat caramel sundae sauce from a jar—*

| | |
|---|---|
| 1 2-ounce package dessert topping mix | 1 6-ounce can ($2/3$ cup) evaporated milk |
| 1 large banana, sliced | 3 to 4 drops bitters |
| * * * | 6 slices pound cake |
| $1/2$ 14-ounce package vanilla caramels (about $1^1/4$ cups) | |

Prepare dessert topping mix according to package directions; fold in banana. Chill. In medium saucepan, combine caramels and evaporated milk. Cook and stir over medium heat till caramels are melted; stir in bitters. To serve, top cake slices with banana mixture then with warm caramel sauce. Makes 6 servings.

## PINK FRUIT DESSERT

1 12-ounce package
(1½ cups) frozen
sliced peaches
1 13½-ounce can
(1½ cups) frozen
pineapple chunks

1 10-ounce package
frozen raspberries,
thawed
Dash bitters

Thaw peaches and pineapple together. To serve, add raspberries. Dash in bitters. Spoon into sherbets. Serves 4 to 6.

**Triple Fruit Dessert:** Follow recipe above but thaw fruits with 1 to 2 teaspoons finely chopped candied ginger; omit bitters. Substitute ½ cup frozen blueberries, thawed and drained for raspberries.

## CHOCO-MINT SHORTCAKES

For each serving, top a slice of toasted pound cake with peppermint ice cream, then pour canned chocolate syrup over all.

## FAST DESSERT IDEAS

• **Special Banana Pudding:** Layer banana pudding, banana slices, and crushed chocolate wafers in parfait glasses.
• **Custard Sauce:** Combine instant vanilla pudding mix and 1½ times the amount of milk called for on package. Serve over fresh or canned fruit.
• **Ice Cream Surprise:** Stir chopped semisweet chocolate pieces or nuts into softened vanilla or chocolate ice cream. Refreeze in paper bake cups.
• **Ice Cream Special:** Scoop ice cream ahead; then roll each scoop in crushed cookies or candy and refreeze.
• **Ice Cream Delight:** Sprinkle vanilla or chocolate ice

cream with instant coffee powder; or, sprinkle pepper-mint ice cream with chocolate malt powder.

- **Quick Upside-down Cake:** Use fruit cocktail for bottom layer and a spice cake or gingerbread mix for top.
- **Ginger Bars:** Bake gingerbread mix in a 13x9x2-inch bak-ing pan. While warm, spread with orange glaze made by blending orange juice and confectioners' sugar to a thin, spreading consistency. Cut in bars.
- **Choco-angel Dessert:** Cube angel cake; fold into choco-late pudding.
- **Ice Cream Treats:** Sandwich peppermint ice cream be-tween slices of cake.
- **Applesauce Cream:** Fold applesauce into sweetened whipped cream. Serve plain or as a topper for warm gingerbread squares prepared from a mix.
- **Apricot Mousse:** Stir strained apricots (baby food) into prepared dessert topping. Sweeten to taste with honey. Spoon into dessert dishes; chill in freezer.
- **Pears Deluxe:** Sauce canned pears with mint-flavored chocolate syrup.
- **Fruit Dessert Tray:** Serve chilled fresh fruits with Cam-embert or other dessert cheese or with whipped cream cheese.
- **Melba Sundaes:** Fill chilled canned peach halves with vanilla ice cream. Top with raspberry topping from a jar.
- **Coconut-mallow Topper:** Stir pineapple juice and flaked coconut into marshmallow creme. Spoon over sherbet.
- **Raspberry-Lemon Sundae:** Top scoops of lemon sherbet with frozen red raspberries, partially thawed.

## STRAWBERRY CREAM

| | |
|---|---|
| 1 3-ounce package cream cheese, softened | Dash salt |
| | 1 cup whipping cream |
| 2 tablespoons sugar | Fresh whole strawberries |

In small mixing bowl, combine cheese, sugar, salt, and 2 *tablespoons* whipping cream; beat till fluffy. Whip re-maining cream; fold into cheese mixture. Spoon over berries. Makes 1³/₄ cups sauce.

## DOUBLE BERRY DESSERT

1 quart fresh
   strawberries
1 8-ounce carton
   strawberry-flavored
   yogurt

¼ cup sugar
3 drops red food
   coloring

Wash and hull berries; spoon into sherbet dishes. Combine remaining ingredients. Drizzle over strawberries. Serves 6.

## QUICK FUDGE SUNDAES

1 6-ounce package
   (1 cup) semisweet
   chocolate pieces
1 6-ounce can
   evaporated milk

½ 1-pint jar marshmallow
   creme
   Vanilla ice cream

Mix chocolate and milk in saucepan. Heat slowly, stirring to blend. Beat in marshmallow creme till blended. Serve warm or cool over ice cream. Makes 2 cups.

## BROWNIE MINT TREATS

1 1-pound package
   fudge brownie mix
½ 1-pint jar marshmallow
   creme

2 tablespoons green
   creme de menthe
   Vanilla ice cream

Prepare brownies according to package directions. Cool slightly; cut into large bars or squares. Blend together marshmallow creme and creme de menthe. To serve, top brownies with a scoop of ice cream. Spoon mint sauce atop. Serves 6.

## PEPPERMINT ALASKAS

3 egg whites
½ teaspoon vanilla
¼ teaspoon cream of tartar
⅓ cup sugar
4 sponge cake dessert cups

4 1½-ounce chocolate-coated peppermint ice cream patties
2 tablespoons crushed peppermint candies

OVEN 500°

Beat first 3 ingredients and dash salt to soft peaks. Gradually add sugar, beating till stiff peaks form. Place cake cups on baking sheet. Top each with ice cream patty and completely cover with meringue, spreading thicker over ice cream and thinner around cake. Be careful to seal edges at bottom. Sprinkle meringue with crushed candies. Bake in extremely hot oven (500°) for 2 to 3 minutes or till browned. Serve immediately. Makes 6 servings.

## WINTER FRUIT COMPOTE

3 firm-ripe pears, quartered and cored
3 baking apples, quartered and cored

2 oranges, peeled and chunked
¼ cup raisins
¾ cup brown sugar

OVEN 350°

Place pears, apples, oranges, and raisins in 2-quart casserole. Combine brown sugar and ½ cup water; pour over fruits. Cover and bake at 350° for 1 hour or till tender. Serve warm or cool. Serves 6.

## FROZEN APRICOT TORTE

1 1-pound 14-ounce can apricots, drained and chopped
½ cup sugar
1 tablespoon lemon juice

1 cup whipping cream, whipped
1 cup soft macaroon crumbs

Combine apricots, sugar, and lemon juice; mix well. Fold in cream. Sprinkle ½ *cup* macaroon crumbs in bottom of

1-quart refrigerator tray; spoon in cream mixture. Top with remaining macaroon crumbs. Freeze firm, about 5 hours. Serves 6 to 8.

## PINEAPPLE FREEZE

1 cup dairy sour cream
1 15-ounce can sweetened *condensed* milk
2 cups milk
1 tablespoon lemon juice
1 8³/₄-ounce can (1 cup) crushed pineapple, drained

Combine sour cream and condensed milk. Stir in milk and lemon juice. Freeze in 1-quart refrigerator tray till partially frozen. Stir in drained pineapple; freeze firm. Makes 1 quart.

## CHERRY PARFAITS

1 cup milk
1 cup dairy sour cream
¹/₄ teaspoon almond extract
1 3⁵/₈- or 3³/₄-ounce package *instant* vanilla pudding mix
1 1-pound 5-ounce can cherry pie filling
Toasted slivered almonds

In mixing bowl, combine milk, sour cream, and almond extract. Add pudding mix and beat with rotary beater till creamy and well blended, about 2 minutes. Fill parfait glasses with alternate layers of pudding, cherry pie filling, and almonds; chill. Garnish with additional toasted slivered almonds. Makes 6 parfaits.

## EMERALD SALAD DESSERT

1 8³/₄-ounce can (1 cup) crushed pineapple
1 3-ounce package lime-flavored gelatin
2 cups miniature marshmallows
1 2-ounce package dessert topping mix

Drain pineapple, reserving syrup. Add water to syrup to make 2 cups; bring to boil; add gelatin and stir to dissolve. Add pineapple; pour into 10x6x1¹/₂-inch dish. Cover immediately with a layer of marshmallows. Chill till gelatin is firm.

Just before serving, prepare topping mix using package directions; spread over marshmallows. Makes 8 to 10 servings.

## BERRY CHEESECAKE PIE

1 8-ounce package
cream cheese,
softened
1 cup sifted
confectioners' sugar
1 teaspoon vanilla

1 cup whipping cream,
whipped
1 9-inch *baked* pastry
shell
1 1-pound 5-ounce can
blueberry pie filling

Beat together cream cheese, sugar, and vanilla till smooth. Fold in whipped cream. Spoon into pastry shell. Spoon pie filling atop. Chill till set.

## APRICOT CREAM PIE

Swirl 1/2 cup dairy sour cream in one 1-pound 6-ounce can apricot pie filling till almost blended. Turn into 9-inch graham-cracker crust. Sprinkle 1 cup flaked coconut, toasted, over filling. Chill thoroughly, about 4 hours, before serving.

## CHERRY CREAM PIE

1 8-ounce package
cream cheese,
softened
1 cup dairy sour cream
1/2 cup milk

1 3³/4- or 3⁵/8-ounce
package *instant* vanilla
pudding mix
1 1-pound 5-ounce can
cherry pie filling
1 9-inch *baked* pastry
shell

Beat first 3 ingredients using slow speed on mixer. Fold in pudding mix. Reserve 1/2 cup cherry filling; marble remainder into cheese mixture. Pour into pie shell; top with remaining cherry filling. Chill well.

# GINGERSCOTCH CAKE

OVEN 350°

Prepare 1 package 2-layer-size butterscotch cake mix using package directions. Stir in ½ cup chopped walnuts, 2 tablespoons chopped candied ginger, and one 1-ounce square semisweet chocolate, grated. Bake in 2 greased and lightly floured 8x1½-inch round pans at 350° for 35 minutes. Cool 10 minutes; remove from pan.

# CHERRY SAUCED CAKE

1 package 2-layer-size
   devil's food cake mix
1 1-pound can pitted
   dark sweet cherries
¼ cup sugar
2 tablespoons
   cornstarch

¼ cup Burgundy
* * *
1 8-ounce package
   cream cheese,
   softened
¼ cup sugar
2 tablespoons milk
¼ teaspoon vanilla

Prepare cake mix according to package directions. Bake in a 13x9x2-inch baking pan using package directions. Cool.

Drain cherries, reserving syrup. In saucepan, blend ¼ cup sugar and cornstarch; gradually add cherry syrup, mixing well. Cook and stir over medium heat till mixture thickens and bubbles. Remove from heat; stir in wine and cherries.

Beat cream cheese, ¼ cup sugar, milk, and vanilla till fluffy. Cut cake into squares. Top each square with a small mound of cream cheese mixture. Then serve warm cherry sauce over all.

# SPICY PUMPKIN CAKE

1 package 2-layer-size
   spice cake mix
½ teaspoon soda
1 cup milk
1 cup canned pumpkin
½ cup chopped walnuts

½ cup dates, finely cut
* * *
1 cup whipping cream
2 tablespoons honey
¼ teaspoon ground
   cinnamon

Combine cake mix and soda; proceed according to package directions substituting milk for the first addition of liquid and pumpkin for the second addition. Fold in nuts and dates. Bake in 2 greased and lightly floured 9x1½-inch round pans according to package directions. Cool; remove from pans. Cool completely.

Whip cream with honey and cinnamon. Fill and frost top of cake. Chill.

## RHUBARB CAKE

| | |
|---|---|
| 3 tablespoons butter, melted | 1 pound rhubarb, finely diced (about 3 cups) |
| ½ cup sugar Few drops red food coloring | 1 package 1-layer-size white cake mix |

OVEN 375°

Combine butter, sugar, and food coloring. Add rhubarb; toss lightly; spread in 8x8x2-inch pan. Prepare cake mix using package directions; pour over fruit. Bake at 375° about 35 minutes or till done.

Immediately run spatula around edge of pan and invert onto serving plate. Before lifting off pan, let syrup drain onto cake for 3 to 5 minutes. Cut while warm. Pass whipped cream. Serves 6 to 8.

## DATE APPLE TORTE

OVEN 375°

Spread one 1-pound 5-ounce can apple pie filling in 9x9x2-inch baking pan. Sprinkle 1 teaspoon grated orange peel over; pour 2 tablespoons orange juice over all. Prepare date filling from one 14-ounce package date bar mix according to package directions. Stir in ½ cup chopped walnuts. Add crumbly mixture from mix and 1 egg; blend. Spread over apples. Bake at 375° for 35 to 40 minutes. Serve with cream or ice cream. Serves 6.

## CRUNCHY PEACH COBBLER

6 fresh peaches, peeled and sliced (4 cups)
1 cup sugar
2 tablespoons lemon juice

1 14-ounce package oatmeal muffin mix
1/4 teaspoon ground nutmeg
1/2 cup butter

OVEN 375°

Combine peaches, sugar, and lemon juice. Turn into 8x8x2-inch baking dish. In mixing bowl, combine muffin mix and nutmeg; cut in butter till like coarse crumbs. Spoon over peaches. Bake in moderate oven (375°) for 40 to 45 minutes. Cut in squares. Serve warm or cool, topped with ice cream. Serves 6 to 8.

## BROILED PARTY CAKE

1 package 2-layer-size yellow cake mix
1 12-ounce jar (1 cup) apricot preserves
1 tablespoon lemon juice

1 3 1/2-ounce can (1 1/3 cups) flaked coconut
1 1/2 cups miniature marshmallows

OVEN 350°

Prepare cake mix using package directions. Bake in greased and floured 13x9x2-inch pan at 350° about 35 minutes. Combine preserves and lemon juice; stir in coconut and marshmallows. Spread atop hot cake. Broil 3 to 4 inches from heat about 1 minute or till golden. Cool.

## CARAMEL TOPPED CAKE

OVEN 350°

Prepare 1 package 1-layer-size yellow cake mix using package directions. Pour into greased 9x9x2-inch pan. Bake at 350° for 25 to 30 minutes. Combine 3/4 cup brown sugar, 1/2 cup quick-cooking rolled oats, 1/4 cup butter, and 1/4 cup milk; bring to boil. Pour over cake. Return to oven for 5 minutes or till bubbly.

## PEACH KUCHEN

1 package 2-layer-size white cake mix
1/2 cup flaked coconut, toasted
1/2 cup butter or margarine

1 1-pound 13-ounce can sliced peaches, drained (3 cups)
2 tablespoons sugar
1/2 teaspoon ground cinnamon
1 cup dairy sour cream
1 slightly beaten egg

OVEN 350°

Combine cake mix and coconut; cut in butter till mixture resembles coarse crumbs. *Lightly* press onto bottom and 1/2 inch up sides of 13x9x2-inch pan. Bake at 350° for 10 to 15 minutes. Arrange peaches over crust. Combine sugar and cinnamon; sprinkle evenly over peaches. Blend sour cream and egg; pour over all. Bake at 350° just till sour cream is set, about 10 minutes. Makes 10 to 12 servings.

## QUICK SANDWICH COOKIES

OVEN 375°

Cut 1 roll refrigerated slice-and-bake sugar cookies into 13 slices of about 3/4-inch thickness. Cut each slice into quarters. Place 2 inches apart on ungreased cookie sheet and bake at 375° for about 9 minutes. Remove from oven.

Top each of *half* the slices with a pecan half (about 1/2 cup total). Top each of the remaining cookies with about 10 semisweet chocolate pieces (about 1/2 cup total). Return to 375° oven for about 1 minute. Remove from oven; spread softened chocolate evenly over the chocolate-topped cookies. Top each with a pecan-topped cookie. Makes 26 sandwich cookies.

## BROWNED BUTTER NUGGETS

1 2 7/8-ounce package whole shelled filberts (about 2 1/2 dozen)
* * *
1/2 cup butter or margarine

1/4 cup sifted confectioners' sugar
1/2 teaspoon vanilla
1 1/4 cups sifted all-purpose flour

OVEN 325°

Toast filberts in 325° oven for 10 minutes. Brown butter in saucepan. Add confectioners' sugar and vanilla. Cool. Blend in flour. Shape a rounded teaspoon of dough around each nut, forming balls. Bake on ungreased cookie sheet at 325° for 20 minutes. Cool slightly on sheet; remove. When cool, sift confectioners' sugar over cookies. Makes about 2½ dozen.

## GLORIFIED GRAHAMS

| | |
|---|---|
| 24 graham-cracker squares | ½ cup brown sugar |
| ½ cup butter or margarine, melted | 1 cup chopped pecans |

OVEN 350°

Line a 15½x10½x1-inch pan with 24 graham-cracker squares. Mix butter and brown sugar; spoon over graham crackers. Sprinkle with nuts. Bake at 350° about 12 minutes. Break into squares. Makes 24.

## RASPBERRY FOLDOVERS

| | |
|---|---|
| 2 sticks pie crust mix | 1 tablespoon milk |
| 1 3-ounce package cream cheese, softened | Raspberry jam |

OVEN 350°

Blend pie crust mix, cream cheese, and milk. Divide dough in half; roll each into a 10-inch square. With pastry wheel, cut each square into sixteen 2½-inch squares; place ½ teaspoon jam in center of each. Pinch only two opposite corners together. Place on greased cookie sheet. Bake at 350° for 10 to 12 minutes. Remove immediately to rack. Sift confectioners' sugar over, if desired. Makes 32.

## LAYER BAR COOKIES

1/2 cup butter or
  margarine
1 cup graham-cracker
  crumbs
1 6-ounce package
  (1 cup) semisweet
  chocolate pieces

1 6-ounce package
  (1 cup) butterscotch
  pieces
1 1/3 cups flaked coconut
1/2 cup chopped walnuts
1 15-ounce can
  sweetened *condensed*
  milk

OVEN 350°

Melt butter in 13x9x2-inch pan. Sprinkle crumbs evenly over butter. Layer with chocolate and butterscotch pieces, coconut, and nuts. Pour milk over all. Bake at 350° for 30 minutes. Cool. Cut in bars.

## GINGER-APPLE BARS

OVEN 375°

Combine one 14-ounce package ginger-bread mix and one 8-ounce can applesauce. Beat 2 minutes at medium speed with electric mixer. Stir in 1/2 cup raisins and one 4-ounce jar (1/2 cup) chopped mixed candied fruits and peels. Spread in greased 15 1/2x10 1/2x1-inch pan. Bake in moderate oven (375°) for 15 minutes.

Prepare one 14-ounce package white creamy-type frosting mix according to package directions, substituting 2 tablespoons lemon juice for *half* the liquid. Spread on cooled cookies. Cut in 1x1 1/2-inch bars. Makes about 8 dozen bars.

## MINT-TOP BROWNIES

1 family-size package
  chocolate brownie mix
1/2 cup chopped walnuts
1 package fluffy white
  frosting mix (for
  2-layer cake)

3 drops red food
  coloring
1/4 cup crushed
  peppermint-stick
  candy

OVEN 350°

Prepare brownie mix following package directions; add nuts. Spread in greased 13x9x2-inch pan. Bake at 350° for 25 minutes. Cool. Prepare frosting mix following package directions; tint pink with food coloring. Spread brownies with frosting. Bake 10 minutes longer. Remove from oven; sprinkle with candy. Cool; cut into 40 bars.

## NO-BAKE ALMOND BALLS

1 6-ounce package (1 cup) semisweet chocolate pieces
1 6-ounce package (1 cup) butterscotch pieces
3/4 cup sifted confectioners' sugar
1/2 cup dairy sour cream
1 teaspoon grated lemon peel
1 3/4 cups vanilla-wafer crumbs
3/4 cup chopped almonds, toasted

Melt chocolate and butterscotch pieces together over hot water; remove from heat. Add sugar, sour cream, peel, and 1/4 teaspoon salt; mix. Blend in crumbs. Chill 20 minutes. Shape into 1-inch balls; roll in chopped nuts. Store in tightly covered container. Makes about 42.

## CARAMEL CANDY

In large saucepan, combine 2 cups sugar, 1/2 cup butter, and one 6-ounce can (2/3 cup) evaporated milk. Bring to rolling boil, stirring frequently. Remove from heat and add one 3 5/8- or 4-ounce package *instant* butterscotch pudding mix and 4 cups quick-cooking rolled oats; mix well. Cook 1 minute more; remove from heat. Cool 15 minutes; drop from teaspoon onto waxed paper-lined tray. Makes about 40. *Note:* Fill saucepan with hot soapy water for easier cleanup.

## EASY MACAROONS

2 8-ounce packages shredded coconut
1 15-ounce can (1 1/3 cups) sweetened *condensed* milk
2 teaspoons vanilla

OVEN 350°

Mix ingredients. Drop from teaspoon onto well-greased cookie sheet. Bake at 350° for 10 to 12 minutes. Cool slightly. Remove to rack. Makes about 4 dozen.

## EASY PEANUT CHEWS

| | |
|---|---|
| 1 stick pie crust mix | 1 slightly beaten egg |
| ¾ cup brown sugar | ½ cup chopped peanuts |
| ½ teaspoon vanilla | |

OVEN 350°

Prepare pie crust mix according to package directions. Blend in brown sugar and vanilla. Add egg and ¼ *cup* chopped peanuts. Spread on well-greased and floured cookie sheet to 13x10-inch rectangle. Top with remaining peanuts.

Bake in moderate oven (350°) for 15 to 17 minutes. *Loosen edges as soon as cookie sheet is removed from oven.* Cool cookies on sheet. Cut cookies in pieces.

## RAISIN OATMEAL COOKIES

| | |
|---|---|
| 1 package 2-layer-size yellow cake mix | ½ teaspoon ground nutmeg |
| 2 cups quick-cooking rolled oats | 1 1-pound 6-ounce can raisin pie filling |
| ½ teaspoon salt | 2 eggs |
| 1 teaspoon ground cinnamon | ¼ cup salad oil |
| | * * * |
| | 1 cup chopped walnuts |

OVEN 350°

Combine all ingredients except nuts in a large bowl. Beat till blended. Stir in the nuts. Drop from a spoon onto a greased cookie sheet, using about 2 tablespoons dough for each. Bake in a moderate oven (350°) for 15 to 17 minutes. Remove from pan. Makes 5 dozen large cookies.

## SCOTCH CRUNCHIES

1 6-ounce package (1 cup) butterscotch pieces

1 6-ounce package (1 cup) semisweet chocolate pieces

1 3-ounce can (2 cups) chow mein noodles

1 cup salted cashews

Melt butterscotch and chocolate pieces together over hot water. Remove from heat. Stir in noodles and cashews. Drop by teaspoon onto waxed paper. Refrigerate till set. Makes about 4 dozen.

## CARAMEL SNAPPERS

144 small pecan halves (about 1 cup)

36 vanilla caramels

½ cup semisweet chocolate pieces, melted

OVEN 325°

Grease cookie sheet. On it arrange pecans, flat side down, in groups of 4. Place 1 caramel on each cluster of pecans. Heat in slow oven (325°) till caramels soften, about 4 to 8 minutes. (Watch carefully; various caramels melt at different rates.)

Remove from the oven; with buttered spatula, flatten caramel over pecans. Cool slightly; remove from pan to waxed paper. Swirl melted chocolate on top. Makes 36 pieces of candy.

## PEANUT CEREAL CANDY

3 cups crisp rice cereal

1 cup salted peanuts

* * *

½ cup sugar

½ cup light corn syrup

¼ cup peanut butter

½ teaspoon vanilla

Mix cereal and peanuts; set aside. Combine sugar and corn syrup. Cook, stirring constantly, till mixture comes to a full rolling boil. Remove from heat.

Stir in peanut butter and vanilla. Immediately pour syrup over cereal mixture, stirring gently to coat. Pat cereal evenly into buttered 8x8x2-inch pan. Cool; cut in 2x1-inch bars. Makes 32 bars.

## EASY CHOCOLATE FUDGE

1/2 cup butter or
   margarine
1 4-ounce package
   *regular* chocolate
   pudding mix
1 3- or 3 1/4-ounce
   package *regular*
   vanilla pudding mix

1/2 cup milk
* * *
1 1-pound package
   sifted confectioners'
   sugar (about 4 3/4 cups)
1/2 teaspoon vanilla
1/2 cup chopped walnuts

In saucepan, melt butter; stir in dry pudding mixes and milk. Bring to boiling; boil for 1 minute, stirring constantly. Remove from heat; beat in sugar. Stir in vanilla and nuts. Pour into buttered 10x6x1 1/2-inch baking dish. Garnish with walnut halves, if desired. Chill before cutting in 1 1/2-inch squares. Makes 24.

## ROCKY ROAD

*Not really a fudge, but the next best thing with pieces of marshmallows and nuts—*

4 4 1/2-ounce milk-
   chocolate bars
3 cups miniature
   marshmallows

3/4 cup coarsely broken
   walnuts

Partially melt chocolate bars over hot water; remove from heat; beat smooth. Stir in marshmallows and nuts. Spread in buttered 8x8x2-inch pan. Chill. Cut when firm.

## PECAN ROLL

1 12-ounce package
   penuche fudge mix
1/2 pound caramels
   (about 28)

1/4 cup milk
1 1/2 cups chopped pecans

Prepare fudge mix according to package directions; cool. Roll into four rolls about 1 inch in diameter. Melt caramels with milk; spread rolls with caramel mixture; roll in pecans. Chill. Cut chilled rolls in 1/2-inch slices. Makes 32.

# ENERGY-SAVING OVEN MEALS

Try an oven meal on a busy day. Just prepare the dishes, slide them into the oven at the appropriate time, and set the oven temperature and timer. (When you use an automatic timer to turn the oven on, omit egg or milk dishes if meal will wait in the oven before baking.) Prepare a molded salad ahead of time (marked with an *), or toss salad greens together at mealtime.

Oven meals save energy by making the most efficient use of oven heat. Position racks before turning on the oven. Warm air is lost when the oven door is opened. If two racks are used, position them to divide the oven in thirds. This allows air to circulate freely for efficient cooking. Do not peek into the oven during cooking just to check on the dinner's progress—this also causes a heat loss. Use the oven window.

When planning menus for oven meals, set oven temperature for the meat dish. Then choose vegetables and a dessert that bake at the same temperature. Accompany with crisp salads or breads. If your oven is too small for some of the following menus, transfer some item to the top of the range.

**OVEN 350°** Salmon Loaf
(pp. 558–559)
Lima-cheese Bake (p. 672)
Carrot Sticks
Lemon Pudding Cake
(p. 395)
Beverage

Stuffed Pepper Cups
(pp. 362–363)
Herb-buttered Bread (p. 75)
*Double Apple Salad (p. 606)
Caramel Topped Cake (p. 85)
Beverage

Beef Mushroom Loaf
(pp. 57–58)
Crisscross Potatoes (p. 71)
*Three-bean Salad (p. 596)
Baked Apples (p. 416)
Beverage

Pork Chops on Rice (p. 59)
Oven-cooked Frozen Broccoli
(p. 659)
Lettuce Wedge—French
Dressing
Chocolate Cake
Beverage

Ham Medley (pp. 370–371)
Oven-cooked Frozen
Green Beans (p. 659)
Tossed Green Salad
Brownie Pudding (p. 395)
Beverage

**OVEN 325°** Roast Leg of Lamb
(p. 432)
Oven-cooked Frozen Peas
(p. 659)
Butter-baked Rice (p. 687)
*Cran-raspberry Ring (p. 605)
Baked Custard (p. 397)
Gingersnaps
Beverage

**OVEN 375°** Special
Hamburger (p. 451)
Baked Tomatoes (p. 691)
Stuffed Baked Potatoes
(p. 685)
*Orange-apricot Freeze
(p. 608)
Apple Betty (p. 419)
Beverage

**OVEN 400°** Orange Chicken
(p. 527)
Potato Salad
Green Beans
Sliced Tomatoes
Peach Cobbler (p. 418)
Beverage

**OVEN 450°** Halibut Royale
(p. 559)
Peas and Onions (p. 681)
Foil-baked Corn (p. 678)
Easy Breadsticks (pp. 73–74)
*Classic Waldorf Salad
(p. 609)
Lemon Sherbet
Sugar Cookies
Beverage

# 3

# APPETIZERS
# AND
# BEVERAGES

# APPETIZERS

## FRUIT CUP COMBINATIONS

• Section 3 oranges; combine with 2 bananas, sliced, and 2 slices canned or fresh pineapple, diced. Sprinkle with lemon juice and sweeten to taste. Chill. If desired, serve in hollowed-out halves of orange shells.

• Combine diced fresh pineapple and halved ripe strawberries. Sift confectioners' sugar over. Chill. Trim with fluff of mint.

• Combine canned fruit cocktail with thin red apple slices, orange sections, and avocado balls. Chill: Or, top fruit cocktail with a scoop of orange or lemon ice.

• Freeze ginger ale to a mush in refrigerator tray. Serve in chilled sherbets; top with chilled drained canned fruit cocktail.

• Cut balls from melon using melon-ball cutter or half-teaspoon measure. Serve very cold, alone or with other fruits.

• Pare ½-inch thick rings of chilled cantaloupe or honeydew melon. Fill centers with watermelon balls or fresh berries. Sprinkle melon with lemon juice.

• Toss melon balls with mixture of sweetened fresh lime juice, finely chopped candied ginger, and a dash of bitters.

• For variety, sweeten fruits with grape juice, grenadine, apricot cordial, orange liqueur or maraschino cherry juice.

## LIME ICEBERGS

| | |
|---|---|
| 2 7-ounce bottles lemon-lime carbonated beverage | 1 egg white |
| | 1 tablespoon sugar |
| | Lime wedges |
| 2 tablespoons lime juice | Mint sprigs |
| 2 to 3 drops green food coloring | |

Mix first 3 ingredients. Freeze just till mushy in 1-quart refrigerator tray. Beat egg white to soft peaks; gradually add sugar, beating to stiff peaks. Fold into lime mixture. Freeze, stirring once before firm. Just before serving, break up with fork till flaky. Pile in sherbets. Top each with lime wedge and mint. Serves 8 to 10.

## GINGER FRUIT COCKTAIL

- 1 fully ripe banana
  Lemon juice
- 1 1-pound can fruit cocktail, drained
- 1 cup fresh strawberries, halved

- 1 cup melon balls
- 1 7-ounce bottle (about 1 cup) ginger ale, chilled
  Bitters (optional)

Peel banana; slice on bias; dip in lemon juice. Combine with remaining fruits. Cover; chill. Just before serving, pour ginger ale over fruit. Dash with bitters. Serves 6.

## OAHU FRAPPE

Bring ½ cup sugar and ¾ cup water to boiling; cook over medium heat 5 minutes. Cool slightly. Add ¾ cup orange juice and one 12-ounce can pineapple juice; freeze hard. To serve, break in small pieces and stir till mushy. Spoon into sherbets. Trim with grated orange peel. Serves 6.

## FROSTED COCKTAIL

- ½ cup sugar
- ⅔ cup lemon juice
- ⅔ cup pineapple juice

- 2 tablespoons lime juice
- 2 unbeaten egg whites
- 4 cups finely crushed ice

Cook sugar and ⅔ cup water 5 minutes; chill. Add remaining ingredients. Pour *half* the mixture into blender container. Blend till light and frothy, 7 or 8 seconds. Repeat. Serve at once in chilled cocktail glasses with short straws. Serves 8 to 10.

## PINEAPPLE-MINT CUP

Drain one 1-pound 14-ounce can (3½ cups) pineapple chunks. Add 1 cup halved and seeded Tokay grapes and ½ cup white after-dinner mints, broken; chill. Spoon into sherbets; pour a little chilled ginger ale over each serving. Serves 8.

## APPETIZER JUICES

• **Two-tone Cocktail:** Fill glasses half full with chilled pineapple juice. Tip glass and *slowly* pour chilled tomato juice down side of glass till full. Serve at once.

• **Tomato Refresher:** Combine $2\frac{1}{2}$ cups tomato juice, 3 tablespoons lemon juice, 1 teaspoon sugar, $\frac{1}{4}$ teaspoon celery salt, and 1 teaspoon Worcestershire sauce; chill. Stir before serving. Float lemon slices atop. Makes five 4-ounce servings.

• **Spiced Juice:** To each cup pineapple-grapefruit juice, add 2 whole cloves and 1 inch stick cinnamon. Simmer 5 minutes.

• **Hot Sherried Consomme:** Heat two $10\frac{1}{2}$-ounce cans condensed consomme, $1\frac{1}{3}$ cups water, and 6 tablespoons dry sherry. Serve warm.

• Combine 2 parts chilled tomato juice and 1 part sauerkraut juice. Serve over ice.

• Combine one 7-ounce bottle lemon-lime carbonated beverage with 1 cup pineapple juice. Dash with bitters.

• Mix equal parts cranberry-juice cocktail and orange juice. Chill.

• Heat canned vegetable-juice cocktail. Stir in 1 teaspoon butter for each cup.

## BROILED GRAPEFRUIT

Cut grapefruit in half crosswise; loosen sections. Cut white membrane out of center of each half. Dot with butter; sprinkle with sugar and dash ground cinnamon. Broil 4 inches from heat 8 to 10 minutes or till tops bubble. Serve hot.

## FRUIT-CRAB COCKTAIL

| | |
|---|---|
| 1 7½-ounce can (1 cup) crab meat, chilled, flaked, and cartilage removed | ½ cup mayonnaise |
| | 2 tablespoons catsup |
| | 1 tablespoon lemon juice |
| 1 1-pound can (2 cups) grapefruit segments, chilled and drained | Dash bottled hot pepper sauce |

Alternate crab meat and grapefruit sections in lettuce-lined glasses. Combine mayonnaise, catsup, lemon juice, and hot pepper sauce; chill. Pour over crab and grapefruit. Makes 8 servings.

## SEAFOOD COCKTAILS

• **Shrimp Cocktail:** Shell freshly cooked shrimp, removing black veins. Chill. Serve in lettuce-lined chilled cocktail cups with Cocktail Sauce.

• **Crab Cocktail:** Flake 1 cup freshly cooked *or* one 7½-ounce can crab meat, removing cartilage. Mix with 1 cup finely chopped celery; chill. Serve in lettuce-lined cocktail cups with Cocktail Sauce.

• **Oyster Cocktail:** Serve shucked oysters, drained and chilled, in lettuce-lined cocktail cups. Spoon on Cocktail Sauce. One pint oysters serves 6.

• **Clams or Oysters on the Half Shell:** Open small cherrystone clams or tiny oysters. With knife, loosen each from shell, leaving in deep half of shell. Serve on bed of crushed ice with Cocktail Sauce.

## COCKTAIL SAUCE

| | |
|---|---|
| ¾ cup chili sauce | 2 teaspoons Worcestershire sauce |
| 2 to 4 tablespoons lemon juice | ½ teaspoon grated onion |
| 1 to 2 tablespoons prepared horseradish | Dash bottled hot pepper sauce |

Combine all ingredients; mix well; add salt to taste. Chill. Serve with Seafood Cocktails. Makes 1¼ cups sauce.

## OYSTERS ROCKEFELLER

24 oysters in shells
 1 tablespoon chopped
   onion
 2 tablespoons snipped
   parsley

 1 tablespoon melted
   butter
 1 cup chopped cooked
   spinach
1/4 cup fine dry bread
   crumbs

OVEN 450°

Open oyster shells. With knife, remove oysters and dry. Wash shells; place each oyster in a deep half shell. Mix onion, parsley, and butter; spread over oysters. Season with salt, pepper, and paprika to taste. Top each with 2 teaspoons spinach and sprinkle with 1/2 teaspoon crumbs. Dot each with 1 teaspoon butter. Heat on bed of rock salt at 450° for 10 minutes. Serves 4.

## CRAB-BACON ROLLS

1/4 cup tomato juice
 1 well beaten egg
 1 7 1/2-ounce can (1 cup)
   crab meat, flaked, and
   cartilage removed
1/2 cup fine dry bread
   crumbs
 1 tablespoon snipped
   parsley

 1 tablespoon lemon
   juice
1/4 teaspoon salt
1/4 teaspoon
   Worcestershire sauce
   Dash pepper
 9 slices bacon,
   cut in half

Mix tomato juice and egg. Add crab, bread crumbs, parsley, lemon juice, salt, Worcestershire, and pepper; mix thoroughly. Roll into 18 fingers, about 2 inches long. Wrap each roll with 1/2 slice bacon; fasten with wooden picks. Broil 5 inches from heat about 10 minutes, turning often to brown evenly. Serve hot. Makes 18 rolls.

## SWEDISH PICKLED SHRIMP

2 to 2¹/₂ pounds fresh
  or frozen shrimp in
  shells
¹/₂ cup celery tops
¹/₄ cup mixed pickling
  spices
1 tablespoon salt
2 cups sliced onion
7 or 8 bay leaves

1¹/₂ cups salad oil
³/₄ cup white vinegar
3 tablespoons capers
  with juice
2¹/₂ teaspoons celery seed
1¹/₂ teaspoons salt
3 drops bottled hot
  pepper sauce

Cover shrimp with boiling water; add celery tops, pickling spices, and 1 tablespoon salt. Cover and simmer 5 minutes. Drain; peel and devein under cold water. Layer shrimp, onion, and bay leaves in shallow baking dish. Combine remaining ingredients. Pour over shrimp. Cover; chill at least 24 hours, spooning marinade over shrimp occasionally. Serves 6.

## APPETIZER KABOBS

String small pieces of favorite appetizer meats, seafood, fruits, or vegetables on bamboo skewers. Broil or grill if desired.

## CAVIAR CANAPES

Serve chilled caviar—black or red—in its own container in a bed of crushed ice. Offer Melba toast, a dash of lemon or lime juice, and a selection of chopped hard-cooked egg yolk and egg white, minced onion, or snipped chives. For variety:
• Stuff mushroom crowns with caviar.
• Scoop a tiny hollow in the top of deviled eggs; fill with red or black caviar.
• Combine cream cheese with red caviar and stuff into celery or artichoke hearts.
• Top halved hard-cooked eggs with a spot of caviar and a little minced onion.

## LOBSTER CANAPES

OVEN 225°

Cut 2½ dozen 2-inch bread rounds from thinly sliced bread. Brush lightly with salad oil. Heat in extremely slow oven (225°) for 1¼ to 1½ hours or till crisp.

Shred one 5-ounce can (1 cup) lobster. Combine with ½ cup canned condensed cream of mushroom soup, 2 tablespoons dry white wine, 1 tablespoon chopped canned pimiento, ¼ teaspoon salt, and few drops bottled hot pepper sauce. Spread mixture on the toasted bread rounds. Sprinkle with ¼ cup buttered fine dry bread crumbs. Broil 2 to 3 minutes.

## TERIYAKI MINIATURES

*Let guests do the cooking—*

| | |
|---|---|
| 1 tablespoon soy sauce | Dash ground ginger |
| 1 tablespoon water | ½ pound lean ground |
| 2 teaspoons sugar | beef |
| ¼ teaspoon instant | ½ cup fine soft bread |
| minced onion | crumbs |
| Dash garlic salt | |

Combine soy sauce, water, sugar, onion, garlic salt, and ginger; let stand 10 minutes. Mix ground beef and bread crumbs; stir in soy mixture: Shape into ¾-inch meatballs. Refrigerate till serving time. Spear on bamboo skewers; cook in deep hot fat (375°) in a metal fondue pot about 1½ minutes. Offer heated catsup and mustard for dunking. Makes 2½ dozen.

## SWEET-SOUR SURPRISES

| | |
|---|---|
| 2 tablespoons cornstarch | 1 tablespoon butter |
| 2 tablespoons sugar | or margarine |
| 1 chicken bouillon cube | * * * |
| ½ cup water | ½ pound tiny meatballs, |
| ⅓ cup vinegar | cooked |
| 1 cup pineapple juice | ½ pound shrimp, cooked |
| 2 tablespoons soy sauce | ½ pound chicken livers, |
| | cooked |

Combine cornstarch, sugar, chicken bouillon cube, water, vinegar, pineapple juice, soy sauce, and butter. Cook and stir till mixture boils; cover and simmer 5 minutes. Group cooked meatballs, shrimp, and chicken livers in sauce. Heat through; serve hot. Makes 1½ cups sauce.

## PICKLED MUSHROOMS

In a small saucepan, combine ⅓ cup red wine vinegar, ⅓ cup salad oil, 1 small onion, thinly sliced and separated in rings, 1 teaspoon salt, 2 teaspoons dried parsley flakes, 1 teaspoon prepared mustard, and 1 tablespoon brown sugar. Bring to boil. Add two 6-ounce cans mushroom crowns, drained; simmer 5 to 6 minutes. Chill in a covered bowl several hours, stirring occasionally. Drain. Makes 2 cups.

## MARINATED ARTICHOKES

2 tablespoons lemon
  juice
2 tablespoons salad oil
  Dash garlic salt
1 tablespoon sugar
¼ teaspoon dried
  oregano, crushed

¼ teaspoon dried
  tarragon, crushed
1 15-ounce can (2 cups)
  artichoke hearts,
  drained

Combine all ingredients and 2 tablespoons water in a bowl. Cover; chill several hours or overnight. Drain and sprinkle with paprika; serve with picks. Makes 2 cups.

## CHICKEN PUFFS

2 tablespoons butter
¼ cup all-purpose flour
1 egg
¼ cup shredded process
  Swiss cheese
2 cups finely chopped
  cooked or canned
  chicken

¼ cup finely chopped
  celery
2 tablespoons chopped
  pimiento
2 tablespoons dry white
  wine
¼ cup mayonnaise

OVEN 400°

Melt butter in ¼ cup *boiling* water. Add flour and dash salt; stir vigorously. Cook and stir till mixture forms a ball that doesn't separate. Remove from heat and cool slightly. Add egg and beat vigorously till smooth. Stir in cheese. Drop dough onto greased baking sheet, using 1 level teaspoon dough for each puff. Bake at 400° about 20 minutes. Remove puffs from oven; cool and split. Combine remaining ingredients, ½ teaspoon salt, and dash pepper; fill each puff with 2 teaspoons.

## LUAU BITES

Cut 10 canned water chestnuts in half; quarter 5 chicken livers. Wrap a piece of each in half slice bacon; fasten with wooden pick. Chill in mixture of ¼ cup soy sauce and 2 tablespoons brown sugar about ½ hour; spoon marinade over occasionally. Drain. Broil 3 inches from heat till bacon is crisp, turning once. Makes 20.

## COCKTAIL WIENERS

Mix one 6-ounce jar (¾ cup) prepared mustard and one 10-ounce jar (1 cup) currant jelly in chafing dish or saucepan over low heat. Slice 1 pound (8 to 10) frankfurters diagonally in bite-size pieces. Add to sauce and heat through. Serve hot.

## SWISS AND FRANK SPIRALS

| | |
|---|---|
| 2 5½-ounce packages cocktail wieners (32 wieners) | 1 8-ounce package refrigerated biscuits (10 biscuits) |
| 32 2-inch strips process Swiss cheese | 2 tablespoons butter or margarine, melted |
| | 2 tablespoons sesame seed |

OVEN 400°

Cut a lengthwise slit in each wiener; insert strip of cheese in each. Quarter 8 biscuits. (Bake remaining with appetizers.) Shape quarters in 4-inch strips. Wind, spiral fashion, around each wiener. Place on baking sheet; brush with butter and sprinkle with sesame. Bake at 400° for 10 minutes, or till browned. Serve warm. Makes 32.

## HOT STEAK CANAPES

Have beef strip sirloin steak or whole tenderloin sliced 1½ to 2 inches thick. Broil 2 to 4 inches from heat to desired doneness. Season. Slice thin and serve hot on thin slices of salty rye bread.

## MARINATED BEEF STRIPS

*Good instead of herring on a relish tray—*

| | |
|---|---|
| 1 pound cooked roast beef | ¾ teaspoon salt<br>Dash pepper |
| 1 small onion, thinly sliced | 1½ tablespoons lemon juice |
| | 1 cup dairy sour cream |

Cut meat in thin strips. Separate onion in rings. Combine beef, onion, salt, and pepper. Sprinkle with lemon juice. Stir in sour cream. Chill. Serve in lettuce-lined dishes. Makes 6 servings.

## HAM AND RYE ROUNDS

OVEN 350°

Score one 3-pound canned ham in 1-inch diamonds. Combine ½ cup brown sugar, ¼ cup dark corn syrup, and 1 tablespoon fruit juice *or* syrup from canned fruit; heat till sugar is dissolved. Bake ham at 350° for 45 minutes glazing 3 or 4 times with brown sugar mixture. Whip ½ cup butter with 2 tablespoons prepared mustard till fluffy. Spread on slices of party rye bread; serve with thin slices of ham.

# LEEK LORRAINE

1 9-inch unbaked pastry shell

1 1³/₄-ounce envelope leek soup mix

1¹/₂ cups milk

¹/₂ cup light cream

3 slightly beaten eggs

6 ounces Swiss cheese, shredded (1¹/₂ cups)

1 teaspoon dry mustard Dash pepper

1 4¹/₂-ounce can deviled ham

2 tablespoons fine dry bread crumbs

OVEN 450°

Bake pastry shell (crimp edges high) at 450° for 7 minutes, or till lightly browned. Remove from oven; reduce oven to 325°.

In a saucepan, combine soup mix and milk. Cook and stir till mixture boils; cool slightly. Stir in cream. Combine eggs, cheese, mustard, and pepper. Slowly stir in soup mixture. Mix deviled ham and bread crumbs. Spread on bottom and sides of pie shell. Pour soup-egg mixture over. Bake at 325° for 45 to 50 minutes or till knife inserted in center comes out clean. Let stand about 10 minutes. Cut tiny wedges and serve while warm.

# BLUE CHEESE BITES

OVEN 400°

Cut one 8-ounce package refrigerated biscuits in quarters. Arrange in two 8-inch round baking dishes. Melt together ¹/₄ cup butter and 3 tablespoons crumbled blue cheese. Pour mixture over biscuit pieces, coating well. Bake at 400° for 12 to 15 minutes, or till golden. Serve hot. Makes 40.

# CHEESE STUFFED APPLES

Beat one 3-ounce package softened cream cheese, 1¹/₃ ounces Camembert cheese, and 1 tablespoon dry white wine with electric or rotary beater till smooth. Core 4 medium apples; scoop out insides leaving shells about ¹/₂ inch thick. Fill with cheese mixture; chill 2 to 3 hours. Cut in wedges.

## STUFFED MUSHROOMS

OVEN 425°

Drain two 6-ounce cans broiled mushroom crowns. Hollow out and chop enough of the pieces to make 3 tablespoons; cook pieces with 1 tablespoon finely chopped onion in 1 teaspoon salad oil. Stir in ¼ cup finely chopped salami, ¼ cup smoked process cheese spread, and 1 tablespoon catsup. Stuff into mushroom crowns; sprinkle with fine soft bread crumbs. Bake at 425° for 6 to 8 minutes.

## PIZZA SNACKS

½ pound Italian sausage
1 teaspoon dried oregano, crushed
1 clove garlic, minced
1 8-ounce package refrigerated biscuits (10 biscuits)

Tomato paste
4 ounces sharp process American cheese, shredded (1 cup)
¼ cup grated Parmesan cheese

OVEN 425°

Brown sausage; drain. Add oregano and garlic. On greased baking sheet, flatten biscuits to 4-inch circles with floured custard cup; leave rim. Fill with tomato paste and sausage. Sprinkle with cheeses. Bake at 425° about 10 minutes.

## CHEESE PUFFS

OVEN 450°

Toast twelve 2-inch bread rounds on one side in broiler. Mix ¼ cup mayonnaise, 1 envelope onion dip mix, and 2 tablespoons grated Parmesan cheese. Fold in 1 stiffly beaten egg white. Spoon onto untoasted side of bread rounds. Bake at 450° about 10 minutes or till golden. Serve hot.

## STUFFED EDAM

Bring 1 round Edam or Gouda cheese to room temperature. Cut a 5- or 6-inch star pattern from heavy paper; pin to top of cheese, anchoring points. Cut around star

pattern with a sharp knife. Remove star; carefully remove
cheese from shell. Whip cheese with electric beater adding enough cream to make spreading consistency. Mound
whipped mixture high in red cheese shell. Chill till serving time. Remove from refrigerator about 1 hour before
serving. Serve with assorted crackers and wedges of apple.

## SNAPPY CHEESE STICKS

1 stick pie crust mix
1/2 cup shredded sharp
   natural Cheddar
   cheese

1/8 teaspoon dry
   mustard
1 teaspoon paprika

OVEN 425°

Prepare pie crust mix according to package directions,
thoroughly mixing in shredded cheese, mustard, and paprika till mixture forms a ball. Roll dough on lightly floured
surface to 12x8-inch rectangle. With pastry wheel or knife,
cut into sticks 1/2 inch wide and 4 inches long. Place on
ungreased baking sheet. Bake in a hot oven (425°) for 10
to 12 minutes or till golden brown. Makes 4 dozen sticks.

## SEEDED CRACKERS

OVEN 350°

Select saltines, rich round crackers, rye wafers, or other
crackers. Brush with melted butter or margarine. Sprinkle
with onion or garlic powder, caraway seed, celery seed,
dillweed, poppy seed, or sesame seed. Heat on baking
sheet at 350° about 5 minutes or till crisp and hot.

## PARMESAN RICE SQUARES

OVEN 300°

In a shallow pan, toss 2 cups bite-size crisp rice squares
in 3 tablespoons melted butter or margarine till coated.
Sprinkle with 1/4 cup grated Parmesan cheese. Toast in
slow oven (300°) about 15 minutes, stirring occasionally.
Cool.

## CURRIED WHEAT SNACKS

6 tablespoons butter
1/2 to 1 teaspoon curry powder
1/4 teaspoon onion salt
1/8 teaspoon ground ginger
3 cups spoon-size shredded wheat biscuits

Melt butter in large skillet. Blend in seasonings. Add shredded wheat and toss to coat with butter. Heat 5 minutes over low heat, stirring frequently. Drain on paper towels. Serve warm. (Or, reheat in oven just before serving.) Makes 3 cups.

## WALNUT SNACK

OVEN 350°

Spread 1 cup walnut halves in shallow pan. Dot with 2 teaspoons butter or margarine. Heat in 350° oven about 15 minutes, stirring occasionally. Remove from oven; sprinkle with 1/2 to 1 teaspoon onion salt. Cool on paper towels.

## DEVILED ALMONDS

In heavy skillet, combine 1 1/2 cups blanched whole almonds, 1/4 cup butter, and 1/4 cup salad oil. Cook and stir over medium heat till golden. Remove almonds and drain on paper towels. Combine 1 tablespoon celery salt, 1/2 teaspoon salt, 1/2 teaspoon chili powder, and 1/8 teaspoon cayenne. Sprinkle over hot almonds; stir to coat. Makes 1 1/2 cups.

## DRIED BEEF LOG

1 8-ounce package cream cheese, softened
1/4 cup grated Parmesan cheese
1 tablespoon prepared horseradish
1/3 cup chopped pimiento-stuffed green olives
2 1/2 ounces dried beef, finely snipped

Blend cream cheese, Parmesan, and horseradish. Stir in olives. On waxed paper, shape mixture in two 6-inch rolls. Wrap and chill several hours or overnight. Roll in snipped beef. Serve with crackers.

## SCRAMBLE

2 pounds mixed salted nuts

1 11-ounce package spoon-size shredded wheat biscuits

1 10$\frac{1}{2}$-ounce package doughnut-shaped oat cereal

1 6-ounce package bite-size crisp rice squares

1 7-ounce package small pretzel twists

1 5$\frac{3}{4}$-ounce can slim pretzel sticks

1 4$\frac{1}{2}$-ounce can pretzel bits

2 cups salad oil

2 tablespoons Worcestershire sauce

1 tablespoon garlic salt

1 tablespoon seasoned salt

OVEN 250°

Mix all ingredients in very large baking pans. Bake at 250° for 2 hours, stirring every 15 minutes. Makes about 9 quarts.

## APPETIZER HAM BALL

Blend two 4$\frac{1}{2}$-ounce cans deviled ham, 3 tablespoons chopped pimiento-stuffed green olives, 1 tablespoon prepared mustard, and bottled hot pepper sauce to taste. Form in ball on serving dish; chill. Combine one 3-ounce package softened cream cheese and 2 teaspoons milk; frost ham ball. Chill; remove from refrigerator 15 minutes before serving. Trim with parsley.

## BRAUNSCHWEIGER GLACE

1 envelope unflavored gelatin

1 10$\frac{1}{2}$-ounce can condensed consomme

$\frac{1}{2}$ pound (1 cup) Braunschweiger

3 tablespoons mayonnaise

1 tablespoon vinegar

1 tablespoon minced onion

Soften gelatin in ½ cup cold water and consomme. Heat to boiling, stirring to dissolve gelatin. Pour into 2-cup mold; chill till firm. Blend remaining ingredients. Spoon out center of firm consomme, leaving ½ inch shell. Fill with meat mixture. Heat spooned-out consomme till melted; pour over meat. Chill firm. Unmold.

## CHICKEN LIVER PATE

1 pound fresh or frozen chicken livers, thawed
Butter or margarine
3 tablespoons mayonnaise
2 tablespoons lemon juice
2 tablespoons butter, softened

1 tablespoon finely chopped onion
8 to 10 drops bottled hot pepper sauce
½ teaspoon salt
½ teaspoon dry mustard
Dash pepper

Cook livers, covered, in small amount of butter, stirring occasionally, till no longer pink. Put livers through a meat grinder; blend with remaining ingredients. Place mixture in a 2-cup mold. Chill several hours; carefully unmold. Garnish with chopped hard-cooked egg, snipped chives, or snipped parsley. Serve with crackers.

## SALMON PARTY LOG

1 1-pound can (2 cups) salmon
1 8-ounce package cream cheese, softened
1 tablespoon lemon juice
2 teaspoons grated onion

1 teaspoon prepared horseradish
¼ teaspoon salt
¼ teaspoon liquid smoke
½ cup chopped pecans
3 tablespoons snipped parsley

Drain and flake salmon, removing skin and bones. Combine salmon with next 6 ingredients; mix thoroughly. Chill several hours. Combine pecans and parsley. Shape salmon mixture in 8x2-inch log; roll in nut mixture; chill well. Pass crackers.

## OLIVE-CHEESE BALL

Blend one 8-ounce package cream cheese, softened, 8 ounces blue cheese, and ¼ cup butter. Stir in ⅔ cup well-drained chopped ripe olives and 1 tablespoon snipped chives. Chill slightly; form in ball. Chill well. Press ⅓ cup chopped walnuts over outside of ball. Serve surrounded with assorted crackers. Makes 3 cups.

## HOT MEXICAN BEAN DIP

1 1-pound 12-ounce can (3¼ cups) pork and beans in tomato sauce, sieved
½ cup shredded sharp process American cheese
1 teaspoon garlic salt
1 teaspoon chili powder
½ teaspoon salt
Dash cayenne pepper
2 teaspoons vinegar
2 teaspoons Worcestershire sauce
½ teaspoon liquid smoke
4 slices bacon, crisp-cooked, drained, and crumbled

Combine all ingredients except bacon; heat through. Top with bacon. Serve with corn chips or potato chips. Makes 3 cups.

## HOT CHEESE AND CRAB DIP

1 10-ounce stick sharp natural Cheddar cheese
1 8-ounce package sliced sharp process American cheese
⅓ cup milk
½ cup dry white wine
1 7½-ounce can crab meat, flaked and cartilage removed

Cut cheeses in small pieces; combine in a saucepan with milk. Stir over low heat till cheeses melt. Stir in wine and crab; heat through. Serve in chafing dish with shredded wheat wafers. Makes 3 cups.

## CLAM CHEESE DIP

1 8-ounce package
  cream cheese, softened
1/2 cup crumbled blue
  cheese
1 tablespoon snipped
  green onion

1/4 teaspoon salt
  Dash bottled hot
  pepper sauce
1 7 1/2-ounce can minced
  clams

Mix first 5 ingredients, beat smooth. Drain clams; add with enough milk to make spreading consistency. Chill; remove from refrigerator 15 minutes before serving. Makes 1 2/3 cups.

## GINGER DIP

1/2 cup mayonnaise
1/2 cup dairy sour cream
1 tablespoon finely
  chopped onion
2 tablespoons snipped
  parsley

2 tablespoons finely
  chopped canned water
  chestnuts
1 tablespoon finely
  chopped candied
  ginger
1 clove garlic, minced
1 1/2 teaspoons soy sauce

Combine mayonnaise and sour cream. Stir in remaining ingredients; chill. Offer sesame crackers or chips. Makes 1 1/4 cups.

## DILL DIP

1 3-ounce package
  cream cheese, softened
1 tablespoon finely
  chopped pimiento-
  stuffed green olives
1 teaspoon grated onion

1/4 teaspoon dried
  dillweed
  Dash salt
1 to 2 tablespoons light
  cream

Combine first 5 ingredients; stir in cream to make mixture of dipping consistency. Chill. Makes about 2/3 cup dip.

## CREAMY ONION DIP

Blend 1¹/₂ cups dairy sour cream and 2 tablespoons packaged *dry* onion soup mix. Stir in ¹/₂ cup crumbled blue cheese and ¹/₃ cup chopped walnuts. Makes 2 cups.

## QUICK COTTAGE DIP

1¹/₂ teaspoons instant minced onion
¹/₂ teaspoon seasoned salt
1 12-ounce carton cream-style cottage cheese

1 tablespoon finely chopped canned pimiento *or* snipped parsley

Combine onion, salt, and cheese. Beat well with electric mixer. Chill several hours. Stir in pimiento or parsley. Serve with celery and carrot strips. Makes 1¹/₂ cups.

## GUACAMOLE

Mash 2 pitted and peeled avocados with fork. Stir in 1 tablespoon grated onion, 1 tablespoon lemon juice, 1 teaspoon salt, and ¹/₄ teaspoon chili powder. Spread ¹/₃ cup mayonnaise over mixture, sealing to edges of bowl; chill. At serving time, blend mayonnaise into mixture. Serve with corn chips and crackers. Makes 1¹/₂ cups.

## TROPICAL FRUIT FLUFF

In small mixer bowl, combine 1 cup dairy sour cream, ¹/₄ cup flaked coconut, 2 tablespoons chopped California walnuts, and 2 tablespoons apricot preserves (cut up any large pieces of apricot); mix well. Stir in enough milk to make mixture dipping consistency; chill. Serve with chilled fruit dippers: grapes, melon, or pineapple.

## HERB CURRY DIP

1 cup mayonnaise or
  salad dressing
½ cup dairy sour cream
1 teaspoon fines herbs,
  crushed
¼ teaspoon salt
⅛ teaspoon curry powder
1 tablespoon snipped
  parsley

1 tablespoon grated
  onion
1½ teaspoons lemon
  juice
½ teaspoon
  Worcestershire sauce
2 teaspoons capers,
  drained

Combine all ingredients in small bowl; mix well. Chill.
Makes 1½ cups.

## ANCHOVY DIP

1 8-ounce package
  cream cheese,
  softened
1 tablespoon anchovy
  paste
1 tablespoon snipped
  green onion tops

2 tablespoons chopped
  pimiento-stuffed
  green olives
1 teaspoon lemon juice
¼ teaspoon
  Worcestershire sauce
1 tablespoon milk

Combine ingredients in small mixer bowl. Beat at medium
speed on electric mixer till light and fluffy. Chill. Makes
2 cups.

# BEVERAGES

## SPARKLE PUNCH

1 ½-ounce envelope
unsweetened lemon-
lime or cherry-flavored
soft drink powder
1 cup sugar

2 cups cold milk
1 quart vanilla ice cream
1 1-point 12-ounce
bottle (3½ cups)
carbonated water

Combine soft drink powder and sugar. Dissolve in milk. Pour into 6 to 8 soda glasses. Add scoops of ice cream. Resting bottle on rim of glass, carefully pour in carbonated water to fill each glass. Stir to muddle slightly. Makes 6 to 8 servings.

## RUBY WINE PUNCH

¾ cup water
¾ cup sugar
6 inches stick cinnamon
1 teaspoon whole cloves
Dash salt

2 cups Burgundy, chilled
1 1-quart bottle
cranberry-apple juice,
chilled

In saucepan, combine water, sugar, cinnamon, cloves, and salt; bring to boil. Reduce heat; simmer 10 minutes. Strain out spices and chill liquid. Combine chilled mixture with wine and cranberry-apple juice. Makes 12 to 14 four-ounce servings.

## APRICOT SWIZZLE

4 teaspoons instant tea
¼ cup sugar
1 12-ounce can (1½
cups) apricot nectar
½ teaspoon bitters

1 6-ounce can (⅔ cup)
frozen lemonade
concentrate, thawed
1 1-pint 12-ounce bottle
(3½ cups) ginger ale,
chilled

Mix tea, sugar, nectar, bitters, and 2 cups cold water; stir till sugar dissolves. Just before serving add concentrate and several ice cubes; stir. Slowly add ginger ale; mix gently. Makes 8 servings.

## RASPBERRY MINT CRUSH

| | |
|---|---|
| ¼ cup sugar | 1 10-ounce package |
| ½ cup lightly packed | frozen red raspberries |
| fresh mint leaves | 1 6-ounce can frozen |
| | lemonade concentrate |

Combine sugar, mint leaves, and 1 cup boiling water; let stand 5 minutes. Add raspberries and concentrate; stir till thawed. Add 2 cups cold water and stir. Serve over ice. Makes 8 servings.

## QUANTITY FRUIT PUNCH

| | |
|---|---|
| 3 quarts pineapple juice | 4 1-pint 12-ounce |
| 1½ cups lemon juice | bottles ginger ale |
| 3 cups orange juice | 2 1-pint 12-ounce |
| ⅓ cup lime juice | bottles carbonated |
| 2½ cups sugar | water |
| 1 cup lightly packed | 1 pint fresh strawberries, |
| fresh mint leaves | quartered |

Combine juices, sugar, and mint; chill. Just before serving, add remaining ingredients; pour over cake of ice in punch bowl. Makes 75 four-ounce servings.

## LEMONADE OR LIMEADE

| | |
|---|---|
| 1 cup sugar | 1 cup lemon or |
| 5 cups cold water | lime juice |

Dissolve sugar in 1 *cup* water and lemon or lime juice. Add remaining cold water. Serve over ice. Makes 6½ cups.

## GOLDEN GLOW PUNCH

1 3-ounce package
orange-flavored
gelatin
1 6-ounce can frozen
pineapple-orange
juice concentrate

4 cups apple juice
1 1-pint 12-ounce bottle
(3½ cups) ginger ale,
chilled

Dissolve gelatin in 1 cup *boiling* water. Stir in pineapple-orange concentrate. Add apple juice and 3 cups cold water. Carefully pour in chilled ginger ale. Makes about 25 four-ounce servings.

## TRADER'S PUNCH

Mix 2 cups orange juice, 2 cups lemon juice, 1 cup grenadine syrup, and ½ cup light corn syrup; chill. Just before serving, carefully add three 1-pint 12-ounce bottles chilled ginger ale. Makes about 4 quarts.

## QUICK PUNCH

Scoop 1 quart sherbet (any fruit flavor) into punch bowl. Carefully add three 1-pint 12-ounce bottles lemon-lime carbonated beverage. Ladle into punch cups. Makes 25 to 30 four-ounce servings.

## RASPBERRY COOLER

1 ½-ounce envelope
unsweetened rasp-
berry-flavored soft
drink powder
¾ cup sugar

½ cup orange juice
¼ cup lemon juice
1 12-ounce can (1½
cups) pineapple juice

Dissolve drink powder and sugar in 4 cups water. Add juices; chill. Makes 1½ quarts.

## CHAMPAGNE PUNCH

Combine two 12-ounce cans pineapple juice; one 6-ounce can frozen orange juice concentrate, thawed; one 6-ounce can frozen lemonade concentrate, thawed; and 4 cups water. Chill thoroughly.

Just before serving, transfer mixture to punch bowl; carefully pour two 4/5-quart bottles chilled champagne down side of bowl. Stir gently. Trim with orange slices. Makes 40 four-ounce servings.

## HOT MULLED CIDER

| | |
|---|---|
| 1/2 cup brown sugar | 1/4 teaspoon salt |
| 1 teaspoon whole allspice | Dash ground nutmeg |
| | 3 inches stick cinnamon |
| 1 teaspoon whole cloves | 2 quarts apple cider |
| | Orange wedges |

Combine sugar, allspice, cloves, salt, nutmeg, cinnamon, and cider in large saucepan. Slowly bring to boiling; cover and simmer 20 minutes. Remove spices. Serve in warmed mugs with a clove-studded orange wedge in each. Serves 8.

## EGGNOG

| | |
|---|---|
| 1/3 cup sugar | 1 teaspoon vanilla |
| 2 egg yolks | Brandy or rum |
| 1/4 teaspoon salt | flavoring to taste |
| 4 cups milk | 1/2 cup whipping cream, |
| 2 egg whites | whipped |
| 3 tablespoons sugar | Ground nutmeg |

Beat 1/3 cup sugar into egg yolks. Add salt; stir in milk. Cook over medium heat, stirring constantly, till mixture coats spoon. Cool. Beat egg whites till foamy. Gradually add 3 tablespoons sugar, beating to soft peaks. Add to custard and mix thoroughly. Add vanilla and flavoring. Chill 3 or 4 hours. Pour into punch bowl or cups. Dot with "islands" of whipped cream; dash with nutmeg. Serves 6 to 8.

## DAIQUIRI PUNCH

2 6-ounce cans frozen
limeade concentrate,
thawed
1 6-ounce can frozen
lemonade concentrate,
thawed

1 6-ounce can frozen
orange juice
concentrate, thawed
1 4/5-quart bottle rum
4 cups carbonated water,
chilled
Ice Ring

Combine concentrates with 8 cups water. Chill. To serve, combine limeade mixture with rum in punch bowl. Carefully pour in carbonated water. Float Ice Ring in punch. Makes 30 five-ounce servings.

*Ice Ring:* Alternate canned pineapple slices, halved, and green maraschino cherries in ring mold. Fill with water; freeze.

## SANGRIA

Cut outer peel from 1 orange into long spiral strip without membrane; place in 2-quart container. Squeeze orange and 1 lemon; add to peel. Slice I unpeeled lemon into thin cartwheels. Add to juice with two 4/5-quart bottles rosé, Burgundy, or other red wine; 1/2 cup sugar; and 3 tablespoons brandy (1 jigger). Stir to dissolve sugar. Chill. Pour into punch bowl or into two pitchers. Add I quart chilled sparkling water. Makes 2 quarts.

## HOT CRANBERRY PUNCH

2 48-ounce bottles
cranberry juice
cocktail (12 cups)
1 cup brown sugar
9 whole cardamom
pods, shelled

4 inches stick cinnamon
1/2 teaspoon ground
allspice
2 cups brandy
1 cup bourbon

In large kettle or Dutch oven mix cranberry juice cocktail and sugar; stir till sugar dissolves. Add spices. Heat to boiling; reduce heat and simmer 15 minutes. Remove from heat; strain through sieve to remove whole spices. Stir in brandy and bourbon. Serve in small mugs. Add a pat of butter, if desired. Makes 20 five-ounce servings.

## COFFEE

- Start with a clean coffee maker. After each use, clean with sudsy hot water and a stiff brush to remove oils that collect on coffee maker. Rinse thoroughly; dry.
- Use fresh, cold water for making coffee.
- Store coffee in an airtight container in a cool place (refrigerator is good).
- Use the right grind of coffee for your coffee maker for best flavor.
- Measure coffee accurately. Allow 2 level measuring tablespoons coffee (or 1 coffee measure) for each ³/₄ measuring cup water. These proportions may vary with individual taste, brand of coffee, and coffee maker. Find the amount that suits you best, then measure each time.
- For best results, use the full capacity of your coffee maker.
- Never boil coffee for best flavor.
- **Percolator Coffee:** Measure cold water into percolator. Measure coffee into basket. Cover; place over heat. Bring to boiling; reduce heat; perk *gently* 6 to 8 minutes. Remove basket; keep coffee hot till ready to serve over *very low heat.*
- **Vacuum Coffee:** Measure cold water into lower bowl; place over heat. Insert filter and correct measure of finely ground coffee in upper bowl. When water boils, insert upper bowl into lower bowl. When water rises to top, stir mixture. Reduce heat. After 2 or 3 minutes, remove from heat. Let coffee return to lower bowl before removing upper bowl.
- **Drip Coffee:** Bring cold water to boiling. Measure coffee into coffee basket; pour boiling water in top water container. Let drip through coffee. Remove basket and water container and stir briskly.
- **Instant Coffee:** For each cup needed, place 1 rounded teaspoon instant coffee powder or crystals and ³/₄ cup

boiling water into coffeepot. Heat over *low* heat 5 minutes. Or, fix coffee right in the cups.
• **Iced Coffee:** Brew coffee using *half* the amount of water as usual. Pour hot into ice-filled tumblers. Or, dissolve 2 rounded teaspoons instant coffee powder in 1/2 glass cold water; add ice.
• **Demitasse:** Make coffee using 3 to 4 tablespoons coffee to 1 cup water. Serve hot in small cups with or without sugar (usually black). Or, dissolve 3 tablespoons instant coffee powder in 2 cups boiling water for six 1/3-cup servings.
• **Cafe au Lait:** Brew coffee regular strength. Heat equal parts of milk and light cream over low heat. Beat with rotary beater till foamy. Transfer to warmed container. Pour hot coffee and hot milk mixture together into serving cups.
• **Swedish Egg Coffee:** In small bowl, combine 1 slightly beaten egg (reserve shell) and 2/3 cup coffee. (If stronger coffee is desired, use 1 cup coffee.) Add 1/2 cup cold water; blend well. Stir in crumbled egg shell. Add to 8 cups boiling water. Heat and stir over high heat till foam disappears, about 4 minutes. Remove from heat; cover; let settle, about 7 to 10 minutes. Serve clear coffee off top, or strain through fine mesh strainer.

## TEA

• **Hot Tea:** You can use black tea, green tea, oolong, and other teas interchangeably, but remember that each will impart its own characteristic flavor.
Place 1 teaspoon loose tea *or* 1 tea bag for each cup desired in teapot heated by rinsing with boiling water. Bring freshly drawn cold water to full rolling boil. Immediately pour over tea. Steep tea 5 minutes. Stir briskly and serve at once.
If weaker tea is desired, dilute by adding a little hot water to each cup. Pass sugar, lemon wedges, and milk or cream.
• **Iced Tea:** Heat 1 quart freshly drawn cold water to full rolling boil; remove from heat. Add 8 to 10 tea bags *or* 3 tablespoons loose tea at once. Let steep, uncovered, 5 minutes. Remove tea bags or strain out loose tea and

add 1 quart fresh cold water. Serve over ice; pass lemon wedges and sugar.

*Note:* Keep at room temperature—refrigeration may cause cloudiness. If tea does cloud, you can restore its amber-clear color by adding a little boiling water.

• **Cold Water Iced Tea:** For 4 servings, place 6 tea bags in 1 quart freshly drawn cold water. Refrigerate overnight. Serve over ice; pass lemon wedges and sugar.

## BREAKFAST COCOA

| | |
|---|---|
| 1/3 cup cocoa (regular-type, dry) | 1/2 cup water |
| | 3 1/2 cups milk |
| 1/3 cup sugar | 1/2 teaspoon vanilla |
| Dash salt | |

In a saucepan, mix cocoa, sugar, and salt; add water. Bring to boiling, stirring constantly. Boil 1 minute. Stir in milk; heat to boiling point (do not boil). Add vanilla; beat with rotary beater just before serving. Float dollops of marshmallow creme atop each serving. Makes 4 cups cocoa.

## HOT CHOCOLATE

| | |
|---|---|
| 2 1-ounce squares unsweetened chocolate | 1/4 cup sugar |
| | Dash salt |
| | 1 cup water |
| | 4 cups milk |

Combine chocolate, sugar, salt, and water in saucepan. Stir over low heat till chocolate melts. Gradually stir in milk; heat slowly just to boiling. Beat with rotary beater. Serve in heated cups. Makes 5 cups.

## CHOCOLATE COFFEE

In saucepan, combine 2 tablespoons instant coffee powder, 1/4 cup sugar, dash salt, two 1-ounce squares unsweetened chocolate, and 1 cup water; stir over low heat till chocolate melts.

Gradually add 3 cups milk, stirring constantly. When piping hot, remove from heat and beat with rotary beater till frothy. Pour into cups and top with dollops of whipped cream. Serves 6.

## MEXICAN CHOCOLATE

Combine 4 cups milk, five 1-ounce squares semisweet chocolate, and three 2-inch cinnamon sticks in saucepan. Cook and stir just till chocolate melts. Remove from heat; remove cinnamon and stir in 1 teaspoon vanilla. Beat with rotary beater till frothy. Serve in warmed mugs with cinnamon stick stirrers. Makes 4 cups.

## CHOCOLATE SYRUP

| | |
|---|---|
| ½ cup sugar | Dash salt |
| ¼ cup cocoa (regular-type, dry) | ½ cup water |
| | 1 teaspoon vanilla |

Mix sugar, cocoa, and salt. Add ½ cup water. Bring to a boil; reduce heat and cook 1 minute. Remove from heat and add vanilla. Cool. Store in refrigerator. Use in Milk Shakes and Sodas below. Or combine 2 tablespoons syrup and 1 cup milk; heat for cocoa.

## MILK SHAKES

Combine 1 cup cold milk and ¼ cup Chocolate Syrup (or other favorite syrup flavors). Add 1 pint vanilla ice cream; mix just to blend. Makes 3⅓ cups.

## MALTED MILK

Add 2 tablespoons malted milk powder to Milk Shakes recipe.

## SODAS

For each serving, pour ¼ cup Chocolate Syrup (or other syrup flavors) and 2 tablespoons milk into a chilled 14- or 16-ounce glass; mix well. Add chilled carbonated water to fill glass ¾ full (about one half of 7-ounce bottle). Stir. Add 1 or 2 scoops vanilla ice cream. Fill glass with carbonated water. Serve with a spoon and straw.

## SPICED TEA

| | |
|---|---|
| 6 cups water | ³/₄ cup orange juice |
| 1 teaspoon whole cloves | 2 tablespoons lemon |
| 1 inch stick cinnamon | juice |
| 2¹/₂ tablespoons black tea | ¹/₂ cup sugar |

\* \* \*

Combine water, cloves, and cinnamon. Heat to boiling. Add tea; cover and steep 5 minutes; strain. Heat orange juice, lemon juice, and sugar to boiling; stir and add to hot tea. Makes 6 to 8 servings.

# WINE GUIDE

Are you confused when it comes to choosing the right type of wine to serve with certain foods? You needn't be because there are no definite rules that must be followed. However, here are some guidelines that will help you enjoy wine to the fullest.

Wines can be divided into four general classes: appetizer, dinner, dessert, and sparkling wines. The name of the class generally indicates the use of each wine.

Appetizer wines, also referred to as aperitifs, are those served before a meal or as a cocktail. Dry wines usually are preferred over the sweeter types. (In reference to wines, dry means "not sweet.")

Dinner wines, also called table wines, include both red and white wines. They usually are served with the main course. Red dinner wines are predominantly dry and rich and sometimes have a tart or astringent characteristic, so they are best with hearty foods. White dinner wines are lighter in flavor and can be very dry and tart or sweet and full-bodied. Serve white wines with delicately flavored foods so that the flavor of the wine does not overpower the entree. Rosé wine is an all-purpose dinner wine, compatible with any food.

Dessert wines are sweeter wines, and they are served as the dessert or as a dessert accompaniment.

Sparkling wines, served either by themselves or as an accompaniment, make any occasion special. They taste equally good before, during, or at the end of a meal.

In cooking, the flavor of wine is meant to be a subtle accent, enhancing the natural food flavors. Feel free to substitute one wine for another in a recipe, but choose a similar wine from the same class. In general, drier wines are used in main dishes, sweeter wines in desserts and sauces.

Store unopened wines away from the sun at a cool, constant temperature (about 60°). Place a corked bottle on its side so that the cork will stay moist.

| WINES | SERVING TEMPERATURE | BEST WITH |
|---|---|---|
| **Appetizer Wines** | | |
| Sherry (dry) Vermouth Flavored Wines | Cool room temperature (60° to 70°) *or* chilled (45° to 55°) | All appetizer foods —canapes, hors d'oeuvres, soups, dips |
| **Red Dinner Wines** | | |
| Burgundy (red) Claret (Bordeaux) Chianti (red) | Cool room temperature (60° to 70°) *except* for Rosé | Hearty foods—all red meats including beef, veal, pork, game; cheese, egg, and pasta dishes; and highly seasoned foods |
| Rosé | Chilled (45° to 50°) | |
| **White Dinner Wines** | | |
| Chablis (White Burgundy) Rhine Sauterne (dry) Chianti (white) | Chilled (45° to 50°) | Light foods— poultry, fish and shellfish, ham, veal |
| **Dessert Wines** | | |
| Port Tokay Muscatel Sauterne (sweet) Sherry (sweet or cream) | Cool room temperature (60° to 70°) | All desserts—fruits, nuts, cakes, dessert cheeses |
| **Sparkling Wines** | | |
| Champagne Sparkling Burgundy Sparkling Rosé Cold Duck | Chilled (40° to 45°) | All foods and occasions |

# 4

pages **129** through **195**

# BREADS

## QUICK BREADS

# YEAST BREADS

## • PERFECT YEAST BREAD TIPS •

Today, breadmaking is easier than ever. A new mixing method lets you mix the active dry yeast with part of the flour, add the warm liquid ingredients, and beat with an electric mixer. However, if you would rather dissolve the yeast, go ahead. You'll have excellent results either way.

For the conventional method of dissolving the yeast, you can use either active dry yeast or compressed yeast. Soften active dry yeast in warm water (110° F) and compressed yeast in lukewarm water (85° F). Both soften in 5 to 10 minutes. If desired, one 0.6 ounce cake of compressed yeast can be substituted for one package active dry yeast.

Sugar provides food for the yeast to grow. It also adds flavor and aids in browning.

Salt is added to the dough for flavor, but it also helps control the growth of the yeast.

Flour forms the basic structure of dough.

• Add all flour to the dough at time of mixing and kneading. Adding flour after the dough rises causes dark streaks and a coarse texture.

• To knead dough, turn out onto a lightly floured surface (picture 1). Curve fingers over dough, pull it toward you, then push down and away with heel of hand. Give dough a quarter turn, fold dough toward you, and push down again. Repeat kneading motions until the dough is smooth, satiny, and elastic. Include the flour used for kneading as part of the measured amount. Add only enough extra flour to make the dough easy to handle. (On humid days, dough will require more flour.)

• Cover dough; let rise in a warm place (80° F) until double. (Place bowl on top rack of cold oven with pan of hot water on lower rack.) During rising, the yeast grows, giving off gas bubbles which cause the dough to rise. A high temperature will kill yeast. A low temperature retards its growth.

- Punch the dough down; pulling edges to the center and turning dough over. Cover; let rest before shaping to make dough easy to handle.
- To shape loaf, roll dough to 12x8-inch rectangle. Starting from narrow edge, roll up tightly. Seal at each turn with fingertips or edge of hand (picture 2). Press down on ends of loaf with sides of hands to make 2 thin sealed strips (picture 3). Fold strips under loaf. (Or, shape dough into a rectangular loaf, pulling ends under until smooth.)
- When dough is ready to bake or shape, fingertips will leave slight indentation (picture 4).

## PERFECT WHITE BREAD

5³/₄ to 6¹/₄ cups all-
    purpose flour
1 package active dry
    yeast

2¹/₄ cups milk
2 tablespoons sugar
1 tablespoon shortening
2 teaspoons salt

OVEN 375°

In large mixing bowl combine 2¹/₂ *cups* of the flour and the yeast. In saucepan heat milk, sugar, shortening, and salt just till warm (115–120°), stirring constantly till shortening almost melts. Add to dry mixture in mixing bowl. Beat at low speed of electric mixer for ¹/₂ minute, scraping sides of bowl constantly. Beat 3 minutes at high speed. By hand, stir in enough of the remaining flour to make a moderately stiff dough. Turn out onto a lightly floured surface and knead till smooth and elastic, 8 to 10 minutes. Shape in a ball.

Place dough in lightly greased bowl, turning once to grease surface. Cover; let rise in warm place till double, about 1¹/₄ hours. Punch dough down; turn out on lightly floured surface. Divide in half.

Shape each in a smooth ball. Cover and let rest 10 minutes. Shape in loaves. Place in two greased 8¹/₂x4¹/₂x 2¹/₂-inch loaf pans. Cover and let rise in warm place till double, 45 to 60 minutes. Bake in moderate oven (375°) about 45 minutes or till done. If tops brown too quickly, cover loosely with foil last 15 minutes. Remove from pans; cool on wire racks. Makes 2 loaves.

## WHOLE WHEAT BREAD

  3 to 3¹/₄ cups
    all-purpose flour
  1 package active dry
    yeast
1³/₄ cups water

¹/₃ cup brown sugar
  3 tablespoons
    shortening
  2 cups whole wheat
    flour

OVEN 375°

In large mixing bowl combine 2 *cups* of the all-purpose flour and the yeast. Heat water, brown sugar, shortening, and 2 teaspoons salt just till warm (115–120°), stirring constantly till shortening almost melts. Add to dry mixture. Beat at low speed of electric mixer for ¹/₂ minute, scraping bowl. Beat 3 minutes at high speed. By hand, stir in whole wheat flour and enough of the remaining all-purpose flour to make a moderately stiff dough. Knead on lightly floured surface till smooth, 8 to 10 minutes. Shape in ball. Place in lightly greased bowl; turn once. Cover; let rise in warm place till double, about 1¹/₂ hours. Punch down; turn out on floured surface.

Divide in half. Cover and let rest 10 minutes. Shape in loaves; place in two greased 8½x4½x2½-inch loaf pans. Cover and let rise till double, about 1¼ hours. Bake in moderate oven (375°) about 45 minutes. If tops brown too quickly, cover loosely with foil last 20 minutes. Makes 2 loaves.

## SUGARPLUM LOAVES

| | |
|---|---|
| 5 to 5¼ cups all-purpose flour | 2 eggs |
| 2 packages active dry yeast | ½ teaspoon vanilla |
| 1⅓ cups milk | 1 cup raisins |
| ½ cup sugar | 1 cup chopped mixed candied fruits and peels |
| ¼ cup shortening | Confectioners' Icing (page 258) |
| 1½ teaspoons salt | |

OVEN 350°

In large mixing bowl combine *2 cups* of the flour and the yeast. Heat milk, sugar, shortening, and salt just till warm (115–120°), stirring constantly till shortening almost melts. Add to dry mixture; add eggs and vanilla. Beat at low speed of electric mixer for ½ minute, scraping bowl. Beat 3 minutes at high speed. By hand, stir in raisins, fruits, and enough remaining flour to make a soft dough. Knead on lightly floured surface till smooth and elastic, 8 to 10 minutes.

Shape in ball. Place in greased bowl; turn once. Cover; let rise in warm place till double, about 1½ hours. Punch down; divide in half. Cover; let rest 10 minutes. Shape into two balls. Place on greased baking sheets; pat tops to flatten slightly. Cover; let rise in warm place till double, about 2 hours. Bake at 350° about 30 minutes. Remove from sheets; cool. Frost with Confectioners' Icing. Decorate with candied cherries, if desired. Makes 2 loaves.

## FRENCH BREAD

7 to 7¹/₄ cups
all-purpose flour
2 packages active dry
yeast
1 tablespoon sugar

1 tablespoon salt
1 tablespoon shortening
Yellow cornmeal
1 egg white

OVEN 375°

In large mixing bowl combine *3 cups* of the flour and the yeast. Heat 2¹/₂ cups water, sugar, salt, and shortening just till warm (115–120°), stirring constantly till shortening almost melts. Add to dry mixture. Beat at low speed of electric mixer for ¹/₂ minute, scraping bowl. Beat 3 minutes at high speed. By hand, stir in enough of the remaining flour to make a soft dough.

Turn out onto lightly floured surface and knead till smooth and elastic, 10 to 12 minutes. Shape into ball. Place in a lightly greased bowl, turning once. Cover; let rise in warm place till double, 1 to 1¹/₂ hours. Punch down; divide in half. Cover; let rest 10 minutes. Roll each half to 15x12-inch rectangle. Starting with long edge, roll up tightly; seal well. Taper ends. Place each loaf diagonally, seam side down, on greased baking sheet sprinkled with cornmeal. Gash tops diagonally every 2¹/₂ inches, ¹/₈ to ¹/₄ inch deep.

Beat egg white just till foamy; add 1 tablespoon water. Brush tops and sides of loaves. Cover; let rise in warm place till double, about 1 hour. Bake in moderate oven (375°) for 20 minutes. Brush again with egg white mixture. Bake about 20 minutes longer. Remove from baking sheets; cool on wire racks. Makes 2 loaves.

## RAISIN LOAVES

OVEN 375°

Use recipe for Perfect White Bread (page 132), increasing sugar to ¹/₃ cup and shortening to ¹/₄ cup. Stir in 2 cups raisins when adding enough remaining flour to make a moderately stiff dough. Continue as directed. Shape dough into 8 small loaves (4¹/₂x2¹/₂x1¹/₂-inch loaf pans) or 2 large loaves. Bake small loaves at 375° for 25 to 30 minutes. Bake large loaves at 375° for 35 to 40 minutes.

While warm, drizzle with Confectioners' Icing (page 258), if desired.

## SOURDOUGH BREAD

*To make Sourdough Starter:* In bowl soften 1 package active dry yeast in ½ cup warm water (110°). Stir in 2 cups warm water, 2 cups all-purpose flour, and 1 tablespoon sugar; beat smooth. Cover with cheesecloth. Let stand at room temperature till bubbly, 5 to 10 days; stir 2 or 3 times a day. (A warmer temperature speeds fermentation.) Store, covered, in refrigerator. To use, bring to room temperature.

| | |
|---|---|
| 1 package active dry yeast | 1 cup Sourdough Starter (room temperature) |
| 5½ to 6 cups all-purpose flour | 2 teaspoons sugar |
| | ½ teaspoon soda |

OVEN 400°

*To make bread:* In large mixing bowl soften yeast in 1½ cups warm water (110°). Blend in 2½ *cups* of the flour, the Starter, sugar, and 2 teaspoons salt. Combine 2½ *cups* of the flour and soda; stir into flour-yeast mixture. Add enough remaining flour to make a stiff dough. Knead on floured surface till smooth and elastic, 5 to 7 minutes. Shape into ball. Place in greased bowl; turn once. Cover; let rise in warm place till double, about 1½ hours. Punch down; divide in half. Cover; let rest 10 minutes. Shape in round loaves. Place on greased baking sheets. With sharp knife, make parallel slashes across tops. Let rise, uncovered, till double, 1 to 1½ hours. Bake at 400° for 35 to 40 minutes. Makes 2 loaves.

*To keep Starter going:* Stir ¾ cup all-purpose flour, ¾ cup water, and 1 teaspoon sugar into remainder of Starter. Let stand at room temperature till bubbly, at least 1 day. Cover and chill for later use. If not used within 10 days, stir in 1 teaspoon sugar. Repeat adding sugar every 10 days.

## CINNAMON SWIRL BREAD

OVEN 375°

Make Perfect White Bread, increasing sugar to $1/3$ cup and shortening to $1/4$ cup. After first rising, roll dough to two 15x7-inch rectangles. Mix $1/2$ cup sugar and 1 tablespoon ground cinnamon; spread *half* over each. Sprinkle $1^1/2$ teaspoons water over each. Roll into loaves. Continue as directed. Bake at 375° for 35 to 40 minutes.

## RYE BREAD

*Shape the dough for this dark bread into oblong loaves or the traditional round loaves—*

| | |
|---|---|
| 3 cups all-purpose flour | 2 cups water |
| 2 packages active dry yeast | $1/2$ cup brown sugar |
| 1 tablespoon caraway seed | 1 tablespoon shortening |
| | 1 teaspoon salt |
| | $2^1/2$ cups rye flour |

OVEN 350°

In large mixing bowl combine $2^1/2$ *cups* of the all-purpose flour, the yeast, and the caraway seed. In saucepan heat together water, brown sugar, shortening, and salt just till warm (115-120°), stirring constantly till shortening almost melts. Add to dry mixture in mixing bowl. Beat at low speed of electric mixer for $1/2$ minute, scraping sides of bowl constantly. Beat 3 minutes at high speed. By hand, stir in the rye flour and enough of the remaining all-purpose flour to make a moderately stiff dough. Turn dough out onto a lightly floured surface and knead until smooth and elastic, 8 to 10 minutes.

Shape into a ball. Place in a lightly greased bowl, turning once to grease the surface. Cover; let rise in warm place till double, about $1^1/2$ hours. Punch down. Turn out onto lightly floured surface. Divide in half. Shape each half into smooth ball. Cover; let rest 10 minutes. Shape into two round loaves and place on two greased baking sheets. (Or, shape into two oblong loaves; place in two greased $8^1/2$x$4^1/2$x$2^1/2$-inch loaf pans.) Cover and let rise in warm place until double, about 40 minutes. Bake in moderate oven (350°) for 40 to 45 minutes or till done. If tops brown too quickly, cover loosely with foil the last 15 minutes. Remove from baking sheets; cool on wire racks. Makes 2 loaves.

## NO-KNEAD OATMEAL BREAD

| | |
|---|---|
| 6¼ cups all-purpose flour | 2 cups water |
| 1 cup quick-cooking rolled oats | ½ cup light molasses |
| | ⅓ cup shortening |
| 2 packages active dry yeast | 1 tablespoon salt |
| | 2 eggs |

OVEN 375°

In large mixing bowl combine 2 *cups* of the flour, the rolled oats, and yeast. In saucepan heat water, molasses, shortening, and salt just till warm (115-120°), stirring constantly till shortening almost melts. Add to dry mixture in mixing bowl; add eggs. Beat at low speed of electric mixer for ½ minute, scraping sides of bowl constantly. Beat 3 minutes at high speed.

By hand, stir in enough remaining flour to make a moderately stiff dough. Beat till smooth, about 10 minutes. Cover and refrigerate dough at least 2 hours or overnight. Turn out on floured surface; shape into 2 loaves. Place in greased 8½x4½x2½-inch loaf pans. Cover; let rise in warm place till double, about 2 hours. Bake in moderate oven (375°) about 40 minutes. If tops brown too quickly, cover loosely with foil last 20 minutes. Makes 2 loaves.

## CARDAMOM BRAID

OVEN 375°

Prepare one 13¾-ounce package hot roll mix according to package directions, adding 2 tablespoons melted butter or margarine, cooled, and ¾ teaspoon ground cardamom *or* 1 teaspoon crushed cardamom seed. Add ½ cup light raisins; mix well. Cover; let rise in warm place till double, about 1 hour. Turn out onto lightly floured surface and knead about 1 minute.

Divide in thirds and shape into balls. Form each ball into a 10-inch rope, tapering ends. Line up ropes, 1 inch apart, on greased baking sheet. Braid loosely, beginning in middle and working toward ends. Pinch ends and tuck under. Cover and let rise in warm place till almost double, about 40 minutes. Brush with milk; sprinkle with sugar. Bake in moderate oven (375°) about 25 minutes. Serve warm. Makes 1 loaf.

## HERB BREAD

3 to 3 1/2 cups all-
   purpose flour
1 package active dry
   yeast
2 teaspoons celery seed
1 teaspoon ground sage

1/2 teaspoon ground
   nutmeg
1 cup milk
2 tablespoons sugar
2 tablespoons shortening
1 egg

OVEN 400°

In mixing bowl combine 1 1/2 cups of the flour, the yeast, celery seed, sage, and nutmeg. Heat milk, sugar, shortening, and 1 1/2 teaspoons salt just till warm (115-120°), stirring constantly till shortening almost melts. Add to dry mixture; add egg. Beat at low speed of electric mixer for 1/2 minute, scraping bowl. Beat 3 minutes at high speed. By hand, stir in enough remaining flour to make a moderately soft dough.

Knead on floured surface till smooth, 5 to 8 minutes. Place in greased bowl; turn once. Cover; let rise in warm place till double, about 1 1/2 hours. Punch down. Cover; let rest 10 minutes. Shape into round loaf. Place in greased 9-inch pie plate. Cover; let rise till double, 45 to 60 minutes. Bake at 400° for 35 minutes. Makes 1.

## CINNAMON CRESCENTS

OVEN 375°

Soften yeast from one 13 3/4-ounce package hot roll mix in 1/2 cup warm water (110°). Stir in 3 eggs; beat well. Add flour mixture from mix and 6 tablespoons softened butter; beat well. Cover; let rise in warm place till double, about 1 hour. Sprinkle 1/2 cup all-purpose flour on board and knead in so that dough is still very soft but not sticky. Divide in half. Cover; let rest 10 minutes. On lightly floured surface roll each half to 12x10-inch rectangle.

Spread *each* with 1 tablespoon softened butter. Mix $1/2$ cup sugar and 1 teaspoon ground cinnamon. Add 1 cup raisins and $1/2$ cup chopped walnuts. Sprinkle *half* over each rectangle. Roll as for jelly roll, starting with long edge; seal. Place, sealed side down, on greased baking sheet, curving ends. Pinch each end to seal. Cover; let rise till almost double, about 30 minutes. Bake at 375° about 25 minutes. Frost, if desired.

# ROLLS AND COFFEE CAKES

- In a mixing bowl stir together a portion of the flour and the undissolved yeast. Add the warm liquid ingredients and begin beating with an electric mixer.
- Most rolls require little or no kneading. To knead, use firm, even strokes.
- The lightest, most tender rolls are made from a dough that is softer than plain bread dough. Roll dough should be as soft as can be handled without sticking to hands or to the working surface.
- Let dough rise in a warm place (80° F). (Place bowl on top rack in cold oven with pan of hot water on lower rack.)
- For crusty rolls, brush tops with milk, water, or egg diluted with milk or water. (You can use egg whites, yolks, or entire egg.) Place 1 to 2 inches apart when baking.
- Tender, more browned crusts result from a swish of melted butter after baking.
- Either serve rolls at once or cool them on wire racks out of drafts.
- To reheat rolls, heat oven to 325°. Place rolls in paper bag; sprinkle bag with water. Warm rolls in oven about 10 minutes.
- To bake fresh rolls daily with little fuss, use Refrigerator Rolls. The dough will keep 3 to 4 days in the refrigerator.

## BASIC ROLL DOUGH

| | |
|---|---|
| 3½ cups all-purpose flour | ¼ cup sugar |
| 1 package active dry yeast | ¼ cup shortening |
| | 1 teaspoon salt |
| 1¼ cups milk | 1 egg |

OVEN 400°

In mixing bowl combine 1½ cups of the flour and the yeast. Heat milk, sugar, shortening, and salt just till warm (115-120°), stirring constantly till shortening almost melts. Add to dry mixture; add egg. Beat at low speed of electric mixer for ½ minute, scraping bowl. Beat 3 minutes at high speed. By hand, stir in remaining flour to make a soft dough. Shape into ball.

Place in lightly greased bowl; turn once to grease surface. Cover; let rise in warm place till double, 1½ to 2 hours. Punch down; turn out on floured surface. Cover; let rest 10 minutes. Shape into desired rolls (see photos). Cover; let rise in warm place till double, 30 to 45 minutes. Bake on greased baking sheets or in greased muffin pans in hot oven (400°) for 10 to 12 minutes. Makes 2 to 3 dozen rolls.

## REFRIGERATOR ROLLS

Prepare Basic Roll Dough. After adding remainder of flour, place dough in lightly greased bowl, turning once to grease surface. Cover and refrigerate at least 2 hours or till needed. (Use within 3 to 4 days.) About 1½ to 2 hours before serving, shape into desired rolls (see photos). Cover; let rise in warm place till double, 1 to 1¼ hours. Follow baking times above.

## POTATO ROLLS

| | |
|---|---|
| 1 small potato, pared and cubed | * * * |
| 1 cup water | 1¼ cups milk |
| 4 to 4½ cups all-purpose flour | ¼ cup sugar |
| | ¼ cup shortening |
| 1 package active dry yeast | 1½ teaspoons salt |
| | 1 egg |

OVEN 400°

In saucepan cook potato, covered, in the water till tender, 10 to 15 minutes. Drain. Mash potato and measure ½ cup mashed potato; set aside. In large mixing bowl combine 2 cups of the flour and yeast. In saucepan heat together milk, sugar, shortening, and salt just till warm (115-120°), stirring constantly till shortening almost melts. Add to dry mixture in mixing bowl; add egg and mashed potato. Beat at low speed of electric mixer for ¹/₂ minute, scraping sides of bowl constantly. Beat 3 minutes at high speed. By hand, stir in enough of the remaining flour to make a soft dough. Turn out onto lightly floured surface and knead till smooth and elastic, 6 to 8 minutes. Shape in a ball. Place in lightly greased bowl, turning once to grease surface. Cover and let rise in warm place till double, about 1 hour.

Punch down; turn out on lightly floured surface. Cover; let rest 10 minutes. Shape into rolls (see photos). Place on greased baking sheets. Cover; let rise in warm place till almost double, about 1 hour. Bake in hot oven (400°) for 10 to 12 minutes. Makes 2 dozen rolls.

**Corkscrew:** Wrap a rope of dough, 8 inches long and ¹/₄ inch thick, around greased wooden clothespin; seal ends.

**Parker House:** Roll dough ¹/₄ inch thick. Cut with floured 2¹/₂-inch round cutter. Brush with melted butter. Make an off-center crease in each round. Fold in half so top overlaps slightly. Place 2 to 3 inches apart.

**Jiffy Cloverleaf:** Using scissors dipped in flour, snip golf-ball-size pieces of dough across top, making 2 cuts at right angles.

**Cloverleaf:** Place three 1-inch balls of dough in each greased muffin pan (fill pan half full). Brush balls with melted butter or margarine.

**Rolling dough for sweet rolls:** Roll a portion of dough into a rectangle, following size given in recipe. Spread filling evenly over dough. Roll up, starting from long side as for jelly roll, and seal seam securely.

**To cut rolls:** Place piece of thread under rolled dough and pull up around sides. Crisscross thread at top, then pull quickly.

## RAISIN-CINNAMON ROLLS

Basic Roll Dough
(½ recipe)
¼ cup sugar
1 teaspoon ground
cinnamon

2 tablespoons butter,
melted
¼ cup raisins

OVEN 375°

On lightly floured surface roll ½ recipe Basic Roll Dough to 16x8-inch rectangle. Mix sugar and cinnamon; add butter. Spread over dough. Sprinkle with raisins. Roll as for jelly roll, starting with long edge; seal. Cut in 1-inch

**Butter Fans:** Roll dough to 27x14-inch rectangle. Brush with melted butter. Cut crosswise in eighteen 1½-inch strips. Pile 6 strips on top of one another; make ends even. Cut each stack into 9 portions. Place, cut side down, in greased muffin pans.

**Bowknots:** Roll dough to 18x10-inch rectangle. Cut strips 10 inches long and ¾ inch wide. Roll each strip lightly under fingers into a pencil-like strand; loosely tie in knot. Place on greased baking sheet.

**Rosettes:** Tuck under loose ends of knot.

**Butterhorns:** Roll dough to a 12-inch circle. Brush with melted butter. Cut into 12 wedges. To shape rolls, begin at wide end of wedge and roll toward point. Place, point down, on greased baking sheet.

**Crescents:** Curve the ends of rolls.

slices. Place, cut side down, in greased 9x9x2-inch baking pan. Cover; let rise in warm place till double, 30 to 45 minutes. Bake in moderate oven (375°) for 20 minutes. Remove from pan. Frost with Confectioners' Icing (page 258), is desired. Makes 16 rolls.

## CARAMEL ROLLS

OVEN 375°

Roll ½ recipe Basic Roll Dough on lightly floured surface to 12x8-inch rectangle. Brush with ¼ cup melted butter; sprinkle with mixture of ¼ cup brown sugar and 1 teaspoon ground cinnamon. Roll as for jelly roll, starting with long edge; seal. Cut in 1-inch slices. In saucepan mix $1/2$ cup brown sugar, $1/4$ cup butter, and 1 tablespoon light corn syrup. Heat slowly, stirring often. Pour into 8x8x2-inch baking pan. Place rolls, cut side down, over mixture. Cover; let rise in warm place till double, 30 to 45 minutes. Bake at 375° about 20 minutes. Cool 2 to 3 minutes; invert on rack; remove pan. Makes 12 rolls.

## ORANGE ROLLS

Prepare recipe for Raisin-Cinnamon Rolls, substituting 2 teaspoons grated orange peel for the cinnamon and omitting the raisins. Continue shaping and baking as directed. Makes 16 rolls.

## GOLDEN PUMPKIN ROLLS

| | |
|---|---|
| 5 to 5$1/2$ cups all-purpose flour | 2 tablespoons shortening |
| 1 package active dry yeast | 1 teaspoon salt |
| 1$1/4$ cups milk | 1 egg |
| 2 tablespoons sugar | $1/2$ cup canned pumpkin |

OVEN 400°

In large mixing bowl combine *2 cups* of the flour and the yeast. Heat milk, sugar, shortening, and salt just till warm (115-120°), stirring constantly till shortening almost melts. Add to dry mixture; add egg and pumpkin. Beat at low speed of electric mixer for $1/2$ minute, scraping bowl. Beat 3 minutes at high speed. By hand, stir in enough remaining flour to make a soft dough. Knead on lightly floured surface till smooth and elastic, 8 to 10 minutes.

Shape in ball. Place in lightly greased bowl; turn once. Cover; let rise in warm place till double, about 1$3/4$ hours. Punch down; turn out on floured surface. Cover; let rest 10 minutes. Form into 32 balls. Place in two greased 9x9x2-inch baking pans. Cover; let rise in warm place till double, about 50 minutes. Bake in hot oven (400°) about 15 minutes. Makes 32 rolls.

# BUTTERHORNS

OVEN 400°

In large mixing bowl combine 2½ cups all-purpose flour and 1 package active dry yeast. Heat 1 cup milk, ½ cup sugar, ½ cup shortening, and 2 teaspoons salt just till warm (115-120°), stirring constantly till shortening almost melts. Add to dry mixture; add 3 eggs. Beat at low speed of electric mixer for ½ minute, scraping bowl. Beat 3 minutes at high speed. By hand, stir in 2 to 2¼ cups all-purpose flour to make a soft dough. Knead on lightly floured surface till smooth and elastic, 5 to 8 minutes. Shape in a ball.

Place in greased bowl; turn once. Cover; let rise in warm place till double, about 2¼ hours. Punch down; divide in thirds. Cover; let rest 10 minutes. On floured surface roll each to a 12-inch circle. Shape into Butterhorns (see photo). Arrange, point down, on greased baking sheets. Brush with melted butter. Cover; let rise till very light, about 1 hour. Bake at 400° for 10 to 12 minutes. Makes 3 dozen rolls.

# ORANGE ROSETTES

OVEN 400°

In large mixing bowl combine 2½ cups all-purpose flour and 1 package active dry yeast. Heat 1¼ cups milk, ½ cup shortening, ⅓ cup sugar, and 1 teaspoon salt just till warm (115-120°), stirring constantly till shortening almost melts. Add to dry mixture; add 2 eggs, 2 tablespoons grated orange peel, and ¼ cup orange juice. Beat at low speed of electric mixer for ½ minute, scraping bowl. Beat 3 minutes at high speed. By hand, stir in 2½ to 3 cups all-purpose flour to make a soft dough.

Knead on lightly floured surface till smooth and elastic, 8 to 10 minutes. Shape in a ball. Place in greased bowl; turn once. Cover; let rise in warm place till double, about 2 hours. Punch down. Cover; let rest 10 minutes. Shape into Rosettes (see photo). Cover; let rise till almost double, about 45 minutes. Bake in hot oven (400°) about 12 minutes. Cool. Frost with Orange Icing. Makes 2 dozen rolls.

*Orange Icing:* Blend 1 cup sifted confectioners' sugar,

1 teaspoon grated orange peel, and 2 tablespoons orange juice.

## BRAN REFRIGERATOR ROLLS

| | |
|---|---|
| 6½ cups all-purpose flour | 1 cup shortening |
| 2 packages active dry yeast | ¾ cup sugar |
| 2 cups water | 2 eggs |
| | 1 cup whole bran |

OVEN 425°

In large mixing bowl combine *3 cups* of the flour and the yeast. Heat water, shortening, sugar, and 2 teaspoons salt just till warm (115-120°), stirring constantly till shortening almost melts. Add to dry mixture; add eggs. Beat at low speed of electric mixer for ½ minute, scraping bowl constantly. Beat 3 minutes at high speed. By hand, stir in whole bran and remaining flour to make a moderately stiff dough. Place in greased bowl; turn once. Cover and refrigerate at least 2 hours or till needed. (Use within 3 to 4 days.)

Shape into Cloverleaves (see photo) or round rolls. Cover; let rise in warm place till double, 1½ to 2 hours. Bake at 425° about 15 minutes. Makes 3½ dozen rolls.

## ENGLISH MUFFINS

| | |
|---|---|
| 5¾ to 6 cups all-purpose flour | 2 cups milk |
| 1 package active dry yeast | ¼ cup shortening |
| | 2 tablespoons sugar |

In large mixing bowl combine 2½ *cups* of the flour and the yeast. Heat milk, shortening, sugar, and 2 teaspoons salt just till warm (115-120°), stirring constantly till shortening almost melts. Add to dry mixture. Beat at low speed of electric mixer for ½ minute, scraping bowl. Beat 3 minutes at high speed. By hand, stir in enough remaining flour to make a moderately stiff dough. Knead on floured surface till smooth, 8 to 10 minutes. Shape in ball.

Place in greased bowl; turn once. Cover; let rise till double, about 1¼ hours. Punch down. Cover; let rest 10 minutes. Roll to ³/₈-inch thickness. Using a 3-inch cutter, cut dough into muffins. Bake on top of range on medium-hot, lightly greased griddle about 30 minutes, turning often. Cool. Split; toast on both sides. Makes 24 muffins.

## HARD ROLLS

*Another time, prepare 1 recipe of French Bread dough. Shape half the dough into Hard Rolls, the rest into a French bread loaf or breadsticks—*

OVEN 400°

Prepare ¹/₂ recipe French Bread dough (page 135). After first rising, turn dough out onto a lightly floured surface. Divide in half. Cover and let rest 10 minutes. Divide each half of dough into 9 portions, making 18 pieces in all. Shape each piece into oval or round roll. Place about 2 inches apart on greased baking sheets sprinkled with yellow cornmeal. Cut shallow crisscross in top of each roll. Combine 1 slightly beaten egg white and 1 table-spoon water. Brush over top and sides of rolls. Or, for crisper crusts, just brush with water. Cover and let rise in warm place till double, 45 to 60 minutes.

When ready to bake, place a large shallow pan on lower rack of oven and fill with boiling water. Bake rolls on upper rack in hot oven (400°) for 15 minutes. Brush again with egg white mixture or water. Bake 10 to 15 minutes longer. For crackly crust, cool in draft. Makes 18 rolls.

## BREADSTICKS

OVEN 400°

Prepare ¹/₂ recipe French Bread dough (page 135). After first rising, divide dough in half. Cover and let rest 10 minutes. Divide each half of dough into 12 pieces. Roll each piece under hands to form a pencil-like rope 12 inches long. Smooth each rope as you work. Place, 1 inch apart, on greased baking sheets sprinkled with yellow cornmeal. Brush with mixture of 1 slightly beaten egg white and 1 tablespoon water. Or, for crisper breadsticks, just brush with water. Let rise, uncovered, in warm place till double, 45 to 60 minutes. Brush again with egg white mixture or water; sprinkle breadsticks with coarse salt, if desired.

When ready to bake, place a large shallow pan on lower rack of oven and fill with boiling water. Bake breadsticks on upper rack in hot oven (400°) for 15 minutes. Brush again with egg white mixture or water. Bake 10 to 15 minutes longer. Remove from baking sheets. Makes 24.

## HOT CROSS BUNS

3½ to 4 cups all-purpose flour
2 packages active dry yeast
½ to 1 teaspoon ground cinnamon
¾ cup milk

½ cup salad oil
⅓ cup sugar
¾ teaspoon salt
3 eggs
⅔ cup dried currants
1 egg white

OVEN 375°

In large mixing bowl combine 2 cups of the flour, the yeast, and cinnamon. Heat milk, oil, sugar, and salt just till warm (115-120°). Add to dry mixture; add eggs. Beat at low speed of electric mixer for ½ minute, scraping bowl. Beat 3 minutes at high speed. By hand, stir in currants and enough of the remaining flour to make a soft dough. Shape into a ball. Place in lightly greased bowl, turning once.

Cover; let rise in warm place till double, about 1½ hours. Punch down; turn out on floured surface. Cover; let rest 10 minutes. Divide in 18 pieces; form into smooth balls. Place on greased baking sheet 1½ inches apart. Cover; let rise till double, 30 to 45 minutes. Cut shallow cross in each; brush tops with slightly beaten egg white (reserve remaining). Bake at 375° for 12 to 15 minutes. Cool slightly; frost (see right). Makes 18 buns.

Pipe on crosses with Frosting: Combine about 1½ cups sifted confectioners' sugar, reserved egg white, ¼ teaspoon vanilla, and dash salt. Add milk, if needed.

## KOLACHE

OVEN 375°

In mixing bowl combine 2 cups all-purpose flour, 1 package active dry yeast, and ¼ teaspoon ground cinnamon. Heat 1 cup milk, ½ cup butter, ¼ cup sugar, and 1 teaspoon salt just till warm (115-120°), stirring constantly till butter almost melts. Add to dry mixture; add 2 eggs and 1 teaspoon grated lemon peel. Beat at low speed of electric mixer for ½ minute, scraping bowl. Beat 3 minutes at high speed. By hand, stir in 1½ to 2¼ cups all-purpose flour to make a moderately soft dough. Knead on floured surface till smooth, 8 to 10 minutes. Shape in ball. Place in greased bowl; turn once. Cover; let rise in warm place till double, 1 to 1½ hours.

Punch down; divide in half. Cover; let rest 10 minutes. Shape each half into 9 balls. Place 3 inches apart on greased baking sheets. Flatten to 3½-inch circles. Cover; let rise till double, about 45 minutes. Make depression in centers; fill with Prune Filling. Bake in moderate oven (375°) for 10 to 12 minutes. Cool. Dust with confectioners' sugar. Makes 18 rolls.

*Prune Filling:* Combine 1 cup pitted prunes and enough water to come 1 inch above prunes. Simmer for 10 to 15 minutes; drain and chop prunes. Stir in ¼ cup sugar and ½ teaspoon ground cinnamon.

## STREUSEL COFFEE CAKE

Basic Roll Dough
1 cup all-purpose flour
$\frac{1}{2}$ cup brown sugar
$\frac{1}{2}$ cup granulated sugar
1 teaspoon ground cinnamon
$\frac{1}{2}$ cup butter or margarine
$\frac{1}{4}$ cup finely chopped nuts
$1\frac{1}{2}$ teaspoons vanilla

OVEN 375°

Prepare dough and let rise once. Divide in thirds. Cover and let rest 10 minutes. Pat each into greased 8x1½-inch round baking pan. Combine flour, sugars, and cinnamon; cut in butter till crumbly. Add nuts. Sprinkle ⅓ mixture over each coffee cake. Cover; let rise till double, 30 to 45 minutes. Bake at 375° about 20 minutes. Immediately drizzle ½ teaspoon vanilla over each coffee cake. Serve warm.


## GOLDEN BUBBLE RING

4 to 4½ cups all-purpose flour
2 packages active dry yeast
1 cup milk
$\frac{1}{2}$ cup sugar
$\frac{1}{2}$ cup shortening
2 eggs
3 tablespoons butter or margarine, melted
$\frac{3}{4}$ cup sugar
1 teaspoon ground cinnamon

OVEN 350°

In large mixing bowl combine 2½ cups of the flour and the yeast. Heat milk, ½ cup sugar, shortening, and 1 teaspoon salt just till warm (115-120°), stirring constantly till shortening almost melts. Add to dry mixture; add eggs. Beat at low speed of electric mixer for ½ minute, scraping bowl. Beat 3 minutes at high speed. By hand, stir in enough remaining flour to make a soft dough. Knead on a lightly floured surface till smooth and elastic, 8 to 10 minutes. Shape in ball. Place in greased bowl; turn once. Cover; let rise in warm place till double, 1 to 1¼ hours. Grease a 10-inch tube pan. Shape dough into 28 balls. Roll each in melted butter, then in mixture of ¾ cup sugar and cinnamon. Arrange in pan; sprinkle with any remaining sugar mixture. Let rise till double, about 1 hour.

Bake at 350° for 35 to 40 minutes. Cool in pan 15 to 20 minutes. Invert on rack; remove pan.

## BRIOCHE

OVEN 375°

Soften 1 package active dry yeast in ¼ cup warm water (110°). Thoroughly cream ½ cup butter, ⅓ cup sugar, and ½ teaspoon salt. Add 1 cup all-purpose flour and ½ cup milk to creamed mixture. Beat 3 eggs and 1 egg yolk together (reserve egg white). Add softened yeast and eggs to creamed mixture; beat well. Add 2½ cups all-purpose flour. By hand, beat for 5 to 8 minutes. Cover; let rise in warm place till double, about 2 hours. Stir down; beat well. Cover and refrigerate overnight.

Stir down and turn out on lightly floured surface. Set aside ¼ of the dough. Cut remaining dough into 6 pieces; form each into 4 balls. With floured hands, tuck under cut edges. Place in greased muffin pans. Cut reserved dough in 4 wedges; divide each into 6 pieces. Shape into 24 small balls. Make indentation in each large ball. Brush holes with water; press small balls into indentations. Cover; let rise in warm place till double, about 30 minutes. Combine 1 slightly beaten egg white and 1 tablespoon sugar; brush tops. Bake in moderate oven (375°) about 15 minutes. Makes 24 rolls.

## ENGLISH TEA RING

2½ to 2¾ cups all-purpose flour
1 package active dry yeast
¾ cup milk
¼ cup sugar
¼ cup shortening
1 egg
½ teaspoon vanilla

1 tablespoon butter or margarine, melted
¼ cup sugar
1 teaspoon ground cinnamon
½ cup chopped walnuts
½ cup chopped mixed candied fruits and peels

OVEN 375°

In large mixing bowl combine 1½ *cups* of the flour and the yeast. Heat milk, ¼ cup sugar, shortening, and 1 teaspoon salt just till warm (115-120°), stirring constantly till shortening almost melts. Add to dry mixture; add egg and vanilla. Beat at low speed of electric mixer for 1/2 minute, scraping bowl. Beat 3 minutes at high speed. By hand, stir in enough remaining flour to make a soft dough.

Knead on floured surface till smooth, 5 to 8 minutes. Shape in ball. Place in greased bowl; turn once. Cover; let rise in warm place till double, 1 1/2 to 2 hours. Punch down. Cover; let rest 10 minutes. Roll to 13x9-inch rectangle. Brush with butter. Mix 1/4 cup sugar and cinnamon; add nuts and fruits. Spread over dough. Roll as for jelly roll, starting from long edge; seal. Shape in a ring on greased baking sheet; seal ends. With scissors, snip 2/3 of the way to center at 1-inch intervals. Turn each section slightly to one side. Cover; let rise till double, 30 to 45 minutes. Bake at 375° for 20 to 25 minutes.

# DOUGHNUTS

## DOUGHNUT TIPS

• Fry doughnuts in deep hot fat (salad oil or shortening) at 375°. If fat is too hot, doughnuts will not be cooked through; if too cool, they will be fat-soaked. Fry just a few at one time to prevent fat from cooling down too quickly.
• Turn doughnuts only once while frying.
• Drain doughnuts on paper towels.
• Give doughnuts a final touch by shaking in a bag of granulated sugar or confectioners' sugar, plain or with spices. Or glaze with thin Confectioners' Icing.

## RAISED DOUGHNUTS

3 to 3½ cups all-
  purpose flour
2 packages active dry
  yeast
¾ cup milk
⅓ cup sugar
¼ cup shortening
2 eggs
  Orange Glaze

In large mixing bowl combine 1½ cups of the flour and the yeast. Heat milk, sugar, shortening, and 1 teaspoon salt just till warm (115-120°), stirring constantly till shortening almost melts. Add to dry mixture; add eggs. Beat at low speed of electric mixer for ½ minute, scraping bowl. Beat 3 minutes at high speed. By hand, stir in enough of the remaining flour to make a moderately soft dough. Knead on a lightly floured surface till smooth and elastic, 5 to 8 minutes. Shape into ball.

Place in greased bowl; turn once. Cover; let rise in warm place till double, 45 to 60 minutes. Punch down; divide in half. Roll to ½-inch thickness. Cut with floured doughnut cutter. Cover; let rise till very light, 30 to 45 minutes. Fry in deep hot fat (375°) about 1 minute on each side or till golden. Drain on paper toweling. If desired, roll warm doughnuts in sugar or frost with Orange Glaze. Makes 18 to 20 doughnuts.

*Orange Glaze:* Mix 2 cups sifted confectioners' sugar, 1 teaspoon grated orange peel, and 3 tablespoons orange juice.

## BUTTERMILK DOUGHNUTS

*Allow doughnuts to stand for a few minutes before frying so that a delicate, thin crust will form. This crust slows absorption of fat—*

| | |
|---|---|
| 4 cups all-purpose flour | 1 cup granulated sugar |
| 4 teaspoons baking powder | 1/4 cup salad oil |
| 3/4 teaspoon salt | 1 teaspoon vanilla |
| 1/4 teaspoon soda | 1 cup buttermilk |
| 2 beaten eggs | Sifted confectioners' sugar |

In bowl stir together the flour, baking powder, salt, and soda. Beat eggs and granulated sugar together till thick and lemon-colored. Stir in oil and vanilla. Add dry ingredients and buttermilk alternately to egg mixture, beginning and ending with dry ingredients. Beat just till blended after each addition. Roll dough out on lightly floured surface to 1/2-inch thickness. Cut with floured doughnut cutter. Fry in deep hot fat (375°) about 1 1/2 minutes on each side or till golden brown. Drain on paper toweling. Cool slightly. Dust with confectioners' sugar. Makes 24.

# TOAST

**Cinnamon Toast:** Toast bread; butter while hot and sprinkle with mixture of 1 part cinnamon to 4 parts sugar. Keep warm in slow oven till serving time.

Keep cinnamon-sugar mixture in a large shaker—it's ready to use!

**French Toast:** Combine 2 slightly beaten eggs, $1/2$ cup milk, and $1/4$ teaspoon salt. Dip day-old bread into milk-egg mixture (enough for 4 to 6 slices of bread). Fry in small amount hot fat till golden brown. Serve hot with maple-flavored syrup, confectioners' sugar, or tart jelly.

**Melba Toast:** Slice bread $1/8$ inch thick; trim crusts; place in slow oven (250°) until toast curls and is golden brown.

**Toasted Croutons:** Dice bread in small squares. Brown in butter in skillet. Season with salt, pepper, and favorite herb.

# QUICK BREADS

- Baking powder, soda, steam, or air, rather than yeast, leaven quick breads.
- Most quick breads are best served hot from the oven—with plenty of butter!
- Nut breads should be stored for at least a day. The flavors will mellow and the loaf will slice more easily.
- After baking, turn nut breads out of pan and cool on rack. Place cooled bread in airtight container, or wrap in foil or clear plastic wrap.
- A crack down the center of a nut loaf is no mistake—it's typical.
- Serve nut breads cut in very thin slices with simple fillings: soft butter, cream cheese, jam or jelly.

## COCOA RIPPLE RING

Cream together ½ cup shortening, ¾ cup sugar, and 2 eggs till light and fluffy. Sift together 1½ cups sifted all-purpose flour, ¾ teaspoon salt, and 2 teaspoons baking powder. Add to creamed mixture alternately with ⅔ cup milk, beating well after each addition. Spoon ⅓ of batter into well-greased 6½-cup ring mold or 9x9x2-inch pan. Mix ⅓ cup pre-sweetened instant cocoa powder and ⅓ cup broken walnuts; sprinkle *half* over batter in pan. Repeat layers, ending with batter. Bake at 350° for 35 minutes. Let stand 5 minutes; turn out of mold. Serve warm.

## BLUEBERRY BUCKLE

| | |
|---|---|
| 1/2 cup shortening | 2 cups fresh blueberries |
| 3/4 cup sugar | 1/2 cup sugar |
| 1 egg | 1/2 cup sifted all-purpose |
| 2 cups sifted all-purpose | flour |
| flour | 1/2 teaspoon ground |
| 2 1/2 teaspoons baking | cinnamon |
| powder | 1/4 cup butter or |
| 1/4 teaspoon salt | margarine |
| 1/2 cup milk | |

OVEN 350°

Thoroughly cream shortening and 3/4 cup sugar; add egg and beat till light and fluffy. Sift together 2 cups flour, baking powder, and salt; add to creamed mixture alternately with milk. Spread in greased 11x7x1 1/2-inch pan. Top with berries. Mix 1/2 cup sugar, 1/2 cup flour, and cinnamon; cut in butter till crumbly; sprinkle over berries. Bake at 350° for 45 minutes. Cut in squares. Serve warm.

## SPICY RAISIN COFFEE CAKE

| | |
|---|---|
| 1/2 cup butter or | 1 teaspoon soda |
| margarine | 1/4 teaspoon salt |
| 1 cup sugar | * * * |
| 2 eggs | 1 cup broken walnuts |
| 1 teaspoon vanilla | 1/2 cup sugar |
| 1 cup dairy sour cream | 1 teaspoon ground |
| 2 cups sifted all-purpose | cinnamon |
| flour | 1 1/2 cups raisins |
| 1 1/2 teaspoons baking | |
| powder | |

OVEN 350°

Cream together butter and 1 cup sugar till fluffy. Add eggs and vanilla; beat well. Blend in sour cream. Sift together flour, baking powder, soda, and salt; stir into creamed mixture; mix well. Spread *half* the batter in greased 9x9x2-inch pan.

Mix nuts, 1/2 cup sugar, and cinnamon; sprinkle *half* over batter. Top with raisins. Spoon on remaining batter.

Top with reserved nut mixture. Bake in moderate oven (350°) for 40 minutes. Serve warm.

## COWBOY COFFEE CAKE

2½ cups sifted all-purpose
    flour
 2 cups brown sugar
 ½ teaspoon salt
 ⅔ cup shortening
 2 teaspoons baking
    powder

½ teaspoon soda
½ teaspoon ground
    cinnamon
½ teaspoon ground
    nutmeg
 1 cup sour milk
 2 beaten eggs

OVEN 375°

Mix flour, sugar, salt, and shortening till crumbly; reserve ½ cup. To remaining crumbs, add baking powder, soda, and spices; mix well. Add milk and eggs; mix well. Pour into 2 greased and floured 8x1½-inch round pans; top with reserved crumbs. Bake at 375° for 25 to 30 minutes. Serve warm. Makes 2 cakes.

## BANANA COFFEE BREAD

½ cup shortening
 1 cup sugar
 2 eggs
¾ cup mashed ripe
    banana

1¼ cups sifted all-purpose
    flour
¾ teaspoon soda
½ teaspoon salt

OVEN 350°

Cream shortening and sugar until fluffy. Add eggs, one at a time, beating well after each. Stir in banana. Sift together dry ingredients; add to banana mixture; mix well. Pour into greased 9x9x2-inch pan. Bake at 350° for 30 to 35 minutes.

## CRANBERRY KUCHEN

OVEN 375°

Combine 1 well-beaten egg, ½ cup sugar, ½ cup milk, and 2 tablespoons salad oil. Sift together 1 cup sifted all-purpose flour, 2 teaspoons baking powder, and ½ teaspoon salt; add to egg mixture. Mix well. Turn into greased 8x8x2-inch pan.

Force ½ pound (2 cups) fresh cranberries through coarse blade of food chopper; dot over batter; top with Crumb Topper. Bake at 375° for 25 to 30 minutes.

*Crumb Topper:* Combine ¾ cup sifted all-purpose flour and ½ cup sugar. Cut in 3 tablespoons butter or margarine.

## KAFFEE KUCHEN

| | |
|---|---|
| ½ cup butter or margarine, softened | 2 teaspoons baking powder |
| 1 cup sugar | ½ teaspoon salt |
| 2 egg yolks | ½ cup milk |
| 1½ cups sifted all-purpose flour | 2 stiffly beaten egg whites |
| | Topper |

OVEN 350°

Cream butter and sugar; beat in egg yolks. Sift together dry ingredients; add alternately with milk, beating after each addition. Fold in egg whites. Pour into greased 9x9x2-inch pan. Sprinkle with Topper. Bake at 350° for 30 minutes. Serve warm.

*Topper:* Mix ⅓ cup flour and ¼ cup brown sugar; cut in 2 tablespoons butter.

## COFFEE CAKE

| | |
|---|---|
| ¼ cup salad oil | ¾ cup sugar |
| 1 beaten egg | 2 teaspoons baking powder |
| ½ cup milk | ½ teaspoon salt |
| 1½ cups sifted all-purpose flour | Spicy Topping |

OVEN 375°

Combine salad oil, egg, and milk. Sift together dry ingredients; add to milk mixture; mix well. Pour into greased 9x9x2-inch pan. Sprinkle with Spicy Topping. Bake at 375° about 25 minutes.

*Spicy Topping:* Combine ¼ cup brown sugar, 1 tablespoon all-purpose flour, 1 teaspoon ground cinnamon, 1 tablespoon melted butter, and ½ cup broken nuts.

## PUMPKIN NUT BREAD

OVEN 350°

In mixing bowl, blend ¾ cup canned pumpkin, ½ cup water, 1 egg, 1 teaspoon ground cinnamon, and ½ teaspoon ground mace. Add one 1-pound 1-ounce package nut quick bread mix; stir till moistened. Turn into greased 9x5x3-inch pan. Bake at 350° for 50 minutes or till done. Remove from pan; cool. If desired, frost with Confectioners' Icing (page 258).

## FRUIT BREAD

| | |
|---|---|
| 2 cups sifted all-purpose flour | * * * |
| ¾ cup sugar | ¼ cup diced candied citron |
| 3 teaspoons baking powder | ¼ cup dried currants |
| ½ teaspoon salt | 2 tablespoons finely diced candied cherries |
| 2 beaten eggs | 2 tablespoons diced candied lemon peel |
| 1 cup milk | ½ cup chopped walnuts |
| 3 tablespoons salad oil | |

OVEN 350°

Sift together flour, sugar, baking powder, and salt. Combine eggs, milk, and salad oil; add to flour mixture, beating well (about ½ minute). Stir in fruits and nuts.

Turn into greased 9x5x3-inch loaf pan. Bake in moderate oven (350°) about 50 minutes or till done. Remove from pan and cool on rack. Wrap and store overnight.

## BOSTON BROWN BREAD

*Traditional with Baked Beans—*

1 cup sifted all-purpose
  flour
1 teaspoon baking
  powder
1 teaspoon soda
1 teaspoon salt
1 cup yellow cornmeal

1 cup stirred whole
  wheat flour
  * * *
3/4 cup dark molasses
2 cups buttermilk *or*
  sour milk
1 cup raisins

OVEN 450°

Sift all-purpose flour with baking powder, soda, and salt;
stir in cornmeal and whole wheat flour. Add remaining
ingredients; beat well. Divide batter among 4 greased and
floured 1-pound food cans. Cover tightly with foil.

Place on rack in deep kettle; pour in boiling water to
1-inch depth. Cover kettle; steam 3 hours, adding more
boiling water if needed. Uncover cans; place in very hot
oven (450°) for 5 minutes. Remove bread from cans. Cool
on rack. Wrap and store overnight. Makes 4 loaves.

## GLAZED LEMON NUT BREAD

*Delicate lemon flavor—fresh as early spring—*

4 tablespoons butter or
  margarine
3/4 cup sugar
2 eggs
2 teaspoons grated
  lemon peel
  * * *
2 cups sifted all-purpose
  flour

2½ teaspoons baking
  powder
1 teaspoon salt
3/4 cup milk
½ cup chopped walnuts
2 teaspoons lemon juice
2 tablespoons sugar

OVEN 350°

Cream together butter or margarine and the 3/4 cup sugar
till light and fluffy. Add eggs and lemon peel; beat well.
Sift together flour, baking powder, and salt; add to
creamed mixture alternately with milk, beating till smooth
after each addition. Stir in walnuts.

Pour into greased 8½x4½x2½-inch loaf dish. Bake in

moderate oven (350°) 50 to 55 minutes or till done. Let cool in pan 10 minutes. Combine lemon juice and 2 tablespoons sugar; spoon over top. Remove from pan; cool. Wrap; store overnight.

## CRANBERRY ORANGE BREAD

| | |
|---|---|
| 2 cups sifted all-purpose flour | 1 teaspoon grated orange peel |
| ¾ cup sugar | ¾ cup orange juice |
| 1½ teaspoons baking powder | 2 tablespoons salad oil |
| 1 teaspoon salt | 1 cup coarsely chopped fresh cranberries |
| ½ teaspoon soda | ½ cup chopped walnuts |
| 1 beaten egg | |

OVEN 350°

Sift together flour, sugar, baking powder, salt, and soda. Combine egg, grated orange peel, orange juice, and salad oil. Add to dry ingredients, stirring just till moistened. Fold in cranberries and walnuts.

Bake in greased 9x5x3-inch loaf pan at 350° for 60 minutes or till done. Remove from pan; cool. Wrap; store overnight.

## PRUNE NUT BREAD

| | |
|---|---|
| 1 cup dried prunes, chopped | 3 teaspoons baking powder |
| 2 teaspoons shredded orange peel | ½ teaspoon salt |
| 1 cup orange juice | ½ teaspoon ground cinnamon |
| 2 cups sifted all-purpose flour | 2 beaten eggs |
| ¾ cup sugar | 2 tablespoons salad oil |
| | ½ cup chopped walnuts |

OVEN 350°

Combine prunes, orange peel, and juice; let stand ½ hour. Sift together dry ingredients. Combine eggs, oil, and prune mixture; add to dry ingredients, mixing well. Add nuts. Turn into greased 9x5x3-inch loaf pan. Bake in moderate oven (350°) for 55 minutes. Remove from pan; cool.

## BEST NUT LOAF

| | |
|---|---|
| 3 cups sifted all-purpose flour | 1½ teaspoons salt |
| 1 cup sugar | 1 beaten egg |
| 4 teaspoons baking powder | 1½ cups milk |
| | 2 tablespoons salad oil |
| | ¾ cup chopped walnuts |

OVEN 350°

Sift together dry ingredients. Combine egg, milk, and salad oil; add to dry ingredients, beating well. Stir in nuts. Turn into greased 9x5x3-inch loaf pan. Bake in moderate oven (350°) about 1 to 1¼ hours or till done. Remove from pan; cool on rack.

## RAISIN ORANGE BREAD

OVEN 325°

Combine 1½ cups raisins and 1½ cups water; bring to boil. Cool to room temperature. Mix 1 slightly beaten egg, 1 cup brown sugar, 2 tablespoons salad oil, and 1 tablespoon grated orange peel. Stir in raisin mixture. Sift together 2½ cups sifted all-purpose flour, 1 teaspoon salt, 2 teaspoons baking powder, and ½ teaspoon soda; add, beating well.

Pour into greased 8½x4½x2½-inch loaf dish. Bake at 325° about 60 minutes.

## MIDGET DATE LOAVES

OVEN 325°

Pour ½ cup boiling water over 8 ounces pitted dates, cut up (1½ cups), and 2 tablespoons shortening; cool to room temperature. Add 1 tablespoon grated orange peel and ½ cup orange juice. Stir in 1 beaten egg. Sift together 2 cups sifted all-purpose flour, ⅓ cup sugar, 1 teaspoon baking powder, 1 teaspoon soda, and ½ teaspoon salt; add to mixture; stir just till mixed.

Stir in ½ cup chopped walnuts. Turn into 4 greased 4½x2¾x2-inch loaf pans.* Bake at 325° for 40 to 45 minutes. Remove from pans; cool. Wrap and store overnight.

*Or, bake in 9x5x3-inch loaf pan 1 hour.

## BANANA NUT BREAD

| | |
|---|---|
| 1/3 cup shortening | 1/2 teaspoon soda |
| 1/2 cup sugar | 1/2 teaspoon salt |
| 2 eggs | 1 cup mashed ripe |
| 1 3/4 cups sifted all-purpose flour | banana |
| | 1/2 cup chopped walnuts |
| 1 teaspoon baking powder | |

OVEN 350°

Cream together shortening and sugar; add eggs and beat well. Sift together dry ingredients; add to creamed mixture alternately with banana, blending well after each addition. Stir in nuts.

Pour into well-greased 9x5x3-inch loaf pan. Bake in moderate oven (350°) 45 to 50 minutes or till done. Remove from pan; cool on rack. Wrap and store overnight.

## ORANGE NUT BREAD

OVEN 350°

Sift together 2 1/4 cups sifted all-purpose flour, 3/4 cup sugar, 2 1/4 teaspoons baking powder, 3/4 teaspoon salt, and 1/4 teaspoon soda. Stir in 3/4 cup chopped walnuts and 1 tablespoon grated orange peel. Mix 1 beaten egg, 3/4 cup orange juice, and 2 tablespoons salad oil; add to dry ingredients, stirring just till moistened.

Pour into greased 8 1/2x4 1/2x2 1/2-inch loaf dish. Bake in moderate oven (350°) 55 minutes or till done. Remove from pan; cool on rack. Wrap and store overnight.

## PERFECT CORN BREAD

| | |
|---|---|
| 1 cup sifted all-purpose flour | 3/4 teaspoon salt |
| | 1 cup yellow cornmeal |
| 1/4 cup sugar | 2 eggs |
| 4 teaspoons baking powder | 1 cup milk |
| | 1/4 cup shortening |

OVEN 425°

Sift flour with sugar, baking powder, and salt; stir in cornmeal. Add eggs, milk, and shortening. Beat with rotary or electric beater till just smooth. (Do not overbeat.) Pour into greased 9x9x2-inch pan. Bake at 425° for 20 to 25 minutes.

**Corn Sticks:** Spoon batter into greased corn-stick pans, filling ²/₃ full. Bake in hot oven (425°) 12 to 15 minutes. Makes 18.

## SPOON BREAD

OVEN 325°

Stir 2 cups milk into 1 cup cornmeal; cook till the consistency of mush. Remove from heat; add 1 cup milk, 2 tablespoons butter, and 1 teaspoon *each* baking powder and salt. Stir a moderate amount into 3 beaten egg yolks; return to mixture. Fold in 3 stiffly beaten egg whites. Bake in greased 2-quart casserole at 325° for 55 minutes. Serve with butter. Serves 6.

## CORN FRITTERS

3 to 4 ears fresh corn *or* one 8³/₄-ounce can whole kernel corn
Milk
1¹/₂ cups sifted all-purpose flour

3 teaspoons baking powder
³/₄ teaspoon salt
1 beaten egg

Cut off tips of kernels, then scrape cobs to make 1 cup cut corn. Drain fresh (or canned) corn, reserving liquid. Add enough milk to liquid to measure 1 cup.

Sift together dry ingredients. Combine egg, milk mixture, and corn. Add to dry ingredients. Mix just till moistened.

Drop batter from tablespoon into deep, hot fat (375°). Fry until golden brown, 3 to 4 minutes. Drain on paper towels. Serve with warm maple syrup. Makes 2 dozen.

# MUFFINS

- Perfect muffins are light and tender with rough, shiny, golden brown crusts. For most muffins, stir batter only a few strokes. If overbeaten, muffins will be tough, have peaks on top, dull crusts, and an uneven, tunneled texture.
- For standard method of mixing muffins: Sift dry ingredients into bowl; make well in center. Combine beaten egg, milk, and salad oil or melted shortening. (Cool melted shortening slightly.) Add to dry ingredients all at once. Stir quickly *just till dry ingredients are moistened.*
- When muffins have to wait, tip to one side in pan—no soggy crusts; keep warm.
- To reheat muffins, wrap in aluminum foil and heat in 400° oven 15 to 20 minutes.
- Make cleanup easy by lining muffin pans with paper bake cups.

## BEST-EVER MUFFINS

| | |
|---|---|
| 1³/₄ cups sifted all-purpose flour | ³/₄ teaspoon salt |
| ¹/₄ cup sugar | 1 well-beaten egg |
| 2¹/₂ teaspoons baking powder | ³/₄ cup milk |
| | ¹/₃ cup salad oil or melted shortening |

OVEN 400°

Sift dry ingredients into bowl; make well in center. Combine egg, milk, and oil. Add all at once to dry ingredients. Stir quickly just till dry ingredients are moistened. Fill greased muffin pans ²/₃ full. Bake at 400° for 20 to 25 minutes. Makes 10.

**Blueberry Muffins:** Prepare batter above. Gently stir in

1 cup fresh *or* thawed and well-drained frozen blueberries.

**Jelly Muffins:** Prepare muffin batter above. Before baking, top batter in each pan with 1 teaspoon tart jelly.

**Low-fat Muffins:** Prepare batter above *except* substitute
skim milk for the whole milk and reduce the salad oil to
1 tablespoon. To further reduce fat, substitute 1 slightly
beaten egg white for the whole, well-beaten egg.

**Raisin or Date Muffins:** Add ½ to ¾ cup raisins,
coarsely cut dates, *or* chopped pecans, walnuts, or peanuts to Best-ever Muffins batter.

**Cheese-caraway Muffins:** Add 4 ounces sharp process
American cheese, shredded (1 cup) and ½ to 1 teaspoon
caraway seed to flour mixture in Best-ever Muffins.

**Sour-milk Muffins:** Add ¼ teaspoon soda and *reduce*
baking powder to 1 teaspoon in Best-ever Muffins. Substitute ¾ cup sour milk or buttermilk for sweet milk.

## BANANA BRAN MUFFINS

| | |
|---|---|
| 1 cup sifted all-purpose flour | 1 well-beaten egg |
| 3 tablespoons sugar | 1 cup mashed *ripe* banana |
| 2½ teaspoons baking powder | ¼ cup milk |
| ½ teaspoon salt | 2 tablespoons salad oil *or* melted shortening |
| 1 cup whole bran | |

OVEN 400°

Sift together flour, sugar, baking powder, and salt. Stir in
bran. Mix remaining ingredients; add all at once to flour
mixture, stirring just to moisten. Fill greased muffin pans
⅔ full. Bake at 400° for 20 to 25 minutes. Makes about
10 muffins.

## OATMEAL MUFFINS

| | |
|---|---|
| 1 cup quick-cooking rolled oats | 3 teaspoons baking powder |
| 1 cup milk | 1/2 teaspoon salt |
| 1 cup sifted all-purpose flour | 1 well-beaten egg |
| 1/3 cup sugar | 1/4 cup salad oil *or* melted shortening |

OVEN 425°

Combine rolled oats and milk; let stand 15 minutes. Sift flour, sugar, baking powder, and salt into bowl. Combine egg, oil, and oatmeal mixture. Add all at once to sifted dry ingredients, stirring just to moisten. Fill greased muffin pans 2/3 full. Bake at 425° for 20 to 25 minutes. Makes about 1 dozen muffins.

## BACON CORNETTES

| | |
|---|---|
| 10 to 12 slices bacon | 3/4 teaspoon salt |
| 1 cup sifted all-purpose flour | 1 cup yellow cornmeal |
| 1/4 cup sugar | 2 well-beaten eggs |
| 4 teaspoons baking powder | 1 cup milk |
| | 1/4 cup salad oil |

OVEN 425°

Cook bacon till crisp; drain and crumble. Sift together next 4 ingredients; stir in cornmeal. Add eggs, milk, and oil. Beat till *just* smooth, about 1 minute (do not over-beat). Stir in bacon. Fill greased muffin pans 2/3 full. If desired, top with a few bits of uncooked bacon. Bake at 425° for 20 to 25 minutes. Makes 12.

## ORANGE CRUNCH MUFFINS

OVEN 400°

Sift together 2 cups sifted all-purpose flour, 1/3 cup sugar, 1 teaspoon baking powder, 1/2 teaspoon soda, and 3/4 teaspoon salt. Stir in 1/2 cup grape nuts cereal. Combine 2 well-beaten eggs, 1 tablespoon grated orange peel, 1 cup orange juice, and 1/3 cup salad oil. Add all at once to dry ingredients, stirring just till moistened. Fill greased muffin pans ²/₃ full. Bake in hot oven (400°) for 20 to 25 minutes. Makes 14 to 16.

## DOUBLE CORN STICKS

| | |
|---|---|
| 1 cup sifted all-purpose flour | 1 cup yellow cornmeal |
| 2 tablespoons sugar | 1 well-beaten egg |
| 2 teaspoons baking powder | 1 8³/₄-ounce can cream-style corn |
| ³/₄ teaspoon salt | ³/₄ cup milk |
| | 2 tablespoons salad oil |

OVEN 425°

Sift flour, sugar, baking powder, and salt together; stir in cornmeal. Blend egg, corn, milk, and salad oil; add to dry ingredients; stir just till moistened. Preheat cornstick pans in oven, then grease generously. Fill pans ²/₃ full. Bake at 425° about 20 minutes. Makes about 18.

## GINGER MUFFINS

OVEN 375°

Cream together ¹/₄ cup shortening and ¹/₄ cup sugar. Beat in 1 egg, then ¹/₂ cup molasses. Sift together 1¹/₂ cups sifted all-purpose flour, ³/₄ teaspoon soda, ¹/₄ teaspoon salt, ¹/₂ teaspoon ground cinnamon, ¹/₂ teaspoon ground ginger, and ¹/₄ teaspoon ground cloves; stir into molasses mixture. Gradually add ¹/₂ cup hot water, beating till smooth. Fill greased muffin pans ²/₃ full. Bake in moderate oven (375°) for 20 to 25 minutes. Makes 1 dozen.

## CHEDDAR BRAN MUFFINS

| | |
|---|---|
| 1 cup whole bran | 1¹/₂ teaspoons baking powder |
| 1¹/₄ cups buttermilk or sour milk | ¹/₂ teaspoon salt |
| ¹/₄ cup shortening | ¹/₄ teaspoon soda |
| ¹/₃ cup sugar | 4 ounces sharp Cheddar cheese, shredded (1 cup) |
| 1 egg | |

* * *

1¹/₂ cups sifted all-purpose flour

OVEN 400°

Soften bran in buttermilk. Cream shortening and sugar till fluffy; beat in egg. Sift together next 4 ingredients. Add to creamed mixture alternately with bran mixture. Stir in cheese. Fill greased muffin pans ²/₃ full. Bake at 400° for 30 minutes. Makes 1 dozen.


## HAWAIIAN MUFFINS

OVEN 400°

Combine one 14-ounce package orange muffin mix and ¹/₂ cup flaked coconut.

Drain one 8³/₄-ounce can crushed pineapple, reserving 1 tablespoon syrup. Add pineapple, 1 beaten egg, and ²/₃ cup milk to dry ingredients. Blend only till dry ingredients are moistened.

Fill greased muffin pans ²/₃ full. Bake in hot oven (400°) for 15 to 20 minutes, or till done.

Beat one 3-ounce package cream cheese till fluffy. Add the 1 tablespoon reserved pineapple syrup; beat well. Serve with hot muffins. Makes 12 to 16.


## COFFEE CAKE MUFFINS

| | |
|---|---|
| 1¹/₂ cups sifted all-purpose flour | ¹/₄ cup brown sugar |
| ¹/₂ cup granulated sugar | ¹/₄ cup chopped walnuts or pecans |
| 2 teaspoons baking powder | 1 tablespoon all-purpose flour |
| ¹/₂ teaspoon salt | 1 teaspoon ground cinnamon |
| ¹/₄ cup shortening | |
| 1 well-beaten egg | 1 tablespoon butter or margarine, melted |
| ¹/₂ cup milk | |

* * *

OVEN 350°

Sift 1¹/₂ cups flour, granulated sugar, baking powder, and salt into mixing bowl; cut in shortening till mixture resembles coarse crumbs. Mix egg and milk; add all at once to flour mixture; stir just till moistened.

Combine brown sugar, nuts, 1 tablespoon flour, cinnamon, and melted butter. Place *half* of batter in greased muffin pans. Sprinkle nut mixture over, then top with remaining batter, filling pans $1/2$ full. Bake at 350° about 20 minutes. Makes 12.

## SPICY FRUIT PUFFS

2 cups sifted all-purpose flour
3 teaspoons baking powder
1 teaspoon salt
$1/2$ teaspoon ground cinnamon
$1/4$ teaspoon ground nutmeg

\* \* \*

1 cup shredded pared apple or $1/2$ cup raisins
$2/3$ cup brown sugar
$1/4$ cup chopped walnuts
2 well-beaten eggs
$2/3$ cup milk
$1/4$ cup salad oil or melted shortening
1 cup whole wheat flakes or bran flakes

OVEN 400°

Sift together first 5 ingredients. Stir in apple or raisins, brown sugar, and nuts. Combine eggs, milk, and oil or melted shortening; add all at once, stirring just to blend. Fold in cereal flakes. Fill greased muffin pans $2/3$ full. Bake at 400° for 15 to 20 minutes. Makes 1 dozen muffins.

## GINGER SUGAR PUFFS

$1/4$ cup butter, softened
$1/2$ cup sugar
1 egg
1 teaspoon grated lemon peel
2 cups sifted all-purpose flour
4 teaspoons baking powder

$1/2$ teaspoon salt
$1/4$ teaspoon ground nutmeg
1 cup milk
$1/2$ cup butter or margarine, melted
$3/4$ cup sugar
2 teaspoons ground ginger

OVEN 375°

Cream $1/4$ cup butter and $1/2$ cup sugar till light and fluffy; beat in egg and lemon peel. Sift together flour, baking powder, salt, and nutmeg; add to creamed mixture alternately with milk, beating after each addition. Fill small greased 2-inch muffin pans $2/3$ full. Bake at 375° for about

15 minutes. While hot, dip muffins quickly into melted butter, then roll in mixture of ³/₄ cup sugar and ginger. Makes 36.

## LEMON TEA MUFFINS

| | |
|---|---|
| 1 cup sifted all-purpose flour | 2 eggs, separated |
| 1 teaspoon baking powder | 3 tablespoons lemon juice |
| ¹/₄ teaspoon salt | 1 teaspoon grated lemon peel |
| ¹/₂ cup butter or margarine | 2 tablespoons sugar |
| ¹/₂ cup sugar | ¹/₄ teaspoon ground cinnamon |

OVEN 375°

Sift together flour, baking powder, and salt. Cream butter and ¹/₂ cup sugar till light and fluffy. Beat egg yolks till thick and lemon-colored; blend well with creamed mixture. Add flour mixture alternately with lemon juice. (Do not over-mix.) Beat egg whites till stiff peaks form. Carefully fold whites and lemon peel into batter. Fill small greased 2-inch muffin pans ²/₃ full. Combine 2 tablespoons sugar and cinnamon; sprinkle about ¹/₂ teaspoon over each muffin. Bake at 375° for 15 to 20 minutes. Makes about 18 muffins.

## MOLASSES CORN MUFFINS

OVEN 375°

Cream ¹/₂ cup shortening and ¹/₂ cup sugar. Beat in 2 eggs, one at a time; stir in ¹/₂ cup molasses and 1 cup milk. Sift together 1 cup sifted all-purpose flour, 3 teaspoons baking powder, and ¹/₂ teaspoon salt. Stir in ¹/₂ cup yellow cornmeal and 1¹/₂ cups whole bran. Add to creamed mixture, stirring just till blended. Fill paper bake cups in muffin pans ²/₃ full. Bake at 375° for 22 to 24 minutes or till done. Makes about 1¹/₂ dozen.

# RUM MUFFINS

1 well-beaten egg
1/2 cup canned
   mincemeat
1/2 cup apple juice
1 14-ounce package
   orange muffin mix

\* \* \*

1 cup sifted
   confectioners' sugar
4 teaspoons milk
1/4 teaspoon rum extract

OVEN 400°

Combine the egg, mincemeat, and apple juice in mixing bowl. Add muffin mix all at once; stir just till blended. Fill greased muffin pans 1/2 full. Bake at 400° for about 15 minutes. Remove from pans immediately. Blend confectioners' sugar with milk and rum extract; drizzle over warm muffins. Makes 12.

# SWEDISH TIMBALE CASES

1 cup sifted all-purpose
   flour
1 tablespoon sugar

1/4 teaspoon salt
1 cup milk
2 well-beaten eggs

Sift flour, sugar, and salt. Add milk to eggs; gradually stir in flour mixture; beat till smooth. Heat timbale iron in deep hot fat (375°) 2 minutes. Drain excess fat from iron; dip into batter to within 1/4 inch of top. Return at once to hot fat. Fry till case is crisp and golden, and slips from iron. Turn upside down to drain. Reheat iron 1 minute; make next case. Makes about 2 dozen. (If batter slips off, iron is too cold; if it sticks, iron is too hot.)

# PEANUT BUTTER MUFFINS

2 cups sifted all-purpose
   flour
1/2 cup sugar
2 1/2 teaspoons baking
   powder
1/2 teaspoon salt
         \* \* \*
1/2 cup chunk-style peanut
   butter

2 tablespoons butter or
   margarine
1 cup milk
2 well-beaten eggs
         \* \* \*
1/4 cup currant jelly,
   melted
1/2 cup finely chopped
   peanuts

OVEN 400°

Sift together flour, sugar, baking powder, and salt. Cut in peanut butter and butter till mixture resembles coarse crumbs. Add milk and eggs all at once, stirring just till moistened. Fill greased muffin pans $2/3$ full. Bake in hot oven (400°) for 15 to 17 minutes. Immediately brush tops with melted jelly; dip in peanuts. Serve hot. Makes $1^1/2$ dozen muffins.

## POPOVERS

*These crispy shells are light as balloons—*

| | |
|---|---|
| 2 eggs | 1 cup milk |
| 1 cup sifted all-purpose flour | 1 tablespoon salad oil |
| | $1/2$ teaspoon salt |

OVEN 475°

In mixing bowl, beat eggs with a rotary beater or electric mixer. Add flour, milk, salad oil, and salt. Beat till smooth.

Fill 6 to 8 *well-greased* custard cups $1/2$ full. Bake in very hot oven (475°) for 15 minutes. Reduce oven to moderate (350°) and bake 25 to 30 minutes longer or till browned and firm. A few minutes before removing from oven, prick with a fork to allow steam to escape.

If you like popovers dry and crisp, turn off oven and leave popovers in oven 30 minutes with door ajar. Serve hot. Makes 6 to 8 large popovers.

**Pecan Popovers:** Stir $1/4$ cup finely chopped pecans into Popover batter before filling custard cups.

# BISCUITS

- Always sift dry ingredients together for even distribution. Uneven distribution of leavening causes yellow or brown flecks.
- Use a pastry blender or blending fork to cut shortening into dry ingredients.
- Kneading biscuits gently 10 to 12 strokes blends all ingredients and assures tall, plump biscuits.
- For crusty biscuits, place ³/₄ inch apart on baking sheet. For soft sides, place biscuits close together in a shallow baking pan. Brush tops with milk or light cream before baking for golden color.
- Cut biscuits may be refrigerated 30 minutes to an hour before baking.
- Drop biscuits use more liquid than rolled biscuits, and should be dropped from a teaspoon onto greased baking sheet.

## BISCUITS SUPREME

OVEN 450°

Mix biscuits according to picture directions on the next page using these ingredients: 2 cups sifted all-purpose flour, 4 teaspoons baking powder, ¹/₂ teaspoon salt, ¹/₂ teaspoon cream of tartar, 2 teaspoons sugar, ¹/₂ cup shortening, and ²/₃ cup milk. Bake on ungreased baking sheet in very hot oven (450°) for 10 to 12 minutes. Makes about 16 medium biscuits.

For biscuits, sift dry ingredients into bowl. Cut in the shortening till like coarse crumbs. Make a well; add milk all at once. Stir quickly with fork just till dough follows fork around bowl. Turn onto lightly floured surface. (Dough should be soft.) Knead gently 10 to 12 strokes. Roll or pat dough 1/2 inch thick. Dip 2 1/2-inch biscuit cutter in flour; cut dough straight down. Bake as directed.

## BAKING POWDER BISCUITS

2 cups sifted all-purpose
flour
3 teaspoons baking
powder

$^1/_2$ teaspoon salt
$^1/_3$ cup shortening
$^3/_4$ cup milk

OVEN 450°

Mix biscuits according to picture directions on previous page. Bake on ungreased baking sheet at 450° about 12 minutes. Makes 10.

**Drop Biscuits:** Increase milk to 1 cup. Drop from teaspoon onto ungreased baking sheet. Bake as above. Makes 12.

**Pinwheel Biscuits:** Roll dough in 18x9x$^1/_4$-inch rectangle; brush with melted butter or margarine; sprinkle with mixture of sugar and ground cinnamon *or* brown sugar and chopped nuts. Beginning at long side, roll as for jelly roll; seal edge; cut in $^1/_2$-inch slices. Bake, cut side down, on greased baking sheet as directed above.

**Cheese Swirls:** Add 1 cup shredded sharp process American cheese and $^1/_2$ teaspoon celery seed to flour mixture before adding milk. Roll dough to 18x9x$^1/_4$-inch rectangle; spread with mixture of 2 tablespoons soft butter or margarine and 1 tablespoon prepared mustard. Sprinkle with 8 slices crumbled, crisp-cooked bacon. Roll and slice as for Pinwheel Biscuits. Bake at 425° about 15 minutes. Makes 30.

**Whole Wheat Biscuits:** Substitute 1 cup whole wheat flour for 1 cup sifted all-purpose flour; mix with sifted dry ingredients. Increase salt to $^3/_4$ teaspoon and baking powder to 4 teaspoons.

**Buttermilk Biscuits:** Sift $^1/_4$ teaspoon soda with flour mixture. Substitute buttermilk for milk in recipe.

## QUICK PECAN ROLLS

OVEN 375°

Mix 1 cup brown sugar, 2 tablespoons dark corn syrup, and $^1/_2$ cup melted butter. Divide among 18 muffin cups; sprinkle with $^2/_3$ cup pecans.

Sift together 3 cups sifted all-purpose flour, 4$^1/_2$ teaspoons baking powder, 1 teaspoon salt, and $1/3$ cup sugar. Cut in $1/2$ cup shortening. Add 2 slightly beaten eggs and $2/3$ cup milk all at once; stir just to blend. Turn out on lightly floured surface; knead 8 to 10 times. Roll into 15x12x$1/4$-inch rectangle. Brush with 2 tablespoons melted butter; sprinkle with mixture of $1/4$ cup granulated sugar and 1 teaspoon ground cinnamon. Roll as for jelly roll; seal edge; cut in $3/4$-inch slices. Place slice, cut side down, in each muffin cup. Bake at 375° for 20 to 25 minutes. Remove from pans immediately. Makes 18.

## FLUFFY DUMPLINGS

| | |
|---|---|
| 1 cup sifted all-purpose flour | $1/2$ teaspoon salt |
| | * * * |
| 2 teaspoons baking powder | $1/2$ cup milk |
| | 2 tablespoons salad oil |

Sift flour, baking powder, and salt together into mixing bowl. Combine milk and salad oil; add all at once to dry ingredients, stirring just till moistened.

Drop from tablespoon atop bubbling stew. Cover tightly; let mixture return to boiling. Reduce heat (don't lift cover); simmer 12 to 15 minutes. Makes 10.

# PANCAKES, WAFFLES

- Stir pancake and waffle batters quickly and only till dry ingredients are moistened (batter will be lumpy).
- Dip up pancake batter with a ¼-cup measure. Use a tablespoon for dollar-size.
- Test heat of griddle or waffle baker by sprinkling with water. If drops dance, heat is just right. Use electric skillet, waffle baker, or griddle for perfect heat control.
- For even baking of waffles, close lid quickly—don't open. Wait for signal light or till steam stops.
- For crisp waffles, allow waffle to remain on grid a few seconds after opening lid, or let bake a little longer.
- Refrigerate any leftover pancake or waffle batter for use the next day.
- Keep baked pancakes and waffles warm for a short time on rack in 250° oven.

## FAVORITE PANCAKES

| | |
|---|---|
| 1¼ cups sifted all-purpose flour | ½ teaspoon salt |
| 3 teaspoons baking powder | 1 beaten egg |
| 1 tablespoon sugar | 1 cup milk* |
| | 2 tablespoons salad oil |

Sift together dry ingredients. Combine egg, milk, and salad oil; add to dry ingredients, stirring just till moistened. Bake on hot griddle. Makes about 12 dollar-size, or eight 4-inch pancakes.

  * For thinner pancakes, add 2 tablespoons milk to batter.

  **Blueberry Pancakes:** When undersides of pancakes are nicely browned, sprinkle about 2 tablespoons drained blueberries over each cake. Turn, brown other side.

**Buttermilk Pancakes:** Substitute buttermilk or sour milk for sweet milk. Add 1/2 teaspoon soda and reduce baking powder to 2 teaspoons. Bake on hot griddle.

**Feather Pancakes:** Reduce flour to 1 cup. Increase baking powder and sugar to 2 tablespoons each. Add dry ingredients to liquid; beat smooth. Bake on hot griddle.

## APPLE PANCAKES

2 cups sifted all-purpose flour
2 tablespoons sugar
4 teaspoons baking powder
1 teaspoon salt
2 well-beaten egg yolks

2 cups milk
2 tablespoons butter, melted
1 cup finely chopped apple
2 stiffly beaten egg whites

Sift together dry ingredients. Combine egg yolks and milk. Pour into dry ingredients; stir well. Stir in butter and apple. Fold in egg whites. Let batter stand a few minutes.

Bake on hot griddle using 1/3 cup batter for each. (Use a spatula to spread batter evenly.) Dot with butter; sprinkle with confectioners' sugar; roll up. Makes 12.

## BUCKWHEAT GRIDDLE CAKES

2 2/3 cups sifted all-purpose flour
1 1/3 cups stirred buckwheat flour
1 teaspoon salt
1 package active dry yeast

2 1/2 cups warm water
3 tablespoons brown sugar
3/4 teaspoon soda
2 tablespoons salad oil

Combine flours and salt. Soften yeast in warm water; stir in *1 tablespoon* brown sugar. Stir into dry ingredients. Mix well. Cover; let stand overnight at room temperature (bowl *must not* be over 1/2 full). The next morning stir batter; add remaining sugar, soda, and oil; mix well. Refrigerate 1 cup batter for starter (keeps several weeks). Bake remaining batter on hot, lightly greased griddle. Makes 16 large pancakes.

*To use starter,* place starter in large bowl; add 2¼ cups warm water, 2¼ cups sifted all-purpose flour, and 1¼ cups buckwheat flour. Stir till smooth. Cover; let stand overnight as before. The next morning, stir batter. Add 2 tablespoons brown sugar, ¾ teaspoon soda, and 2 tablespoons salad oil. Again reserve 1 cup batter for starter. Bake remaining batter as above.

## CORNMEAL GRIDDLE CAKES

1½ cups yellow cornmeal
¼ cup all-purpose flour
1 teaspoon soda
1 teaspoon salt
1 teaspoon sugar
2 cups buttermilk

2 tablespoons salad oil
1 slightly beaten egg yolk
1 stiffly beaten egg white

Mix dry ingredients. Add buttermilk, oil, and egg yolk; blend well. Fold in egg white. Let stand 10 minutes. Bake on hot griddle. Makes 16 four-inch pancakes.

## CREPES

1 cup sifted all-purpose flour
1½ cups milk

2 eggs
1 tablespoon salad oil

In bowl, combine all ingredients and ¼ teaspoon salt; beat till smooth. Lightly grease a 6-inch skillet or crepe pan; heat. Remove from heat; spoon in about 2 tablespoons batter. Spread batter evenly. Return to heat; brown on one side only. To remove, invert pan over paper toweling. Repeat with remaining batter to make 16 crepes, greasing pan occasionally.

Fill with creamed meat mixture; roll up and keep warm. Or, fill with sweetened fruit; top with whipped cream, if desired.

## BLINTZ PANCAKES

Sift together 1 cup sifted all-purpose flour, 1 tablespoon sugar, and ½ teaspoon salt. Add 1 cup dairy sour cream, 1 cup small-curd cottage cheese, and 4 well-beaten eggs;

stir just till combined. Bake on hot, greased griddle. Stack cakes; serve with Blueberry Sauce. Makes about 24.

## JIFFY ORANGE PANCAKES

Combine 1 beaten egg, 1 cup light cream, and $\frac{1}{4}$ cup frozen orange juice concentrate. Add 1 cup packaged pancake mix; stir to remove most lumps. Bake on greased griddle. Serve with warm Orange Sauce (page 187). Makes 18 pancakes.

When uppersides of pancakes are bubbly all over, a few bubbles have burst, and edges begin to appear dry, cakes are ready to turn. A quick flip with a broad spatula makes the job easy. Turn only once.

## EVERYDAY WAFFLES

1$\frac{3}{4}$ cups sifted all-purpose flour
3 teaspoons baking powder
$\frac{1}{2}$ teaspoon salt
2 beaten egg yolks
1$\frac{3}{4}$ cups milk
$\frac{1}{2}$ cup salad oil or melted shortening
2 stiffly beaten egg whites

Sift together dry ingredients. Combine yolks, milk, and oil; stir into dry ingredients. Fold in whites, leaving a few fluffs. Bake. Makes three 10-inch waffles.

**Buttermilk Waffles:** Substitute 2 cups buttermilk for sweet milk. Add $\frac{1}{2}$ teaspoon soda and reduce baking powder to 2 teaspoons. Continue as above.

**Ham Waffles:** Sprinkle 2 tablespoons chopped cooked ham over each waffle before baking.

**Cheese Waffles:** Add $\frac{1}{2}$ cup shredded process cheese to batter before baking.

**Corn Waffles:** Reduce milk to 1¼ cups; add 1 cup canned cream-style corn.

**Pecan Waffles:** Sprinkle 2 tablespoons broken pecans atop waffle before baking.

## PEANUT BUTTER WAFFLES

To 1 cup packaged pancake mix, add 2 tablespoons sugar, ⅓ cup chunk-style peanut butter, 1 egg, 1 cup milk, and 2 tablespoons salad oil. Beat almost smooth. Bake in preheated waffle baker. Makes 8.

## CORNMEAL WAFFLES

| | |
|---|---|
| 1 cup sifted all-purpose flour | 1 cup yellow cornmeal |
| 2 teaspoons baking powder | 2 beaten egg yolks |
| 1 teaspoon soda | 2 cups buttermilk |
| 1 teaspoon sugar | ¼ cup salad oil |
| ½ teaspoon salt | 2 stiffly beaten egg whites |

Sift first 5 ingredients; stir in cornmeal. Mix yolks, milk, and oil; add to dry ingredients. Fold in whites. Bake. Makes 12.

## DESSERT WAFFLES

| | |
|---|---|
| 2 well-beaten eggs | ¼ cup butter or margarine, melted |
| 1 cup light cream | |
| 1¼ cups sifted cake flour | 2 stiffly beaten egg whites |
| ½ teaspoon salt | |
| 3 teaspoons baking powder | |

Blend whole eggs and cream. Sift together dry ingredients; stir in. Add butter. Fold in whites. Bake. Makes three 10-inch waffles. Top with ice cream or fruit.

**Chocolate Waffles:** Sift 6 tablespoons cocoa (regular-type, dry) and ½ cup sugar with dry ingredients. Use ¾ cup cream and add ¼ teaspoon vanilla.

**Polka-dot Waffles:** Sprinkle ½ cup semisweet chocolate pieces and ⅓ cup chopped pecans over batter in baker.

**Orange Waffles:** Add 1 tablespoon grated orange peel. Pass Orange Butter.

## TASTY BRAN WAFFLES

Sift together 1 cup sifted all-purpose flour, ¼ cup sugar, 1 teaspoon baking powder, ½ teaspoon soda, and ¼ teaspoon salt into mixing bowl. Stir in 1 cup buttermilk *or* sour milk and 2 beaten egg yolks. Stir in 1 cup whole bran cereal and 6 tablespoons butter, melted. Fold in 2 stiffly beaten egg whites. Bake in preheated waffle baker. Makes 4 or 5 large waffles.

*Note:* Or bake pancakes on hot greased griddle using ¼ cup batter for each.

## "OH BOY" WAFFLES

Sift together 2¼ cups sifted all-purpose flour, 4 teaspoons baking powder, ¾ teaspoon salt, and 1½ tablespoons sugar. Mix 2 beaten eggs, 2¼ cups milk, and ½ cup salad oil; add all at once to dry ingredients, beating only till moistened. Bake in preheated baker. Makes 10 to 12.

## PANCAKE, WAFFLE TOPPERS

**Maple Syrup:** Mix 1 cup light corn syrup, ½ cup brown sugar, and ½ cup water; cook; stir till dissolved. Add dash maple flavoring and 1 tablespoon butter.

**Whipped Butter:** Beat ½ cup butter with electric mixer till fluffy.

**Orange Butter:** Add 1 tablespoon confectioners' sugar and ¼ teaspoon grated orange peel to Whipped Butter.

**Honey Butter:** Gradually add ¼ cup honey to Whipped Butter; beat smooth. Add 2 teaspoons grated orange peel.

**Cranberry-orange Butter:** Place 1 small unpeeled orange (diced), ¼ cup raw cranberries, and ¼ cup sugar in electric blender. Blend 40 seconds; fold into Whipped Butter.

**Blueberry Sauce:** Cook and stir one 1-pound can blueberries and 2 teaspoons cornstarch till mixture thickens and bubbles. Add 1 teaspoon lemon juice.

**Lingonberry Sauce:** Combine ¾ cup sugar and 1 tablespoon cornstarch. Stir in 2 cups *undrained* lingonberries

(about ¹/₂ cup liquid). Cook and stir till mixture boils.
Cook 1 minute longer.

**Orange Sauce:** Combine ¹/₂ cup butter, 1 cup sugar, ¹/₂
cup frozen orange juice concentrate. Bring to boil; stir
occasionally.

## FRIED CORNMEAL MUSH

Bring to boil 2³/₄ cups water. Combine 1 cup cornmeal,
1 cup cold water, 1 teaspoon salt, and 1 teaspoon sugar;
gradually add to boiling water, stirring constantly. Cook till
thick, stirring frequently. Cover, cook over *low* heat 10 to
15 minutes. Pour into 7¹/₂x3³/₄x2¹/₄-inch loaf pan. Cool;
chill several hours or overnight. Turn out; cut in ¹/₂-inch
slices. Fry slowly in hot fat; turn once. When browned,
serve with butter and syrup. Serves 6.

# SANDWICHES

• For good sandwiches, use day-old bread of firm texture. Spread softened butter or margarine on bread to prevent fillings from soaking sandwiches.
• To keep sandwiches fresh, wrap and refrigerate. Add lettuce, tomato, cucumber, or bacon just before serving. (Wrap these items separately for box lunches.)
• Tea sandwich fillings may be the same as for other sandwiches. Choose a variety of flavors, colors, textures, and shapes, making sandwiches small. Trim with parsley, sieved egg yolk, or chopped nuts.
• Freeze bread slices for easier cutting of fancy shapes—edges will be smooth.

## WATERCRESS PINWHEELS

*Try this pretty sandwich idea with a variety of your favorite fillings—*

| | |
|---|---|
| 1 loaf unsliced white sandwich bread | 2 3-ounce packages cream cheese, softened |
| 1 cup snipped watercress | |

Cut bread lengthwise in slices ³/₈-inch thick; remove crusts. Combine watercress, cheese, and dash salt. Spread ¹/₄ cup filling on each slice. Roll up, starting at narrow end. Wrap in foil; chill. Slice pinwheels ³/₈-inch thick. Makes 24.

## FROSTED RIBBON LOAF

| | |
|---|---|
| 1 unsliced sandwich loaf | 1 cup Egg Salad Filling |
| Butter or margarine, softened | 4 3-ounce packages cream cheese, softened |
| 1 cup Ham Salad Filling | 1/3 cup milk |
| 1 tomato, peeled and thinly sliced | Snipped parsley |

Slice bread lengthwise in 4 layers; trim crusts. Butter layers. Spread first layer with Ham Salad Filling, arrange tomato slices on second layer, and spread Egg Salad Filling on third layer. Assemble loaf using 2 spatulas to support layers. Wrap in foil; chill. At serving time, beat cream cheese with milk till fluffy. Frost top and sides of loaf*. Sprinkle frosted loaf with snipped parsley. Makes 10 slices.

* Or, frost early; cover loosely; chill.

**Ribbon Sandwiches:** Assemble Ribbon Loaf with 2 or 3 fillings (such as cream cheese with pineapple, pimiento cheese with chopped ripe olives, honey and peanut butter, or crab meat and mayonnaise). Wrap in foil; chill. Slice; serve unfrosted.

## HAM SALAD FILLING

| | |
|---|---|
| 1 cup ground fully cooked ham | 2 tablespoons drained pickle relish |
| 1/3 cup finely chopped celery | 1/2 teaspoon prepared horseradish |
| | 1/4 cup mayonnaise |

Combine all ingredients. Spread between buttered bread slices. Makes 1 1/2 cups.

## EGG SALAD FILLING

| | |
|---|---|
| 4 hard-cooked eggs, chopped | 2 tablespoons finely chopped green onion |
| 1/3 cup chopped pimiento-stuffed green olives | 2 teaspoons prepared mustard |
| | 1/4 cup mayonnaise |

Combine all ingredients. Spread between buttered bread slices. Makes 1½ cups.

## APPETIZER PIE

| | |
|---|---|
| 1 hard-cooked egg, finely chopped | 1 8-ounce package cream cheese, softened |
| 1 tablespoon mayonnaise Dash dried dillweed | 2 tablespoons crumbled blue cheese |
| 1 4½-ounce can deviled ham | 2 medium unpared cucumbers, scored |
| 1 teaspoon prepared horseradish | 1 6- or 7-inch round loaf rye bread, unsliced |
| 1 teaspoon prepared mustard | 1 2-ounce jar caviar (optional) |

*Egg Filling:* Combine egg, mayonnaise, dill, and dash salt. *Ham Filling:* Combine ham, horseradish, and mustard. *Cheese Filling:* Beat cheeses till fluffy. Slice the cucumber thin; cut slices in half. Cut four ½-inch horizontal slices from center of rye loaf. Spread with mayonnaise. For each pie: Spread Egg Filling in center of slice. Ring with Ham Filling, then Cheese Filling. Overlap cucumber atop cheese. Add band of caviar between cucumber and ham. Serve in wedges. Makes 4 pies.

## JIGSAW SANDWICHES

Soften one 3-ounce package cream cheese; blend in 1 tablespoon milk, 1 teaspoon Worcestershire sauce, and 4 or 5 slices crisp-cooked bacon, crumbled. Cut 2-inch rounds with cookie cutters from white, whole wheat, and rye sliced sandwich loaves. (For smooth edges, freeze breads first, then cut while frozen.) Spread *half* of the rounds (use a variety of breads) with cheese mixture. Top with remaining rounds made into the following:

**Double Rounds:** With small hors d'oeuvre cutters, cut shapes from centers of rounds. Fit together contrasting breads.

**Stripes:** Cut rounds in three strips, making center strip widest. Fit large strip between two smaller strips of contrasting bread; hold together with a bit of cheese.

**Checkerboards:** Cut rounds in fourths. Fit together contrasting breads; spread cheese on edges to hold together.

## TEATIME SANDWICHES

Soften two 3-ounce packages cream cheese. Blend in $1/3$ cup mayonnaise and 2 tablespoons crumbled blue cheese. Add $1/2$ cup finely chopped nuts, $1/4$ teaspoon salt, $1/4$ teaspoon grated onion, and $1/2$ teaspoon Worcestershire sauce; mix well. Chill. Spread on lightly buttered bread rounds. Makes $1^{1}/3$ cups.

## SPRING SANDWICH PUFF

Butter 6 slices toasted white bread. Place buttered side up on baking sheet. Top each slice with 2 tomato slices, 1 slice sharp process American cheese, and a few cooked asparagus spears. Beat 3 egg yolks till thick and lemon-colored; add dash salt, dash pepper, and 1 tablespoon French salad dressing. Fold into 3 stiffly beaten egg whites; spoon over asparagus. Bake at 350° for 15 minutes or till egg mixture is lightly browned. Makes 6 servings.

## CLUB SANDWICH

3 slices toasted sandwich bread
Butter or margarine
Lettuce
Sliced cooked chicken or turkey
Mayonnaise or salad dressing
2 or 3 thin slices tomato
2 or 3 slices cooked bacon

Spread toast with butter. Top first slice with lettuce and chicken or turkey. Spread with mayonnaise. Top with second toast slice. Add tomato and bacon. Top with third toast slice. Anchor with 4 wooden picks. Cut diagonally in quarters. Makes 1.

## HAM SALAD ON RYE

 1 recipe Ham Salad
 Filling
10 slices buttered rye
 bread

 5 slices Swiss cheese
 5 slices tomato

Prepare Ham Salad Filling according to recipe directions; chill. Spread on 5 slices bread. Top each with cheese slice, then tomato slice; sprinkle with salt. Top with remaining bread. Makes 5 sandwiches.

## SUBMARINE SANDWICHES

Brown giant brown-and-serve French rolls (about 8 inches long) according to package directions. Split rolls lengthwise, *but don't cut quite through.* Scoop out some of centers. Spread generously with prepared mustard, garlic butter, and/or mayonnaise with curry powder. Line bottoms of rolls with leaf lettuce. Pile on slices of corned beef, boiled ham, Bologna, salami, pickled tongue, chicken, tuna, and herring as desired. Add slices of American and Swiss cheese, onion, green and ripe olive, and dill pickle. Anchor sandwich with wooden picks. Makes one large serving.

## BROILED LUNCHEON MEAT SANDWICHES

Combine 4 ounces (1 cup) shredded sharp process American cheese, 3 tablespoons mayonnaise or salad dressing, and 2 tablespoons chopped green onion. Cut one 12-ounce can luncheon meat in 12 thin slices. Lightly spread 6 slices toasted bread with prepared mustard; top each with 2 slices luncheon meat. Spread with cheese mixture. Broil 4 inches from heat about 3 minutes or till cheese melts. Makes 6 open-face sandwiches.

## BROILER TUNA BURGERS

Combine one 6½- or 7-ounce can tuna, flaked, 2 tablespoons chopped onion, 2 tablespoons chopped sweet pickle, and ¼ cup mayonnaise or salad dressing.
  Split and toast 5 hamburger buns; butter bottom

halves; spread with tuna mixture. Top each with slice of sharp process American cheese. Broil 5 inches from heat 4 minutes or till cheese melts. Add bun toppers. Makes 5 sandwiches.

## GRILLED REUBENS

Spread 6 slices pumpernickel or rye bread with ½ cup Thousand Island dressing. Top each with 1 slice Swiss cheese, 2 tablespoons well-drained sauerkraut, thin slices cooked or canned corned beef, and a second bread slice. Butter tops and bottoms of sandwiches. Grill on both sides till hot and cheese melts. Makes 6 sandwiches.

## SKILLETBURGERS

| | |
|---|---|
| 1 pound ground beef | 1 8-ounce can tomato |
| 1 cup chopped onion | sauce |
| 1 cup chopped celery | ¼ teaspoon chili powder |
| 1 10¾-ounce can | Dash bottled hot |
| condensed tomato | pepper sauce |
| soup | 8 to 10 sandwich buns, |
| | split and toasted |

Brown ground beef in a skillet. Add onion and celery; cook till tender but not brown. Add soup, tomato sauce, chili powder, pepper sauce, and ¾ teaspoon salt. Simmer, uncovered, about 30 minutes. Spoon into buns. Makes 8 to 10.

## WIENER DOUBLES

Slit frankfurters lengthwise, *not quite through*. Spread cut surfaces with prepared mustard. Stuff with cheese strips, pineapple chunks, baked beans, drained sauerkraut, pickle relish, or mashed potatoes. Wrap each frank with bacon; fasten ends with wooden picks. Broil, stuffed side down on broiler rack, 3 to 4 inches from heat, about 5 minutes. Turn and broil 3 to 5 minutes longer. Serve in toasted buns.

## SALAD SANDWICH TOWER

For each serving, butter large round slice of rye bread. Place, buttered side up, on plate. Add lettuce, then slices of Swiss cheese, and chicken or turkey. Pour Chili Mayonnaise (page 618) over all. Top with tomato slice, hard-cooked egg slice, *hot* cooked bacon, ripe olives, and parsley.

## CHICKEN-FRUIT SANDWICHES

Drain one 8³/₄-ounce can crushed pineapple, reserving syrup. Combine pineapple, 2 cups chopped, cooked chicken, one 3-ounce package softened cream cheese, 2 tablespoons snipped parsley, and 1/2 teaspoon salt. Blend in 2 or 3 tablespoons reserved syrup. Spread on 6 slices buttered white bread, using 1/3 cup for each. Top with lettuce. Cover with 6 slices buttered white bread. Makes 6 sandwiches.

## SANDWICH IDEAS

• Add avocado slices to bacon, lettuce, and tomato sandwiches. Serve open-face with Thousand Island Dressing.
• Add cole slaw with a little prepared mustard to corned beef on rye sandwiches.
• Spread French bread slices with butter and prepared mustard. Spoon on baked beans and top with shredded sharp process cheese. Broil till cheese melts.
• Blend softened cream cheese with orange marmalade, cranberry jelly, or crushed pineapple. Spread on nut bread.
• Spread 2 tablespoons seasoned ground beef on sliced bread. Broil about 3 minutes.
• Blend softened cream cheese with chopped pimiento-stuffed green olives or finely chopped candied ginger. Good for celery stuffing, too.
• Scramble eggs. Add finely chopped onion, chopped green pepper, and diced ham. Serve on toast.
• Arrange thinly sliced radishes on buttered whole wheat bread.
• Spread peanut butter on buttered bread. Add crumbled cooked bacon, jelly, pickle slices, or sliced banana.

- Arrange thinly sliced onion or pickle on buttered bread. Spoon baked beans combined with chili sauce atop.
- Mix flaked tuna, crab, or lobster with finely chopped celery, mayonnaise, and a few drops lemon juice.
- Moisten sardines and chopped hard-cooked egg with lemon juice.
- Spark ground beef with one or more of the following ingredients: Worcestershire sauce, chopped onion, chopped green pepper, soy sauce and ginger, mustard, catsup, pickle relish, barbecue sauce, or prepared horse-radish. Add before forming patties.
- Toast bread on one side. Top untoasted side with cheese and tomato slices. Broil to melt cheese; top with cooked bacon.
- Layer liverwurst, lettuce, and sliced tomato on buttered whole wheat bread. Add onion slice, if desired.
- Chop hard-cooked eggs and pimiento-stuffed green olives; add mayonnaise. Spread on rye bread; add leaf lettuce.
- Mix diced cooked chicken, chopped celery and sweet pickle, and mayonnaise.
- Mix cottage cheese, finely chopped onion and green pepper, salt, and paprika.

# 5

# COOKIES
# AND CAKES
## Frostings and Fillings

# COOKIES

- Shiny cookie sheets, 2 inches shorter and narrower than oven, will help cookies brown evenly.
- Baked cookies should be cooled on racks—this prevents sogginess. Use a cool sheet to bake remaining batches.
- Prevent excessive spreading of cookies by chilling dough; dropping onto cooled cookie sheet; baking at correct temperature; and mounding dough when dropped.
- Molded cookies can be flattened with the bottom of a glass which has been dipped in sugar or flour; crisscrossed with the tines of a fork; or pressed with thumb.
- For rolled cookies, roll a small amount of dough at a time, keeping rest chilled. Use pastry cloth and stockinette for rolling pin. Roll from center to edge as for pie crust. Use lightly floured cutter. Start cutting at edge, working toward center.
- For best results with a cookie press, keep dough pliable to obtain well defined patterns. Chill dough if it becomes soft.
- Store soft cookies in a tightly covered jar; tuck in an apple wedge if they become dry. Keep crisp cookies in a jar with a loose-fitting lid to retain freshness.

## CHOCOLATE CHIPPERS

| | |
|---|---|
| $\frac{1}{2}$ cup shortening | $\frac{3}{4}$ teaspoon salt |
| $\frac{1}{2}$ cup granulated sugar | $\frac{1}{2}$ teaspoon soda |
| $\frac{1}{4}$ cup brown sugar | 1 6-ounce package |
| 1 egg | (1 cup) semisweet |
| 1 teaspoon vanilla | chocolate pieces |
| 1 cup sifted all-purpose flour | $\frac{1}{2}$ cup broken nuts |

OVEN 375°

Cream shortening, sugars, egg, and vanilla till light and fluffy. Sift together dry ingredients; stir into creamed mixture; blend well. Add chocolate and nuts.

Drop from teaspoon 2 inches apart on a greased cookie sheet. Bake in moderate oven (375°) 10 to 12 minutes. Remove from sheet immediately. Makes 3 dozen.

## OATMEAL COOKIES

| | |
|---|---|
| 1 cup shortening | 1 teaspoon salt |
| 1½ cups brown sugar | 1 teaspoon ground |
| 2 eggs | cinnamon |
| ½ cup buttermilk or | 1 teaspoon ground |
| sour milk* | nutmeg |
| 1¾ cups sifted all-purpose | 3 cups quick-cooking |
| flour | rolled oats |
| 1 teaspoon soda* | 1 cup raisins |
| 1 teaspoon baking | ½ cup chopped walnuts |
| powder* | |

OVEN 400°

Cream shortening, sugar, and eggs together till light and fluffy. Stir in buttermilk. Sift together dry ingredients; stir into creamed mixture. Stir in oats, raisins, and nuts. Drop from tablespoon 2 inches apart on lightly greased cookie sheet. Bake in hot oven (400°) about 8 minutes. Cool slightly; remove from pan. Makes about 60.

 * Or use sweet milk; reduce soda to ¼ teaspoon; use 2 teaspoons baking powder.

## SPICY HERMITS

| | |
|---|---|
| ½ cup shortening | ½ teaspoon ground |
| 1 cup brown sugar | cinnamon |
| 1 egg | ¼ teaspoon salt |
| 1½ cups sifted all-purpose | ¼ teaspoon ground |
| flour | nutmeg |
| 1 tablespoon instant | ¼ teaspoon ground |
| coffee powder | cloves |
| ½ teaspoon soda | ¾ cup raisins |
| | ½ cup broken walnuts |

OVEN 375°

Thoroughly cream shortening and sugar. Add egg; beat well. Stir in 2 tablespoons water. Sift together dry ingredients; add to creamed mixture. Stir in raisins and nuts. Drop from teaspoon 2 inches apart on lightly greased cookie sheet. Bake at 375° for 10 minutes. Makes 42.

## COCONUT KISSES

3 egg whites
1/2 teaspoon vanilla
1 cup granulated sugar
2 cups cornflakes
1 3 1/2-ounce can (1 1/3 cups) flaked coconut

1/2 cup chopped nuts
2 1-ounce squares semisweet chocolate
2 teaspoons shortening

OVEN 350°

Beat egg whites with dash salt and vanilla to soft peaks; gradually add sugar; beat stiff. Stir in cereal, coconut, and nuts.

Drop from teaspoon onto well-greased cookie sheet. Bake at 350° for 18 to 20 minutes. Remove cookies immediately. If they stick to pan, return to oven to soften.

Melt chocolate and shortening together; drizzle atop cookies. Makes 3 1/2 dozen.

## COCONUT MACAROONS

2 egg whites
Dash salt
1/2 teaspoon vanilla

2/3 cup granulated sugar
1 3 1/2-ounce can (1 1/3 cups) flaked coconut

OVEN 325°

Beat egg whites with dash salt and the vanilla till soft peaks form. Gradually add sugar, beating till stiff. Fold in coconut.

Drop by rounded teaspoon onto greased cookie sheet. Bake in slow oven (325°) about 20 minutes. Makes about 1 1/2 dozen.

## GUMDROP COOKIES

OVEN 375°

Thoroughly cream together 1/2 cup shortening, 1/2 cup brown sugar, and 1/2 cup granulated sugar. Add 1 egg and 1/2 teaspoon vanilla; beat well. Sift together 3/4 cup sifted all-purpose flour, 1/2 teaspoon baking powder, 1/4 teaspoon soda, and 1/4 teaspoon salt; add to creamed mixture.

Stir in 3/4 cup quick-cooking rolled oats, 1/2 cup flaked coconut, and 1/2 cup gumdrops, cut in small pieces. Drop from teaspoon onto ungreased cookie sheet. Bake in moderate oven (375°) about 10 to 12 minutes. Makes 3 dozen cookies.

## MOCHA FROSTED DROPS

1/2 cup shortening
2 1-ounce squares
    unsweetened
    chocolate
1 cup brown sugar
1 egg
1 teaspoon vanilla
1/2 cup buttermilk or sour
    milk
1 1/2 cups sifted all-purpose
    flour
1/2 teaspoon baking
    powder
1/2 teaspoon soda
1/4 teaspoon salt
1/2 cup chopped walnuts
1 6-ounce package
    (1 cup) semisweet
    chocolate pieces
    Mocha Frosting

OVEN 375°

Melt shortening and unsweetened chocolate together in a saucepan. Cool 10 minutes. Stir in the brown sugar. Beat in the egg, vanilla, and buttermilk or sour milk.

Sift together dry ingredients and add to chocolate mixture. Stir in nuts and chocolate pieces. Drop from teaspoon on greased cookie sheet. Bake at 375° about 10 minutes. Remove from pan and cool. Frost with Mocha Frosting. Top with walnut half, if desired. Makes 3 1/2 dozen.

*Mocha Frosting:* Cream 1/4 cup butter, 2 tablespoons cocoa (regular-type, dry), 2 teaspoons instant coffee powder, and dash salt. Beat in 2 1/2 cups sifted confectioners' sugar, 1¹/₂ teaspoons vanilla, and enough milk for spreading consistency.

## PECAN CRISPIES

¹/₂ cup butter or margarine
6 tablespoons brown sugar
6 tablespoons granulated sugar
1 egg
¹/₂ teaspoon vanilla

1¹/₄ cups sifted all-purpose flour
1 teaspoon baking powder
¹/₄ teaspoon each soda and salt
1 cup chopped pecans

OVEN 375°

Cream butter and sugars till light. Beat in egg and vanilla. Sift together dry ingredients; blend into creamed mixture. Stir in nuts. Drop from teaspoon on ungreased cookie sheet. Bake at 375° about 10 minutes. Cool cookies slightly before removing from pan. Makes 2¹/₂ dozen.

## ORANGE DROP COOKIES

³/₄ cup shortening
¹/₄ cup butter or margarine
1¹/₂ cups brown sugar
2 beaten eggs
2 tablespoons grated orange peel
¹/₄ cup orange juice
1 teaspoon vanilla

1 cup buttermilk or sour milk
3¹/₂ cups sifted all-purpose flour
2 teaspoons baking powder
1 teaspoon soda
¹/₄ teaspoon salt
1 cup chopped nuts

OVEN 350°

Thoroughly cream together shortening, butter, and brown sugar. Beat in eggs, orange peel, orange juice, vanilla, and buttermilk. Sift together dry ingredients; add to creamed mixture. Add nuts. Drop from teaspoon onto greased cookie sheet. Bake at 350° for 15 minutes. Makes 6 dozen.

## LEMON TEA COOKIES

1 1/2 teaspoons vinegar
1/2 cup milk
1/2 cup butter or
  margarine
3/4 cup granulated sugar
1 egg
1 teaspoon shredded
  lemon peel

1 3/4 cups sifted all-purpose
  flour
1 teaspoon baking
  powder
1/4 teaspoon each soda
  and salt
Lemon Glaze

OVEN 350°

Stir vinegar into milk. Cream butter and sugar till fluffy.
Beat in egg and peel. Sift dry ingredients; add to creamed
mixture alternately with milk; beat after each addition.
Drop from teaspoon 2 inches apart on ungreased cookie
sheet. Bake at 350° for 12 to 14 minutes. Remove at once;
brush with Lemon Glaze. Makes 48 cookies.

*Lemon Glaze:* Combine 3/4 cup granulated sugar and 1/4
cup lemon juice.

## DROP SUGAR COOKIES

Prepare Sugar Cookies (page 215) but omit 1/2 cup flour.
Drop from teaspoon onto cookie sheet. If desired, flatten
each by pressing with fork tines. Bake at 375° about 10
to 12 minutes. Makes 48 cookies.

## JAM THUMBPRINTS

2/3 cup butter
1/3 cup sugar
2 egg yolks
1 teaspoon vanilla
1 1/2 cups sifted all-purpose
  flour

2 slightly beaten egg
  whites
3/4 cup finely chopped
  walnuts
1/3 cup cherry or
  strawberry preserves

OVEN 350°

Cream butter and sugar till fluffy. Add egg yolks, vanilla,
and 1/2 teaspoon salt; beat well. Gradually add flour, mixing well. Shape in 3/4-inch balls; dip in egg whites, then
roll in nuts. Place 1 inch apart on greased cookie sheet.
Press down centers with thumb. Bake at 350° for 15 to

17 minutes. Cool slightly; remove from pan and cool on rack. Just before serving, fill centers with preserves. Makes 36.

## BUTTERSCOTCH COOKIES

| | |
|---|---|
| 1/2 cup butter or margarine | 1 1/3 cups sifted all-purpose flour |
| 2/3 cup brown sugar | 3/4 teaspoon soda |
| 1 egg | 3/4 teaspoon vanilla |
| | 1/3 cup chopped walnuts |

OVEN 375°

Melt butter in 2-quart saucepan; add sugar and mix well. Add egg; beat till light colored. Sift flour with soda; stir into egg mixture. Add vanilla and nuts. Chill. Roll in small balls. Bake on ungreased cookie sheet at 375° for 7 to 10 minutes. Remove at once. Makes 3 dozen.

## GINGERSNAPS

OVEN 375°

Cream 3/4 cup shortening, 1 cup brown sugar, 1/4 cup molasses, and 1 egg till fluffy. Sift together 2 1/4 cup sifted all-purpose flour, 2 teaspoons soda, 1/2 teaspoon salt, 1 teaspoon ground ginger, 1 teaspoon ground cinnamon, and 1/2 teaspoon ground cloves; stir into molasses mixture.

Form in small balls. Roll in granulated sugar; place 2 inches apart on greased cookie sheet. Bake in moderate oven (375°) 12 minutes. Makes about 5 dozen.

## PEANUT BUTTER COOKIES

| | |
|---|---|
| 1/2 cup butter or margarine | 1/2 teaspoon vanilla |
| 1/2 cup peanut butter | 1 1/4 cups sifted all-purpose flour |
| 1/2 cup granulated sugar | |
| 1/2 cup brown sugar | 3/4 teaspoon soda |
| 1 egg | 1/4 teaspoon salt |

OVEN 375°

Thoroughly cream butter, peanut butter, sugars, egg, and vanilla. Sift together dry ingredients; blend into creamed mixture. Shape in 1-inch balls; roll in granulated sugar. Place 2 inches apart on ungreased cookie sheet. Press 5 peanut halves atop each or crisscross with fork tines. Bake at 375° for 10 to 12 minutes. Cool slightly; remove from pan. Makes 4 dozen.

## CHOCOLATE CRINKLES

OVEN 350°

Thoroughly cream ½ cup shortening, 1⅔ cups granulated sugar, and 2 teaspoons vanilla. Beat in 2 eggs, then two 1-ounce squares unsweetened chocolate, melted.

Sift together 2 cups sifted all-purpose flour, 2 teaspoons baking powder, and ½ teaspoon salt; add alternately with ⅓ cup milk. Add ½ cup chopped walnuts.

Chill 3 hours. Form in 1-inch balls; roll in confectioners' sugar. Place on greased cookie sheet 2 to 3 inches apart. Bake in moderate oven (350°) for 15 minutes. Cool slightly; remove from pan. Makes 48.

## SANDIES

| | |
|---|---|
| 1 cup butter or margarine | 2 teaspoons vanilla |
| ⅓ cup granulated sugar | 2 cups sifted all-purpose flour |
| 2 teaspoons water | 1 cup chopped pecans |

OVEN 325°

Cream butter and sugar; add 2 teaspoons water and vanilla; mix well. Blend in flour and nuts; chill 4 hours. Shape in balls or fingers. Bake on ungreased cookie sheet at 325° about 20 minutes. Remove from pan; cool slightly; roll in confectioners' sugar. Makes about 3 dozen cookies.

## VANILLA CRISPS

| | |
|---|---|
| 1/2 cup butter or margarine | 2 teaspoons vanilla |
| 1/2 cup shortening | 2 eggs |
| 1 cup granulated sugar | 2 1/2 cups sifted all-purpose flour |

OVEN 375°

Cream butter, shortening, and sugar. Add vanilla and 1/2 teaspoon salt. Add eggs, beating well. Stir in flour; mix well. Drop from teaspoon 2 inches apart on ungreased cookie sheet. (Or, chill dough; shape into 1-inch balls.) Flatten with floured glass. Bake at 375° for 8 to 10 minutes. Remove immediately and cool on rack. Makes 84.

## SPRITZ

| | |
|---|---|
| 1 1/2 cups butter or margarine | 1/2 teaspoon almond extract |
| 1 cup granulated sugar | 4 cups sifted all-purpose flour |
| 1 egg | 1 teaspoon baking powder |
| 2 tablespoons milk | |
| 1 teaspoon vanilla | |

OVEN 400°

Thoroughly cream butter and sugar. Add egg, milk, vanilla, and almond extract; beat well. Sift flour and baking powder; add gradually to creamed mixture, mixing till smooth. Do not chill. Force through cookie press onto ungreased cookie sheet. Bake at 400° for 8 minutes; cool. Makes 72.

## PFEFFERNUESSE

OVEN 375°

In saucepan, combine 3/4 cup light molasses and 1/2 cup butter. Cook and stir till butter melts. Cool to room temperature.

Stir in 2 beaten eggs. Sift together 4 1/2 cups sifted all-purpose flour, 1/2 cup granulated sugar, 1 1/4 teaspoons soda, 1 1/2 teaspoons ground cinnamon, 1/2 teaspoon ground cloves, 1/2 teaspoon ground nutmeg, and dash pepper. Add to molasses mixture; mix well. Chill well.

Shape dough into 1-inch balls. Bake on greased cookie sheet at 375° for 12 minutes. Cool; roll in confectioners' sugar. Makes 4½ dozen.

## GUMDROP GEMS

| | |
|---|---|
| 1 cup butter or margarine | 1 teaspoon soda |
| 1½ cups sifted confectioners' sugar | 1 teaspoon cream of tartar |
| 1 teaspoon vanilla | ¼ teaspoon salt |
| 1 egg | 1 cup small gumdrops, sliced* |
| 2½ cups sifted all-purpose flour | |

OVEN 375°

Cream butter, confectioners' sugar, and vanilla; beat in egg. Sift together flour, soda, cream of tartar, and salt; gradually stir into creamed mixture; mix well.

Shape dough into roll 2 inches in diameter and 12 inches long. Wrap in waxed paper; chill several hours or overnight.

Cut ¼-inch-thick slices. Place on ungreased cookie sheet. Decorate tops with gumdrop slices. Bake in a moderate oven (375°) about 12 minutes or till lightly browned. Cool slightly before removing from pan. Makes about 4 dozen cookies.

* Remove black candies.

## REFRIGERATOR CRISPS

| | |
|---|---|
| 1 cup shortening | 1 teaspoon ground cinnamon |
| ½ cup granulated sugar | ¼ teaspoon ground nutmeg |
| ½ cup brown sugar | |
| 1 egg | ¼ teaspoon ground cloves |
| 2 tablespoons milk | |
| 2¼ cups sifted all-purpose flour | ½ cup finely chopped walnuts |
| ½ teaspoon soda | |
| ½ teaspoon salt | |

OVEN 375°

Cream together shortening and sugars; add egg and milk; beat well. Sift together dry ingredients; stir into creamed mixture. Add nuts. Shape in rolls 2¹/₂ inches in diameter. Wrap in waxed paper; chill well.

Slice about ¹/₄ inch thick. Place 1 inch apart on lightly greased cookie sheet. Bake in moderate oven (375°) for 5 to 7 minutes or till delicately browned. Remove at once to rack. Makes about 4¹/₂ dozen.

## OATMEAL ROUNDS

1¹/₂ cups sifted all-purpose flour
¹/₂ teaspoon soda
³/₄ teaspoon salt
³/₄ cup brown sugar

1¹/₂ cups quick-cooking rolled oats
¹/₂ cup shortening
¹/₂ cup butter or margarine
1 teaspoon vanilla

OVEN 350°

Sift together flour, soda, and salt; stir in sugar and oats. Cut in shortening and butter till crumbly. Combine 2 tablespoons cold water and vanilla; sprinkle over mixture, tossing lightly till moistened. Shape into a roll 2 inches in diameter. Wrap in waxed paper; chill. Slice *thinly*. Bake on greased cookie sheet at 350° for 8 to 10 minutes. Makes 3-3¹/₂ dozen.

## LEMON PECAN DAINTIES

OVEN 350°

Thoroughly cream ³/₄ cup butter and 1 cup granulated sugar. Add 1 egg, 1 teaspoon grated lemon peel, and 1 tablespoon lemon juice; beat well. Sift together 2 cups sifted all-purpose flour, 1 teaspoon baking powder, and ¹/₂ teaspoon salt; add to creamed mixture, mixing well. Stir in 1 cup finely chopped pecans. Shape in rolls 2 inches in diameter. Chill thoroughly.

Slice very thin and place on ungreased cookie sheet. Bake in a moderate oven (350°) for 10 to 12 minutes. Cool slightly before removing from pan. Makes 5 dozen.

## PECAN TASSIES

OVEN 325°

Let one 3-ounce package cream cheese and ½ cup butter soften; blend together. Stir in 1 cup sifted all-purpose flour. Chill 1 hour. Shape in 2 dozen 1-inch balls; place in ungreased 1¾-inch muffin pans; press dough against bottom and sides.

Beat together 1 egg, ¾ cup brown sugar, 1 tablespoon softened butter, 1 teaspoon vanilla, and dash salt just till smooth. Divide ⅓ cup coarsely broken pecans among "tarts"; add egg mixture. Top with ⅓ cup coarsely broken pecans. Bake at 325° for 25 minutes or till filling is set. Cool; remove from pans. Makes 2 dozen.

## APPLE-OATMEAL COOKIES

| | |
|---|---|
| 1 cup finely diced unpared apple | 2 teaspoons baking powder |
| ¼ cup raisins | 1 teaspoon ground cinnamon |
| ¼ cup chopped pecans | |
| ½ cup granulated sugar | ½ teaspoon each salt and cloves |
| 1 cup butter or margarine | ½ cup milk |
| 1 cup brown sugar | 2 cups quick-cooking rolled oats |
| 2 eggs | |
| 2 cups sifted all-purpose flour | |

OVEN 375°

In saucepan, combine fruits, nuts, granulated sugar, and 2 tablespoons water. Cook and stir till thick and apple is tender, about 10 minutes. Cream butter and brown sugar till fluffy. Beat in eggs. Sift together dry ingredients; add alternately with milk to creamed mixture. Stir in oats.

Reserve ¾ cup dough. Drop remainder from teaspoon onto greased cookie sheet; make depression in centers; top with apple filling and dab of reserved dough. Bake at 375° for 10 to 12 minutes. Makes 36.

## JAM SHORTBREAD COOKIES

1 cup shortening
1/2 cup granulated sugar
1/2 cup brown sugar
2 egg yolks
3 tablespoons milk
2 teaspoons vanilla
2 2/3 cups sifted all-purpose
    flour

2 teaspoons cream of
    tartar
1 teaspoon soda
1/2 teaspoon salt
1/2 cup raspberry
    preserves

OVEN 350°

Cream shortening and sugars; beat in yolks, milk, and vanilla. Sift together dry ingredients; add to creamed mixture. Chill 1 hour. On well-floured surface roll *half* the dough at a time to 1/8 inch thick; cut with 2-inch cutter; cut small hole in center of *half*. Place 1/2 teaspoon preserves on each plain cookie; top with cut out one; seal edges. Bake on ungreased cookie sheet at 350° for 10 to 12 minutes. Makes 12.

## DATE-FILLED COOKIES

1 cup shortening
1/2 cup granulated sugar
1/2 cup brown sugar
1 egg
3 tablespoons milk
1 teaspoon vanilla

3 cups sifted all-purpose
    flour
1/2 teaspoon salt
1/2 teaspoon soda
Date Filling

OVEN 375°

Cream shortening and sugars till fluffy; add egg, milk, and vanilla; beat well. Sift together dry ingredients; add to creamed mixture; mix well. Chill 1 hour.

On floured pastry cloth, roll *half* the dough at a time about 1/8 inch thick. Cut with 2 1/2-inch round cutter. Place about 1 teaspoon Date Filling on each cookie. Top with another cookie; press edges with tip of inverted teaspoon or pinch together to seal. Bake on ungreased cookie sheet at 375° for 10 to 12 minutes. Makes 3 dozen.

*Date Filling:* Combine 2 cups chopped dates, 1/3 cup sugar, 1/4 teaspoon salt, and 1/2 cup water. Bring to boiling; reduce heat; cover and simmer 5 minutes, stirring often. Add 2 tablespoons lemon juice. Cool.

## APRICOT FOLDOVERS

| | |
|---|---|
| ½ cup butter or margarine | 1⅓ cups sifted all-purpose flour |
| 4 ounces sharp process American cheese, grated (1 cup) | 2 tablespoons water |
| | * * * |
| | 1 cup dried apricots |
| | 1 cup granulated sugar |

OVEN 375°

Cream butter and cheese till light. Blend sifted flour into creamed mixture. Add water and mix well. Chill 4 to 5 hours.

Meanwhile, cook apricots according to package directions. Drain well. Stir sugar into hot fruit; cook and stir till mixture boils and becomes smooth; cool.

Divide chilled dough in half. Roll each *half* to 10-inch square; cut in 2½-inch squares. Place 1 teaspoon apricot filling on each square; fold over and seal. Bake on ungreased cookie sheet at 375° for 8 to 10 minutes. Makes 2½ dozen cookies.

## • COOKIE TRIMS •

Before baking, sprinkle sugar cookies with colored sugar, candy decorettes, gumdrops, or crushed hard peppermint candy.

Use Ornamental Frosting (page 260) for pastry tube decorations. Or, use Confectioners' Icing (page 258) made stiff enough to hold its shape for designs when put through tube.

To pipe wavy lines or frosting borders, use a plain pastry tube tip with fine opening. To make frosting rosettes, use a star tip. A ribbon effect comes from a leaf tip.

If you don't have a pastry tube, a paper cone will do the trick.

For a glaze, use a pastry brush to coat cookies with thin Confectioners' Icing (page 258).

For edgings or borders, brush edges of cookies with light corn syrup; dip in colored sugar or candy decorettes.

Roll gumdrops between waxed paper—sprinkle sugar over bottom sheet of paper and top of candy. Cut shapes with tiny cutter. Fasten to cookie with light corn syrup.

## CHINESE ALMOND COOKIES

*Serve these traditional cookies with hot tea—*

2³/₄ cups sifted all-purpose flour
1 cup granulated sugar
¹/₂ teaspoon soda
¹/₂ teaspoon salt

1 cup butter, margarine, or lard
1 slightly beaten egg
1 teaspoon almond extract
¹/₃ cup whole almonds

OVEN 325°

Sift flour, sugar, soda, and salt together into bowl. Cut in butter till mixture resembles cornmeal. Add egg and almond extract; mix well.

Shape dough into 1-inch balls and place 2 inches apart on ungreased cookie sheet. Place an almond atop each cookie and press down to flatten slightly. Bake in slow oven (325°) 15 to 18 minutes. Cool on rack. Makes 4¹/₂ dozen cookies.

## SUGAR COOKIES

²/₃ cup shortening
³/₄ cup granulated sugar
1 teaspoon vanilla
1 egg
4 teaspoons milk

2 cups sifted all-purpose flour
1¹/₂ teaspoons baking powder
¹/₄ teaspoon salt

OVEN 375°

Thoroughly cream shortening, sugar, and vanilla. Add egg and milk; beat till light and fluffy. Sift together dry ingredients; blend into creamed mixture. Divide dough in half. Cover and chill at least 1 hour.

On lightly floured surface, roll to ¹/₈ inch thickness.* Cut in desired shapes with cutters. Bake on ungreased cookie sheet at 375° about 8 to 10 minutes. Cool slightly; remove. Makes about 3 dozen.

\* Chill other half till ready to use.

## LEBKUCHEN

| | |
|---|---|
| 1 egg | $^1/_2$ teaspoon soda |
| $^3/_4$ cup brown sugar | $^1/_2$ teaspoon ground |
| $^1/_2$ cup honey | cloves |
| $^1/_2$ cup dark molasses | $^1/_2$ teaspoon ground |
| 3 cups sifted all-purpose | allspice |
| flour | $^1/_2$ cup slivered almonds |
| $1^1/_4$ teaspoons ground | $^1/_2$ cup chopped mixed |
| nutmeg | candied fruits and |
| $1^1/_4$ teaspoons ground | peels, finely diced |
| cinnamon | Lemon Glaze |

OVEN 350°

Beat egg; add sugar; beat till fluffy. Stir in honey and molasses. Sift together dry ingredients; add to first mixture; mix well. Stir in nuts, fruits, and peels. Chill several hours. On floured surface, roll $^1/_4$ inch thick; cut in $3^1/_2$x2-inch rectangles. Bake on greased cookie sheet at 350° about 12 minutes. Cool slightly; remove from pan. While warm, brush with Lemon Glaze. Makes 24.

*Lemon Glaze:* Combine 1 slightly beaten egg white, 1 tablespoon lemon juice, $^1/_2$ teaspoon grated lemon peel, dash salt, and $1^1/_2$ cups sifted confectioners' sugar.

## ROLLED GINGER COOKIES

| | |
|---|---|
| 1 cup shortening | $1^1/_2$ teaspoons soda |
| 1 cup granulated sugar | $^1/_2$ teaspoon salt |
| 1 egg | 2 to 3 teaspoons ground |
| 1 cup molasses | ginger |
| 2 tablespoons vinegar | 1 teaspoon ground |
| 5 cups sifted all-purpose | cinnamon |
| flour | 1 teaspoon ground |
| | cloves |

OVEN 375°

Cream shortening and sugar. Beat in egg, molasses, and vinegar. Sift together dry ingredients; blend in. Chill 3 hours.

Roll dough $^1/_8$ inch thick on lightly floured surface. Cut in shapes. Place 1 inch apart on greased cookie sheet.

Bake at 375° for 5 to 6 minutes. Cool slightly; remove to rack. Makes about 5 dozen.

## FIG BARS

1 cup shortening
1/2 cup granulated sugar
1/2 cup brown sugar
1 egg
1/4 cup milk
1 teaspoon vanilla

3 cups sifted all-purpose flour
1/2 teaspoon salt
1/2 teaspoon soda
Fig Filling

OVEN 375°

Cream shortening and sugars. Add egg, milk, and vanilla; beat well. Sift together dry ingredients. Stir into creamed mixture. Chill at least 1 hour.

On well-floured surface roll 1/4 of dough at a time into 8x12-inch rectangle. Cut crosswise in six 2-inch strips. Spread about 2 tablespoons Fig Filling down center of three strips. Moisten edges and top with remaining strips. Press lengthwise edges together with floured fork. Cut in 2-inch lengths. Bake on ungreased cookie sheet at 375° about 10 minutes. Makes 4 dozen.

*Fig Filling:* Combine 2 cups finely chopped dried figs, 1/2 cup granulated sugar, 1 cup orange juice, and dash salt. Cook, stirring occasionally, till mixture is thick, about 5 minutes. Cool.

## APRICOT BARS

1 1/2 cups sifted all-purpose flour
1 teaspoon baking powder
1/4 teaspoon salt

1 1/2 cups quick-cooking rolled oats
1 cup brown sugar
3/4 cup butter or margarine
3/4 cup apricot preserves

OVEN 375°

Sift together dry ingredients; stir in oats and sugar. Cut in butter till crumbly; pat 2/3 of crumbs in 11x7x1 1/2-inch pan. Spread with preserves; top with remaining crumbs. Bake in moderate oven (375°) about 35 minutes. Cool. Makes 2 1/2 dozen.

## SCOTCH SHORTBREAD

OVEN 300°

Cream 1 cup butter and ¹/₂ cup granulated sugar till light and fluffy. Stir in 2¹/₂ cups sifted all-purpose flour. Chill several hours. Divide in half. On ungreased cookie sheet pat each half into 7-inch circle. With fork prick each mound deeply to make 16 pie-shaped wedges. (Or on floured surface, roll ¹/₄ to ¹/₂ inch thick. Cut in 2x¹/₂-inch strips or with 1³/₄-inch cutter.)

Bake on ungreased cookie sheet at 300° about 30 minutes. Cool slightly; remove from pan. Makes 32 wedges or 42 cookies

## MOLASSES CAKE BARS

| | |
|---|---|
| ¹/₂ cup shortening | ¹/₄ teaspoon soda |
| ¹/₂ cup granulated sugar | 1 teaspoon instant |
| 1 egg | coffee powder |
| ¹/₂ cup light molasses | 1 teaspoon ground |
| 1¹/₂ cups sifted all-purpose | cinnamon |
| flour | ¹/₂ teaspoon ground |
| ¹/₂ teaspoon salt | cloves |
| 1¹/₂ teaspoons baking | |
| powder | |

OVEN 350°

Cream shortening and sugar; add egg; beat well. Mix in molasses and ¹/₂ cup water. Sift together remaining ingredients. Stir into creamed mixture. Pour into greased 13x9x2-inch pan. Bake at 350° for 25 minutes. While warm frost with Confectioners' Icing. Cool; cut 24 squares.

## FUDGE BROWNIES

| | |
|---|---|
| ¹/₂ cup butter or | 1 cup granulated sugar |
| margarine | 2 eggs |
| 2 1-ounce squares | 1 teaspoon vanilla |
| unsweetened | ³/₄ cup sifted all-purpose |
| chocolate, melted and | flour |
| cooled | ¹/₂ cup chopped walnuts |

OVEN 350°

In medium saucepan melt butter and chocolate. Remove from heat; stir in sugar. Blend in eggs one at a time. Add vanilla. Stir in flour and nuts; mix well. Spread in greased 8x8x2-inch baking pan. Bake at 350° for 30 minutes. *Be careful not to overbake.* Cool. Cut into 16 squares.

## TOFFEE BARS

OVEN 350°

Thoroughly cream 1 cup butter, 1 cup brown sugar, 1 egg yolk, and 1 teaspoon vanilla. Add 2 cups sifted all-purpose flour; mix well. Stir in one 6-ounce package (1 cup) semisweet chocolate pieces and 1 cup chopped walnuts. Pat into ungreased 15½x10½x1-inch baking pan. Bake at 350° for 18 to 20 minutes. While warm, cut in bars. Cool. Makes 48 bars.

## CHOCOLATE SYRUP BROWNIES

½ cup butter, softened
1 cup sugar
4 eggs
1 1-pound can chocolate-flavored syrup (1½ cups)

1¼ cups sifted all-purpose flour
1 cup chopped walnuts
Quick Frosting

OVEN 350°

Cream together butter and sugar; beat in eggs. Blend in syrup and flour; stir in nuts. Pour into greased 13x9x2-inch baking pan. Bake at 350° for 30 to 35 minutes. Cool slightly; top with Quick Frosting. Cool; cut into bars. Makes 32 brownies.

*Quick Frosting:* Mix ⅔ cup sugar, 3 tablespoons milk, and 3 tablespoons butter. Bring to boil; boil 30 seconds. Remove from heat; stir in ½ cup semisweet chocolate pieces till melted. Mixture will be thin.

## BUTTERMILK BROWNIES

| | |
|---|---|
| 1 cup butter or margarine | 1 teaspoon soda |
| 1/3 cup cocoa (regular-type, dry) | 1/2 teaspoon salt |
| | 2 slightly beaten eggs |
| 2 cups sifted all-purpose flour | 1/2 cup buttermilk |
| | 1 1/2 teaspoons vanilla |
| 2 cups sugar | Frosting |

OVEN 375°

In saucepan, combine butter, cocoa, and 1 cup water. Bring to boil; stir constantly. Remove from heat. In large bowl, sift together flour, sugar, soda, and salt; stir in eggs, buttermilk, and vanilla. Add cocoa mixture; mix till blended. Pour into greased 15 1/2x10 1/2x1-inch baking pan. Bake at 375° for 20 minutes. Immediately pour Frosting over brownies; spread evenly. Cool; cut into bars. Makes 60.

Frosting: In saucepan, mix 1/4 cup butter, 3 tablespoons cocoa (regular-type, dry), and 3 tablespoons buttermilk. Cook and stir till boiling; remove from heat. Beat in 2 1/4 cups sifted confectioners' sugar, 1/2 cup chopped walnuts, and 1/2 teaspoon vanilla.

## CHEESE-MARBLED BROWNIES

OVEN 350°

Melt one 6-ounce package (1 cup) semisweet chocolate pieces and 6 tablespoons butter or margarine over low heat; stir constantly. Cool. Gradually add 1/3 cup honey to 2 beaten eggs. Blend in chocolate mixture and 1 teaspoon vanilla. Sift together 1/2 cup sifted all-purpose flour and 1/2 teaspoon baking powder. Add to chocolate mixture; stir just till dry ingredients are moistened. Pour half of the batter into greased 9x9x2-inch baking pan. Bake at 350° for 10 minutes. Pour Cheese Filling over partially baked layer. Carefully spoon remaining brownie batter over filling; swirl slightly with cheese. Bake at 350° for 30 to 35 minutes. Cool; cut into bars. Makes 24 brownies.

Cheese Filling: In mixing bowl cream together one 8-ounce package softened cream cheese and 1/2 cup sugar; beat in 1 egg and dash salt. Stir in 1/2 cup chopped nuts.

## CINNAMON-RAISIN BARS

<sup>1</sup>/<sub>2</sub> cup butter or
   margarine
1 cup brown sugar
1<sup>1</sup>/<sub>2</sub> cups sifted all-purpose
   flour
<sup>1</sup>/<sub>2</sub> teaspoon soda

<sup>1</sup>/<sub>2</sub> teaspoon salt
1<sup>1</sup>/<sub>2</sub> cups quick-cooking
   rolled oats
Raisin Filling
Cinnamon Icing

OVEN 350°

Cream butter and sugar. Sift together dry ingredients; stir into creamed mixture. Add oats and 1 tablespoon water. Mix until crumbly. Firmly pat *half* the mixture in greased 13x9x2-inch baking dish. Spread with Raisin Filling. Mix remaining crumbs and 1 tablespoon water; spoon over filling; pat smooth. Bake in moderate oven (350°) about 35 minutes. Cool. Drizzle with Cinnamon Icing. Makes 2<sup>1</sup>/<sub>2</sub> dozen.

*Raisin Filling:* Combine <sup>1</sup>/<sub>4</sub> cup granulated sugar and 1 tablespoon cornstarch in saucepan. Stir in 1 cup water and 2 cups raisins. Cook over medium heat till thickened and bubbly. Cool.

*Cinnamon Icing:* Mix 1 cup sifted confectioners' sugar with <sup>1</sup>/<sub>4</sub> teaspoon ground cinnamon. Stir in enough milk, about 1 tablespoon, for drizzling consistency.

## BUTTERSCOTCH BARS

<sup>1</sup>/<sub>2</sub> cup butter or
   margarine
2 cups brown sugar
2 eggs
1 teaspoon vanilla
2 cups sifted all-purpose
   flour

2 teaspoons baking
   powder
<sup>1</sup>/<sub>4</sub> teaspoon salt
1 cup shredded coconut
1 cup chopped walnuts

OVEN 350°

In a 2-quart saucepan melt the butter over low heat. Remove pan from heat and stir in brown sugar. Add the eggs, one at a time, beating well after each addition. Stir in the vanilla.

Sift together dry ingredients; add with coconut and nuts to brown sugar mixture; mix thoroughly. Spread in greased 15½x10½x1-inch pan. Bake in a moderate oven (350°) about 25 minutes. Cut in bars while warm. Remove from pan when almost cool. Makes 3 dozen.

## COCONUT DIAMONDS

6 tablespoons butter, softened
¼ cup granulated sugar
¼ teaspoon salt
1 cup sifted all-purpose flour
2 eggs
1 teaspoon vanilla

1 cup brown sugar
2 tablespoons all-purpose flour
½ teaspoon salt
1 cup flaked coconut
½ cup coarsely chopped walnuts

OVEN 350°

Cream together butter, ¼ cup sugar, and ¼ teaspoon salt. Stir in 1 cup flour. Pat onto bottom of 9x9x2-inch pan. Bake at 350° for 15 minutes or till lightly browned.

Meanwhile, beat eggs slightly; add vanilla. Gradually add brown sugar, beating just till blended. Add 2 tablespoons flour and ½ teaspoon salt. Stir in coconut and nuts. Spread over baked layer. Bake 20 minutes longer or till wooden pick comes out clean. Cool. Cut in diamonds. Makes 1½ dozen.

## CEREAL-PEANUT BARS

Combine ½ cup light corn syrup, ¼ cup brown sugar, and dash salt in saucepan. Bring to full boil. Stir in 1 cup peanut butter. Remove from heat. Stir in 1 teaspoon vanilla, 2 cups crisp rice cereal, 1 cup cornflakes, slightly crushed, and one 6-ounce package (1 cup) semisweet chocolate pieces. Press into buttered 9x9x2-inch pan. Chill 1 hour. Cut in bars; store in refrigerator. Makes 2 dozen.

## DATE ORANGE BARS

OVEN 350°

Cream ¼ cup butter and ½ cup brown sugar till fluffy. Add 1 egg and 1 teaspoon grated orange peel; beat well. Sift together 1 cup sifted all-purpose flour, ½ teaspoon baking powder, and $\frac{1}{2}$ teaspoon soda; add to creamed mixture. Stir in $\frac{1}{4}$ cup milk, $\frac{1}{4}$ cup orange juice, $\frac{1}{2}$ cup chopped walnuts, and $\frac{1}{2}$ cup chopped dates.

Spread in greased 11x7x1$\frac{1}{2}$-inch pan. Bake at 350° for 25 minutes. Cool; sprinkle with confectioners' sugar. Makes 24.

# CAKES

- Cakes are grouped in three classes: with shortening (conventional and quick-mix cakes), without shortening (angel and sponge cakes), and combination angel and shortening types (chiffon cake).
- In these recipes, double-acting baking powder and regular-type all-purpose flour (unless cake flour is specified) are used. To substitute one flour for the other, use the following formula: 1 cup minus 2 tablespoons sifted all-purpose flour equals 1 cup sifted cake flour.
- When a recipe calls for shortening, don't use butter, margarine, lard, or oils. Margarine may be substituted for butter; all should be at room temperature when they are used.
- Use fresh eggs. Eggs will separate more easily when cold, but the whites will whip up better if at room temperature.
- Check accuracy of oven regulator occasionally. Preheat oven to the correct temperature before mixing cake.
- An electric mixer makes for better creaming and beating. The average number of vigorous strokes by hand needed to combine dry and liquid ingredients is 250 to 300. Cakes with high proportions of sugar or fat should be beaten more.
- Always let melted chocolate cool slightly before blending into the creamed mixture. Scrape the sides of bowl frequently.
- When adding dry ingredients alternately with liquid, begin and end with dry ingredients, beating smooth after each.
- For a shortening-type cake, grease and lightly flour bottoms of pans, or line bottoms with waxed or baking pan

liner paper. Push batter to sides of pan. Tap pans lightly
to remove large bubbles.
• Place pans as near the center of oven as possible. Don't
let pans touch each other or sides of oven. Do not place
pans directly under each other. If necessary, stagger the
pans on two shelves.
• Cool shortening layer cakes in pan about 10 minutes,
loaf cakes, 15 minutes; loosen edges. Place inverted rack
on cake; turn all over; lift off pan. Put second rack over
cake. Turn cake so top is up.

## • SHORTENING CAKES •

To bake a moist, velvety shortening-type cake, follow
the recipe carefully. Accurate measuring assures correct
proportion of ingredients and a perfect cake. Any devia-
tion in measuring can cause many of the problems listed
below.

Be sure to sift the flour, both all-purpose and cake
flour, before you measure it, then sift again when combining the flour with the other dry ingredients.

Cream shortening and sugar till light and fluffy or till
sugar is dissolved. This is important as it incorporates air
and gives cake a light texture. For other information, see
Test Kitchen Tips on this page. If problems still exist, check
the following:

**Coarse texture**
  Insufficient creaming
  Oven too slow

**Heavy, compact texture**
  Oven too slow
  Extreme overbeating

**A dry cake**
  Overbeaten egg whites
  Overbaking

**Thick, heavy crust**
  Baking too long
  Oven too hot

**Hump or cracks on top**
  Oven too hot

**Moist, sticky crust**
  Insufficient baking

**Cake falling**
  Oven too slow
  Insufficient baking
  Too much batter in pan
  Moving cake during baking

**Poor volume**
  Pan too large
  Oven too hot

A shortening-type cake is done when a cake tester or wooden pick inserted in center comes out clean. The cake will also shrink slightly from sides of baking dish or pan.

## HIGH-ALTITUDE CHANGES

If you live in a high altitude area (3,000 feet above sea level or above), you may find that many cakes will tend to fall and give unpredictable results. The chart below will help you make adjustments in the ingredient proportions. Make the adjustment for all 3 ingredients listed. Since each recipe is different, you may have to experiment a few times with each recipe to discover the best proportions. Where two amounts appear, try smaller amount first then adjust if necessary.

### • HIGH-ALTITUDE CAKE BAKING •

| Ingredients | 3,000 feet | 5,000 feet | 7,000 feet |
|---|---|---|---|
| Liquid: add for each cup | 1 to 2 tablespoons | 2 to 4 tablespoons | 3 to 4 tablespoons |
| Baking powder: decrease for each teaspoon | 1/8 teaspoon | 1/8 to 1/4 teaspoon | 1/4 teaspoon |
| Sugar: decrease for each cup | 0 to 1 tablespoon | 0 to 2 tablespoons | 1 to 3 tablespoons |

## YELLOW CAKE

2/3 cup butter or margarine
1 3/4 cups sugar
2 eggs
1 1/2 teaspoons vanilla

3 cups sifted cake flour
2 1/2 teaspoons baking powder
1 teaspoon salt
1 1/4 cups milk

OVEN 350°

Cream butter. Add sugar gradually, creaming till light. Add eggs and vanilla and beat till fluffy. Sift dry ingredients together; add to creamed mixture alternately with milk, beating after each addition. Beat 1 minute. Bake in 2 greased and lightly floured 9x1½-inch round pans at 350° for 30 to 35 minutes. Cool 10 minutes; remove from pans. Cool.

## BEST TWO-EGG CAKE

OVEN 375°

Cream ½ cup shortening and 1½ cups sugar till light, 12 to 15 minutes at medium-high speed on electric mixer. Add 1 teaspoon vanilla and 2 eggs, one at a time, beating well after each. Sift 2¼ cups sifted cake flour with 2½ teaspoons baking powder and 1 teaspoon salt. Add to creamed mixture alternately with 1 cup plus 2 tablespoons milk, beating after each addition. Bake in 2 greased and floured 9x1½-inch round pans at 375° for 20 to 25 minutes.

## BUSY-DAY CAKE

| | |
|---|---|
| ⅓ cup shortening | ½ teaspoon salt |
| 1¾ cups sifted cake flour | 1 egg |
| ¾ cup sugar | ¾ cup milk |
| 2½ teaspoons baking powder | 1½ teaspoons vanilla |

OVEN 375°

Place shortening in mixing bowl. Sift in dry ingredients. Add egg and *half* the milk; mix till flour is moistened. Beat 2 minutes at medium speed on electric mixer. Add remaining milk and vanilla; beat 2 minutes longer. Bake in greased and lightly floured 9x9x2-inch baking pan at 375° about 25 minutes or till done.

## CITRUS YELLOW CAKE

OVEN 375°

Combine ⅔ cup shortening, 1 tablespoon grated orange peel, and 1½ teaspoons grated lemon peel; mix well.

Gradually add 1½ cups sugar; cream till light and fluffy. Add 3 eggs, one at a time, beating well after each.

Sift together 2½ cups sifted cake flour, 2½ teaspoons baking powder, and ¾ teaspoon salt. Add to creamed mixture alternately with 2 tablespoons lemon juice and ¾ cup milk, beating smooth after each addition. Turn into 2 greased and lightly floured 9x1½-inch round baking pans. Bake in moderate oven (375°) for 25 to 30 minutes. Cool 10 minutes; remove from pans. Cool.

## PINEAPPLE UPSIDE-DOWN CAKE

| | |
|---|---|
| 1 8½-ounce can sliced pineapple | ½ cup granulated sugar |
| 3 tablespoons butter or margarine | 1 egg |
| | 1 teaspoon vanilla |
| ½ cup brown sugar | 1 cup sifted all-purpose flour |
| 4 maraschino cherries, halved | 1¼ teaspoons baking powder |
| * * * | ¼ teaspoon salt |
| ⅓ cup shortening | |

OVEN 350°

Drain pineapple, reserving syrup. Halve pineapple slices. Melt butter in 8x8x2-inch baking pan. Add brown sugar and 1 *tablespoon* of the reserved pineapple syrup. Add water to remaining syrup to make ½ cup. Arrange pineapple in bottom of pan. Place cherry half in center of each slice.

Cream together shortening and granulated sugar till light and fluffy. Add egg and vanilla; beat till fluffy. Sift together flour, baking powder, and salt; add to creamed mixture alternately with the ½ *cup* reserved pineapple syrup, beating after each addition. Spread over pineapple. Bake in moderate oven (350°) for 40 to 45 minutes. Cool 5 minutes; invert on plate. Serve warm.

## LOAF POUND CAKE

| | |
|---|---|
| 3/4 cup butter or margarine | 3 eggs |
| 1/2 teaspoon grated lemon peel | 1 1/4 cups sifted all-purpose flour |
| 3/4 cup sugar | 1/2 teaspoon baking powder |
| 1 teaspoon vanilla | 1/4 teaspoon salt |

OVEN 350°

Cream butter and peel; gradually add sugar, creaming till light, about 6 minutes at medium speed on electric mixer. Add vanilla, then eggs, one at a time, beating well after each. Sift together dry ingredients; stir in. Grease *bottom* only of 9x5x3-inch pan; turn in batter. Bake at 350° for 50 minutes or till done. Cool in pan. Sift confectioners' sugar lightly on top.

## DATE CAKE

| | |
|---|---|
| 1/2 pound pitted dates, coarsely chopped (1 1/2 cups) | 1 egg |
| 1 cup boiling water | 1 1/2 cups sifted all-purpose flour |
| 1/2 cup shortening | 1 teaspoon soda |
| 1 cup sugar | 1/4 teaspoon salt |
| 1 teaspoon vanilla | 1/2 cup chopped walnuts |

OVEN 350°

Combine dates with water; cool to room temperature. Cream shortening and sugar till light. Add vanilla and egg; beat well. Sift flour, soda, and salt together; add to creamed mixture alternately with date mixture, beating after each addition. Stir in nuts. Bake in greased and lightly floured 13x9x2-inch baking pan at 350° about 25 to 30 minutes. If desired, serve with a dollop of whipped cream.

## CHOCO-DATE CAKE

Prepare Date Cake, sifting 2 tablespoons cocoa (regular-type, dry) with dry ingredients and omitting nuts from batter. Turn into greased and lightly floured 13x9x2-inch baking pan. Sprinkle with ½ cup chopped walnuts and ½ cup semisweet chocolate pieces. Bake as above.

## SPICE NUT CAKE

| | |
|---|---|
| 2 cups sifted all-purpose flour | ¾ teaspoon ground cinnamon |
| 1 cup granulated sugar | ⅔ cup shortening |
| 1 teaspoon baking powder | ¾ cup brown sugar |
| 1 teaspoon salt | 1 cup buttermilk or sour milk |
| ¾ teaspoon soda | 3 eggs |
| ¾ teaspoon ground cloves | ½ cup finely chopped walnuts |

OVEN 350°

Sift together first 7 ingredients. Add shortening, brown sugar, and buttermilk. Mix till all flour is moistened. Beat 2 minutes at medium speed on electric mixer. Add eggs; beat 2 minutes more. Stir in nuts. Bake in 2 greased and lightly floured 9x1½-inch round pans in moderate oven (350°) for 30 to 35 minutes or till done. Cool 10 minutes; remove from pans. Cool completely. Fill and frost with Penuche Frosting (see page 259).

## NUTMEG FEATHER CAKE

| | |
|---|---|
| ¼ cup butter or margarine | 1 teaspoon soda |
| ¼ cup shortening | 1 teaspoon baking powder |
| 1½ cups sugar | 1½ to 2 teaspoons ground nutmeg |
| ½ teaspoon vanilla | ¼ teaspoon salt |
| 3 eggs | 1 cup buttermilk or sour milk |
| 2 cups sifted all-purpose flour | |

OVEN 350°

Cream together butter and shortening; gradually add sugar, creaming till light. Add vanilla, then eggs one at a time, beating well after each. Sift together dry ingredients; add to creamed mixture alternately with buttermilk, beating after each addition. Pour into greased and lightly floured 13x9x2-inch pan. Bake in moderate oven (350°)

for 30 minutes or till done. Cool completely in pan. Top with Broiled Coconut Topper (see page 261).

## GINGERBREAD

| | |
|---|---|
| ½ cup shortening | ¾ teaspoon soda |
| ½ cup sugar | ½ teaspoon ground |
| 1 egg | ginger |
| ½ cup light molasses | ½ teaspoon ground |
| 1½ cups sifted all-purpose | cinnamon |
| flour | ½ cup boiling water |
| ¾ teaspoon salt | |

OVEN 350°

Cream shortening and sugar till light. Add egg and molasses; beat thoroughly. Sift together dry ingredients. Add to creamed mixture alternately with water, beating after each addition. Bake in greased and lightly floured 8x8x2-inch pan at 350° for 35 to 40 minutes or till done. Serve warm.

## BANANA CAKE

OVEN 350°

Place 2 teaspoons lemon juice in measuring cup. Add milk to make ⅔ cup. Sift 2⅓ cups sifted all-purpose flour, 1⅔ cups sugar, 1¼ teaspoons baking powder, 1 teaspoon soda, and 1 teaspoon salt into large mixing bowl. Add ⅔ cup shortening, ⅔ cup mashed fully ripe bananas, and sour milk; mix until all flour is dampened. Beat vigorously 2 minutes. Add 2 eggs; beat 2 minutes longer. Stir in ⅔ cup chopped walnuts. Bake in 2 greased and floured 9x1½-inch round pans in 350° oven 35 minutes. Cool 10 minutes in pans. Remove; cool.

## CARROT-PINEAPPLE CAKE

OVEN 350°

Sift together into large mixing bowl 1½ cups sifted all-purpose flour, 1 cup sugar, 1 teaspoon baking powder, 1 teaspoon soda, 1 teaspoon ground cinnamon, and ½ teaspoon salt. Add ⅔ cup salad oil, 2 eggs, 1 cup finely shredded carrot, 1/2 cup crushed pineapple (with syrup), and 1 teaspoon vanilla. Mix till moistened; beat 2 minutes at medium speed on electric mixer. Bake in greased and lightly floured 9x9x2-inch pan in moderate oven (350°) about 35 minutes or till done. Cool 10 minutes; remove from pan. Cool. Frost with Cream Cheese Frosting (see page 258).

## APPLESAUCE CAKE

1/2 cup butter or
  margarine
2 cups sugar
2 eggs
2 1/2 cups sifted all-purpose
  flour
1 1/2 teaspoons soda
1 teaspoon salt
1 teaspoon ground
  cinnamon

1/2 teaspoon ground
  nutmeg
1/4 teaspoon ground
  allspice
1 1/2 cups canned
  applesauce
1/2 cup raisins
1/2 cup chopped pecans

OVEN 350°

Cream butter; gradually add sugar, creaming till light. Add eggs, beating well after each. Sift together dry ingredients. Add alternately to creamed mixture with applesauce. Stir in raisins and nuts. Turn batter into greased and lightly floured 13x9x2-inch pan. Bake at 350° about 45 minutes or till done. Cool in pan.

## WHITE CAKE SUPREME

3/4 cup shortening
1 1/2 cups sugar
1 1/2 teaspoons vanilla
2 1/4 cups sifted cake flour
3 teaspoons baking
  powder

1 teaspoon salt
1 cup milk
5 stiffly beaten egg
  whites

OVEN 375°

Cream shortening and sugar till light. Add vanilla and mix well. Sift together flour, baking powder, and salt. Add to creamed mixture alternately with milk, beating after each addition. Gently fold in egg whites. Bake in 2 greased and lightly floured 9x1½-inch round pans in moderate oven (375°) for 18 to 20 minutes or till done. Cool 10 minutes; remove from pans. Cool thoroughly and frost.

## LADY BALTIMORE CAKE

Prepare White Cake Supreme. Fill with *Lady Baltimore Filling:* Add ⅓ cup candied cherries, chopped, and ¼ cup *each* chopped figs, raisins, and chopped pecans to ⅓ of Seven-minute Frosting (page 256). Frost with remaining frosting.

## PETITS FOURS

*Petits Fours make dainty tea cakes for a party—*

| | |
|---|---|
| ¼ cup butter or margarine | 2 cups sifted cake flour |
| ¼ cup shortening | 3 teaspoons baking powder |
| 1 cup sugar | ¼ teaspoon salt |
| ½ teaspoon vanilla | ¾ cup milk |
| ¼ teaspoon almond extract | ¾ cup (6) egg whites |
| | ¼ cup sugar |

OVEN 350°

Cream together butter and shortening. Gradually add 1 cup sugar, creaming till light. Stir in vanilla and almond extract. Sift together flour, baking powder, and salt. Add to creamed mixture alternately with milk, beating well after each addition. Beat egg whites till foamy; gradually add ¼ cup sugar, beating till soft peaks form. Fold into batter. Turn into greased and lightly floured 13x9x2-inch pan. Bake at 350° for 35 to 40 minutes. Cool 10 minutes; remove from pan. Cool completely.

## PETITS FOURS ICING

| | |
|---|---|
| 3 cups granulated sugar | 1 teaspoon vanilla |
| ¼ teaspoon cream of tartar | Sifted confectioners' sugar (about 2½ cups) |
| | Food coloring |

In covered 2-quart saucepan, bring granulated sugar, cream of tartar, and 1½ cups hot water to boil. Uncover;

continue cooking to thin syrup (226°). Cool at room temperature, not over ice water, to lukewarm (110°). Add vanilla and confectioners' sugar till icing is of pouring consistency. Tint with food coloring.

*Assemble:* Cut cooled cake in 1½-inch diamonds, squares, or circles using a stiff paper pattern. Place cake on rack with cookie sheet below. Spoon icing evenly over cakes. Let dry; add another coat. Decorate with various decorations: sliced almonds, snipped marshmallow flowers, or frosting flowers using Ornamental Frosting (page 260).

## COCOA FUDGE CAKE

| | |
|---|---|
| ¾ cup butter or margarine | 2¼ cups sifted cake flour |
| 1½ cups sugar | ½ cup cocoa (regular-type, dry) |
| 3 eggs, separated | 3 teaspoons baking powder |
| 1½ teaspoons vanilla | |
| 1 teaspoon red food coloring | |

OVEN 350°

Cream butter and sugar till light. Add egg *yolks*, one at a time, beating well after each. Add vanilla and food coloring. Sift together dry ingredients. Add to creamed mixture alternately with 1 cup cold water, beating after each addition. Beat egg whites to stiff peaks; fold into batter. Bake in 2 greased and floured 9x1½-inch round pans at 350° for 25 minutes.

## CHOCOLATE FUDGE CAKE

OVEN 350°

In saucepan, combine 1 slightly beaten egg, ⅔ cup sugar, ½ cup milk, and three 1-ounce squares unsweetened chocolate. Cook and stir over medium heat till chocolate melts and mixture comes just to boiling; cool. Cream 1 cup sugar and ½ cup shortening till light. Add 1 teaspoon vanilla and 2 eggs, one at a time, beating well after each. Sift together 2 cups sifted cake flour, 1 teaspoon soda, and ½ teaspoon salt. Add to creamed mixture alternately with

1 cup milk, beating after each addition. Blend in chocolate mixture. Bake in 2 greased and floured 9x1½-inch round pans at 350° for 25 to 30 minutes.

## PRIZE CHOCOLATE CAKE

OVEN 350°

Cream together ⅔ cup shortening and 1¼ cups sugar till light. Blend in 1½ teaspoons vanilla and three 1-ounce squares unsweetened chocolate, melted and cooled. Add 3 eggs, one at a time; beat well after each. Sift together 1½ cups sifted all-purpose flour and ¾ teaspoon each soda and salt. Add to creamed mixture alternately with 1¼ cups sour milk; beat after each. Bake in greased and floured 13x9x2-inch baking pan at 350° for 35 to 40 minutes.

## DEVIL'S FOOD CAKE

½ cup shortening
1¾ cups sugar
1 teaspoon vanilla
3 eggs, separated
2½ cups sifted cake flour
½ cup cocoa (regular-type, dry)

1½ teaspoons soda
1 teaspoon salt
1⅓ cups cold water
Sea Foam Frosting (see page 257)
Shadow Icing (see page 261)

OVEN 350°

Cream shortening and 1 cup of the sugar till light. Add vanilla and egg *yolks*, one at a time, beating well after each. Sift together dry ingredients; add to creamed mixture alternately with cold water, beating after each addition. Beat egg whites till soft peaks form; gradually add ¾ cup sugar, beating till stiff peaks form. Fold into batter; blend well. Bake in 2 greased and lightly floured 9x1½-inch round baking pans at 350° for 30 to 35 minutes. Fill and frost with Sea Foam Frosting. Prepare Shadow Icing; drizzle around edge of frosted cake.

## FEATHERY FUDGE CAKE

$^2/_3$ cup butter or
 margarine
$1^3/_4$ cups sugar
1 teaspoon vanilla
2 eggs

$2^1/_2$ 1-ounce squares unsweetened chocolate,
 melted and cooled
$2^1/_2$ cups sifted cake flour
$1^1/_4$ teaspoons soda
$^1/_2$ teaspoon salt
$1^1/_4$ cups icy cold water

OVEN 350°

Cream butter. Gradually add sugar, creaming till light.
Add vanilla and eggs, one at a time, beating after each.
Blend in chocolate. Sift together flour, soda, and salt.
Add to creamed mixture alternately with water, beating
after each addition. Turn into 2 greased and lightly floured
9x1$^1/_2$-inch round baking pans. Bake at 350° for 30 to 35
minutes.

## SWEET CHOCOLATE CAKE

1 4-ounce bar sweet
 cooking chocolate
$^1/_2$ cup butter or
 margarine
1 cup sugar
3 eggs, separated

1 teaspoon vanilla
$1^3/_4$ cups sifted cake flour
1 teaspoon soda
$^1/_2$ teaspoon salt
$^2/_3$ cup buttermilk

OVEN 350°

Combine chocolate with $^1/_3$ cup water; stir over low heat
till chocolate melts. Cool. Cream butter; gradually add
sugar, creaming till light. Add egg *yolks,* one at a time,
beating well after each. Blend in vanilla and chocolate
mixture. Sift together dry ingredients. Add to creamed
mixture alternately with buttermilk, beating after each
addition. Beat egg whites to stiff peaks; fold into batter.
Bake in 2 greased and lightly floured 8x1$^1/_2$-inch round
pans at 350° for 30 to 35 minutes. Cool. Fill and frost with
Coconut Frosting (page 261).

## CHOCOLATE MARBLE CAKE

$^{1}/_{2}$ cup butter or
    margarine
1 cup sugar
1 teaspoon vanilla
3 eggs
2 cups sifted cake flour
2$^{1}/_{2}$ teaspoons baking
    powder
$^{1}/_{4}$ teaspoon salt

$^{2}/_{3}$ cup milk
1 1-ounce square un-
    sweetened chocolate,
    melted and cooled
2 tablespoons hot water
$^{1}/_{8}$ teaspoon red food
    coloring
$^{1}/_{4}$ teaspoon soda

OVEN 350°

Cream butter and sugar till light. Add vanilla and eggs, one at a time, beating well after each. Sift together flour, baking powder, and salt; add to creamed mixture alternately with milk; beat after each addition. Combine remaining ingredients; stir into a *third* of the batter. Alternate light and dark batters by spoonfuls in greased and lightly floured 9x5x3-inch loaf pan. Zigzag spatula through batter. Bake at 350° for 55 to 60 minutes. Cool 15 minutes; remove from pan. Cool.

## BLACK FOREST CAKE

OVEN 350°

Beat 2 egg whites till soft peaks form. Gradually add $^{1}/_{2}$ cup sugar, beating till stiff peaks form. Sift together 1$^{3}/_{4}$ cups sifted cake flour, 1 cup sugar, $^{3}/_{4}$ teaspoon soda, and 1 teaspoon salt into mixing bowl. Add $^{1}/_{3}$ cup salad oil and $^{1}/_{2}$ cup milk; beat 1 minute at medium speed on electric mixer. Scrape bowl often.

Add $^{1}/_{2}$ cup milk, 2 egg yolks, and two 1-ounce squares unsweetened chocolate, melted and cooled. Beat 1 minute longer, scraping bowl frequently. Gently fold in egg whites. Pour into two greased and lightly floured 9x1$^{1}/_{2}$-inch round pans. Bake in moderate oven (350°) for 30 to 35 minutes. Cool 10 minutes; remove from pans. Cool thoroughly. Split each layer in half making 4 thin layers. Set aside.

*Cherry Filling:* Combine one 1-pound 4-ounce can pitted tart red cherries, drained, $^{1}/_{2}$ cup port wine, 1 tablespoon kirsch, and 3 drops almond extract. Chill 3 to 4 hours or overnight. Drain thoroughly.

*Chocolate Mousse:* Combine three 1-ounce squares semisweet chocolate and 3 tablespoons kirsch in top of double boiler; stir over, *not touching,* boiling water till chocolate melts and mixture is smooth. Slowly stir into 1 well-beaten egg. Whip 1 cup whipping cream and 2 tablespoons sugar; fold into chocolate. Chill 2 hours.

Prepare Butter Frosting (see page 258). Chill 30 minutes.

*To assemble:* Spread 1/2 cup Butter Frosting on the cut side of a cake layer. With remaining frosting, form one ridge 1/2 inch wide and 3/4 inch high around outside edge of same cake layer; make another ridge 2 inches from outside edge. Chill 30 minutes. Fill spaces with Cherry Filling. Spread second cake layer with Chocolate Mousse and place unfrosted side atop first. Chill 30 minutes. Whip 2 cups whipping cream with 2 tablespoons sugar and 1 teaspoon vanilla. Spread third cake layer with 1 1/2 *cups* whipped cream and place atop second layer. Top with fourth cake layer. Reserving 1/4 cup whipped cream, frost sides with remainder. Sift confectioners' sugar over top. Garnish with dollops of whipped cream, maraschino cherries, and chocolate curls. Chill 2 hours.

## EVERYDAY CUPCAKES

| | |
|---|---|
| 1/2 cup shortening | 1/2 teaspoon salt |
| 1 3/4 cups sifted all-purpose flour | 1 egg |
| | 3/4 cup milk |
| 1 cup sugar | 1 teaspoon vanilla |
| 2 1/2 teaspoons baking powder | |

OVEN 375°

Place shortening in mixing bowl. Sift in dry ingredients. Add egg and *half* the milk; mix till flour is moistened. Beat 2 minutes at low speed on electric mixer. Add remaining milk and vanilla; beat 1 minute longer. Fill paper bake cups in muffin pans half full. Bake at 375° for 18 to 20 minutes or till done. Cool; frost with Jelly Frosting (see page 260). Makes 1 1/2 dozen cupcakes.

# PEANUT BUTTER CUPCAKES

OVEN 375°

Cream ¹/₂ cup chunk-style peanut butter and ¹/₃ cup shortening. Gradually add 1¹/₂ cups brown sugar, beating till light. Add 1 teaspoon vanilla and 2 eggs, one at a time, beating till fluffy. Sift together 2 cups sifted all-purpose flour, 2 teaspoons baking powder, and ¹/₂ teaspoon salt; add alternately with 1 cup milk, beating after each addition. Fill paper bake cups in muffin pans half full. Bake at 375° for 15 to 20 minutes. Cool; frost with peanut butter. Makes about 2 dozen cupcakes.

# COCONUT TOPPED CUPCAKES

OVEN 400°

Sift together 2¹/₄ cups sifted cake flour, 1 cup sugar, 3 teaspoons baking powder, and 1 teaspoon salt into bowl; make a well in center. Add in order: ¹/₃ cup salad oil, ¹/₂ cup milk, and 1¹/₂ teaspoons vanilla; blend. Beat 1 minute at medium speed on electric mixer. Add ¹/₂ cup milk and 2 egg yolks; beat 1 minute. Beat 2 egg whites till soft peaks form; gradually add ¹/₂ cup sugar. Beat till *very stiff peaks* form; fold into batter. Fill paper bake cups in muffin pans half full. Top with one 3¹/₂-ounce can flaked coconut. Bake at 400° about 12 to 15 minutes. Makes about 3 dozen cupcakes.

# FUDGE CUPCAKES

²/₃ cup brown sugar
¹/₃ cup milk
2 1-ounce squares unsweetened chocolate
²/₃ cup brown sugar
¹/₃ cup shortening

1 teaspoon vanilla
2 eggs
1¹/₃ cups sifted all-purpose flour
1 teaspoon soda
¹/₂ teaspoon salt
¹/₂ cup milk

\* \* \*

OVEN 375°

Combine ²/₃ cup brown sugar, ¹/₃ cup milk, and chocolate in saucepan. Stir over very low heat till chocolate melts; cool. Gradually add ²/₃ cup brown sugar to shortening, creaming till sugar is dissolved. Add vanilla and eggs, one at a time, beating well after each. Sift together flour, soda, and salt. Add to creamed mixture alternately with $1/2$ cup milk, beating after each addition. Stir in chocolate mixture. Fill paper bake cups in muffin pans half full. Bake in moderate oven (375°) about 20 minutes. Makes about 2 dozen cupcakes.

## MOCHA CUPCAKES

| | |
|---|---|
| $1/2$ cup shortening | $1/2$ teaspoon soda |
| 1 cup sugar | $1/4$ teaspoon salt |
| 1 egg | $1/2$ cup cocoa (regular- |
| 1 teaspoon vanilla | type, dry) |
| $1^1/3$ cups sifted all-purpose flour | * * * |
| 1 teaspoon baking powder | $1/2$ cup milk |
| | $1^1/2$ teaspoons instant coffee powder |

OVEN 375°

Cream shortening and sugar till light. Add egg and vanilla; beat well. Sift together the next 5 ingredients. Add to creamed mixture alternately with milk, beating after each addition. Dissolve coffee powder in $1/2$ cup hot water; stir into batter. Fill paper bake cups in muffin pans $2/3$ full. Bake in moderate oven (375°) for 20 minutes. Cool and frost. Makes about 18 cupcakes.

## LIGHT FRUITCAKE

1 cup butter or margarine
1 cup sugar
4 eggs
3 cups sifted all-purpose flour
1 teaspoon baking powder
1/4 cup light corn syrup
1/4 cup orange juice
1/4 cup dry white wine
1 teaspoon lemon extract
3/4 pound (1 1/2 cups) candied cherries, chopped

1 cup light raisins
1/2 pound (1 cup) candied pineapple, chopped
1/4 pound (1/2 cup) chopped mixed candied fruits and peels
1/4 pound (1/2 cup) candied lemon peel, chopped
1/4 pound (1/2 cup) candied orange peel, chopped
1 cup chopped walnuts

OVEN 275°

Cream butter and sugar till light; add eggs, one at a time, beating well after each. Sift flour and baking powder together. Combine corn syrup, orange juice, wine, and lemon extract; add to creamed mixture alternately with flour mixture. Mix well. Combine chopped fruits, peels, and nuts; fold into batter. Pour into 1 well-greased 5 1/2-cup ring mold and 6 well-greased 4 1/2 x 2 1/2 x 1 1/2-inch loaf pans. (*Or,* turn into 1 well-greased 5 1/2-cup ring mold and 1 well-greased 10 x 3 1/2 x 2 1/2-inch loaf pan.) Bake at 275° 60 to 70 minutes, or till done. Cool in pans; turn out of pans. Wrap in several layers of wine moistened cheesecloth. Overwrap with foil. Store in cool place at least one week. Remoisten cheesecloth as needed.

## FRUITCAKE POINTERS

• Cool fruitcakes in pans, then turn out.
• Store cakes in foil, clear plastic wrap, or airtight container. Keep in cool place. If desired, wrap cakes in brandy-, wine-, or juice-soaked cloth, then in foil. Store cakes wrapped in juice-soaked cloth in refrigerator. Moisten cloth once a week.
• For thin slices, chill before cutting.
• Make fruitcakes 3 to 4 weeks ahead for a blended and mellow flavor.

## DARK FRUITCAKE

3 cups sifted all-purpose flour
2 teaspoons baking powder
2 teaspoons ground cinnamon
1 teaspoon salt
1/2 teaspoon ground nutmeg
1/2 teaspoon ground allspice
1/2 teaspoon ground cloves
1 1-pound package (2 1/2 cups) mixed candied fruits and peels
1 15-ounce package (3 cups) raisins

1 8-ounce package (1 1/2 cups) whole candied cherries
1 8-ounce package (1 1/3 cups) pitted dates, snipped
1 cup slivered almonds
1 cup pecan halves
1/2 cup candied pineapple, chopped
4 eggs
1 3/4 cups brown sugar
1 cup orange juice
3/4 cup butter or margarine, melted and cooled
1/4 cup light molasses

OVEN 300°

Sift flour, baking powder, cinnamon, salt, nutmeg, allspice, and cloves into large mixing bowl. Add candied fruits and peels, raisins, candied cherries, dates, almonds, pecans, and candied pineapple. Mix till fruits and nuts are well coated. Beat eggs till foamy. Gradually add brown sugar, beating till well combined. Blend in orange juice, butter or margarine, and light molasses. Add to fruit mixture; stir till well combined.

Grease one 5 3/4x3 1/4x2 1/4-inch loaf pan, one 8 1/2x4 1/2x 2 1/2-inch loaf pan, and one 10x3 1/2x2 1/2-inch loaf pan. Line bottom and sides of pans with strips of brown paper; grease paper. Turn batter into prepared pans, filling each about 3/4 full. Bake at 300° till done. (Allow about 1 1/2 hours for the 5 3/4x3 1/4x2 1/4-inch pan and about 2 hours for the other two pans.) Cover all pans with foil after 1 hour. Cool thoroughly; remove from pans. Wrap in several layers of wine- or fruit juice-moistened cheesecloth. Overwrap with foil. Store in refrigerator. Remoisten cheesecloth as needed if cakes are kept longer than one week.

## • HOW TO MAKE
## HIGH, LIGHT CHIFFON CAKES •

A chiffon cake combines the lightness of an angel cake with the richness of a shortening-type cake. Keep in mind these tips when preparing a chiffon cake.

• The volume of a chiffon cake depends upon beating egg whites till very stiff peaks form—when a spatula is pulled through, a clear path should remain.

• When beating egg whites, be sure the beaters are free of grease. Avoid using plastic mixing bowls as they retain a greasy film. This is important as grease will inhibit the volume of beaten egg whites, therefore, the volume of the cake.

• To fold batter into stiffly beaten egg whites, use rubber spatula with down-up-over motion; turn bowl as you work. Fold gently; don't stir.

• A chiffon cake is done when it springs back when pressed lightly with finger.

• Turn chiffon cakes upside down as they come from oven until cool. This keeps the cake from shrinking or falling. A carbonated beverage bottle makes a convenient stand for a tube pan.

• To remove from pan, loosen cake around sides and center tube with spatula or knife. Turn upside down; remove pan.

## MARBLE CHIFFON CAKE

OVEN 325°

Sift together 2¼ cups sifted cake flour, 1½ cups sugar, 3 teaspoons baking powder, and 1 teaspoon salt. Make well in center of dry ingredients and add in order: ½ cup salad oil, 7 egg yolks, ¾ cup cold water, and 1 teaspoon vanilla. Beat till satin smooth. In large bowl, beat 7 egg whites with ½ teaspoon cream of tartar till *very stiff peaks* form.

Pour egg yolk mixture in thin stream over entire surface of egg whites, gently folding to blend. Remove $1/3$ of batter to separate bowl. Blend together $1/4$ cup boiling water, 2 tablespoons sugar, and two 1-ounce squares unsweetened chocolate, melted; cool. Gently fold chocolate mixture into $1/3$ portion of batter. Spoon *half* the light batter into *ungreased* 10-inch tube pan; top with *half* the chocolate batter. Repeat layers. With narrow spatula, swirl gently through batters to marble. Leave definite areas of light and dark batter.

Bake in slow oven (325°) about 65 minutes or till cake tests done. Invert cake in pan; cool. Frost with a chocolate frosting.

Sift dry ingredients into a mixing bowl and make a well in the center. Add in order: salad oil, egg yolks, liquids, and flavorings. Beat till batter is satin smooth. In large bowl, beat egg whites till very stiff peaks form. Pour egg yolk batter in thin stream over entire surface of egg whites, gently folding to blend. Don't stir. Turn into *ungreased* tube pan. For a marble cake, gently swirl narrow spatula through batter to blend. Leave definite areas of light and dark batter.

## MAPLE CHIFFON CAKE

2¼ cups sifted cake flour
¾ cup granulated sugar
3 teaspoons baking powder
1 teaspoon salt

* * *

¾ cup brown sugar
½ cup salad oil
5 egg yolks

¾ cup cold water
2 teaspoons maple flavoring
1 cup (8) egg whites
½ teaspoon cream of tartar
1 cup finely chopped walnuts

OVEN 350°

Sift first 4 ingredients together into mixing bowl; stir in brown sugar. Make a well in dry ingredients. Add in order: salad oil, egg yolks, water, and flavoring. Beat till satin smooth. Beat egg whites with cream of tartar till *very stiff peaks* form. Pour batter in thin stream over entire surface of egg whites; fold in gently. Fold in nuts. Bake in *ungreased* 10-inch tube pan at 350° for 1 hour. Invert pan; cool. Frost with Golden Butter Frosting (see page 259).

## ORANGE SUNSHINE CAKE

*As light and delicate as a sunny spring day—*

¾ cup (8) egg yolks
⅔ cup sugar
1 teaspoon grated orange peel
½ cup orange juice
1 cup sifted cake flour

1 cup (8) egg whites
1 teaspoon cream of tartar
½ teaspoon salt
⅔ cup sugar

OVEN 325°

Beat egg yolks till thick and lemon-colored; gradually add ⅔ cup sugar, beating till thick. Combine orange peel and orange juice; add to egg mixture alternately with cake flour.

Beat egg whites with cream of tartar and salt till soft peaks form. Gradually add ⅔ cup sugar, beating till stiff peaks form. Gently fold into egg yolk mixture. Bake in *ungreased* 10-inch tube pan in slow oven (325°) for about 1 hour and 10 to 15 minutes. Invert; cool.

## PINEAPPLE CHIFFON CAKE

OVEN 350°

Sift together 2¼ cups sifted cake flour, 1½ cups sugar, 3 teaspoons baking powder, and 1 teaspoon salt into bowl. Make well in center and add in order: ½ cup salad oil, 5 egg yolks, and ¾ cup pineapple juice. Beat until satin smooth.

In large mixing bowl, beat 1 cup (8) egg whites with ½ teaspoon cream of tartar till *very stiff peaks* form. Pour batter in thin stream over entire surface of egg whites; fold in gently. Bake in *ungreased* 10-inch tube pan in moderate oven (350°) for 1 hour or until done. Invert; cool.

Split cooled cake into 2 layers. Fill with part of Pineapple-whipped Topping; frost top and sides with remainder.

*Pineapple-whipped Topping:* Thoroughly drain one 1-pound 4½-ounce can crushed pineapple, chilled. Fold drained pineapple into 2 cups whipping cream, whipped.

## CHOCOLATE CHIFFON CAKE

| | |
|---|---|
| 4 1-ounce squares unsweetened chocolate, melted | 1 teaspoon salt |
| | ½ cup salad oil |
| | 7 egg yolks |
| ¼ cup sugar | ¾ cup cold water |
| 2¼ cups sifted cake flour | 1 teaspoon vanilla |
| 1½ cups sugar | ½ teaspoon cream of |
| 3 teaspoons baking | tartar |
| powder | 7 egg whites |

OVEN 325°

Thoroughly blend melted chocolate, ½ cup boiling water, and ¼ cup sugar; cool. Sift together flour, 1½ cups sugar, baking powder, and salt into bowl. Make well in center of dry ingredients. Add in order: salad oil, egg yolks, water, and vanilla. Beat until satin smooth.

Stir chocolate mixture into batter. In large mixing bowl, combine cream of tartar and egg whites; beat till *very stiff peaks* form. Pour chocolate batter in thin stream over entire surface of egg whites; fold in gently. Bake in *un-*

*greased* 10-inch tube pan in slow oven (325°) for 1 hour and 5 minutes. Invert pan; cool.

## MOCHA CHIFFON CAKE

4 teaspoons instant
coffee powder
2¼ cups sifted cake flour
1½ cups sugar
3 teaspoons baking
powder
1 teaspoon salt
½ cup salad oil

5 egg yolks
1 teaspoon vanilla
3 1-ounce squares
semisweet chocolate,
coarsely grated
1 cup (8) egg whites
½ teaspoon cream of
tartar

OVEN 325°

Dissolve coffee powder in ¾ cup water; set aside. Sift dry ingredients into a bowl; make well in center. Add in order: oil, yolks, vanilla, and coffee. Beat till satin smooth. Stir in chocolate. Beat egg whites with cream of tartar to *very stiff peaks*. Pour batter in thin stream over egg whites; fold in gently. Bake in *ungreased* 10-inch tube pan in slow oven (325°) for 1 hour and 10 minutes. Invert pan; cool.

## GOLDEN CHIFFON CAKE

2¼ cups sifted cake flour
1½ cups sugar
3 teaspoons baking
powder
1 teaspoon salt
       * * *
½ cup salad oil
5 egg yolks

¾ cup water
1 teaspoon vanilla
2 teaspoons grated
lemon peel
½ teaspoon cream of
tartar
1 cup (8) egg whites

OVEN 325°

Sift together first 4 ingredients into bowl; make well in center. Add in order next 5 ingredients. Beat till satin smooth. Add cream of tartar to egg whites; beat till *very stiff peaks* form. Pour batter in thin stream over entire surface of egg whites; fold in gently. Bake in *ungreased* 10-inch tube pan in a slow oven (325°) for 1 hour and

10 minutes. Invert pan; cool. Frost with Seven-minute Frosting (see page 256) tinted with few drops yellow food coloring. Sprinkle with yellow tinted coconut.

## • PERFECT ANGEL AND SPONGE CAKES •

For angel and sponge cakes, the air incorporated into the batter is the leavening agent. Beating the egg whites and egg yolks, gently folding in the sugar-flour mixture, and an accurate oven temperature help to incorporate and keep air in the batter. Remember these tips when preparing an angel or sponge cake:
• Do not grease pan, unless specified.
• Angel and sponge cakes are done when they spring back to the touch.
• For a brown crust, remove cake from pan when completely cooled. The longer these cooled cakes are kept in the pan, the more crust will adhere to the pan.
• Beat egg yolks until they are thick and *literally* lemon-colored.

For problems, check the following list:

**Tough cake**
Oven too hot
Overmixing

**Coarse texture**
Underbeaten egg whites
Insufficient mixing

**Egg layer at bottom**
Underbeaten egg yolks

**Undersized cake**
Underbeaten or overbeaten egg whites
Overmixing
Too large a pan
Oven too hot
Removing cake from pan before cooling

**Sticky crust**
Insufficient baking

Invert angel and sponge cakes in pan as they come from the oven. A carbonated beverage bottle makes a handy stand.

## ANGEL CAKE

1 cup sifted cake flour
³/₄ cup sugar
1¹/₂ cups (12) egg whites
1¹/₂ teaspoons cream of tartar

¹/₄ teaspoon salt
1¹/₂ teaspoons vanilla
³/₄ cup sugar

OVEN 375°

Sift flour with ³/₄ cup sugar 2 times; set aside. Beat egg whites with cream of tartar, salt and vanilla till stiff enough to form soft peaks but still moist and glossy. Add remaining ³/₄ cup sugar, 2 tablespoons at a time, continuing to beat till egg whites hold stiff peaks.

Sift about ¹/₄ of flour mixture over whites; fold in. Repeat, folding in remaining flour by fourths. Bake in *ungreased* 10-inch tube pan at 375° for 35 to 40 minutes or till done. Invert cake in pan; cool.

## CHOCOLATE ANGEL CAKE

Prepare Angel Cake, substituting ³/₄ cup sifted cake flour and ¹/₄ cup cocoa (regular-type, dry) for 1 cup sifted cake flour. Sift cocoa with flour and sugar 2 times.

## ANGEL LOAF CAKE

| | |
|---|---|
| 1/2 cup sifted cake flour | Dash salt |
| 1/4 cup sugar | 1 teaspoon vanilla |
| * * * | 1/4 teaspoon almond |
| 3/4 cup (6) egg whites | extract |
| 1/2 teaspoon cream of | 1/2 cup sugar |
| tartar | |

OVEN 375°

Sift flour with 1/4 cup sugar 2 times; set aside. Beat egg whites with cream of tartar, salt, vanilla, and almond extract till stiff enough to form soft peaks but still moist and glossy. Add remaining 1/2 cup sugar, 2 tablespoons at a time, continuing to beat until egg whites hold stiff peaks. Sift about 1/3 of flour mixture over whites; fold in. Repeat, folding in remaining flour in two additions.

Bake in *ungreased* 9x5x3-inch loaf pan in moderate oven (375°) for 25 minutes or until done. Invert cake in pan; cool.

## DAISY MARBLE CAKE

| | |
|---|---|
| 1 cup sifted cake flour | 1 1/2 teaspoons finely |
| 1/2 cup sugar | shredded orange peel |
| 1 1/3 cups (10) egg whites | 4 drops yellow food |
| 1 1/4 teaspoons cream of | coloring |
| tartar | 4 well-beaten egg yolks |
| 1/4 teaspoon salt | 2 tablespoons sifted |
| 1 cup sugar | cake flour |
| | 1/2 teaspoon vanilla |

OVEN 375°

Sift 1 cup flour with 1/2 cup sugar. Beat egg whites with cream of tartar and salt till soft peaks form. Gradually add 1 cup sugar, beating till stiff peaks form. Sift about 1/4 of flour mixture over whites; fold in lightly. Repeat, folding in remaining flour mixture by thirds.

Divide batter into 2 parts. Add orange peel and food coloring to egg yolks; beat till very thick and lemon-colored. Fold egg-yolk mixture and 2 tablespoons flour into *half* of the batter. Fold the vanilla into *other half* of batter. Spoon batters alternately into *ungreased* 10-inch tube pan. Bake in moderate oven (375°) about 35 minutes or till done. Invert cake in pan; cool.

## HOT-MILK SPONGE CAKE

| | |
|---|---|
| 1 cup sifted all-purpose flour | 1/2 cup milk |
| 1 teaspoon baking powder | 2 tablespoons butter |
| 1/4 teaspoon salt | 2 eggs |
| | 1 cup sugar |
| | 1 teaspoon vanilla |

OVEN 350°

Sift together flour, baking powder, and salt. Heat milk and butter till butter melts; keep hot. Beat eggs till thick and lemon-colored, about 3 minutes on high speed of electric mixer. Gradually add sugar, beating constantly at medium speed for 4 to 5 minutes. Add sifted dry ingredients to egg mixture; stir just till blended. Stir in hot milk mixture and vanilla; blend well. Turn batter into greased and floured 9x9x2-inch pan. Bake at 350° for 25 to 30 minutes. Don't invert; cool in pan.

## BUTTER SPONGE

| | |
|---|---|
| 1 cup sifted cake flour | 1/4 cup butter or |
| 1 teaspoon baking powder | margarine |
| | * * * |
| 1/2 cup milk | 6 egg yolks |
| | 1 cup sugar |
| | 1/2 teaspoon vanilla |

OVEN 350°

Sift together flour and baking powder. Heat milk and butter till butter melts; keep hot. Beat egg yolks till thick and lemon-colored; gradually add sugar, beating constantly. Add vanilla. Add flour mixture; stir just till mixed. Gently stir in the hot milk mixture. Bake in greased and floured 9x9x2-inch pan at 350° for 30 to 35 minutes. Don't invert; cool in pan.

## ORANGE SPONGE CAKE

OVEN 325°

Combine 1¹/₃ cups sifted cake flour and ¹/₃ cup sugar. Beat 6 egg yolks till thick and lemon-colored. Add 1 tablespoon grated orange peel and ¹/₂ cup orange juice; beat till very thick. Gradually add ²/₃ cup sugar and ¹/₄ teaspoon salt, beating constantly. Sift flour mixture over egg yolk mixture, a little at a time, folding just till blended. Wash beaters. Beat 6 egg whites with 1 teaspoon cream of tartar till soft peaks form. Gradually add ¹/₂ cup sugar, beating till stiff peaks form. Thoroughly fold yolk mixture into whites. Bake in *ungreased* 10-inch tube pan at 325° about 55 minutes. Invert cake in pan; cool.

## PINEAPPLE FLUFF CAKE

OVEN 325°

Beat 6 egg yolks till thick and lemon-colored. Add ¹/₂ cup pineapple juice and 1 tablespoon lemon juice; beat till well combined. Sift 1¹/₂ cups sifted cake flour, 1 teaspoon baking powder, and ³/₄ cup sugar together 2 times. Add to yolk mixture. Wash beaters. Beat 6 egg whites with ¹/₄ teaspoon salt till soft peaks form. Gradually add ³/₄ cup sugar, beating till stiff peaks form. Fold batter into egg whites. Bake in *ungreased* 10-inch tube pan at 325° about 1 hour. Invert; cool.

## JELLY ROLL

| | |
|---|---|
| 4 egg yolks | ²/₃ cup sifted cake flour |
| ¹/₃ cup sugar | 1 teaspoon baking |
| ¹/₂ teaspoon vanilla | powder |
| 4 egg whites | ¹/₄ teaspoon salt |
| ¹/₂ cup sugar | |

OVEN 375°

Beat egg yolks till thick and lemon-colored; gradually beat in ¹/₃ cup sugar; add vanilla. Beat egg whites till soft peaks form; gradually add ¹/₂ cup sugar and beat till stiff peaks form. Fold yolks into whites. Sift together flour, baking powder, and salt; fold into egg mixture.

Spread batter evenly in greased and lightly floured 15$\frac{1}{2}$x 10$\frac{1}{2}$x1-inch jelly roll pan. Bake in moderate oven (375°) about 10 to 12 minutes or till done.

Immediately loosen sides and turn out on towel sprinkled with sifted confectioners' sugar. Starting at narrow end, roll cake and towel together; cool on rack.

Unroll; spread with favorite filling. Roll up. Makes ten 1-inch slices.

## CHOCOLATE ROLL

Prepare Jelly Roll, sifting $\frac{1}{4}$ cup cocoa (regular-type, dry) with other dry ingredients. Fill cake with 1 cup whipping cream, whipped; roll. Frost with Chocolate Gloss. Chill till serving time.

Or, fill with 1 quart ice cream, softened to spreading consistency. Roll and freeze.

## CHOCOLATE GLOSS

| | |
|---|---|
| $\frac{1}{2}$ cup sugar | Dash salt |
| 1$\frac{1}{2}$ tablespoons cornstarch | 1$\frac{1}{2}$ tablespoons butter or |
| 1 1-ounce square un- | margarine |
| sweetened chocolate | $\frac{1}{2}$ teaspoon vanilla |

Combine sugar and cornstarch; add chocolate, salt, and $\frac{1}{2}$ cup water. Cook and stir till thickened and bubbly and chocolate melts. Remove from heat; add butter and vanilla. While hot, frost rolled cake.

## SNOW-CAPPED LEMON ROLL

| | |
|---|---|
| 4 egg yolks | 4 egg whites |
| $\frac{2}{3}$ cup sugar | $\frac{2}{3}$ cup sifted cake flour |
| $\frac{1}{2}$ teaspoon grated lemon peel | $\frac{1}{4}$ teaspoon salt |
| | Lemon Filling |
| 1 tablespoon lemon juice | Meringue |

OVEN 350°

Beat egg yolks till thick and lemon-colored. Gradually add $\frac{1}{3}$ *cup* sugar, beating constantly. Stir in lemon peel and juice. Beat egg whites till soft peaks form; gradually add remaining 1/3 cup sugar and beat till stiff peaks form.

Gently fold yolks into whites. Sift together flour and salt; fold into egg mixture. Spread batter evenly in greased and floured 15 1/2 x10 1/2 x1-inch jelly roll pan. Bake at 350° about 15 minutes. Loosen sides; immediately turn out on towel sprinkled with confectioners' sugar. Starting at narrow end, roll cake and towel together; cool. Prepare Lemon Filling (see page 263). Unroll cake; spread with filling. Roll again. Spread Meringue over top and sides of cake roll. Bake at 350° for 12 to 15 minutes. Makes 10 servings.

*Meringue:* Beat 2 egg whites till soft peaks form. Gradually add 1/4 cup sugar, beating till stiff peaks form.

## WALNUT CREAM ROLL

OVEN 375°

Beat 4 egg yolks till thick and lemon-colored. Combine 4 egg whites, 1 teaspoon vanilla, and 1/2 teaspoon salt. Beat till soft peaks form; gradually add 1/2 cup sugar, beating till stiff peaks form. Fold egg yolks into whites; carefully fold in 1/4 cup sifted all-purpose flour and 1/2 cup finely chopped walnuts. Spread batter evenly in greased and floured 15 1/2 x10 1/2 x1-inch jelly roll pan. Bake in moderate oven (375°) for 12 minutes or till done.

Immediately loosen sides and turn out on towel sprinkled with confectioners' sugar. Starting at narrow end, roll cake and towel together; cool on rack. Unroll; spread with 1 cup whipping cream, sweetened and whipped. Roll cake; chill.

## • HOW TO FROST AND CUT CAKES
## THE PROFESSIONAL WAY •

• When frosting layer cakes, begin with completely cooled layers. Brush away loose crumbs and position the first layer top side *down* on the serving plate. (To keep serving plate clean, see page 256.) Frost the top of the first layer with about ¼ of the frosting. When using a soft, fluffy frosting, spread frosting almost to the edge of the cake. The second cake layer, when positioned on top, will cause the frosting to flow to the edge. When using firmer frostings, such as a butter frosting, spread frosting just to the edge of the cake.

• Position the second layer top side *up* on the filling. Holding spatula vertically, spread a thin frosting layer around the side of the cake. (Crumbs behave if you cover them with a thin layer first.) With more frosting, finish sides of cake. Cover top with remaining frosting, joining frosted sides at edge. Make swirls or design on surface with spatula.

• When frosting three or more layers, position the first two layers the same as above. Always place the top layer top side *up* on the filling for pretty finish to cake.

• For tube cakes, place top side down on serving plate and frost or glaze cake. Or, lightly sift confectioners' sugar over top of cake. With the cake in this position it is easier to frost and cut.

• When cutting a foam-type cake, use a cake breaker or knife with serrated blade. For a cake breaker, press prongs gently through cake, turn handle away from slice till cake separates. If using a knife, cut with a gentle back-and-forth motion.

• To cut a frosted layer cake, use a sharp thin-bladed knife. Insert point of knife into cake, keeping point down and handle up. Slice with up-and-down motion, pulling knife toward you. Occasionally dip blade in warm water or wipe with a damp cloth to keep free of frosting and crumbs.

To keep your serving plate clean while frosting, place 3 or 4 strips waxed paper over edges of plate. Place cake on plate and frost. Pull paper out after decorating cake. Frost cupcakes the easy way. Simply dip the top of each cupcake into a Seven-minute type frosting. Twirl the cake slightly and then quickly turn right side up.

• To split a cake layer, place wooden picks in side of cake for a guide. With a sharp thin-bladed knife cut cake. Or, place a string around cake crossing the two ends in front. Pull ends of thread in opposite directions drawing thread through cake.

## SEVEN-MINUTE FROSTING

|  |  |
|---|---|
| 2 unbeaten egg whites | 1/3 cup cold water |
| 1 1/2 cups granulated sugar | Dash salt |
| 2 teaspoons light corn syrup *or* 1/4 teaspoon cream of tartar | 1 teaspoon vanilla |

Place all ingredients except vanilla in top of double boiler (don't place over boiling water); beat 1/2 minute at low speed on electric mixer to blend. Place over, *not touching,* boiling water. Cook, beating constantly, till frosting forms stiff peaks, *about* 7 minutes *(don't overcook)*. Remove from boiling water. If desired, pour into mixing bowl. Add vanilla; beat till of spreading consistency, about 2 minutes. Frosts tops and sides of two 8- or 9-inch layers.

**Peppermint-stick Frosting:** Prepare Seven-minute Frosting adding a few drops red food coloring with vanilla. Trim cake with crushed peppermint-stick candy.

**Sea Foam Frosting:** Prepare Seven-minute Frosting substituting 1 1/2 cups brown sugar for granulated sugar.

**Chocolate Frosting:** Prepare Seven-minute Frosting *folding* in two 1-ounce squares unsweetened chocolate, melted and cooled, just before frosting cake.

**Tropical Frosting:** Drain one 8 3/4-ounce can pineapple tidbits, reserving 1/3 cup syrup. Prepare Seven-minute Frosting substituting the reserved pineapple syrup for cold water. Add 1 teaspoon grated lemon peel instead of vanilla. Garnish cake with pineapple tidbits.

## SOUR CREAM FROSTING

| | |
|---|---|
| 1 6-ounce package semi-<br>sweet chocolate pieces | 1 teaspoon vanilla<br>2 1/2 to 2 3/4 cups sifted |
| 1/4 cup butter | confectioners' sugar |
| 1/2 cup dairy sour cream | |

Melt chocolate and butter; cool slightly. Blend in cream, vanilla, and 1/4 teaspoon salt. Slowly beat in sugar till spreading consistency. Frosts two 9-inch layers.

## FLUFFY WHITE FROSTING

Combine 1 cup granulated sugar, 1/3 cup water, 1/4 teaspoon cream of tartar, and dash salt in saucepan. Bring to boiling, stirring till sugar dissolves. Very slowly add sugar syrup to 2 unbeaten egg whites in mixing bowl, beating constantly with electric mixer till stiff peaks form, about 7 minutes. Beat in 1 teaspoon vanilla. Frosts tops and sides of two 8- or 9-inch layers or one 10-inch tube cake.

## CONFECTIONERS' ICING

Add light cream to 2 cups sifted confectioners' sugar for spreading consistency. Add dash salt and 1 teaspoon vanilla.

## BUTTER FROSTING

| | |
|---|---|
| 6 tablespoons butter | Light cream (about |
| 1 1-pound package | ¼ cup) |
| confectioners' sugar, | 1½ teaspoons vanilla |
| sifted (about 4¾ cups) | |

Cream butter; gradually add about *half* the sugar, blending well. Beat in 2 *tablespoons* cream and vanilla. Gradually blend in remaining sugar. Add enough cream to make of spreading consistency. Frosts two 8- or 9-inch layers.

*Note:* For a more creamy frosting, beat in 1 egg *instead* of the first 2 tablespoons of light cream. After blending in the remaining confectioners' sugar, beat in just enough cream to make frosting the desired spreading consistency.

**Orange Butter Frosting or Lemon Butter Frosting:** Prepare Butter Frosting creaming butter and 2 teaspoons grated orange peel *or* ½ teaspoon grated lemon peel. Substitute orange *or* lemon juice for the cream; blend in enough to make of spreading consistency.

**Chocolate Butter Frosting:** Prepare Butter Frosting adding two 1-ounce squares unsweetened chocolate, melted and cooled with the vanilla.

**Mocha Butter Frosting:** Prepare Butter Frosting creaming butter with ¼ cup cocoa (regular-type, dry) and ½ teaspoon instant coffee powder.

## CREAM CHEESE FROSTING

| | |
|---|---|
| 1 3-ounce package | 1 teaspoon vanilla |
| cream cheese, | 2 cups sifted |
| softened | confectioners' sugar |
| 1 tablespoon butter, | |
| softened | |

In small mixing bowl, combine cream cheese, butter, and vanilla. Beat at low speed on electric mixer till light.

Gradually add sugar, beating till fluffy. If necessary, add milk to make of spreading consistency. Stir in $1/2$ cup chopped nuts, if desired. Frosts one 8- or 9-inch square cake.

## GOLDEN BUTTER FROSTING

Melt $1/2$ cup butter or margarine in saucepan; keep over low heat till golden brown. Watch carefully to prevent scorching. Remove from heat. Place 4 cups sifted confectioners' sugar in mixing bowl. Beat in melted butter. Add 1 teaspoon vanilla or $1/2$ to 1 teaspoon maple flavoring. Blend in light cream till of spreading consistency, about $1/4$ cup. Makes enough to frost one 10-inch tube cake.

## PENUCHE FROSTING

Melt $1/2$ cup butter or margarine; add 1 cup brown sugar. Bring to boiling; cook and stir 1 minute or till slightly thick. Cool 15 minutes.

Add $1/4$ cup hot milk and beat smooth. Beat in enough of $3^1/4$ cups sifted confectioners' sugar for spreading consistency. Frosts two 8- or 9-inch layers.

## CARAMEL CANDY FROSTING

Combine $1/4$ pound (16) vanilla caramels and $1/4$ cup water in $1^1/2$-quart saucepan. Melt caramels over low heat, stirring occasionally. Cool to room temperature.

Cream 3 tablespoons butter or margarine; add dash salt. Add 2 cups sifted confectioners' sugar alternately with caramel sauce, blending till frosting is smooth and creamy. Add 2 tablespoons chopped walnuts. Chill till of spreading consistency, about 30 minutes. Frosts one 9-inch square cake or 1 dozen cupcakes.

## ROYAL FROSTING

*Make-ahead decorations harden for easy use—*

Combine 3 egg whites, at room temperature, one 1-pound package confectioners' sugar, sifted (about $4^3/4$ cups), 1 teaspoon vanilla, and $1/2$ teaspoon cream of tartar. Beat with electric mixer 7 to 10 minutes or till frosting is very stiff. Keep frosting covered with damp cloth at all times to prevent crust from forming. Makes 3 cups.

Make flowers with pastry tube on silicone paper or waxed paper. Let dry 8 hours before peeling off paper. Dab a little frosting on bottom of each flower to attach to top or sides of cake.

## ORNAMENTAL FROSTING

In electric mixer, blend 1 cup shortening and 1 teaspoon vanilla. Slowly add 4 cups sifted confectioners' sugar; beat just till combined. Stir in about 1½ tablespoons milk. Make trial flower to check frosting consistency. Add a few drops more milk if frosting is too stiff.

Tint to desired color. Make flowers with pastry tube on silicone paper or waxed paper; place on cookie sheet. Harden in refrigerator or freezer 1 hour. Transfer to cake with spatula. Work fast to keep flowers cold. Makes about 2¼ cups.

## BOILED FROSTING

| | |
|---|---|
| 2 cups sugar | Dash salt |
| ¾ cup water | 2 stiffly beaten egg |
| 1 tablespoon light corn | whites |
| syrup or ¼ teaspoon | 1 teaspoon vanilla |
| cream of tartar | |

Cook first 4 ingredients over low heat, stirring till sugar dissolves. Cover pan 2 to 3 minutes to dissolve sugar crystals on sides of pan. Uncover; cook to soft ball stage (240°). Gradually add hot syrup to egg whites, beating constantly with electric mixer. Add vanilla; beat till spreading consistency, about 6 minutes. If too thin, let stand 3 minutes to set up slightly; stir once or twice. Frosts two 8- or 9-inch layers.

## JELLY FROSTING

Combine ½ cup jelly, 1 unbeaten egg white, 2 tablespoons sugar, and dash salt in top of double boiler. Cook over boiling water, beating constantly till stiff peaks form.

Remove from heat. Beat till spreading consistency, about 2 minutes. Frosts two 8-inch layers or 24 cupcakes.

## UNCOOKED FROSTING

Combine 1 unbeaten egg white, 1/2 cup corn syrup, 1/2 teaspoon vanilla, and dash salt. Beat with electric mixer till of fluffy spreading consistency. Frosts one 8- or 9-inch square cake or a loaf cake. Serve within a few hours or refrigerate.

## COCONUT FROSTING

| | |
|---|---|
| 1 6-ounce can evaporated milk | 1 slightly beaten egg |
| | 1 teaspoon vanilla |
| 2/3 cup sugar | 1 1/3 cups flaked coconut |
| 1/4 cup butter or margarine | 1/2 cup chopped pecans |

In saucepan combine milk, sugar, butter, egg, and dash salt. Cook and stir over medium heat till mixture thickens and bubbles, about 12 minutes. Add remaining ingredients. Cool. Frosts top of 13x9x2-inch cake or two 8-inch layers.

## BROILED COCONUT TOPPER

Cream 1/4 cup butter and 1/2 cup brown sugar. Add 2 tablespoons milk; mix well. Stir in 1 cup flaked or shredded coconut. Spread over warm 8- or 9-inch square cake. Broil 4 to 5 inches from heat, about 3 minutes or till golden brown. Serve warm.

## SHADOW ICING

In a small saucepan melt one 1-ounce square unsweetened chocolate with 1/2 teaspoon shortening over low heat. Pour the chocolate from the tip of a teaspoon in a steady stream around the edge of a cake frosted with Seven-minute or Boiled Frosting, letting chocolate run down sides of cake to form "icicles" of varying lengths.

## FUDGE FROSTING

| | |
|---|---|
| 2 1-ounce squares un-sweetened chocolate | 1 cup milk |
| 3 cups sugar | 1/4 cup butter or margarine |
| 3 tablespoons light corn syrup | 1 teaspoon vanilla |

Butter sides of heavy 3-quart saucepan. In it combine first 4 ingredients and 1/4 teaspoon salt. Cook and stir over low heat till sugar dissolves and chocolate melts. Cook to soft ball stage (234°) without stirring. Remove from heat; add butter and cool to warm (110°) without stirring. Add vanilla; beat till mixture is of spreading consistency. Frosts two 9-inch layers.

## FAST FUDGE FROSTING

| | |
|---|---|
| 1 1-pound package confectioners' sugar, sifted | 1/4 teaspoon salt |
| | 1/3 cup boiling water |
| 1/2 cup cocoa (regular-type, dry) | 1/3 cup butter, softened |
| | 1 teaspoon vanilla |

Combine sugar, cocoa, and salt. Add water and butter; blend. Add vanilla. Frosts tops and sides of two 8- or 9-inch layers.

## ROCKY-ROAD FROSTING

| | |
|---|---|
| 2 1-ounce squares un-sweetened chocolate | 2 cups sifted confectioners' sugar |
| 1 cup miniature marshmallows | 1 teaspoon vanilla |
| 1/4 cup butter or margarine | 1 cup miniature marshmallows |
| | 1/2 cup broken walnuts |

In small saucepan, combine chocolate, 1 cup marsh-mallows, butter, and 1/4 cup water. Cook and stir over low heat till the chocolate and marshmallows are melted. Cool slightly. Add confectioners' sugar and vanilla; beat till smooth and thick enough for spreading consistency, about 2 minutes. Stir in 1 cup marshmallows and nuts. Frosts top of 13x9x2-inch cake.

## PINEAPPLE TOPPER

2 egg yolks
3 tablespoons sugar
1/3 cup pineapple juice
1 cup miniature
   marshmallows

1/4 teaspoon vanilla
1/2 cup whipping cream,
   whipped

Beat egg yolks and sugar until thick and lemon-colored. Add pineapple juice. Cook and stir over low heat until thick, about 6 minutes. Remove from heat; add marshmallows. Chill. Fold in vanilla and whipped cream. Makes 1 2/3 cups.

## LEMON FILLING

3/4 cup sugar
2 tablespoons cornstarch
   Dash salt
3/4 cup cold water
2 slightly beaten egg
   yolks

1 teaspoon grated lemon
   peel
3 tablespoons lemon
   juice
1 tablespoon butter or
   margarine

In saucepan, combine sugar, cornstarch, and salt; gradually add water. Stir in egg yolks, lemon peel, and juice. Cook and stir over medium heat till thickened and bubbly. Boil 1 minute; remove from heat. Stir in butter. Cool to room temperature without stirring. Makes 1 1/3 cups.

**Lime Filling:** Prepare Lemon Filling substituting 1 teaspoon grated lime peel and 3 tablespoons lime juice for lemon peel and lemon juice. Add I drop green food coloring with the butter.

**Orange Filling:** Prepare Lemon Filling, substituting 3/4 cup orange juice for 3/4 cup water and the 3 tablespoons lemon juice. Omit 1 teaspoon grated lemon peel.

## DATE-NUT FILLING

Combine 1 1/2 cups pitted dates, cut up, 1 cup water, 1/3 cup sugar, and 1/4 teaspoon salt in saucepan; bring to boiling. Cook and stir over low heat about 4 minutes or till thick. Remove from heat; cool to room temperature. Fold in 1/4 cup chopped walnuts. If desired, fold in 1/4 cup Seven-minute Frosting. Makes about 1 1/2 cups.

## CREAM FILLING

| | |
|---|---|
| ⅓ cup granulated sugar | 1¼ cups milk |
| 3 tablespoons all-purpose flour | 1 beaten egg |
| | 1 tablespoon butter |
| ¼ teaspoon salt | 1 teaspoon vanilla |

In saucepan, combine sugar, flour, and salt. Gradually add milk; mix well. Cook and stir over medium heat till mixture thickens and boils; cook and stir 2 minutes longer. Very gradually stir the hot mixture into the egg; return to saucepan. Cook and stir till mixture just boils. Stir in butter and vanilla; cover surface with waxed paper or clear plastic wrap. Cool. (Don't stir during cooling.) Makes 1½ cups.

**Butterscotch Filling:** Prepare Cream Filling, substituting ⅓ cup brown sugar for ⅓ cup granulated sugar. Increase butter to 2 tablespoons.

**Chocolate Filling:** Prepare Cream Filling, increasing granulated sugar to ½ cup. Add one 1-ounce square unsweetened chocolate, cut up, with milk.

## EASY VANILLA FILLING

Prepare one 3- or 3¼-ounce package *regular* vanilla pudding mix according to package directions, *but use only 1¾ cups milk.* Cover surface and chill.

## FRENCH CUSTARD FILLING

| | |
|---|---|
| ⅓ cup sugar | 1 slightly beaten egg yolk |
| 1 tablespoon all-purpose flour | 1 teaspoon vanilla |
| 1 tablespoon cornstarch | ½ cup whipping cream, whipped |
| ¼ teaspoon salt | |
| 1½ cups milk | |

In saucepan, combine sugar, flour, cornstarch, and salt. Gradually stir in milk. Cook and stir till mixture thickens and boils; cook and stir 2 to 3 minutes longer. Stir a little hot mixture into egg yolk; return to hot mixture. Cook and stir till mixture just boils. Add vanilla; cool. Beat smooth; fold in whipped cream.

# 6

# CANDIES

• **Thermometer test:** Check candy thermometer in boiling water. If it doesn't register 212°, add or subtract the same number of degrees in recipe. Clip thermometer to pan after syrup boils (bulb must be covered with liquid, not just foam).

• **Cold-water test:** Remove pan from heat. Drop a little syrup into small bowl of very cold (but not ice cold) water. Form into ball (see chart below).

• **Fudge repair:** If smooth but too stiff, knead till softened; press into buttered pan or form roll; slice. If fudge doesn't set, stir in ¼ cup milk and recook.

## REMARKABLE FUDGE

Butter sides of heavy 3-quart saucepan. Add 4 cups granulated sugar, one 14½-ounce can evaporated milk, and 1 cup butter. Cook over medium heat to soft ball stage (236°), stirring often. Remove from heat. Stir in one 12-ounce package semisweet chocolate pieces (not imitation) till almost melted. Stir in one 7-ounce jar marshmallow creme, 1 teaspoon vanilla, and 1 cup broken walnuts. Beat till chocolate melts. Pour into buttered 13x9x2-inch pan. Score while warm; cut when firm.

## BLUE RIBBON FUDGE

Butter sides of heavy 2-quart saucepan. In it combine 2 cups granulated sugar, one 6-ounce can evaporated milk, two 1-ounce squares unsweetened chocolate, dash salt, and 1 teaspoon light corn syrup. Cook and stir over medium heat till chocolate melts and sugar dissolves. Cook to soft ball stage (236°). Immediately remove from heat. Add 2 tablespoons butter *without stirring*. Cool to lukewarm (110°). Add 1 teaspoon vanilla and beat vigorously till fudge stiffens and loses its gloss. Quickly stir in ½ cup chopped walnuts. Push from pan (don't scrape sides) into buttered shallow pan. Score while warm; cut when firm.

## OPERA FUDGE

Butter sides of a heavy 2-quart saucepan. In it combine 2 cups granulated sugar, 1/2 cup milk, 1/2 cup light cream, 1 tablespoon light corn syrup, and 1/2 teaspoon salt. Cook over medium heat, stirring constantly, till sugar dissolves and mixture boils. Cook to soft ball stage (238°). Immediately remove from heat; cool to lukewarm (110°) *without stirring*. Add 1 tablespoon butter and 1 teaspoon vanilla. Beat vigorously till fudge stiffens and loses its gloss. Quickly stir in 1/4 cup chopped candied cherries. Spread in buttered 9x5x3-inch pan. Score while warm; cut when firm.

## • TEMPERATURES AND TESTS FOR CANDY •

| TEMPERATURES (at Sea Level) | STAGE | COLD-WATER TEST |
|---|---|---|
| 230° to 234°F | Thread | Syrup dropped from spoon spins 2-inch thread. |
| 234° to 240°F | Soft ball | Syrup can be shaped into a ball but flattens when removed from water. |
| 244° to 248°F | Firm ball | Syrup can be shaped into a firm ball which does not flatten when removed from water. |
| 250° to 266°F | Hard ball | Syrup forms hard ball, although it is pliable. |
| 270° to 290°F | Soft crack | Syrup separates into threads that are not brittle. |
| 300° to 310°F | Hard crack | Syrup separates into hard, brittle threads. |

# • EASY STEPS TO PERFECT FUDGE •

**1** Butter sides of heavy, high-sided saucepan, top to bottom. Then when fudge bubbles up, grains of sugar can't cling and unwanted crystals won't be able to form.

**2** Stir fudge till it comes to boiling and *all* sugar is dissolved. One sugar crystal can start a chain reaction. Wait to clip on candy thermometer till mixture boils.

**3** Check temperature often after 220°—it will climb fast after this point. Most accurate check is with a candy thermometer. Double check with cold-water test.

**4** Add butter and let fudge cool *undisturbed* to 110° (bottom of pan should feel comfortably warm). Add extract; start beating vigorously. Don't stop too soon.

**5** Pour at just the right moment—fudge will seem to stiffen and lose its gloss. Add nuts at this point. *Push* mixture from pan with rubber spatula—*don't scrape* pan.

**6** Score fudge while warm, using tip of knife. (Dip knife in water when necessary.) Press a nut half on each square if desired. Cut when candy is cool and firm.

# NOUGAT

Grease 9x5x3-inch pan lightly, then dust with cornstarch. In a large saucepan, combine 1½ cups granulated sugar and 1 tablespoon cornstarch. Add 1 cup light corn syrup and ½ cup water. Cook and stir till sugar dissolves. Continue cooking to soft crack stage (286°), stirring occasionally to prevent sticking.

Meanwhile, beat 2 egg whites to stiff peaks. Slowly pour syrup over egg whites beating constantly with electric mixer. Beat till mixture becomes stiff. Fold in ⅔ cup chopped candied cherries. Pack candy into loaf pan. Cut in 1-inch squares.

# BROWN SUGAR NUT ROLL

| | |
|---|---|
| 2 cups granulated sugar | ¼ cup light corn syrup |
| 1 cup brown sugar | 1 cup chopped pecans |
| 1 cup evaporated milk | |

Butter sides of heavy 2-quart saucepan. In it combine sugars, milk, corn syrup, and dash salt. Stir over medium heat till sugars dissolve and mixture boils. Cook to soft ball stage (236°) stirring frequently. Immediately remove from heat; cool to lukewarm (110°); *do not* stir.

Beat till candy begins to hold its shape. Turn out on buttered surface. Knead till it can be shaped, keeping hands well buttered. Shape in two 7-inch rolls; roll immediately in chopped nuts, pressing to coat well. Wrap and chill. Cut ½-inch slices. Makes about 28 pieces of candy.

*Note:* Mixture will curdle while cooking, but becomes smooth when you beat it.

# QUICK WALNUT PENUCHE

Melt ½ cup butter or margarine in saucepan; add 1 cup brown sugar. Cook over low heat 2 minutes, stirring constantly. Add ¼ cup milk and continue cooking and stirring till mixture comes to boiling. Remove from heat. Cool. Gradually add 1¾ to 2 cups confectioners' sugar till mixture is of fudge consistency. Stir in 1 cup chopped walnuts. Spread candy in buttered 8x8x2-inch pan. Chill. Cut in squares. Makes about 36 pieces of candy.

## PENUCHE

| | |
|---|---|
| 1½ cups granulated sugar | 2 tablespoons butter or |
| 1 cup brown sugar | margarine |
| ⅓ cup light cream | 1 teaspoon vanilla |
| ⅓ cup milk | ½ cup broken walnuts or |
| | pecans |

Butter sides of heavy 2-quart saucepan. In it combine sugars, cream, milk, and butter. Heat over medium heat, stirring constantly, till sugars dissolve and mixture comes to boiling. Cook to soft ball stage (238°), stirring only if necessary. Immediately remove from heat and cool to lukewarm (110°). *Do not* stir. Add vanilla. Beat vigorously till candy becomes very thick and starts to lose its gloss. Quickly stir in nuts and spread in buttered shallow pan. Score while warm; cut when firm.

## PEANUT BUTTER FUDGE

Butter sides of heavy 2-quart saucepan. In it combine 2 cups granulated sugar and ⅔ cup milk. Stir over medium heat till sugar dissolves and mixture boils. Cook to soft ball stage (234°). Remove from heat; quickly add ½ of pint jar marshmallow creme, 1 cup chunk-style peanut butter, one 6-ounce package (1 cup) semisweet chocolate pieces, and 1 teaspoon vanilla; blend. Pour into buttered 9x9x2-inch pan. Score; cut when firm.

## DIVINITY

| | |
|---|---|
| 2½ cups granulated sugar | 2 egg whites |
| ½ cup light corn syrup | 1 teaspoon vanilla |

In 2-quart saucepan, combine sugar, corn syrup, ¼ teaspoon salt, and ½ cup water. Cook to hard ball stage (260°) stirring only till sugar dissolves. Meanwhile, beat egg whites to stiff peaks. Gradually pour syrup over egg whites, beating at high speed on electric mixer. Add vanilla and beat till candy holds its shape, 4 to 5 minutes. Quickly drop from a teaspoon onto waxed paper. Makes about 40 pieces.

## SEA FOAM

| | |
|---|---|
| 1³/₄ cups light brown sugar | 2 egg whites |
| ³/₄ cup granulated sugar | 1 teaspoon vanilla |
| ¹/₄ cup light corn syrup | ¹/₂ cup broken pecans |
| ¹/₄ teaspoon salt | (optional) |

Butter sides of heavy 2-quart saucepan. In it combine sugars, corn syrup, salt, and ¹/₂ cup water. Cook, stirring constantly, till sugars dissolve and mixture comes to boiling. Cook to hard ball stage (260°), without stirring. Remove from heat. Immediately beat egg whites till stiff peaks form. Pour hot syrup in a thin stream over beaten egg whites, beating constantly at high speed on electric mixer. Add vanilla. Continue beating till mixture forms soft peaks and begins to lose its gloss, about 10 minutes. Stir in nuts. Let stand about 2 minutes; drop by rounded teaspoons onto waxed paper. Makes 2 to 3 dozen pieces.

## FONDANT

| | |
|---|---|
| 2 cups granulated sugar | ¹/₈ teaspoon cream of |
| 1¹/₂ cups boiling water | tartar *or* 2 tablespoons |
| | light corn syrup |

Butter sides of heavy 1¹/₂-quart saucepan. In it combine sugar, water, and cream of tartar or syrup. Stir over medium heat till sugar dissolves and mixture boils. Cook without stirring to soft ball stage (238°). Immediately pour on platter. *Do not* scrape pan. Cool till candy feels only slightly warm to the touch, about 30 minutes; *do not move* candy. Using spatula or wooden spoon, scrape candy from edge of platter toward center, then work till creamy and stiff. Knead with fingers till free from lumps. Wrap; place in covered container to ripen 24 hours. Tint, flavor, and shape. Or, use to stuff dates, prunes, or figs and roll in confectioners' sugar.

**Vanilla Fondant:** Knead in 1 tablespoon soft butter and 1 teaspoon vanilla.

**Pink Peppermint Fondant:** Knead in 10 drops peppermint extract and 4 drops red food coloring.

## CARAMELS

| | |
|---|---|
| 1 cup butter or margarine | 1 cup light corn syrup |
| 1 pound (2¼ cups) brown sugar | 1 15-ounce can sweetened condensed milk |
| Dash salt | 1 teaspoon vanilla |

Melt butter in heavy 3-quart saucepan. Add sugar and salt; stir thoroughly. Stir in corn syrup; mix well. Gradually add milk, stirring constantly. Cook and stir over medium heat to firm ball stage (245°), 12 to 15 minutes. Remove from heat; stir in vanilla. Pour into buttered 9x9x2-inch pan. Cool and cut into squares.

**Chocolate Caramels:** Add two 1-ounce squares unsweetened chocolate with milk. Makes about 2½ pounds.

## RAISIN CARAMELS

Place 1 cup raisins in buttered 8x8x2-inch pan. Combine ¾ cup butter or margarine and 1 cup brown sugar in saucepan; cook and stir to hard ball stage (254°). Pour over raisins. Top with ½ cup semisweet chocolate pieces, spreading as they melt. Chill till firm; cut in pieces.

## CHOCOLATES

Dip caramels, nuts, candied fruits, or molded fondant in chocolate. (Mold fondant centers a day or two earlier so fondant won't leak through chocolate.) Don't attempt chocolate dipping on a hot or damp day. Work in a room temperature of 65°.

Use at least 1 pound grated candy-making chocolate. Place in double boiler over *hot, not boiling* water (115° to 120°), with water touching pan. Stir constantly till melted. Exchange hot water for cold in bottom of double boiler; stir and cool chocolate to 83°. Exchange cold water for warm (85°).

Working rapidly, drop desired center into chocolate, roll to coat, and lift out with fork. Draw fork across rim of pan to remove excess chocolate; place on waxed paper-lined baking sheet, bring "string" of chocolate across top. (If chocolate becomes too stiff, heat as at first.)

## CREAMY PRALINES

| | |
|---|---|
| 2 cups granulated sugar | 1¹/₂ tablespoons butter |
| ³/₄ teaspoon soda | 2 cups pecan halves |
| 1 cup light cream | |

Combine sugar and soda in 3¹/₂-quart saucepan; mix well. Stir in cream. Bring to boiling over medium heat, stirring constantly. Reduce heat; cook and stir to soft ball stage (234°). (Mixture caramelizes slightly.) Remove from heat; add butter. Stir in pecans; beat till thick, 2 to 3 minutes. Drop from tablespoon onto waxed paper. (If candy becomes too stiff, add a tablespoon hot water.) Makes 30.

## SMALL MINTS

Cook 2 cups granulated sugar, ¹/₂ cup water, and ¹/₂ cup light corn syrup in 2-quart saucepan; stir till sugar dissolves. Cook to thread stage (232°) without stirring. Add ¹/₈ teaspoon cream of tartar; beat with wire whip till creamy. Add a few drops flavored oil and food coloring. Drop from teaspoon onto waxed paper forming patties. (Keep pan over hot water.) Store tightly covered. Makes about 60.

## MARSHMALLOWS

| | |
|---|---|
| 2 envelopes (2 tablespoons) unflavored gelatin | 1 cup granulated sugar |
| | 1 cup light corn syrup |
| | 1 egg white |

Soften gelatin in ¹/₂ cup cold water. In 2-quart saucepan, combine sugar, corn syrup, and ¹/₃ cup water. Cook to soft ball stage (240°) stirring only till sugar dissolves. Remove from heat; stir in gelatin to dissolve. Let cool 10 minutes. Beat egg white to stiff peaks. Slowly add syrup, beating on high speed of electric mixer till candy stands in soft peaks. Pour onto plain brown paper and spread in 12x10-inch rectangle. Let stand overnight. Dust with confectioners' sugar; turn over on another piece of paper. Moisten brown paper to remove from candy. Cut in desired size pieces. Makes 1¹/₂ pounds.

## SALT WATER TAFFY

| | |
|---|---|
| 2 cups granulated sugar | $^1/_4$ teaspoon oil of |
| 1 cup light corn syrup | peppermint |
| $1^1/_2$ teaspoons salt | 7 drops green food |
| 2 tablespoons butter | coloring |

Combine sugar, syrup, salt, and 1 cup water in 2-quart saucepan. Cook slowly, stirring constantly, till sugar dissolves. Cook to hard ball stage (265°) without stirring. Remove from heat; stir in remaining ingredients. Pour into buttered $15^1/_2$x$10^1/_2$x1-inch pan. Cool till comfortable to handle. Butter hands; gather taffy into a ball and pull. When candy is light in color and gets hard to pull, cut in fourths; pull each piece into long strand about $^1/_2$ inch thick. With buttered scissors, quickly snip in bite-size pieces. Wrap each piece in waxed paper. Makes $1^1/_4$ pounds.

## MOLASSES TAFFY

Butter sides of heavy 3-quart saucepan. In it combine 2 cups granulated sugar, 1 cup light molasses, and $^1/_4$ cup water. Heat slowly, stirring constantly, till sugar dissolves. Bring to boiling; add 2 teaspoons vinegar; cook to soft crack stage (270°).

Remove from heat; add 2 tablespoons butter and sift in $^1/_2$ teaspoon soda; stir to mix. Pour into buttered $15^1/_2$x$10^1/_2$x1-inch pan. Use spatula to turn edges to center. Cool till comfortable to handle. Butter hands; gather taffy into ball and pull with fingertips. When light tan color and hard to pull, cut in fourths. Pull each piece into long strand about $^1/_2$ inch thick. With buttered scissors, quickly snip in bite-size pieces. Wrap each piece in clear plastic wrap. Makes $1^1/_2$ pounds.

## GLAZED ALMONDS

Combine 1 cup whole almonds, $^1/_2$ cup sugar, and 2 tablespoons butter in heavy skillet. Cook over medium-low heat, *stirring constantly*, till almonds are coated and sugar is golden brown, about 15 minutes. Stir in $^1/_2$ teaspoon vanilla. Spread nuts on aluminum foil. Cool. Break into 2- or 3-nut clusters. Sprinkle lightly with salt.

## PEANUT BRITTLE

| | |
|---|---|
| 2 cups granulated sugar | 1 tablespoon butter |
| 1 cup light corn syrup | 1 teaspoon soda |
| 2 cups raw Spanish peanuts | |

Heat and stir sugar, syrup, and 1 cup water in heavy 3-quart saucepan till sugar dissolves. Cook over medium heat to soft ball stage (234°). Add nuts and ½ teaspoon salt. Cook to hard crack stage (305°), stirring often. Remove from heat. Quickly stir in butter and soda. Pour at once onto 2 well-buttered 15½x10½x1-inch pans, spreading with spatula. If desired, cool slightly and pull with forks to stretch thin. Break up when cold. Makes 1½ pounds.

## ALMOND BUTTER CRUNCH

| | |
|---|---|
| 1 cup butter or margarine | ½ cup coarsely chopped toasted almonds |
| 1 cup sugar | 4 ounces milk chocolate, chopped (¾ cup) |
| 1 tablespoon light corn syrup | ½ cup finely chopped toasted almonds |

Melt butter in heavy 2-quart saucepan. Add sugar. Stir over medium heat till sugar dissolves. Add 3 tablespoons water and corn syrup. Cook over medium heat, stirring often, to soft crack stage (290°), about 12 minutes. (Watch carefully after 280°.) Remove from heat; quickly stir in coarse nuts. Spread on buttered baking sheet. Immediately sprinkle chocolate over top; let stand a few minutes. Spread evenly. Sprinkle with fine nuts. Chill to firm. Break in pieces. Makes 1¼ pounds.

## COFFEE WALNUTS

Combine 1 cup brown sugar, ½ cup granulated sugar, ½ cup dairy sour cream, and 1 tablespoon instant coffee powder in saucepan. Cook and stir to soft ball stage (236°). Remove from heat; stir in 1 teaspoon vanilla. Add 3 cups walnut halves; stir gently to coat. Separate nuts on buttered cookie sheet. Makes 4 cups.

# CINNAMON APPLES

| | |
|---|---|
| 6 crisp, medium apples | 2 cups light corn syrup |
| 6 wooden skewers | 1/4 teaspoon red food |
| * * * | coloring |
| 1 1/3 cups granulated sugar | 10 drops oil of cinnamon |

Wash and dry the apples; remove stems. Insert skewer into blossom end of each apple. Combine sugar, corn syrup, and food coloring in top of double boiler. Cook directly over low heat stirring till sugar dissolves, about 4 minutes. Cover and cook slowly 8 minutes. Uncover. Cook without stirring to hard crack stage (300°). Stir in flavoring. Place top of double boiler over boiling water in lower part.

Turn each apple in syrup to coat. Twirl apple to spread coating evenly—let excess syrup drip back into pan. Set apples on buttered cookie sheet. If syrup thickens, reheat over direct heat. Makes 6 apples.

• **Lollipops:** Prepare syrup recipe above for 2 dozen. When syrup reaches 300°, remove from heat and let stand a few minutes to thicken slightly (or use remaining syrup from Cinnamon Apples). Arrange wooden skewers 5 inches apart on buttered cookie sheet. Drop hot syrup from tip of tablespoon over the skewers to form 2- to 3-inch candy circles.

# CANDIED ORANGE PEEL

| | |
|---|---|
| 6 medium oranges | 2 cups sugar |
| 1 tablespoon salt | |

Cut peel of each orange in sixths; loosen from pulp with bowl of spoon. Remove most of white membrane from peel. Add salt and peel to 4 cups water. Weight with a plate to keep peel under water; let stand overnight. Drain; wash thoroughly. Cover with cold water; heat to boiling. Drain. Repeat 3 times (helps remove bitter taste).

With shears, cut peel in strips. In saucepan, combine peel (about 2 cups), sugar, and 1/2 cup water. Heat and stir till sugar dissolves. Cook slowly till peel is translucent. Drain; roll in granulated sugar. Dry on rack. Makes 2 to 2 1/2 cups.

## OLD-TIME POPCORN BALLS

2 cups granulated sugar
1½ cups water
½ teaspoon salt
½ cup light corn syrup
1 teaspoon vinegar
1 teaspoon vanilla
5 quarts popped corn

Butter sides of saucepan. In it combine sugar, water, salt, syrup, and vinegar. Cook to hard ball stage (250°). Stir in vanilla. Slowly pour over popped corn, stirring just to mix well. Butter hands lightly; shape balls. Makes 15 to 20 balls.

## CARAMEL POPCORN BALLS

¼ cup butter or
   margarine
1 cup brown sugar
½ cup light corn syrup
½ 15-ounce can (⅔ cup)
   sweetened *condensed*
   milk
½ teaspoon vanilla
5 quarts popped corn

In saucepan, combine butter, sugar, and corn syrup. Stir well and bring to boiling over medium heat. Stir in condensed milk; simmer, stirring constantly, till mixture comes to soft ball stage (234° to 238°). Stir in vanilla. Pour over popped corn and stir to coat. Butter hands lightly; shape popcorn into balls about 3½ inches in diameter. Makes about 15.

## POPCORN POPS

4 quarts popped corn
   (⅔ cup unpopped)
1 cup peanuts
1 cup light molasses
1 cup granulated sugar
1 teaspoon salt

Combine popped corn and peanuts in large bowl or pan. In 2-quart saucepan, combine molasses, sugar, and salt; cook over medium heat to hard ball stage (260°). Pour syrup slowly over popped corn and nuts, stirring till mixture is well coated. Press into 5-ounce cold-drink cups. Insert a wooden skewer in each; let cool. Push on bottoms of cups to remove. Makes 16.

## NO-BAKE FRUIT SQUARES

1 cup raisins
1/2 cup dried apricots
1/3 cup dried figs
1 cup pitted dates
1/2 cup candied orange
peel

1/4 cup candied cherries
1 cup chopped walnuts
2 to 3 tablespoons
orange juice
Confectioners' sugar

Grind together fruits and nuts. Mix in enough juice to hold together. Press into greased 8x8x2-inch pan. Chill overnight. Cut; sift sugar atop. Makes 24.

## ANGEL SWEETS

1 6-ounce package
(1 cup) semisweet
chocolate pieces
2 tablespoons butter or
margarine
1 egg

1 cup sifted
confectioners' sugar
1 cup chopped walnuts
2 cups miniature
marshmallows
1/2 cup flaked coconut

Melt chocolate and butter over low heat. Remove from heat; blend in egg. Stir in sugar, nuts, and marshmallows, blending well. Shape into 1-inch balls; roll in coconut. Chill. Makes about 48.

## STUFFED DATES

3 tablespoons butter,
softened
3 tablespoons light corn
syrup
1/2 teaspoon shredded
orange peel

1/2 teaspoon vanilla
1/4 teaspoon salt
2 1/3 cups sifted
confectioners' sugar
Walnut halves
48 pitted dates

Cream butter; blend in syrup, peel, vanilla, and salt. Add sugar all at once; mix in, first with spoon, then by kneading with hands. Place mixture on board; knead till smooth. Wrap in foil; chill 24 hours. Wrap each nut with about 1/2 teaspoon candy and stuff into date. Makes 48.

# 7

# CANNING
# AND FREEZING

# CANNING

Home canning is one of the easiest and most satisfying ways to ensure having your favorite fruits, vegetables, and meats year-round. Canning halts spoilage of fresh foods by heating the food in sealed containers. The heat destroys the troublesome organisms and the sealed containers prevent recontamination.

**Jars and lids:** Use only standard mason jars and the lids designed to fit them. Jars and lids must be flawless. Discard jars with chips or cracks. Always use new self-sealing lids or rubber rings.

Wash jars and lids, except those with sealing compound, in sudsy water and rinse thoroughly. Then, pour boiling water over the jars and allow them to stand in hot water until ready to fill. Follow the manufacturer's directions for washing flat metal lids with sealing compound.

The flat metal lid with sealing compound and metal screw band is the most popular type of cap for home-canned products. This lid is self-sealing. Do not tighten the band after processing.

Follow the manufacturer's directions for washing and sealing rubber rings and porcelain-lined zinc caps.

**Canners:** For canning to be effective, you must have the proper combination of temperature and time. While 212° in the boiling water bath is sufficient to destroy harmful organisms in high-acid foods, you must process low-acid foods at 240° to achieve the same result. In order to do this you'll need a pressure canner for low-acid foods such as vegetables, meat, and fish (see page 306).

**Filling the jars:** For most foods, you may use either raw-pack or hot-pack method.

*Raw Pack:* Pack the uncooked food into containers. Add boiling syrup or water.

*Hot Pack:* Partially cook food before packing, then add boiling liquid.

The following steps apply to both raw pack and hot pack:

1. Pack foods into hot jars, leaving the headspace—room at the top—specified for each product. Shake jars gently.

2. Ladle boiling liquid over the food, leaving the specified headspace.

3. Gently work blade of spatula or knife around inside filled jar to eliminate air bubbles. Add more boiling liquid if needed.

4. Wipe off rim of jar with a damp cloth. Bits of food or syrup on the rim could prevent a perfect seal after processing.

5. Prepare lids following manufacturer's directions. For flat metal lid, place compound side down. Add metal band and screw down until it is firm and tight.

6. Transfer filled jar to canner. Complete filling, covering, and placing each jar in canner before filling another.

**Testing for seal:** To test jar with flat lid, press center of lid on cooled jar. If the dip in lid holds, jar is sealed. Other types of caps won't leak when jar is tipped. If jar isn't sealed, check for flaws, repack, and reprocess with a new lid the full length of time. Or, refrigerate food and serve it within a day or two.

**Storing jars:** Remove screw bands from flat metal lids. Label with contents and date. Store in cool, dry, dark place.

**Detecting spoilage:** Leakage, patches of mold, foamy or murky appearance, bulging lids, and off-odor are signs of spoilage. If the canned food doesn't look or smell right, don't use it. Boil meats and vegetables, except tomatoes, uncovered, at least 10 minutes (20 minutes for corn and spinach) before tasting or using.

## • ALTITUDE CORRECTION •

For water bath, add 1 minute to processing for each 1,000 feet above sea level when the time specified is 20 minutes or less. Add 2 minutes to processing for each 1,000 feet above sea level if the time called for is more than 20 minutes.

## WATER-BATH CANNING

Water-bath canning is recommended for most fruits; the high-acid vegetables such as tomatoes and ripe pimiento peppers; sauerkraut; and all pickles and relishes. Use either a raw-pack or a hot-pack method.

1. Set water-bath canner containing a rack on kitchen range. Fill with 4 to 5 inches water, cover, and start heating water over high heat. Also, start heating additional water in a teakettle to use to fill canner after jars are in place.

2. Prepare the sugar syrup if it is to be used (see page 289). Keep syrup warm but not boiling till ready to fill jars.

3. Prepare fruits or vegetables to be canned following recipe directions.

4. Refer to directions on pages 283–284 when you are ready to fill jars.

5. When the water in the canner is hot, fill each jar and place on rack in canner. Make sure jars do not touch. Replace the cover on canner each time you add a jar.

6. When the last jar has been added, check water level in the canner. Using the boiling water that was heated in teakettle, fill canner so water is 1 to 2 inches over tops of jars. Place cover on canner. Heat water to a brisk rolling boil.

7. Now, start counting the processing time given in recipe. (Some pickle recipes will start timing as soon as jars are placed in water.) Make altitude adjustment, if needed (see opposite page).

8. Adjust heat under canner so water boils gently during entire processing time. Add boiling water from teakettle if water level drops. If the water stops boiling when you add water, stop counting processing time, turn up heat, and wait for a full boil before resuming counting.

9. When processing time is up, turn heat off under canner. Remove hot jars with a jar lifter or long-handled tongs.

Have water heating in canner on range. As each jar is filled and closed, place on canner rack, using jar lifter or tongs.

Add hot water to bring level in canner 1 or 2 inches over tops of jars. Cover canner; heat water to a brisk rolling boil.

When processing time is up, transfer hot jars to rack to cool. Area should be draft-free. Allow air to circulate around jars.

A dip in the lid identifies a sealed jar. You may also tap the lid with a metal spoon and listen for a ringing sound.

# CANNING FRUITS

## CANNING PROCEDURE

Most fruits may be canned in two ways: raw pack (cold) or hot pack (precooked).

1. Wash jars; rinse. Wash caps according to manufacturer's directions. Place jars in hot water till ready to use —no need to sterilize jars; processing does that. Place water-bath canner on heat with 4 to 5 inches water. Cover; start heating on high heat.

2. Prepare fruit following directions given in chart or recipe.

3. Pack fruit into jars using raw or hot pack method. Use syrup to suit sweetness of the fruit and your taste.

*Raw pack:* (May be used for all fruits except apples and applesauce.) Pack fruit firmly into jars. Leave ¹/₂-inch headspace at top of jar. Pour in boiling syrup, still leaving ¹/₂-inch headspace.

*Hot pack:* (May be used for all fruits.) Precook fruit in syrup according to directions in chart on opposite page. Pack boiling hot fruit loosely into jars, leaving ¹/₂-inch headspace. Cover with boiling syrup, still leaving ¹/₂-inch headspace.

4. Chase out air bubbles from filled jars by working blade of knife down sides of jars. Add more liquid if needed, but keep the original headspace.

5. Adjust jar caps: For self-sealing caps, wipe sealing edge of jar with clean cloth to remove food particles; put flat metal lid on jar with sealing compound next to glass and screw band tight. Fit wet rubber ring on jar with zinc caps; wipe jar rim and ring with clean cloth; partially seal by screwing zinc caps down firmly, then turn caps back ¹/₄ inch.

6. Lower jars on rack into water bath canner (see photos

on page 286). Be sure jars do not touch. Cover. Count time when water comes to rolling boil. Keep boiling gently during entire processing time. Add more *boiling* water if needed to keep jars covered. Process for time on pages 289–291. Note altitude and water bath instructions, pages 284 and 285.

7. Follow instructions for sealing and cooling on pages 283–286.

• Choose fresh, firm fruits for canning.

• Sort fruits according to size and ripeness—they cook more evenly that way.

• Wash fruits thoroughly under running water or through several changes of water.

• Handle fruits gently to avoid bruising.

• Use ascorbic acid color keeper to treat fruits that darken easily during preparation. It's found at the grocer's and is the same product used in freezing fruits.

## CANNED FRUIT YIELD

Generally, for 1 quart canned fruit use the following amount fresh fruit as purchased:

| Fruit | Pounds |
| --- | --- |
| Apples | 2¹/₂ to 3 |
| Berries, except strawberries | 1¹/₂ to 3 |
| Cherries (if canned unpitted) | 2 to 2¹/₂ |
| Peaches | 2 to 3 |
| Pears | 2 to 3 |
| Plums | 1¹/₂ to 2¹/₂ |

Work blade of knife down sides of jar to chase out air bubbles. This keeps liquid above fruit—no dark spots on top. Note ¹/₂-inch headspace between fruit-liquid mixture and top of jar for proper sealing. Overlap peach halves hollow side down for pretty effect and best use of jar space.

| | Preparation of Fruit | Water bath in minutes (pints) | Water bath in minutes (quarts) |
|---|---|---|---|
| Fruit | **Thin Syrup**—2 cups sugar to 4 cups water. Yield 5 cups. **Medium Syrup**—3 cups sugar to 4 cups water. Yield 5½ cups. **Heavy Syrup**—4¾ cups sugar to 4 cups water. Yield 6½ cups. (Boil sugar and water together 5 minutes. Skim if needed. Figure ½ to 1½ cups sugar for each quart jar.) | | |
| Apples | *Hot Pack:* Wash, pare, core, and cut in pieces. While preparing, treat to prevent darkening with ascorbic acid color keeper following package directions for fresh-cut fruit. Boil in syrup or water 5 minutes. Pack hot; cover with boiling syrup or water leaving ½-inch headspace. Adjust lids; process in boiling water bath. | 15 | 20 |
| | *Applesauce:* Prepare sauce; heat to simmering; pack hot into hot jars leaving ½-inch headspace. Adjust lids; process in boiling water bath. | 20 | 20 |
| Apricots Peaches Pears | *Raw Pack:* Wash and peel fruit (dip peaches and apricots in boiling water, then in cold water for easier peeling) or omit peeling apricots, if desired. Halve or slice; pit or core. While preparing, use ascorbic acid color keeper following package directions for fresh-cut fruit. Pack into hot jars; cover with boiling syrup leaving ½-inch headspace. Adjust lids; process in boiling water bath. | 25 | 30 |
| | *Hot Pack:* Prepare as above. Heat through in syrup. Pack hot into hot jars; cover with boiling syrup leaving ½-inch headspace. Adjust lids; process in boiling water bath. | 20 | 25 |

| Fruit | Preparation of Fruit | Water bath in minutes (pints) | Water bath in minutes (quarts) |
|---|---|---|---|
| Berries (except strawberries) | *Raw Pack:* Use for raspberries, other soft berries. Wash fruit; drain. Fill hot jars. Cover with boiling syrup leaving ¹/₂-inch headspace. Adjust lids; process in boiling water bath. | 10 | 15 |
| | *Hot Pack:* Use for firm berries. Wash; drain. Add ¹/₂ cup sugar to each quart berries. Bring to boil in covered pan; shake pan to keep berries from sticking. Pack hot into hot jars leaving ¹/₂-inch headspace. Adjust lids; process in boiling water bath. | 10 | 15 |
| Cherries | *Raw Pack:* Wash, stem, and pit, if desired. Fill hot jars. Cover with boiling syrup leaving ¹/₂-inch headspace. Adjust lids; process in boiling water bath. | 20 | 25 |
| | *Hot Pack:* Wash; remove pits, if desired. Add ¹/₂ cup sugar to each quart fruit. Add a little water only to *unpitted* cherries. Cover; bring to boiling. Pack hot into hot jars leaving ¹/₂-inch headspace. Adjust lids; process in boiling water bath. | 10 | 15 |
| Plums | *Raw Pack:* Wash; prick skins if canning whole fruit. Halve and pit freestone plums, if desired. Pack into hot jars. Cover with boiling syrup leaving ¹/₂-inch headspace. Adjust lids; process in boiling water bath. | 20 | 25 |
| | *Hot Pack:* Prepare as above. Bring to boil in syrup. Pack hot into hot jars; add | 20 | 25 |

| | | 10 | 10 |
| | | 5 | 5 |

boiling syrup leaving ¹/₂-inch headspace. Adjust lids; process in boiling water bath.

**Rhubarb** — Wash; cut rhubarb into ¹/₂-inch pieces. Pack into hot jars, leaving ¹/₂-inch headspace. Cover with boiling thin syrup, leaving ¹/₂-inch headspace. Adjust lids; process in boiling water bath.

**Fruit juices** — Wash fruit; pit, if desired. Crush fruit; heat to simmering; strain through cheesecloth bag. Add sugar, if desired (1 cup per gallon of juice). Heat to simmering. Fill hot jars with hot juice leaving ¹/₂-inch headspace. Adjust lids; process in boiling water bath.

## APPLE BUTTER

| | |
|---|---|
| 6 pounds tart apples | 2 teaspoons ground |
| 6 cups cider or apple | cinnamon |
| juice | 1/2 teaspoon ground |
| 3 cups sugar | cloves |

Core and quarter unpared apples. In 4- to 6-quart kettle, combine apples and cider. Cook about 30 minutes, or till soft. Pass through food mill. Boil gently 30 minutes; stir often. Add sugar and spices. Cook and stir over low heat till sugar dissolves. Boil gently, stirring frequently, till of desired thickness. Ladle hot butter into hot jars, leaving 1/2-inch headspace. Adjust lids. Process in boiling water bath (half-pints) 10 minutes. Makes 8 half-pints.

## APRICOT-ORANGE BUTTER

| | |
|---|---|
| 2 pounds apricots | 3 tablespoons frozen |
| 1 1/2 cups sugar | orange juice |
| 3/4 cup honey | concentrate, thawed |

Pit and slice apricots; measure 6 cups. Cook apricots in 1/2 cup water, covered, 5 to 10 minutes, or till soft. Press through food mill; measure 3 cups. In 4- to 6-quart kettle or Dutch oven, combine apricot puree, sugar, and honey. Bring to full boil; reduce heat and simmer gently, stirring constantly, 12 to 15 minutes. Stir in orange juice concentrate. Pour into hot jars, leaving 1/2-inch headspace. Adjust lids. Process in boiling water bath (half-pints) 10 minutes. Makes 4 half-pints.

## PINEAPPLE SPEARS

Prepare Medium Syrup (see page 289); keep hot but not boiling. Wash two 4 1/2-pound pineapples thoroughly. Remove crowns. Pare pineapples; remove eyes. Quarter; remove core. Cut fruit in spears that are 1/2-inch shorter than pint jars.

In 4- to 6-quart kettle, bring spears and syrup to boiling. Boil about 7 minutes. Pack hot fruit into hot pint jars. Cover with boiling syrup; leave 1/2-inch headspace. Adjust lids. Process in boiling water bath (pints) 30 minutes. Makes 3 pints.

# FRUIT BOWL

5 cups Thin Syrup
(page 289)
2 3-pound pineapples
2 pounds seedless
green grapes

2 pounds fully ripe
apricots
Ascorbic acid color
keeper

Prepare syrup; keep hot but not boiling. Wash pineapples. Remove crowns. Slice and pare pineapples; remove eyes and cores. Cut pineapple into chunks. Wash and drain grapes. Remove stems. Wash and drain apricots; halve and pit. While preparing apricots, add color keeper.

Simmer pineapple chunks in hot syrup 5 to 10 minutes, or till almost tender. Add apricots and grapes; simmer fruit about 5 minutes, or till heated through. Pack hot fruit into hot jars, leaving 1-inch headspace. Cover with boiling syrup, leaving $^1/_2$-inch headspace. Adjust lids. Process fruit in boiling water bath (pints) 20 minutes; (quarts) 25 minutes. Makes 8 pints.

*Before serving:* If desired, add $^1/_4$ cup maraschino cherry halves to each pint fruit mixture. Chill thoroughly.

# FRUIT COCKTAIL

$5^1/_2$ cups Medium Syrup
(page 289)
1 2-pound pineapple
3 pounds peaches
3 pounds pears

1 pound dark sweet
cherries
1 pound seedless
green grapes
Ascorbic acid color
keeper

Prepare syrup; keep hot but not boiling. Wash fruits. Remove crown from pineapple; pare and cut pineapple in tidbits, removing eyes and center core (measure 3 cups). Pare and pit peaches; cube (measure $8^1/_2$ cups). Pare and core pears; cube (measure $6^1/_2$ cups). While preparing peaches and pears, add color keeper. Halve and pit cherries (measure $2^1/_2$ cups). Stem green grapes (measure 3 cups).

In 4- to 6-quart kettle, combine all fruit. Add hot syrup; bring to boiling. Pack hot fruit into hot jars; leave $^1/_2$-inch headspace. Cover fruit with boiling syrup; leave $^1/_2$-inch headspace. Adjust lids. Process in boiling water bath (pints and quarts) 30 minutes. Makes 9 pints.

## APPLE-CHERRY JUICE

3 pounds apples          ½ cup sugar
4 cups tart red cherries

Wash and core apples. Wash and pit cherries. Grind fruit through food chopper, using a fine blade. In a 4- to 6-quart kettle or Dutch oven, bring fruit and 3 cups water to boiling, stirring occasionally. Reduce heat; cook slowly about 10 minutes. Strain through clean muslin or several thicknesses of cheesecloth. Let juice stand 1 to 2 hours to let sediment settle.

Pour off juice. Add sugar and a few drops red food coloring to juice; heat. Pour hot juice into hot jars; leave ½-inch headspace. Adjust lids. Process in boiling water bath (pints) 15 minutes. Makes 3 pints.

## GRAPE JUICE CONCENTRATE

6 pounds Concord          1½ cups sugar
  grapes

Wash grapes; remove from stems. Measure 14 cups grapes. Combine grapes and 2 cups water in 6-quart kettle; cover. Heat to boiling; cook slowly about 30 minutes, or until very tender. Remove from heat; strain through muslin or cheesecloth. Let juice stand 24 hours in refrigerator. Strain again. Combine grape juice and sugar in large kettle; heat to boiling. Pour hot juice into hot jars, leaving ½-inch headspace. Adjust lids. Process in boiling water bath (pints) 10 minutes. Makes 3 pints.

*Before serving:* Dilute grape juice concentrate with water to taste; chill well.

## WHOLE CRANBERRY SAUCE

Combine 6¾ cups sugar and 6 cups water in an 8- to 10-quart kettle or Dutch oven; stir to dissolve sugar. Heat mixture to boiling; boil 5 minutes. Add 3 pounds (12 cups) fresh cranberries; cook about 5 minutes, or till skins pop. Remove from heat. Pack hot cranberry sauce into hot jars, leaving 1/2-inch headspace. Adjust lids. Process in boiling water bath (pints) 5 minutes. Makes 6 pints.

## APRICOT NECTAR

| | |
|---|---|
| 2 pounds apricots | 1 cup sugar |
| 5 cups water | |

Pit and slice apricots; measure 6 cups fruit. In 8- to 10-quart kettle or Dutch oven, combine apricots and water. Cook 5 to 10 minutes, or till soft. Press apricots through food mill. Measure about 7 cups puree; add sugar. Heat and stir till sugar is dissolved and mixture is heated through. Pour hot juice into hot jars, leaving 1/2-inch headspace. Adjust lids. Process in boiling water bath (pints or quarts) 10 minutes. Makes 4 pints.

*Before serving:* Chill and shake well.

## STRAWBERRY SYRUP

Wash and hull 6 pints strawberries. Put strawberries in blender container to mash; blend thoroughly. In 8- to 10-quart kettle or Dutch oven, combine strawberries and 7 cups sugar. Heat to full boil; reduce heat. Boil gently 10 minutes. Strain juice through jelly bag; drain several hours or overnight. Return juice to kettle and heat. Pour hot syrup into hot jars, leaving 1/2-inch headspace. Adjust lids. Process in boiling water bath (half-pints) 10 minutes. Makes 5 to 6 half-pints.

## MINTED PEARS

| | |
|---|---|
| 5 cups Thin Syrup (see page 289) | 2/3 cup green creme de menthe |
| 7 pounds pears | Green food coloring |
| Ascorbic acid color keeper | (optional) |

Prepare syrup; keep hot but not boiling. Wash, pare, halve, and core pears. While preparing fruit, add color keeper. In 4- to 6-quart kettle or Dutch oven, stir creme de menthe into syrup. Add food coloring, if desired. Add pears; heat 2 to 3 minutes. Pack hot pears into hot jars, leaving 1/2-inch headspace. Cover with hot syrup, leaving 1/2-inch headspace. Adjust lids. Process in boiling water bath (pints) 25 minutes; (quarts) 30 minutes. Makes 7 pints.

# PICKLES

- Use *unwaxed* cucumbers for pickling; remove all blossoms.
- Use pure granulated pickling salt. *Or*, substitute *uniodized* table salt.
- Choose a high-grade cider vinegar for all but light pickles—use white vinegar for them. Acidity of vinegar should be 4 to 6 percent (40 to 60 grain).
- Do not use copper, brass, galvanized, or iron utensils for making pickles.
- Common causes of poor products: Shriveling is produced by too strong a salt, sugar, or vinegar solution, overcooking, or overprocessing. Too little salt or acid, insufficient processing, or poor sealing causes soft pickles. Hollow pickles are due to not-fresh cucumbers.

## CANNING PROCEDURE

1. Wash jars; rinse. Wash caps according to manufacturer's directions. Place jars in hot water till ready to use —no need to sterilize; processing does that. Place water bath canner on heat with 4 to 5 inches water.

2. Prepare pickles according to recipes on the following pages.

3. Fill hot jars firmly, but be sure the liquid fills in around product. Leave 1/2-inch headspace between food-liquid mixture and top of jar. Remove air bubbles from filled jars by working blade of knife down sides of jars. Add more liquid, if needed, but keep the same headspace.

4. Adjust jar caps: For self-sealing caps, wipe sealing edge of jar with clean cloth to remove food particles; put flat metal lid on jar with sealing compound next to glass

and screw band tight. Fit wet rubber ring on jar with zinc caps; wipe jar rim and ring with clean cloth; partially seal by screwing zinc caps down firmly, then turning the caps back 1/4 inch.

5. Process immediately in boiling water bath (see instructions, page 285) using times indicated in recipes. Note high altitude changes, page 284.

6. For sealing and cooling, follow instructions on pages 283–286.

## SWEET PICKLES

Select 9 1/2 pounds of 3- to 4-inch cucumbers (about 150). Wash and cover cucumbers with hot salt brine made from 1 cup granulated pickling salt to each 2 quarts water. Cool; cover with large plate or lid with weight atop to keep cucumbers in brine. Let stand for 7 days in cool place.

Drain; cover with hot water; let stand 24 hours. Drain; again cover with hot water; let stand 24 hours. Drain; split cucumbers. Combine 12 cups sugar, 8 cups cider vinegar, 1 1/2 teaspoons celery seed, 8 sticks stick cinnamon, and 1 cup prepared horseradish. Bring to boil; slowly pour over cucumbers. Drain syrup from cucumbers each morning for 4 days; reheat and slowly pour over cucumbers. Let cool in syrup before covering.

The last morning, remove cinnamon and bring cucumbers and syrup to boil. Pack cucumbers and syrup into hot jars, leaving 1/2-inch headspace. Adjust lids. Process in boiling water bath for 5 minutes (start counting time after water returns to boiling). Makes about 13 pints.

## CRISP PICKLE SLICES

*(bread-and-butter type)*

| | |
|---|---|
| 4 quarts sliced unpared medium cucumbers | 1/3 cup granulated pickling salt |
| 6 medium white onions, sliced (6 cups) | 5 cups sugar |
| 2 green peppers, sliced (1 2/3 cups) | 3 cups cider vinegar |
| | 1 1/2 teaspoons turmeric |
| 3 cloves garlic | 1 1/2 teaspoons celery seed |
| | 2 tablespoons mustard seed |

Combine cucumber, onion, green pepper, and whole garlic cloves. Add salt; cover with cracked ice; mix thoroughly. Let stand 3 hours; drain well. Remove garlic. Combine remaining ingredients; pour over cucumber mixture. Bring to boil.

Fill hot jars, leaving 1/2-inch headspace; adjust lids. Process in boiling water bath for 5 minutes (start timing when water returns to boiling). Makes 8 pints.

## DILL PICKLES

*For each quart:*

| | |
|---|---|
| 1/2 pound 4-inch cucumbers (5-6) | 2 cups water |
| 3 or 4 heads fresh dill | 1 cup cider vinegar |
| 1 teaspoon mustard seed | 1 tablespoon granulated pickling salt |

Scrub cucumbers; pack loosely in hot quart jars, leaving 1/2-inch headspace. For each quart, add dill and mustard seed. Make a brine by combining water, vinegar, and salt. Bring to boiling. Slowly pour hot brine over cucumbers, leaving 1/2-inch headspace. Adjust lids. Process in boiling water bath for 20 minutes (start timing as soon as jars are placed in water).

**Kosher Dill Pickles:** Follow recipe above *except* omit mustard seed; add 1 clove garlic and 1 small piece hot red pepper (optional) to each quart. Prepare a brine using 2 1/4 cups water, 3/4 cup vinegar, and 1 tablespoon pickling salt. Bring to boiling. Slowly pour hot brine over cucumbers. Process as above.

## WATERMELON PICKLES

| | |
|---|---|
| 2 pounds watermelon rind | 1 tablespoon broken stick cinnamon |
| 1/4 cup granulated pickling salt | 1 1/2 teaspoons whole cloves |
| 2 cups sugar | 1/2 lemon, thinly sliced |
| 1 cup white vinegar | |

Trim dark green and pink parts from rind; cut in 1-inch squares. Measure 6 cups. Soak overnight in solution of salt and 1 quart water (it may take more to cover). Drain;

rinse rind; cover with cold water. Cook about 25 minutes or till just tender.

Meanwhile, combine sugar, vinegar, 1 cup water, and spices. Simmer 10 minutes; strain. Add (drained) rind and lemon. Simmer, covered, about 25 minutes or till rind is clear; fill hot jars with rind and syrup, leaving ½-inch headspace. Adjust lids; process in boiling water bath 5 minutes (start timing when water returns to boil). Makes 4 half-pints.

## SWEET-SOUR PICKLES

Wash 3½ pounds 2½-inch cucumbers (about 50). Dissolve ½ cup granulated pickling salt in 4 cups boiling water; pour over cucumbers. Let stand in liquid till cool; drain. Combine 1½ quarts cider vinegar, 3 cups sugar, 2 cups water, and 1 tablespoon mixed pickling spices; bring to boil. Slowly pour over cucumbers; let stand 24 hours. Bring cucumbers and syrup to boil; pack in hot jars, leaving ½-inch headspace. Adjust lids. Process in boiling water bath for 5 minutes, (start timing when water returns to boil). Makes 5 pints.

## MUSTARD PICKLES

Break 1 large head cauliflower in flowerets. Cut 1 quart small green tomatoes in wedges, 3 green peppers in strips, and 1½ pounds 2-inch cucumbers in halves lengthwise. Peel 3 cups pickling onions. Combine washed vegetables; cover with a mixture of 1 cup granulated pickling salt and 4 cups water; let stand in cool place overnight.

Drain; cover with boiling water; let stand 10 minutes; drain. Combine 2 cups sugar, 1 cup all-purpose flour, ½ cup dry mustard, 1 tablespoon turmeric, 5 cups cider vinegar, and 5 cups water. Cook and stir till thick and bubbly. Add vegetables; cook till tender. Fill hot jars, leaving ½-inch headspace; adjust lids. Process in boiling water bath for 5 minutes (time when water returns to boil). Makes 10 pints.

## VEGETABLE RELISH

Wash vegetables to be used. Using coarse blade, grind 12 green peppers (5 cups), 7 large onions (4 cups), 1 medium head cabbage (4 cups), 10 green tomatoes (4 cups), and 6 sweet red peppers (1½ cups).

Sprinkle with ½ cup granulated pickling salt; let stand overnight. Rinse and drain. Combine 6 cups sugar, 2 tablespoons mustard seed, 1 tablespoon celery seed, 1½ teaspoons turmeric, 4 cups cider vinegar, and 2 cups water. Pour over vegetables. Bring to boil; boil gently 5 minutes.

Fill hot jars, leaving ½-inch headspace; adjust lids. Process in boiling water bath 5 minutes (start timing when water returns to boil). Makes 9 pints.

## CORN RELISH

*Capture the flavor of fresh corn in a jar—*

Husk 16 to 20 ears fresh corn. Cook in boiling water 5 minutes; plunge into cold water. Drain; cut corn from cobs (8 cups cut corn). Do not scrape cobs.

Combine 4 cups chopped celery, 2 cups chopped sweet red pepper, 2 cups chopped green pepper, 1 cup chopped onion, 2 cups *each* sugar, vinegar, and water, 2 tablespoons salt, and 2 teaspoons celery seed in a large saucepan. Bring to boil; boil, uncovered, 5 minutes; stir occasionally.

Blend ¼ cup all-purpose flour, 2 tablespoons dry mustard, and 1 teaspoon turmeric with ½ cup cold water. Add along with corn to boiling mixture. Return to boiling; cook and stir 5 minutes.

Pack loosely while boiling hot into hot pint jars, leaving ½-inch headspace. Adjust jar lids. Process in boiling water bath 15 minutes (count time when water returns to boil). Makes 7 pints.

## DILLY GREEN TOMATOES

Wash 5 pounds small, firm, green tomatoes; slice tomatoes ¼ inch thick. Pack loosely into hot quart jars, leaving ½-inch headspace. To *each quart* add: 3 or 4 heads fresh dill *or* 2 tablespoons dillseed, 1 clove garlic, and 1 whole clove. Combine 1 quart vinegar, 1 quart water, and $\frac{1}{3}$ cup granulated pickling salt. Bring to boil; slowly pour boiling liquid over tomatoes, leaving $\frac{1}{2}$-inch headspace. Adjust lids. Process in boiling water bath 20 minutes (start timing as soon as jars are placed in water). Makes 5 quarts.

## SPICED PEACHES

Combine 5 cups sugar, 2 cups water, 1 cup vinegar, 12 inches stick cinnamon, broken, and 2 teaspoons whole cloves. Heat to boiling. Into syrup drop enough small peeled peaches to fill 2 or 3 pints.

Heat peaches in syrup about 5 minutes. Pack hot fruit in hot pint jars; add syrup, leaving $\frac{1}{2}$-inch headspace; adjust lids. Process in boiling water bath 20 minutes (count time after water returns to boil). Seven pounds fruit yields about 9 pints.

## CHILI SAUCE

| | |
|---|---|
| 1 peck (12 to 14 pounds) tomatoes | 3 green peppers, ground (about 2$\frac{1}{2}$ cups) |
| 1 pound (about 2 bunches) celery, chopped (about 4 cups) | 6 inches stick cinnamon |
| | 1$\frac{1}{2}$ teaspoons ground cloves |
| 1 quart small onions, ground (about 2$\frac{1}{2}$ cups) | 1 tablespoon dry mustard |
| | 2 pounds brown sugar (4$\frac{1}{2}$ cups) |
| | 1 quart cider vinegar |

Scald tomatoes; peel, core, and slice in chunks into large kettle. Cook 15 minutes; drain off *half* (about 6 cups) the juice (use for drinking or cooking). Add celery, onion, and green pepper; simmer about 1$\frac{1}{2}$ hours. Tie cinnamon in cloth; add with remaining ingredients and $\frac{1}{4}$ cup salt. Continue cooking 1$\frac{1}{2}$ hours. Remove cinnamon. Fill hot pint jars, leaving $\frac{1}{2}$-inch headspace; adjust lids. Process in boiling water bath 5 minutes (start timing when water returns to boil). Makes 9 pints.

# TOMATO CATSUP

In small saucepan, combine 1¹/₂ teaspoons whole cloves, 1¹/₂ inches broken stick cinnamon, 1 teaspoon celery seed, and 1 cup white vinegar. Cover; bring to boil. Remove from heat; let stand.

Wash, core, and quarter 8 pounds (25 medium) tomatoes into large kettle. Add 1 medium onion, chopped, and ¹/₄ teaspoon cayenne. Bring to boil; cook 15 minutes stirring occasionally. Put tomatoes through food mill or a coarse sieve.

Add 1 cup sugar to tomato juice. Bring to boil, then *simmer* briskly 1¹/₂ to 2 hours, or till mixture is reduced by half (measure depth with ruler at start and end).

Strain spiced vinegar mixture into tomato mixture; discard spices. Add 4 teaspoons salt. Simmer about 30 minutes, or till of desired consistency. Stir often.

Fill hot pint jars, leaving ¹/₂-inch headspace; adjust lids. Process in boiling water bath 5 minutes (count time after water returns to boil). Makes 2 pints.

# CANNING VEGETABLES

With the exception of tomatoes, vegetables do not have natural acidity. This means that you must process them in a pressure canner to destroy the heat-resistant bacteria, which could cause food poisoning. This rule applies to all low-acid vegetables except those made into pickles, relishes, and sauerkraut. These foods are prepared with vinegar and/or brine, which makes water-bath canning a safe way to process them.

## CANNED TOMATOES

To loosen skins, dip tomatoes in boiling water ½ minute; dip quickly in cold water. Cut out stem ends and peel. Follow either raw or hot pack method.

*Raw pack:* Pack tomatoes in hot jars, pressing gently to fill spaces. Leave ½-inch headspace. Add no water. Add 1 teaspoon lemon juice to each quart or ½ teaspoon to each pint. Add ½ teaspoon salt to each quart or ¼ teaspoon to each pint. Adjust lids. Process in boiling water bath (pints) 35 minutes; (quarts) 45 minutes.

*Hot pack:* Quarter peeled tomatoes. Bring to boiling, stirring constantly but gently. Pack hot tomatoes into hot jars, leaving ½-inch headspace. Add 1 teaspoon lemon juice to each quart or ½ teaspoon to each pint. Add ½ teaspoon salt to each quart or ¼ teaspoon to each pint. Adjust lids. Process in boiling water bath (pints or quarts) 10 minutes.

## TOMATO JUICE

Thoroughly wash tomatoes; remove stem ends and cut tomatoes in pieces. Slowly cook tomatoes, covered, about 15 minutes, or until soft. Stir often to prevent sticking. Press through food mill or sieve to extract juice. Return juice to kettle. Add 1 teaspoon lemon juice for each quart or ½ teaspoon for each pint. Add ½ teaspoon salt for each quart or $1/4$ teaspoon for each pint. Bring to boiling. Pour hot juice into hot jars, leaving $1/2$-inch headspace. Adjust lids. Process in boiling water bath (pints) 10 minutes; (quarts) 15 minutes.

## SAUERKRAUT

Use 5 pounds fully matured cabbage. Wash, quarter, core, and finely shred. Sprinkle with $3^1/2$ tablespoons salt; mix well. Let stand 30 to 60 minutes. Firmly pack into room-temperature jars; leave 2-inch headspace. Fill with cold water; leave $1/2$-inch headspace. Adjust lids; screw band tight. Place jars on jelly-roll pan to catch brine that overflows. Keep cabbage covered with brine. If necessary, open jars and add more brine made by dissolving $1^1/2$ tablespoons salt in 1 quart water.

Sauerkraut is ready to can in 6 to 8 weeks. Clean rims of jars; replace lids if sealer appears damaged; screw band tight. Set in water bath canner filled with cold water (should extend 2 inches above jars). Bring slowly to boiling. Process (pints or quarts) 30 minutes. Makes 7 pints.

## CANNING PROCEDURE
## (LOW-ACID VEGETABLES)

1. Wash jars and lids (see page 287).
2. Wash and trim vegetables as directed.
3. Pack into jars, using either method:

*Raw pack:* You can pack asparagus, lima and green beans, carrots, corn, and peas by this method. Pack firmly into hot jars (loosely pack limas, corn, and peas). Leave $1/2$-inch headspace (1 inch for limas, corn—both whole kernel and cream-style—and peas). Pour boiling water into jars, leaving the headspace specified.

*Hot pack:* You can pack any vegetable by this method. Precook for time indicated. Pack boiling vegetables loosely into hot jars, leaving $1/2$-inch headspace (1 inch for limas, corn, peas, and sweet potatoes). Pour boiling cooking liquid or water into jars; leave the headspace specified.

4. Remove air bubbles by working knife down sides, keeping liquid above food. Add liquid, if needed; leave headspace.

5. Add the amount of salt specified.

6. Adjust jar caps (pages 283 and 287).

7. Process immediately in pressure canner (see page 306). Note high altitude changes (page 315). Check seal (page 284).

## PRESSURE CANNING

Pressure canning is absolutely necessary for processing garden vegetables, including corn, beans of all kinds, carrots, beets, and greens, plus all meats, poultry, and fish. Remember to boil these foods at least 10 minutes before tasting or serving (20 minutes for corn or spinach).

1. Well before canning day, read instruction booklet packed with canner. Have spring-dial gauge checked for accuracy (check with your county Extension Service for nearest testing location).

2. Assemble canner and basket. Set canner on kitchen range and add 2 or 3 inches boiling water. Turn heat on low.

3. Prepare vegetables or meats.

4. Refer to directions on pages 283 and 284.

5. As each jar is filled, place it in the canner. Be sure jars do not touch.

6. Cover and lock canner. Turn heat up to high. When steam starts to come from the open vent or pet cock, reduce heat so steam flows freely at moderate rate. Let steam flow steadily for 10 minutes.

7. Close vent; bring up pressure. Refer to your manual for specific instructions.

8. Turn heat up to high, maintain heat till you reach 10 pounds pressure. Then, adjust heat to maintain a constant pressure. If pressure drops, stop counting processing time till pressure is regained.

9. Count processing time from the moment 10 pounds pressure is reached.

10. Remove canner from heat and set it out of drafts on a wire rack or wooden board. Allow pressure to return to normal of its own accord. This will take 20 to 25 minutes. Do not run water over canner.

11. Pressure is down when dial gauge registers zero

and the safety plug is normal, or when no steam is visible when weight gauge is nudged gently. Remove regulators or open pet cock and unlatch cover of canner. Lift cover away from you.

12. If food is still boiling vigorously in jars, wait a few minutes before removing jars. Cool jars 2 to 3 inches apart on wooden board in draft-free area.

**Pressure cookers** may be used to process pints if pan has accurate gauge and operates at 10 pounds pressure. Allow 20 minutes longer than time in pressure canner.

On canners with the spring-dial gauge, wait until the indicator returns to zero before removing the pressure regulator.

On canners with a weight gauge, let canner cool before nudging the gauge gently. If no steam is visible, lift off gauge.

Carefully unlatch the cover of the canner. Lift cover so that it opens away from you to avoid a blast of hot steam.

| Vegetables | Preparation of Vegetables<br>Precook; pack into jar with hot cooking water to 1/2 inch from top unless otherwise specified; add 1/2 teaspoon salt to each quart. Or pack raw into jars; cover with boiling water leaving the amount of headspace specified; add 1/2 teaspoon salt to each quart. | Pressure canner minutes at 10 lbs. (Pints) | Pressure canner minutes at 10 lbs. (Quarts) |
|---|---|---|---|
| Asparagus | Wash; trim off scales and tough ends; cut in 1-inch pieces.<br>*Hot pack:* Cook in boiling water 3 minutes; pack hot. Add salt, boiling cooking liquid; leave 1/2-inch headspace. Adjust lids; process.<br>*Raw pack:* Pack tightly into jars; add salt; cover with boiling water. Leave 1/2-inch headspace; adjust lids; process. | 25 | 30 |
| | | 25 | 30 |
| Beans<br>Green<br>and Wax | Wash; trim ends; cut in 1-inch pieces.<br>*Hot pack:* Cook 5 minutes in boiling water. Pack hot; add salt, hot cooking liquid; leave 1/2-inch headspace. Adjust lids; process.<br>*Raw pack:* Pack in jars; add salt; cover with boiling water. Leave 1/2-inch headspace; adjust lids; process. | 20 | 25 |
| | | 20 | 25 |
| Beans<br>Lima | *Hot pack:* Shell and wash young beans; cover with boiling water; bring to boil. Pack loosely to 1 inch from top of jar. Add salt and boiling water; leave 1-inch headspace; adjust lids; process.<br>*Raw pack:* Shell and wash young beans; pack lima beans loosely to 1 inch from top of pint jar; 1 inch from top of quart jar. Add salt and boiling water; leave 1-inch headspace; adjust lids; process. | 40 | 50 |
| | | 40 | 50 |

| | | |
|---|---|---|
| Beets | Wash, leaving on root and 1 inch of tops. Cover with boiling water; pre-cook about 15 minutes. Slip off skins and trim; cube or slice large beets. Pack hot. Add salt and boiling water. Leave ½-inch headspace. Adjust lids; process. | 30  35 |
| Carrots | *Hot pack:* Wash and pare; slice or dice. Cover with boiling water and bring to boil. Pack hot; add salt and boiling cooking liquid. Leave ½-inch headspace. Adjust lids, process. | 25  30 |
| | *Raw pack:* Wash; pare; slice or dice. Pack tightly into jars; add salt, boil-ing water. Leave ½-inch headspace, adjust lids; process. | 25  30 |
| Corn Whole kernel | Cut corn from cob; do not scrape cob. *Hot pack:* Add 2 cups boiling water per 1 quart of corn; bring to boil. Pack hot corn loosely. Add salt and boiling hot cooking liquid leaving 1-inch headspace. Adjust lids; process. | 55  85 |
| | *Raw pack:* Pack corn loosely to 1 inch from top. Add salt. Cover with boiling water leaving 1-inch headspace. Adjust lids; process. | 55  85 |
| Cream-style | Cut corn from cob, cutting only about half the kernel; scrape cob. *Hot pack:* Follow directions above; pack hot corn in pints only. *Raw pack:* Follow directions above packing to 1 inch from top of *pint* jars. Fill with boiling water; leave 1-inch headspace. | 85  95 |

| Vegetables | Preparation of Vegetables<br>Precook; pack into jar with hot cooking water to 1/2 inch from top unless otherwise specified; add 1/2 teaspoon salt to each quart. Or pack raw into jars; cover with boiling water leaving the amount of headspace specified; add 1/2 teaspoon salt to each quart. | Pressure canner minutes at 10 lbs. (Pints) | Pressure canner minutes at 10 lbs. (Quarts) |
|---|---|---|---|
| Greens,<br>all<br>kinds | Wash thoroughly; cut out tough stems and midribs. Steam in cheesecloth bag till well wilted, 10 minutes. Pack hot greens loosely. Add 1/4 teaspoon salt to pints and 1/2 teaspoon salt to quarts; cover with boiling water. Leave 1/2-inch headspace; adjust lids; process. | 70 | 90 |
| Mushrooms | Wash thoroughly; trim stems. Slice or leave small mushrooms whole. Steam 4 minutes or heat gently, covered, without liquid 15 minutes. Pack hot in pint jars; add 1/4 teaspoon salt per pint. For good color use ascorbic acid color keeper (follow label directions). Cover with boiling water. Leave 1/2-inch headspace; adjust lids; process. | 30 | |
| Peas<br>Green | *Hot pack:* Shell; wash. Cover with boiling water; bring to boil. Pack hot peas loosely to 1 inch from top of jar. Add salt and boiling water. Leave 1-inch headspace; adjust lids; process.<br>*Raw pack:* Shell and wash peas. Pack loosely to 1 inch from top of jar. Add salt; cover with boiling water leaving 1-inch headspace. Adjust lids; process. | 40 | 40 |

| | | | |
|---|---|---|---|
| Potatoes New White | Wash; precook 10 minutes; remove skins. Pack hot; add salt; cover with boiling water. Leave 1-inch headspace. Adjust lids; process. | 30 | 40 |
| Sweet | *Dry pack:* Wash; precook in boiling water 20 to 30 minutes. Remove skins; cut up. Pack hot to 1 inch from top; press gently; add no liquid or salt. Leave 1-inch headspace. Adjust lids; process. | 65 | 95 |
| | *Wet pack:* Wash; boil till skins slip off easily. Remove skins; cut potatoes in pieces. Pack hot to 1 inch from top. Add salt. Cover with boiling water leaving 1-inch headspace. Adjust lids; process. | 55 | 90 |
| Pumpkin Squash Winter | Wash; remove seeds; pare and cube. Barely cover with water; bring to boil. Pack hot. Add salt; cover with boiling cooking liquid. Leave ½-inch headspace; adjust lids; process. | 55 | 90 |

## • SAFETY REMINDER •

Before tasting or using home-canned vegetables, boil, uncovered, at least 10 minutes (20 minutes for corn or spinach). Add water to avoid sticking.

## CANNED VEGETABLE YIELD

Purchase or pick the following amounts of fresh vegetables to get 1 quart canned:

| Vegetable | Pounds |
|-----------|--------|
| Asparagus | 2$\frac{1}{2}$ to 4$\frac{1}{2}$ |
| Beans, lima in pods | 3 to 5 |
| Beans, snap green | 1$\frac{1}{2}$ to 2$\frac{1}{2}$ |
| Beets, without tops | 2 to 3$\frac{1}{2}$ |
| Carrots, without tops | 2 to 3 |
| Corn, sweet, in husks | 3 to 6 |
| Peas, green, in pods | 3 to 6 |
| Squash, winter | 1$\frac{1}{2}$ to 3 |
| Sweet potatoes | 2 to 3 |
| Tomatoes | 2$\frac{1}{2}$ to 3$\frac{1}{2}$ |

## SUCCOTASH

4 cups shelled lima beans

6 to 8 medium ears sweet corn, cut from cob

Wash and drain beans. Combine beans and corn in kettle; add 4 cups water. Bring to boil; cook 5 minutes. Pack hot vegetables loosely into hot jars, leaving 1-inch headspace. Add $\frac{1}{4}$ teaspoon salt per pint. Pour in boiling cooking liquid; leave 1-inch headspace. Adjust lids. Process in pressure canner at 10 pounds pressure (pints) 55 minutes; (quarts) 85 minutes. Makes 4 pints.

*Before serving:* Boil these vegetables 20 minutes *before* tasting or using. If desired, add $\frac{1}{2}$ cup light cream and 2 tablespoons butter to each pint of succotash.

## BEANS IN TOMATO SAUCE

| | |
|---|---|
| 2 pounds (4 cups) dry navy beans | 1 tablespoon Worcestershire sauce |
| 3 quarts cold water | 1 tablespoon sugar |
| 3 cups tomato juice | 1/2 teaspoon salt |
| 1 6-ounce can tomato paste | Few drops bottled hot pepper sauce |
| 1/2 cup chopped onion | 2 teaspoons salt |
| 1/4 cup chopped green pepper | 1/4 pound salt pork, cut in pieces |

Rinse beans; add to 3 quarts cold water in 8- to 10-quart kettle or Dutch oven. Bring to boiling; simmer 2 minutes. Remove from heat; cover and let beans stand 1 hour.

Meanwhile, in large saucepan combine tomato juice, tomato paste, onion, green pepper, Worcestershire sauce, sugar, the 1/2 teaspoon salt, and hot pepper sauce. Cover and bring to boiling. Reduce heat; simmer tomato mixture 5 to 10 minutes.

Add the 2 teaspoons salt to beans and soaking water; cover and bring to boiling. Drain. Add salt pork to drained beans. Pack hot mixture into hot jars, filling jars 3/4 full. Fill with boiling tomato mixture, leaving 1-inch headspace. Adjust lids. Process in pressure canner at 10 pounds pressure (pints) 80 minutes; (quarts) 100 minutes. Makes 6 pints.

## • SAFETY REMINDER •

Before tasting or using home-canned vegetables, boil, uncovered, at least 10 minutes (20 minutes for corn or spinach). Add water to avoid sticking.

## TROPICAL BEETS

Wash 2 pounds beets, leaving on root and 1 inch of tops. Cover with boiling water; simmer 15 minutes. Slip off skins and trim; slice beets (about 5 cups).

In 4- to 6-quart kettle or Dutch oven, combine 2 cups water and 3/4 cup brown sugar. Stir till sugar dissolves. Add 2 cups fresh pineapple tidbits. Simmer 5 minutes. Add beets and heat through.

Pack hot beet slices and pineapple tidbits into hot jars, leaving 1/2-inch headspace. Add 1 teaspoon lemon juice and 1/4 teaspoon salt to each pint. Cover with boiling syrup, leaving 1/2-inch headspace. Adjust lids. Process in pressure canner at 10 pounds pressure (pints) 30 minutes; (quarts) 40 minutes. Makes 4 pints.

*Before serving:* In saucepan, boil beets with pineapple at least 10 minutes *before* tasting or using. For each pint, blend 1 tablespoon cold water into 2 teaspoons cornstarch. Stir into beet mixture with 1 tablespoon butter. Cook, stirring constantly, till mixture thickens.

## CABBAGE BORSCH

Wash 5 pounds tomatoes. Peel, remove stem ends and cores, and quarter tomatoes. Use a small spoon to scrape out excess seeds, if desired. In 4- to 6-quart kettle, combine tomatoes with 8 cups coarsely shredded cabbage, 6 cups water, 2 cups chopped onion, 2 medium apples, pared, cored, and cut in pieces, 2 tablespoons instant beef bouillon granules, 2 tablespoons sugar, 2 tablespoons lemon juice, 1 teaspoon salt, and dash pepper.

Bring the cabbage mixture to boiling. Boil, uncovered, for 5 minutes. Ladle the hot cabbage mixture into hot jars, leaving 1/2-inch headspace. Adjust the lids. Process in a pressure canner at 10 pounds pressure (pints) 45 minutes; (quarts) 55 minutes. Makes 8 pints.

## VEGETABLE SOUP

| | |
|---|---|
| 2 cups chopped, peeled tomatoes | 3 cups cubed, pared potatoes |
| 4 teaspoons instant beef bouillon granules | 3 cups sliced carrots |
| 1 tablespoon Worcestershire sauce | 2 1/2 cups cut green beans |
| | 2 cups corn cut from cob |
| 1/2 teaspoon chili powder | 1 cup chopped celery |
| | 1/2 cup chopped onion |

In large kettle, mix first 4 ingredients, 3 cups water, and 2 teaspoons salt; heat. Add vegetables; boil 5 minutes. Pour hot soup into hot jars; leave 1-inch headspace. Adjust lids. Process in pressure canner at 10 pounds pressure (pints) 55 minutes; (quarts) 85 minutes. Makes 6 pints.

*Before serving:* Boil 1 pint soup 10 to 15 minutes *before* tasting or using; add ½ cup water to soup mixture.

## MIXED VEGETABLES

Pare and chop 1½ pounds carrots. Husk and silk 10 or 11 medium ears sweet corn. Cut corn from cobs. Trim ends from 1½ pounds green beans; cut green beans in 1-inch pieces. In large kettle, combine carrots, corn, and green beans with 4 cups shelled lima beans. Cover with boiling water. Bring to boiling. Pack hot vegetables into hot jars; leave 1-inch headspace. Add ½ teaspoon salt per pint. Cover with boiling cooking liquid; leave 1-inch headspace. Adjust lids. Process in pressure canner at 10 pounds pressure (pints) 55 minutes. Makes 11 pints.

## • CORRECT FOR ALTITUDE •

Pounds of pressure in recipes apply up to 2,000 feet above sea level. Adjust for type of gauge as follows:

*Spring-dial gauge:* For each extra 2,000 feet add 1 pound pressure.

*Weight gauge:* Above 2,000 feet use 15 pounds pressure instead of 10. **Do not raw pack vegetables for processing at altitudes above 6,000 feet.**

# CANNING MEAT, POULTRY, AND FISH

Wash jars and lids using manufacturer's directions. Pack meat following methods below. Adjust caps (see pages 283 and 284). Process immediately in *pressure canner* (see pages 306–307), using times below. Note altitude corrections (page 315) and after processing instructions, page 284. *Boil all meats at least 10 minutes before tasting.*

| Food | Preparation of Food | Pressure canner minutes at 10 lbs. (Pints) | Pressure canner minutes at 10 lbs. (Quarts) |
|---|---|---|---|
| Meat Beef Veal Lamb Pork Venison | Chill meat immediately after slaughter. Wipe meat with a clean, damp cloth. Cube meat or cut meat into jar-length pieces so grain of meat runs the length of the jar. Remove gristle, bones, and as much fat as possible. *Raw pack:* Pack loosely into hot jars, leaving 1-inch headspace. Add 1/2 teaspoon salt to each quart jar, if desired. Do not add liquid. Adjust the lids and process in pressure canner. *Hot pack:* Simmer the meat in a small amount of water in a covered pan till medium-done; stir occasionally. Season the meat lightly with salt. Or, brown the meat in a small amount of fat. Season the meat lightly with salt. Pack the meat loosely into hot jars, leaving 1-inch headspace. Fill with boiling water or broth, leaving 1-inch headspace. Adjust lids. Process in pressure canner. | 75 75 | 90 90 |
| Poultry Chicken Duck Turkey Game Birds | Rinse chilled, dressed poultry in cold water. Pat dry with a clean cloth. Cut up chicken or small game birds; remove visible fat. Pack by raw-pack method. Simmer or roast unstuffed larger birds just till meat can be removed from bone and pack by hot-pack method. *Raw pack:* Do not remove bones (except breastbone, if desired). Pack raw chicken pieces or small game bird pieces loosely into hot jars as follows: place the thighs and drumsticks with skin next to glass and fit breast pieces | bone-in 65 | 75 |

| Food | Preparation of Food | Pressure canner minutes at 10 lbs. (Pints) | Pressure canner minutes at 10 lbs. (Quarts) |
|---|---|---|---|
| | into center, leaving 1-inch headspace. Add ½ teaspoon salt to each quart jar, if desired. Do not add liquid. Adjust lids and process. *Hot pack:* Remove meat from bones of cooked chicken, if desired, but do not remove skin. If not boned, pack cooked chicken pieces loosely into hot jars as above. Cut other precooked boned poultry into pieces. Pack loosely into hot jars, leaving 1-inch headspace. Add ½ teaspoon salt to each quart jar, if desired. Cover with boiling water or broth, leaving 1-inch headspace. Adjust lids. Process in pressure canner. | boned 75<br>bone-in 65 | 90<br>75 |
| Fish<br>Bass<br>Mackerel<br>Salmon<br>Trout | Rinse well-cleaned fish in fresh water. Split, but do not remove backbone. Remove skin, if desired. Make brine solution, using 1 cup salt and 1 gallon water. Soak the fish in brine for 30 to 60 minutes, depending upon the thickness of the fish. Drain and rinse fish; discard brine.<br>*Raw pack:* Cut fish into pieces about 1 inch shorter than jar length. Pack fish so that the skin side of the pieces is next to the glass. Alternate head and tail ends if small fish are being packed. Pack fish into hot jars, leaving 1-inch headspace. Do not add liquid or oil. Add ½ teaspoon salt to each quart jar, if desired. Adjust lids. Process in pressure canner. | 100 | 100 |

# ITALIAN MEAT SAUCE

| | |
|---|---|
| 12 pounds tomatoes | 2 bay leaves |
| 2 tablespoons sugar | * * * |
| 1 tablespoon dried oregano, crushed | 1 pound ground beef |
| | 2 cups chopped onion |
| 1 tablespoon dried thyme, crushed | 1 cup chopped green pepper |
| 1 tablespoon salt | 2 cloves garlic, minced |
| 1/2 teaspoon pepper | |

Remove stem ends and cores and chop tomatoes. Measure about 24 cups. Let chopped tomatoes stand in colander for a few minutes to drain off excess liquid.

In 8- to 10-quart kettle or Dutch oven, combine drained, chopped tomatoes, sugar, oregano, thyme, salt, pepper, and bay leaves. Boil tomato mixture gently, uncovered, for 1 hour. Strain through food mill; measure about 11 cups tomato puree. Return puree to kettle. Boil gently, uncovered, about 1 hour, or till mixture is of desired consistency.

Meanwhile, in skillet cook ground beef, chopped onion, chopped green pepper, and garlic till meat is browned and onion and green pepper are tender; drain off excess fat. Add meat mixture to tomato puree in kettle and heat through.

Pack hot meat sauce into hot jars, leaving 1-inch headspace. Adjust lids. Process in pressure canner at 10 pounds pressure (pints) 75 minutes; (quarts) 90 minutes. Makes 5 pints.

*Before serving:* Boil meat sauce, uncovered, for at least 10 minutes *before* tasting or using. Serve Italian Meat Sauce over hot cooked spaghetti. Pass grated Parmesan cheese, if desired.

## • SAFETY REMINDER •

Always boil home-canned meat, poultry, or fish, uncovered, for at least 10 minutes before tasting or using. Add water as needed to prevent sticking. Do not taste cold from the jar.

## CHICKEN A LA KING

In 8- to 10-quart kettle or Dutch oven, place two 5-pound stewing chickens, cut in pieces. Cover with water. Add 1 cup chopped celery, 1/2 cup chopped onion, and 1 clove garlic, minced. Bring to boiling. Reduce heat; simmer, covered, about 2 hours, or till chicken is barely tender. Cool.

Remove chicken from broth. Remove skin and bones from chicken; cube meat. Remove excess fat from broth; reserve 1 cup fat. Strain broth; reserve 8 cups. Melt fat; blend in 1 1/3 cups all-purpose flour and 4 teaspoons salt. Add reserved broth; cook and stir till bubbly. Add chicken, 2 cups sliced fresh mushrooms, 1 cup chopped canned pimiento, and 1/2 cup chopped green pepper. Simmer 5 minutes. Pack into hot jars; leave 1-inch headspace. Adjust lids. Process in pressure canner at 10 pounds pressure (pints) 65 minutes. Makes 9 pints.

*Before serving:* Boil chicken, uncovered, at least 10 minutes *before* tasting or using. Add milk till of desired consistency.

## HOMEMADE MINCEMEAT

| | |
|---|---|
| 1 pound beef stew meat | 1/2 cup diced candied fruits and peels |
| 4 pounds apples, pared, cored, and cut up | 1 teaspoon grated orange peel |
| 4 ounces suet | 1 cup orange juice |
| 1 15-ounce package raisins | 1 teaspoon grated lemon peel |
| 2 1/2 cups sugar | 1/4 cup lemon juice |
| 2 1/2 cups water | 1/2 teaspoon ground nutmeg |
| 1 8-ounce package currants | 1/4 teaspoon ground mace |

Simmer beef, covered, in water about 2 hours, or till tender. Cool. Put through coarse blade of food chopper with apples and suet. Combine with remaining ingredients in large kettle. Add 1 teaspoon salt. Cover; simmer 1 hour; stir often.

Pack hot mincemeat into hot jars; leave 1-inch headspace. Adjust lids. Process in pressure canner at 10 pounds pressure (pints or quarts) 20 minutes. Makes 6 pints.

# JAMS AND JELLIES

- Straight-sided glasses are suitable for jelly and make it easy to slip jelly out in a molded shape. For jams and preserves, use any type of canning jar.
- A very large kettle, 8- to 10-quart size, is needed to allow room for boiling.
- To extract juice for jelly, place prepared fruit in damp jelly bag or fruit press. For clear jelly, do not squeeze the bag.
- A double boiler is handy for melting paraffin and keeping it hot without overheating. Do not use paraffin to seal soft jams and preserves.
- Jams and jellies will fade if stored too long or in too warm a place.
- Fruit floating in jam may be caused by: underripe fruit, insufficient crushing of fruit, undercooking, pouring into containers too soon after removing from heat.
- Stirring jam often and skimming off foam for 5 minutes after cooking will help prevent floating fruit. Stir gently.
- Use jams, jellies within a few months.

## CANNING PROCEDURE

1. Wash jelly glasses or jars in warm, soapy water; rinse. Sterilize jars by boiling in water 10 minutes; let stand in hot water till needed; drain. Prepare lids following manufacturer's directions.

2. Prepare jelly or jam according to recipes on the following pages. Note the description of the jelly test on page 322.

3. Pour hot jelly mixture into hot sterilized jars to within ½ inch of top. Cover at once with hot paraffin ⅛ inch thick. Prick any air bubbles. (Standard 6-ounce jelly glass takes 1 tablespoon paraffin.)

*Or,* pour preserves and soft jams into canning jars, filling to top. Wipe top and threads of jar with clean, damp cloth. Place lids with sealing compound next to jar rim. Screw metal bands down tightly.

4. Let jams and jellies cool on rack or thick cloth overnight. Cover jelly glasses with metal or paper lids. Label to show name of product and date. Store in a cool, dry, dark place.

**Jellies** are made from fruit juice, are clear, and firm enough to hold their shape.

**Jams** contain slightly crushed or ground fruit and are usually softer than jelly.

**Conserves** are jams made from a mixture of fruits, usually including citrus fruit; raisins and nuts are often added.

**Marmalade** is a tender jelly with pieces of fruit distributed throughout; it commonly contains citrus fruits.

**Preserves** are whole fruits or large pieces of fruit in a thick, jellied syrup.

**To test jelly** without added pectin for doneness, dip large cool metal spoon into mixture; lift 12 inches above kettle. Tilt so syrup runs over side. At jelly stage, liquid will stop flowing in stream and divide into 2 distinct drops that run together and sheet from edge of spoon. On thermometer, the temperature should register 8° higher than the boiling point of water. (Find the temperature at which water boils in your area—it differs with altitude.) For *jams* without added pectin, the temperature should be 9° higher.

## POOR PRODUCT CAUSES

• *Cloudy* jelly may be caused by: pouring jelly mixture into glasses too slowly; allowing jelly mixture to stand before pouring; straining juice improperly, causing pulp in the juice; using green fruit which makes jelly set too fast.

• *Crystals* throughout the jelly may be caused by too much sugar or cooking the mixture too little, too slowly, or too long. Crystals due to evaporation of liquid may appear on top of jelly after it has been opened and allowed to stand.

• *Weeping* jelly may result from sealing with too thick a layer of paraffin on top or storing in a warm place.

• *Stiff* jelly may be due to overcooking or too much pectin.

## MINT OR BASIL JELLY

| | |
|---|---|
| 2 cups water | 6 drops green food |
| 1 cup white vinegar | coloring |
| 1 cup fresh mint *or* basil leaves (lightly packed) | 6½ cups sugar |
| | 1 6-ounce bottle liquid fruit pectin |

Combine first five ingredients in large saucepan; bring to boil. Add fruit pectin; heat to a *full rolling boil* and *boil hard 1 minute*. Remove leaves. Pour liquid into hot sterilized glasses. Seal immediately with paraffin. Makes 7 cups.

## MINT-APPLE JELLY

| | |
|---|---|
| 4 cups canned apple juice | 6 drops green food coloring |
| 1 1¾-ounce package powdered fruit pectin | 1 cup fresh mint leaves (lightly packed) |
| | 4½ cups sugar |

Combine apple juice, pectin, food coloring, and mint leaves in very large kettle. Bring to *hard boil*. Stir in sugar. Bring again to *rolling boil; boil hard 1 minute,* stirring constantly. Remove from heat; remove leaves. Pour into hot sterilized jars; seal. Makes six ½-pint jars.

## CRAN-PINEAPPLE JELLY

3 cups cranberry-juice
   cocktail
1 7½-ounce can (1 cup)
   pineapple juice

⅓ cup lemon juice
1 1¾-ounce package
   powdered fruit pectin
5 cups sugar

Combine fruit juices with pectin in very large saucepan; stir over high heat till mixture boils hard. At once, stir in the sugar. Bring to a *full rolling boil; boil hard 1 minute,* stirring constantly.

Remove from heat; skim off foam. Pour into hot sterilized jelly glasses; seal at once. Fills 6 to 8 jelly glasses.


## CINNAMON-APPLE JELLY

3 pounds tart apples
3 cups sugar
1 drop oil of cinnamon

6 drops red food
   coloring

Wash fruit; do not pare or core. Cut in eighths, removing blemishes. Barely cover with water; simmer until soft.

Strain juice through jelly bag. Measure 4 cups juice into large kettle. Add sugar; stir till dissolved. Bring to *full rolling boil* over high heat. Boil hard till syrup sheets off spoon, about 8° above the boiling point of water. Remove from heat; skim off foam quickly. Add cinnamon and coloring. Pour into hot sterilized glasses. Seal immediately with paraffin. Makes three ½-pints.


## APRICOT-PINEAPPLE JAM

1 11-ounce package
   (2 cups) dried apricots
1 1-pound 4½-ounce
   can crushed
   pineapple (undrained)

½ lemon, sliced and
   quartered
4 cups sugar

Rinse apricots. Simmer, covered, in 2½ cups water until tender. Mash apricots; add pineapple, lemon, and sugar. Simmer, stirring frequently, until thick and clear, about 45 minutes. Ladle into hot sterilized jars; seal. Makes about six ½-pint jars.

## STRAWBERRY JAM

2 pints fresh strawberries  
7 cups sugar  

½ 6-ounce bottle liquid fruit pectin

Wash berries; slice in half lengthwise or quarter large berries. Measure 4 cups into large saucepan; add 1 *cup* sugar; mix carefully; let stand 15 minutes. Add remaining sugar; mix well. Bring to *full rolling boil; boil hard 1 minute,* stirring constantly.

Remove from heat; stir in pectin. Stir and skim alternately 5 minutes to prevent floating fruit. Ladle into hot sterilized jars; seal at once. Makes seven ½-pint jars.

## CHERRY-STRAWBERRY JAM

1 1-pound 4-ounce can pitted tart red cherries (water pack)  
1 10-ounce package frozen sliced strawberries, thawed  

4½ cups sugar  
3 tablespoons lemon juice  

\* \* \*  

½ 6-ounce bottle liquid fruit pectin

Drain cherries, reserving juice. Chop cherries; measure and add enough reserved juice to make 2 cups. Combine fruits, sugar, and lemon juice in large saucepan. Bring to *full rolling boil; boil hard 1 minute,* stirring constantly.

Remove from heat; stir in pectin at once. Skim off foam. Stir and skim for 5 minutes. Ladle quickly into hot sterilized jars. Seal. Makes six ½-pint jars.

## FROZEN STRAWBERRY JAM

Thaw two 10-ounce packages frozen strawberries. Put through food mill or mash. Add 3½ cups sugar; mix well. Let stand 20 minutes, stirring occasionally.

When sugar has dissolved, add ½ 6-ounce bottle liquid fruit pectin; stir 3 minutes. Ladle into hot sterilized jars or clean freezer containers. Cover and let stand 24 hours, or till set. Seal with paraffin.

Store jam up to 6 weeks in the refrigerator or up to 1 year in the freezer. Makes four ½-pint jars jam.

## PEACH-RUM JAM

3 pounds fully ripe
peaches, scalded,
peeled, and finely
chopped (4 cups
chopped)

1 1³/₄-ounce package
powdered fruit pectin
5 cups sugar
¼ cup light rum

Combine chopped peaches and fruit pectin in a *very large* saucepan or Dutch oven. Place over high heat and bring to a full rolling boil, stirring constantly. Immediately add all the sugar and stir. Again bring to a *full rolling boil* and *boil hard for 1 minute,* stirring constantly.

Remove from heat; stir in rum; skim off foam. Stir and skim for 5 minutes to cool slightly and prevent fruit from floating. Ladle into hot sterilized jars. Seal at once. Makes about six ¹/₂-pint jars.

## PEACH-PLUM JAM

2 pounds ripe peaches
1¹/₂ pounds fully ripe
Italian prune plums

1 1³/₄-ounce package
powdered fruit pectin
5¹/₂ cups sugar

Peel and pit peaches; chop very fine. Pit plums; chop very fine. Mix fruits; measure 4¹/₂ cups into large saucepan.

Place saucepan of fruit over high heat. Add pectin. Stir till mixture comes to a hard boil. At once, stir in sugar. Bring to a *full rolling boil* and *boil hard 1 minute,* stirring constantly. Remove from heat.

Skim and stir for 5 minutes. Ladle quickly into hot sterilized glasses. Seal at once. Makes ten 6-ounce glasses.

## DOUBLE BERRY JAM

Wash and crush 1 quart *each* fresh blueberries and fresh red raspberries; measure 4 cups (fill last cup with water, if necessary) into large saucepan.

Add 7 cups sugar; heat to *full rolling boil; boil hard 1 minute,* stirring constantly. Remove from heat. Stir in ¹/₂ 6-ounce bottle liquid fruit pectin. Skim. Pour into 8 hot sterilized ¹/₂-pint jars. Seal at once.

## RASPBERRY-RHUBARB JAM

2 10-ounce packages
frozen raspberries,
thawed
1 pound fresh rhubarb,
cut in 1-inch pieces
(4 cups)

1 1³/₄-ounce package
powdered fruit pectin
5 cups sugar

In Dutch oven or large kettle, combine fruits. Stir in the
pectin. Place over high heat, stirring till mixture reaches
a hard boil. Immediately stir in sugar. Bring to a *full rolling boil; boil hard 1 minute,* stirring constantly. Remove
from heat. Using metal spoon, skim off foam; stir and
skim for 5 minutes. Quickly ladle into 6 hot sterilized
¹/₂-pint jars; seal.

## GINGERED RHUBARB JAM

4 cups diced fresh
rhubarb
3 cups sugar
3 tablespoons finely
snipped candied
ginger

2 tablespoons lemon
juice
Few drops red food
coloring

Combine rhubarb with next 3 ingredients in large saucepan; let stand about 15 minutes, or till sugar is moistened
by juice. Cook over medium-high heat, stirring frequently
till thick and clear, 12 to 15 minutes. Skim off foam; add
red food coloring, if desired. Ladle into hot sterilized jars;
seal. Makes three ¹/₂-pints.

## SPICED GRAPE JAM

1¹/₂ pounds Concord
grapes
1 tablespoon grated
orange peel
1 cup water

2¹/₄ cups sugar
¹/₄ teaspoon ground
cinnamon
¹/₈ teaspoon ground
cloves

Wash grapes; separate skins from pulp. Reserve skins.
Cook pulp in 3-quart saucepan until soft; sieve to remove
seeds.

Add orange peel and water; cook 10 minutes. Add grape skins; bring to boil. Add sugar and spices; cook over medium-low heat until thick. Pour into hot sterilized jars; seal. Makes about three ½-pints.

## APRICOT JAM

| | |
|---|---|
| 3 pounds fully ripe apricots | 3 cups sugar |
| ⅓ cup water | 2 tablespoons lemon juice |

Wash, peel, and pit apricots. Chop fruit; measure 4½ cups. In large kettle or Dutch oven, combine apricots and water. Bring to boiling. Cover and simmer 5 to 10 minutes, or till apricots are tender; stir frequently. Add sugar and lemon juice; mix well. Stir till sugar dissolves.

Bring to a *full rolling boil*. Cook 7 to 8 minutes till desired thickness; stir constantly. Remove from heat. Quickly skim off foam. Pour at once into hot sterilized jars; seal. Makes six ½-pints.

## PLUM JAM

Wash and pit 3 pounds red plums. Put through food chopper using coarse blade (5 cups). Add 4 cups sugar; let stand 1 hour. Cook over high heat 8 minutes, or till mixture gives jelly test. Pour into 5 hot sterilized ½-pint jars; seal.

Ladle jams and jellies into hot sterilized jars with the aid of a handy wide-mouth funnel— no drips or spills outside the jars.

# ORANGE MARMALADE

| 4 medium oranges | 6 cups sugar |
| 1 medium lemon | 1/2 6-ounce bottle liquid |
| 1/4 teaspoon soda | fruit pectin |

Remove fruit peels; scrape off excess white. Cut peels in very fine shreds. Add 1 1/2 cups water and soda; bring to boil; cover and cook slowly 10 minutes.

Remove white membrane on fruit; section fruit, working over bowl to catch juice. Combine pulp, reserved juice, and peel; cover; cook slowly 20 minutes.

Measure 3 cups; add sugar. Bring to boil; cook 5 minutes. Remove from heat; add fruit pectin. Skim and stir 5 minutes. Pour into hot sterilized glasses; seal. Makes six 8-ounce glasses.

# KUMQUAT MARMALADE

Slice 1 pint fresh kumquats in paper-thin circles (remove seeds as needed) to measure 2 1/2 cups slices. Cover with 4 cups water; let stand overnight. In 6-quart kettle, boil mixture 30 minutes. Measure into 3-quart saucepan. For *each cup* fruit mixture, add 1 cup sugar.

Return to heat. Cook to *full rolling boil;* boil hard till mixture sheets off spoon, about 3 minutes. Stir in 1 tablespoon lemon juice. Ladle into hot sterilized jars; seal immediately. Makes 1 pint.

# BLUEBERRY MARMALADE

Remove peel from 1 medium orange and 1 lemon. Scrape excess white from peel; cut peel in *very fine* shreds. Place in very large saucepan. Add 3/4 cup water. Bring to boil; simmer, covered, 10 minutes; stir occasionally. Remove white membrane on fruit; finely chop pulp (discard seeds). Add to peel with 3 cups crushed blueberries. Cover; simmer 12 minutes. Add 5 cups sugar. Bring to *full rolling boil;* boil hard 1 minute, stirring constantly. Remove from heat; immediately stir in 1/2 6-ounce bottle liquid fruit pectin. Skim off foam; stir and skim for 7 minutes. Ladle into hot sterilized jars. Seal at once. Makes six 1/2-pints.

## APPLE-PEACH CONSERVE

2 cups chopped, pared,
   tart apples
2 cups chopped, peeled
   peaches

$1/3$ cup lemon juice
3 cups sugar

Combine all ingredients. Cook slowly for 20 minutes. Pour into hot sterilized jars. Seal at once. Makes about four $1/2$-pints.

## PLUM CONSERVE

2 pounds Italian plums
1 cup seedless raisins
1 medium orange

3 cups sugar
$1/2$ cup coarsely chopped
   walnuts

Pit plums. Grind all fruits; add sugar; bring to boil. Cook till thick, about 10 minutes. Stir in nuts. Pour into hot sterilized jars. Seal at once. Makes six $1/2$-pints.

## GRAPE CONSERVE

Wash 4 pounds Concord grapes; separate skins from pulp; reserve skins. Cook pulp till soft; sieve to remove seeds. Squeeze $1^{1}/2$ cups orange juice and $1/2$ cup lemon juice; reserve peels from 2 oranges and 1 lemon. Scrape excess white from the orange and lemon peels. Slice peel very thin; cover with water and cook, uncovered, till tender; drain.

Add grape skins, 8 cups sugar, juices, and peels to grape pulp. Boil till mixture is thick and sheets from spoon, about 35 to 40 minutes. Add 1 cup broken walnuts. Pour into hot sterilized jars. Seal at once. Makes ten $1/2$-pints.

## PEACH CONSERVE

Quarter and seed 5 oranges (don't pare); peel and pit 18 peaches. Put both fruits through food chopper, using coarse blade. Measure fruit into large pan; add $1^{1}/2$ cups sugar for each cup fruit. Cook rapidly till mixture sheets from spoon; stir often. Add 1 cup chopped maraschino cherries. Pour into hot sterilized glasses; seal at once. Makes twelve 6-ounce glasses.

# FREEZING FRUITS

## FREEZING PROCEDURE

The intended use determines which freezing method is best. Use syrup pack fruits for dessert; sugar pack for cooking. Unsweetened fruit is generally lower quality but is handy for special diet cookery.

1. *Preparation:* Freeze fresh, ripe fruit. Prepare fruits for syrup or sugar pack as indicated on chart, pages 334–336. Unsweetened pack method is on page 332.

2. *Packaging:* Moisture-vaporproof containers are essential. Rigid containers are: glass, aluminum, plastic, or heavily waxed cardboard. Bags and sheets made of moisture-vaporproof materials such as heavy foil, cellophane, plastic, or laminated papers are suitable. Pack fruit tightly into containers to eliminate air.

3. *Sealing:* Leave headspace—room between the packed fruit and top of the container (see chart at right)—for food to expand during freezing. Place piece of crumpled parchment paper atop fruit in container to hold fruit under juice. Follow manufacturer's directions for sealing containers. Label with contents and date.

4. *Freezing:* Freeze at 0° or below in small batches. Keep fruits stored at this temperature until ready to use. Most fruits may be stored 8 to 12 months. Do not refreeze.

# FROZEN FRUIT YIELD

Generally the following amount of fruit as purchased yields 1 pint frozen fruit.

| Fruit | Amount |
| --- | --- |
| Apples | 1¼ to 1½ pounds |
| Apricots | ⅔ to ¾ pound |
| Berries* | 1⅓ to 1½ pints |
| Peaches | 1 to 1½ pounds |
| Pears | 1 to 1¼ pounds |
| Plums | 1 to 1½ pounds |
| Raspberries | 1 pint |
| Rhubarb | ⅔ to 1 pound |
| Strawberries | ⅔ quart |

*Includes blackberries, blueberries, boysenberries, elderberries, and loganberries.

## UNSWEETENED PACK

*Apples:* Wash, pare, and core. Dissolve ½ teaspoon ascorbic acid color keeper in 1 quart water. Pour ½ cup of this water into freezer container. Slice apples into container. Press down; cover with water. Leave ½-inch headspace. Seal; freeze.

*Blueberries:* Use directions for syrup pack (see page 334); replace syrup with water. Leave ½-inch headspace. Freeze.

*Peaches or Strawberries:* Wash. Cut as desired. Pack; cover with water containing 1 teaspoon ascorbic acid color keeper per quart. Leave ½-inch headspace in pints; 1-inch headspace in quarts. Seal; freeze.

*Plums or Raspberries:* Wash; drain. Pack whole; leave ½-inch headspace. Freeze.

*Rhubarb:* Wash, trim, and cut into 1- or 2-inch pieces or in lengths to fit container. Cook in boiling water 1 minute; cool quickly in cold water. Pack; cover with cold water. Leave ½-inch headspace. Seal; label; freeze.

## SYRUP PROPORTIONS

For syrup pack fruit; Add sugar to boiling water; stir to dissolve; chill. Figure $1/2$ to $2/3$ cup syrup per pint packaged fruit.

| Syrup | Sugar (cups) | Water (cups) | Yield (cups) |
|---|---|---|---|
| Thin | 2 | 4 | 5 |
| Medium | 3 | 4 | $5^1/2$ |
| Heavy | $4^3/4$ | 4 | $6^1/2$ |
| Very Heavy | 7 | 4 | $7^3/4$ |
| Extra Heavy | $8^3/4$ | 4 | $8^2/3$ |

## HEADSPACE

Leave the following headspace between fruit mixture and top of container:

| Syrup or Sugar Pack | | | |
|---|---|---|---|
| Wide top opening | | Narrow top opening | |
| Pint | Quart | Pint | Quart |
| $1/2$ inch | 1 inch | $3/4$ inch | $1^1/2$ inches |

See Unsweetened Pack for headspace.

| Fruit | Syrup Pack | Sugar Pack |
|-------|-----------|-----------|
| Apples | Wash, pare, and core. Add 1/2 teaspoon ascorbic acid color keeper per quart Medium Syrup. Slice apples into 1/2 cup cold syrup in container. Press down; cover with syrup; leave headspace. Seal; label; freeze. | Wash, pare, core, and slice. Steam 1 1/2 to 2 minutes; cool; drain. Sprinkle 1/2 cup sugar over each quart of fruit; stir. Pack tightly into containers, leaving headspace. Seal; label; freeze. |
| Apricots | Wash, halve, and pit. Peel and slice, if desired. If not peeled, cook in boiling water 1/2 minute; cool; drain. Add 3/4 teaspoon ascorbic acid color keeper to each quart Medium Syrup. Pack fruit tightly into containers. Cover with cold syrup; leave headspace. Seal; label; freeze. | Wash, halve, and pit. Peel and slice, if desired. If not peeled, cook in boiling water 1/2 minute; cool; drain. Dissolve 1/4 teaspoon ascorbic acid color keeper in 1/4 cup cold water; sprinkle over 1 quart apricots. Mix 1/2 cup sugar with each quart fruit; stir till dissolved. Pack into containers, pressing down till juice covers fruit. Leave headspace; seal; label; freeze. |
| Blueberries Elderberries Huckleberries | Wash; drain. Steam 1 minute; cool quickly. Pack into containers; cover with cold Medium Syrup. Leave headspace; seal; freeze. | Wash; drain. Steam 1 minute; cool. To 1 quart berries, add 2/3 cup sugar; mix. Place in containers; leave headspace. Seal; label; freeze. |
| Cherries, sour | Stem, wash, drain, and pit. Pack into containers; cover with cold Very Heavy or Extra Heavy Syrup, depending on tartness. Leave headspace; seal; label; freeze. | Stem; wash; drain; pit. To each quart fruit add 3/4 cup sugar; mix till dissolved. Pack into containers, leaving headspace. Seal; label; freeze. |

| | |
|---|---|
| Cherries, sweet | Stem, wash, drain, and pit if desired. Add 1/2 teaspoon ascorbic acid color keeper to each quart Medium Syrup. Pack fruit into containers; cover with syrup, leaving headspace. Seal; label; freeze. |
| Melons | Halve, remove seeds, and peel. Cut into slices, cubes, or balls; pack into containers. Cover with cold Thin Syrup, leaving headspace. Seal; label; freeze. |
| Peaches | Wash, pit, and peel (for smooth look, don't scald). Add 1/2 teaspoon ascorbic acid color keeper per quart Medium Syrup. Slice peaches into 1/2 cup syrup in container or leave in halves; press fruit down; add syrup to cover; leave headspace; seal; freeze. |
| Pears | Wash, pare, halve or quarter, and remove cores. Cook in boiling Medium Syrup for 1 to 2 minutes; drain; cool. Pack pears into containers. Add 3/4 teaspoon ascorbic acid color keeper per quart Medium Syrup; cover fruit with syrup, leaving headspace. Seal; label; freeze. |

Wash, pit, and peel (for smooth look, don't scald). Halve or slice. Dissolve 1/4 teaspoon ascorbic acid color keeper in 1/4 cup cold water. Sprinkle over 1 quart fruit; add 2/3 cup sugar; mix well. Pack into containers; leave headspace. Seal; label; freeze.

| Fruit | Syrup Pack | Sugar Pack |
|---|---|---|
| Plums | Wash, pit, halve or quarter; pack into containers. Add 1/2 teaspoon ascorbic acid color keeper to each quart Medium or Heavy Syrup, depending on tartness. Cover fruit with syrup; leave headspace. Seal; label; freeze. | Wash; drain. Pit, halve or quarter. To 1 pound fruit add 2/3 cup sugar; mix. Place in containers; leave headspace. Seal; label; freeze. |
| Raspberries Blackberries Boysenberries Strawberries | Wash and drain. Remove hulls and slice or leave strawberries whole. Place in containers; cover with cold Medium or Heavy Syrup; leave headspace. Seal; label; freeze. | Wash and drain. Remove hulls and slice or leave strawberries whole. Add 3/4 cup sugar to each quart berries; mix carefully. Place in containers; leave headspace. Seal; label; freeze. |
| Rhubarb | Wash, trim, cut into 1- or 2-inch pieces or in lengths to fit container. Cook in boiling water 1 minute; cool in cold water. Pack into containers; cover with cold Medium Syrup; leave headspace; seal; label; freeze. | |

# FREEZING VEGETABLES

## FREEZING PROCEDURE

1. *Preparation:* Select fresh, tender vegetables. Lettuce and other salad greens, green onions, cucumbers, celery, tomatoes, and radishes should not be frozen since they lose crispness and texture. Wash, trim, and sort vegetables according to size following the chart on opposite page.

2. *Blanch* vegetables to prevent any off-flavors (see directions on page 338).

3. *Packaging:* Moisture-vaporproof containers are essential. Rigid containers might be glass, aluminum, plastic, or heavily waxed cardboard. Bags and sheets made of moisture-vaporproof materials such as heavy foil, cellophane, plastic, or laminated papers are suitable. Pack vegetables tightly to eliminate air.

4. *Sealing:* Leave $1/2$-inch headspace—room between packed vegetable and top of container to allow food to expand. Follow manufacturer's directions for sealing containers. Label with contents and date.

5. *Freezing:* Freeze at 0° or below in small batches. Keep stored at this temperature until ready to use, up to 8 to 12 months. *Never refreeze vegetables.*

## FROZEN VEGETABLE YIELD

Generally, the following amount of vegetable, as purchased, yields 1 pint frozen.

| Vegetable | Pounds |
|---|---|
| Asparagus | 1 to $1^1/2$ |
| Beans, limas in pods | 2 to $2^1/2$ |
| Beans, snap green | $2/3$ to 1 |
| Beets, without tops | $1^1/4$ to $1^1/2$ |
| Broccoli | 1 |
| Brussels sprouts | 1 |
| Carrots, without tops | $1^1/4$ to $1^1/2$ |

| Vegetable | Pounds |
|---|---|
| Cauliflower | 1⅓ |
| Corn, sweet in husks | 2 to 2½ |
| Peas | 2 to 2½ |
| Spinach | 1 to 1½ |
| Squash, summer | 1 to 1¼ |
| Squash, winter | 1½ |
| Sweet potatoes | ⅔ |

## BLANCHING VEGETABLES

Blanching vegetables before freezing stops enzyme action. It also helps retain fresh flavor and appearance. Water blanching is best for most vegetables. Broccoli, sweet potatoes, and winter squash may be blanched using steam or water method.

*Water blanching.* Place 1 pound prepared fresh vegetable in wire-mesh basket. Immerse in 1 gallon rapidly boiling water in large kettle. Cover and boil for time indicated in chart on opposite page. Allow 1 minute longer boiling time at 5,000 or more feet above sea level.

Remove promptly when time is up. Chill quickly by putting basket of vegetables into a pan of *cold* or *ice* water. Change water frequently. Allow about as much time for cooling as for blanching. Drain well.

*Steam blanching.* Use kettle with tight lid and rack 3 inches off bottom. Add water 1 to 2 inches deep; bring to rapid boil. Keep heat high. Place vegetables in single layer in basket; lower onto rack. Cover and steam for time in chart. Steam 1 minute longer at 5,000 or more feet above sea level. Remove vegetables and cool in ice water, as for water blanching.

Give vegetables an icy water bath when blanching time ends. Cool for the same number of minutes as they were blanched.

| Vegetable | Preparation | Blanching Boiling water | Steam (on rack over boiling water) |
|---|---|---|---|
| Asparagus | Wash. Trim; cut to package length or in 2-inch pieces. Sort according to stalk thickness. | Small stalks—2 min. Large stalks—4 min. | |
| Beans, green | Wash; remove ends. Cut in 1- or 2-inch pieces, or French cut. | 3 min. | |
| lima | Shell. Or leave in pods and shell after blanching. | Small—2 min. Large—4 min. | |
| Beets | Wash and sort according to size; leave 1/2 inch stems. Cook till tender. Peel; cut up. | Small—25 to 30 min. Medium—45 to 50 min. | |
| Broccoli | Wash; peel stalks; trim; cut into medium pieces 5-6 inches long, no thicker than 1 1/2 inches. | 3 min. | 5 min. |
| Brussels sprouts | Cut from stem; wash carefully. Remove outer leaves. Sort according to size. | Small—3 min. Large—5 min. | |

| Vegetable | Preparation | Blanching Boiling water | Steam (on rack over boiling water) |
|---|---|---|---|
| Carrots | Wash; scrape or pare. Cut into 1/4-inch slices or leave whole if small and tender. | Sliced—2 min. Whole—5 min. | |
| Cauliflower | Wash; cut into 1-inch pieces. | 3 min. | |
| Corn, on cob | Husk, remove silk, wash, and sort. Don't use over-mature corn. | Small ears—7 min. Medium ears—9 min. Large ears—11 min. | |
| kernel | Blanch ears; cool, then cut off corn. | 4 min. | |
| Greens Beet or chard Kale Mustard Spinach Collards | Wash thoroughly. Cut and discard thick stems and imperfect leaves. | 2 min. 2 min. 2 min. 2 min. 3 min. | |
| Mixed vegetables | Prepare. Blanch separately for times given; mix to-gether after cooling. | | |

| | | | |
|---|---|---|---|
| Peas | Shell peas. Discard starchy peas. | 1½ min. | |
| Potatoes, sweet | Cook till almost tender with jackets on. Cool; pare and slice. Dip in solution of ¼ cup lemon juice to 1 quart water. Or mash; mix 2 tablespoons lemon juice with each quart. | Cook 30-40 min. | Cook 45-60 min. |
| Rutabagas and Turnips | Wash, cut off tops, peel, and cut into ½-inch cubes. | 2 min. | |
| Squash, summer | Wash. Cut in ½-inch slices. | 3 min. | |
| winter | Cut into pieces; remove seeds. Cook till soft; remove pulp; mash. Cool quickly. | Cook 15 min. | Cook about 20 min. |

## • 4 SIMPLE STEPS TO ASSURE PROPER FREEZER PACKAGING •

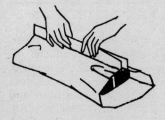

Use suitable wrapping 1½ times as long as needed to go around food. Put food in center of wrap.

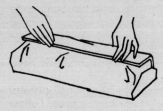

Join sides of wrapper at top; fold edges down in series of locked folds; press wrap against food.

Crease ends into points. Press wrap to remove air. Be sure the coated side of paper is next to food.

Turn ends under; secure ends and the folded seam with freezer tape. Label with contents and date.

# FREEZING MEAT, FISH

Select high quality meat and fish for freezing. Remember, freezing cannot improve the quality of the products.

Meat, poultry, and fish are usually frozen uncooked. However, cooked meats can be wrapped and frozen, too. Freeze meat, both the cuts purchased at a retail store and the carcass meat slaughtered at home or at a locker plant, while it is fresh and in the peak of condition. Follow directions given on chart (page 344).

*Packaging and wrapping:* Keep packages small for rapid freezing; make them family-sized units. Separate individual portions of chops or fillets with 2 layers of waxed paper for easy separation, then wrap in moisture-vaporproof material.

Package ground meat in freezer cartons or plastic bags, or form into patties.

Use moisture-vaporproof materials for wrap to prevent "freezer burn"—drying out of meat on surfaces. Follow wrapping instructions in the drawings above. Exclude all air from packages by pressing wrap against food and wrapping tightly. Seal with freezer tape. Label with contents, weight or servings, and date.

*Freeze at 0° or below:* Place packages next to a refrigerated surface in freezer. Separate unfrozen food from food already frozen. Freeze in small batches.

Keep frozen at 0° or below—fluctuations above 0° can cause loss of quality. Do not freeze smoked meats for more than 1 month—quality deteriorates rapidly. Limit storage time—see chart on the following pages.

Thaw unopened in the refrigerator. Use promptly. Do not refreeze.

| Food | Preparation for freezing | Storage time at 0°<br>How to thaw and use |
|------|--------------------------|--------------------------------------------|
| Meat | Have meat cut in desired meat cuts. Avoid packing more bone than necessary. Wrap tightly in moisture-vaporproof material. Seal, label, and freeze at 0° or below. | Beef: 6 to 12 months<br>Lamb and Veal: 6 to 9 months<br>Pork: 3 to 6 months<br>Ground meat: 3 to 4 months<br>Ham: 2 months<br>Thaw in refrigerator in original wrap. See pgs. 427–485 for cooking information. |
| Poultry | Select young, tender birds that are well-finished. Chill cleaned, dressed birds. Wrap and freeze giblets separately. Disjoint and cut up bird or leave whole. Wrap bird or pieces in moisture-waterproof material. Seal, label, and freeze. Never freeze stuffed poultry. | Chicken: 12 months<br>Turkey, Duck, Goose: 6 months<br>Giblets: 3 months<br>Thaw in refrigerator in original wrap. See pgs. 525–554 for cooking information. |
| Fish | Dress and wash fish as for cooking. Dip in solution of ²/₃ cup salt to 1 gallon water for 30 seconds. Wrap in moisture-vaporproof material. Seal, label, and freeze. | Fish: 6 to 9 months<br>Thaw in refrigerator in original wrap or cook frozen allowing extra cooking time. See pgs. 555–564 for cooking information. |
| Shellfish | Oysters, clams, and scallops: Shuck; freeze immediately. Pack in freezer containers leaving ½ inch headspace. Seal, label, freeze. | Oysters, Clams, and Scallops: 3 months<br>Thaw in refrigerator in original wrap. See pgs. 561–568 for cooking information. |

*Crabs and lobsters:* Cook as for eating; chill in refrigerator. Remove meat from shell. Wrap in moisture-vaporproof material. Seal, label, and freeze.

*Shrimp:* Freeze uncooked either in shells or shelled. Remove heads. Wrap in moisture-vaporproof material. Seal, label, freeze.

Crabs and Lobsters: 1 month
Thaw in refrigerator in original wrap. See pgs. 566–570 for cooking information.

Shrimp: 3 months
Cook shrimp while still frozen. See pgs. 562 and 565–566 for cooking information.

| | | |
|---|---|---|
| **Whole eggs** | Wash eggs. Break into bowl. Stir with fork just to break yolks; mix well with whites; don't whip in air. To each cup eggs, add 1 tablespoon sugar or corn syrup or 1 teaspoon salt. Mix; sieve. Pack in freezer containers in amounts for one cake, scrambled eggs for one meal, etc. Skim air bubbles off surface. Leave ½ inch headspace in pints. Seal. Label with date, measure, and number of eggs, what was added, and intended use. Freeze. | Whole eggs: 6 to 8 months<br>Thaw completely in unopened container in refrigerator; use promptly. Allow for sugar, corn syrup, or salt, which was added during preparation for freezing; otherwise use same as fresh eggs. About 2½ tablespoons equal 1 egg. |
| **Egg yolks** | Wash eggs. Separate into bowl. Stir with fork to break yolks. To each cup yolks, add 2 tablespoons sugar or corn syrup, or 1 teaspoon salt. Blend carefully; do not whip in air; sieve. Package as above. | Egg yolks: 6 to 8 months<br>Thaw completely in unopened container; use promptly. Allow for sugar, corn syrup, or salt; otherwise use same as fresh yolks. About 1 tablespoon equals 1 yolk. |
| **Egg whites** | Wash eggs. Separate into bowl. Do not stir or add anything to whites. Package same as for whole eggs above. | Egg whites: 6 to 8 months<br>Thaw completely in unopened container; use promptly, same as fresh whites. About 1½ tablespoons equal 1 egg white. |

| Food | Preparation for freezing | Storage time at 0° How to thaw and use |
|------|--------------------------|----------------------------------------|
| Butter | Select fresh, high-quality butter. Wrap in moisture-vaporproof material; seal, label, and freeze. | Butter or margarine: 3 to 6 months. Thaw unopened in package. Use same as fresh. |
| Ice cream | Seal in freezer container or overwrap carton with moisture-vaporproof material; seal. Homemade becomes grainy when stored. | Commercial ice cream: 3 weeks Remove from freezer shortly before serving. |
| Whipped cream mounds | Whip whipping cream with sugar and flavoring. Drop from spoon in mounds on waxed paper-lined baking sheet; freeze firm. Place in freezer container. Seal, label, and freeze. | Whipped cream mounds: 3 months Place frozen mounds on servings of dessert. Let stand at room temperature 20 minutes. |

# FREEZING COOKED FOOD

- Don't oversalt or overseason. Slightly decrease garlic, green pepper, and celery as they intensify in flavor when frozen.
- Don't overcook foods. Undercook rice (use converted rice) and noodles. Cook vegetables and meats till barely tender.
- Don't freeze potatoes in main dishes.
- Add crumb toppers at reheating time.
- Use fat sparingly in sauces—it doesn't blend in well when reheated.
- Freeze in family-size portions.
- Cool quickly before packaging. Place pan of cooked food in sink containing ice water; cool food to room temperature.
- Never attempt to refreeze food.

## FREEZING PROCEDURE

1. Prepare food as indicated on chart (pages 349 to 355).

2. Package properly. Wrap with moisture-vaporproof materials such as cellophane, polyester, and polyethylene films, clear plastic wrap, freezer-weight aluminum foil, and laminated wrap. Or, use freezer containers with wide top openings.

Allow headspace when packing semi-liquid foods—room for food to expand.

To save freezer space and free dish for reuse, line casserole with heavy foil, leaving long ends. Fill. Seal. Place container in freezer. When food is frozen, remove from container. Label and store. Reheat in same casserole, foil and all.

3. Seal and label with contents; date.

4. Freeze at 0° or below.

| Food | Preparation for freezing | How to serve | Storage time |
|---|---|---|---|
| **Breads:** | | | |
| Baking powder biscuits | Bake as usual; cool. Seal in freezer container, or wrap in foil and seal. | Thaw in package in 300° oven about 20 minutes. | 2 months |
| Doughnuts | Fry; cool; wrap and seal. | Reheat in oven. | 2 to 4 weeks |
| Muffins | Bake as usual; cool. Seal in freezer container, or wrap in foil and seal. | Thaw in package at room temperature 1 hour or in 300° oven about 20 minutes. | 2 months |
| Yeast breads | Bake as usual; cool quickly. Wrap and seal. | Thaw, wrapped, at room temperature 3 hours. | 2 months |
| Yeast rolls | Use either plain or sweet dough recipe. Bake as usual; cool quickly. Wrap in foil and seal. Freeze at once. | Thaw baked rolls in package at room temperature or in 250° to 300° oven about 15 minutes. Use at once. | 2 months |
| | Or partially bake at 325° about 15 minutes; do not let brown. Cool, wrap, and freeze at once. | Thaw partially baked rolls 10 to 15 minutes at room temperature. Unwrap; bake in very hot oven (450°) for 5 to 10 minutes. Serve at once. | 2 months |

| Food | Preparation for freezing | How to serve | Storage time |
|---|---|---|---|
| **Cakes:**<br>General | *Baked.* Remove from pan; cool thoroughly. If you frost cake, freeze it before wrapping. Wrap; seal. If desired, place in sturdy container. Freeze at once. (Unfrosted cakes freeze better. Frosted and filled cakes may become soggy.) | Thaw in wrapping at room temperature (2 to 3 hours for large cake, 1 hour for layers). If frosted or filled, thaw loosely covered in the refrigerator. | Unfrosted 6 months<br><br>Frosted 2 months |
| Cupcakes | Bake as usual; cool. If frosted, freeze before wrapping. Seal in freezer container or wrap and seal. Freeze. (Unfrosted cupcakes freeze better.) | Thaw, wrapped, at room temperature 40 minutes. If frosted, thaw loosely covered in refrigerator. | 2 months |
| Sponge and angel food | Bake as usual; cool thoroughly. If frosted, freeze it before wrapping. If desired, place in sturdy container. | Thaw in package 2 to 3 hours at room temperature. If frosted, thaw loosely covered in refrigerator. | 1 month |
| Cake frostings and fillings | *Recommended for freezing:* Frostings with confectioners' sugar and fat, cooked-candy type with honey or corn syrup, fudge, penuche, fruit, nut. Seal in freezer containers; freeze. | Thaw in refrigerator. | 2 months |

| | | |
|---|---|---|
| | *Not recommended:* Soft frostings, boiled icings, 7-minute frosting, cream fillings. | |
| **Cookies:**<br>Unbaked | Pack dough in freezer containers; seal.<br>*Not recommended:* Meringue-type cookies. | Thaw in package at room temperature till dough is soft. Bake as usual. | 6 to 12 months |
| | Bar cookies. Spread dough in baking pan; wrap and seal. Freeze. | Bake without thawing. | |
| | Refrigerator cookies. Shape into roll; wrap and seal. Freeze. | Thaw slightly at room temperature. Slice roll; bake. | |
| Baked | Bake as usual; cool thoroughly. Pack in freezer containers with waxed paper between layers and in air spaces. Seal. Freeze. | Thaw in package at room temperature. | 6 to 12 months |
| **Pastry** | Pastry and graham-cracker shells freeze satisfactorily. Roll out dough; fit it into pie plates. Bake, if desired. Wrap and seal. | Thaw baked at 325° 8 to 10 minutes. Unbaked frozen pastry baked same as fresh. | 2 months |
| **Pies:**<br>Fruit, general | *Unbaked:* Treat light-colored fruits with ascorbic acid color keeper to prevent darken- | Unwrap; cut vent holes in top crust. Without thawing, bake at | 2 months |

| Food | Preparation for freezing | How to serve | Storage time |
|---|---|---|---|
| | ing. Prepare pie as usual but don't slit top crust. Use glass or metal pie plate. Cover with inverted paper plate. Wrap and seal. If desired, place in sturdy container. Freeze at once. | 450° to 475° for 15 to 20 minutes, then at 375° till done. *Berry, cherry:* Unwrap; cut vent holes in top crust. Without thawing, bake at 400°. | |
| Apple, unbaked | *Baked:* Bake as usual in glass or metal pie plate. Cool. Package as above. | Thaw in package at room temperature or in 300° oven. | 2 months |
| | Use firmer varieties of apples. Steam slices 2 minutes, cool, and drain; or treat with ascorbic acid color keeper. Prepare and package as above. | Unwrap; cut vent holes in top crust; bake in hot oven (425°) about 1 hour. | 2 months |
| Peach, unbaked | To keep color bright, treat with ascorbic acid color keeper. Prepare and package as above. | Unwrap; cut vent holes in top crust. Bake, without thawing, at 400° for 1 hour. | 2 months |
| Chiffon | Chocolate and lemon freeze satisfactorily. | Thaw in the refrigerator. | 2 weeks |
| Deep-dish fruit pies | Use deep pie plates. | Bake or thaw same as two-crust pies above. | 2 months |

| | | |
|---|---|---|
| **Main dishes** Casseroles: Poultry, fish, or meat with vegetable or pasta | Cool mixture quickly. Turn into freezer container or casserole. Cover tightly. Seal, label, and freeze. | If frozen in oven-proof container, uncover. Bake at 400° for 1 hour for pints, 1¾ hours for quarts, or till hot. Or steam over hot water in double boiler top. | 2 to 4 months |
| **Creamed Dishes** Chicken, turkey, fish, or seafood | Cool quickly. Freeze any except those containing hard-cooked egg white. Don't overcook. Use fat sparingly when making sauce. This helps prevent separation of sauce when reheating. Cover tightly. Seal, label, and freeze. | Heat without thawing in top of double boiler, stirring occasionally. If sauce separates, stir till smooth. About 30 minutes is needed to thaw and heat 1 pint of creamed mixture. | |
| Meatballs with tomato sauce | Cook till done; cool quickly. Ladle into jars or freezer containers, allowing headspace. Seal, label, and freeze. | Stir frequently over low heat or occasionally in top of double boiler. Or defrost overnight in refrigerator. Heat in saucepan. | 3 months |
| Meat pies and scalloped dishes | Cook meat till tender. Cook vegetables till almost tender. Cool quickly. Put in baking dish. Top with pastry, or freeze pastry separately. Wrap tightly. Seal, label, and freeze. | Bake frozen pies with pastry topper at 400° for 45 minutes for pints and 1 hour for quarts, or till hot and crust is browned. | 2 to 3 months |

| Food | Preparation for freezing | How to serve | Storage time |
|---|---|---|---|
| Roast beef, pork, other meats, poultry | Do not freeze fried meats or poultry. Prepare as for serving. Remove excess fat and bone. Cool quickly. Wrap tightly. Best to freeze small pieces or slices; cover with broth, gravy, or sauce. Wrap tightly, seal, label, and freeze. | Thaw large pieces of meat in the refrigerator before heating. Heat meat in sauces in top of double boiler. | 2 to 4 months |
| Spaghetti sauce | Cool sauce quickly; ladle into jars or freezer containers, allowing headspace. Seal, label, and freeze. | Heat over low heat or in top of double boiler stirring frequently. | 2 to 3 months |
| **Vegetables** | | | |
| Baked beans with tomato sauce | Chill mixture quickly. Package in moisture-vaporproof container. Cover tightly. | Partially thaw in package. Heat in casserole or top of double boiler. | 6 months |
| Spanish rice | Use converted rice. Cook till rice is tender, but not mushy. Cool quickly. Package. Seal, label, and freeze. | Heat in top of double boiler about 50 minutes. Add a little water if needed. | 3 months |
| **Stews and Soups** | Select vegetables that freeze well. Omit potatoes. Onions lose flavor. Green pepper and garlic become more intense in flavor. Omit | Heat quickly from frozen state. Do not overcook. Separate with fork as it thaws. Do not stir | 2 to 4 months |

| | | |
|---|---|---|
| | salt and thickening if stew is to be kept longer than 2 months. Do not completely cook vegetables. Cool quickly, wrap. Seal, label, and freeze. | enough to make the mixture mushy. |
| **Sandwiches** | *These freeze well:* Cream cheese, hard-cooked egg yolk, sliced or ground meat and poultry, tuna or salmon, peanut butter. Spread slice of bread with softened butter; fill; place second buttered bread slice atop. Wrap tightly. Seal; label with contents and date; freeze.<br><br>*Not recommended:* Lettuce, celery, toma-toes, cucumber, watercress, whites of hard-cooked eggs, jelly, mayonnaise. | Thaw sandwiches in wrapping at room temperature about 3 hours. Serve immediately. 2 weeks |

# 8

# CASSEROLES AND ONE-DISH MEALS

## ITALIAN MEAT SAUCE

| | |
|---|---|
| 1 cup chopped onion | 1 tablespoon brown sugar |
| 1 pound ground beef | 1 teaspoon salt |
| 2 cloves garlic, minced | 1½ teaspoons dried oregano, crushed |
| 1 1-pound 14-ounce can tomatoes, cut up | ¼ teaspoon dried thyme, crushed |
| 1 1-pound can tomatoes, cut up | 1 bay leaf |
| 1 6-ounce can tomato paste | Hot cooked spaghetti |
| ¼ cup snipped parsley | Shredded Parmesan cheese |

In Dutch oven, combine onion, meat, and garlic; cook till meat is browned and onion is tender. Skim off excess fat; add next 9 ingredients and 2 cups water. Simmer, uncovered, 3 hours, or till sauce is thick; stir occasionally. Remove bay leaf. Serve over hot spaghetti. Pass bowl of shredded Parmesan cheese. Makes 6 servings.

## SPAGHETTI AND MEATBALLS

| | |
|---|---|
| ¾ cup chopped onion | 1 teaspoon sugar |
| 1 clove garlic, minced | 1½ teaspoons salt |
| 3 tablespoons salad oil | ½ teaspoon pepper |
| 2 1-pound cans (4 cups) tomatoes, cut up | 1½ teaspoons dried oregano, crushed |
| 2 6-ounce cans tomato paste | 1 bay leaf |
| 2 cups water | Italian Meatballs |
| | Hot cooked spaghetti |

Cook onion and garlic in oil till tender but not brown. Stir in next 8 ingredients. Simmer, uncovered, 30 minutes; remove bay leaf. Add meatballs. Loosely cover; cook 30 minutes. Serve over spaghetti. Pass Parmesan cheese, if desired. Serves 8.

## • HOW TO COOK SPAGHETTI, MACARONI, AND NOODLES •

A *large* pan filled with plenty of water is important to cook any pasta. Three quarts of water is the minimum for cooking 8 ounces of pasta. To season, add 1 teaspoon salt for each quart of water. The addition of a teaspoon of salad oil to the water helps prevent pasta from sticking together and water from boiling over.

When water boils vigorously, add pasta. Don't cover. Keep water boiling; stir at the start to prevent sticking. Cook till tender, but still firm. Drain at once.

No need to break long spaghetti—hold a handful at one end, dip the other into the water. As it softens, curl it around in pan till immersed. One pound spaghetti serves 6 to 8.

## ITALIAN MEATBALLS

*For a variation, serve with mushroom sauce—*

Soak 4 bread slices in $\frac{1}{2}$ cup water 2 to 3 minutes; add 2 eggs and mix well. Mix with 1 pound ground beef, $\frac{1}{4}$ cup grated Parmesan cheese, 2 tablespoons snipped parsley, 1 teaspoon salt, $\frac{1}{4}$ teaspoon dried oregano, crushed, and dash pepper.

With wet hands, form meat mixture into small balls (about 24). Brown slowly in 2 tablespoons hot salad oil. Add meatballs to sauce, simmer, loosely covered, for 30 minutes as directed for Spaghetti and Meatballs. Makes 8 servings.

## BISCUIT PIZZA CRUST

| | |
|---|---|
| 1 package active dry yeast | 2$\frac{1}{2}$ cups packaged biscuit mix |
| $\frac{3}{4}$ cup warm water | Olive oil or salad oil |

OVEN 425°

Soften yeast in warm water (110°). Add biscuit mix; beat vigorously for 2 minutes. Dust surface with biscuit mix, knead dough till smooth (25 strokes). Divide dough in half and roll each piece of dough to a 12-inch circle.

Place dough circles on greased baking sheets; crimp edges. Brush dough with oil. Fill with desired toppers. Bake at 425° for 15 minutes, or till crusts are done. Makes two 12-inch pizza crusts.

## SAUSAGE PIZZA

In skillet, break 1 pound Italian sausage in bits. Cook slowly until lightly browned, about 10 minutes, stirring occasionally; drain off fat. Drain one 1-pound can tomatoes, reserving 1/2 cup juice. Cut tomatoes in small pieces and layer on two 12-inch pizza-dough circles. Sprinkle with salt and pepper; then cover with one 6-ounce package mozzarella cheese, *thinly* sliced and torn in pieces. Drizzle *each* with 1 tablespoon olive oil. Sprinkle with the lightly browned sausage.

Combine one 6-ounce can tomato paste, reserved tomato juice, 2 cloves garlic, minced, 1 tablespoon crushed dried oregano, and 1 tablespoon whole basil. Mix well; spread over sausage. Dash generously with salt and pepper. Scatter 1/4 cup grated Parmesan *or* Romano cheese atop. Drizzle *each* with 1 tablespoon olive oil. Bake as for crust. Makes 2 pizzas.

## PIZZA TOPPERS

For creative cooking with a jiffy flair, start with packaged pizza mix. Spread canned pizza sauce atop; oregano and basil are compatible herbs to add. Top with your own fix-ups.

For salami pizza, sprinkle generously atop with small pieces of salami; shake Parmesan cheese overall. Try anchovy pizza with wedges of mozzarella cheese. Season pepperoni pizza with anise seed.

## LASAGNE

1 pound Italian sausage
1 clove garlic, minced
1 tablespoon whole basil
1½ teaspoons salt
1 1-pound can tomatoes
2 6-ounce cans tomato paste

---

10 ounces lasagne noodles
2 eggs

3 cups fresh Ricotta or cream-style cottage cheese
½ cup grated Parmesan or Romano cheese
2 tablespoons parsley flakes
1 teaspoon salt
½ teaspoon pepper
1 pound mozzarella cheese, sliced very thin

OVEN 375°

Brown meat slowly; spoon off excess fat. Add next 5 ingredients and 1 cup water. Simmer, covered, 15 minutes; stir often. Cook noodles in boiling salted water till tender; drain; rinse. Beat eggs; add remaining ingredients, except mozzarella.

Layer *half* the noodles in 13x9x2-inch baking dish; spread with *half* the Ricotta filling; add *half* the mozzarella cheese and *half* the meat sauce. Repeat. Bake at 375° about 30 minutes (or assemble early and refrigerate; bake 45 minutes). Let stand 10 minutes before serving. Serves 8 to 10.

## STUFFED PEPPER CUPS

OVEN 350°

Cut off tops of 6 medium green peppers; remove seeds and membrane. Precook green pepper cups in boiling salted water about 5 minutes; drain. (For crisp peppers, omit precooking.) Sprinkle inside of cups generously with salt.

Cook 1 pound ground beef and ⅓ cup chopped onion till meat is lightly browned. Season with ½ teaspoon salt and dash pepper. Add one 1-pound can tomatoes, ½ cup water, ½ cup uncooked long-grain rice, and 1 teaspoon Worcestershire sauce. Cover and simmer till rice is tender, about 15 minutes. Stir in 4 ounces sharp process American cheese, shredded (1 cup). Stuff peppers; stand upright in

10x6x1½-inch baking dish. Bake, uncovered, at 350° for 20 to 25 minutes. Serves 6.

## CHILI CON CARNE

1 pound ground beef
1 cup chopped onion
¾ cup chopped green pepper
1 1-pound can (2 cups) tomatoes, broken up
1 1-pound can (2 cups) dark red kidney beans, drained
1 8-ounce can tomato sauce
1 teaspoon salt
1 to 2 teaspoons chili powder
1 bay leaf

In heavy skillet, cook meat, onion, and green pepper till meat is lightly browned and vegetables are tender. Stir in remaining ingredients. Cover and simmer for 1 hour. Remove bay leaf. Makes 4 servings.

## HAMBURGER-CHEESE BAKE

1 pound ground beef
½ cup chopped onion
2 8-ounce cans tomato sauce
1 teaspoon sugar
¾ teaspoon salt
¼ teaspoon garlic salt
¼ teaspoon pepper
4 cups uncooked medium noodles
1 cup cream-style cottage cheese
1 8-ounce package cream cheese, softened
¼ cup dairy sour cream
⅓ cup sliced green onion
¼ cup chopped green pepper
¼ cup shredded Parmesan cheese

OVEN 350°

In large skillet, cook meat and onion till meat is lightly browned and onion is tender. Stir in tomato sauce, sugar, salt, garlic salt, and pepper. Remove from heat. Meanwhile, cook noodles according to package directions; drain. Combine cottage cheese, cream cheese, sour cream, green onion, and green pepper.

Spread *half* the noodles in 11x7x1½-inch baking pan; top with a little of the meat sauce. Cover with cheese mixture. Add remaining noodles and meat sauce. Sprinkle with Parmesan cheese. Bake at 350° for 30 minutes. Makes 8 to 10 servings.

## HAMBURGER PIE

1 pound ground beef
1/2 cup chopped onion
      * * *
1/2 teaspoon salt
    Dash pepper
1 1-pound can (2 cups)
    cut green beans,
    drained

1 10³/4-ounce can
    condensed tomato
    soup
5 medium potatoes,
    cooked*
1/2 cup warm milk
1 beaten egg
2 ounces process
    American cheese,
    shredded (1/2 cup)

OVEN 350°

In large skillet, cook meat and onion till meat is lightly browned and onion is tender. Add salt and pepper. Add drained beans and soup; pour into greased 1¹/2-quart casserole. Mash potatoes while hot; add milk and egg. Season with salt and pepper. Spoon in mounds over casserole. Sprinkle potatoes with cheese. Bake in moderate oven (350°) for 25 to 30 minutes. Makes 4 to 6 servings.

*Or prepare 4 servings packaged instant mashed potatoes according to package directions except *reserve the milk.* Add egg and season with salt and pepper to taste. Add enough reserved milk so potatoes are stiff enough to hold shape.

## HAMBURGER-CORN BAKE

OVEN 350°

In large skillet, cook 1¹/2 pounds ground beef and 1 cup chopped onion till meat is lightly browned and onion is tender. Stir in one 12-ounce can whole kernel corn, drained, one 10¹/2-ounce can condensed cream of chicken soup, one 10¹/2-ounce can condensed cream of mushroom soup, 1 cup dairy sour cream, 1/4 cup chopped canned pimiento, 3/4 teaspoon salt, and 1/4 teaspoon pepper. Mix well.

Stir in 6 ounces (3 cups) medium noodles, cooked and drained. Turn mixture into 2½-quart casserole. Combine 1 cup soft bread crumbs and 2 tablespoons melted butter or margarine; sprinkle atop. Bake at 350° for 45 minutes, or till hot. Makes 8 to 10 servings.

## SAUCY MEATBALL SUPPER

Combine 1½ pounds ground beef, ½ cup chopped onion, 2 eggs, ¼ cup milk, 1 teaspoon salt, dash pepper, 1 cup (2 slices) soft bread crumbs, 2 tablespoons snipped parsley, and ½ teaspoon dried oregano, crushed; mix well. Shape in 1-inch balls. In large skillet, brown meatballs in a little shortening on all sides.

Drain off excess fat. Combine one 11-ounce can condensed Cheddar cheese soup, ½ cup water, and ¼ cup dry white wine. Add to meat in skillet. Cook, covered, over low heat 15 to 20 minutes. Serve over hot cooked spaghetti. Serves 6.

## TAMALE PIE

1 pound ground beef
1 cup chopped onion
1 cup chopped green pepper
2 8-ounce cans tomato sauce
1 12-ounce can (1½ cups) whole kernel corn, drained
½ cup pitted ripe olives, chopped
1 clove garlic, minced
1 tablespoon sugar

1 teaspoon salt
2 to 3 teaspoons chili powder
Dash pepper

* * *

6 ounces sharp process American cheese, shredded (1½ cups)
¾ cup yellow cornmeal
½ teaspoon salt
2 cups cold water
1 tablespoon butter or margarine

OVEN 375°

Cook meat, onion, and green pepper in a large skillet till meat is lightly browned and vegetables are tender. Stir in tomato sauce, corn, olives, garlic, sugar, the 1 teaspoon salt, chili powder, and pepper. Simmer 20 to 25 minutes, or until thick. Add cheese; stir till melted. Turn into greased 9x9x2-inch baking dish.

Stir cornmeal and 1/2 teaspoon salt into cold water. Cook, stirring constantly, till thick. Add butter or margarine; mix well. Spoon over hot meat mixture.

Bake casserole in moderate oven (375°) about 40 minutes. Makes 6 servings.

## EASY MEXICALI DINNER

1 pound ground beef
1/2 cup chopped onion
6 ounces (3 cups) medium noodles, cooked and drained
1 1-pound can tomatoes
1 6-ounce can tomato paste

6 ounces sharp process American cheese, shredded (1 1/2 cups)
1/2 cup sliced ripe olives
1 teaspoon salt
1/4 teaspoon dried basil, crushed
1/8 teaspoon pepper

OVEN 350°

Cook meat and onion in large skillet till onion is tender. Stir in noodles, tomatoes, tomato paste, 1 *cup* shredded cheese, olives, and seasonings. Turn into 2-quart casserole. Top with remaining cheese. Bake at 350° for 45 minutes. Serves 6.

## INSIDE-OUT RAVIOLI

1 pound ground beef
1/2 cup chopped onion
1 clove garlic, minced
1 10-ounce package frozen chopped spinach
1 1-pound can spaghetti sauce with mushrooms
1 8-ounce can tomato sauce
1 6-ounce can tomato paste

1/2 teaspoon salt
Dash pepper
1 7-ounce package (2 cups) shell *or* elbow macaroni, cooked and drained
4 ounces sharp process American cheese, shredded (1 cup)
1/2 cup soft bread crumbs
2 well-beaten eggs
1/4 cup salad oil

OVEN 350°

Brown first 3 ingredients in large skillet. Cook spinach using package directions. Drain, reserving liquid; add water to make 1 cup. Add spinach liquid and next 5 ingredients to meat mixture. Simmer 10 minutes. Combine spinach with macaroni and remaining ingredients; spread in 13x9x2-inch baking dish. Top with meat sauce. Bake at 350° for 30 minutes. Let stand 10 minutes. Serves 8 to 10.

## MEATBALLS AND SPAETZLE

German Meatballs
1 10½-ounce can condensed beef broth
1 3-ounce can chopped mushrooms, drained (½ cup)
½ cup chopped onion

1 cup dairy sour cream
1 tablespoon all-purpose flour
½ to 1 teaspoon caraway seed
Spaetzle

*German Meatballs:* Combine 1 pound ground beef, 1 egg, ¼ cup fine dry bread crumbs, ¼ cup milk, 1 tablespoon snipped parsley, ½ teaspoon salt, ¼ teaspoon poultry seasoning, and dash pepper. Shape in twenty-four 1½-inch balls.

In skillet, brown meatballs; drain off excess fat. Add broth, mushrooms, and onion. Simmer, covered, 30 minutes. Blend cream, flour, and seed; stir into broth. Cook and stir till thick. Serve with Spaetzle. Serves 5 or 6.

*Spaetzle:* Sift together 2 cups sifted all-purpose flour and 1 teaspoon salt. Add 2 beaten eggs and 1 cup milk; beat well. Place in coarse-sieved colander. Hold over large kettle of rapidly boiling salted water. Press batter through colander. Cook and stir 5 minutes; drain. Sprinkle with mixture of ¼ cup fine dry bread crumbs and 2 tablespoons melted butter.

## BEST OVEN HASH

1 cup coarsely ground cooked beef
1 cup coarsely ground cooked potatoes
¼ cup coarsely ground onion
¼ cup snipped parsley

2 teaspoons Worcestershire sauce
1 6-ounce can (⅔ cup) evaporated milk
¼ cup fine dry bread crumbs
1 tablespoon butter or margarine, melted

OVEN 350°

Mix first 6 ingredients, 1 teaspoon salt, and dash pepper. Turn into 1-quart casserole. Mix crumbs and butter; sprinkle atop. Bake at 350° for 30 minutes. Serves 4.

## FRENCH RAGOUT

| | |
|---|---|
| 1½ cups sliced onion | 1 lemon slice |
| 3 tablespoons butter | 1½ cups diced potatoes |
| 1 beef bouillon cube | 1½ cups sliced carrots |
| 1½ cups water | 12 dried prunes |
| 2 cups cubed cooked beef | ¾ teaspoon salt |
| ¾ cup leftover or canned gravy | 1 tablespoon cornstarch |

Cook onion in butter until just tender. Add remaining ingredients except cornstarch. Bring to a boil; cover; simmer 25 minutes. Blend ¼ cup cold water with the cornstarch. Stir into beef mixture. Bring to a boil, stirring constantly. Simmer, uncovered, 5 minutes. Makes 4 servings.

## CORNED BEEF AND NOODLES

OVEN 350°

Cook 4 ounces (2 cups) medium noodles according to package directions; drain. In saucepan, melt 3 tablespoons butter or margarine; stir in 3 tablespoons all-purpose flour. Add 2¼ cups milk; cook quickly, stirring constantly, till mixture thickens and bubbles. Stir in 1 tablespoon prepared horseradish, 2 teaspoons salt, 1 teaspoon prepared mustard, and dash pepper. Add one 10-ounce package frozen peas, thawed, and noodles. Turn into 10x6x1½-inch baking dish. Arrange one 12-ounce can corned beef, cut in 6 slices, over noodles. Bake at 350° for 30 minutes. Serves 5 or 6.

## HOMEMADE NOODLES

Combine 1 beaten egg, 2 tablespoons milk, and ½ teaspoon salt. Add enough sifted all-purpose flour to make stiff dough, about 1 cup. Roll very thin on floured surface; let stand 20 minutes. Roll up loosely; slice ¼ inch wide; unroll, spread out and let dry 2 hours. (If desired, store in container until needed.)

Drop into boiling soup or boiling, salted water and cook, uncovered, about 10 minutes. Makes 3 cups cooked noodles.

## VEAL ROLLS DIVAN

3 slices bacon
1½ cups packaged herb-seasoned stuffing mix
6 thin veal steaks, pounded ⅛ inch thick
1 tablespoon salad oil
2 10-ounce packages frozen broccoli spears, thawed

1 chicken bouillon cube
½ cup boiling water
1 10½-ounce can condensed cream of mushroom soup
⅓ cup milk
1 4½- or 5-ounce can shrimp, drained

OVEN 350°

In skillet, cook bacon till crisp; drain; reserve drippings. Prepare stuffing according to package directions, using drippings and melted butter to make ¼ cup. Crumble bacon; stir into stuffing. Sprinkle veal with salt. Place ⅓ cup stuffing on each steak; roll and tie securely. Add oil to same skillet; brown veal. Arrange meat and broccoli in 12x7½x2-inch baking dish.

Dissolve crushed bouillon cube in boiling water; pour over meat. Cover with foil; bake at 350° for 1 hour. Combine soup, milk, and shrimp; heat through. Before serving, remove ties from meat; pour soup mixture over meat rolls. Garnish plates with radish roses. Makes 6 servings.

## CHOPSTICK VEAL BAKE

1½ pounds veal steak, ½ inch thick
2 tablespoons salad oil
1½ cups sliced celery
1 cup chopped onion
1 cup diced green pepper
3 tablespoons chopped canned pimiento

½ cup uncooked long-grain rice
1 10½-ounce can condensed cream of mushroom soup
1 cup milk
2 tablespoons soy sauce
1 3-ounce can (2 cups) chow mein noodles

OVEN 350°

Cut meat in 2x$\frac{1}{2}$-inch strips. Brown in hot oil. Add remaining ingredients except noodles. Turn into 2-quart casserole. Cover; bake at 350° for 1$\frac{1}{4}$ to 1$\frac{1}{2}$ hours; stir occasionally. Uncover last 5 minutes; sprinkle with noodles. Serves 8.

## PORK CHOW MEIN

Cook 1 pound pork, cut in *thin* strips, in 1 tablespoon salad oil till done, about 10 minutes. Remove from skillet. Cook 3 cups thin bias-cut celery slices, 1 cup sliced onion, and one 6-ounce can sliced mushrooms, drained, in 2 tablespoons salad oil till crisp-tender, stirring often. Blend 3 tablespoons cornstarch and $\frac{1}{4}$ cup cold water; add one 10$\frac{1}{2}$-ounce can condensed beef broth and $\frac{1}{4}$ cup soy sauce; stir into vegetables. Add meat, one 1-pound can bean sprouts, drained, and one 5-ounce can water chestnuts, drained and sliced. Cook and stir till thickened. Serve over rice or heated chow mein noodles. Serves 4 or 5.

## HAM-CHEESE DELIGHT

OVEN 350°

Cook $\frac{1}{2}$ cup finely chopped onion in 1 tablespoon butter till tender. Add 2 cups finely chopped cooked ham, 3 slightly beaten eggs, 1 cup shredded sharp process American cheese, $\frac{2}{3}$ cup fine cracker crumbs, 1$\frac{1}{2}$ cups milk, and dash pepper. Mix well; turn into a 10x6x1$\frac{1}{2}$-inch baking dish. Bake at 350° for 45 to 50 minutes. Serves 6.

## HAM MEDLEY

OVEN 350°

Melt $\frac{1}{4}$ cup butter; add 1 cup chopped celery and $\frac{1}{2}$ cup each chopped green pepper and onion; cook till tender. Blend in $\frac{1}{4}$ cup flour, $\frac{1}{2}$ teaspoon salt, and dash pepper. Stir in 2$\frac{1}{2}$ cups milk and 3 cups cream-style cottage cheese; cook and stir till boiling. Add 4 cups cubed cooked ham and 8 ounces noodles, cooked and drained. Turn into 3-quart casserole. Mix 2 tablespoons melted butter and $1/2$ cup fine dry bread crumbs; sprinkle atop. Bake at 350° for 1 hour. Serves 10 to 12.

## HAM-SQUASH SKILLET

| | |
|---|---|
| 1 pound ground cooked ham | 2 tablespoons prepared mustard |
| 1 egg | 1 medium acorn squash |
| $1/2$ cup soft bread crumbs | $1/2$ cup brown sugar |
| $1/4$ cup finely chopped onion | 2 tablespoons butter, softened |

Combine first 5 ingredients; form into 5 patties. Brown in hot fat; remove from skillet. Cut squash crosswise in 5 rings; halve. Place in skillet; season. Add 2 or 3 tablespoons water. Combine brown sugar and butter; dot over squash. Cover; cook till tender, 15 to 20 minutes, turning once. Uncover; add meat. Cook 5 minutes more, basting often. Serves 5.

## TENDERLOIN-NOODLE BAKE

OVEN 350°

Cook 6 ounces noodles; rinse; drain. Slowly brown $1\frac{1}{2}$ pounds pork tenderloin, sliced $1/2$ inch thick, in hot fat. Season with $1/2$ teaspoon salt and dash pepper. Combine noodles, Cheese Sauce, and 3 tablespoons *each* chopped green pepper and canned pimiento. Turn into 10x6x1$\frac{1}{2}$-inch baking dish; top with meat. Bake at 350° for 30 minutes. Serves 6.

*Cheese Sauce:* Melt 3 tablespoons butter. Blend in 3 tablespoons flour, $3/4$ teaspoon salt, and dash pepper. Add 1 cup milk. Cook quickly, stirring, till thickened and bubbly; remove from heat. Add $1/2$ cup crumbled blue cheese; stir to melt.

## CANTONESE CASSEROLE

| | |
|---|---|
| 1 10-ounce package frozen French-style green beans | 2 cups cubed cooked ham |
| 1 tablespoon butter | 1 5-ounce can water chestnuts, drained and thinly sliced |
| 1 tablespoon all-purpose flour | |
| 3/4 cup milk | 1 cup buttered soft bread crumbs (about 1 1/2 slices) |
| 2 tablespoons soy sauce | |
| 1 cup dairy sour cream | Paprika |

OVEN 350°

Pour boiling water over beans to separate; drain well. In saucepan, melt butter; blend in flour. Stir in milk and soy sauce; cook, stirring constantly, over medium heat till thick and bubbly. Stir in sour cream, cubed ham, beans, and water chestnuts. Pour into greased 10x6x1 1/2-inch baking dish. Sprinkle crumbs atop; dash with paprika. Bake at 350° for 30 minutes, or till hot. Serves 6.

## PORK CHOP SPANISH RICE

| | |
|---|---|
| 5 pork chops, 1/2-inch thick | 1/4 cup chopped green pepper |
| 2 tablespoons shortening | 1 1-pound 12-ounce can (3 1/2 cups) tomatoes |
| 1 teaspoon salt | |
| 1/2 teaspoon chili powder | 5 green pepper rings |
| Dash pepper | 2 ounces sharp process American cheese, shredded (1/2 cup) |
| 3/4 cup uncooked long-grain rice | |
| 1/2 cup chopped onion | |

Trim excess fat from chops. Slowly brown chops in melted shortening about 15 to 20 minutes; drain off excess fat.

Combine salt, chili powder, and pepper; sprinkle over meat. Add rice, onion, and chopped green pepper. Pour tomatoes over. Cover and cook over low heat 35 minutes, stirring occasionally. Add green pepper rings and cook 5 minutes longer, or till rice and meat are tender. Sprinkle with cheese. Makes 5 servings.

## SPANISH TOMATO RICE

In a 10-inch skillet, cook 8 slices bacon till crisp; remove. Pour off *half* the fat. In remaining fat, cook 1 cup finely chopped onion, and 1/4 cup chopped green pepper till tender but not brown.

Add one 1-pound can tomatoes, 1 1/2 cups water, 3/4 cup uncooked long-grain rice, 1/2 cup chili sauce, 1 teaspoon salt, 1 teaspoon brown sugar, 1/2 teaspoon Worcestershire sauce, and dash pepper. Cover and simmer 35 to 40 minutes. Crumble bacon on top. Serves 6.

## SAUSAGE SQUASH SPECIAL

1 pound bulk pork
    sausage
1 clove garlic, crushed
4 cups sliced summer
    squash
1/2 cup dry bread crumbs
1/2 cup grated Parmesan
    cheese

1/2 cup milk
1 tablespoon snipped
    parsley
1/2 teaspoon salt
1/2 teaspoon dried
    oregano, crushed
2 beaten eggs

OVEN 325°

Cook sausage and garlic till meat is brown; drain off excess fat. Cook squash, covered, in small amount of water till tender; drain. Stir squash and next 6 ingredients into meat; fold in eggs. Transfer to 10x6x1 1/2-inch baking dish. Bake at 325° for 25 to 30 minutes. Makes 4 to 6 servings.

## MEAT-MACARONI SUPPER

OVEN 350°

In medium skillet, melt 2 tablespoons butter or margarine; cook 1/2 cup chopped onion in butter till tender but not brown. Stir in one 10 3/4-ounce can condensed cream of celery soup, one 8-ounce can (1 cup) tomatoes, cut up, 1/4 teaspoon dried thyme, crushed, and dash pepper.

Add 1/2 7-ounce package (1 cup) elbow macaroni, cooked and drained, one 12-ounce can luncheon meat, cut in 1x1 1/2-inch strips, and 1/4 cup chopped green pepper. Turn into 1 1/2-quart casserole. Top with 1/4 cup shredded process American cheese. Bake, uncovered, at 350° for 35 to 40 minutes. Serves 4 to 6.

## CLASSIC CHICKEN DIVAN

2 10-ounce packages frozen broccoli spears
1/4 cup butter or margarine
6 tablespoons all-purpose flour
2 cups chicken broth
1/2 cup whipping cream
3 tablespoons dry white wine
3 chicken breasts, halved and cooked
1/4 cup grated Parmesan cheese

OVEN 350°

Cook broccoli using package directions; drain. Melt butter; blend in flour, 1/2 teaspoon salt, and dash pepper. Add chicken broth; cook and stir till mixture thickens and bubbles. Stir in cream and wine.

Place broccoli crosswise in 12x7 1/2 x2-inch baking dish. Pour *half* the sauce over. Top with chicken. To remaining sauce, add cheese; pour over chicken; sprinkle with additional Parmesan cheese. Bake at 350° for 20 minutes, or till heated through. Then broil just till sauce is golden, about 5 minutes. Serves 6.

## CHICKEN CURRY

1 tablespoon butter
1 cup finely chopped pared apple
1 cup sliced celery
1/2 cup chopped onion
1 clove garlic, minced
2 tablespoons cornstarch
2 to 3 teaspoons curry powder
3/4 cup cold chicken broth
2 cups milk
2 cups diced cooked chicken
1 3-ounce can sliced mushrooms, drained (1/2 cup)

In saucepan, melt butter; add apple, celery, onion, and garlic. Cook till onion is tender. Combine cornstarch, curry, 3/4 teaspoon salt, and broth. Stir into onion mixture; add milk. Cook and stir till mixture thickens and bubbles. Stir in chicken and mushrooms. Heat through. Serve over hot cooked rice and pass condiments—raisins, shredded coconut, chopped peanuts, and chutney; *or* serve in East Indian Rice Ring. Serves 5 or 6.

## • RICE RINGS •

**Glamorous Rice Ring:** Combine 3 cups hot cooked rice and $1/4$ cup snipped parsley. Press lightly in greased $5^{1}/2$-cup ring mold (or custard cups). Unmold at once on platter. Fill with creamed mixture.

**Confetti Rice Ring:** Cook one 10-ounce package frozen peas according to package directions; drain. Combine 4 cups hot cooked rice, peas, 3 tablespoons chopped canned pimiento, and 2 tablespoons butter, melted. Press lightly in greased $5^{1}/2$-cup ring mold. Unmold at once on hot platter.

**East Indian Rice Ring:** In skillet, melt $1/4$ cup butter; cook $1/2$ cup chopped onion and $1/4$ cup slivered almonds till golden. Add $1/2$ cup light raisins; heat till plump. Add to 6 cups hot cooked rice; mix gently. Press mixture lightly into greased $6^{1}/2$-cup ring mold. Unmold at once on platter. Fill with Chicken Curry; top with coconut.

## CHICKEN BUYING GUIDE

• One $3^{1}/2$-pound ready-to-cook chicken yields 3 cups diced cooked chicken.
• Two whole chicken breasts (10 ounces each) yield $1^{1}/2$ to 2 cups diced cooked chicken, or 12 thin slices cooked chicken.

## HERBED CHICKEN BAKE

1 6-ounce package long-
  grain and wild rice mix
3 large chicken breasts,
  boned and halved
  lengthwise
1/4 cup butter or
  margarine
1 10½-ounce can
  condensed cream of
  chicken soup

3/4 cup sauterne
1/2 cup sliced celery
1 3-ounce can sliced
  mushrooms, drained
  (1/2 cup)
2 tablespoons chopped
  canned pimiento

OVEN 350°

Prepare rice mix using package directions. Season chicken with salt and pepper; in skillet, brown slowly in butter. Spoon rice into 1½-quart casserole; top with chicken, skin side up. Add soup to skillet; slowly add sauterne, stirring till smooth. Add remaining ingredients; bring to boil; pour over chicken. Cover; bake at 350° for 25 minutes. Uncover; bake 15 to 20 minutes, or till tender. Serves 6.


## CHICKEN FRIED RICE

1 cup diced cooked
  chicken
1 tablespoon soy sauce
1 cup uncooked long-
  grain rice
1/3 cup salad oil
2½ cups chicken broth
1/2 cup coarsely chopped
  onion

1/4 cup finely chopped
  green pepper
1/4 cup thinly sliced celery
2 slightly beaten eggs
1 cup finely shredded
  lettuce or Chinese
  cabbage

Combine chicken, soy sauce, and 1/2 teaspoon salt. Let stand 15 minutes. Cook rice in hot oil in skillet over medium heat till golden brown; stir frequently. Reduce heat; add chicken with soy sauce and broth. Simmer, covered, 20 to 25 minutes, or till rice is tender. Remove cover last few minutes. Stir in onion, green pepper, and celery. Cook, uncovered, over medium heat till liquid is absorbed. Push rice mixture to sides of skillet. Add eggs;

cook till almost set; blend into rice. Stir in lettuce; serve at once with soy sauce. Serves 6.

## CHICKEN ALMOND

2 cups skinned uncooked chicken breasts cut in thin strips (about 2 whole breasts)

¼ cup shortening or salad oil

2 5-ounce cans bamboo shoots, drained and diced

2 cups diced celery

1 cup diced bok choy (Chinese chard) or romaine

2 5-ounce cans water chestnuts, drained and sliced

3 cups chicken broth

2 tablespoons soy sauce

* * *

⅓ cup cornstarch

½ cup cold water

½ cup toasted halved almonds

Hot cooked rice

In large heavy skillet, quickly cook chicken strips in hot shortening. Add diced bamboo shoots, celery, bok choy or romaine, water chestnuts, chicken broth, and soy sauce; mix thoroughly. Bring to boiling; cover and cook over low heat 5 minutes or till crisp-tender. Slowly blend cornstarch into ½ cup cold water; add to chicken mixture. Cook, stirring constantly, till mixture thickens and bubbles. Salt to taste. Garnish with toasted almonds. Serve immediately over hot cooked rice. Makes 6 servings.

*Note:* High heat and quick stirring are essential; avoid overcooking.

## CLUB CHICKEN CASSEROLE

OVEN 350°

In saucepan, melt ¼ cup butter or margarine; blend in ¼ cup all-purpose flour. Add one 14½-ounce can (1⅔ cups) evaporated milk, 1 cup chicken broth, and ½ cup water; cook quickly, stirring constantly, till mixture thickens and bubbles. Add 3 cups cooked long-grain rice, 2½ cups diced cooked chicken, one 3-ounce can sliced mushrooms, drained, ⅓ cup chopped green pepper, ¼ cup chopped canned pimiento, and 1½ teaspoons salt.

Pour into greased 2-quart casserole. Bake, uncovered, in moderate oven (350°) for 40 minutes, or until heated through. If desired, top with ¼ cup toasted slivered almonds. Makes 8 to 10 servings.

## TUNA-NOODLE CASSEROLE

OVEN 425°

Cook 6 ounces (3 cups) medium noodles using package directions; drain. Combine noodles, one 6½- or 7-ounce can tuna, drained, ½ cup mayonnaise, 1 cup sliced celery, ⅓ cup chopped onion, ¼ cup chopped green pepper, ¼ cup chopped canned pimiento, and ½ teaspoon salt. Blend one 10½-ounce can condensed cream of celery soup and ½ cup milk; heat through. Add 4 ounces sharp process American cheese, shredded (1 cup); heat and stir till cheese melts. Add to noodle mixture. Turn into 2-quart casserole. If desired, top with ½ cup toasted slivered almonds. Bake, uncovered, at 425° for 20 minutes. Makes 6 servings.

## CHOPSTICK TUNA

1 10½-ounce can
  condensed cream of
  mushroom soup
2 cups chow mein
  noodles

1 6½- or 7-ounce can
  tuna, drained and
  flaked
1 cup sliced celery
½ cup toasted cashews
¼ cup chopped onion

OVEN 375°

Combine soup and ¼ cup water. Add 1 *cup* of the chow mein noodles, dash pepper, and remaining ingredients. Toss lightly; turn into 10x6x1½-inch baking dish. Sprinkle remaining noodles atop. Bake at 375° for 30 minutes. Serves 4 or 5.

## SWEET-SOUR TUNA

Drain one 8¾-ounce can pineapple tidbits, reserving syrup. In saucepan, combine ⅓ cup of the pineapple syrup, pineapple tidbits, 1 cup green pepper strips, 1 vegetable bouillon cube, and $1/2$ cup water. Heat to boiling; simmer 5 minutes. Mix 3 tablespoons sugar and 1 tablespoon cornstarch; stir in remaining pineapple syrup, 1 tablespoon vinegar, and 1 teaspoon soy sauce. Stir into pineapple mixture. Cook and stir till mixture thickens and bubbles. Add one $6^{1}/_{2}$- or 7-ounce can tuna, drained, and 1 tablespoon butter. Heat through; serve over one 3-ounce can (2 cups) chow mein noodles, warmed. Serves 3 or 4.

## RICE AND TUNA PIE

2 cups cooked rice
1 tablespoon chopped onion
2 tablespoons butter
$1/4$ teaspoon dried marjoram, crushed
1 slightly beaten egg
1 $9^{1}/_{4}$-ounce can tuna, drained
3 beaten eggs

4 ounces process Swiss cheese, shredded (1 cup)
1 cup milk
$1/4$ teaspoon salt
Dash pepper
$1/4$ teaspoon dried marjoram, crushed
1 tablespoon chopped onion

OVEN 350°

For rice shell, combine first 5 ingredients; press onto bottom and sides of lightly buttered 10-inch pie plate or 10x6x1$1/2$-inch baking dish. Sprinkle tuna evenly over rice shell. Combine remaining ingredients; pour over tuna. Bake at 350° for 50 to 55 minutes, or till knife inserted off center comes out clean. Garnish with pimiento, if desired. Makes 6 servings.

## COMPANY CREAMED TUNA

2 tablespoons finely chopped onion
3 tablespoons butter
3 tablespoons all-purpose flour
$1/4$ teaspoon salt
$1^{1}/_{4}$ cups milk
$1/2$ cup dairy sour cream

1 $6^{1}/_{2}$- or 7-ounce can tuna, drained
3 tablespoons dry white wine
2 tablespoons snipped parsley
Toasted slivered almonds
Pastry shells

Cook onion in butter till tender but not brown. Blend in flour, salt, and dash pepper. Add milk all at once; cook quickly, stirring constantly, until mixture thickens and bubbles. Stir in sour cream. Add tuna, wine, and parsley. Heat through. Sprinkle with toasted almonds, if desired. Serve in pastry shells or spoon over hot buttered toast points. Makes 4 servings.

## SALMON OR TUNA PIE

| | |
|---|---|
| 2 beaten eggs | ³/₄ teaspoon dried basil, crushed |
| ¹/₂ cup milk | |
| ¹/₄ cup chopped onion | ¹/₄ teaspoon salt |
| 2 tablespoons snipped parsley | 1 1-pound can salmon, or 2 6¹/₂- or 7-ounce cans tuna |
| 1 tablespoon butter, melted | 1 stick pie crust mix |

OVEN 425°

Combine eggs, milk, onion, parsley, butter, and seasonings. Break salmon into chunks, removing bones and skin. Add to egg mixture. Pour into well-greased 8-inch pie plate. Prepare pie crust mix according to package directions. Roll ¹/₈ inch thick; cut circle using bottom of 8-inch pie plate as a guide. Cut the circle into 6 wedges; arrange atop seafood mixture. Bake at 425° about 25 minutes, or till done. Serve at once. Serve with creamed peas. Serves 6.

## SWISS AND CRAB QUICHE

*A main dish cheese and seafood pie—*

| | |
|---|---|
| 4 ounces natural Swiss cheese, shredded (1 cup) | 3 beaten eggs |
| | 1 cup light cream |
| | ¹/₂ teaspoon salt |
| 1 9-inch *unbaked* pastry shell | ¹/₂ teaspoon grated lemon peel |
| 1 7¹/₂-ounce can crab meat, drained, flaked, and cartilage removed | ¹/₄ teaspoon dry mustard |
| | Dash ground mace |
| | ¹/₄ cup sliced almonds |
| 2 green onions, sliced (with tops) | |

OVEN 325°

Arrange cheese evenly over bottom of pastry shell. Top with crab meat; sprinkle with green onions. Combine eggs, cream, salt, lemon peel, dry mustard, and mace. Pour evenly over crab meat. Top with sliced almonds. Bake in slow oven (325°) for about 45 minutes, or till set. Remove from oven and let stand 10 minutes before serving. Makes 6 servings.

## SCALLOP CASSEROLE

2 12-ounce packages frozen scallops
1/4 cup chopped onion
2 tablespoons butter
1 10 1/2-ounce can condensed cream of mushroom soup
1/2 cup milk
1/2 to 1 teaspoon curry powder
Dash pepper

1 cup shredded sharp process American cheese
1 1-pound can French-style green beans, drained
1 cup soft bread crumbs
2 tablespoons butter or margarine, melted

OVEN 425°

Simmer scallops in boiling salted water 3 to 4 minutes; drain. Cook onion in 2 tablespoons butter till tender but not brown. Add soup, milk, curry powder, pepper, and 1/2 cup of the cheese; stir till cheese melts. Slice cooked scallops crosswise; combine with drained green beans in 10x6x1 1/2-inch baking dish. Pour soup mixture over. Sprinkle with remaining cheese, bread crumbs, and 2 tablespoons butter. Bake in hot oven (425°) for 15 to 20 minutes. Makes 6 servings.

## SEAFOOD PILAF

3/4 cup uncooked long-
   grain rice
2 tablespoons butter
1 3-ounce can (2/3 cup)
   broiled sliced
   mushrooms
1 10 1/2-ounce can
   condensed chicken
   with rice soup

1 7 1/2-ounce can crab
   meat, drained, flaked,
   and cartilage removed
1 4 1/2-ounce can shrimp,
   drained
1/4 cup dry white wine
1 tablespoon instant
   minced onion

OVEN 350°

In skillet, brown rice in butter. Add mushrooms with liquid, remaining ingredients, and 1/4 cup water. Turn into 1 1/2-quart casserole. Bake, covered, at 350° for 55 minutes. Fluff with fork; bake, uncovered, 5 minutes. Serves 6.

## SHRIMP CURRIED EGGS

OVEN 350°

Cut 8 hard-cooked eggs in half lengthwise; remove yolks and mash. Mix with 1/3 cup mayonnaise, 1/2 teaspoon salt, 1/2 teaspoon paprika, 1/4 teaspoon curry powder, and 1/4 teaspoon dry mustard.

Refill egg whites; place in 10x6x1 1/2-inch baking dish. Melt 2 tablespoons butter; blend in 2 tablespoons all-purpose flour. Add one 10 1/2-ounce can condensed cream of celery soup and 3/4 cup milk; cook and stir till bubbly. Add 2 ounces sharp natural Cheddar cheese, shredded (1/2 cup), and 1 cup frozen, cooked shrimp; stir to melt cheese. Stir in 1/4 teaspoon curry powder. Pour over eggs. Mix 1 cup soft bread crumbs with 1 tablespoon butter, melted; sprinkle around edge of mixture. Bake at 350° for 15 to 20 minutes, or till hot. Makes 6 to 8 servings.

## SAUSAGE-EGG CASSEROLE

| | |
|---|---|
| 1 pound bulk pork<br>   sausage | 2 cups milk |
| 4 hard-cooked eggs | 1 1-pound can (2 cups)<br>   whole kernel corn, |
| ¼ cup butter or<br>   margarine | drained |
| ¼ cup all-purpose flour | 1 cup soft bread crumbs |

OVEN 375°

Cook sausage; drain. Slice 2 *of the eggs* into 1½-quart casserole. In saucepan, melt butter; blend in flour, ½ teaspoon salt, and dash pepper. Add milk all at once. Cook, stirring constantly, till mixture thickens and bubbles. Stir sausage and corn into sauce; pour over eggs. Slice remaining eggs; arrange atop mixture. Sprinkle with crumbs; bake at 375° for 30 minutes, or till heated through. Serves 6.

## SWISS PIE

*Flavored with bacon and onion—*

| | |
|---|---|
| 6 slices bacon | 12 ounces natural Swiss |
| 1 cup chopped onion | cheese, cut in ¼-inch |
| ¾ cup dairy sour cream | cubes (2½ cups) |
| 2 slightly beaten eggs | 1 9-inch *unbaked* pastry |
| ¼ teaspoon salt | shell |
| Dash pepper | |

OVEN 375°

Cook bacon till crisp. Drain bacon, reserving drippings. Crumble bacon; set aside. Cook onion in drippings till tender but not brown; drain. Blend in sour cream, slightly beaten eggs, salt, and pepper. Add the cubed cheese and crumbled bacon. Pour mixture into pastry shell.

Bake at 375° for 25 minutes, or till knife inserted off center comes out clean. Serve at once. Serves 6 to 8.

## CLASSIC CHEESE STRATA

8 slices day-old bread
6 ounces sharp process American cheese, sliced
4 eggs
2½ cups milk

¼ cup finely chopped onion
1½ teaspoons salt
½ teaspoon prepared mustard

OVEN 325°

Trim crusts from 4 *slices* of the bread; cut in half diagonally. Use trimmings and remaining 4 slices *untrimmed* bread to cover bottom of a 9-inch square baking dish. Top with cheese. Arrange the 8 trimmed bread "triangles" in 2 rows atop cheese. (Points should overlap bases of preceding "triangles.") Beat eggs; blend in remaining ingredients and dash pepper; pour over bread. Cover; let stand 1 hour at room temperature or several hours in refrigerator. Bake at 325° for 1 hour, or till knife inserted off center comes out clean. Let stand 5 minutes. Makes 6 servings.

## CLASSIC CHEESE FONDUE

French bread *or* hard rolls
1 tablespoon cornstarch
¼ cup kirsch *or* dry sherry
1 clove garlic, halved
2 cups sauterne

½ pound gruyere cheese, shredded (2 cups)
1½ pounds *natural* Swiss cheese, shredded (6 cups)
¼ teaspoon ground nutmeg
Dash pepper

Cut bread into bite-size pieces, with each piece having a crust on one side. Stir cornstarch into kirsch till well dissolved. Rub inside of heavy saucepan with garlic. Add sauterne; warm till air bubbles rise and cover surface. (Don't cover or boil.)

Remember to stir vigorously all the time from now on. Add a handful of combined cheeses, keeping heat medium (*do not* boil). When melted, toss in another handful. After all cheese is blended and is bubbling gently and while still stirring vigorously, add seasonings and kirsch mixture. Quickly transfer to earthenware fondue pot; keep warm. (If fondue becomes thick, add a little warm sauterne.)

Spear bread cube with fondue fork so crust is on outside. Dip into fondue; swirl to coat. The swirling is important to keep fondue in motion. Serves 10.

## WELSH RAREBIT

6 ounces sharp process American cheese, shredded (1½ cups)
¾ cup milk
1 teaspoon dry mustard
1 teaspoon Worcestershire sauce
Dash cayenne
1 well-beaten egg

In heavy saucepan, heat cheese and milk over very low heat, stirring constantly till cheese melts and sauce is smooth. Add next 3 ingredients. Stir about 1 cup of the hot mixture into egg; return to hot mixture. Cook and stir over very low heat till mixture thickens and bubbles. Serve at once over hot toast points with broiled tomato slices. Makes 4 servings.

## MACARONI AND CHEESE

OVEN 350°

Cook 1½ cups elbow macaroni in boiling salted water till tender; drain. In saucepan, melt 3 tablespoons butter; blend in 2 tablespoons all-purpose flour, ½ teaspoon salt, and dash pepper. Add 2 cups milk; cook and stir till thick and bubbly. Add ¼ cup finely chopped onion (optional) and 8 ounces sharp process American cheese, cubed (2 cups); stir till melted.

Mix cheese sauce with macaroni. Turn into 1½-quart casserole. Sprinkle 1 sliced tomato with salt; arrange atop. Bake at 350° for 35 to 40 minutes, or till heated through. Makes 6 servings.

## HUNGARIAN NOODLE BAKE

4 ounces fine noodles
1/4 cup finely chopped onion
1 clove garlic, minced
1 tablespoon butter
1 12-ounce carton (1 1/2 cups) cream-style cottage cheese

1 cup dairy sour cream
1 teaspoon Worcestershire sauce
Dash bottled hot pepper sauce
2 teaspoons poppy seed

OVEN 350°

Cook noodles in large amount boiling salted water till tender; drain. Cook onion and garlic in butter till tender. Combine noodles and onion mixture with remaining ingredients, 1/2 teaspoon salt, and dash pepper. Turn into greased 10x6x1 1/2-inch baking dish. Bake at 350° for 25 minutes, or till hot. Sprinkle with paprika. Pass grated Parmesan cheese. Makes 6 servings.

## GOLDEN CHEESE BAKE

OVEN 350°

Simmer 3 cups shredded carrots, 2/3 cup long grain rice, and 1/2 teaspoon salt in 1 1/2 cups water, covered, for 25 minutes. *Do not drain.* Stir in 1 1/2 cups shredded process American cheese, 1 cup milk, 2 beaten eggs, 2 tablespoons instant minced onion, and 1/4 teaspoon pepper. Bake in 1 1/2-quart casserole, uncovered, at 350° about 1 hour. Top with 1/2 cup shredded process American cheese. Heat till cheese melts. Serves 6.

## NOODLES ROMANO

1/4 cup butter or margarine, softened
2 tablespoons dried parsley flakes
1 teaspoon dried basil, crushed
1 8-ounce package cream cheese, softened
1/8 teaspoon pepper

2/3 cup boiling water
8 ounces fettucini, thin noodles, *or* spaghetti
1 clove garlic, minced
1/4 cup butter or margarine
3/4 cup shredded *or* grated Romano *or* Parmesan cheese

Combine ¼ cup butter or margarine, parsley flakes, and basil; blend in cream cheese and pepper; stir in ⅔ cup boiling water; blend mixture well. Keep warm over pan of hot water.

Cook noodles in large amount boiling salted water till just tender; drain. Cook garlic in ¼ cup butter 1 to 2 minutes; pour over noodles; toss lightly and quickly to coat well. Sprinkle with *½ cup of the cheese;* toss again. Pile noodles on warm serving platter; spoon warm cream cheese mixture over; sprinkle with remaining ¼ cup cheese; garnish with additional parsley, if desired. Makes 6 servings.

## MACARONI-CHEESE PUFF

OVEN 325°

Cook ½ cup small elbow macaroni in boiling salted water till tender; drain. Combine 1½ cups milk, 6 ounces sharp process American cheese, shredded (1½ cups), and 3 tablespoons butter; cook and stir over low heat till cheese is melted. Stir small amount of hot mixture into 3 beaten egg yolks; return to hot mixture; blend thoroughly. Add cooked macaroni, 1 cup soft bread crumbs, ¼ cup chopped canned pimiento, 1 tablespoon snipped parsley, and 1 tablespoon grated onion.

Beat 3 egg whites and ¼ teaspoon cream of tartar till stiff peaks form. Gently fold into macaroni mixture. Pour into *ungreased* 1½-quart souffle dish. Bake in a slow oven (325°) for 1 hour, or till set. Serve immediately. Makes 6 servings.

# 9

# DESSERTS

## VANILLA PUDDING

*Delicious served with fresh or canned fruit—*

| | |
|---|---|
| ³/₄ cup sugar | 2 slightly beaten egg |
| 2 tablespoons cornstarch | yolks *or* 1 well-beaten |
| ¹/₄ teaspoon salt | egg |
| 2 cups milk | 2 tablespoons butter or |
| | margarine |
| | 1 teaspoon vanilla |

In saucepan, blend sugar, cornstarch, and salt; add milk. Cook and stir over medium heat till thickened and bubbly. Cook and stir 2 minutes more. Remove from heat. Stir small amount of hot mixture into yolks (or beaten egg); return to hot mixture; cook and stir 2 minutes more. Remove from heat; blend in butter and vanilla. Pour into sherbet dishes; chill. Makes 4 or 5 servings.

**Chocolate Pudding:** Follow directions for Vanilla Pudding, increasing sugar to 1 cup. Add two 1-ounce squares unsweetened chocolate along with the milk.

**Butterscotch Pudding:** Follow directions for Vanilla Pudding, substituting brown sugar for the granulated sugar. Increase the amount of butter or margarine to 3 tablespoons.

## BREAD PUDDING

| | |
|---|---|
| 2 slightly beaten eggs | ¹/₄ teaspoon salt |
| 2¹/₄ cups milk | 2 cups 1-inch day-old |
| 1 teaspoon vanilla | bread cubes |
| ¹/₂ teaspoon ground | ¹/₂ cup brown sugar |
| cinnamon | ¹/₂ cup raisins |

OVEN 350°

Combine eggs, milk, vanilla, cinnamon, and salt; stir in bread cubes. Stir in brown sugar and raisins. Pour mixture into 8x1³/₄-inch round ovenware cake dish. Place pan in larger shallow pan on oven rack; pour hot water into larger pan 1 inch deep. Bake at 350° about 45 minutes or till knife inserted halfway between center and edge comes out clean. Makes 6 servings.

## FLUFFY TAPIOCA PUDDING

| | |
|---|---|
| 1 quart milk | 3 slightly beaten egg |
| 1/4 cup quick-cooking | yolks |
|     tapioca | 1 1/2 teaspoons vanilla |
| 1/2 cup sugar | 3 stiffly beaten egg |
| 1/4 teaspoon salt | whites |

Combine milk, tapioca, sugar, and salt; let stand 5 minutes. Add egg yolks. Bring to boiling, stirring constantly. Remove from heat (mixture will be thin); add vanilla.

Put 1/3 of beaten egg whites in large bowl; slowly stir in tapioca mixture. Fold in remaining egg whites, leaving little "pillows" of egg white. Chill. Pile into sherbets. Garnish with tart jelly. Serves 8 to 10.


## SNOW PUDDING

| | |
|---|---|
| 3/4 cup sugar | 1 teaspoon grated |
| 1 envelope unflavored | lemon peel |
|     gelatin | 1/4 cup lemon juice |
| 1/4 teaspoon salt | 2 egg whites |
| 1 1/4 cups cold water | |

In saucepan, combine sugar, unflavored gelatin, and salt; add 1/2 cup of the cold water. Stir over low heat till dissolved. Remove from heat; add remaining 3/4 cup cold water, lemon peel, and lemon juice. Chill till partially set. Turn into large bowl; add egg whites. Beat with electric mixer till mixture begins to hold its shape. Chill till firm in eight 6-ounce custard cups. Unmold; pass Custard Sauce (page 651).


## COTTAGE PUDDING

OVEN 350°

Cream well 1/2 cup shortening and 3/4 cup sugar; add 1 egg and 1/4 teaspoon lemon extract; beat well. Sift together 1 3/4 cups sifted all-purpose flour, 2 1/2 teaspoons baking powder, and 1/2 teaspoon salt.

Add to creamed mixture alternately with 2/3 cup milk, beating after each addition. Bake in lightly greased and floured 9x9x2-inch baking pan at 350° for 40 to 45 minutes or till cake tests done. Serve warm with Cherry or Lemon Sauce (page 653).

## GLORIFIED RICE

1 8³/₄-ounce can crushed pineapple
²/₃ cup packaged precooked rice
2 teaspoons lemon juice
1¹/₂ cups miniature marshmallows

1 ripe banana, sliced
1 cup whipping cream, whipped
2 tablespoons chopped maraschino cherries

Drain pineapple, reserving syrup. In saucepan, combine uncooked rice, ²/₃ cup water, pineapple syrup, and ¹/₂ teaspoon salt. Stir to moisten rice. Bring quickly to boil; cover; simmer 5 minutes.

Remove from heat; let stand 5 minutes. Add pineapple and lemon juice; cool. Stir in marshmallows and banana. Fold in cream and cherries; chill. Serves 8.

## CHILLED PRUNE WHIP

Combine 1¹/₂ cups dried prunes and 1¹/₂ cups water in saucepan; bring to boiling. Cover and simmer 10 minutes; cool in liquid; drain. Snip prunes from pits in small pieces; set aside. Beat 3 egg whites and ¹/₄ teaspoon salt to soft peaks. Gradually add ¹/₃ cup sugar; beat to stiff peaks. Combine prunes and 2 tablespoons lemon juice; beat till well blended. Fold into egg whites with ¹/₄ cup chopped pecans. Spoon into 6 to 8 sherbets; chill.

## RICE PUDDING

3 slightly beaten eggs
2 cups milk
1¹/₂ cups cooked rice
¹/₂ cup sugar

¹/₂ cup raisins
1 teaspoon vanilla
Ground cinnamon

OVEN 325°

In bowl, combine eggs, milk, rice, sugar, raisins, vanilla, and ¹/₂ teaspoon salt; mix well. Bake in 10x6x2-inch baking dish at 325° for 25 minutes. Stir. Sprinkle with cinnamon. Continue baking till knife inserted halfway between center and edge comes out clean, 20 to 25 minutes longer. Serve warm or chilled with light cream, if desired. Serves 6.

## POTS DE CREME

Break up two 4-ounce packages sweet cooking chocolate. Put *half* of chocolate in blender container. Cover; blend till grated. Repeat with remaining chocolate. In saucepan, mix 2 cups light cream, 2 tablespoons sugar, dash salt, and chocolate. Stir over low heat till blended, smooth, and *slightly thick*. Slowly pour into 6 beaten egg yolks, beating well. Stir in 1 teaspoon vanilla. Pour into 10 pots de creme cups or *small* sherbets. Cover; chill till firm. Serves 10.

## TWO-BERRY PARFAITS

| | |
|---|---|
| 1 10-ounce package frozen raspberries, thawed | 2 cups strawberries, sliced |
| ¼ cup sugar | 2 teaspoons lemon juice |
| 2 tablespoons cornstarch | 1 quart vanilla ice cream |
| | 1 cup dairy sour cream |

Drain raspberries, reserving syrup. Add enough water to syrup to make 1 cup. In saucepan, combine sugar and cornstarch; stir in syrup. Add strawberries. Cook and stir over medium-high heat till mixture thickens and boils. Remove from heat; stir in raspberries and lemon juice; chill. In parfait glasses, layer ice cream, berry sauce, sour cream, and berry sauce. Repeat layers. Makes 6 to 8 servings.

## COFFEE-MALLOW TOWERS

| | |
|---|---|
| 24 regular marshmallows (about 3 cups) | 1 cup whipping cream, whipped |
| 1 tablespoon instant coffee crystals | ½ cup chocolate-wafer crumbs |

In medium saucepan, combine marshmallows, 1 cup water, and coffee crystals. Cook and stir over medium heat till marshmallows melt. Chill till partially set; fold in whipped cream. (If mixture thins, chill about 20 minutes till partially reset.) In parfait glasses, alternate coffee mixture and crumbs, beginning and ending with coffee mixture; chill. Top with whipped cream and chocolate curls. Makes 4 servings.

## BROWNIE PUDDING

1 cup sifted all-purpose flour
3/4 cup granulated sugar
2 tablespoons cocoa (regular-type, dry)
2 teaspoons baking powder
1/2 teaspoon salt

1/2 cup milk
2 tablespoons salad oil
1 teaspoon vanilla
1/2 cup chopped walnuts
3/4 cup brown sugar
1/4 cup cocoa (regular-type, dry)
1 3/4 cups hot water

OVEN 350°

Sift together first 5 ingredients; add milk, oil, and vanilla; mix till smooth. Stir in nuts. Pour into greased 8x8x2-inch baking pan. Combine remaining ingredients; pour over batter. Bake at 350° about 40 minutes. Makes 6 to 8 servings.

## LEMON PUDDING CAKE

3/4 cup sugar
1/4 cup sifted all-purpose flour
3 tablespoons butter, melted
1 teaspoon grated lemon peel

1/4 cup lemon juice
1 1/2 cups milk
3 well-beaten egg yolks
3 stiffly beaten egg whites

OVEN 350°

Combine sugar, dash salt, and flour; stir in melted butter, lemon peel, and juice. Combine milk and egg yolks; add to lemon mixture. Fold in egg whites. Pour into 8x8x2-inch baking pan. Place in larger pan on oven rack. Pour hot water into larger pan, 1 inch deep. Bake at 350° for 40 minutes. Serve warm or chilled. Serves 9.

## DATE-NUT PUDDING

OVEN 350°

Beat 3 eggs 1 minute; beat in ¾ cup sugar. Sift together ¼ cup sifted all-purpose flour, 1 teaspoon baking powder, and ¼ teaspoon salt; fold into egg mixture. Fold in 1 cup chopped dates and ½ cup chopped walnuts. Bake in greased 8x8x2-inch baking pan at 350° about 40 minutes. Serve warm with ice cream. Serves 9.

## REGAL PLUM PUDDING

| | |
|---|---|
| 4 slices bread, torn up | 2 teaspoons ground cinnamon |
| 1 cup milk | |
| 2 slightly beaten eggs | 1 teaspoon ground cloves |
| 1 cup light brown sugar | |
| ¼ cup orange juice | 1 teaspoon ground mace |
| 6 ounces finely chopped suet | 2 cups raisins |
| 1 teaspoon vanilla | 1 cup pitted dates, cut up |
| 1 cup sifted all-purpose flour | ½ cup chopped mixed candied fruits and peels |
| 1 teaspoon soda | |
| ½ teaspoon salt | ½ cup broken walnuts |

Soak bread in milk; beat. Stir in next 5 ingredients. Sift together dry ingredients; add fruits and nuts; mix well. Stir in bread mixture. Pour into well-greased 2-quart mold. Cover with foil; tie with string.

Place on rack in deep kettle; add boiling water, 1 inch deep. Cover; steam 3½ hours, adding water if needed. Cool 10 minutes; unmold. Serve warm with Hard Sauce (page 652). Serves 12.

## GRAHAM CRACKER PUDDING

| | |
|---|---|
| ¼ cup shortening | 2 cups fine graham-cracker crumbs |
| ⅓ cup sugar | |
| 1 teaspoon vanilla | 1 teaspoon baking powder |
| 1 egg yolk | |
| ½ cup raisins or chopped dates | ⅔ cup milk |
| ¼ cup chopped walnuts | 1 stiffly beaten egg white |

OVEN 350°

Cream shortening, sugar, and vanilla; add egg yolk; beat well. Stir in fruit and nuts. Mix crumbs, baking powder, and ¼ teaspoon salt. Add to creamed mixture alternately with milk. Fold in egg white. Fill six greased 6-ounce custard cups. Bake at 350° for 25 to 30 minutes. Serve warm with Lemon Sauce or whipped cream.

## BAKED CUSTARD

| | |
|---|---|
| 3 slightly beaten eggs | 2 cups milk, scalded |
| ¼ cup sugar | ½ teaspoon vanilla |

OVEN 325°

Combine eggs, sugar, and ¼ teaspoon salt. Slowly stir in lightly cooled milk and vanilla. Fill six 6-ounce custard cups*; set in shallow pan on oven rack. Pour hot water into pan, 1 inch deep. Bake at 325° for 40 to 45 minutes, or till knife inserted off-center comes out clean. Serve warm or chilled. To unmold chilled custard, first loosen edge; then slip point of knife down side to let air in. Invert.

*For one large custard, bake in 1-quart casserole about 60 minutes.

For delicate stirred custard, cook just till mixture evenly coats a metal spoon. Remove from heat; cool immediately.

To test doneness of baked custard, insert knife halfway between center and edge. A clean knife indicates custard is done.

## CARAMEL CUSTARD

Melt 12 vanilla caramels in 1/4 cup milk over low heat, stirring constantly. Divide sauce among six 5-ounce custard cups. Prepare Baked Custard (page 397); pour over sauce; bake. Serve warm, or chill and unmold.

## STIRRED CUSTARD

Combine ingredients except vanilla as for Baked Custard (page 397). Cook in double boiler, placing pan over, *not touching*, boiling water; stir constantly. When custard coats metal spoon, remove from heat (page 397). Cool at once—place pan in cold water; stir 1 to 2 minutes; add vanilla. Chill. Serves 6.

## CREME BRULEE

Prepare Stirred Custard using light cream instead of milk. Cook 2 minutes *after* it coats spoon; cool and stir in vanilla. Pour into 1-quart shallow baking dish; chill. Sift 1/2 cup brown sugar over. Set in shallow pan of ice cubes and cold water. Broil 5 inches from heat 1 to 2 minutes or till bubbly crust forms. Serve warm or chilled.

## BERRY FLOATING ISLAND

|  |  |
|---|---|
| Poached Meringues | Milk |
| 3 eggs | 1 1/2 teaspoons vanilla |
| 2 egg yolks | 2 cups strawberries |
| 1/2 cup sugar | |

*Poached Meringues:* Beat 2 egg whites with dash salt to soft peaks. Gradually add 1/4 cup sugar, beating to stiff peaks. In skillet, heat 3 cups milk to simmer. Drop meringue onto milk in 6 mounds. Cook slowly uncovered, till set, about 5 minutes. Lift from milk; drain on paper towels.

Beat 3 eggs and 2 egg yolks slightly; add sugar and dash salt. Stir in 3 cups slightly cooled milk (from meringues plus extra). Cook in double boiler, placing pan over, *not touching*, boiling water; stir constantly. When custard coats metal spoon, remove from heat; cool quickly. Add vanilla. Place berries in dish; pour custard over. Top with meringues. Chill. Serves 6.

## MERINGUE SHELL

3 egg whites
1 teaspoon vanilla

¼ teaspoon cream of
tartar
1 cup sugar

OVEN 275°

Have egg whites at room temperature. Add vanilla, cream of tartar, and dash salt. Beat to soft peaks. *Gradually* add sugar, beating till very stiff peaks form. (Meringue will be glossy.)

Cover baking sheet with plain ungreased brown paper. Using 9-inch round cake pan as guide, draw circle on paper. Spread meringue over circle. Shape into shell with back of spoon, making bottom ½ inch thick and sides about 1¾ inches high. Bake at 275° for 1 hour. Turn off heat and let dry in oven (door closed) at least 2 hours. Fill with ice cream and sauce, or fresh fruit. Makes 8 servings.

## INDIVIDUAL MERINGUES

OVEN 275°

Make meringue as for Meringue Shell above. Cover baking sheet with plain ungreased brown paper. Draw 8 circles, 3½ inches in diameter; spread each with ⅓ cup meringue. Using back of spoon, shape into shells; form a hollow in center.

Bake meringues at 275° for 1 hour. For crisper meringues, turn off heat and let dry in oven (door closed) about 1 hour.

Fill with ice cream, pudding mixtures, or fresh fruit. Makes 8 servings.

To make 3½ inch circles, use a compass or trace around a jar lid. Use a spoon to shape meringue mixture into shells.

## CHEESECAKE SUPREME

Crust:
- ¾ cup all-purpose flour
- 3 tablespoons sugar
- ½ teaspoon grated lemon peel

Filling:
- 3 8-ounce packages cream cheese
- ¼ teaspoon vanilla
- ¼ teaspoon grated lemon peel
- 1 cup sugar

- 6 tablespoons butter
- 1 slightly beaten egg yolk
- ¼ tsp. grated lemon peel
- 2 tablespoons all-purpose flour
- ¼ teaspoon salt
- 2 eggs
- 1 egg yolk
- ¼ cup milk
- Strawberry Glaze

OVEN 400°

*Crust:* Combine the first 3 ingredients. Cut in the butter till crumbly. Add egg yolk and vanilla; mix well. Pat ⅓ of dough on bottom of 8-inch spring-form pan (sides removed). Bake at 400° about 7 minutes or till golden; cool. Butter sides of pan; attach to bottom. Pat remaining dough on sides of pan to height of 1¾ inches.

*Filling:* Let the cream cheese stand at room temperature to soften (1 to 1½ hours). Beat till creamy; add vanilla and lemon peel. Mix sugar, flour, and salt; gradually blend into cheese. Add eggs and egg yolk all at once; beat just till blended. Gently stir in milk.

Turn into crust-lined pan. Bake at 450° for 10 minutes; reduce heat to 300°; bake 55 minutes or till center appears set. Remove from oven; cool 15 minutes; loosen sides of cheesecake from pan with spatula. Cool ½ hour more; remove sides of pan. Cool 2 hours longer. Meanwhile, prepare Strawberry Glaze. Place 1 cup halved fresh strawberries on cooled cheesecake. Pour glaze over strawberries. Chill 2 hours. Makes 12 servings.

*Strawberry Glaze:* Crush ¾ cup fresh strawberries; add ½ cup water. Cook 2 minutes; sieve. In saucepan, combine ⅓ cup sugar and 4 teaspoons cornstarch; gradually stir in berry mixture. Bring to boil; stir constantly. Cook and stir till thick and clear. (Add few drops red food coloring, if needed.) Cool to room temperature.

## LEMON CHEESECAKE

Crumb Crust
1 cup sugar
2 envelopes unflavored gelatin
1/4 teaspoon salt
1 6-ounce can (2/3 cup) evaporated milk
2 beaten egg yolks
1 teaspoon grated lemon peel

2 12-ounce cartons (3 cups) cream-style cottage cheese, sieved
2 tablespoons lemon juice
1 teaspoon vanilla
2 egg whites
1 cup whipping cream, whipped

*Crumb Crust:* In bowl, mix 1 cup zwieback crumbs, 1/4 cup sugar, 3/4 teaspoon ground cinnamon, 1/4 teaspoon ground nutmeg, and 1/4 cup butter, melted. Mix till crumbly. Reserve 1/4 cup for garnish; press remainder on bottom and sides of buttered 9-inch spring-form pan. Chill.

In a saucepan, combine 3/4 *cup* sugar, gelatin, and salt. Stir in evaporated milk, then egg yolks. Cook and stir over low heat till gelatin dissolves. Add lemon peel; cool at room temperature for 30 minutes. Stir in cottage cheese, lemon juice, and vanilla. Chill, stirring occasionally, till mixture mounds. Beat egg whites to soft peaks; gradually add 1/4 cup sugar, beating to stiff peaks. Fold into gelatin mixture. Fold in whipped cream. Pour into chilled crust; sprinkle with reserved crumbs. Chill overnight. Serves 8.

## COMPANY CHEESECAKE

OVEN 375°

Combine 1 3/4 cups fine graham-cracker crumbs, 1/4 cup finely chopped walnuts, 1/2 teaspoon ground cinnamon, and 1/2 cup butter, melted. Press on bottom and up 2/3 of sides of 9-inch spring-form pan.

Beat smooth 3 well-beaten eggs, two 8-ounce packages cream cheese, softened, 1 cup sugar, 1/4 teaspoon salt, 2 teaspoons vanilla, and 1/4 teaspoon almond extract.

Blend in 3 cups dairy sour cream. Pour into crust. Bake at 375° about 35 minutes or just till set; cool. Chill 4 to 5 hours. (Filling will be soft.) Serves 12 to 16.

## CHOCOLATE CHARLOTTE RUSSE

Soften 1 envelope (1 tablespoon) unflavored gelatin in ¼ cup cold water. Melt three 1-ounce squares unsweetened chocolate in ½ cup water over low heat, stirring constantly. Remove from heat; add softened gelatin; stir to dissolve. Beat 4 egg yolks till thick and lemon-colored; gradually beat in ½ cup sugar. Add 1 teaspoon vanilla and dash salt. Gradually stir in chocolate mixture. Cool to room temperature; stir till smooth.

Beat 4 egg whites and ½ teaspoon cream of tartar to soft peaks. Gradually add ¼ cup sugar, beating to stiff peaks. Fold into chocolate mixture. Fold in 1 cup whipping cream, whipped.

Split 16 whole ladyfingers lengthwise. Line bottom and sides of 9-inch spring-form pan (cut about ½ inch off bottoms of ladyfingers that stand around sides). Fill with *half* the chocolate mixture. Add another layer of split ladyfingers. Add remaining chocolate mixture. Sprinkle toasted slivered almonds atop, if desired. Chill 8 hours or overnight. Remove sides. Makes 12 to 16 servings.

## BERRY MERINGUE TORTE

| | |
|---|---|
| 1½ cups vanilla-wafer crumbs | 1 pint fresh red raspberries, slightly sweetened |
| ¼ cup butter, melted | |
| 2 tablespoons sugar | 1 2-ounce package dessert topping mix |
| 4 egg whites | |
| ½ cup sugar | 1 tablespoon lemon juice |

OVEN 325°

Combine crumbs, butter, and the 2 tablespoons sugar; mix well. Press firmly in bottom of 9x9x2-inch baking pan. Beat egg whites to soft peaks; gradually add the ½ cup sugar, beating to stiff peaks.

Swirl meringue over crust. Bake at 325° for 12 to 15 minutes; cool. Spread berries over meringue. Prepare dessert topping mix according to package directions. Gently stir in lemon juice. Spread over berries; chill. Cut in 9 squares.

## CHOCOLATE MINT DESSERT

2 tablespoons butter
½ cup graham-cracker crumbs
½ cup sugar
1 envelope unflavored gelatin
2 tablespoons cornstarch
2 cups milk
3 slightly beaten egg yolks

3 egg whites
¼ cup sugar
½ cup whipping cream, whipped
1½ teaspoons creme de menthe syrup
2 1-ounce squares unsweetened chocolate, melted

Melt butter; stir in crumbs. Reserve 1 tablespoon; spread remainder in 10x6x1½-inch dish. Mix sugar, gelatin, and cornstarch; add milk. Cook and stir to boiling. Add small amount hot mixture to egg yolks; return to hot mixture; cook 1 minute. Cool till partially thickened.

Beat egg whites to soft peaks; gradually add ¼ cup sugar, beating to stiff peaks. Fold into custard; then fold in whipped cream. Add syrup to 1½ *cups* of mixture. Stir chocolate into remaining mixture; spread *half* over crumbs. Cover with mint layer, then rest of chocolate. Top with reserved crumbs. Chill firm. Serves 6.

## STRAWBERRY SQUARES

1 cup sifted all-purpose flour
¼ cup brown sugar
½ cup chopped walnuts
½ cup butter, melted
2 egg whites

1 cup granulated sugar
2 cups sliced strawberries*
2 tablespoons lemon juice
1 cup whipping cream

OVEN 350°

Mix first 4 ingredients; bake in shallow pan at 350° for 20 minutes; stir occasionally. Sprinkle ⅔ *crumbs* in 13x9x2-inch pan. Combine egg whites, granulated sugar, berries, and lemon juice. Beat at high speed about 10 minutes. Whip cream; fold in. Spoon over crumbs. Top with remaining crumbs. Freeze 6 hours. Serves 12.

*Or 10-ounces frozen berries, thawed. Reduce granulated sugar to ⅔ cup.

## PINEAPPLE CREAM LOAF

<table>
<tr><td>1/2 cup butter or margarine</td><td>1 8³/4-ounce can crushed pineapple, drained (³/4 cup)</td></tr>
<tr><td>1¹/2 cups sifted confectioners' sugar</td><td>1 cup dairy sour cream</td></tr>
<tr><td>2 egg yolks</td><td>2 stiffly beaten egg whites</td></tr>
<tr><td>1/2 teaspoon lemon extract</td><td>8 ladyfingers, split lengthwise</td></tr>
</table>

Cream butter and sugar together till fluffy. Add egg yolks, one at a time, beating after each. Stir in lemon extract and pineapple; fold in sour cream and egg whites. Line bottom of 9x5x3-inch loaf pan with *half* the ladyfingers; top with *half* the pineapple mixture; repeat layers. Chill 6 to 8 hours. Makes 8 to 10 servings.

## AMBROSIA

<table>
<tr><td>1 13¹/2-ounce can frozen pineapple chunks, thawed</td><td>1 cup seedless grapes or halved grapes, seeded</td></tr>
<tr><td>1 ripe banana, peeled</td><td>²/3 cup flaked coconut</td></tr>
<tr><td>3 medium oranges, sectioned</td><td>1/2 cup ginger ale (optional)</td></tr>
</table>

Drain thawed pineapple, reserving syrup. Slice peeled banana on bias, dipping into pineapple syrup. Arrange *half* of each fruit in bowl; top with *half* the coconut, then rest of fruit. Pour pineapple syrup over; chill. At serving time, pour ginger ale over top, if desired. Top with remaining coconut. Makes 4 to 6 servings.

## RUBY FRUIT COMPOTE

Drain one 1-pound 4-ounce can frozen pitted tart red cherries, thawed, and one 10-ounce package frozen raspberries, thawed, reserving syrups. Add enough water to syrups to make 2¹/2 cups. Blend 1¹/2 tablespoons cornstarch, dash salt, and syrup mixture. Cook and stir till thick and bubbly. Add 1 tablespoon lemon juice. Stir in drained fruits and 2 cups fresh whole strawberries. Chill.

Spoon into sherbets; top with sour cream, if desired.
Makes 8 servings.

## FREEZING ICE CREAM

Pour ice cream mixture into freezer can (cool mixture
first, if cooked). Fill can only ⅔ full. Fit can into freezer.
If using electric ice cream freezer, follow manufacturer's
directions.

Adjust dasher and cover. Pack crushed ice and rock
salt around can, using 6 parts ice to 1 part salt. Turn
dasher slowly till ice partially melts and forms brine—add
more ice and salt to maintain ice level. Turn handle constantly till crank turns hard. Remove ice to below lid of
can; remove lid and dasher.

*To ripen ice cream:* Plug opening in lid. Cover can with
several thicknesses of waxed paper or foil for tight fit;
replace lid. Pack more ice and salt (use 4 parts ice to 1
part salt) around can to fill freezer. Cover freezer with
heavy cloth or newspapers. Let ice cream ripen about
4 hours.

## VANILLA ICE CREAM

| | |
|---|---|
| 4 eggs | 3 cups whipping cream |
| 2½ cups sugar | 2½ tablespoons vanilla |
| 7 cups milk | ½ teaspoon salt |

Beat eggs till light. Add sugar gradually, beating till thick.
Add remaining ingredients; mix well. Freeze in 5-quart
ice cream freezer. Makes 1 gallon.

## VANILLA CUSTARD ICE CREAM

| | |
|---|---|
| ¾ cup sugar | 2 cups milk |
| 2 tablespoons all-purpose flour | 2 beaten eggs |
| | 2 cups whipping cream |
| ¼ teaspoon salt | 1½ tablespoons vanilla |

Combine sugar, flour, and salt; gradually stir in milk.
Cook and stir over low heat till thick. Add small amount
of hot mixture to eggs; mix well; return to hot mixture.
Cook and stir 1 minute. Chill.

Stir in cream and vanilla. Freeze in ice cream freezer. Makes 1¹/₄ quarts.

## COFFEE ICE CREAM

Make Vanilla Custard Ice Cream page 405; use 1¹/₂ teaspoons vanilla. Add 1¹/₂ tablespoons instant coffee powder with vanilla.

## CHOCO-ALMOND VELVET

Combine ²/₃ cup canned chocolate syrup, ²/₃ cup sweetened *condensed* milk, 2 cups whipping cream, and ¹/₂ teaspoon vanilla; chill. Whip to soft peaks. Fold in ¹/₃ cup toasted slivered almonds. Freeze firm in refrigerator tray. Serves 8 to 10.

## STRAWBERRY ICE CREAM

| | |
|---|---|
| 1 envelope unflavored gelatin | 2 cups crushed strawberries |
| 2 well-beaten egg yolks | 2 cups whipping cream |
| ³/₄ cup sugar | 2 egg whites |
| ¹/₄ teaspoon salt | ¹/₄ cup sugar |
| 1¹/₂ teaspoons vanilla | |

Soften gelatin in ¹/₄ cup cold water. Dissolve over hot water. Combine next 6 ingredients; add gelatin; mix well. Freeze in refrigerator trays. Beat egg whites to soft peaks; gradually add ¹/₄ cup sugar, beating to stiff peaks. Break frozen mixture in chunks; beat till fluffy with electric mixer. Fold in egg whites. Return to *cold* trays; freeze firm. Serves 8 to 10.

## PEPPERMINT ICE CREAM

| | |
|---|---|
| 1 envelope unflavored gelatin | 1 9-ounce package peppermint stick candy, crushed (1¹/₄ cups) |
| ¹/₂ cup cold milk | |
| 1¹/₂ cups milk, scalded | 2 cups whipping cream, whipped |

Soften gelatin in cold milk; dissolve in hot milk. Add $1/4$ teaspoon salt and all but $1/4$ cup candy to hot milk; stir to dissolve. Freeze in refrigerator tray. Break up; beat smooth with electric mixer. Fold in cream and reserved candy. Tint pink. Freeze in refrigerator tray. Serves 6 to 8.

## PEACH ICE CREAM

| | |
|---|---|
| 2 cups finely chopped peaches | 1 cup whipping cream, whipped |
| $1/4$ cup sugar | $1/3$ cup slivered almonds, toasted |
| 1 15-ounce can ($1^1/3$ cups) sweetened *condensed* milk | |

To peaches, add sugar and $1/4$ cup water; mash. Add 1 to 2 drops *each* red and yellow food coloring. Drain, reserving juice. Add water to juice to make $3/4$ cup. Combine peaches, juice, and milk; pour into refrigerator trays. Freeze till firm. Break into chunks; beat fluffy with electric mixer. Fold in whipped cream and nuts. Return to trays. Freeze firm. Serves 8 to 10.

## REFRIGERATOR VANILLA ICE CREAM

| | |
|---|---|
| 1 rennet tablet | $1^1/4$ teaspoons vanilla |
| 1 cup light cream | 1 cup whipping cream, whipped |
| $1/2$ cup sugar | |

Crush rennet tablet in 1 tablespoon cold water; dissolve. Combine the light cream and sugar; heat slowly till warm (110°), not hot. Stir in rennet mixture. Add vanilla; stir quickly for a few seconds. Pour into refrigerator tray. Let mixture stand at room temperature for 10 minutes.

Freeze firm. Break in chunks with wooden spoon; turn into chilled bowl; beat smooth with electric mixer. Fold in whipped cream. Return quickly to *cold* tray; freeze firm. Makes 4 to 6 servings.

## LEMON SHERBET

Combine $3/4$ cup sugar, dash salt, and 1 cup water; bring to boiling; simmer 5 minutes. Cool. Add $1/2$ cup light cream, then ¹/₂ cup lemon juice. Pour into refrigerator tray; freeze till firm.

Beat 2 egg whites to soft peaks; gradually add ¹/₄ cup sugar, beating to stiff peaks. Break frozen mixture into chunks with wooden spoon; turn into chilled bowl. Beat with electric or rotary beater till smooth. Fold in egg whites. Return quickly to *cold* tray; freeze firm. Serves 6.

## PINEAPPLE SHERBET

| | |
|---|---|
| ¹/₂ envelope (1¹/₂ teaspoons) unflavored gelatin | ³/₄ cup sugar |
| | 1 8³/₄-ounce can (1 cup) crushed pineapple |
| 2 tablespoons cold water | 1 teaspoon vanilla |
| 2 cups buttermilk *or* sour milk | 1 egg white |
| | ¹/₄ cup sugar |

Soften gelatin in cold water; dissolve over hot water. Combine buttermilk *or* sour milk, ³/₄ cup sugar, pineapple, vanilla, and gelatin; mix well. Turn into refrigerator tray. Freeze till firm.

Break in chunks; turn into chilled bowl; beat smooth with electric or rotary beater. Beat egg white to soft peaks; gradually add ¹/₄ cup sugar, beating to stiff peaks. Fold into pineapple mixture. Return to *cold* tray. Freeze firm. Serves 4 to 6.

## TUTTI-FRUTTI TORTONI

Stir 1 pint vanilla ice cream to soften. Add ¹/₄ cup chopped mixed candied fruits and peels, ¹/₄ cup raisins, and 1¹/₄ teaspoons rum flavoring. Spoon into 4 to 5 paper bake cups set in a muffin pan. Top each with a maraschino cherry half and whole toasted almonds. Freeze till firm.

## BAKED ALASKA

OVEN 500°

Trim a 1-inch-thick piece of sponge *or* layer cake 1 inch larger on all sides than 1 quart *or* 2 pints brick-style ice cream*; place cake on plate. Center ice cream on cake (place pints side by side). Cover; freeze firm. At serving time, beat 5 egg whites with 1 teaspoon vanilla and ¹/₂ teaspoon cream of tartar till soft peaks form. Gradually add ⅔ cup sugar, beating till stiff peaks form. Transfer cake with ice cream to baking sheet; spread with egg white mixture, sealing to edges of cake all around. Swirl to make peaks. Bake at 500° till golden, about 3 minutes. Slice; serve immediately. Makes 8 servings.

*Note:* If using half of ½ gallon ice cream, cut in half lengthwise.

## PUFF PASTRY

Chill 1 cup butter or margarine. Reserve 2 tablespoons; chill. Work remaining chilled butter with back of wooden spoon just till pliable. Pat or roll between sheets of waxed paper to 8x6-inch rectangle. Chill at least 1 hour in refrigerator or 20 minutes in freezer. (Chill utensils before each use.)

Cut reserved 2 tablespoons butter into 1¾ cups sifted all-purpose flour till mixture resembles coarse meal. Gradually add ½ cup ice water, tossing with fork to make stiff dough. Shape in ball. Knead on *lightly* floured surface till smooth and elastic, about 5 minutes. Cover dough; let rest 10 minutes.

On lightly floured surface, roll dough in 15x9-inch rectangle. Peel waxed paper from one side of chilled butter; invert on half of dough. Remove waxed paper on top. Fold dough over to cover butter. Seal edges of dough. Wrap in waxed paper; chill thoroughly (1 hour).

Unwrap dough. On *lightly* floured surface, roll to 15x9-inch rectangle. (Roll from center just to edges.) Brush off excess flour; fold in thirds, then turn dough and fold in thirds again. Press edges to seal. Wrap and chill at least 1 hour. Repeat rolling, folding, and thorough chilling 2 or 3 times more. Shape Napoleons.

## NAPOLEONS

OVEN 450°

Roll Puff Pastry into 14x8-inch rectangle, ⅜ inch thick. Cut off all edges. Prick dough well with fork. Cut in sixteen 3½x2-inch rectangles. Place on baking sheets covered with 3 or 4 thicknesses of paper towels. Chill well. Brush with mixture of 1 slightly beaten egg white and 1 table-spoon ice water.

Bake at 450° for 6 minutes, then at 300° for 25 to 30 minutes, till lightly browned and crisp. Remove from pan; cool on rack. (If baked ahead, place on baking sheet covered with 4 thicknesses of paper towels; heat at 300° about 10 minutes.) Separate each pastry into layers. Spread between layers with French Custard Filling (page 264); glaze tops with thinned Confectioners' Icing (page 258). Makes 16.

## ITALIAN SPUMONI

1¹/₂ pints vanilla ice cream
Rum flavoring to taste
6 maraschino cherries
1¹/₂ pints pistachio ice cream
¹/₃ cup chopped pistachio nuts

³/₄ cup whipping cream
¹/₃ cup instant cocoa (dry)
1 10-ounce package frozen red raspberries, thawed
¹/₂ cup whipping cream
¹/₄ cup sifted confectioners' sugar

Chill 2-quart metal mold in freezer. Stir vanilla ice cream just to soften; stir in rum flavoring. Refreeze till work-able. Spread quickly in layer over bottom and sides of mold, bringing ice cream all the way to top. (If it tends to slip, refreeze till workable.) Circle cherries around bottom. Freeze.

Stir pistachio ice cream to soften; stir in nuts. Refreeze till workable. Quickly spread over first layer. Freeze.

Combine ³/₄ cup cream and cocoa; whip to peaks. Quickly spread over pistachio layer. Freeze. Drain berries (discard syrup); sieve. Mix ¹/₂ cup cream, sugar, and dash salt; whip to peaks. Fold in berry pulp. Pile into mold; smooth top. Cover with foil. Freeze 6 hours. Peel off foil. Invert on chilled plate. Rub mold with hot towel; lift off mold. Cut in wedges to serve. Makes 12 to 16 servings.

## CREAM PUFFS

| | |
|---|---|
| ½ cup butter or margarine | 1 cup sifted all-purpose flour |
| 1 cup boiling water | ¼ teaspoon salt |
| | 4 eggs |

OVEN 400°

Melt butter in 1 cup boiling water. Add flour and salt all at once; stir vigorously. Cook and stir till mixture forms a ball that doesn't separate. Remove from heat; cool slightly. Add eggs, one at a time, beating after each till smooth.

Drop by heaping tablespoons 3 inches apart on greased cookie sheet. Bake at 400° till golden brown and puffy, about 30 minutes. Remove from oven; split. Cool on rack. Makes 10.

## RASPBERRY BOMBE

| | |
|---|---|
| 3 pints red raspberry sherbet | Dash salt |
| 2 pints pink peppermint or strawberry ice cream | ¼ cup finely chopped mixed candied fruits and peels |
| * * * | ¼ cup finely chopped almonds, toasted |
| 1 cup whipping cream | Rum flavoring to taste |
| 3 tablespoons confectioners' sugar | |

Chill a 2½-quart metal mold in freezer. Stir sherbet just to soften. With chilled spoon, quickly spread over bottom and sides of mold; be sure sherbet comes to top. (If it slips down, refreeze in mold till workable.) Freeze firm.

Stir the ice cream just to soften. Quickly spread over raspberry layer, covering completely. Freeze firm. Whip cream with sugar and salt to soft peaks. Fold in fruits, nuts, and flavoring. Pile into center of mold, smoothing top. Cover with foil; freeze 6 hours or overnight. Peel off foil. Invert mold on *chilled* plate. Rub mold with hot damp towel to loosen; lift off mold. Serves 12 to 16.

## ECLAIRS

Mix dough as directed for Cream Puffs (page 411). Put through a pastry tube or paper cone making 4-inch strips, ³/₄ inch wide on greased cookie sheet. Bake, split, and cool as for Cream Puffs. Frost with chocolate icing. Fill with double recipe of French Custard Filling (page 264) just before serving. Makes 14 eclairs.

## CHOCOLATE SOUFFLE

OVEN 325°

Beat 3 egg yolks till thick and lemon-colored; set aside. In saucepan, melt 2 tablespoons butter. Stir in 2 tablespoons all-purpose flour and ¼ teaspoon salt. Add ³/₄ cup milk all at once. Cook, stirring constantly, till mixture is thickened and bubbly. Stir moderate amount of hot mixture into beaten egg yolks; mix well. Return to remaining hot mixture in saucepan; cook and stir 2 minutes. Remove from heat.

Stir together two 1-ounce squares unsweetened chocolate, melted and cooled, ¼ cup sugar, and 2 tablespoons hot water. Stir chocolate mixture into egg mixture.

Beat 3 egg whites and ½ teaspoon vanilla till soft peaks form; gradually add ¼ cup sugar, beating to stiff peaks. Fold the egg whites into chocolate mixture. Turn into 1¹/₂-quart souffle dish. Bake at 325° till knife inserted just off-center comes out clean, 55 to 60 minutes. Serve immediately with sweetened whipped cream. Serves 6.

## ORANGE SOUFFLE

OVEN 325°

Melt ¼ cup butter; blend in ¹/₃ cup all-purpose flour and dash salt. Add 1 cup milk. Cook and stir till thickened and bubbly. Remove from heat; stir in 1 teaspoon grated orange peel and ½ cup orange juice. Beat 6 egg yolks till thick and lemon-colored (5 minutes). Slowly add orange mixture to egg yolks; stir constantly.

Beat 6 egg whites to soft peaks. Gradually add ¼ cup sugar, beating to stiff peaks. Carefully fold orange mixture into whites. Pour into *ungreased* 2-quart souffle dish with foil collar. (Measure foil to go around dish; fold in thirds. Butter well; sprinkle with sugar. Extend collar 2 inches above dish; fasten with tape.)

Bake at 325° for 1 hour and 15 minutes or till knife inserted halfway between center and edge comes out clean. Serve at once with Orange Sauce. Serves 8 to 10.

*Orange Sauce:* Combine ½ cup sugar, 2 tablespoons cornstarch, and dash salt. Stir in 1½ cups orange juice. Cook and stir till thick and boiling. Remove from heat; add 1 tablespoon butter and 1 orange, sectioned and diced. Serve warm.

## CHOCOLATE-MINT FONDUE

1 15-ounce can sweetened condensed milk

1 1-pint jar marshmallow creme

1 6-ounce package semisweet chocolate pieces

⅓ cup crushed butter mints

¼ cup milk

2 tablespoons creme de cacao

Apple or banana dippers

In saucepan, combine first 4 ingredients. Cook and stir over low heat till chocolate melts. Stir in milk and creme de cacao. Transfer to fondue pot; place over fondue burner. Spear dipper with fondue fork; dip into fondue. Makes 6 to 8 servings.

## CHERRY PUFF

OVEN 325°

Drain a 1-pound 4-ounce can pitted tart red cherries (water pack), reserving ½ cup liquid. Chop cherries; add liquid, ½ cup sugar, and 2 tablespoons quick-cooking tapioca. Cook and stir till thickened. Beat 2 egg whites, ¼ teaspoon cream of tartar, and dash salt to soft peaks; gradually add ⅓ cup sugar, beating to stiff peaks. Beat 2 egg yolks till thick and lemon-colored. Fold yolks into whites. Sift ⅓ cup sifted cake flour over; fold in. Pour cherry mixture into 8x8x2-inch baking dish. Pour batter over. Bake at 325° for 30 minutes. Serve warm with ice cream. Serves 6.

## LEMON-ANGEL DESSERT

Mix 1/2 cup sugar, 1 envelope unflavored gelatin, and dash salt; add 2 beaten eggs and 1/2 cup water. Cook and stir till gelatin dissolves and mixture thickens slightly. Remove from heat; stir in one 6-ounce can frozen lemonade concentrate, thawed, and few drops yellow food coloring. Chill till just partially set. Chill one 14 1/2-ounce can evaporated milk *icy cold;* whip in chilled bowl. Fold into gelatin mixture. Rub brown crumbs from 10-inch angel cake. Tear cake into bite-size pieces. Cover bottom of 10-inch tube pan with thin layer of gelatin mixture. Arrange 1/3 of cake on top. Pour 1/3 remaining gelatin over. Repeat twice. Chill firm. Unmold. Serves 12.

## KONA COFFEE TORTE

1 1/2 tablespoons instant coffee powder
1 cup cold water
6 egg yolks
2 cups sugar
* * *
2 cups sifted all-purpose flour

3 teaspoons baking powder
1/4 teaspoon salt
1 teaspoon vanilla
1 cup ground walnuts
6 stiffly beaten egg whites
Orange Filling
Mocha Frosting

OVEN 325°

Dissolve coffee powder in 1 cup cold water. Beat yolks till light and fluffy. Gradually add sugar, beating till thick. Sift together dry ingredients; add to yolks alternately with coffee, beating after each addition. Add vanilla and nuts. Fold in stiffly beaten egg whites.

Bake in 3 paper-lined 9x1 1/2-inch round pans in slow oven (325°) for 30 minutes or till done. Cool 10 minutes. Remove from pans; cool. Fill cake with Orange Filling; frost top with Mocha Frosting.

*Orange Filling:* Cream 1 cup butter or margarine. Add 2 cups sifted confectioners' sugar; cream well. Beat in 2 teaspoons cocoa (regular-type, dry), 1/2 teaspoon instant coffee powder, and 2 tablespoons *each* cold water and orange juice.

*Mocha Frosting:* Mix 2 cups sifted confectioners' sugar,

2 teaspoons cocoa (regular-type, dry), and $\frac{1}{2}$ teaspoon instant coffee powder; add 2 tablespoons cold water, 3 tablespoons butter, melted, and $\frac{1}{2}$ teaspoon vanilla. Beat till frosting is of spreading consistency.

## BROWNIE TORTE

OVEN 325°

Beat 3 egg whites, $\frac{1}{2}$ teaspoon vanilla, and dash salt to soft peaks. Gradually add $\frac{3}{4}$ cup sugar; beat to stiff peaks. Fold in $\frac{3}{4}$ cup fine chocolate-wafer crumbs and $\frac{1}{2}$ cup chopped walnuts. Spread in buttered 9-inch pie plate. Bake in a slow oven (325°) for 35 minutes. Cool well; top with sweetened whipped cream; chill 3 to 4 hours. Trim with chocolate curls.

## LEMON ANGEL TORTE

OVEN 450°

*Torte Shell:* Beat 4 egg whites with electric mixer till foamy. Add $\frac{1}{4}$ teaspoon *each* salt and cream of tartar. Gradually beat in $\frac{3}{4}$ cup sugar, beating to very stiff peaks, about 7 minutes. Spread in *well-buttered* 9-inch pie plate. Place in 450° *preheated* oven; turn off heat. Let stand in closed oven 5 hours or overnight (don't peek).

*Filling:* In top of double boiler, beat 4 egg yolks till thick and lemon-colored. Gradually beat in 1 tablespoon grated lemon peel, 3 tablespoons lemon juice, $\frac{1}{2}$ cup sugar, and dash salt. Stir over boiling water till thick, 8 minutes; cover; cool.

Whip 1 cup whipping cream. Spread *half* the cream in shell. Spoon in Filling; cover Filling and entire shell with rest of cream. Chill 5 hours or overnight. Serves 8.

## APPLE DUMPLINGS

2 cups water
1½ cups sugar
¼ teaspoon ground cinnamon
¼ teaspoon ground nutmeg
8 drops red food coloring
¼ cup butter or margarine

2 cups sifted all-purpose flour
2 teaspoons baking powder
1 teaspoon salt
¾ cup shortening
½ cup milk
6 small, whole apples, pared and cored

OVEN 375°

For syrup, mix first 5 ingredients; cook 5 minutes. Remove from heat; add butter.

Sift together dry ingredients; cut in shortening till mixture resembles coarse crumbs. Add milk all at once; stir just till flour is moistened. On lightly floured surface, roll to 18x12-inch rectangle.

Cut in six 6-inch squares. Place apple on each. Sprinkle apples generously with additional sugar, cinnamon, and nutmeg; dot with additional butter. Moisten edges of pastry. Bring corners to center and pinch edges together. Place 1 inch apart in ungreased 13x9x2-inch baking pan. Pour syrup over dumplings. Bake at 375° for 35 to 40 minutes. Serve warm with cream. Makes 6 servings.

## BAKED APPLES

OVEN 350°

Core 6 large baking apples; pare strip from top of each. Place in 10x6x1½-inch baking dish. Fill apples with ¾ cup raisins or chopped dates.

Combine I cup brown sugar, 1 cup water, 2 tablespoons butter, ½ teaspoon ground cinnamon, and ½ teaspoon ground nutmeg; bring to boil. Pour hot syrup around apples. Bake uncovered at 350° about 60 minutes, basting occasionally. Serve warm with cream. Serves 6.

## STRAWBERRY SHORTCAKE

Shortcake
3 to 4 cups sugared
  sliced strawberries

1 cup whipping cream,
  whipped

*Shortcake:* Sift together 2 cups sifted all-purpose flour, 2 tablespoons sugar, 3 teaspoons baking powder, and ½ teaspoon salt. Cut in ½ cup butter till mixture resembles coarse crumbs. Mix 1 beaten egg and ⅔ cup milk; add all at once to dry mixture; stir just enough to moisten.

Spread dough in greased 8x1½-inch round pan, building up edges slightly. Bake at 450° for 15 to 18 minutes. Remove from pan; cool on rack 5 minutes. Split in 2 layers; lift top off carefully. Butter bottom layer. Spoon berries and cream between layers and over top. Serve warm.

## SPONGE SHORTCAKE

OVEN 350°

Sift together 1 cup sifted all-purpose flour, 1 teaspoon baking powder, and ¼ teaspoon salt. Beat 2 eggs till thick and lemon-colored, about 3 minutes at high speed on mixer. Gradually add 1 cup sugar, beating at medium speed 5 minutes.

By hand, quickly fold dry ingredients into egg mixture. Add 2 tablespoons butter to ½ cup *hot* milk. Stir into batter with 1 teaspoon vanilla. Blend well. Pour into paper-lined 8x8x2-inch baking pan. Bake at 350° for 25 to 30 minutes. Cool in pan 15 minutes; remove from pan. Top with sweetened fruit and whipped cream.

## INDIVIDUAL SHORTCAKES

OVEN 450°

Prepare dough for Strawberry Shortcake except decrease milk to ½ cup. Knead gently on floured surface for ½ minute. Pat or roll to ½ inch thickness. Cut 6 biscuits with floured 2½-inch cutter. Bake on ungreased baking sheet at 450° about 10 minutes. Split; butter bottom layers. Fill and top with fresh fruit and whipped cream. Serve warm. Serves 6.

## FRUIT COBBLERS

OVEN 400°

For biscuit topper, sift together 1 cup sifted all-purpose flour, 2 tablespoons sugar, 1 1/2 teaspoons baking powder, and 1/4 teaspoon salt. Cut in 1/4 cup butter till mixture resembles coarse crumbs. Combine 1/4 cup milk and 1 beaten egg. Add to dry mixture; stir just to moisten.

Prepare Cherry, Peach, Apple, or Rhubarb filling. Pour filling into 8 1/4x1 3/4-inch round baking dish. Immediately spoon on biscuit topper in 6 mounds. Bake at 400° for 20 to 25 minutes. Serve warm with cream or ice cream. Makes 6 servings.

**Cherry:** Combine one 1-pound 4-ounce can pitted tart red cherries (water pack) with juice, 1/2 cup sugar, 1 tablespoon quick-cooking tapioca, and few drops red food coloring in a saucepan. Let stand 5 minutes. Cook and stir till slightly thickened and bubbly, about 5 minutes. Stir in 1 tablespoon butter or margarine.

**Peach:** Combine 1 1/2 tablespoons cornstarch, 1/4 teaspoon ground mace, 1/2 cup brown sugar, and 1/2 cup water in saucepan. Cook and stir till thickened. Add 4 cups sliced peaches, 1 tablespoon lemon juice, and 1 tablespoon butter. Cook till peaches are hot, about 5 minutes.

**Apple:** Combine 1 cup sugar, 2 tablespoons all-purpose flour, 1/2 teaspoon ground cinnamon, and 1/4 teaspoon ground nutmeg. Toss with 6 cups sliced pared apples. Cook and stir over medium heat till almost tender, about 7 minutes.

**Rhubarb:** Combine 1 cup sugar, 2 tablespoons cornstarch, 1/4 teaspoon ground cinnamon, 1 tablespoon each water and butter, and 4 cups 1-inch slices rhubarb. Bring to boil. Cook and stir 1 minute.

## APPLE BETTY

4 cups sliced pared tart apples *or* 1 1-pound 2-ounce can pie-sliced apples, drained
¼ cup orange juice
1 cup sugar

¾ cup sifted all-purpose flour
½ teaspoon ground cinnamon
¼ teaspoon ground nutmeg
½ cup butter

OVEN 375°

Mound apples in buttered 9-inch pie plate; sprinkle with orange juice. Combine sugar, flour, spices, and dash salt; cut in butter till mixture is crumbly; sprinkle over apples. Bake at 375° for 45 minutes or till apples are tender and topping is crisp. Serve warm with cream. Serves 6.

## CHERRIES JUBILEE

1 1-pound can (2 cups) pitted dark sweet cherries
¼ cup sugar

2 tablespoons cornstarch
¼ cup brandy, kirsch, or cherry brandy
Vanilla ice cream

Drain cherries; reserve syrup and add water to make 1 cup. In saucepan, blend sugar and cornstarch; gradually add syrup. Mix well. Stir over medium heat till thick and bubbly. Remove from heat; stir in cherries. Turn into silver or heat-proof bowl. Heat brandy. Ignite brandy and pour or ladle over cherry mixture. Blend into sauce. Serve at once over ice cream. Makes 2 cups sauce.

## HOT FRUIT COMPOTE

1 1-pound package dried prunes
1⅓ cups dried apricots
1 13½-ounce can (1⅔ cups) pineapple chunks, undrained

1 1-pound 5-ounce can cherry pie filling
¼ cup dry white wine

OVEN 350°

Arrange first 3 fruits in 9x9x2-inch baking dish. Combine pie filling, 2 cups water, and wine; pour over fruit. Cover; bake at 350° for 1½ hours. Serve warm. Serves 8.

## SWEDISH FRUIT SOUP

1 11-ounce package (1³/₄ cups) mixed dried fruits
¹/₂ cup light raisins
3 to 4 inches stick cinnamon
4 cups water
1 medium unpared orange, thinly sliced and halved

1 1-pint 2-ounce can (2¹/₄ cups) pineapple juice
¹/₂ cup currant jelly
¹/₄ cup sugar
2 tablespoons quick-cooking tapioca
¹/₄ teaspoon salt

In a large saucepan, combine mixed fruits, raisins, cinnamon, and water. Bring to boiling; simmer, uncovered, till fruits are tender, about 30 minutes. Add remaining ingredients. Bring to a boil; cover; cook over low heat 15 minutes longer, stirring occasionally. Remove stick cinnamon. Serve warm or chilled. Serves 8 to 10.

## HOW TO COOK DRIED FRUIT

Rinse fruit and cover with water 1 inch above fruit in saucepan. Cover; simmer gently for time specified in chart. If desired, add sugar last 5 minutes of cooking.

To plump raisins, cover with water in saucepan. Bring to boiling; remove from heat; let stand covered 5 minutes.

| Dried Fruit | Cooking Time in Minutes* | Sugar/Cup Uncooked Fruit |
| --- | --- | --- |
| Apples | 20 to 30 | 4 tablespoons per cup |
| Apricots | 20 to 25 | 3 to 4 tablespoons per cup |
| Figs | 40 to 45 | 1 tablespoon per cup |
| Mixed Fruits | 25 to 30 | 2 to 3 tablespoons per cup |

| Dried Fruit | Cooking Time in Minutes* | Sugar/Cup Uncooked Fruit |
|---|---|---|
| Peaches | 30 to 35 | 3 to 4 tablespoons per cup |
| Pears | 30 to 35 | 3 to 4 tablespoons per cup |
| Prunes | 25 to 30 | 2 tablespoons per cup |

* Some dried fruits are processed to cut cooking time. See cooking directions on package.

# 10

# MEATS

423

## Cooking Methods

Cook tender meat cuts by dry heat; less tender cuts by
moist heat (liquid used).

Dry-heat Methods | Moist-heat Methods
--- | ---

Dry-heat Methods
- Roasting
- Broiling
- Panbroiling
- Panfrying
- Rotisserie cooking

Moist-heat Methods
- Braising
- Cooking in liquid
  - Stewing
  - Soup-making
- Pressure cooking

**Roasting:** Season meat. Insert meat thermometer. Place
roast, fat side up, on rack in an open roasting pan. (Rib
bones may serve as a rack.) Meat browns as it cooks. *Do
not* cover, add water, or baste. Roast at 325°. See roasting
chart, pages 430–432. Let meat stand 15 minutes before
carving. Carve across the grain. Often referred to as
"baked" when cooking ham.

**Broiling:** Preheat broiler or do not preheat broiler according to directions for range. Slash fat edge of meat.
Place meat on cold rack of broiler pan. See broiling chart,
page 440.

**Panbroiling:** Place meat in heavy skillet or on griddle.
Do not add fat or water. Brown slowly on both sides.
Cook, uncovered, over medium heat; turn occasionally.
Remove fat as it accumulates. See cooking time, pages
440 and 451.

**Panfrying:** In heavy skillet, brown slowly on both sides
in small amount of shortening. Season. Cook, uncovered,
over medium heat, turning occasionally.

**Braising:** Coat meat with all-purpose flour, if desired.
Brown slowly on all sides in hot shortening. Pour off fat.
Season. Add a very small amount of water (or other
liquid). Cover *tightly*. Cook at low temperature or in slow
oven.

**Cooking in liquid:** Cover large less tender cuts of meat

with liquid. Season, if desired. Cover and simmer till tender.

**Stewing:** Cut meat in uniform 1- to 2-inch cubes; coat with flour. Brown slowly in hot shortening, if desired. Season. Add liquid just to cover meat. Cover pan tightly and simmer. Add vegetables just long enough before serving to be cooked. Remove meat and vegetables; thicken juices.

**Soup-making:** Follow directions for stewing, but add large amount *cold* water. (This extracts the meat flavor.) Cover; simmer 2 or 3 hours. Add vegetables last half of cooking time.

## MEAT THERMOMETER

A meat thermometer is the best guide to determine the degree of doneness. Insert in center of raw roast so bulb reaches the thickest part of the lean meat, and does not rest in fat or on bone. When thermometer registers desired internal temperature (see roasting chart, pages 430–432) push thermometer into the meat a little farther. If temperature drops, continue cooking the roast to correct temperature.

## ROAST BEEF TENDERLOIN

OVEN 425°

Remove surface fat and connective tissue from one 4- to 6-pound whole beef tenderloin. Season; tuck under small end. Brush meat with salad oil. Roast according to chart, opposite page. Serves 6 to 8.

## BRAISED FLANK STEAK

Score one 1- to 1½-pound beef flank steak; coat with all-purpose flour. Brown in hot shortening. Season. Add ½ cup hot water. Cover; cook over low heat or in moderate oven (350°) about 1½ hours. Serves 3 to 4.

# • HOW MUCH MEAT TO SERVE •

| Meat | Servings per pound |
|---|---|
| Boneless meat (ground, stew, or variety meat) | 4-5 |
| Cuts with little bone (beef round or ham center cuts, lamb or veal cutlets) | 3-4 |
| Cuts with medium amount of bone (whole or end cuts of beef round, bone-in ham; loin, rump, rib, or chuck roasts; steaks and chops) | 2-3 |
| Cuts with much bone (shank, brisket, plate, spareribs, breast of lamb or veal) | 1-2 |

# ROASTING TIME AND TEMPERATURE CHART

*Roast meat at constant oven temperature of 325° unless otherwise indicated.*

| Cut | Approximate Weight (Pounds) | Internal Temperature on Removal from oven | Approximate Cooking Time (Total Time) |
|---|---|---|---|
| **Beef** | | | |
| Rib Roast | 4 to 6 | 140° (rare) | 2¼ to 2¾ hrs. |
| | | 160° (medium) | 2¾ to 3¼ hrs. |
| | | 170° (well done) | 3¼ to 3½ hrs. |
| Rib Roast | 6 to 8 | 140° (rare) | 2½ to 3 hrs. |
| | | 160° (medium) | 3 to 3½ hrs. |
| | | 170° (well done) | 3¾ to 4 hrs. |
| Boneless Rib Roast | 5 to 7 | 140° (rare) | 3¼ to 3½ hrs. |
| | | 160° (medium) | 3¾ to 4 hrs. |
| | | 170° (well done) | 4½ to 4¾ hrs. |
| Boneless Rolled Rump Roast | 4 to 6 | 150° to 170° | 2 to 2½ hrs. |
| Tip Roast | 3½ to 4 | 140° to 170° | 2 to 2¾ hrs. |
| Rib Eye (Delmonico) Roast (Roast at 350°) | 4 to 6 | 140° (rare) | 1½ to 1¾ hrs. |
| | | 160° (medium) | 1¾ hrs. |
| | | 170° (well done) | 2 hrs. |
| Tenderloin Roast (Roast at 425°) | 4 to 6 | 140° (rare) | 45 min. to 1 hr. |
| **Veal** | | | |
| Leg Roast | 5 to 8 | 170° | 2¾ to 3¾ hrs. |

| | Pounds | Internal Temperature | Approximate Roasting Time |
|---|---|---|---|
| Loin Roast | 4 to 6 | 170° | 2½ to 3 hrs. |
| Boneless Shoulder Roast | 4 to 6 | 170° | 3½ to 3¾ hrs. |
| **Fresh Pork** | | | |
| Loin Center Roast | 3 to 5 | 170° | 2½ to 3 hrs. |
| Sirloin Roast | 5 to 7 | 170° | 3½ to 4¼ hrs. |
| Loin Blade Roast | 3 to 4 | 170° | 2¼ to 2¾ hrs. |
| Boneless Top Loin Roast | 3 to 4 | 170° | 2½ to 3 hrs. |
| Blade Boston Roast | 4 to 6 | 170° | 3 to 4 hrs. |
| Arm Picnic | 5 to 8 | 170° | 3 to 4 hrs. |
| Leg (fresh ham) | 10 to 16 | 170° | 4½ to 6 hrs. |
| Leg, half (fresh ham) | 5 to 7 | 170° | 3½ to 4½ hrs. |
| **Smoked Pork** | | | |
| Ham (cook-before-eating) | | | |
| whole | 10 to 14 | 160° | 3½ to 4 hrs. |
| half | 5 to 7 | 160° | 2½ to 3 hrs. |
| shank or rump portion | 3 to 4 | 160° | 2 to 2¼ hrs. |
| Ham (fully-cooked) | | | |
| whole | 10 to 14 | 140° | 2½ to 3 hrs. |
| half | 5 to 7 | 140° | 1¾ to 2¼ hrs. |
| whole, boneless | 8 to 10 | 140° | 2 to 2¼ hrs. |
| half, boneless | 4 to 5 | 140° | 1½ to 2 hrs. |
| Picnic Shoulder (cook-before-eating) | 5 to 8 | 170° | 3 to 4 hrs. |

| Cut | Approximate Weight (Pounds) | Internal Temperature on Removal from oven | Approximate Cooking Time (Total Time) |
|---|---|---|---|
| **Lamb** | | | |
| Leg, whole | 5 to 7 | 140° (rare) | 1¾ to 2¼ hrs. |
| | | 160° (medium) | 2 to 3 hrs. |
| | | 170° to 180° (well done) | 2½ to 3½ hrs. |
| Leg, half | 3 to 4 | 160° (medium) | 1¼ to 1¾ hrs. |
| Square Cut Shoulder | 4 to 6 | 160° (medium) | 1¾ to 2½ hrs. |
| Boneless Shoulder | 3 to 5 | 160° (medium) | 1¾ to 3 hrs. |

# BEEF CUTS

## and How To Cook Them

Locate wholesale cuts on drawing, identify their retail pieces in the same numbered picture, then note cooking methods.

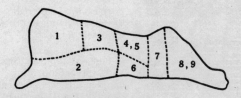

**1.** Boneless Chuck Eye Roast, upper left. Arm Pot Roast, right. Blade (7-bone) Roast, lower left. *Braise.*

**2.** Corned Boneless Brisket, top; *cook in liquid.* Plate Short Ribs, right; *braise, cook in liquid.* Shank Cross Cuts, left; *braise, cook in liquid.*

**3.** Rib Roast, upper left. Boneless Rib Roast, right. Rib Eye (Delmonico) Roast, lower left. *Roast.*

**4.** Boneless Top Loin (New York Strip or Strip) Steak, upper left. Tenderloin Steak, right. Rib Eye (Delmonico) Steak (section 3 on drawing), lower left. *Broil, panbroil, or panfry these beef cuts.*

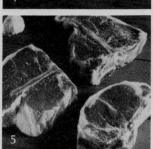

**5.** T-Bone Steak, upper right. Top Loin Steak, lower right. Porterhouse Steak, left. *Broil, panbroil, panfry.*

**6.** Scored Flank Steak, upper left. Rolled Flank Steak, upper right. Flank Steak Rolls, bottom. *Braise, broil (high quality).*

**7.** Sirloin Steak, upper right. Boneless Sirloin Steak, lower left. *Broil, panbroil, or panfry these beef steaks.*

**8.** Upper left to lower right: Round Tip Roast; *braise, roast (high quality)*. Bottom Round Steak; *braise, panfry*. Round Bone. Top Round Steak; *braise, panfry*.

**9.** Boneless Rump Roast, upper right. Rump Roast, lower left. *Braise, or roast high-quality samples of these cuts.*

## ROAST PEPPERED RIB EYE

1 5- to 6-pound boneless beef rib eye roast
½ cup coarsely cracked pepper
½ teaspoon ground cardamom

1 tablespoon tomato paste
1 teaspoon paprika
½ teaspoon garlic powder
1 cup soy sauce
¾ cup vinegar

OVEN 300°

Trim excess fat from meat. Combine pepper and cardamom; rub all over meat and press in with heel of palm. Place meat in shallow baking dish. Combine tomato paste, paprika, and garlic powder; gradually add soy, then vinegar. Carefully pour mixture over meat; marinate in refrigerator overnight. Baste with marinade several times while marinating.

Remove meat from marinade. Let stand at room temperature 1 hour. Wrap meat in foil; place in shallow pan. Roast in slow oven (300°) 2 hours for medium-rare. Open foil; ladle out and reserve drippings. Brown roast, uncovered, at 350° while making Gravy. Makes 8 to 10 servings.

*Gravy:* Strain pan drippings; skim off excess fat. To 1 cup meat juices, add 1 cup water; bring to boiling. Add a little marinade, if desired. Serve roast *au jus,* or thicken gravy with 1½ tablespoons cornstarch mixed with ¼ cup cold water.

To carve beef rib roast, have butcher remove backbone or saw across base of ribs. Remove backbone when cooked.

Stand roast on side with ribs to carver's left. Steady with fork and slice across meat to ribs. Loosen slice by cutting along bone.

## STUFFED TENDERLOIN

OVEN 325°

Split and flatten slightly one 3-pound beef tenderloin. In 6 tablespoons butter, cook ½ cup *each* chopped onion and celery. Stir in 3 cups soft bread crumbs and one 6-ounce can sliced mushrooms, drained.

Spread mixture over half the meat. Bring second side over; fasten edges with skewers. Season meat with salt and pepper; top with 3 bacon slices. Roast, uncovered, in shallow pan at 325° about 1¼ hours till rare or medium-rare. Serves 6 to 8.

# BRAISED TIP ROAST

OVEN 350°

Sprinkle one 3- to 4-pound beef round tip roast lightly with 2 tablespoons all-purpose flour and rub in. In Dutch oven, brown slowly on all sides in 2 tablespoons shortening. Season with 2 teaspoons salt and $1/4$ teaspoon pepper. Add 1 medium onion, sliced, 2 bay leaves, 1 clove garlic, minced, and $1/2$ cup hot water. Cover and cook in moderate oven (350°) about 2 hours or till meat is almost tender.

Add 8 small onions, peeled, 8 medium carrots, pared, and 8 small potatoes, pared. Sprinkle vegetables with $1^1/2$ teaspoons salt. Cover and cook $1^1/2$ hours or till meat and vegetables are tender. Thicken liquid for Gravy (page 484). Makes 6 to 8 servings.

# TO BROWN MEAT

Use trimmed fat from meat for browning instead of shortening, if desired. Heat trimmings. When about 2 tablespoons melted fat accumulates, remove trimmings. This is enough to brown a 3- or 4-pound beef pot roast. For a rich brown color, coat pot roast with all-purpose flour. Brown slowly on all sides in hot fat.

# BEEF POT ROAST

Coat one 3- to 4-pound beef pot roast with all-purpose flour. In Dutch oven, large skillet, or roasting pan, brown pot roast slowly on all sides in 2 tablespoons hot shortening or salad oil. Season with salt and pepper. Remove from heat, then add $1/2$ cup water. Cover tightly and cook slowly $2^1/2$ hours, or till tender. Add water if needed to prevent sticking.

If desired, add small potatoes, pared and halved, small whole onions, and medium carrots, pared and cut in 1-inch pieces, the last 45 to 60 minutes of cooking. Thicken juices in pan for Pot Roast Gravy, (page 484). Makes 6 to 8 servings.

## POT ROAST VARIATIONS

• Use tomato juice instead of the $\frac{1}{2}$ cup water for cooking liquid in Beef Pot Roast. Prepare Pot Roast Gravy (page 484), *except* add tomato juice to pan juices instead of water to make $1\frac{1}{2}$ cups liquid. Slowly blend an additional $\frac{1}{3}$ cup tomato juice into the flour. Season with salt, pepper, and $\frac{1}{2}$ teaspoon Worcestershire sauce.

• Slice 2 small onions over meat after browning. Add 2 bay leaves and 5 whole cloves. Use $\frac{1}{4}$ cup vinegar and $\frac{1}{4}$ cup water as the cooking liquid. Cook as directed for Beef Pot Roast.

• After browning, season pot roast with salt, pepper, and 1 tablespoon dillseed. Top meat with 2 medium onions, sliced. Serve with Sour Cream Gravy (pages 484–485).

• Mix one 8-ounce can (1 cup) tomato sauce, 1 cup water, 1 envelope *dry* onion soup mix, 1 teaspoon caraway seed, and 2 bay leaves. Pour over meat after browning. Cook as directed for Beef Pot Roast. Thicken liquid as for Pot Roast Gravy, *using only* 2 tablespoons all-purpose flour.

## BEEF WITH DUMPLINGS

| | |
|---|---|
| 1 3- to 4-pound beef pot roast | 1 teaspoon salt |
| 2 tablespoons shortening | $\frac{1}{2}$ teaspoon mixed pickling spices |
| 1 1-pound can tomatoes | $\frac{1}{4}$ teaspoon pepper |
| $\frac{1}{4}$ cup wine vinegar | 1 tube refrigerated biscuits (10 biscuits) |
| $\frac{1}{4}$ cup water | 1 tablespoon snipped parsley |
| 1 clove garlic, minced | |
| 1 teaspoon sugar | |

Trim excess fat from roast. In Dutch oven or large skillet, slowly brown meat on all sides in hot shortening. Add next 8 ingredients. Cover; cook slowly 2 to $2\frac{1}{2}$ hours, or till meat is tender. Place biscuits on meat; sprinkle with parsley. Cover tightly and steam 15 minutes, or till "dumplings" are done. Remove meat and dumplings to warm platter. Make Pot Roast Gravy (page 484) *except* add water to juices to make $2\frac{1}{2}$ cups. Makes 6 to 8 servings.

# FRUITED POT ROAST

| | |
|---|---|
| 1  3- to 4-pound beef pot roast | ¹/₂ cup red Burgundy |
| 2  tablespoons shortening | 1  clove garlic, minced |
| ¹/₂ cup finely chopped onion | 1  11-ounce package mixed dried fruit (1³/₄ cups) |
| ¹/₃ cup finely chopped carrot | 3  tablespoons all-purpose flour |

Trim excess fat from meat. In Dutch oven or large skillet, brown meat in hot shortening. Season with 1¹/₂ teaspoons salt and ¹/₄ teaspoon pepper. Add next 4 ingredients. Cover; cook over low heat 1¹/₂ hours.

Meanwhile, pour 1¹/₂ cups hot water over fruit; let stand 1 hour. Drain fruit, reserving liquid. Place fruit on meat. Cover; cook 45 minutes more. Remove meat and fruit to platter. Skim fat from pan juices. Add reserved liquid to juices to make 1¹/₂ cups. Blend flour and ¹/₃ cup cold water; stir into liquid. Cook and stir till thick and bubbly. Makes 6 servings.

# BROILED BEEF STEAK

Have a beef porterhouse, T-bone, top loin, sirloin, or tenderloin (filet mignon) steak cut 1 to 2 inches thick. Slash fat edge (not into meat) at 1-inch intervals.

Place steak on cold rack in broiler pan. Broil 1- to 1¹/₂-inch thick steaks so surface of meat is 3 inches from heat, thicker cuts 4 to 5 inches from heat. (Check range instruction booklet.) Broil about *half* of time indicated on Broiling Chart (page 440); season with salt and pepper, if desired. Turn with tongs; broil for remaining time; season.

*Doneness test:* Slit center; note inside color: red—rare; pink—medium; gray—well.

**Planked Steak:** Broil 1¹/₂-inch thick steak (see Broiling Chart (page 440) *except* reduce timing 7 minutes from second side). Place on seasoned plank (brush with oil; heat in 300° oven, 1 hour). Pipe or spoon border of Duchess Potatoes (page 686) around edge of plank. Oil exposed wood. (If desired, make extra potato cups; fill with hot cooked vegetables just before serving.) Broil 4 inches from heat 5 to 7 minutes, or till potatoes brown and meat is done.

**Tenderized Steak:** Choose beef round or chuck steak, 1 inch thick. Use instant meat tenderizer according to label directions. Broiling time is slightly less.

**Panbroiled Steak:** Select steak as for broiling, 1 inch thick. Place in cold heavy skillet. *Do not add shortening* (unless very lean cuts are used). Brown both sides. Cook, uncovered, over medium-high heat, turning occasionally. Total cooking time is about 9 to 10 minutes for rare; 11 to 12 minutes for medium; about 20 minutes for well-done. Season, if desired.

## • BROILING CHART •

| Thickness of Steak | Rare | Medium (total time in minutes) | Well-done |
|---|---|---|---|
| 1 inch | 8 to 10 | 12 to 14 | 18 to 20 |
| 1½ inch | 14 to 16 | 18 to 20 | 25 to 30 |
| 2 inch | 20 to 25 | 30 to 35 | 40 to 45 |

## LONDON BROIL

Score one 1- to 1¼-pound *top-quality* beef flank steak. Place in shallow pan. Combine ⅓ cup salad oil, 1 teaspoon vinegar, and 1 small clove garlic, minced; pour over steak. Cover; let stand at room temperature 2 to 3 hours; turn several times.

Place steak on cold rack in broiler pan. Broil, 3 inches from heat, for 4 to 5 minutes; season with salt and pepper. Turn; broil 4 to 5 minutes more (for medium-rare); season. To serve, carve in *very thin* slices diagonally across grain. Serves 4 or 5.

## STUFFED FLANK STEAKS

$^1/_3$ cup chopped onion
2 tablespoons butter
4 cups dry bread cubes
$^1/_2$ teaspoon poultry
   seasoning
2 1$^1/_2$-pound beef flank
   steaks, scored
1 1-pound can tomatoes

$^1/_4$ cup chopped onion
$^1/_4$ cup catsup
$^1/_4$ cup chopped green
   pepper
1 3-ounce can sliced
   mushrooms, drained
   ($^1/_2$ cup)

In skillet, cook $^1/_3$ cup onion in butter till tender. Add bread cubes, poultry seasoning, $^1/_2$ teaspoon salt, and dash pepper; toss till bread is lightly toasted. Sprinkle with $^1/_4$ to $^1/_2$ cup water to moisten. Spread stuffing over steaks and roll up lengthwise as for jelly roll; fasten with wooden picks and lace with string.

Roll in flour; brown all sides in small amount hot shortening. Season with salt and pepper. Add tomatoes, $^1/_4$ cup chopped onion, catsup, and $^1/_2$ teaspoon salt. Cover; simmer 1$^1/_2$ to 2 hours or till tender. Add remaining ingredients last 15 minutes. Remove steaks to warm platter. Mix 1 tablespoon flour with 2 tablespoons cold water till smooth. Stir into sauce; cook till thick and bubbly. Serves 6 to 8.

## BEEF CUBED STEAKS

Lightly grease hot skillet. Cook beef cubed steaks over high heat, 1 minute on each side; season. Remove steaks. Swirl a *little* water in pan. Pour juices over steaks.

## CHICKEN-FRIED STEAK

1$^1/_2$ pounds beef top round
   steak, $^1/_2$ inch thick
1 beaten egg
1 tablespoon milk

1 cup fine cracker
   crumbs
$^1/_4$ cup salad oil

Pound steak $^1/_4$ inch thick; cut in serving pieces. Blend egg and milk. Dip meat in egg mixture, then in crumbs. Slowly brown meat in hot oil, turning once. Cover; cook over low heat 45 to 60 minutes till tender. Season with salt and pepper. Serves 6.

## CHEESE ROUND STEAK

Coat one 2-pound beef round steak, $1/2$ inch thick, with a mixture of $1/4$ cup flour, $1/2$ teaspoon salt, and $1/4$ teaspoon garlic salt. Pound meat to $1/4$ inch thickness; cut into 6 to 8 pieces.

In skillet, brown slowly in 3 tablespoons hot shortening. Add 1 cup hot water and $1/4$ cup chopped onion. Cover; simmer 1 hour, or till tender. Sprinkle with $1/2$ cup shredded sharp process American cheese and 2 tablespoons snipped parsley. Cover; heat to melt cheese. Serves 6 to 8.

## SWISS STEAK

| | |
|---|---|
| $1/4$ cup all-purpose flour | $1/2$ cup chopped onion |
| 2 pounds beef round steak, 1 inch thick | 1 1-pound can tomatoes |
| 3 tablespoons shortening | 2 tablespoons chopped green pepper |

Combine flour, 1 teaspoon salt, and $1/4$ teaspoon pepper; pound into meat. In large skillet, brown meat on both sides in hot shortening.* Top with onion and tomatoes, cut up. Cover; cook over low heat about $1^1/2$ hours, or till tender. Add green pepper; cook 15 minutes more. Skim off excess fat. Thicken juices if desired. Season to taste. Makes 6 servings.

*Or, transfer to 12x7$1/2$x2-inch baking dish. Cook covered at 350° for $1^1/2$ hours. Uncover; add green pepper and cook 15 minutes, basting meat occasionally.

## PANFRIED ROUND STEAK

Cut $1^1/2$ pounds beef round steak, $1/2$ inch thick, into 5 pieces. Use instant meat tenderizer according to label directions. *Do not use salt.* Coat meat immediately with all-purpose flour. Cook quickly in small amount hot shortening, just till browned; turn occasionally. Serves 5.

# DEVILED SWISS STEAK

¹/₄ cup all-purpose flour
2 teaspoons dry mustard
1 3-pound beef round
steak, cut 1 inch thick
2 tablespoons salad oil

1 4-ounce can
mushroom stems
and pieces
1 tablespoon
Worcestershire sauce

Combine flour, 1¹/₂ teaspoons salt, ¹/₄ teaspoon pepper, and dry mustard. Sprinkle mixture over round steak and pound into meat with meat mallet. In heavy skillet, brown steak slowly on both sides in hot oil. Drain off excess fat.

Drain mushrooms; reserve liquid. Add water if needed to make ¹/₂ cup. Add mushroom liquid and Worcestershire to meat in skillet. Cover tightly and cook over low heat for 1¹/₄ to 1¹/₂ hours, or till tender. During the last few minutes, add mushrooms and heat through. Skim any fat from pan juices before serving. Garnish with parsley, if desired. Serves 6 to 8.

Pound round steak with a meat mallet. The pounding breaks up tough fibers and works seasoned flour into the meat.

## OLD-TIME BEEF STEW

2 pounds beef stew
  meat, cut in
  1½-inch cubes
2 tablespoons shortening
1 teaspoon
  Worcestershire sauce
1 clove garlic
1 medium onion, sliced
1 or 2 bay leaves
1 tablespoon salt
1 teaspoon sugar
½ teaspoon paprika

¼ teaspoon pepper
  Dash ground allspice
  *or* cloves
6 carrots, pared and
  quartered
4 potatoes, pared and
  quartered
1 pound small white
  onions
3 tablespoons all-
  purpose flour

In Dutch oven, thoroughly brown meat in 2 tablespoons hot shortening, turning often. Add 2 cups hot water and next 9 ingredients. Cover; simmer for 1½ hours, stirring occasionally to keep from sticking. Remove bay leaves and garlic. Add vegetables. Cover and cook 30 to 45 minutes, or till vegetables are tender.

Slowly blend ⅓ cup cold water into the 3 tablespoons flour. Stir slowly into hot stew mixture. Cook and stir till bubbly. Cook and stir 3 minutes longer. Serve stew in bowls. Makes 6 to 8 servings.

## SAUERBRATEN

In large bowl or crock, combine 2 medium onions, sliced, ½ lemon, sliced, 2½ cups water, 1½ cups red wine vinegar, 12 whole cloves, 6 bay leaves, 6 whole peppercorns, 1 tablespoon sugar, 1 tablespoon salt, and ¼ teaspoon ground ginger. Add one 4-pound beef rump roast, turning to coat. Cover and refrigerate about 36 hours; turn meat at least twice daily. Remove meat; wipe dry. Strain; reserve marinade.

In Dutch oven, brown meat in 2 tablespoons hot shortening; add strained marinade. Cover and cook slowly 2 hours, or till tender. Remove meat. For each cup of gravy: Combine ¾ cup meat juices and ¼ cup water; add ⅓ cup broken gingersnaps. Cook and stir till thick. Serves 10.

# BEEF STROGANOFF

Cut 1 pound beef sirloin into ¼-inch strips. Combine 1 tablespoon flour and ½ teaspoon salt. Coat meat with flour mixture. Heat skillet, then add 2 tablespoons butter or margarine. When melted, add sirloin strips and brown quickly on both sides. Add one 3-ounce can sliced mushrooms, drained, ½ cup chopped onion, and 1 clove garlic, minced; cook 3 or 4 minutes, or till onion is crisp-tender.

Remove meat and mushrooms from pan. Add 2 table-spoons butter or margarine to pan drippings; blend in 3 tablespoons all-purpose flour. Add 1 tablespoon tomato paste. Stir in 1¼ cups cold beef stock or one 10½-ounce can condensed beef broth. Cook and stir over medium-high heat till thickened and bubbly.

Return browned meat and mushrooms to skillet. Stir in 1 cup dairy sour cream and 2 tablespoons dry white wine; cook slowly till heated through. Do not boil. Keep warm over hot water. Serve over hot buttered noodles. Makes 4 or 5 servings.

# BEEF FONDUE

| | |
|---|---|
| Salad oil | Wine-Mushroom |
| 1½ pounds trimmed beef | Sauce, page 642 |
| tenderloin, cut in | Garlic Butter, page 642 |
| ¾-inch cubes | Horseradish Sauce, |
| Bordelaise Sauce, | page 645 |
| page 644 | Mustard Sauce, |
| Caper Butter, page 642 | pages 644–645 |

Pour salad oil in saucepan or beef fondue cooker to no more than ½ capacity or to depth of about 2 inches. Heat to 425° on range (don't let oil smoke). Transfer to cooker; place over alcohol burner or canned heat. Have beef cubes at room temperature in serving bowl.

Set out small bowls of several or all of the special but-ters and sauces. Each guest spears a beef cube with fondue fork, then holds it in the hot oil until cooked to desired doneness—it doesn't take long to learn the length of time. Then transfer the meat to a dinner fork and dip it in a sauce on plate. Makes 4 servings.

## BRAISED SHORT RIBS

3 pounds beef short ribs
All-purpose flour
2 tablespoons shortening

1 medium onion, sliced
Onion Gravy

Trim excess fat from ribs. Roll ribs in flour. In Dutch oven, brown in hot shortening; spoon off fat. Season with 1 teaspoon salt and dash pepper. Add onion and 1/2 cup water. Cover and simmer for 2 to 2 1/2 hours, or till tender, adding more water if needed. (Or, cover and cook in moderate oven [350°] for 2 to 2 1/2 hours, or till tender.) Remove meat to warm platter; keep hot while preparing gravy. Serve gravy with short ribs. Makes 6 servings.

*Onion Gravy:* Skim fat from meat juices, reserving 2 tablespoons fat. Measure juices and add water to make 2 cups; set aside. Brown 3 tablespoons sugar in reserved fat. Add 2 medium onions, thinly sliced; cook, stirring constantly, till tender. Push onions to one side. Add 3 tablespoons all-purpose flour; brown slightly. Stir in meat juices, 2 tablespoons vinegar, and 1/4 teaspoon Kitchen Bouquet sauce. Return to heat; cook, stirring constantly, till gravy thickens and bubbles. Boil 2 to 3 minutes more. Season with salt and pepper.

## CORNED BEEF DINNER

Place one 3- to 4-pound corned beef brisket in Dutch oven; barely cover with hot water. Add 1/2 cup chopped onion, 2 cloves garlic, minced, and 2 bay leaves. Cover; simmer 3 to 4 hours, or till tender.

Remove meat from liquid; keep warm. Add 6 medium potatoes, pared, and 6 small carrots, pared. Cover; bring to boiling; cook 5 minutes. Add 6 cabbage wedges and cook 25 minutes longer.

If desired, glaze meat while vegetables cook. To glaze, spread fat side of meat lightly with prepared mustard. Sprinkle with mixture of 3 tablespoons brown sugar and dash ground cloves. Bake in shallow pan in moderate oven (350°) about 15 minutes. For carving instructions, see picture opposite. Makes 6 servings.

Slice corned beef across grain, ¹/₈ to ¹/₄ inch thick. Since the grain goes in several directions, carve from two sides.

## CREAMED DRIED BEEF

| | |
|---|---|
| 4 ounces dried or smoked dried beef,* torn | 1 cup milk |
| 2 tablespoons butter | ¹/₂ teaspoon Worcestershire sauce |
| 2 tablespoons all-purpose flour | Toast points |

Cook dried beef in butter till edges frizzle. Push meat to one side; blend flour into butter. Add milk all at once. Cook, stirring constantly, till thick and bubbly, gradually incorporating dried beef. Add Worcestershire and dash pepper. Spoon over buttered toast. Serves 3.

*If dried beef is extra salty, let stand a few minutes in boiling water. Drain on paper towels before cooking in the butter.

## FRESH BRISKET FEAST

Place one 3- to 3¹/₂-pound fresh boneless beef brisket in Dutch oven. Halve 2 onions; stick a whole clove into each onion half. Add onions with cloves to meat with 2 branches celery, 4¹/₂ teaspoons salt, and ¹/₂ teaspoon whole peppercorns.

Barely cover with water. Cover; simmer 3 to 3¹/₂ hours. Add 6 medium carrots, pared, the last 20 minutes of cooking. Discard onions and celery. Serves 8 to 10.

## APPLESAUCE BEEF LOAF

OVEN 350°

Combine 1 beaten egg, 1½ cups soft bread crumbs (2 slices bread), ½ cup applesauce, ¼ cup finely chopped celery, 2 tablespoons finely chopped onion, 1 teaspoon Dijon-style mustard, ½ teaspoon salt, and dash pepper. Add 1 pound ground beef and mix thoroughly. Shape mixture into a round loaf in an 8x8x2-inch baking pan.

With a spoon, make a crater-like depression in top of loaf. Combine ½ cup applesauce, 1 tablespoon brown sugar, 1½ teaspoons vinegar, and ½ teaspoon Dijon-style mustard; pour into depression. Bake at 350° for 1 hour. Makes 4 or 5 servings.

## BERRY-GLAZED LOAVES

OVEN 350°

Combine 1 beaten egg, ⅓ cup milk, ⅓ cup quick-cooking rolled oats, 2 tablespoons finely chopped onion, ½ teaspoon salt, and dash pepper. Add 1 pound ground beef and ¼ pound bulk pork sausage; mix thoroughly. Shape into 5 individual loaves. Place in 13x9x2-inch baking dish. Combine one 8-ounce can whole cranberry sauce, 3 tablespoons brown sugar, and 2 teaspoons lemon juice; set aside.

Bake at 350° for 30 minutes. Spoon on sauce; bake 15 minutes more. Remove loaves to warm platter. Skim fat from sauce; pour some sauce over meat loaves; pass remaining. Makes 5 servings.

## FAVORITE BEEF LOAF

| | |
|---|---|
| 2 beaten eggs | 2 tablespoons chopped green pepper |
| 1 8-ounce can tomato sauce | 1 teaspoon salt |
| ½ cup medium cracker crumbs | Dash dried thyme, crushed |
| ¼ cup finely chopped onion | Dash dried marjoram, crushed |
| | 1½ pounds ground beef |

OVEN 350°

Combine first 8 ingredients. Add ground beef; mix well. Shape mixture into a loaf in 12x7½x2-inch baking dish. Bake at 350° about 1¼ hours. Makes 6 to 8 servings.

## TWIN MEAT LOAVES

3 cups soft bread cubes (about 4 slices cut in ½-inch cubes)
¾ cup milk
2 eggs

* * *

¼ cup finely chopped onion
¼ cup finely chopped celery
1 tablespoon Worcestershire sauce

1½ teaspoons salt
⅛ teaspoon pepper
½ teaspoon poultry seasoning
1½ pounds ground beef
½ pound ground pork

* * *

¼ cup chili sauce or ¼ cup catsup and 2 tablespoons corn syrup

OVEN 350°

Soak bread cubes in milk. Add eggs; beat with rotary beater. Add onion, celery, Worcestershire sauce, salt, pepper, and poultry seasoning; mix thoroughly. Add meats; mix well. Form into 2 loaves. Place in 13x9x2-inch baking pan. Bake, uncovered, in moderate oven (350°) for 1 hour.

For glaze, spread loaves with chili sauce or spread with mixture of the catsup and corn syrup. Bake 15 minutes longer. Makes 8 to 10 servings.

## ITALIAN MEAT LOAF

OVEN 350°

In large bowl, combine 2 eggs, one 6-ounce can (⅔ cup) tomato paste, ½ cup medium cracker crumbs (about 11 crackers), ½ cup finely chopped onion, ¼ cup finely chopped green pepper, ¾ teaspoon salt, and dash pepper. Add 1½ pounds ground beef; mix well. Pat *half* the mixture into bottom of an 8x8x2-inch baking pan.

Combine ½ cup medium cracker crumbs, one 12-ounce carton (1½ cups) small-curd cottage cheese, one 3-ounce can chopped mushrooms, drained (½ cup), 1 tablespoon snipped parsley, and 1/4 teaspoon dried oregano, crushed. Spread mixture evenly over meat in pan. Top with remaining meat mixture.

Bake in moderate oven (350°) for 50 minutes. Let meat loaf stand 10 minutes before serving. Makes 8 servings.

## SWEDISH MEATBALLS

| | |
|---|---|
| 3/4 pound lean ground beef | 1/4 cup finely snipped parsley |
| 1/2 pound ground veal | 1 1/4 teaspoons salt |
| 1/4 pound ground pork | Dash pepper |
| 1 1/2 cups soft bread crumbs | Dash ground ginger |
| 1 cup light cream | Dash ground nutmeg |
| 1/2 cup chopped onion | 2 tablespoons butter |
| 1 tablespoon butter | Gravy |
| 1 egg | |

Have meats ground together twice. Soak bread in cream about 5 minutes. Cook onion in 1 tablespoon butter till tender.

Mix egg, crumb mixture, onion, parsley, salt, pepper, and spices; add meats. Beat 5 minutes at medium speed on electric mixer, or mix by hand till well combined. Shape into 1 1/2-inch balls (mixture will be soft—for easier shaping, wet hands or chill mixture first). Brown in 2 tablespoons butter. Remove from skillet. Prepare Gravy; add meatballs. Cover; cook *slowly* 30 minutes; baste often. Makes 30.

*Gravy:* Melt 2 tablespoons butter in skillet with drippings. Stir in 2 tablespoons all-purpose flour. Add 1 beef bouillon cube dissolved in 1 1/4 cups boiling water and 1/2 teaspoon instant coffee powder. Cook and stir till thickened and bubbly.

## • SOY PRODUCTS •

Soy-based products, such as textured vegetable protein, extend ground meat by stretching protein value and volume of ground meat while still keeping the meat's flavor.

Textured vegetable protein is available already mixed with ground meat or in a granular form ready to blend with meat. To make your own mixture, use 1 pound ground meat; add soy protein with the amount of liquid specified in label directions to yield about 1½ pounds.

## HAMBURGERS

**Panbroiled:** Shape 1 pound ground beef into 4 patties, ¾-inch thick. Heat skillet sizzling hot; sprinkle skillet lightly with salt. Cook burgers over high heat 5 minutes; turn and cook 4 to 5 minutes. Partially cover if meat spatters.

**Broiled:** Combine 1 pound ground beef, ½ teaspoon salt, dash pepper, and ¼ cup finely chopped onion (optional). Shape burgers into 4 patties, ¾-inch thick. Broil 3 inches from heat 6 minutes; turn and broil 4 minutes or till done.

## SPECIAL HAMBURGERS

| | |
|---|---|
| 1 pound ground beef | ¼ cup catsup |
| 2 tablespoons finely chopped green pepper | 1 tablespoon prepared horseradish |
| ¼ cup chopped onion | ½ teaspoon dry mustard |

OVEN 375°

Combine ingredients and ½ teaspoon salt; mix well. Form into 4 to 6 patties. Broil as above, *or* place in greased shallow baking dish; bake at 375° for 30 minutes.

## SWEET-SOUR MEATBALLS

Combine 1 beaten egg, 1 cup soft bread crumbs, 2 tablespoons chopped onion, 2 tablespoons milk, and ¾ teaspoon salt. Add 1 pound ground beef-textured vegetable protein mixture; mix well. Shape into 24 one-inch balls. In large skillet, brown meatballs in 2 tablespoons hot shortening. Drain off fat. Drain one 8¼-ounce can pineapple tidbits, reserving syrup; set pineapple aside. Add water to reserved syrup to make ¾ cup. Combine syrup mixture, one 8-ounce can whole cranberry sauce, ½ cup bottled barbecue sauce, ¼ teaspoon salt, and dash pepper. Pour over meatballs. Bring to boiling. Cover; simmer

15 to 20 minutes. Blend ¼ cup cold water into 1 tablespoon cornstarch; stir into skillet. Cook and stir till thick. Add pineapple and ½ cup green pepper strips. Simmer, covered, till pepper is barely tender. Serve over hot cooked rice. Serves 6.

# VEAL CUTS
## and How To Cook Them

Locate wholesale cuts on drawing, identify their retail pieces in the same numbered picture, then note cooking methods.

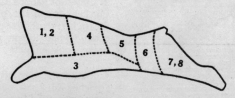

**1.** Boneless Shoulder Roast, upper right; *roast, braise.* Arm Roast, left; *roast, braise.* Arm Steak, lower right; *braise or panfry this veal cut.*

**2.** Blade Roast, upper right. Mock Chicken Legs, left. Blade Steak, lower right. *Braise, panfry.*

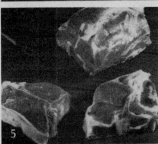

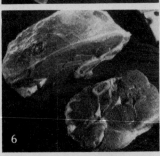

**3.** Cubes for Kabobs (City Chicken), top; *braise, panfry.* Breast, left; *roast, braise, cook in liquid.* Riblets, right; *braise, cook in liquid.*

**4.** Rib Roast, upper left; *roast.* Frenched Rib Roast, upper right; *roast.* Rib Chops, bottom; *braise, panfry.*

**5.** Loin Roast, top; *roast.* Loin Chop, left; *braise, panfry.* Loin Kidney Chop, lower right; *braise, panfry.*

**6.** Sirloin Roast, upper left; *roast.* Sirloin Steak, lower right; *braise or panfry this veal cut.*

**7.** Rump Roast, upper right; *roast, braise.* Boneless Rump Roast, left; *roast, braise.* Round Steak, lower right; *braise or panfry this veal steak.*

**8.** Round Steak (cut thick), upper right; *braise*. Round Roast, lower left; *roast or braise this veal roast.*

**9.** Veal Loaf, upper left; *bake*. Ground Veal Patties (wrapped with bacon), right; *panfry, braise, broil.*

## VEAL ROAST

OVEN 325°

Season a bone-in veal loin or leg roast, or a boneless veal shoulder roast. Place, fat side up, on rack in open pan. Lay 5 bacon slices over top. Insert meat thermometer (see page 428). Roast according to time and temperature chart, pages 430–431. Let stand 15 minutes before carving.

## STUFFED BREAST OF VEAL

OVEN 325°

Have meatman bone one 3-pound veal breast. Cut off triangular end and skewer to larger piece to make an even rectangle. Sprinkle with salt. Spread Sausage-apple Stuffing on half of meat. Fold other half over; fasten with metal skewers. Place on rack in shallow pan. Cover with foil and bake at 325° for 2 hours. Uncover and lay 5 bacon slices over top. Roast, uncovered, 1 hour more or till well done. Serves 6 to 8.

*Sausage-apple stuffing:* In skillet, cook ½ pound bulk pork sausage till lightly browned; drain. Combine 1 cup soft bread crumbs, 1 cup medium coarse cracker crumbs, 1 cup chopped tart apple, ¼ cup hot water, 2 tablespoons chopped onion, ½ teaspoon salt, dash pepper, and the drained sausage; mix well. Makes 2¾ cups.

## VEAL CHOPS

Dip 4 veal chops, ½ to ¾ inch thick, in flour*; brown in hot shortening; season with salt and pepper. Add ½ cup water. Cover; cook slowly about 45 minutes, or till done, adding more water if necessary during cooking. Makes 4 servings.

*Or, dip chops into mixture of 1 slightly beaten egg and 1 tablespoon water, then into ¼ cup fine cracker crumbs.

## BRAISED VEAL SHOULDER

OVEN 325°

Brown one 5- to 6-pound boneless veal shoulder roast on all sides in hot shortening. Season with salt and pepper. Place in roasting pan; add ½ cup water. Cover; cook at 325° for 2 to 2½ hours, or till tender. Vegetables may be added last 45 minutes. Makes 10 to 12 servings.

## VEAL SCALLOPINI

| | |
|---|---|
| 1½ pounds veal round steak | ½ cup tomato sauce |
| ¼ cup all-purpose flour | 2 tablespoons chopped green pepper |
| 1 teaspoon paprika | 4 ounces medium noodles |
| 1 3-ounce can broiled sliced mushrooms | Parmesan cheese |
| 1 teaspoon beef-flavored gravy base | |

OVEN 350°

Pound meat thoroughly with meat mallet. Cut into serving pieces. Coat with flour seasoned with ½ teaspoon salt, dash pepper, and paprika. Brown in a little hot shortening. Put in 9x9x2-inch baking dish.

Drain mushrooms, reserving liquid. Add water to mushroom liquid to make ½ cup; heat to boiling. Stir in beef-flavored gravy base and pour over meat.

Bake, covered, at 350° for 30 minutes. Combine tomato sauce, green pepper, and mushrooms; pour over meat and bake, uncovered, for 15 minutes more.

Meanwhile, cook noodles until tender in large amount boiling salted water; drain. Baste meat with sauce just before serving. Sprinkle with Parmesan cheese. Serve with hot buttered noodles. Serves 4 to 6.

## VEAL STEW 'N DUMPLINGS

Have 1½ pounds veal cut in 1-inch cubes. Coat meat with all-purpose flour. Brown slowly in small amount of hot shortening in Dutch oven. Add 4 cups tomato juice, 2 teaspoons salt, and 4 to 6 drops bottled hot pepper sauce. Cover and simmer for 1 hour. Add 1 cup diced pared potatoes, ½ cup sliced celery, and ½ cup chopped onion; cover and cook 30 minutes, or till vegetables are almost tender. Meanwhile, prepare Corn-meal Dumplings. Drop by rounded tablespoons onto *hot bubbling* stew. Cover tightly; steam 10 minutes (don't lift cover). Serves 6.

*Corn-meal Dumplings:* Combine one 10-ounce package corn bread mix and 2 tablespoons snipped parsley. Then, prepare mix according to package directions, *except* reduce milk to ⅓ cup.

## CITY CHICKEN

2 pounds veal, cut in
   1½-inch cubes
⅔ cup fine cracker
   crumbs
1½ teaspoons salt
1 teaspoon paprika
¾ teaspoon poultry
   seasoning

1 slightly beaten egg
2 tablespoons milk

\* \* \*

3 tablespoons shortening
1 chicken bouillon cube
½ cup boiling water

OVEN 350°

Thread veal cubes onto 6 short skewers. Combine crumbs, salt, paprika, and poultry seasoning. Combine egg and milk. Dip meat in egg mixture, then in crumbs. Brown slowly on all sides in hot shortening. Dissolve bouillon cube in boiling water; add to meat. Cover and bake at 350° for 45 minutes. Uncover; bake 30 minutes. Makes 6 servings.

## VEAL AND HAM BIRDS

2 to 2¹/₂ pounds veal round steak or cutlets, ¹/₄ inch thick
8 slices boiled ham
4 slices process Swiss cheese (4 ounces)
1 slightly beaten egg
2 tablespoons water

¹/₂ cup fine dry bread crumbs
1 10¹/₂-ounce can condensed cream of mushroom soup
2 tablespoons dry white wine
¹/₂ cup milk

OVEN 350°

Have meatman cut veal into 8 serving pieces and put through tenderizer. Or, at home pound each piece to about ¹/₈-inch thickness. Top each veal slice with a ham slice. Cut cheese in narrow strips and place a few stacks on each ham slice. Roll meat around cheese; secure with picks.

Dip rolls in mixture of egg and water; roll in crumbs to coat. Place seam side down in 13x9x2-inch baking dish. Combine soup, wine, and milk; heat till bubbly. Pour sauce around rolls.

Cover baking dish with foil; bake at 350° for 50 minutes. Uncover; bake 10 minutes or till crumbs are crisp. Makes 8 servings.

## VEAL PARMIGIANO

3 tablespoons butter
½ cup cornflake crumbs
¼ cup grated Parmesan cheese
1 pound veal cutlets or round steak, about ¼ inch thick
1 slightly beaten egg

1 8-ounce can tomato sauce
½ teaspoon dried oregano, crushed
½ teaspoon sugar
Dash onion salt
2 thin slices mozzarella cheese, halved (4 ounces)

OVEN 400°

Melt butter in 10x6x1½-inch baking dish in 400° oven. Combine crumbs, Parmesan, ½ teaspoon salt, and dash pepper. Cut veal in serving pieces; dip in egg, then in crumb mixture. Place in baking dish. Bake at 400° for 20 minutes. Turn meat; bake 15 to 20 minutes more or till tender.

Meanwhile, combine tomato sauce, oregano, sugar, and onion salt; heat to boiling, stirring frequently. Pour sauce over meat. Top with cheese. Return to oven to melt cheese. Serves 4.

## WIENER SCHNITZEL

1½ pounds veal round steak or cutlets, ½ inch thick
¼ cup all-purpose flour
1 beaten egg

1 tablespoon milk
1 cup fine dry bread crumbs
¼ cup salad oil
Lemon wedges

Cut meat into 4 pieces; pound ¼ to ⅛ inch thick. Cut small slits around edges to prevent curling. Coat meat with flour seasoned with 1 teaspoon salt and ¼ teaspoon pepper. Combine egg and milk. Dip floured cutlets in egg mixture, then in bread crumbs. Cook meat in hot salad oil for 2 to 3 minutes on each side, or till tender. Serve with lemon. Serves 4.

**Wiener Schnitzel a la Holstein:** Prepare Wiener Schnitzel. In skillet, fry 4 eggs in butter till whites are set. Add 1 tablespoon water. Cover; cook till eggs are done. Place one cooked egg on each veal cutlet. Sprinkle with snipped parsley.

# PORK CUTS

## and How To Cook Them

Locate wholesale cuts on drawing, identify their retail pieces in the same numbered picture, then note cooking methods.

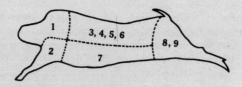

**1.** Blade Boston Roast, top; *roast.* Smoked Shoulder Roll, left; *roast, cook in liquid.* Blade Steak, right; *braise, broil, panfry.*

**2.** Smoked Arm Picnic Roast, top; *roast, cook in liquid.* Canned Arm Picnic, left; *roast.* Smoked Hocks (cross cut), right; *roast, cook in liquid.*

**3.** Rib Crown Roast, top; *roast*. Center Loin Roast, right; *roast*. Rib Chops (stuffed); *roast, braise*.

**4.** Sirloin Roast, upper right; *roast*. Whole Tenderloin, left; *roast, braise, broil, panfry*. Loin Chop, lower right; *braise, panfry, or broil this pork chop*.

**5.** Loin Blade Roast, upper right; *roast*. Back Rib, upper left; *roast, braise*. Country-Style Rib, lower left; *roast, braise*. Rib Chop, lower right; *braise, panfry, broil*.

**6.** Canadian-Style Bacon, upper left; *roast*. Sliced Canadian-Style Bacon, lower left; *broil, panbroil, panfry*. Boneless Top Loin Roast, upper right; *roast*. Loin Butterfly Chop; *braise, broil, panfry*.

**7.** Spareribs, left; *roast, braise, cook in liquid*. Salt Pork, upper right; *cook in liquid (for seasoning), panbroil, panfry*. Bacon: Slab, middle right; Sliced, lower right; *broil, panbroil, panfry*.

**8.** Smoked Ham: Shank Portion, left; *roast, cook in liquid.* Rump Portion, upper right; *roast, cook in liquid.* Center Slice, lower right; *broil, panbroil, panfry, roast.*

**9.** Boneless Smoked Ham Roll, upper left; *roast.* Country-Style Ham; Shank Portion, right; *cook in liquid and roast.* Canned Ham, lower left; *roast.*

## CROWN ROAST OF PORK

OVEN 325°

Have one 5½- to 6-pound pork rib crown roast (14 to 16 ribs) made from strip of pork loin (backbone removed). Have roast tied securely around loin area as well as near bones, and have ends of ribs "frenched" (meat removed from about a one-inch section). Season. Place in shallow roasting pan, bone ends up*; wrap tips in foil. Insert meat thermometer in loin, making sure it does not rest on bone.

Roast, uncovered, at 325° about 2½ to 3 hours, or till thermometer reads 170°. An hour before meat is done, fill center with Corn Stuffing. To carve, slice between ribs allowing one rib per serving.

*Or, if roast is to be filled after roasting with potatoes or other vegetables, place rib bones down forming a rack.

Have backbone loosened from ribs of pork loin roast. Rub salt, pepper, and sage over fat side; insert meat thermometer in center of meat. See roasting chart, pages 430–432.

## CORN STUFFING

Mix one 1-pound 1-ounce can cream-style corn, one 12-ounce can vacuum packed whole kernel corn, drained, 1 beaten egg, 1 cup soft bread crumbs, 1/4 cup each chopped onion and green pepper, 2 tablespoons chopped canned pimiento, 1 teaspoon salt, and dash pepper. Fill roast 1 hour before done. Place remaining stuffing in casserole. Dot with butter; bake alongside crown roast at 325°.

## STUFFED PORK SHOULDER

1 4- to 5-pound boneless
  pork arm picnic for
  stuffing

Poultry seasoning
Celery Stuffing,
page 538

OVEN 325°

Rub outside of meat and pocket with poultry seasoning; sprinkle with salt and pepper. Lightly stuff with Celery Stuffing. (Cut pocket larger to hold more stuffing or bake remaining in casserole last hour.) Skewer and lace closed. Roast, uncovered, fat side up on rack in shallow roasting pan at 325° for 3 to 3¾ hours, or till well done. Make gravy. Serves 12 to 15.

Stuff pork chops lightly. Close opening with wooden picks or skewers, poking them in at a slight angle so meat will lie flat in baking dish. Lace with string; tie.

## SMOKED PORK DINNER

OVEN 350°

Place one 2-pound smoked pork shoulder roll (butt) in Dutch oven; cover with cold water. Bring just to boiling; simmer for 2 hours or till tender. Remove from water. Slice; spread with prepared mustard.

In 13x9x2-inch baking dish, arrange meat and onion slices alternately. Place one 1-pound 1-ounce can vacuum packed sweet potatoes around edges; top with ¼ cup brown sugar and drizzle with ¼ cup butter, melted. Bake, covered, at 350° for 1 hour. Uncover; bake 30 minutes longer. Makes 8 servings.

## FRUIT STUFFED PORK

8 double-rib pork chops, with pockets cut for stuffing
2 cups small dry bread cubes
1 cup finely chopped unpared apple
1 cup shredded sharp process American cheese
¼ cup light raisins
¼ cup butter, melted
¼ cup orange juice
½ teaspoon salt
¼ teaspoon ground cinnamon

OVEN 350°

Sprinkle salt and pepper over chops. Combine bread cubes, apple, cheese, raisins, butter, orange juice, ½ teaspoon salt, and cinnamon. Stuff mixture into pockets. Press edges of pockets together to seal. Bake at 350° for 1½ hours, or till chops are tender. Makes 8 servings.

## PIZZA PORK CHOPS

6 double-rib pork chops, about 1¼ inches thick
1 cup packaged herb-seasoned stuffing mix
¼ cup chopped onion
¼ to ½ teaspoon dried oregano, crushed
⅓ cup water

2 tablespoons butter or margarine
1 10½-ounce can pizza sauce
1 8-ounce can tomato sauce
3 slices sharp process American cheese, halved diagonally

OVEN 350°

Have pocket cut on *bone side* of pork chops. Trim off excess fat. Combine stuffing mix, onion, and oregano. Prepare stuffing mixture according to label directions, *using only ⅓ cup water and 2 tablespoons butter or margarine.* Lightly stuff pockets of chops. Season chops with salt and pepper. Place in 13x9x2-inch baking dish.

Combine pizza sauce and tomato sauce; pour over meat. Cover tightly with foil. Bake at 350° for 1½ hours, or till well done. Remove foil. Top with halved cheese slices. Makes 6 servings.

## BARBECUED PORK CHOPS

6 pork chops, 1 inch thick
1 8-ounce can tomato sauce
½ cup catsup

1 teaspoon Worcestershire sauce
½ teaspoon onion salt
½ teaspoon liquid smoke

Trim excess fat from chops. Cook trimmings in heavy skillet till 1 tablespoon fat accumulates. Discard trimmings. Brown chops slowly on both sides in hot fat. Drain off fat. Season chops with salt and pepper. For sauce, combine tomato sauce, catsup, Worcestershire, onion salt, and liquid smoke; pour over chops. Cover and simmer about 1 hour, or till tender, turning occasionally. Makes 6 servings.

## CHICKEN-FRIED PORK CHOPS

| | |
|---|---|
| 6 pork chops, ¹/₂ inch thick | ²/₃ cup fine dry bread crumbs *or* cracker crumbs |
| 1 beaten egg | 2 tablespoons shortening |
| 1 tablespoon milk | ¹/₂ teaspoon salt |

Trim excess fat from chops. Combine beaten egg and milk. Dip pork chops in egg mixture, then in bread crumbs or cracker crumbs. In heavy skillet, brown chops on both sides in hot shortening. Season with salt. Add ¹/₄ cup water. Cover and cook over low heat for 30 to 45 minutes, or till tender. Lift chops occasionally to prevent sticking. For crisp coating, remove cover the last 15 minutes. Makes 6 servings.

## BRAISED PORK

Trim excess fat from ³/₄- to 1-inch thick pork chops. Cook trimmings in heavy skillet till small amount of fat accumulates. Discard trimmings. Brown chops slowly on both sides in hot fat; drain off excess fat. Season chops with salt and pepper. Add a little hot water, if desired. Cover tightly; cook over low heat for 45 to 60 minutes, or till tender. Make gravy from pan juices, if desired.

## CANADIAN-STYLE BACON

**Broiled:** Slice Canadian-style bacon ¹/₄-inch thick; slash edges. Place on cold broiler rack. Broil 3 to 4 inches from heat, 1 to 2 minutes on each side.

**Panbroiled:** Slash edges of ¹/₄-inch thick Canadian-style bacon slices. Preheat skillet; brush lightly with oil. Brown bacon quickly, about 2 to 3 minutes per side.

**Baked:** Place one 2-pound piece Canadian-style bacon in shallow baking pan; spread Tangy Mustard Glaze (page 471) over. Bake, uncovered, at 325° for 1¹/₄ hours. Baste with glaze every 15 minutes. Heat remaining glaze and pass. Serves 8.

## SAUSAGE-STUFFING BAKE

1½ pounds bulk pork
   sausage
1 cup packaged herb-
   seasoned stuffing mix
1 cup finely chopped
   pared tart apple
½ cup finely chopped
   celery

¼ cup finely chopped
   onion
2 tablespoons snipped
   parsley
2 tablespoons chili sauce
¼ teaspoon dry mustard
¼ teaspoon pepper

OVEN 375°

Shape sausage in 12 patties, ¼ inch thick. Prepare stuffing according to package directions, *using ¼ cup water and 2 tablespoons butter.* Add apple, celery, onion, parsley, chili sauce, mustard, and pepper; toss well.

Arrange *6 of the sausage patties* in shallow baking pan. Top each with ½ cup stuffing, then another patty; hold with wooden pick through center. Bake at 375° about 45 minutes, or till done. Garnish with crab apples, if desired. Makes 6 servings.

## TENDERLOINS IN CREAM

6 pork tenderloin patties
   *or* pork cutlets
3 tablespoons all-
   purpose flour

2 to 3 tablespoons
   shortening
¾ cup light cream

Sprinkle meat with flour; season. In large skillet, brown meat in hot shortening. Add cream; cover; simmer 40 minutes, or till tender. Trim with parsley. Serves 6.

## BACON

**Fried:** Put bacon strips in unheated skillet. Cook over moderately low heat for 6 to 8 minutes, turning often. Drain. For crisp bacon, spoon off fat while cooking.

**Broiled:** Separate bacon slices and place on cold rack of broiler pan. Broil 3 to 5 inches from heat till desired doneness; turn only once. Watch closely.

Bacon the easy way—cooked in the oven. Place separated slices of bacon on cold rack in shallow baking pan. Bake at 400° for 10 minutes—no turning or draining.

## SAUSAGE

**Patties:** Buy or shape bulk pork sausage in a roll; cut in thin patties. Place in a cold skillet. Cook slowly 15 to 20 minutes, turning once. Drain thoroughly.

**Links:** Place in cold skillet; add ¼ cup cold water. Cover and cook slowly 5 minutes; drain. Uncover and cook slowly 12 to 14 minutes, turning with tongs till all sides are brown. Do not prick.

## STUFFED PORK TENDERLOIN

OVEN 325°

Have 2 pork tenderloins of equal size split open lengthwise (do not cut through); flatten. Season. Spread Mushroom Stuffing (page 538) over one; lay other on top. Season with salt and pepper and top with 4 bacon slices. Place on rack in open roasting pan. Roast in a slow oven (325°) for 1½ hours. Makes 8 servings.

## SWEET-SOUR PORK

1½ pounds lean pork, cut in 2x½-inch strips
2 tablespoons hot shortening
1 chicken bouillon cube
1 1-pound 4½-ounce can pineapple chunks
¼ cup brown sugar
2 tablespoons cornstarch
¼ cup vinegar
1 tablespoon soy sauce
1 medium green pepper, cut in strips
¼ cup thinly sliced onion
Hot cooked rice

Brown pork slowly in hot shortening. Add 1 cup water, bouillon cube, and ¼ teaspoon salt; mix well. Cover and simmer till tender, about 1 hour. Meanwhile, drain pineapple, reserving syrup. Combine brown sugar and cornstarch; add reserved pineapple syrup, vinegar, soy sauce, and ½ teaspoon salt. Cook and stir over medium-high heat till thickened and bubbly.

Remove from heat. Add sauce to pork; mix well. Stir in pineapple, green pepper, and onion. Cook over low heat 2 to 3 minutes or till vegetables are tender-crisp. Serve over rice. Makes 6 servings.

## ORANGE-GLAZED RIBS

4 pounds pork spareribs, cut in serving-sized pieces
⅔ cup orange marmalade
3 tablespoons soy sauce

2 tablespoons lemon juice
¾ teaspoon ground ginger
Orange slices

OVEN 450°

Place spareribs, meaty side down, in shallow roasting pan. Bake at 450° for 30 minutes. Remove meat from oven; drain off excess fat. Turn ribs meaty side up. Reduce oven temperature to 350°; continue baking 30 minutes longer.

Combine orange marmalade, soy sauce, lemon juice, and ground ginger; blend well. Spoon *half* of the mixture over spareribs. Bake 30 minutes longer, or till tender, spooning remaining sauce over ribs occasionally. Garnish with orange slices, if desired. Makes 4 servings.

## OVEN BARBECUED RIBS

OVEN 350°

Simmer, covered, 4 pounds pork back ribs, cut in serving pieces, in enough salted water to cover about 1 hour, or till nearly tender.

Meanwhile, in saucepan melt 1 tablespoon butter; add 1 clove garlic, crushed, and cook 4 to 5 minutes. Add ½ cup catsup, ⅓ cup chili sauce, 2 tablespoons brown sugar, 2 tablespoons chopped onion, 1 tablespoon Worcestershire sauce, 1 tablespoon prepared mustard, 1 teaspoon celery seed, ¼ teaspoon salt, dash bottled hot pepper sauce, and 3 thin lemon slices. Bring to boiling. Drain ribs; place in shallow pan; pour boiling sauce over. Bake at 350° for 20 minutes, basting often with sauce. Makes 6 to 8 servings.

## SPARERIBS WITH KRAUT

| | |
|---|---|
| 3 pounds pork spareribs | 1½ cups tomato juice |
| 1 1-pound 11-ounce can (3½ cups) sauerkraut | 2 tablespoons brown sugar |
| 1 cup finely chopped unpared tart apple | 2 teaspoons caraway seed |
| 1 cup shredded carrot | |

Cut ribs in pieces; season with 2 teaspoons salt and ¼ teaspoon pepper; place in Dutch oven and brown well. Combine kraut (including liquid) with remaining ingredients; spoon over ribs. Simmer, covered, 1¾ hours, or till ribs are done, basting with juices several times during the last hour. Skim off excess fat. Makes 6 servings.

## ITALIAN PICNIC ROAST

| | |
|---|---|
| 1 5- to 6-pound smoked pork arm picnic roast | 6 garlic cloves, quartered |
| | ¾ cup cider vinegar |

OVEN 350°

Remove skin from picnic. Place in 10-quart Dutch oven; cover with water; add garlic and vinegar. Cover; simmer 2½ to 3 hours. Remove from liquid. Bake in shallow pan at 350° for 15 to 20 minutes. Makes 8 to 12 servings.

## HAM WITH MUSTARD GLAZE

| | |
|---|---|
| 1 ham | 2 tablespoons fruit juice |
| ½ cup brown sugar | Whole cloves |
| ½ teaspoon dry mustard | |

OVEN 325°

Place ham, fat side up, on rack in shallow pan. Do not cover or add water. Score ham fat in diamonds (cut only

¼-inch deep). (A strip of heavy paper, 12x2 inches, makes an easy guide for cutting parallel lines.) Insert meat thermometer (see page 428). Roast in slow oven (325°) according to chart, page 431. Meanwhile, prepare Tangy Mustard Glaze. The last 30 minutes of cooking time, spoon fat from pan. Stud ham with whole cloves. Spoon glaze over ham. Continue baking, basting occasionally.

*Tangy Mustard Glaze:* Combine brown sugar, dry mustard, and fruit juice.

## HAM CROQUETTES

Melt 3 tablespoons butter; blend in ¼ cup all-purpose flour. Add ¾ cup milk all at once. Cook and stir till thick and bubbly; cook and stir I minute. Remove from heat. Add 2 cups coarsely ground cooked ham, 1 teaspoon grated onion, and 2 teaspoons prepared mustard; blend well. Chill well. Shape into 8 to 10 balls. Roll in ¾ cup fine dry bread crumbs. Shape into cones, handling lightly. Dip into mixture of 1 beaten egg and 2 tablespoons water; roll in crumbs again. Fry in deep hot fat (365°) for 1½ to 2 minutes, till heated through. Drain. Serve with Creamy Egg Sauce. Makes 4 or 5 servings.

*Creamy Egg Sauce:* Melt 2 tablespoons butter; blend in 2 tablespoons all-purpose flour, ¼ teaspoon salt, and dash white pepper. Add 1 cup milk. Cook and stir till thick. Add 1 hard-cooked egg, chopped.

## HAM PATTIES

Combine 2 cups ground cooked ham, ½ cup soft bread crumbs, ¼ cup chopped green onion, ⅓ cup milk, 1 slightly beaten egg, and dash pepper. Shape into 4 patties. Brown slowly in small amount hot shortening. Heat and stir I cup dairy sour cream just till hot. Top patties with sour cream and snipped green onion tops. Serves 4.

## HAM LOAF

OVEN 350°

Combine 1 slightly beaten egg, ½ cup milk, ⅔ cup medium cracker crumbs, ¼ cup chopped onion, and dash pepper. Add 1 pound ground ham and 1 pound ground pork; mix well. Press into 8½x4½x2½-inch loaf dish, then turn out into shallow baking dish. Bake at 350° for 1½ hours. Spoon Tangy Mustard Glaze (page 471) over last 30 minutes. Serves 8.

## TO COOK HAM SLICES

| HAM SLICES | TOTAL MINUTES | |
| --- | --- | --- |
| | Broil | Panfry |
| Fully cooked, bone-in, 1 inch thick | 14 to 16 | 16 to 18 |
| Cook-before-eating, bone-in, 1 inch thick | 18 to 20 | 20 to 22 |

**Broiled:** Slash fat edge of ham at 1-inch intervals to prevent meat from curling during cooking. Place meat on cold rack in broiler pan. Broil according to chart above, about 3 inches from heat.

**Panfried:** In heavy skillet, cook ham in small amount hot shortening over medium heat according to chart; turn occasionally.

# • CARVE CLOVE-STUDDED
## BAKED HAM WITH A FLOURISH •

To carve a ham: With shank to right, cut 2 or 3 long slices from *thin* side and stand ham on this base (top picture).

Anchor with meat fork. Remove a small wedge 6 inches from shank end. At large end, cut down to leg in front of bone that angles upward (find bone with skewer), and cut to leg bone. Run knife along leg bone (middle picture). Lift this cushion of ham to cutting surface. Place, cut side down, and slice (bottom picture). Return ham to first position; slice both ends.

# LAMB CUTS
## and How To Cook Them

Locate wholesale cuts on drawing, identify their retail pieces in the same numbered picture, then note cooking methods.

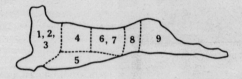

**1.** Whole Shoulder; Square Cut, upper right; *roast.* Boneless Shoulder Roast (netted), lower left; *roast, braise.*

**2.** Boneless Cushion Shoulder Roast, top; *roast.* Boneless Blade (Saratoga) Chops, bottom; *broil, panbroil, panfry, braise.*

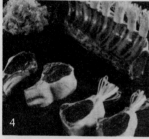

**3.** Blade Chop, upper left; *broil, panbroil, panfry, braise.* Arm Chop, lower left; *broil, panbroil, panfry, braise.* Lamb Shanks, right; *braise, cook in liquid.*

**4.** Frenched Rib Roast, upper right; *roast.* Rib Chops, left; *broil, panbroil, panfry.* Frenched Rib Chops, lower right; *broil, panbroil, panfry.*

**5.** Top to bottom: Riblets; *braise, cook in liquid, grill.* Spareribs; *braise, roast.* Stuffed Chops; *roast, braise.*

**6.** Loin Roast, upper left; *roast.* Loin Chop, upper right; *broil, panbroil, panfry.* Loin Double (English) Chop, lower left; *broil, panbroil, panfry.*

**7.** Boneless Loin Double Roast, upper left; *roast.* Lamb Cubes for Kabobs, upper right; *broil.* Boneless Loin Double (English) Chop, lower left; *broil, panbroil, panfry.*

**8.** Leg Sirloin Half Roast, upper left; *roast*. Leg Sirloin Chop, lower left; *broil, panbroil, panfry, roast*. Leg Center Slice, lower right (section 9 on drawing); *broil, panbroil, panfry*.

**9.** Leg American-Style Roast, upper left. Leg Frenched-Style Roast, right. Boneless Leg Roast (netted), lower left. *Roast*.

## LAMB STEW

1½ pounds boneless lamb, cut in 1-inch cubes
1 clove garlic, minced
4 medium carrots, cut in 2-inch lengths
6 tiny onions
3 small potatoes, pared, cubed
½ teaspoon dried basil, crushed
1 10-ounce package frozen peas
2 tablespoons snipped parsley

Coat meat with flour. In large saucepan, brown meat in small amount hot shortening. Add 3 cups water, garlic, 2 teaspoons salt, and ¼ teaspoon pepper. Cover; simmer 1 hour, or till meat is almost tender. Add carrots, onion, potatoes, and basil; cook, uncovered, 20 minutes, or till done. Add peas and parsley. Cook 5 minutes. Season with salt and pepper. Serves 6.

## BARBECUED LAMB RIBLETS

In large skillet, brown 3 to 4 pounds lamb riblets, cut in serving pieces. Skim off fat. Season with salt and pepper; top with slices of 1 lemon. Combine ³/₄ cup catsup, ³/₄ cup water, ¹/₂ cup chopped onion, 3 tablespoons Worcestershire sauce, 2 tablespoons brown sugar, 1 tablespoon vinegar, ³/₄ teaspoon salt, and dash bottled hot pepper sauce; pour over meat. Cover and simmer 1¹/₂ hours, or till meat is tender. Skim off fat. Makes 6 servings.

## HERBED LAMB SHANKS

In large skillet, brown 4 lamb shanks (about 2¹/₂ pounds) in 1 tablespoon butter. Add 1¹/₂ cups water and 1 teaspoon salt. Cover skillet tightly; cook over low heat for 1 hour. In small skillet, melt 2 tablespoons butter; blend in ¹/₄ cup all-purpose flour. Cook and stir over low heat till mixture is browned. Add to meat; cook and stir till gravy is thickened.

Add ¹/₂ cup water, 1 tablespoon snipped parsley, 1 clove garlic, minced, ¹/₈ teaspoon dried marjoram, crushed, and dash ground mace. Cover and cook about 1 hour more, till meat is tender. Serve on hot cooked noodles. Spoon on a little gravy; pass remaining. Makes 4 servings.

## BROILED LAMB CHOPS

Slash fat edges of lamb loin, rib, or arm chops cut ³/₄ inch thick. Broil 3 inches from heat 5 to 6 minutes. Turn; broil 5 to 6 minutes, or till done.

For snappy flavor, brush once or twice on each side with Italian dressing.

## LAMB CHOPS SUPREME

- 6 lamb arm or sirloin chops, 1/2 inch thick
- 1 10 1/2-ounce can condensed consomme
- 1/2 cup chopped celery
- 1/2 cup sliced green onion
- 1/2 teaspoon dried thyme, crushed
- 1 3-ounce can broiled chopped mushrooms
- 3 tablespoons all-purpose flour
- 1 tablespoon dried parsley flakes

In large skillet, slowly brown chops in small amount hot shortening; sprinkle with salt and pepper. Drain off fat. Add consomme, celery, green onion, and thyme. Cover; simmer 40 to 45 minutes, or till meat is tender. Stack chops to one side. Drain mushrooms, reserving liquid. Stir and blend mushroom liquid slowly into flour. Gradually stir flour mixture into consomme in skillet; cook and stir till thickened and bubbly. Add drained mushrooms and parsley; heat through. Makes 6 servings.

## LAMB WITH DILL SAUCE

Combine 1 beaten egg, 1/2 cup quick-cooking rolled oats, 1/4 cup finely chopped onion, 1 teaspoon salt, 1/4 teaspoon dried thyme, crushed, and dash pepper. Add 1 1/2 pounds ground lamb; mix well. Shape into 6 patties. Wrap 1 slice bacon around each; fasten with wooden pick. Broil 5 inches from heat 10 minutes; turn and broil 5 minutes more. Serve with Dill Sauce. Serves 6.

*Dill Sauce:* Cook 1 tablespoon finely chopped onion in 1 tablespoon butter till tender. Blend in 2 teaspoons all-purpose flour, 2 tablespoons grated Parmesan cheese, 1/2 teaspoon dried dillweed, 1/2 teaspoon paprika, and dash salt. Add 1 cup milk all at once. Cook and stir till bubbly.

# • TO CARVE A LEG OF LAMB
## THE PROFESSIONAL WAY •

1. With shank on right, cut 2 or 3 slices from thin side parallel to bone; turn leg to rest on this base. Anchor with fork.

2. Beginning at shank end, cut ¼-inch slices down to leg bone. Continue cutting till bone pointing upward is reached.

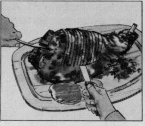

3. With fork still in place, start at shank end again and cut along leg bone to release horseshoe-shaped slices of lamb.

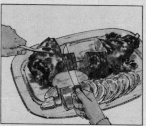

4. Carve 10 to 12 slices from a 6- to 7-pound leg of lamb. Tip roast on its side in order to carve the remaining meat.

## LAMB SHOULDER ROLL

1 4- to 5-pound lamb
  shoulder roast
3 tablespoons all-
  purpose flour

1 tablespoon dry
  mustard
1/2 teaspoon salt
1 cup currant jelly

Have roast boned and rolled. Place on rack in open roasting pan. Mix flour, mustard, salt, and 1/4 teaspoon pepper; blend in 1/2 cup cold water. Spread over meat. Insert meat thermometer. Roast according to chart, page 432. Spread with jelly the last hour; baste every 15 minutes. Serves 8.

## SAUCED LAMB KABOBS

Drain one 1-pound 1-ounce jar purple plums, reserving 1/4 cup syrup. Pit and sieve plums. Combine reserved syrup, sieved plums, 2 to 4 tablespoons lemon juice, 1 tablespoon soy sauce, 1 teaspoon Worcestershire sauce, 1/2 clove garlic, crushed, and 1/2 teaspoon dried basil, crushed. Marinate 1 pound boneless lamb, cut in 1-inch cubes, in mixture in refrigerator overnight. Thread meat on skewers; season with 1/2 teaspoon salt and dash pepper. Broil 4 inches from heat 10 to 12 minutes; turn and baste often. Heat marinade 5 minutes; serve with meat. Serves 4.

## BROILED VENISON STEAKS

Brush four 1/2-inch-thick venison steaks from leg, rib, or loin chops of young animal with 2 tablespoons salad oil. Let stand 15 minutes. Broil steaks 3 inches from heat for 7 to 10 minutes; turn. Broil on other side for 7 to 10 minutes. Combine 1/4 cup melted butter or margarine, 1 tablespoon onion juice, and dash salt; brush on broiled steaks. Makes 4 servings.

## HASENPFEFFER

Cut one 1- to 2-pound ready-to-cook rabbit into serving pieces. Mix 3 cups water, 1 cup vinegar, 1/2 cup sugar, 1 medium onion, sliced, 1 teaspoon mixed pickling spices, 2 teaspoons salt, and 1/4 teaspoon pepper. Add rabbit;

refrigerate 2 days. Remove meat; dry (reserve 1 *cup* marinade).

Place 2 tablespoons all-purpose flour and meat in plastic bag; shake to coat. In skillet, brown meat in 2 tablespoons hot salad oil. Gradually add reserved marinade. Cover; simmer for 45 to 60 minutes, or till meat is tender (add water, if necessary). Remove meat. Thicken liquid for gravy, if desired. Makes 2 or 3 servings.

## TO COOK FRANKFURTERS

**In water:** Cover frankfurters with cold water; bring to boiling. Simmer 5 minutes.

**Panfried:** Score frankfurters, making shallow (1/4-inch) diagonal cuts 1 inch apart, if desired. In skillet, brown frankfurters in 1 tablespoon hot butter or margarine for 5 minutes. Do not overbrown.

## CONEY ISLANDS

Cook 10 frankfurters in water (see directions above). Place franks into 10 heated frankfurter buns; top with prepared mustard and chopped onion, if desired. Spoon hot Coney Sauce atop. Makes 10 servings.

*Coney Sauce:* In skillet, brown 1/2 pound ground beef slowly but thoroughly, breaking with fork till fine. Add 1/4 cup water, 1/4 cup chopped onion, 1 clove garlic, minced, one 8-ounce can tomato sauce, 1/2 teaspoon chili powder, and 1/2 teaspoon salt. Simmer, uncovered, 10 minutes, or till heated through. Makes 1 1/3 cups.

## BEEF AND KIDNEY PIE

OVEN 450°

Combine 1 beef kidney, 4 cups warm water, and 1 tablespoon salt; soak 1 hour; drain. Cover with cold water. Bring to boil; simmer 20 minutes. Drain; remove membrane and hard parts. Cut in 1/2-inch cubes.

Coat 1 pound beef round steak, cut in 1/2-inch cubes, with 1/4 cup all-purpose flour. In Dutch oven, brown steak in 3 tablespoons hot oil. Add 1 medium onion, sliced, 2 cups water, and 1 teaspoon Worcestershire sauce. Cover; simmer 30 minutes, or till tender. Mix 1/2 cup cold water, 1/4 cup all-purpose flour, 1 teaspoon salt, and dash pepper. Stir into hot mixture. Cook and stir till bubbly. Add kidney; heat. Pour into 1 1/2-quart casserole.

Prepare pastry according to directions on pages 491–492 using 1 1/2 cups all-purpose flour, 1/2 teaspoon salt, 1/2 cup shortening, and 4 to 5 tablespoons cold water. Roll in circle 1/2 to 1 inch larger than casserole. Place atop *hot* meat mixture; turn under edge and flute. Cut slits for escape of steam. Brush with milk. Bake at 450° for 20 to 25 minutes. Serves 6.

## CREAMED SWEETBREADS

Cover 1 pound sweetbreads with 1 quart water, 1/2 teaspoon salt, and 1 tablespoon vinegar. Simmer 20 minutes, or till tender. Drain; cube, removing white membrane.

In a saucepan, melt 1/4 cup butter over low heat. Blend in 3 tablespoons all-purpose flour, 1/2 teaspoon salt, and dash pepper. Add 2 cups milk all at once. Cook quickly, stirring constantly, till mixture thickens and bubbles. Add sweetbreads and one 10-ounce package frozen peas with mushrooms, cooked and drained. Heat through, stirring gently. Serve over toast points or pastry shells. Serves 6.

## CHICKEN-FRIED HEART

Slice one 2-pound beef heart,* 1/2 inch thick. Coat with seasoned flour. Brown on all sides in small amount hot shortening. Add small amount hot water; cover tightly. Cook slowly about 2 hours, or till tender. Add more water, if needed. Serves 6.

*Or, use veal, pork, or lamb hearts.

## LIVER

Remove membrane and veins from 1 pound calves liver, 3/8- to 1/2-inch thick.

**Panfried:** Dip slices of liver in seasoned flour. Brown quickly on one side in 1/4 cup hot shortening, about 1 minute; turn, cook 2 to 3 minutes. Don't overcook. Serves 4.

**Broiled:** Dip slices of liver in 2 tablespoons butter, melted, or French salad dressing. Broil 3 inches from heat for 3 minutes. Turn, top with bacon slices; broil 3 minutes longer, turn bacon once. Serves 4.

**Braised:** Dip slices in ¼ cup flour seasoned with salt and pepper. Brown quickly on both sides in 3 to 4 tablespoons hot shortening. Reduce heat. Add 1 beef bouillon cube dissolved in ½ cup boiling water and 1 medium onion, thinly sliced. Cook over low heat 15 to 20 minutes. Serves 4.

## LIVER LOAF

OVEN 350°

Cover 1 pound calves liver with hot water; simmer 5 minutes. Drain; reserve 1 cup stock. Put liver and 1 medium onion, quartered, through medium blade of food chopper. Add 1 pound ground pork, 1 cup soft bread crumbs, 1 teaspoon salt, dash pepper, I teaspoon Worcestershire sauce, ½ teaspoon celery salt, 2 beaten eggs, and reserved stock. Form loaf in 8½x4½x2½-inch baking dish; top with 3 slices bacon, halved. Bake at 350° for 1 hour. Drain off excess fat. Let stand 10 minutes. Serves 8.

## GINGER-SAUCED TONGUE

Place one 2- to 4-pound smoked beef tongue in Dutch oven; cover with water. Add 1 medium onion, sliced, 1 teaspoon whole cloves, 1 teaspoon whole black peppercorns, and 4 bay leaves. Cover; simmer till tender, allowing 1 hour *per pound*. Remove meat; strain and reserve 1 cup liquid for sauce. Cut off bones and gristle from large end; slit skin on underside from large end to tip; peel off. Slice meat on a slant. Serve with hot Gingersnap Sauce. Makes 4 servings per pound.

*Gingersnap Sauce:* Crush 5 gingersnaps; combine with ⅓ cup brown sugar, ⅓ cup raisins, ¼ cup vinegar, and reserved liquid. Cook and stir till mixture is smooth.

## PERFECT PAN GRAVY

Remove roast to hot platter. Leaving crusty bits in pan, pour meat juices and fat into large measuring cup. Skim off fat, reserving 3 to 4 tablespoons. For 2 cups gravy, return reserved fat to pan. Stir in ¼ cup all-purpose flour. Blend fat and flour. Cook and stir over low heat till bubbly.

*Remove pan from the heat.* Add 2 cups liquid (meat juices plus water, milk, or giblet broth) all at once; blend well. Season with salt and pepper. If desired, add a dash of dried thyme, crushed, and a few drops Kitchen Bouquet sauce. Return pan to heat. Simmer and stir 2 to 3 minutes. Makes 6 to 8 servings.

**Giblet Gravy:** Remove turkey roast to hot platter. Prepare Perfect Pan Gravy *except* add giblet broth (page 533) to juices to make 2 cups liquid. Add chopped cooked giblets. Continue as directed above.

## HURRY-UP GRAVY

Remove meat from roasting pan. Skim off excess fat from meat juices. Pour ¼ cup water into pan. Stir well to loosen crusty bits on bottom of pan. Blend in one 10½-ounce can condensed cream of chicken soup *or* cream of mushroom soup. Heat and stir over low heat. Thin with more water, if necessary. Makes about 1½ cups.

## POT ROAST GRAVY

Lift pot roast to hot platter. Skim most of fat from pan juices. Add water to juices to make 1½ cups. Put ⅓ cup cold water in shaker; add 3 tablespoons all-purpose flour; shake well. Stir into juices; cook and stir till gravy is bubbly. Season with salt and pepper. Simmer 2 to 3 minutes; stir occasionally. Makes about 2 cups.

## SOUR CREAM GRAVY

Remove pot roast from pan. Skim fat from pan juices. Measure pan juices; add water if necessary to make 1½ cups. Blend 1 cup dairy sour cream and 3 tablespoons all-purpose flour; gradually stir juices into sour cream mixture. Return to pan. Cook and stir till thickened and bubbly. Season with salt and pepper. Makes 3 cups gravy.

# MEAT PRICE CHART

Find the best meat buys by using the Meat Price Chart to compare cost per serving. Run your finger across one of the rows. The chart shows that ground beef at $.89 a pound is $.30 a serving, but a boneless beef roast at $1.69 a pound is just $.28 a serving. Even though the roast costs more per pound, it costs less per serving.

Since the chart is designed to help you stretch meat, the portions may be smaller than you are accustomed to serving (each is based on about 2½ ounces of cooked meat).

| Price per pound | Cost per Serving of Boneless and Lean Meat (6 servings per pound) | Cost per Serving of Meat with Some Bone or Fat (3 servings per pound) | Cost per Serving of Meat with Much Bone or Fat (2 servings per pound) |
|---|---|---|---|
| $ .59 | $ .10 | $ .20 | $ .30 |
| .69 | .12 | .23 | .35 |
| .79 | .13 | .26 | .40 |
| .89 | .15 | .30 | .45 |
| .99 | .17 | .33 | .50 |
| 1.09 | .18 | .36 | .55 |
| 1.19 | .20 | .40 | .60 |
| 1.29 | .22 | .43 | .65 |
| 1.39 | .23 | .46 | .70 |
| 1.49 | .25 | .50 | .75 |
| 1.59 | .27 | .53 | .80 |
| 1.69 | .28 | .56 | .85 |
| 1.79 | .30 | .60 | .90 |

| | Boneless Beef and Pork Roasts, Beef Flank Steak, Boneless Ham, Stew Meat, Liver, Heart, Tongue, Canadian-style Bacon, Frankfurters, Bologna, other Luncheon Meat, Canned Fish and Seafood | Round Steak, Beef Sirloin, Beef Blade Roast, Smoked Pork Shoulder Roll, Pork Shoulder Steaks, Ham with Bone in, Ground Meat, Fresh Fish and Seafood, Lamb, and Pork Chops | Poultry, Bulk Pork Sausage, Country-style Ribs, Beef Short Ribs, Lamb Shanks, Ham Shanks, and Oxtail |
|------|------|------|------|
| 1.89 | .32 | .63 | .95 |
| 1.99 | .33 | .66 | 1.00 |
| 2.09 | .35 | .70 | 1.05 |
| 2.19 | .37 | .73 | 1.10 |
| 2.29 | .38 | .76 | 1.15 |
| 2.39 | .40 | .80 | 1.20 |
| 2.49 | .42 | .83 | 1.25 |
| 2.59 | .43 | .86 | 1.30 |

# 11

pages **489** through **520**

# PASTRY AND PIES

489

# PASTRY

## PLAIN PASTRY

*For one single-crust pie or 4 to 6 tart shells:*

1½ cups sifted all-purpose
    flour
½ teaspoon salt

½ cup shortening
4 to 5 tablespoons cold
    water

*For one 8-, 9-, or 10-inch double-crust or lattice-top pie,
two 8-, 9-, or 10-inch single-crust pies, or 6 to 8 tart shells:*

2 cups sifted all-purpose
    flour
1 teaspoon salt

⅔ cup shortening
5 to 7 tablespoons cold
    water

Sift flour and salt together; cut in shortening with pastry
blender till pieces are the size of small peas. (For extra
tender pastry, cut in *half* the shortening till like cornmeal.
Cut in remaining till like small peas.) Sprinkle 1 tablespoon water over part of mixture. Gently toss with fork
(picture 1); push to side of bowl. Repeat till all is moistened. Form into a ball. (For double-crust and lattice-top
pies, divide dough for lower and upper crust and form
into balls.) Flatten on lightly floured surface by pressing
with edge of hand 3 times across in both directions (picture 2). Roll from center to edge till ⅛ inch thick.

    *To bake single-crust pie shells:* Fit pastry into pie plate;
trim ½ to 1 inch beyond edge; fold under and flute edge
by pressing dough with forefinger against wedge made
of finger and thumb of other hand (picture 3). Prick bottom and sides well with fork. (If filling and crust are
baked together, *do not prick.*) Bake at 450° for 10 to 12
minutes or till golden.

    *For lattice-top pie:* Trim lower crust ½ inch beyond
edge of pie plate. Roll remaining dough ⅛ inch thick.

Cut strips of pastry ½ to ¾ inch wide with pastry wheel or knife. Lay strips on filled pie at 1-inch intervals. Fold back alternate strips as you weave cross strips. Trim lattice even with outer rim of pie plate; fold lower crust over strips. Seal; flute edge.

*For double-crust pie:* Trim lower crust even with rim of pie plate. Cut slits in top crust. Lift pastry by rolling it over rolling pin; then unroll loosely over well-filled pie. Trim ½ inch beyond edge. Tuck top crust under edge of lower crust. Flute edge of pastry as desired.

If edge of crust browns too quickly, fold strip of foil around rim of crust, covering fluted edge.

## TART SHELLS

OVEN 425°

Prepare pastry; roll till dough is 1/8 inch thick. Cut in 5- or 6-inch circles. Fit into tart pans; press out bubbles. Trim 1/2 inch beyond edge; turn under; flute. Prick bottom and sides. (Or fit 5-inch circles over inverted custard cups; pinch together 4 corners; prick.) Bake at 425° for 10 to 12 minutes, or till golden.

## OIL PASTRY

2 cups all-purpose flour
1 1/2 teaspoons salt
1/2 cup salad oil
5 tablespoons cold water

Sift together flour and salt. Pour salad oil and cold water into measuring cup (*do not stir*). Add all at once to the flour mixture. Stir lightly with fork. Form into 2 balls; flatten dough slightly.

Roll each between two 12-inch squares of waxed paper. (First dampen the table slightly so paper won't slip.) When dough is rolled in circle to edges of paper, it will be right thickness for crust.

Peel off top sheet of waxed paper and fit dough, paper side up, into pie plate. Remove paper. Finish pie shell following directions for single- or double-crust pies on opposite page. Makes enough pastry for one 8- or 9-inch double-crust pie.

## GRAHAM-CRACKER CRUST

OVEN 375°

Combine 1 1/4 cups fine graham-cracker crumbs, 1/4 cup sugar, and 6 tablespoons butter or margarine, melted; mix. Press firmly into 9-inch pie plate. Bake in a moderate oven (375°) for 6 to 9 minutes or till edges are browned; cool. For unbaked crust, chill 45 minutes; fill.

## VANILLA-WAFER CRUST

Mix together 1 1/2 cups fine vanilla-wafer crumbs (36 wafers) and 6 tablespoons butter or margarine, melted. Press firmly into a 9-inch pie plate. Chill till set.

To shape a crumb crust more evenly, heap the crumbs in a 9-inch pie plate. Press an 8-inch pie plate into the crumb mixture.

## CHOCOLATE-WAFER CRUST

Mix together 1½ cups fine chocolate-wafer crumbs and 6 tablespoons butter or margarine, melted. Press firmly into 9-inch pie plate. Chill till set.

## GINGERSNAP CRUST

OVEN 375°

Mix 1½ cups fine gingersnap crumbs and ¼ cup softened butter or margarine. Press firmly into buttered 9-inch pie plate. Bake at 375° about 9 minutes. Cool.

## ZWIEBACK CRUST

Mix 1½ cups zwieback crumbs, 3 tablespoons sugar, and 3 tablespoons butter or margarine, melted. Press into buttered 9-inch pie plate. Chill till set.

## COCONUT CRUST

OVEN 325°

Combine one 3½-ounce can (1⅓ cups) flaked coconut and 2 tablespoons butter or margarine, melted. Press into 9-inch pie plate. Bake at 325° for 15 minutes, or till coconut is light golden brown.

# CORNFLAKE CRUST

Combine 1 cup crushed cornflakes *or* crisp rice cereal *or* cornflake crumbs with ¼ cup sugar and ⅓ cup butter, melted. Press firmly in 9-inch pie plate. Chill.

**Fluted Edge:** Trim pastry ½ inch beyond rim; fold under to make double edge.

Use a knife handle or your index finger to make the indentations. The thumb and index finger of your other hand are a wedge to push against to make the scallop around the knife handle. If you like, pinch curved edges into definite points.

**Woven Lattice Top:** Trim lower crust ½ inch beyond rim. Cut pastry strips ½ to ¾ inch wide and 12 inches long.

Lay strips on pie at 1-inch intervals. Fold back alternate strips to help you weave crosswise strips over and under. Trim lattice strips even with outer rim of pie plate. Fold lower crust over strips. Seal; crimp edge as desired.

**Wedge Cutouts:** Trim bottom crust even with edge of pie plate. Roll top crust in circle. Cut in wedges with pastry cutter. Cut a design on each piece to keep from puffing. Place wedges on pie. Seal rim edges with tines of fork.

**Zigzag Edge:** Trim pastry ½ to 1 inch beyond edge of pie plate; fold under to make plump rim of pastry.

Press dough between thumb and bent finger, pushing slightly forward on slant with finger and pulling back with thumb. Place thumb in dent left by finger; repeat around edge of pie shell.

**Speedy Spiral:** Cut long ¾-inch-wide strips; moisten ends; join. Twist strip; swirl in spiral from center, covering pie.

**Scalloped Edge:** Trim pastry ½ inch beyond rim; fold under to make double edge. Using a round-bowled measuring tablespoon, press against thumb and index finger of other hand. Or press a beverage can opener into edge, curved side down.

**Easy Lattice:** Cut dough in ½-inch strips; twist half the strips and lay 1 inch apart across pie. Twist and place remaining strips in opposite direction in diamond pattern. Secure ends of strips into rim of crust as you flute the edge.

## PINEAPPLE CREAM PIE

3/4 cup sugar
1/4 cup all-purpose flour
1/2 teaspoon salt
1 1-pound 4 1/2-ounce can (2 1/2 cups) crushed pineapple, undrained
1 cup dairy sour cream
1 tablespoon lemon juice

2 slightly beaten egg yolks

\* \* \*

1 9-inch *baked* pastry shell
Meringue (2 egg whites, see above)

OVEN 350°

In saucepan, combine sugar, flour, and salt. Stir in undrained pineapple, sour cream, and lemon juice till thoroughly blended. Cook and stir till mixture thickens and bubbles; cook and stir 2 minutes. Remove from heat. Stir a moderate amount of hot mixture into egg yolks; return to hot mixture, stirring constantly. Cook and stir 2 minutes more. Spoon hot mixture into cooled pastry shell. Spread meringue atop pie, sealing meringue to edge of pastry. Bake at 350° for 12 to 15 minutes, or till golden. Cool before cutting.

## MERINGUE

*For one 9-inch pie:*

3 egg whites
1/2 teaspoon vanilla

1/4 teaspoon cream of tartar
6 tablespoons sugar

*For one 8-inch pie:*

2 egg whites
1/2 teaspoon vanilla

1/4 teaspoon cream of tartar
4 tablespoons sugar

OVEN 350°

Beat egg whites with vanilla and cream of tartar till soft peaks form. Gradually add sugar, beating till stiff and glossy peaks form and all sugar is dissolved. Spread meringue over hot filling, sealing to edge of pastry. Bake at 350° for 12 to 15 minutes, or till meringue is golden. Cool. For Meringue Shell, see page 399.

*Note:* Before cutting a meringue-topped pie, dip knife in water—no need to dry.

## PUMPKIN MERINGUE PIE

3/4 cup sugar
3 tablespoons cornstarch
1/2 teaspoon salt
1/2 to 1 teaspoon ground cinnamon
1/4 to 1/2 teaspoon ground nutmeg
1/2 teaspoon ground ginger

1/4 teaspoon ground cloves
1 cup canned pumpkin
2 cups milk
3 slightly beaten egg yolks
1 9-inch *baked* pastry shell
Meringue (3 egg whites, see above)

OVEN 350°

In saucepan, mix sugar, cornstarch, salt, and spices. Gradually stir in pumpkin and milk. Cook and stir till mixture thickens and bubbles; cook and stir 2 minutes. Remove from heat. Stir a moderate amount of hot mixture into egg yolks; return to hot mixture, stirring constantly. Cook and stir 2 minutes more. Spoon hot mixture into cooled pastry shell. Spread meringue atop pie, sealing meringue to edge of pastry. Bake at 350° for 12 to 15 minutes, or till golden. Cool before cutting.

## • HOW TO COOK CREAM PIE FILLINGS •

Both cooking time and temperature are important when preparing cream pie fillings. Under- and over-cooking cause runny fillings. Set a timer for exact minutes specified in recipe. Cook fillings over moderately high heat. Too high a heat cooks mixture too quickly; too low a heat results in excessively long cooking.

## BANANA-APRICOT PIE

OVEN 350°

Combine 2 cups snipped dried apricots and 1 1/2 cups water. Cover; simmer 10 minutes or till tender. Combine 1 1/4 cups sugar, 1/4 cup all-purpose flour, and 1/4 teaspoon salt; stir into apricot mixture. Cook mixture till boiling, stirring constantly; boil 2 minutes, stirring constantly.

Stir a moderate amount of hot mixture into 3 beaten egg yolks; return to hot mixture. Cook and stir till boiling. Stir in 2 tablespoons butter or margarine.

Place 2 medium bananas, sliced (2 cups) in bottom of one 9-inch *baked* pastry shell, cooled. Top with apricot filling. Prepare Meringue (3 egg whites, page 497). Spread meringue over filling; seal to edge. Bake in moderate oven (350°) for 12 to 15 minutes. Cool before serving.

## LEMON MERINGUE PIE

1½ cups sugar
  3 tablespoons cornstarch
  3 tablespoons all-purpose flour
     Dash salt
1½ cups hot water

    * * *

  3 slightly beaten egg yolks

  2 tablespoons butter or margarine
 ½ teaspoon grated lemon peel
 ⅓ cup lemon juice
  1 9-inch *baked* pastry shell, cooled
     Meringue (3 egg whites, page 497)

OVEN 350°

In saucepan, mix 1½ cups sugar, cornstarch, flour, and salt. Gradually add hot water, stirring constantly. Cook and stir over moderately high heat till mixture comes to boiling. Reduce heat; cook and stir 2 minutes longer. Remove from heat.

Stir a moderate amount of hot mixture into egg yolks, then return to hot mixture. Bring to boiling and cook 2 minutes, stirring constantly. Add butter and lemon peel. Slowly add lemon juice, mixing well. Pour into pastry shell. Spread meringue over filling; seal to edge. Bake at 350° for 12 to 15 minutes. Cool before cutting.

*Note:* For creamier filling, cook and stir first 5 ingredients 8 minutes over low heat after mixture comes to boiling. Blend in egg yolks as above; cook 4 minutes after mixture boils.

Add a moderate amount of hot mixture to the beaten egg yolks. Blend well; then return to hot mixture immediately. Cook.

Pour hot cooked filling into a cooled baked pastry shell. No need to cool the filling before topping with the fluffy meringue.

## VANILLA CREAM PIE

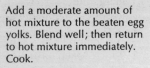

| | |
|---|---|
| ³/₄ cup sugar | 2 tablespoons butter |
| ¹/₃ cup all-purpose flour *or* 3 tablespoons cornstarch | 1 teaspoon vanilla |
| | 1 9-inch *baked* pastry shell |
| ¹/₄ teaspoon salt | Meringue (3 egg whites, page 497) |
| 2 cups milk | |
| 3 slightly beaten egg yolks | |

OVEN 350°

In saucepan, combine sugar, flour or cornstarch, and salt; gradually stir in milk. Cook and stir over medium high heat till bubbly. Cook and stir 2 minutes. Remove from heat. Stir a moderate amount hot mixture into yolks; immediately return to hot mixture; cook 2 minutes, stirring constantly. Remove from heat. Add butter and vanilla. Pour into cooled baked pastry shell. Spread meringue atop pie and bake at 350° for 12 to 15 minutes. Cool.

Or, omit meringue and serve with whipped cream. (To prevent skin from forming on surface of filling, put waxed paper directly on top of hot filling.)

## CHOCOLATE CREAM PIE

Prepare Vanilla Cream Pie, increasing sugar to 1 cup. Chop two 1-ounce squares unsweetened chocolate; add with milk. Top with Meringue and bake as directed.

## BANANA CREAM PIE

Slice 3 bananas into cooled *baked* 9-inch pastry shell. Top with Vanilla Cream Pie filling and Meringue. Bake as directed.

## BUTTERSCOTCH PIE

Substitute brown sugar for granulated sugar in Vanilla Cream Pie filling. Increase butter to 3 tablespoons. Top with Meringue and bake as directed.

## COCONUT CREAM PIE

Add 1 cup flaked coconut to Vanilla Cream Pie filling. Top with Meringue; sprinkle with 1/3 cup coconut. Bake.

## STRAWBERRY PARFAIT PIE

| | |
|---|---|
| 1 3-ounce package strawberry-flavored gelatin | 1 cup sliced fresh strawberries |
| 1 pint vanilla ice cream | 1 9-inch *baked* pastry shell, cooled |

Dissolve gelatin in 1 1/4 cups boiling water. Add ice cream by spoonfuls; stir till melted. Chill till mixture mounds slightly when dropped from spoon. Gently fold in sliced strawberries. Turn into pastry shell. Chill till firm. If desired, trim with whipped cream and extra strawberries.

## CHERRY BURGUNDY PIE

| | |
|---|---|
| 1 1-pound can pitted dark sweet cherries | 1 teaspoon lemon juice |
| 1 3-ounce package cherry-flavored gelatin | 3 tablespoons red Burgundy |
| 1 pint vanilla ice cream | 1 9-inch *baked* pastry shell, cooled |

Drain cherries, reserving syrup. Add enough water to syrup to make 1 cup; heat to boiling. Dissolve gelatin in boiling liquid. Add ice cream by spoonfuls, stirring till melted. Blend in lemon juice and wine. Chill till mixture mounds when spooned. Quarter cherries; fold into mixture. Chill again, if necessary to mound before piling into shell. Chill till firm.

## STRAWBERRY FROZEN PIE

1 8-ounce package
  cream cheese,
  softened
1 cup dairy sour cream

2 10-ounce packages
  frozen sliced
  strawberries, thawed
1 9-inch graham-cracker
  crust

Blend cream cheese and sour cream. Reserve 1/2 cup berries (and syrup); add remaining berries and syrup to cheese mixture. Pour into crust. Freeze firm. Remove from freezer 5 minutes before serving. Cut in wedges; serve topped with reserved strawberries in syrup.

## FUDGE RIBBON PIE

2 1-ounce squares
  unsweetened
  chocolate
1 6-ounce can
  evaporated milk
  (2/3 cup)
1 cup sugar
2 tablespoons butter or
  margarine
1 teaspoon vanilla
1 quart peppermint ice
  cream

1 9-inch *baked* pastry
  shell, cooled
3 egg whites
1/2 teaspoon vanilla
1/4 teaspoon cream of
  tartar
6 tablespoons sugar
1/4 cup crushed
  peppermint-stick
  candy

OVEN 475°

In saucepan, combine chocolate and evaporated milk. Cook and stir over low heat till chocolate is melted, about 15 minutes. Stir in the 1 cup sugar and butter. Cook over medium heat till thickened, 5 to 8 minutes longer, stirring occasionally. Stir in 1 teaspoon vanilla. Cool.

Spoon *half* of the ice cream in the cooled pastry shell. Cover with *half* the cooled chocolate sauce; freeze. Repeat with remaining ice cream and sauce. Cover and freeze overnight or till firm.

Prepare meringue by beating egg whites with 1/2 teaspoon vanilla and cream of tartar till soft peaks form. Gradually add 6 tablespoons sugar, beating till stiff and glossy peaks form. Fold *3 tablespoons* of the crushed candy into the meringue. Remove pie from freezer. Spread meringue over chocolate layer; seal to edge. Sprinkle top with remaining 1 tablespoon crushed candy. Place pie on old, unfinished, wooden cutting board. Bake at 475° for 4 to 5 minutes, or till golden. Serve at once.

## PERFECT APPLE PIE

6 to 8 tart apples, pared, cored, and thinly sliced (6 cups)*
3/4 to 1 cup sugar
2 tablespoons all-purpose flour

1/2 to 1 teaspoon ground cinnamon
Dash ground nutmeg
Pastry for 2-crust 9-inch pie
2 tablespoons butter

OVEN 400°

If apples lack tartness, sprinkle with about 1 tablespoon lemon juice. Combine sugar, flour, spices, and dash salt; mix with apples. Line 9-inch pie plate with pastry. Fill with apple mixture; dot with butter. Adjust top crust, cutting slits for escape of steam; seal. Sprinkle with sugar. Bake at 400° for 50 minutes or till done.

*Or, use two 1-pound 4-ounce cans (about 5 cups) pie-sliced apples, drained.

## APPLE CRUMB PIE

2/3 cup sugar
2 tablespoons all-purpose flour
3/4 teaspoon ground cinnamon
6 to 8 tart apples, pared, cored, and sliced (6 cups)

1 9-inch *unbaked* pastry shell
1/2 cup all-purpose flour
1/4 cup sugar
1/4 cup butter

OVEN 400°

Combine first 3 ingredients; stir into apples. Turn into pastry shell. Combine remaining flour and sugar; cut in butter till crumbly. Sprinkle over apples. Bake at 400° for 45 to 50 minutes or till done. If pie browns too quickly, cover edge with foil.

## APPLE CUSTARD PIE

OVEN 375°

Pare, core, and cut 6 to 8 tart apples in eighths (6 cups). Arrange in 9-inch *unbaked* pastry shell. Combine ³/₄ cup sugar, 3 tablespoons all-purpose flour, and ¹/₂ teaspoon salt. Stir in ¹/₄ cup light cream. Pour mixture over apples. Sprinkle with ground cinnamon. Cover loosely with foil. Bake at 375° for 1 hour. Remove foil; bake 15 minutes or till apples are done. Serve warm with Cheddar cheese, if desired.

## RED CHERRY PIE

³/₄ cup juice from cherries
1 cup sugar
2 tablespoons quick-cooking tapioca
3 cups canned pitted tart red cherries (water pack)

10 drops red food coloring
3 to 4 drops almond extract

Pastry for 9-inch lattice-top pie
1 tablespoon butter

OVEN 400°

Combine first 6 ingredients and dash salt; let stand 20 minutes. Line 9-inch pie plate with pastry; fill with cherry mixture. Dot with butter. Adjust lattice crust; crimp edge high. Bake in hot oven (400°) for 50 to 55 minutes.

## FRESH CHERRY PIE

OVEN 375°

Prepare pastry for 9-inch lattice-top pie; line 9-inch pie plate with pastry. Combine 4 cups fresh pitted tart red cherries, 1 cup sugar, 3 tablespoons quick-cooking tapioca, 1 tablespoon cherry brandy, 1 teaspoon grated lemon peel, and dash salt. Let stand 20 minutes. Turn into pastry-lined pie plate; dot with butter. Adjust lattice top; seal. Bake at 375° for 55 to 60 minutes.

## TWO-CRUST CHERRY PIE

1½ cups sugar
4 tablespoons cornstarch
¾ cup juice from cherries
3 cups canned pitted tart red cherries (water pack)

1 tablespoon butter
¼ teaspoon red food coloring
Pastry for 2-crust 9-inch pie

OVEN 400°

Combine ¾ *cup* sugar with cornstarch. Stir in cherry juice. Cook over medium heat, stirring occasionally, till mixture thickens and bubbles; cook 1 minute longer. Add remaining sugar, cherries, butter, and food coloring. (Mixture will be very thick.) Let stand while preparing pastry. Line 9-inch pie plate with pastry; fill. Adjust top crust, cutting slits for escape of steam; seal. Bake at 400° for 55 minutes.

## CHERRY-RASPBERRY PIE

1 10-ounce package frozen red raspberries, thawed
1 1-pound 4-ounce can frozen pitted tart red cherries, thawed
¾ cup sugar

3 tablespoons cornstarch
¼ teaspoon salt
Few drops red food coloring
* * *
Pastry for 2-crust 9-inch pie

OVEN 425°

Drain thawed raspberries and cherries (reserve syrup); add enough cherry syrup to raspberry syrup to make 1 cup. Blend sugar, cornstarch, and salt in saucepan; stir in syrup and food coloring until smooth. Add cherries. Cook and stir over low heat till thickened. Stir in raspberries. Line 9-inch pie plate with pastry. Add hot filling. Adjust top crust, cutting slits for escape of steam; seal. Bake in hot oven (425°) 30 to 35 minutes, or till golden.
*Note:* Two cups pitted fresh ripe tart red cherries may

be substituted for the frozen cherries. Add water to raspberry syrup to make 1 cup liquid.

## HOMEMADE MINCEMEAT PIE

OVEN 400°

Simmer 1 pound beef neck, covered, in water to cover till tender, about 3 hours. Cool and drain; put meat through coarse blade of food chopper with ½ pound suet and 2 pounds tart red apples, which have been pared, cored, and cubed.

In large kettle, blend with 2½ cups sugar, 2½ cups dried currants, 4½ cups raisins, ½ cup chopped mixed candied fruits and peels, 1½ teaspoons grated orange peel, 1 teaspoon grated lemon peel, ¼ cup lemon juice, 1 cup orange juice, 2½ cups water, 1½ teaspoons salt, ½ teaspoon ground nutmeg, and ¼ teaspoon ground mace. Cover; simmer 1 hour. Makes 12 cups of mincemeat filling.

Use 2 cups for 8-inch pie, 3 cups for 9-inch pie. Freeze remaining mincemeat in pie-sized portions. Fill pastry-lined pie plate; adjust top crust; cut slits in top. Seal. Bake at 400° for 35 to 40 minutes.

## RHUBARB PIE

OVEN 400°

Combine 4 cups 1-inch slices rhubarb, 1⅔ cups sugar, ⅓ cup all-purpose flour, and dash salt; let stand 15 minutes.

Meanwhile, prepare pastry for 2-crust 9-inch pie; line 9-inch pie plate with pastry. Fill with rhubarb mixture. Dot with 2 tablespoons butter. Adjust top crust; cut slits; seal; flute. Bake at 400° for 50 minutes.

## RHUBARB CUSTARD PIE

OVEN 400°

Mix 1½ cups sugar, ¼ cup all-purpose flour, ¼ teaspoon ground nutmeg, and dash salt. Add to 3 beaten eggs; beat smooth. Stir in 4 cups 1-inch slices rhubarb.

Prepare pastry for 9-inch lattice-top pie. Line 9-inch pie plate with pastry. Fill with rhubarb mixture. Dot with 2 tablespoons butter. Adjust lattice top; seal. Bake at 400° for 50 minutes.

## CONCORD GRAPE PIE

OVEN 400°

Slip skins from 1½ pounds (4 cups) Concord grapes; set skins aside. Bring pulp to boil; reduce heat; simmer, uncovered, 5 minutes. Sieve to remove seeds. Add skins.

Mix 1 cup sugar, ⅓ cup all-purpose flour, and ¼ teaspoon salt. Add 1 tablespoon lemon juice, 2 tablespoons butter, melted, and grape mixture. Pour into 9-inch *unbaked* pastry shell. Bake at 400° for 25 minutes. Meanwhile, sift ½ cup all-purpose flour with ½ cup sugar. Cut in ¼ cup butter till crumbly. Sprinkle atop pie. Bake 15 minutes more.

## FRESH GOOSEBERRY PIE

OVEN 400°

Stem and wash 3 cups fresh gooseberries; crush ½ cup. Mix crushed berries with 1½ cups sugar, 3 tablespoons quick-cooking tapioca, and ¼ teaspoon salt. Cook and stir till bubbly; cook 2 minutes more. Add remaining whole berries. Prepare pastry for 2-crust 9-inch pie. Line 9-inch pie plate with pastry; fill. Dot with 2 tablespoons butter. Adjust top crust; cut slits; seal. Bake at 400° for 35 minutes.

## PEACH PIE

OVEN 400°

Prepare pastry for 9-inch lattice-top pie. Combine ¾ to 1 cup sugar, 3 tablespoons all-purpose flour, ¼ teaspoon ground nutmeg or cinnamon, and dash salt. Add to 5 cups sliced fresh peaches; mix.

Line 9-inch pie plate with pastry; fill. Dot with 2 tablespoons butter or margarine. (Dash with extra spice, if desired.) Adjust lattice crust; seal; crimp edges. Bake in a hot oven (400°) for 45 to 50 minutes or till done. Serve warm with whipped cream or ice cream.

## GOLDEN PEACH PIE

| | |
|---|---|
| 2 1-pound cans sliced cling peaches | 1 tablespoon lemon juice |
| 1/2 cup sugar | 1/2 teaspoon grated orange peel |
| 2 tablespoons all-purpose flour | 1/8 teaspoon almond extract |
| 1/4 teaspoon ground nutmeg | Pastry for 2-crust 9-inch pie |
| 2 tablespoons butter or margarine | |

OVEN 400°

Drain peaches, reserving 1/3 cup syrup. Combine sugar, flour, nutmeg, and dash salt. Add reserved syrup. Cook, stirring constantly, till thick and bubbly.

Add butter, lemon juice, peel, and extract, then peaches. Line 9-inch pie plate with pastry; fill. Adjust top crust, cutting slits for escape of steam. Seal. Bake at 400° for 40 to 45 minutes.

## BLUEBERRY PIE

OVEN 400°

Prepare pastry for 2-crust 9-inch pie. Combine 4 cups fresh blueberries with 3/4 to 1 cup sugar, 3 tablespoons all-purpose flour, 1/2 teaspoon grated lemon peel, 1/2 teaspoon ground cinnamon or nutmeg, and dash salt. Line 9-inch pie plate with pastry. Fill. Sprinkle with 1 teaspoon lemon juice; dot with 1 tablespoon butter. Adjust top crust, cutting slits for escape of steam. Seal. Bake at 400° for 35 to 40 minutes. Serve warm, if desired.

## BLUEBERRY STRATA PIE

1 1-pound can
blueberries
1 8³/₄-ounce can (1 cup)
crushed pineapple
1 8-ounce package
cream cheese,
softened
3 tablespoons sugar
1 tablespoon milk

¹/₂ teaspoon vanilla
1 9-inch *baked* pastry
shell, cooled
¹/₄ cup sugar
2 tablespoons cornstarch
¹/₄ teaspoon salt
1 teaspoon lemon juice
¹/₂ cup whipping cream,
whipped

Drain fruits, reserving syrups. Blend cream cheese and next 3 ingredients. Reserve 2 tablespoons pineapple; stir remainder into cheese mixture. Spread over bottom of pastry shell; chill. Blend ¹/₄ cup sugar, cornstarch, and salt. Combine reserved syrups; measure 1¹/₄ cups; blend into cornstarch mixture. Cook and stir till thickened. Stir in blueberries and lemon juice; cool. Pour over cheese layer; chill. Top with whipped cream and reserved pineapple.

## MARMALADE PLUM PIE

1¹/₂ pounds fresh Italian
plums
¹/₃ cup water
³/₄ cup sugar
2 tablespoons cornstarch

¹/₄ teaspoon salt
2 tablespoons butter
Pastry for 2-crust
9-inch pie
¹/₃ cup orange marmalade

OVEN 425°

Pit and quarter plums (about 3 cups). Combine plums and water. Bring to boiling and cook 3 to 4 minutes. Combine sugar, cornstarch, and salt; stir into plum mixture. Cook slowly till thickened and bubbly, stirring constantly; remove from heat. Stir in butter; cool.

Line 9-inch pie plate with pastry; spread bottom with orange marmalade. Fill with plum mixture. Adjust top crust, cutting slits for escape of steam; seal; flute edge. Bake at 425° for 30 to 35 minutes.

## RAISIN CRISSCROSS PIE

1 cup brown sugar
3 tablespoons cornstarch
1½ cups water
2 cups raisins
1 teaspoon grated
  orange peel
½ teaspoon grated
  lemon peel

⅓ cup orange juice
3 tablespoons lemon
  juice

\* \* \*

½ cup broken walnuts
Pastry for 9-inch
lattice-top pie

OVEN 400°

In saucepan, combine sugar, cornstarch, water, raisins, orange and lemon peel, and orange and lemon juices. Cook, stirring constantly, over medium heat until mixture thickens and bubbles. Stir in nuts. Set mixture aside to cool.

Line 9-inch pie plate with pastry. Pour in raisin filling. Adjust lattice top; seal; flute edge. Brush top with milk and sprinkle with sugar. Bake in hot oven (400°) 30 to 35 minutes.

## FRESH FRUIT TARTS

2 slightly beaten egg
  yolks
2 cups milk
1 3-ounce package
  *regular* vanilla
  pudding mix
2 3-ounce packages
  cream cheese

\* \* \*

2 egg whites
¼ cup sugar
8 baked tart shells,
  3½ inches in
  diameter, cooled
Fresh fruits

Combine beaten egg yolks and milk. Cook pudding mix according to package directions using the egg-milk mixture as the liquid. Remove from heat. Cut cream cheese in pieces and add to hot pudding; beat till cheese is melted. Let mixture cool about 10 minutes.

Beat egg whites to soft peaks; gradually add sugar beating to stiff peaks. Fold egg whites into pudding. Spoon into tart shells; chill. Just before serving, spoon sugared fresh strawberries, blueberries, or peach halves over tarts. Makes 8 servings.

## PEAR CRUMBLE PIE

6 medium Bartlett pears, pared

3 tablespoons lemon juice

1/2 cup sugar

2 tablespoons all-purpose flour

1 teaspoon grated lemon peel

1 9-inch *unbaked* pastry shell

Crumble Topping

3 slices sharp process American cheese

OVEN 400°

Slice 5 pears; cut remaining pear in sixths. Sprinkle pears with lemon juice. Mix sugar, flour, and peel; stir into sliced pears. Spoon into pastry shell. Arrange pear wedges atop sliced pears. Sprinkle with Crumble Topping. Bake at 400° for 45 minutes or till pears are tender. Remove from oven. Cut cheese slices in half diagonally and arrange on pie. Serve warm.

*Crumble Topping:* Mix 1/2 cup all-purpose flour, 1/2 cup sugar, 1/2 teaspoon each ground ginger and cinnamon, and 1/4 teaspoon ground mace. Cut in 1/4 cup butter or margarine till crumbly.

## STRAWBERRY-RHUBARB PIE

OVEN 400°

Combine 1 1/2 cups sugar, 3 tablespoons quick-cooking tapioca, 1/4 teaspoon salt, and 1/4 teaspoon ground nutmeg. Add 1 pound rhubarb, cut in 1/2-inch pieces (3 cups), and 1 cup sliced fresh strawberries. Mix to coat fruit. Let stand 20 minutes.

Meanwhile, prepare pastry for 9-inch lattice-top pie. Line 9-inch pie plate with pastry. Fill with fruit mixture. Dot with 1 tablespoon butter or margarine. Adjust lattice top; seal. Bake in a hot oven (400°) for 35 to 40 minutes.

## STRAWBERRY GLAZE PIE

Crush 1 cup fresh strawberries and cook with 1 cup water about 2 minutes; sieve.

Combine 3/4 cup sugar and 3 tablespoons cornstarch; stir into berry juice. Cook and stir till thickened and bubbly. Add few drops red food coloring. Place 2½ cups fresh strawberries in *baked* and cooled 9-inch pastry shell. Pour *half* the sauce over. Repeat layers with 2½ cups berries and remaining sauce. Chill.

## • HINTS FOR MAKING PERFECT, FLUFFY CHIFFON PIES •

For a smooth chiffon pie, it's important that the gelatin be just the right consistency– partially set but still pourable.

For a picture pretty and full chiffon pie that looks fluffy, chill the completed filling mixture until it mounds slightly.

## LEMON CHIFFON PIE

1 envelope unflavored gelatin
1 cup sugar
1/2 teaspoon salt
4 egg yolks
1/3 cup lemon juice

1 teaspoon grated lemon peel
4 egg whites
1/2 cup whipping cream, whipped
1 9-inch *baked* pastry shell, cooled

In saucepan, combine gelatin, 1/2 *cup* of the sugar, and salt. Beat together yolks, lemon juice, and 2/3 cup water. Stir into gelatin mixture. Stir over medium heat till mixture comes to a boil and gelatin dissolves. Remove from heat and stir in peel. Chill; stir occasionally till partially set. Beat egg whites till soft peaks form. Gradually add remaining sugar, beating till stiff peaks form. Fold in gelatin mixture. Fold in whipped cream. Pile into cooled pastry shell. Chill till firm.

## STRAWBERRY CHIFFON PIE

| | |
|---|---|
| 1 pint fresh strawberries | 2 egg whites |
| 1/2 cup sugar | 1/4 cup sugar |
| 1 envelope unflavored gelatin | 1/2 cup whipping cream, whipped |
| 2/3 cup cold water | 1 9-inch *baked* pastry shell, cooled |
| 1 tablespoon lemon juice | |

Crush strawberries (about 1 cup); add 1/2 cup sugar; let stand 30 minutes.

Soften gelatin in water; dissolve over low heat; cool. Add strawberries, lemon juice, and dash salt. Chill, stirring occasionally, till partially set.

Beat egg whites to soft peaks; gradually add 1/4 cup sugar, beating till stiff peaks form. Fold in strawberry mixture, then whipped cream. Chill till mixture mounds. Pile into cooled shell. Chill firm, about 5 hours. Trim with whipped cream.


## PEANUT BRITTLE PIE

| | |
|---|---|
| 2/3 cup brown sugar | 2 egg whites |
| 1 envelope (1 tablespoon) unflavored gelatin | 2 tablespoons granulated sugar |
| Dash salt | 1/2 cup crushed peanut brittle |
| 1 3/4 cups milk | 1/2 cup whipping cream, whipped |
| 2 slightly beaten egg yolks | 1 9-inch *baked* pastry shell, cooled |
| 2 tablespoons butter | |
| 1 teaspoon vanilla | |

In saucepan, combine brown sugar, gelatin, and salt. Stir in milk and egg yolks. Cook and stir over medium heat till gelatin dissolves and mixture thickens slightly. Add butter and vanilla. Chill, stirring occasionally, till partially set.

Beat egg whites to soft peaks; gradually add sugar; beat to stiff peaks. Fold in gelatin mixture, peanut brittle, and whipped cream. Chill till mixture mounds. Pile into cooled shell; chill till firm.

## PUMPKIN CHIFFON PIE

1 envelope unflavored gelatin
1/2 cup sugar
1/2 teaspoon salt
1/2 teaspoon ground cinnamon
1/2 teaspoon ground allspice
1/4 teaspoon ground ginger
1/4 teaspoon ground nutmeg

3/4 cup milk
2 slightly beaten egg yolks
1 cup canned pumpkin
2 egg whites
1/4 cup sugar
1/2 cup whipping cream, whipped
1 9-inch graham-cracker crust

Combine first 7 ingredients in saucepan. Stir in milk, egg yolks, and pumpkin. Cook and stir over medium heat till mixture boils and gelatin dissolves. Remove from heat and chill till partially set.

Beat egg whites till soft peaks form. Gradually add sugar and beat to stiff peaks. Fold into pumpkin mixture with whipped cream. Pile into crust. Chill till firm.

## CHOCOLATE CHIFFON PIE

1 envelope unflavored gelatin
3 egg yolks
1/3 cup sugar
1/4 teaspoon salt
1 teaspoon vanilla

2 1-ounce squares unsweetened chocolate
1/2 cup water
3 egg whites
1/2 cup sugar
1 9-inch *baked* pastry shell, cooled

Soften gelatin in 1/4 cup cold water. Beat egg yolks till thick and lemon-colored. Gradually beat in the 1/3 cup sugar; add salt and vanilla. Combine chocolate and 1/2 cup water; stir over low heat till blended. Add softened gelatin; stir to dissolve. Immediately beat chocolate mixture into egg yolks. Chill, stirring occasionally, till mixture is partially set.

Beat egg whites to soft peaks. Gradually add 1/2 cup sugar, beating to stiff peaks. Fold small amount of egg whites into chilled chocolate mixture. Then spoon about *half* the chocolate mixture over remaining egg whites; fold in just till blended. Repeat with remaining chocolate. If necessary, chill till mixture mounds when spooned. Pile into cooled shell. Chill till firm. Garnish with whipped cream.

## BRAZILIAN PIE

In saucepan, combine $1/3$ cup sugar, 1 envelope (1 tablespoon) unflavored gelatin, 1 tablespoon instant coffee powder, $1/4$ teaspoon ground nutmeg, and dash salt.

Combine 3 slightly beaten egg yolks and one $14^1/2$-ounce can ($1^2/3$ cups) evaporated milk. Add to gelatin mixture. Cook and stir till gelatin dissolves and mixture thickens slightly. Add $1/2$ teaspoon vanilla. Chill, stirring occasionally, till partially set. Beat smooth.

Beat 3 egg whites till soft peaks form. Gradually add $1/3$ cup sugar, beating to stiff peaks. Fold in gelatin mixture. Pile into baked and cooled 9-inch pastry shell. Chill firm. Spread pie with $1/2$ cup whipping cream, whipped; sprinkle with 3 tablespoons grated unsweetened chocolate.

## BLACK BOTTOM PIE

$1/2$ cup sugar
1 tablespoon cornstarch
2 cups milk, scalded
4 beaten egg yolks
1 teaspoon vanilla
1 6-ounce package (1 cup) semisweet chocolate pieces
1 9-inch *baked* pastry shell

\* \* \*

1 envelope (1 tablespoon) unflavored gelatin
$1/4$ cup cold water
$1/2$ teaspoon rum extract *or* 2 tablespoons light rum
4 egg whites
$1/2$ cup sugar

Combine $1/2$ cup sugar and cornstarch. Slowly add milk to egg yolks. Stir in sugar mixture. Cook and stir over medium heat till custard thickens and coats a spoon. ᴇmove from heat; add vanilla. To 1 *cup* of the custard, ᴵd the chocolate and stir till melted. Pour into pastry sɦell; chill.

Meanwhile, soften gelatin in cold water; add to remaining *hot* custard. Stir until dissolved. Stir in extract. Chill till slightly thickened. Beat egg whites till soft peaks form. Gradually add ½ cup sugar; beat till stiff peaks form. Fold in custard-gelatin mixture. Chill if necessary till mixture mounds. Pile over chocolate layer; chill till set. Trim with nuts.

## CUSTARD PIE

| | |
|---|---|
| 4 slightly beaten eggs | 2½ cups milk, scalded |
| ½ cup sugar | 1 9-inch *unbaked* pastry |
| ¼ teaspoon salt | shell |
| ½ teaspoon vanilla | Ground nutmeg |

OVEN 350°

Blend eggs, sugar, salt, and vanilla. Gradually stir in scalded milk. Pour into pastry shell. Sprinkle with nutmeg.

Bake in moderate oven (350°) 35 to 40 minutes or till knife inserted halfway between center and edge comes out clean. Cool on rack; then chill.

*Note:* If desired, omit nutmeg; sprinkle ½ cup flaked coconut atop unbaked filling.

An easy way to fill a pie shell with no spills—pour filling into measuring cup. Place pastry shell on oven rack, then fill.

To test a custard pie for doneness, insert a knife halfway between center and edge of pie. If done, knife will come out clean.

## SLIPPED CUSTARD PIE

OVEN 350°

Prepare filling for Custard Pie. Place buttered 8-inch pie plate in shallow baking pan. Fill pie plate with custard (pour extra into custard cups and bake with pie filling). Fill baking pan with cold water to depth of 1/4 inch. Bake at 350° for 35 to 40 minutes or till knife comes out clean. Remove pie to cooling rack. When cool, carefully run spatula around edge. Shake plate gently to loosen custard. Hold custard just above far rim of *baked* 9-inch pastry shell; gently slip into shell. Chill.

## PUMPKIN PIE

1 1/2 cups canned pumpkin
3/4 cup sugar
1/2 teaspoon salt
1 to 1 1/4 teaspoons ground cinnamon
1/2 to 1 teaspoon ground ginger
1/4 to 1/2 teaspoon ground nutmeg

1/4 to 1/2 teaspoon ground cloves

\* \* \*

3 slightly beaten eggs
1 1/4 cups milk
1 6-ounce can (2/3 cup) evaporated milk
1 9-inch *unbaked* pastry shell

OVEN 400°

Combine pumpkin, sugar, salt, and spices. Blend in eggs, milk, and evaporated milk. Pour into pastry shell (have edges crimped high because amount of filling is generous). Bake in hot oven (400°) 50 minutes, or till knife inserted halfway between center and edge comes out clean. Cool.

## CHESS PIE

1/2 cup butter or margarine
2 cups sugar
1 tablespoon all-purpose flour
1 tablespoon yellow cornmeal

5 well-beaten eggs
1 cup milk
1 teaspoon vanilla
2 tablespoons lemon juice
1 *unbaked* Rich Pastry Shell

OVEN 350°

Cream butter and sugar; beat in flour and cornmeal. Add eggs, milk, vanilla, and lemon juice; beat well. Pour into pastry shell. Bake in moderate oven (350°) 55 to 60 minutes, or till knife comes out clean.

*Rich Pastry Shell:* Sift together 1 cup sifted all-purpose flour, ¼ teaspoon salt, and ¼ teaspoon baking powder. Cut in 6 tablespoons butter or margarine till the size of small peas.

Gradually add 3 to 4 tablespoons milk, mixing till dough can be formed into a ball. Roll out and fit into 9-inch pie plate (have edges crimped high because amount of filling is generous).

## COCONUT TARTS

*Filling will remind you of pecan pie—*

| | |
|---|---|
| 3 beaten eggs | 1 teaspoon vanilla |
| 1½ cups sugar | 1 3½-ounce can (1⅓ |
| ½ cup butter or | cups) flaked coconut |
| margarine, melted | 8 *unbaked* tart shells |
| 4 teaspoons lemon juice | |

OVEN 350°

Combine eggs, sugar, butter or margarine, lemon juice, and vanilla; stir in coconut. Pour into unbaked tart shells. Bake in moderate oven (350°) 40 minutes or till a knife inserted just off-center comes out clean. Cool. Makes enough filling for eight 3¼-inch tarts (or one 9-inch pie).

## RAISIN PIE

| | |
|---|---|
| 6 eggs | ¼ cup butter or |
| 1½ cups of sugar | margarine, melted |
| ½ teaspoon ground | 1½ cups raisins |
| cinnamon | ½ cup coarsely chopped |
| ½ teaspoon ground | walnuts |
| nutmeg | 1 9-inch unbaked pastry |
| ¼ teaspoon salt | shell |
| ¼ cup lemon juice | |

OVEN 375°

Combine eggs, sugar, spices, salt, lemon juice, and butter. Stir in raisins and nuts. Pour into pastry shell. Bake in moderate oven (375°) 35 to 40 minutes or till filling is set in center. Cool.

## SOUTHERN PECAN PIE

OVEN 350°

Beat 3 eggs thoroughly with ²/₃ cup sugar, dash salt, 1 cup dark corn syrup, and ¹/₃ cup butter or margarine, melted. Add 1 cup pecan halves. Pour into 9-inch *unbaked* pastry shell.

Bake in moderate oven (350°) 50 minutes or till knife inserted halfway between center and edge comes out clean. Cool.

# 12

# POULTRY, FISH, AND EGGS

# POULTRY

## PERFECT FRIED CHICKEN

| | |
|---|---|
| 1/3 cup all-purpose flour | 1 2 1/2- to 3-pound |
| 1 teaspoon paprika | ready-to-cook broiler- |
| 1 teaspoon salt | fryer chicken, cut up |
| | Shortening for frying |

Combine flour, paprika, salt, and 1/4 teaspoon pepper in paper or plastic bag; add 2 or 3 pieces of chicken at a time and shake. Heat shortening (1/4 inch deep in skillet) till a drop of water sizzles. Brown meaty pieces first, then add remaining pieces (don't crowd). Brown one side; turn with tongs. When lightly browned, 15 to 20 minutes, reduce heat; cover tightly. (If cover isn't tight, add 1 tablespoon water.) Cook 30 to 40 minutes, or till tender. Uncover last 10 minutes. Makes 4 servings.

*Note:* Add 1/2 cup fine dry bread crumbs to flour for more crusty coating.

## CHICKEN SUPREME

OVEN 350°

Sprinkle 3 large chicken breasts, cut in halves lengthwise, or 6 small chicken breasts with 3/4 teaspoon seasoned salt. Dash with paprika. Place in 12x7 1/2x2-inch baking dish. Dissolve 1 chicken bouillon cube in 1 cup boiling water; add 1/4 cup dry white wine, 1/2 teaspoon instant minced onion, 1/4 teaspoon curry powder, and dash pepper. Pour over chicken. Cover with foil. Bake at 350° for 30 minutes. Uncover; bake 45 minutes till tender.

Remove chicken to warm serving platter. Strain pan juices; reserve for sauce. Blend 2 tablespoons all-purpose flour and 1/4 cup cold water in saucepan; slowly stir in reserved pan juices. Cook and stir over low heat till sauce thickens; boil and stir 3 to 4 minutes. Add one 3-ounce can sliced mushrooms, drained (1/2 cup); heat through.

Spoon over chicken breasts (reserving some sauce to pass) and garnish with watercress. Makes 6 servings.

## MARYLAND FRIED CHICKEN

   1 slightly beaten egg
1¼ cups milk
  ⅔ cup fine cracker
      crumbs
  ½ teaspoon salt

1 2½- to 3-pound
     ready-to-cook broiler-
     fryer chicken, cut up
3 to 4 tablespoons
     shortening

Combine egg and ¼ *cup* of the milk. Mix cracker crumbs, salt, and dash pepper. Dip chicken pieces into egg mixture, then roll in crumbs. In heavy skillet, brown chicken in hot shortening; turn with tongs. Add remaining 1 cup milk. Cover tightly and simmer 35 minutes; uncover and cook about 10 minutes, or till tender. From pan drippings make Cream Gravy (page 533). Makes 4 servings.

## OVEN FRIED CHICKEN

OVEN 375°

Cut up one 2½- to 3-pound ready-to-cook broiler-fryer chicken. Dip pieces in ½ cup melted butter; roll in mixture of 2 cups crushed potato chips (*or* 2 cups crushed barbecue chips, or crushed cornflakes, or 3 cups crisp rice cereal, crushed), ¼ teaspoon garlic salt, and dash pepper. Place pieces, skin side up, not touching, in greased large shallow baking pan. Sprinkle with remaining butter and crumbs. Bake at 375° about 1 hour, or till done. Do not turn. Makes 4 servings.

**Chicken Parmesan:** Prepare Oven Fried Chicken, except roll pieces in mixture of 1 cup crushed packaged herb-seasoned stuffing mix, ⅔ cup grated Parmesan cheese, and ¼ cup snipped parsley. Serves 4.

## OVEN HERB CHICKEN

OVEN 375°

Cut up one 2½- to 3-pound ready-to-cook broiler-fryer chicken. Combine 1 envelope onion salad dressing mix, ½ cup butter or margarine, softened, and 1 teaspoon

paprika. With spatula, spread mixture over chicken pieces, then roll in ³/₄ cup fine dry bread crumbs. Sprinkle with paprika. Bake, skin side up, in greased large shallow baking pan at 375° for 1 hour, or till done. Do not turn. Makes 4 servings.

## ORANGE CHICKEN

2 2¹/₂- to 3-pound ready-to-cook broiler-fryer chickens, cut up
2 slightly beaten eggs
¹/₃ cup orange juice
1 cup fine dry bread crumbs

1 teaspoon salt
1 teaspoon paprika
1 teaspoon shredded orange peel
6 tablespoons butter

OVEN 400°

Dip chicken pieces into mixture of eggs and orange juice, then into mixture of bread crumbs, salt, paprika, and shredded peel. Melt butter in large shallow baking pan in 400° oven. Remove pan from oven. Turn chicken in butter to coat; arrange skin side down (don't crowd). Bake at 400° for 30 minutes. Turn chicken. Bake 30 minutes more. If necessary, cover with foil last 10 minutes. Makes 6 servings.

## SWEET-SOUR CHICKEN

OVEN 425°

In small saucepan, combine 1 tablespoon cornstarch and 1 tablespoon cold water. Add ¹/₂ cup sugar, ¹/₂ cup soy sauce, ¹/₄ cup vinegar, 1 clove garlic, minced, ¹/₂ teaspoon ground ginger, and ¹/₄ teaspoon coarsely ground pepper. Cook, stirring constantly, over medium heat till mixture thickens and bubbles. Brush two 2- to 2¹/₂-pound ready-to-cook broiler-fryer chickens, split in halves lengthwise, with soy mixture. Place chicken halves, skin side down, in greased shallow baking pan.

Bake in hot oven (425°) for 30 minutes. Brush with soy mixture every 10 minutes. Turn chicken skin side up. Bake 30 minutes, brushing occasionally with soy mixture. Drain one 1-pound 4-ounce can pineapple spears or chunks;

add pineapple to chicken halves in baking pan during the last 10 minutes of baking. Serves 4.

## BASIC BROILED CHICKEN

Select two ready-to-cook broiler-fryer chickens (not over 2½ pounds each); split each chicken in half lengthwise or quarter. Brush with salad oil or melted shortening. Season to taste with salt and pepper.

Place, skin side down, in broiler pan (no rack). Broil 5 to 7 inches from heat about 20 minutes, or till lightly browned. Brush occasionally with oil. Turn; broil 20 minutes longer. When drumstick moves easily, chicken is done. Makes 4 servings.

## ISLAND BROILED CHICKEN

| | |
|---|---|
| ½ cup salad oil | ½ teaspoon dried |
| 3 tablespoons lemon | oregano, crushed |
| juice | ¼ teaspoon salt |
| 1½ tablespoons soy sauce | ⅛ teaspoon pepper |
| 1 small clove garlic, | 2 2-pound ready-to- |
| minced | cook broiler-fryer |
| | chickens, cut in half |

Combine salad oil, lemon juice, soy sauce, garlic, oregano, salt, and pepper for marinating sauce. Seal chicken and sauce in plastic bag. Marinate in refrigerator 4 to 5 hours, turning several times.

Place, skin side down, in broiler pan (without rack). Broil 5 to 7 inches from heat about 25 minutes, or till lightly browned. Brush occasionally with sauce. Turn; broil 15 to 20 minutes. Serves 4.

## BARBECUED CHICKEN

OVEN 325°

In skillet, slowly brown one 2½- to 3-pound ready-to-cook broiler-fryer chicken, cut up, in ¼ cup salad oil. Place in 12x7½x2-inch baking dish. To skillet, add ½ cup chopped onion and ¼ cup chopped celery; cook till tender. Add ½ cup catsup, ⅓ cup water, 2 tablespoons lemon juice, 1 tablespoon each brown sugar, Worcestershire sauce, vinegar, and prepared mustard. Season. Simmer 15 minutes; skim off excess fat. Pour sauce over chicken. Bake, uncovered, at 325° for 1¼ hours, or till done, basting 3 or 4 times. Serves 3 or 4.

## CHICKEN A LA KING

In saucepan, melt ¼ cup butter, margarine, or chicken fat; blend in ⅓ cup all-purpose flour and ½ teaspoon salt. Add 1 cup chicken broth and 1 cup milk all at once. Cook, stirring constantly, till sauce is thick and bubbly. Add 2 cups diced cooked chicken, one 3-ounce can sliced mushrooms, drained, and ¼ cup chopped canned pimiento. Heat through. Serve over toast points. Makes 5 servings.

## CHICKEN CACCIATORE

In skillet, brown one 2½- to 3-pound ready-to-cook broiler-fryer chicken, cut up, in ¼ cup hot salad oil. Remove chicken. In same skillet, cook 2 medium onions, cut in ¼ inch slices, and 2 cloves garlic, minced, till tender, but not brown. Return chicken to skillet.

Combine one 1-pound can tomatoes, one 8-ounce can tomato sauce, 1 teaspoon salt, ¼ teaspoon pepper, 1 teaspoon dried oregano or basil, crushed, ½ teaspoon celery seed, and 1 or 2 bay leaves. Pour mixture over chicken. Cover and simmer 30 minutes. Stir in ¼ cup dry white wine. Cook chicken, uncovered, 15 minutes longer or till tender; turn occasionally. Remove bay leaves; skim off excess fat. Ladle sauce over chicken in dish. Makes 4 servings.

## CHICKEN PARISIENNE

| | |
|---|---|
| 6 medium chicken breasts | 1 3-ounce can sliced mushrooms, drained (½ cup) |
| ½ cup dry white wine | Paprika |
| 1 10½-ounce can condensed cream of mushroom soup | 1 cup dairy sour cream Hot cooked rice |

OVEN 350°

Place chicken breasts, skin side up, in 12x7½x2-inch baking dish; sprinkle with salt. Blend wine into mushroom soup; add mushrooms and pour over chicken. Bake at 350° for 1 to 1¼ hours. Remove chicken to platter; sprinkle with paprika. Pour sauce into saucepan; blend in sour cream and heat gently till hot. Serve sauce over chicken and hot cooked rice. Makes 6 servings.

**1** Cut the skin between thighs and body of chicken with a sharp 6-inch paring knife. Grasping one leg of chicken in each hand, lift until hips are free from the body.

**2** To remove the legs and thigh pieces, cut between hip joint and body close to bones in back of the chicken. Follow the same procedure to remove the other leg.

**3** If desired, separate the thigh and leg. Locate the knee joint by bending thigh and leg together. Cut through this joint to separate thigh and leg. Cut second leg.

# CHICKEN KIEV

Have 4 large chicken breasts boned, skinned, and halved lengthwise. Place chicken breasts, boned side up, between two pieces of clear plastic wrap. Pound from center out to form cutlets not quite 1/4 inch thick. Peel off wrap; season with salt.

**4** To remove the wings, pull the wing away from body. Start cutting on the inside of the wing just over the joint. Cut down through joint. Remove other wing.

**5** Divide the body by placing bird on neck end and cutting along the breast end of the ribs to the neck. Separate the breast and back section, cutting through the joints. Bend back piece in half to break at joint; cut through at this point with knife.

**6** To bone breast, cut through white cartilage at V of neck. In each hand, grasp small bones on either side of breast. Bend each side of breast back; push up with fingers to snap out breastbone. If not boned, cut breast in two just below breastbone.

Sprinkle 2 tablespoons snipped parsley over cutlets. Chill 1/4 pound stick butter. Cut butter into 8 sticks; place a stick at end of each cutlet. Roll meat as for jelly roll, tucking in sides. Press seam to seal well.

Coat each roll with all-purpose flour and dip in mixture of 1 beaten egg and 1 tablespoon water, then roll in 1/2 cup fine dry bread crumbs. Chill thoroughly, at least 1 hour. Fry chicken rolls in deep hot fat (375°) about 5 minutes, or till golden brown. Makes 4 to 8 servings.

## SPANISH PAELLA

1/4 cup all-purpose flour
1 teaspoon salt
Dash pepper
1 2 1/2- to 3-pound ready-to-cook broiler-fryer chicken, cut up
1/4 cup olive or salad oil
2 carrots, pared and sliced lengthwise
2 medium onions, quartered
1 celery branch with leaves
2 cups chicken broth
1 clove garlic, crushed

1/4 cup diced canned pimiento
1/2 teaspoon salt
1/4 teaspoon ground oregano
1/4 teaspoon ground saffron
2/3 cup uncooked long-grain rice

* * *

1 9-ounce package frozen artichoke hearts, thawed
3/4 pound shelled raw shrimp
12 *small* clams in shells

Combine flour, 1 teaspoon salt, and pepper in plastic or paper bag. Add a few chicken pieces at a time; shake to coat. In heavy skillet, brown chicken in hot oil about 20 minutes. Transfer to large kettle.

Add next 10 ingredients; simmer, covered, 30 minutes. Add artichoke hearts, shrimp, and clams in shells; simmer, covered, 15 to 20 minutes longer. Serves 6 to 8.

## CHICKEN PIE

Pastry for 2-crust pie
1/2 cup chopped onion
6 tablespoons butter
1/2 cup all-purpose flour
1 teaspoon salt
3 cups chicken broth
3 cups cubed cooked
chicken

1 10-ounce package
frozen peas and
carrots, cooked,
drained
1/4 cup chopped canned
pimiento

Roll out pastry on lightly floured surface, 1/4 inch thick. Cut to fit tops of six individual casseroles. Bake on ungreased baking sheet at 450° for 10 to 12 minutes.

Cook onion in butter till tender, but not brown. Blend in flour and salt. Add broth all at once. Cook and stir till thick and bubbly; add remaining ingredients. Heat till bubbly. Pour into 6 heated individual casseroles. Place pastry on hot filling just before serving. Makes 6 servings.

## CREAM GRAVY

1 1/2 cups milk
3 tablespoons all-
purpose flour

1 teaspoon salt
Dash pepper
3 tablespoons drippings*

In a screw top jar, shake *half* of the milk with flour, salt, and pepper; stir into drippings in pan. Add remaining milk. Cook, stirring constantly, till thick and bubbly. Cook 2 to 3 minutes more. Makes 1 1/2 cups.

*Fry chicken in half butter or margarine and half shortening. Make gravy in same skillet incorporating the crusty bits.

## TO COOK GIBLETS

Place giblets, except liver, in saucepan. Add water just to cover giblets; salt lightly. Add a few celery leaves and onion slices to water, if desired. Cover; simmer for 1 to 2 hours for chicken giblets (2 hours for turkey giblets). Add the liver and continue to simmer for 5 to 10 minutes for chicken liver (20 to 30 minutes for turkey liver). Cool giblets in broth; remove and chop. Use broth and giblets in Cream Gravy, or Giblet Gravy (page 484), or stuffing.

## STEWED CHICKEN

1 5- to 6-pound ready-to-cook stewing chicken, cut up, *or* 2 large broiler-fryer chickens, cut up
2 sprigs parsley
4 celery branches, cut up
1 carrot, pared and sliced
1 small onion, cut up
2 teaspoons salt
¼ teaspoon pepper

Place chicken pieces in Dutch oven or large kettle with enough water to cover (about 2 quarts). Add remaining ingredients. Cover; bring to boiling and cook over low heat about 2½ hours, or till tender. Leave chicken on bones in liquid for Chicken with Dumplings. Or, remove meat from bones. This will yield about 5 cups diced cooked chicken for salads or casseroles.

## CHICKEN WITH DUMPLINGS

Stewed Chicken
1 cup sifted all-purpose flour
2 teaspoons baking powder
½ teaspoon salt
½ cup milk
2 tablespoons salad oil
Chicken Gravy

Prepare Stewed Chicken, above. When chicken is almost tender, sift together flour, baking powder, and salt. Combine milk and oil; add to dry ingredients; stir just to moisten. Drop from tablespoon directly onto chicken in boiling stock. (Do not let batter drop in liquid.) Cover tightly; return to boiling. Reduce heat (don't lift cover); simmer 12 to 15 minutes, or till done. Remove dumplings and chicken to hot platter; keep hot while preparing Chicken Gravy. Pour gravy over chicken and dumplings. Garnish with parsley. Makes 6 to 8 servings.

*Chicken Gravy:* Strain broth from Stewed Chicken. Measure 1 quart broth into medium saucepan. Heat to boiling. Combine ½ cup all-purpose flour and 1 cup cold water; gradually add to broth, mixing well. Cook, stirring constantly, till mixture is thick and bubbly. Season with 1½ teaspoons salt and ⅛ teaspoon pepper.

# COQ AU VIN

4 slices bacon, cut in small pieces

2 tablespoons chopped onion

1 2½- to 3-pound ready-to-cook broiler-fryer chicken, cut up

8 shallots or small whole onions

½ cup coarsely chopped carrot

1 clove garlic, minced

2 tablespoons brandy (cognac)

1 pint fresh mushrooms, sliced

2 tablespoons butter

3 to 4 sprigs parsley

1 medium bay leaf

¼ teaspoon dried thyme

1 celery branch with leaves, cut up

2 cups red Burgundy

OVEN 350°

In a skillet, brown bacon pieces and chopped onion; remove. Add chicken pieces and brown slowly in bacon drippings; remove chicken. Add shallots, carrot, garlic, and brandy; cook about 3 minutes. Cook mushrooms in butter.

For Bouquet Garni, combine parsley, bay leaf, thyme, and celery in a tea ball or cheesecloth bag. Place in a 2-quart casserole. Arrange chicken, vegetables, and mushrooms in layers. Add wine to the skillet; heat to boiling and stir to loosen the crusty brown bits. Pour mixture over casserole. Cover; bake at 350° for 2 hours. Remove Bouquet Garni. Makes 4 servings.

# CHICKEN CROQUETTES

Melt 3 tablespoons butter; blend in ¼ cup all-purpose flour. Add ½ cup milk and ½ cup chicken broth. Cook and stir till mixture thickens and bubbles. Cook and stir 1 minute. Add 1 tablespoon snipped parsley, 1 teaspoon lemon juice, 1 teaspoon grated onion, ¼ teaspoon salt, and dash each paprika, nutmeg, and pepper. Cool. Add 1½ cups finely diced cooked chicken; salt to taste. Chill thoroughly.

With wet hands, shape mixture into 8 balls (scant ¼ cup). Roll in ¾ cup fine crumbs (crackers or dry bread). Lightly shape balls into cones. Dip into mixture of 1 beaten egg and 2 tablespoons water; roll in crumbs. Fry in deep hot fat (365°) for 2½ to 3 minutes. Drain. Serves 4.

## CHICKEN CHIP BAKE

OVEN 425°

Combine 2 cups cubed cooked chicken, 2 cups sliced celery, ¾ cup mayonnaise or salad dressing, ⅓ cup toasted slivered almonds, 2 tablespoons lemon juice, 2 teaspoons grated onion, and ½ teaspoon salt. Pile chicken mixture lightly in 8¼x1¾-inch round ovenware cake dish. Sprinkle with 2 ounces process American cheese, shredded (½ cup), then 1 cup crushed potato chips. Bake at 425° for 20 minutes, or till hot. Makes 6 servings.

## CHICKEN LIVERS AND RICE

| | |
|---|---|
| 1⅓ cups packaged precooked rice | 4 ounces sharp natural Cheddar cheese, shredded (1 cup) |
| ½ pound chicken livers, cut up and browned in butter | 2 tablespoons Burgundy |
| | 2 tablespoons butter |
| 1 10-ounce package frozen chopped spinach, thawed | ½ teaspoon salt |
| | Dash pepper |

OVEN 350°

Cook rice according to package directions. Combine rice, browned chicken livers, and remaining ingredients. Turn into 1½-quart casserole. Bake, covered, in moderate oven (350°) for 25 minutes. Garnish with more shredded cheese. Serves 5 or 6.

## SAUCY CHICKEN SQUARES

OVEN 350°

Combine 2 cups soft bread crumbs, 2 cups chicken broth, 4 beaten eggs, ⅓ cup chopped celery, ¼ cup chopped canned pimiento, 2 tablespoons finely chopped onion, ½ teaspoon salt, and ¼ teaspoon poultry seasoning. Stir in 3 cups chopped cooked chicken and 1 cup cooked long-grain rice. Turn chicken mixture into 9x9x2-inch baking pan. Bake in moderate oven (350°) for 45 to 50 minutes. Cut in squares; serve with hot Mushroom Sauce. Makes 8 servings.

*Mushroom Sauce:* In small saucepan, blend one 10¾-ounce can condensed cream of mushroom soup and ¼ cup milk; stir over low heat till heated through.

## CALICO CHICKEN

Combine 2 cups dairy sour cream and ½ envelope (¼ cup) *dry onion soup mix;* chill. Place two 2½- to 3-pound ready-to-cook broiler-fryer chickens, cut up, in Dutch oven. Add 2 cups water, 1 cup dry white wine, 1 teaspoon salt, dash pepper, and ½ teaspoon dried basil, crushed. Cover; cook chicken over low heat about 1 hour, or till tender.

Meanwhile, cook 2 cups long-grain rice, following package directions. Remove chicken from broth; cool. Cut in large pieces. Cook liquid in Dutch oven, uncovered, till reduced to 1½ cups.

Blend in one 10½-ounce can condensed cream of mushroom soup, ¼ cup chopped canned pimiento, and ¼ cup snipped parsley. Stir in sour cream mixture, chicken, and rice. Cook and stir just till heated. Makes 10 to 12 servings.

## CHICKEN STRATA

| | |
|---|---|
| 6 slices day-old white bread | ¾ teaspoon salt |
| | Dash pepper |
| 2 cups cubed cooked chicken *or* turkey | 2 slightly beaten eggs |
| | 1½ cups milk |
| ½ cup chopped onion | 1 10½-ounce can condensed cream of mushroom soup |
| ½ cup finely chopped celery | |
| ¼ cup chopped green pepper | ½ cup shredded sharp process American cheese |
| ½ cup mayonnaise | |

OVEN 325°

Butter 2 *slices* bread; cut in ½-inch cubes and set aside. Cut remaining bread in 1-inch cubes; place *half of unbuttered* cubes in bottom of 8x8x2-inch baking dish. Combine chicken, vegetables, mayonnaise, and seasonings. Spoon over bread cubes.

Sprinkle remaining *unbuttered* cubes over chicken mixture. Combine eggs and milk; pour over all. Cover and chill 1 hour or overnight. Spoon soup over top. Sprinkle with buttered cubes. Bake at 325° for 60 minutes, or till set. Sprinkle cheese over top last few minutes of baking. Let stand few minutes before serving. Makes 6 servings.

## BREAD STUFFING

| | |
|---|---|
| 3 tablespoons chopped onion | 1/4 teaspoon pepper |
| 1/4 cup butter or margarine | 1/2 teaspoon poultry seasoning |
| 4 cups dry bread cubes (about 7 slices cut in 1/2-inch cubes) | 1/2 teaspoon ground sage |
| 1/4 teaspoon salt | 2 to 4 tablespoons water *or* chicken broth |

Cook onion in butter. Combine with bread and seasonings. Toss with enough liquid to moisten. Makes 3 cups stuffing, or enough stuffing for 4- to 5-pound chicken. Double recipe for 10-pound turkey.

**Giblet Stuffing:** Cook giblets till tender in lightly salted water to cover (page 533). Drain and chop giblets. Prepare Bread Stuffing, adding chopped giblets; use giblet broth as liquid.

**Chestnut Stuffing:** Cover 3 cups (1 pound) fresh chestnuts in shells with water; simmer 15 minutes. Drain. Make gash in shells with sharp knife; peel off while warm. Chop nuts. Prepare Bread Stuffing, cooking 1 cup chopped celery with the onion in 6 *tablespoons* butter. Add chestnuts. Increase salt to 1 teaspoon; use 1/4 cup turkey *or* chicken broth as liquid.

**Mushroom Stuffing:** Prepare Bread Stuffing adding one 6-ounce can sliced mushrooms, drained, *or* 1 cup sliced fresh mushrooms cooked in butter; toss.

**Raisin Stuffing:** Prepare Bread Stuffing adding 3/4 cup raisins to bread mixture.

**Celery Stuffing:** Prepare Bread Stuffing. Add 1 1/2 cups finely chopped celery (cook in butter, if desired).

## OYSTER STUFFING

Cook 1 bay leaf and $\frac{1}{2}$ cup each chopped celery and onion in $\frac{1}{4}$ cup butter till tender. Discard bay leaf. Add 6 cups dry bread cubes and 1 tablespoon snipped parsley to butter mixture; mix thoroughly. Add 2 beaten eggs, 1 pint raw oysters, chopped, 1 teaspoon poultry seasoning, 1 teaspoon salt, and dash pepper. Add milk to oyster liquor to make $\frac{1}{4}$ to $\frac{1}{3}$ cup; add enough liquid to stuffing to moisten. Makes enough stuffing for a 10-pound turkey.

## HERB STUFFING

| | |
|---|---|
| 12 cups slightly dry bread cubes | 1 teaspoon dried thyme, crushed |
| $\frac{1}{3}$ cup snipped parsley | 1 teaspoon dried rosemary, crushed |
| $\frac{1}{3}$ cup finely chopped onion | 6 tablespoons butter, melted |
| $1\frac{1}{2}$ teaspoons salt | 1 cup canned chicken broth (not condensed) |
| 1 teaspoon ground sage | |

Combine all ingredients except broth. Add broth; toss lightly to mix. Makes 8 cups or enough stuffing for one 12-pound turkey.

## CORN BREAD STUFFING

OVEN 350°

In skillet, cook $\frac{1}{2}$ pound bacon (8 to 10 slices) till crisp; drain, reserving $\frac{1}{4}$ cup drippings. Crumble bacon; set aside. To skillet, add 1 cup chopped celery, $\frac{1}{4}$ cup chopped onion, and $\frac{1}{2}$ cup water. Cover; cook till barely tender, about 7 minutes.

Combine bacon, reserved drippings, vegetable mixture, 3 cups coarse corn bread crumbs, 6 slices toasted bread, cubed, $\frac{1}{2}$ teaspoon rubbed sage, and 1 cup chicken or turkey broth; toss well. Bake, covered, in a $1\frac{1}{2}$-quart casserole at 350° for 30 minutes. Makes 8 servings, or enough stuffing for an 8-pound turkey.

## ORANGE STUFFING

2 cups finely diced celery
1/4 cup butter, melted
3 cups toasted bread cubes (about 5 slices cut in 1/2-inch cubes)
1 teaspoon grated orange peel

2/3 cup diced orange sections (2 medium oranges)
1/2 teaspoon salt
1/2 teaspoon poultry seasoning
1 beaten egg

Cook celery in butter till tender but not brown. Add remaining ingredients and dash pepper; toss lightly. Makes enough stuffing for a 5-pound duckling.

## STORING AND THAWING

**To store:** Fresh poultry can be wrapped loosely in waxed paper or clear plastic wrap and stored in the refrigerator for several days. Remove giblets, wrap loosely, and cook as soon as possible. Do not chop fresh poultry until ready to use.

Remove stuffing and meat from bones of cooked poultry as soon as possible. Chill; cover and wrap stuffing, meat, and gravy separately. Follow freezing directions for cooked poultry on page 353.

**Thawing in brown paper bag:** Leave turkey in original wrap. Place frozen turkey in brown paper bag or wrap in 2 to 3 layers of newspaper. Thaw at room temperature. Thawing will take 20 to 24 hours for birds under 12 pounds and up to 24 to 30 hours for birds over 12 pounds. Check turkey often during last hours of thawing.

**Cold water thawing:** Leave turkey in original wrap or place in plastic bag. Place frozen turkey in cold water. Change the water frequently. Thawing will take 30 minutes to 1 hour for small chickens and up to 6 to 8 hours for large turkeys. Never use warm or hot water.

**Refrigerator thawing:** Leave in original wrap and place on tray or drip pan. Thaw in refrigerator for 2 to 3 days. Once thawed, cook at once or keep refrigerated only a short time before cooking.

# CHICKEN GLOSSARY

*Broiler-fryer or fryer:* Young tender birds that weigh 1½ to 3½ pounds ready to cook. A broiler-fryer may be roasted, simmered, baked, fried, grilled, or broiled.

*Capon:* Large 4- to 7-pound ready-to-cook birds with large amount of tender and flavorful white meat; usually roasted.

*Roaster:* Tender birds that weigh 3½ to 5 pounds ready to cook.

*Stewing chicken:* Mature, less tender birds weighing 2½ to 5 pounds, having more fat. Cook in large amount of liquid.

*Cornish game hen:* The smallest, youngest member of the chicken family, weighing 1½ pounds or less. Roast, broil, or fry.

---

### How much to buy for one serving

CHICKEN:

| | |
|---|---|
| Broiler-fryer | ¼ to ½ bird |
| Capon, roaster, stewing | about ½ pound |
| Cornish game hens | 1 bird |

TURKEY:

| | |
|---|---|
| 5 to 12 pounds | ¾ to 1 pound |
| 12 to 24 pounds | ½ to ¾ pound |
| uncooked boneless roast | ⅓ pound |

| | |
|---|---|
| DUCK, domestic | about 1 pound |
| GOOSE, domestic | about 1 pound |

---

## • HOW TO PREPARE
## POULTRY FOR ROASTING •

 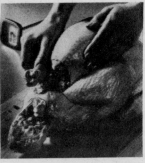

Stuff and close wishbone cavity. Place bird, neck end down, in bowl. Lightly spoon in stuffing —do not pack; shake down.

Push drumsticks under band of skin at tail. Or, if band of skin is not present, tie the legs securely together and to the tail.

## • ROASTING OF DOMESTIC BIRDS
## AND HOW TO TEST FOR DONENESS •

**Stuff** bird just before roasting. Allow about ¾ cup stuffing per pound ready-to-cook weight. Rinse bird and pat dry. Rub inside of cavities with salt, if desired. Spoon some of the stuffing loosely into wishbone cavity; skewer neck skin to back. Then, lightly spoon stuffing into large cavity. If opening has band of skin across tail, push drumsticks under band; if not present, tie legs together and to tail. Twist wing tips under back of turkey.

For unstuffed bird, sprinkle inside with salt. Stuff loosely with quartered onions and celery, if desired. Roast according to chart. Discard stuffing before serving.

**To roast:** Place, breast up, on rack in shallow roasting pan. Rub skin thoroughly with salad oil. If meat thermometer is used, insert in center of inside thigh muscle not touching bone. For turkey, "cap" loosely with foil, pressing it lightly at drumstick and breast ends. Avoid having foil touch top or sides. Roast in uncovered pan (unless specified) according to chart.

When bird is about ⅔ done, cut band of skin or string between legs and tail. Continue roasting till done.

**Test for doneness:** About 20 minutes before roasting time is up, test bird. The thickest part of drumstick should feel very soft when pressed between fingers protected with paper towels, and drumstick should move up and down and twist easily in socket. Meat thermometer should register 185°. Remove bird from oven; let stand 15 minutes before carving.

| Poultry | Ready-To-Cook Weight | Oven Temp. |
| --- | --- | --- |
| Chicken | 1½-2 lbs. | 375° |
| | 2-2½ lbs. | 375° |
| | 2½-3 lbs. | 375° |
| | 3-4 lbs. | 375° |
| Capon | 4-7 lbs. | 375° |
| Turkey | 6-8 lbs. | 325° |
| | 8-12 lbs. | 325° |
| | 12-16 lbs. | 325° |
| | 16-20 lbs. | 325° |
| | 20-24 lbs. | 325° |
| Foil-wrapped Turkey | 8-10 lbs. | 450° |
| | 10-12 lbs. | 450° |
| | 14-16 lbs. | 450° |
| | 18-20 lbs. | 450° |
| | 22-24 lbs. | 450° |
| Cornish Game Hen | 1-1½ lbs. | 375° |

| Roasting Time Stuffed and Unstuffed | Special Instructions |
| --- | --- |
| $^3/_4$-1 hr.<br>1-1$^1/_4$ hrs.<br>1$^1/_4$-1$^1/_2$ hrs.<br>1$^1/_2$-2 hrs. | Brush dry areas of skin occasionally with pan drippings. Cover loosely with foil. |
| 1$^1/_2$-2 hrs. | Same as above. |
| 3$^1/_2$-4 hrs.<br>4-4$^1/_2$ hrs.<br>4$^1/_2$-5$^1/_2$ hrs.<br>5$^1/_2$-6$^1/_2$ hrs.<br>6$^1/_2$-7$^1/_2$ hrs. | Cover loosely with foil. Last 45 minutes, cut band of skin or string between legs and tail; uncover and continue roasting till done. Baste, if desired. |
| 2$^1/_4$-2$^1/_2$ hrs.<br>2$^1/_2$-3 hrs.<br>3-3$^1/_4$ hrs.<br>3$^1/_4$-3$^1/_2$ hrs.<br>3$^1/_2$-3$^3/_4$ hrs. | Place trussed turkey, breast up, in center of greased, wide heavy foil. Bring ends of foil up over breast; overlap fold and press up against ends of turkey. Place bird in shallow pan (no rack). Open foil last 20 minutes to brown turkey. |
| 1$^1/_2$ hrs. | Roast loosely covered for 30 minutes, then 60 minutes uncovered, or till done. If desired, occasionally baste with melted butter or a glaze the last hour. |

## • HOW TO CARVE A TURKEY
### LIKE AN EXPERT •

Remove bird from oven about 15 minutes before carving and keep warm. Place bird on carving board or on platter protected with a board. Have drumsticks to carver's right. First carve side toward guests. Grasp leg with fingers and pull away from body. Cut through meat between thigh and backbone (drawing 1). With knife tip, disjoint leg bone from backbone.

Holding leg vertically, large end down, slice meat parallel to bone and under some tendons, turning leg for even slices. Or, first separate thigh and drumstick. Slice thigh meat by cutting slices parallel to bone. Slice drumstick as above.

Before carving white meat, make a deep horizontal cut into breast close to wing (drawing 2). (Note that wing tips have been folded behind back before roasting so that carving can be done more easily without removing wings.)

Cut thin, even slices from top of breast down to horizontal cut (drawing 3). Final smaller slices can follow curve of breast bone. If desired, cut an opening through thin meat where thigh was removed to reach stuffing. Repeat each step with the other side of the bird. Complete carving.

# OVEN FRIED TURKEY

*No browning, no turning, no carving—*

| | |
|---|---|
| 3 cups packaged herb-seasoned stuffing mix | Salt<br>Pepper |
| 1 4- to 6-pound ready-to-cook fryer-roaster turkey, cut up | $3/4$ cup butter or margarine, melted |

OVEN 350°

Crush stuffing finely (will be about $1\frac{1}{2}$ cups). Sprinkle turkey pieces with salt and pepper. Brush with melted butter or margarine; roll in stuffing crumbs. Place pieces, skin side up (don't crowd), in greased large shallow baking pan. Drizzle with any remaining butter or margarine. Cover pan with foil. Bake in moderate oven (350°) for 1 hour. Uncover and bake 30 to 45 minutes, or till tender. Serves 6 to 8.

# TURKEY-NOODLE BAKE

OVEN 350°

Blend $1\frac{1}{2}$ cups milk into one $10\frac{1}{2}$-ounce can condensed cream of mushroom soup; stir in 3 beaten eggs. Add 3 ounces (about 2 cups) fine noodles, cooked and drained, 2 cups cubed cooked turkey, 1 cup soft bread crumbs ($1\frac{1}{2}$ slices), 4 ounces sharp process American cheese, shredded (1 cup), $\frac{1}{4}$ cup chopped green pepper, $\frac{1}{4}$ cup butter or margarine, melted, and 2 tablespoons chopped canned pimiento. Turn into $12x7\frac{1}{2}x2$-inch baking dish.

Bake in moderate oven (350°) for 30 to 40 minutes, or till knife inserted off center comes out clean. Cut in squares to serve. Makes 6 to 8 servings.

## HAM-TURKEY PIE

2½ cups cooked long-
   grain rice
  2 beaten eggs
 ¼ cup butter or
   margarine, melted
 ⅛ teaspoon pepper
      * * *
 ¼ cup butter or
   margarine
  5 tablespoons all-
   purpose flour
 ¼ teaspoon pepper

2 cups chicken broth
1 cup chopped fully
  cooked ham
1 cup chopped cooked
  turkey
½ cup chopped
  mushrooms
¼ cup chopped green
  onion
3 tablespoons snipped
  parsley

OVEN 350°

To prepare rice shell, thoroughly combine cooked rice, beaten eggs, ¼ cup melted butter or margarine, and ⅛ teaspoon pepper. Press rice mixture firmly into an ungreased 9-inch pie plate. Set aside.

In a saucepan, melt remaining ¼ cup butter or margarine; blend in flour and ¼ teaspoon pepper. Add chicken broth all at once. Cook over medium heat, stirring constantly, till mixture thickens and bubbles. Remove from heat. Stir in chopped ham, chopped turkey, mushrooms, green onion, and snipped parsley; mix thoroughly.

Pour ham-turkey mixture into prepared rice shell. Bake in a moderate oven (350°) for 40 minutes. Let pie stand about 5 minutes before serving. Makes 6 servings.

## TURKEY HASH—OVEN-STYLE

1½ cups coarsely ground
   cooked turkey
  1 cup cubed cooked
   potato
  1 5⅓-ounce can
   evaporated milk
   (⅔ cup)
 ¼ cup finely snipped
   parsley
 ¼ cup finely chopped
   onion

1 teaspoon
  Worcestershire sauce
½ teaspoon salt
¼ teaspoon ground sage
  Dash pepper
    * * *
¼ cup finely crushed
  saltine crackers
  (about 7 crackers)
1 tablespoon butter or
  margarine, melted

OVEN 350°

In a mixing bowl, stir together turkey, potato, evaporated milk, parsley, finely chopped onion, Worcestershire sauce, salt, sage, and dash pepper. Turn mixture into a greased 1-quart casserole.

Toss together saltine cracker crumbs and melted butter; sprinkle crumb mixture evenly over hash. Bake in a moderate oven (350°) till heated through, about 30 minutes. Makes 4 servings.

## TURKEY-TOMATO BAKE

1/2 cup chopped onion
1/2 chopped celery
1 tablespoon butter or margarine
1 1-pound 1-ounce can whole kernel corn, drained
1 1/2 cups chopped cooked turkey

1 10 3/4-ounce can condensed tomato soup
1/3 cup catsup
1 ounce process American cheese, shredded (1/4 cup)
1 9-ounce package frozen French-fried crinkle-cut potatoes

OVEN 425°

In a skillet, cook onion and celery in butter till vegetables are tender but not brown. Stir in the corn, turkey, soup, catsup, and cheese. Turn into an 8x8x2-inch baking dish. Arrange potatoes over top. Bake, uncovered, in a hot oven (425°) for 25 minutes. Makes 6 servings.

## TURKEY-ALMOND BAKE

1 8-ounce package frozen mixed vegetables in onion sauce
Milk
1 6-ounce package noodles with chicken-almond mix

1 1/2 to 2 cups cubed cooked turkey
2 tablespoons butter
2 1/3 cups boiling water
1/2 cup crushed potato chips

OVEN 375°

Prepare vegetables following package directions, *except use milk*. Combine vegetables, noodles from mix, dry sauce from mix, turkey, and butter. Add boiling water; mix well. Pour into 1½-quart casserole. Cover; bake in moderate oven (375°) for 25 minutes. Uncover; stir well. Sprinkle with potato chips and almonds from the mix; bake 5 to 10 minutes more. Let stand 5 minutes before serving. Serves 4.

## TURKEY SPOON BREAD

Spoon Bread
½ cup chopped onion
¼ cup chopped green pepper
1 clove garlic, minced
1 tablespoon salad oil
1 15-ounce can tomato sauce

1½ to 2 cups diced cooked turkey
1 to 1½ teaspoons chili powder
1 teaspoon sugar
½ teaspoon salt

OVEN 350°

Prepare Spoon Bread. Cook onion, pepper, and garlic in hot oil just till tender. Stir in remaining ingredients. Simmer, covered, 15 minutes. Serve over wedges of Spoon Bread. Makes 4 to 6 servings.

*Spoon Bread:* In a saucepan, gradually stir ⅔ cup yellow cornmeal into 2 cups milk. Cook and stir till thickened. Add 1 cup shredded process American cheese, 1 tablespoon butter, ¾ teaspoon baking powder, ½ teaspoon salt, and ¼ teaspoon paprika. Stir till cheese melts. Gradually add a moderate amount of hot mixture to 2 beaten egg yolks; beat well and return to hot mixture. Beat 2 egg whites till stiff; fold into cornmeal mixture. Turn into greased 9-inch pie plate. Bake at 350° for 40 to 45 minutes.

## STUFFED CORNISH HENS

2/3 cup long-grain rice
3 tablespoons butter
2 cups water
2 teaspoons instant chicken bouillon granules
3/4 cup chopped fresh cranberries
3 tablespoons sugar

1 teaspoon grated orange peel
2 tablespoons orange juice
4 1-pound ready-to-cook Cornish game hens
Orange Glaze

OVEN 375°

In a saucepan, cook rice in butter 5 minutes, stirring often. Stir in water and bouillon granules. Bring to boiling; reduce heat. Cover; cook over low heat till rice is tender, about 20 minutes.

Stir in berries, sugar, peel, and orange juice. Salt cavity of birds. Stuff each with cranberry mixture; push drumsticks under band of skin at tail or tie to tail. Place birds on rack in shallow roasting pan. Cover loosely with foil. Roast in a 375° oven for 30 minutes. Uncover; roast 1 hour longer. Brush occasionally with Orange Glaze. Serves 4.

*Orange Glaze:* Combine 1/4 cup orange juice and 3 tablespoons melted butter.

## PHEASANT WITH APPLES

Coat two 1 1/2- to 3-pound ready-to-cook pheasants, cut up, with mixture of 1/4 cup all-purpose flour, 1 teaspoon salt, and 1/4 teaspoon pepper. In a skillet, lightly brown pheasant pieces in 6 tablespoons butter or margarine. Add 3/4 cup sauterne; simmer, covered, 35 to 55 minutes, or till tender. Remove pheasant to serving platter; keep warm. Reserve pan drippings.

Beat 3/4 cup light cream with 3 egg yolks. Slowly stir egg mixture into reserved pan drippings in skillet; cook and stir over medium heat just till mixture is smooth and thickened. *Do not boil.* Pour sauce over pheasants. Garnish platter with Sauteed Apples. Makes 4 to 5 servings.

*Sauteed Apples:* In a skillet, melt 3 tablespoons butter or margarine. Add 2 apples, cored and sliced into wedges.

Sprinkle with 1 teaspoon sugar; cook apples, turning often, till lightly browned.

## ROAST DOMESTIC GOOSE

OVEN 350°

Remove excess fat from body cavity of a 7- to 9-pound ready-to-cook goose. Sprinkle cavity with salt and pepper. Stuff, if desired. Tuck legs under band of skin or tie legs to tail. Twist wing tips under back of goose. Place, breast side up, on rack in shallow roasting pan. *Do not rub with oil.* Prick legs and wings. Loosely cap with foil. Roast at 350° till internal temperature at thigh registers 185°, for 2½ to 3 hours; spoon off fat several times.

## BROILED CORNISH HEN

Split one 1- to 1½-pound ready-to-cook Cornish game hen in half lengthwise. Place, skin side down, in broiler pan (no rack). Brush with melted butter. Season with salt and pepper. Broil 7 inches from heat for 15 minutes. Brush occasionally with butter. Turn, broil 15 minutes longer, or till done. Makes 2 servings.

## SQUAB

OVEN 400°

**To roast:** Sprinkle inside of four 12- to 14-ounce ready-to-cook squabs with salt. Brown giblets; add to *half* recipe Bread Stuffing (page 538). Stuff squab; rub skin with butter or lay bacon slices over breast. Roast, breast up, on rack in shallow pan in hot oven (400°) for 40 to 50 minutes, or till tender. Makes 4 servings.

**To broil:** Cook as for Broiled Cornish Hen. Broil 5 to 7 inches from heat for *total* of 20 to 30 minutes. Serve on buttered toast. Allow 1 bird per serving.

## SMOTHERED QUAIL

In skillet, brown four 4- to 6-ounce ready-to-cook quail, split in halves lengthwise in ¼ cup butter. Season with salt and pepper. Top with ½ cup chopped onion; add

½ cup light cream. Cover and simmer about 30 minutes, or till tender. Remove quail to a warm platter. Blend 2 tablespoons cold water into 1 teaspoon cornstarch; add to pan drippings. Simmer and stir till thickened and bubbly. Pour gravy over quail. Makes 4 servings.

## ROAST PHEASANT

OVEN 350°

Roast only young birds—feet are still gray with rounded and flexible spurs. Salt inside of one 1- to 3-pound ready-to-cook pheasant. Stuff, if desired (pages 538–540). Tie legs together and to tail; place, breast up, on rack in shallow roasting pan. Lay bacon slices over breast. Roast, uncovered, at 350° for 1 to 2½ hours, or till tender. Allow 1 to 1½ pounds per serving.

## ROAST DOMESTIC DUCK

OVEN 375°

Remove wing tips and first joint from one 3- to 5-pound ready-to-cook domestic duck. Sprinkle inside with salt. Stuff lightly with Orange Stuffing (page 540), or celery and 1 quartered tart apple. Prick skin all over. *Do not rub with oil.* Tie legs together and to tail; place, breast up, on rack in shallow pan. Don't add water. Roast, uncovered, at 375° for 1½ to 2 hours. Increase temperature to 425° for 15 minutes longer, or till done. Serves 3 or 4.

*Note:* If desired, roast duck in electric skillet. Place, breast up, on rack in skillet (325°). Prick skin. Cover; cook about 2 hours. Before testing for doneness, unplug skillet and *let cool 5 minutes.* Then, remove the cover of the skillet *carefully.*

## ROAST WILD DUCK, GOOSE

OVEN 400°

Salt inside of ready-to-cook wild duck or goose. Stuff loosely with quartered onions and apples. Tie legs together and to tail; place, breast side up, on rack in shallow pan. Do not brush *duck* with oil. For *goose*, lay bacon slices over breast or rub with oil. Roast, uncovered, at 400°. Roast a 1- to 2-pound duck, 60 to 90 minutes. For a 2- to 4-pound goose allow 1½ to 3 hours; 4- to 6-pounds allow 3 to 4 hours. Cap loosely with foil if necessary to prevent excess browning. Discard stuffing. Allow 1 to 1½ pounds per serving.

*Note:* If bird has had a fish diet or may be old, stuff loosely with pared carrot or quartered potato; precook in simmering water about 10 minutes. Discard stuffing. Prepare and roast as above.

# FISH

## STUFFED FLOUNDER

¼ cup chopped onion
¼ cup butter or
   margarine
1 3-ounce can broiled
   chopped mushrooms,
   drained (reserve liquid)
1 7½-ounce can crab
   meat, drained and
   cartilage removed
½ cup coarse saltine
   cracker crumbs
2 tablespoons snipped
   parsley
½ teaspoon salt

Dash pepper
2 pounds flounder
   fillets (8)
3 tablespoons butter
3 tablespoons
   all-purpose flour
¼ teaspoon salt
   Milk
⅓ cup dry white wine
4 ounces process Swiss
   cheese, shredded
   (1 cup)
½ teaspoon paprika

OVEN 400°

In skillet, cook onion in ¼ cup butter till tender, but not brown. Stir mushrooms into skillet with flaked crab, cracker crumbs, parsley, ½ teaspoon salt, and pepper. Spread over flounder fillets. Roll fillets and place, seam side down, in 12x7½x2-inch baking dish. In saucepan, melt 3 tablespoons butter. Blend in flour and ¼ teaspoon salt. Add enough milk to mushroom liquid to make 1½ cups. Add with wine to saucepan. Cook and stir until thickened and bubbly. Pour over fillets.

Bake in hot oven (400°) for 25 minutes. Sprinkle with cheese and paprika. Return to oven. Bake 10 minutes longer, or till fish flakes easily with fork. Serves 8.

## FISH-FRY POINTERS

• Use large pan to avoid crowding fish.
• Turn fish once when crisp and golden. For fillets, brown skin side last.

- Thaw frozen fish before frying. Separate pieces and cut in uniform size.
- After frying, drain fish immediately on paper towels to remove excess fat.

## OVEN FRIED FISH

| | |
|---|---|
| 1 pound fish fillets or steaks | ½ cup fine dry bread crumbs |
| ½ cup milk | 2 tablespoons butter or margarine, melted |

OVEN 500°

Cut fillets in serving pieces. Dip in milk and roll in bread crumbs. Place in well-greased baking pan; sprinkle with salt and pepper.

Drizzle melted butter or margarine over fish and bake in an extremely hot oven (500°) 10 to 12 minutes, or till fish flakes easily with fork. Makes 3 to 4 servings.

## DEEP-FAT FRIED FISH

Use 2 pounds fresh or frozen fish fillets, steaks, or pan-dressed fish. Thaw frozen fish. Cut into 6 portions. Combine 1 egg and 2 tablespoons water. Combine 1¼ cups fine saltine cracker crumbs and dash pepper. Dip fish into egg; roll in crumbs. Place in single layer in fryer basket. Fry in deep, hot fat (350°) 3 to 5 minutes, or till fish flakes easily. Drain. Makes 6 servings for fillets or steaks; 4 servings for pan-dressed fish.

## FRIED FISH

Wash cleaned fresh- or salt-water fish; dry thoroughly. Dip in 1 beaten egg mixed with 1 tablespoon water, then in bread crumbs, seasoned all-purpose flour, or cornmeal.

Brown fish in ¼ inch hot fat on one side; turn; brown on other side.

Small fish may be fried whole. Larger fish should be boned and cut in steaks or fillets before they are fried.

## BROILED FISH

Cut 2 pounds fish fillets or steaks into 6 portions. Place in a single layer on greased rack of broiler pan. Tuck under any thin edges. Melt 2 tablespoons butter. Brush *half* the butter over fish. Season with 1 teaspoon salt and dash pepper. Broil 4 inches from heat 10 to 15 minutes, or till fish flakes easily, brushing once with remaining butter. Serves 6.

## STUFFED WHITEFISH

| | |
|---|---|
| 1 3-pound dressed whitefish *or* other fish, boned | 1 12-ounce can whole kernel corn, drained |
| 1/4 cup chopped onion | 1 cup soft bread crumbs |
| 3 tablespoons chopped green pepper | 2 tablespoons chopped canned pimiento |
| 1 tablespoon butter | 1/8 teaspoon dried thyme, crushed |
| | 2 tablespoons salad oil |

OVEN 350°

Sprinkle inside of fish with salt. Place in well-greased shallow pan. Cook onion and pepper in butter. Stir in next 4 ingredients and 1/2 teaspoon salt. Stuff fish loosely. Brush with oil; cover with foil. Bake at 350° 45 to 60 minutes. Serves 6.

## SALMON STEAKS

OVEN 350°

Place 4 salmon steaks, 1 inch thick, in shallow baking pan. Blend 1/3 cup melted butter, 1 teaspoon Worcestershire sauce, 1 teaspoon grated onion, and 1/4 teaspoon paprika; brush some lightly on fish. Sprinkle with salt. Bake at 350° for 25 to 30 minutes. Pass remaining sauce. Serves 4.

## STEAMED FISH

Use 1 pound fish fillets *or* steaks, *or* one 3-pound dressed fish. Bring 2 cups water to boiling in 10-inch skillet or fish poacher with tight fitting cover. Sprinkle fish with 1 teaspoon salt. Place on greased rack in pan so that fish does not touch water. Cover pan tightly; steam till fish flakes easily when tested with a fork—fillets, 3 to 4 minutes; steaks, 6 to 8 minutes; dressed, 20 to 25 minutes.

## QUICK TUNA CURRY

Cook ⅓ cup chopped onion, ¼ cup chopped green pepper, and 1 clove garlic, minced, in 2 tablespoons butter till tender, but not brown. Stir in 1 cup dairy sour cream, 1 teaspoon curry powder, and salt and pepper to taste. Add one 6½- or 7-ounce can tuna, drained and broken in bite-size pieces. Heat slowly, stirring often, just till hot (do not boil). Serve over hot rice dotted with raisins. Serves 4 or 5.

## TUNA SALAD BAKE

OVEN 400°

Combine one 10½-ounce can condensed cream of chicken soup, 1 cup diced celery, ¼ cup finely chopped onion, ½ cup mayonnaise or salad dressing, ½ teaspoon salt, and dash pepper. Fold in one 6½- or 7-ounce can tuna, drained and flaked, and 3 hard-cooked eggs, sliced. Turn into 1½-quart casserole. Sprinkle with 1 cup crushed potato chips. Bake in hot oven (400°) for 35 minutes. Makes 6 servings.

## SALMON LOAF

| | |
|---|---|
| 1 1-pound can salmon, drained and flaked | 1 tablespoon butter, melted |
| 2 cups soft bread crumbs | ½ teaspoon salt |
| 1 tablespoon chopped onion | ½ cup milk |
| | 1 slightly beaten egg |
| | Piquant Sauce |

OVEN 350°

In a bowl, combine salmon, crumbs, chopped onion, butter, and salt. Combine milk and egg; add to salmon mixture and mix thoroughly. Shape into a loaf on a greased shallow baking pan or in 7½x3¾x2¼-inch loaf pan. Bake at 350° for 35 to 40 minutes. Serve with Piquant Sauce or creamed peas. Makes 3 or 4 servings.

*Piquant Sauce:* Cook 2 tablespoons chopped green onion in 3 tablespoons butter till tender, but not brown. Blend in 2 tablespoons all-purpose flour, $1/2$ teaspoon dry mustard, $1/2$ teaspoon salt, and dash pepper. Add $1^1/4$ cups milk and 1 teaspoon Worcestershire sauce. Cook, stirring constantly, till sauce thickens and bubbles.

## HADDOCK-SHRIMP BAKE

2 pounds frozen haddock fillets, slightly thawed
1 $10^1/2$-ounce can condensed cream of potato soup
$3/4$ cup milk
1 cup frozen, cooked shrimp

$1/4$ cup butter, melted
$1/2$ teaspoon grated onion
$1/2$ teaspoon Worcestershire sauce
$1/4$ teaspoon garlic salt
$1^1/4$ cups rich round cracker crumbs (30 crackers)

OVEN 375°

Place fish in greased 13x9x2-inch baking dish. Heat soup and milk. Stir in shrimp. Spread over fish. Bake at 375° for 20 minutes. Combine remaining ingredients *except* crumbs; mix in crumbs. Sprinkle over fish. Bake 10 minutes. Serves 6 to 8.

## HALIBUT ROYALE

OVEN 450°

In shallow dish, combine 3 tablespoons lemon juice, 1 teaspoon salt, and $1/2$ teaspoon paprika. Add 6 halibut steaks and marinate for 1 hour, turning steaks after 30 minutes. Cook $1/2$ cup chopped onion in 2 tablespoons butter till tender, but not brown. Place steaks in greased 10x6x1$1/2$-inch baking dish. Top with 6 green pepper strips and sprinkle with onion. Bake at 450° about 10 minutes. Serves 6.

## HERB-BAKED FISH

OVEN 350°

Thaw 1 pound frozen haddock, halibut, or cod fillets. Place in 10x6x1½-inch baking dish. Dot with 1 tablespoon butter.

Thoroughly blend 1 cup milk and 2 tablespoons all-purpose flour. Cook over medium heat, stirring constantly, till sauce thickens and bubbles. Cook and stir 1 minute longer. Stir in ¼ teaspoon salt, ¼ teaspoon garlic salt, ⅛ teaspoon pepper, ⅛ teaspoon dried thyme, crushed, dash dried oregano, crushed, and ¼ cup chopped green onion.

Pour sauce over fish. Sprinkle lightly with paprika. Bake, uncovered, at 350° for 20 to 25 minutes. Makes 4 servings.


## FLOUNDER PROVENCALE

| | |
|---|---|
| 6 flounder fillets (1½ pounds) | 1 3-ounce can chopped mushrooms, drained (½ cup) |
| 4 tablespoons butter | |
| ¼ cup chopped onion | ¼ cup dry white wine |
| 1 clove garlic, minced | 6 lemon wedges |
| 1 1-pound can tomatoes, cut up | Parsley sprigs |

Dot each fillet with 2 teaspoons butter. Sprinkle with salt and paprika. Roll up fillets; fasten with wooden picks. Place fillet rolls in skillet. Add onion and next 4 ingredients. Cover tightly and simmer about 15 minutes, or till fish flakes. Remove fish to warm platter; keep hot. Simmer sauce until slightly thickened. Spoon sauce over fish rolls. Garnish with lemon wedges and parsley sprigs. Makes 6 servings.


## CODFISH BALLS

| | |
|---|---|
| ½ pound salt codfish | 2 tablespoons butter or margarine |
| 3 cups diced raw potatoes | |
| 1 beaten egg | ¼ teaspoon pepper |

Freshen codfish by soaking in water several hours or overnight. Dice. Cook potatoes and codfish in boiling water till potatoes are tender; drain. Beat with electric mixer and add egg, butter or margarine, and pepper; beat thoroughly.

Drop by heaping tablespoons (about the size of golf balls) into deep, hot fat (375°). Fry about 2 to 3 minutes, or till golden brown, turning once. Drain. Makes 30.

## STEAMED CLAMS

Thoroughly wash 5 dozen soft-shelled clams in shells (oval shape). Cover with salt water ($^1/_3$ cup salt to 1 gallon cold water); let stand 15 minutes; rinse. Repeat twice. Place clams on rack in kettle with 1 cup hot water; cover tightly and steam just till shells open, about 5 minutes. Cut out and serve on half shell with melted butter. Makes 4 servings.

## CRAB-ARTICHOKE BAKE

OVEN 375°

Drain and flake two $7^1/_2$-ounce cans crab meat; toss with 1 cup cubed process Swiss cheese, $^1/_3$ cup chopped green pepper, $^1/_4$ cup finely chopped onion, and 1 teaspoon salt. Blend $^1/_2$ cup mayonnaise and 2 teaspoons lemon juice; toss with crab mixture.

Remove small center leaves of 5 cooked artichokes, leaving a cup. Remove chokes. Fill artichokes with crab salad. Place in 12x7$^1/_2$x2-inch baking dish. Pour hot water around them $^1/_4$-inch deep. Cover and bake at 375° for 35 minutes. Serves 5.

## CLAM-STUFFED SHRIMP

| | |
|---|---|
| 1 pound large raw shrimp in shells (about 16 shrimp) | 2 tablespoons snipped parsley |
| 3/4 cup rich round cracker crumbs | 1/8 teaspoon garlic powder |
| 3 tablespoons butter, melted | 1/8 teaspoon salt |
| | Dash pepper |
| 1 7- or 7 1/2-ounce can minced clams, drained | 1/3 cup dry white wine |

OVEN 350°

Shell and devein shrimp. Slit each along vein side about halfway through. Combine crumbs and butter. Stir in clams, parsley, garlic powder, salt, and pepper. Stuff each shrimp. Arrange in 12x7 1/2x2-inch baking dish. Bake at 350° for 18 to 20 minutes; baste with wine. Serves 4.

## CRAB-SHRIMP BAKE

OVEN 350°

Combine 1 cup cleaned cooked shrimp (cut large shrimp in half lengthwise), 1 cup diced celery, 1/4 cup chopped green pepper, 2 tablespoons finely chopped onion, one 7 1/2-ounce can crab meat, drained, flaked, and cartilage removed, 1/2 teaspoon salt, dash pepper, 1 teaspoon Worcestershire sauce, and 3/4 cup mayonnaise.

Turn into 1-quart casserole or individual bakers. Combine 1 cup soft bread crumbs with 1 tablespoon butter, melted. Sprinkle atop casserole. Bake at 350° for 30 to 35 minutes for casserole, 20 to 25 minutes for individual bakers, or till hot. Serves 4.

## SCALLOPED FISH

1 1-pound package frozen fish fillets, thawed and cut in 1-inch pieces
2 cups water
¼ cup finely chopped onion
¼ cup finely chopped green pepper
1 tablespoon butter or margarine, melted
2 beaten eggs
1½ cups milk

1½ cups coarsely crumbled saltine crackers (20 crackers)
1 1-pound can peas and carrots, drained
1 tablespoon lemon juice
2 teaspoons Worcestershire sauce
⅛ teaspoon pepper
2 ounces sharp process American cheese, shredded (½ cup)

OVEN 350°

Place fish in water. Simmer, covered, 3 minutes; drain well. Cook onion and green pepper in butter till tender. Combine eggs, milk, and cracker crumbs. Stir in fish, onion, green pepper, peas and carrots, lemon juice, Worcestershire, and pepper. Turn mixture into 2-quart casserole. Bake in a moderate oven (350°) till set, about 50 minutes. Sprinkle with cheese; bake 5 minutes longer. Serves 6.

## BAKED SEAFOOD SALAD

OVEN 350°

Mix one 7½-ounce can crab meat, flaked and cartilage removed, one 4½-ounce can shrimp, drained, 1½ cups chopped celery, ¼ cup chopped green pepper, ¼ cup chopped onion, and ¼ cup chopped canned pimiento.

Blend together ¾ cup dairy sour cream, ¼ cup mayonnaise, 1 tablespoon lemon juice, ½ teaspoon Worcestershire sauce, ½ teaspoon salt, and dash pepper; stir into seafood mixture. Spoon into 10x6x1½-inch baking dish. Combine 1 cup soft bread crumbs and 1 tablespoon butter or margarine, melted; sprinkle atop casserole. Bake in a moderate oven (350°) for 20 to 25 minutes. Makes 4 to 6 servings.

## SCALLOP-CHEESE BAKE

| | |
|---|---|
| 1 pound fresh or frozen scallops | 2 tablespoons grated Parmesan cheese |
| 1 tablespoon finely chopped onion | 2 tablespoons chopped canned pimiento |
| 3 tablespoons butter | 1 tablespoon snipped parsley |
| 3 tablespoons all-purpose flour | 2 ounces sharp process American cheese, shredded ($1/2$ cup) |
| $1/8$ teaspoon pepper | |
| $1/2$ cup milk | |
| 1 3-ounce can chopped mushrooms, drained | $1 1/2$ cups crushed potato chips |

OVEN 350°

Thaw frozen scallops; rinse. Cover scallops with cold water. Bring to boiling; reduce heat and simmer 2 minutes. Drain, reserving 1 cup of the liquid. Slice scallops about $1/4$ inch thick.

Cook onion in butter till tender. Blend in flour and pepper. Add reserved cooking liquid and milk. Cook and stir till thickened. Remove from heat. Stir in mushrooms, Parmesan, pimiento, parsley, and scallops. Turn into $1 1/2$-quart casserole; sprinkle with shredded cheese; top with potato chips. Bake at 350° for 20 to 25 minutes. Makes 5 or 6 servings.


## CLAM FRITTERS

| | |
|---|---|
| 2 well-beaten egg yolks | 2 teaspoons snipped parsley |
| $1/2$ cup milk | 1 teaspoon salt |
| 2 $7 1/2$-ounce cans minced clams, drained | $1/2$ teaspoon pepper |
| 1 cup fine dry bread crumbs | 2 stiffly beaten egg whites |
| | Salad oil |

Combine first 7 ingredients. Fold in egg whites. Drop batter from a tablespoon into skillet containing $1/4$ inch hot oil. Fry, turning once. Garnish with orange slices, if desired. Makes 6 servings.

# SHRIMP ARITHMETIC

## SHRIMP IN 1 POUND

| Size | Number of raw shrimp in shell from 1 pound |
|---|---|
| Jumbo-size | 15 to 18 |
| Average-size | 26 to 30 |
| Tiny | 60 or more |

## BUY IN SHELL OR SHELLED

| Amount needed | Amount to buy |
|---|---|
| For each 1 cup cleaned cooked shrimp | 12 ounces raw shrimp in shell *or* 7 or 8 ounces frozen shelled shrimp *or* 1 4½- or 5-ounce can shrimp |

## FRESH COOKED SHRIMP

Combine 6 cups water, 2 tablespoons salt, 2 tablespoons vinegar, 2 bay leaves, 1 teaspoon mixed pickling spices, and 2 branches celery; bring to boiling.

Add 2 pounds fresh or frozen shrimp, in shells, or peeled and cleaned. Heat to boiling, then lower heat and simmer gently till shrimp turn pink, about 1 to 3 minutes. Drain. If cooked in shell, peel shrimp; remove vein that runs down back.

*Note:* When cooking shrimp for highly seasoned dishes, omit vinegar and spices.

## FRENCH FRIED SHRIMP

| | |
|---|---|
| 1 cup sifted all-purpose flour | 1 cup ice water |
| ½ teaspoon sugar | 2 tablespoons salad oil |
| ½ teaspoon salt | 2 pounds fresh or frozen shrimp in shells |
| 1 slightly beaten egg | |

Combine ingredients except shrimp; beat smooth. Shell shrimp, leaving last section and tail intact. Butterfly shrimp by cutting almost through at center back without severing tail end; remove black vein.

Dry shrimp well. Dip into batter; fry in deep hot fat

(375°) till golden. Drain. Serve with Cocktail Sauce (page 100).

## SHRIMP DE JONGHE

| | |
|---|---|
| 1/2 cup butter or margarine | 1/2 cup dry white wine |
| 2 cloves garlic, minced | 2 cups soft bread crumbs |
| 1/3 cup snipped parsley | 4 cups cleaned cooked shrimp |
| 1/2 teaspoon paprika Dash cayenne | |

OVEN 350°

Melt butter; add garlic, parsley, paprika, cayenne, and wine; mix. Stir in bread crumbs. Place shrimp in 12x7 1/2x 2-inch baking dish. Spread butter mixture over.

Bake in moderate oven (350°) 25 minutes, or till crumbs brown. Sprinkle with more snipped parsley. Serves 6 to 8.

## DEEP FRIED OYSTERS OR SCALLOPS

Drain oysters or scallops; dry between paper towels. Roll in all-purpose flour seasoned with salt and pepper. Dip into mixture of 1 beaten egg and 1 tablespoon water, then fine dry bread crumbs. Fry golden in deep hot fat (375°) about 2 minutes. Drain on paper towels. Serve hot; pass Tartare Sauce (page 647).

## SCALLOPED OYSTERS

| | |
|---|---|
| 1 pint oysters | 3/4 cup light cream |
| 2 cups medium-coarse cracker crumbs (46 crackers) | 1/2 teaspoon salt |
| | 1/4 teaspoon Worcestershire sauce |
| 1/2 cup butter, melted | |

OVEN 350°

Drain oysters, reserving 1/4 cup liquor. Combine crumbs and butter. Spread a *third* of crumbs in 8x1 1/2-inch round pan. Cover with *half* the oysters. Sprinkle with pepper. Using another *third* of the crumbs, spread a second layer; cover with remaining oysters. Sprinkle with pepper.

Combine cream, reserved oyster liquor, salt, and Worcestershire sauce. Pour over oysters. Top with remaining crumbs. Bake in moderate over (350°) about 40 minutes, or till done. Makes 4 servings.

## PANFRIED SCALLOPS

| | |
|---|---|
| 1 pound fresh or frozen scallops | 1/2 teaspoon salt<br>Dash pepper |
| 2 tablespoons all-purpose flour | 1/4 cup butter or margarine |

Thaw frozen scallops. Dry scallops with paper toweling. Combine flour, salt, and pepper. Dip scallops in seasoned flour to coat. Melt butter in skillet. Add scallops; cook over medium heat, turning often, for 5 to 8 minutes, or till browned and opaque in appearance. Serve with lemon wedges, if desired. Serves 3 or 4.

## FRIED SOFT-SHELL BLUE CRAB

Sprinkle 8 cleaned soft-shell blue crabs with salt. Roll in a mixture of 1/2 cup fine saltine cracker crumbs and 1 tablespoon all-purpose flour. Dip in mixture of 1 slightly beaten egg and 1/2 cup milk; roll in crumbs and flour again. Heat a small amount of salad oil in a skillet. Fry crabs in hot fat 3 to 5 minutes on each side, depending on size of crabs. Drain. Serves 4.

*To Deep-fat Fry:* Fry coated crabs in deep, hot fat (350°) 4 minutes, or till golden. Drain thoroughly on paper toweling.

## BOILED HARD-SHELL CRAB

Wash and scrub live hard-shell blue crabs. Bring enough salted water to boiling in a large kettle to completely cover the crabs. Plunge live crabs into the water. Cover and return to boiling. Reduce heat and simmer 15 minutes. Drain. When cool enough to handle, remove meat as follows: Break off large claws. Pull off top shell. Cut or break off the legs. Remove all the spongy parts—gills, stomach, and intestines. Remove the semitransparent membrane covering the meat in the body. Rinse. Remove small apron-shaped piece on bottom of crab and the projecting mouth parts opposite this piece. Break body in half. Remove meat with fingers, nutpick, small fork, or knife. To remove meat from claws, first crack the different segments of claws and break the shell. Allow about 3 or 4 blue crabs for each serving.

## CORN-OYSTER SCALLOP

OVEN 350°

Combine one 1-pound can (2 cups) cream-style corn, one 10¼-ounce can condensed oyster stew, 1 cup coarsely crushed saltine crackers (22 crackers), 1 cup milk, 1 slightly beaten egg, ¼ cup finely chopped celery, 1 tablespoon finely chopped canned pimiento, ¼ teaspoon salt, and dash pepper. Mix ingredients thoroughly. Pour into a greased 1½-quart casserole.

Combine 2 tablespoons butter, melted, and ½ cup coarsely crushed crackers (11 crackers); sprinkle atop. Bake at 350° for 1 hour, or till knife inserted off center comes out clean. Makes 6 servings.

## LOBSTER NEWBURG

| | |
|---|---|
| 6 tablespoons butter or margarine | 3 tablespoons dry white wine |
| 2 tablespoons all-purpose flour | 2 teaspoons lemon juice |
| 1½ cups light cream | ¼ teaspoon salt |
| 3 beaten egg yolks | Paprika |
| 1 5-ounce can (1 cup) lobster, broken in large pieces | Pastry Petal Cups |

Melt butter in skillet; blend in flour. Add cream all at once. Cook, stirring constantly, till sauce thickens and bubbles.

Stir small amount of hot mixture into egg yolks; return to hot mixture; cook, stirring constantly, till thickened. Add lobster; heat through. Add wine, lemon juice, and salt. Sprinkle with paprika. Serve in Pastry Petal Cups or over toast points. Makes 4 or 5 servings.

*Pastry Petal Cups:* Make Plain Pastry (pages 491–492) or use piecrust mix. Roll ⅛ inch thick; cut in 2¼-inch rounds. In each of 5 muffin cups, place one round in bottom and overlap 4 rounds on sides; press together. Prick. Bake at 450° for 10 to 12 minutes. Cool. A recipe that calls for 1½ cups flour will make 5 pastry cups.

**Crab Meat Newburg:** Substitute 1 cup flaked, cooked crab meat for lobster.

**Shrimp Newburg:** Substitute 2 cups cleaned cooked shrimp for the lobster.

## LOBSTER

**Boiled:** Select active live lobsters. Plunge into enough boiling salted water to cover. Bring to boil; reduce heat and simmer 20 minutes. Remove at once. Place on back. With sharp knife, cut in half lengthwise. Remove black vein that runs to tip of tail. Discard all organs in body section near head except red coral roe (in females only) and brownish-green liver. Crack claws. Serve with cups of melted butter. Or, chill and use meat in salads.

**Broiled:** Select active live lobsters. Plunge into enough boiling salted water to cover. Cook 2 minutes. Remove from pan; place lobster on back on cutting board. With sharp knife, split lengthwise from head to tail. Cut off head, if desired. Using scissors, snip out under shell membrane on tail section. Discard all organs in body section except brownish-green liver and red coral roe (in females only). Remove black vein that runs down to tail. Crack claws.

Place on broiler pan, shell side up; broil 5 inches from heat 7 minutes. Turn; flatten open to expose meat. Brush with 1 tablespoon butter, melted. Season with salt and pepper. Broil 7 to 8 minutes more. Serve with melted butter and lemon wedges. Allow 1 to 1½ pound lobster per serving.

## ROCK LOBSTER TAILS

**Boiled:** Drop frozen rock lobster tails into boiling salted water to cover. Bring to boil; simmer 3 ounce tail 3 to 4 minutes, 6 ounce tail 8 minutes, and 8 ounce tail

11 minutes. Drain. Prepare to serve (see pictures 2 and 3). Pass melted butter. Or, chill and use meat for salads or casseroles.

**Broiled:** With sharp knife, cut down through center of hard top shell of frozen tail. Cut through meat, but not through under shell. Spread open, butterfly-style, so meat is on top. Place tails on broiler pan, shell side down. Dash few drops bottled hot pepper sauce into melted butter; brush over meat.

Broil 4 inches from heat. Broil 6 to 8 ounce tail 17 minutes. Avoid overcooking. Meat is done when it loses its translucency and can be flaked with a fork. To serve, loosen meat by inserting fork between shell and meat. Pass melted butter and lemon.

Lift live lobsters by taking hold of them just behind the eyes. Then, plunge headfirst into a pot of boiling salted water.

Drain boiled lobster tails. With scissors, cut away thin underside membrane—cut down each side and remove under shell.

To remove cooked meat, grasp tail. Insert index finger between shell and meat; pull firmly, separating shell and meat.

# EGG COOKERY

### FRIED EGGS

In a skillet, melt a small amount of butter, margarine, or bacon fat. Add eggs; season with salt and pepper. When the whites are set and edges cooked, add $1/2$ teaspoon water per egg. Cover skillet and cook eggs to desired doneness.

### CODDLED EGGS

Place room-temperature eggs gently into boiling water. Remove from heat; cover and let stand 1 to $1^1/_2$ minutes for Caesar Salad, or 4 to 6 minutes for desired doneness. Promptly cool in cold water.

### SHIRRED (BAKED) EGGS

OVEN 325°

Butter ramekins or custard cups. Break one egg into each; dash with salt and pepper. To each, add 1 teaspoon light cream. Set cups in shallow baking pan; pour hot water around them to depth of 1 inch. Bake in slow oven (325°) about 20 minutes, or till the eggs are firm.

If desired, after 15 minutes of baking, top each egg with shredded sharp process American cheese. Return eggs to oven and bake 5 to 10 minutes longer.

For brunch or hearty breakfast, bake two eggs at a time in shallow individual casseroles, adding two precooked link sausages to each casserole.

## POACHED EGGS

Add water to a saucepan to depth of 3 to 4 inches; bring just to boiling. Stir simmering water to make a swirl, and slip egg from saucedish into middle of the swirl. (Be sure to follow the motion of the swirl with saucedish so egg goes into water in same direction.) Reduce heat to low and cook egg for 3 to 5 minutes, depending on desired doneness. Remove egg from water with slotted spoon. Serve on buttered toast or English muffin, split and toasted. Or, prepare Poached Eggs for Eggs Benedict.

## EGGS BENEDICT

For each serving, split and toast an English muffin; top with thin slice broiled ham. Place a poached egg on ham. Prepare Classic Hollandaise (page 640) and pour over all. Serve immediately.

## BACON-HOMINY SCRAMBLE

Cook 4 slices bacon till crisp; drain, reserving 2 table-spoons drippings. Lightly brown one 1-pound 4-ounce can golden hominy, drained, in reserved drippings.

Beat together 4 eggs, $1/2$ teaspoon salt, and dash pepper. Add to hominy and cook till eggs are just set, stirring frequently. Season with salt and pepper. Crumble bacon over top. Makes 6 servings.

## BASIC SCRAMBLED EGGS

6 eggs
$1/3$ cup milk or light cream
$1/4$ to $1/2$ teaspoon salt

2 tablespoons butter, margarine, or bacon fat

Beat eggs, milk, salt, and dash pepper with fork. (Mix slightly for eggs with streaks of yellow and white; mix well for a uniform yellow.) Heat butter, margarine, or bacon fat in skillet till just hot enough to make a drop of water sizzle. Pour in egg mixture. Turn heat low. Don't disturb mixture till it starts to set on bottom and sides, then lift and fold over with spatula so uncooked part goes to bottom.

Cook for 4 to 5 minutes, until eggs are cooked throughout, but still glossy and moist. Remove from heat immediately. Makes 3 or 4 servings.

**Herb Scrambled Eggs:** Prepare Basic Scrambled Eggs adding 1 tablespoon snipped parsley or chives and dash dried thyme, crushed, to the seasoned egg-milk mixture. Continue as in recipe above.

**Cheese Scrambled Eggs:** Prepare Basic Scrambled Eggs adding one 3-ounce package cream cheese with chives, cut into pieces, to the seasoned egg-milk mixture. Continue as in recipe above.

**Fluffy Scrambled Eggs:** Prepare Basic Scrambled Eggs omitting butter. Cook egg mixture in top of double boiler, stirring with spoon. Water in bottom should only simmer and not touch top pan. (Takes twice as long as in skillet.)

**Deviled Scrambled Eggs:** In skillet, cook 1 tablespoon chopped onion in 2 tablespoons butter, margarine, or

bacon fat till tender. Prepare Basic Scrambled Eggs adding
1/2 teaspoon dry mustard, 1 tablespoon snipped parsley,
1/4 teaspoon Worcestershire sauce, and one 2-ounce can
chopped mushrooms, drained, to the seasoned egg-milk
mixture. Add to onion in skillet. Continue as in recipe
above.

**Cheese and Onion Scrambled Eggs:** Prepare Basic
Scrambled Eggs, cooking till eggs begin to set; sprinkle
with 1/4 cup shredded sharp process American cheese.
Continue cooking just till eggs are cooked and cheese
melts. Trim with 2 tablespoons chopped green onion
tops.

## SOFT-COOKED OR HARD-COOKED EGGS

Place eggs in saucepan and cover with cold water, at
least 1 inch above eggs; rapidly bring to boiling.

**Soft-cooked Eggs:** Cover pan tightly; remove from heat.
Leave eggs in water 2 to 4 minutes, for desired doneness.
For more than 4 eggs, don't turn off heat, but cook, covered, just *below simmering* for 4 to 6 minutes. Promptly
cool in cold water.

**Hard-cooked Eggs:** When water boils, reduce heat at
once to keep water just *below simmering*. Cover and
cook eggs for 15 to 20 minutes. Cool immediately in
cold water to prevent yolk darkening. To shell hard-
cooked eggs, crack shell all over, then roll gently between palms of hands to loosen. Start to peel from large
end.

## CREAMED EGGS

6 hard-cooked eggs
1½ cups Medium White
 Sauce (page 645)

4 slices hot buttered
 toast
 Paprika or snipped
 parsley

Cut eggs in fourths and add to White Sauce; stir carefully. Serve over toast. Sprinkle with paprika or parsley. Serves 4.

## GOLDENROD EGGS

Prepare Creamed Eggs, except reserve yolks and add chopped whites to Sauce; pour over toast. Press yolks through sieve; sprinkle atop creamed whites.

## DEVILED EGGS

Halve hard-cooked eggs lengthwise; remove yolks and mash with desired combination of seasonings, below. Refill whites.

1. For 6 eggs, use ¼ cup mayonnaise, 1 teaspoon vinegar, 1 teaspoon prepared mustard, ⅛ teaspoon salt, and dash pepper.

2. For 5 eggs, use 2 tablespoons mayonnaise, 2 tablespoons chopped ripe olives, 2 teaspoons vinegar, 1 teaspoon prepared mustard, and salt and pepper to taste.

3. Other combinations may include: horseradish, anchovies, parsley, chopped onions or chives, flaked seafood, chopped stuffed green olives, crumbled crisp bacon.

## ROSY PICKLED EGGS

1 cup juice from canned
 pickled beets
1 cup vinegar
1 clove garlic
1 medium bay leaf

2 teaspoons mixed
 pickling spices
½ teaspoon salt
12 hard-cooked eggs
1 small onion, sliced and
 separated into rings

In large bowl, combine beet juice, vinegar, 4 cups water, garlic, bay leaf, pickling spices, and salt; mix well. Add eggs and onion rings; cover and refrigerate for several days. Makes 12 pickled eggs.

## CRISPY EGGS AND BACON

| | |
|---|---|
| 6 slices bacon | 1/3 cup milk or light |
| 1/2 cup small croutons | cream |
| 6 eggs | |

Cook bacon till crisp; drain and crumble coarsely. Reserve bacon drippings. Measure 1 tablespoon reserved drippings into skillet. Add croutons; heat and stir till brown and crisp; remove from skillet.

Add another 1 tablespoon drippings to skillet. Slightly beat eggs, milk, 1/4 teaspoon salt, and dash pepper; pour into skillet. Cook and stir till almost set. Gently stir in crumbled bacon and croutons. Cook till just set. Makes 4 to 6 servings.

## DENVER SCRAMBLE

| | |
|---|---|
| 1 cup finely chopped fully cooked ham | 2 tablespoons chopped green pepper |
| 1 2-ounce can mushroom stems and pieces, drained | 2 tablespoons butter or margarine, melted |
| 1/4 cup chopped onion | 8 beaten eggs |
| | 1/3 cup milk |

In a skillet, cook ham, mushrooms, onion, and green pepper in butter or margarine till vegetables are tender but not brown, about 5 minutes. Combine beaten eggs and milk; add to ham mixture in skillet. Cook till eggs are set throughout but still moist, 5 to 8 minutes, folding eggs over with wide spatula so uncooked part goes to the bottom. Makes 6 servings.

## FRANK-EGG SCRAMBLE

| | |
|---|---|
| 4 or 5 frankfurters | 1/2 medium green pepper, |
| 1 tablespoon sugar | cut in 1/4-inch-wide |
| 1 tablespoon soy sauce | strips |
| 1/2 medium onion, sliced and separated into rings | 6 beaten eggs |

Slice franks diagonally into ¹/₂-inch-wide pieces. In skillet, brown franks. Remove from heat; push to one side. Stir in sugar and soy. Add vegetables. Cook, covered, till vegetables are crisp-tender, about 3 minutes. Pour eggs over. Cook and stir till eggs are set. Serves 4 to 6.

## CHEESE FONDUE BAKE

OVEN 325°

Combine 3 slightly beaten egg yolks, 1¹/₂ cups soft bread crumbs, 8 ounces sharp process American cheese, shredded (2 cups), 1 cup scalded milk, ¹/₂ teaspoon dry mustard, ¹/₄ teaspoon salt, and dash pepper. Fold in 3 stiffly beaten egg whites. Pour into 10x6x1¹/₂-inch baking dish. Bake in slow oven (325°) about 35 to 40 minutes, or till firm. Makes 6 servings.

## EGG CROQUETTES

| | |
|---|---|
| ³/₄ cup Thick White Sauce, cooled (page 645) | 1 tablespoon minced onion |
| 8 hard-cooked eggs, ground | 1 teaspoon salt |
| | 1 teaspoon prepared mustard |
| 3 tablespoons chopped pimiento | 2 slightly beaten eggs |
| 1 tablespoon snipped parsley | 1¹/₄ cups fine cracker crumbs |

Combine White Sauce and next 6 ingredients; mix well. Chill several hours. Form in croquettes, using ¹/₄ cup for each.* Mix beaten eggs and 2 tablespoons water. Roll croquettes in crumbs; dip into egg mixture; roll in crumbs again. Chill 20 minutes. Fry in deep hot fat (365°) till golden brown, about 2 to 3 minutes. Drain on absorbent paper. Makes 10 to 12.

* Or, form into patties; coat and chill. Cook in skillet in a little butter. Brown the patties about 3 minutes on each side.

## SPANISH EGGS

| | |
|---|---|
| 1/2 cup chopped onion | 6 hard-cooked eggs |
| 3 tablespoons butter | 1/4 cup mayonnaise |
| 3 tablespoons all-purpose flour | 1 teaspoon prepared mustard |
| 2 teaspoons sugar | 3/4 cup fine dry bread crumbs |
| 1 1-pound 12-ounce can tomatoes | 2 tablespoons butter, melted |
| 1 small bay leaf | |

OVEN 425°

In skillet, cook onion in 3 tablespoons butter till tender. Blend in flour, sugar, 3/4 teaspoon salt, and dash pepper. Add tomatoes and bay leaf. Cook till thick and bubbly, stirring constantly. Remove bay leaf. Pour into 10x6x1 1/2-inch baking dish.

Halve eggs lengthwise. Remove yolks and mash. Mix with mayonnaise, mustard, 1/8 teaspoon salt, and dash pepper; refill egg whites. Put in dish. Combine crumbs and melted butter; sprinkle atop. Bake at 425° for 10 minutes, or till hot. Serve over buttered noodles or toast. Serves 6.

## EGGS A LA KING

| | |
|---|---|
| 2 cups Medium White Sauce (page 645) | 1/2 cup cooked or canned peas |
| 2 tablespoons catsup | 2 tablespoons chopped canned pimiento |
| 1/4 teaspoon salt | 6 thick tomato slices |
| 6 hard-cooked eggs, sliced | 6 slices buttered toast |
| 1 6-ounce can sliced mushrooms, drained (1 cup) | |

Combine White Sauce, catsup, and salt. Add sliced eggs, mushrooms, peas, and pimiento; heat thoroughly. Sprinkle tomato slices lightly with salt; broil 2 to 3 minutes. Place tomatoes on toast; spoon sauce over all. Makes 6 servings.

## EASY EGGS A LA KING

In saucepan, cook ½ cup chopped celery, ¼ cup chopped green pepper, and ¼ cup finely chopped onion in 2 tablespoons hot salad oil till tender. Add one 10½-ounce can condensed cream of celery soup, ½ cup milk, and 1 cup diced process American cheese; heat and stir till cheese melts. Add 4 hard-cooked eggs, chopped, and 6 pimiento-stuffed green olives, sliced; heat. Spoon over hot buttered toast. Trim with egg slices. Makes 4 servings.

## WINE EGGS MORNAY

Lightly brown 6 thin slices cooked ham in butter. Split 3 English muffins in half; toast and butter. Place a ham slice on each muffin half. Poach 6 eggs; place atop each ham slice. Season. Pour Wine Mornay Sauce over eggs; sprinkle with 1 tablespoon finely chopped green pepper and 1 tablespoon snipped chives. Serves 6.

*Wine Mornay Sauce:* Melt 3 tablespoons butter; blend in 3 tablespoons all-purpose flour, ½ teaspoon salt, ⅛ teaspoon ground nutmeg, and dash pepper. Add 1¼ cups light cream all at once. Cook quickly, stirring constantly, till mixture thickens and bubbles. Stir in ¼ cup dry white wine; add ⅓ cup shredded process Swiss cheese and stir to melt.

## SWISS ONION BAKE

| | |
|---|---|
| 2 tablespoons butter or margarine | 1 10½-ounce can condensed cream of chicken soup |
| 2 cups sliced onion | ¾ cup milk |
| 6 hard-cooked eggs, sliced | ½ teaspoon prepared mustard |
| 6 ounces process Swiss cheese, shredded (1½ cups) | 6 slices French bread, cut ½ inch thick and buttered |

OVEN 350°

In skillet, melt butter. Add onion; cook till tender. Spread onion in bottom of 10x6x1½-inch baking dish. Top with sliced eggs; sprinkle with shredded cheese.

In saucepan, combine soup, milk, and mustard; heat and stir till smooth. Pour over casserole, being sure some goes to bottom. Place bread slices on top, overlapping a little. Bake in moderate oven (350°) for 35 minutes, or till hot. Broil a few minutes to toast bread. Serves 6.

## PUFFY SANDWICH OMELET

| | |
|---|---|
| 1 egg | Dash pepper |
| 2 egg yolks | 2 teaspoons butter or |
| 2 slices bacon, crisp-cooked, drained, and crumbled | margarine |
| | 2 slices white bread, toasted and buttered |
| 1 tablespoon light cream | 2 stiffly beaten egg |
| Dash salt | whites |

OVEN 350°

Beat together the whole egg, egg yolks, bacon, cream, salt, and pepper with a fork till just combined. In small skillet, melt butter. Add egg mixture; cook quickly till set but still glossy.

Fold cooked eggs in half; cut into 2 pieces. On baking sheet, place *each half* of the egg mixture on a slice of toast. Cover both sandwiches entirely with egg whites. Sprinkle with salt and pepper. Bake in moderate oven (350°) till golden, about 10 minutes. Makes 2 sandwiches.

## EGGS FLORENTINE

| | |
|---|---|
| 1 10-ounce package frozen chopped spinach, cooked and drained | * * * |
| | 1 tablespoon milk |
| | 2 teaspoons instant minced onion |
| 1 11-ounce can condensed Cheddar cheese soup | 1 teaspoon prepared mustard |
| 4 eggs | ½ cup plain croutons |

OVEN 350°

Combine spinach and *half* of the soup. Spoon into 4 individual casseroles; spread evenly on bottom and up sides. Break one egg into each dish. Bake at 350° for 20 to 25 minutes, or till eggs are set. In saucepan, heat and stir remaining soup, milk, onion, and mustard. Spoon over eggs. Garnish with croutons. Makes 4 servings.

## CHIPPED BEEF PUFF

4 ounces dried beef, snipped
¼ cup butter or margarine
3 tablespoons all-purpose flour
Dash pepper
2 cups milk
2 tablespoons chopped canned pimiento

1 3-ounce can sliced mushrooms, drained (½ cup)

* * *

3 egg whites
¼ teaspoon salt
3 egg yolks
⅓ cup shredded process American cheese

OVEN 375°

Cook dried beef in butter over low heat, stirring till slightly crisp and frizzled. Blend in flour and pepper. Stir in milk all at once; cook and stir till mixture thickens and bubbles. Stir in pimiento and mushrooms. Pour into 10x 6x1½-inch baking dish. Keep hot in moderate oven (375°).

Meanwhile, beat egg whites with salt till stiff peaks form. Beat yolks till thick and lemon-colored. Fold yolks into whites; fold in cheese. Pour over hot beef mixture. Bake at 375° for 15 to 20 minutes, or till golden brown. Makes 4 or 5 servings.

## FLUFFY OMELET

4 egg whites
¼ teaspoon salt
4 egg yolks

1 tablespoon butter
Cheese Sauce, page 647

OVEN 325°

Beat whites till frothy; add 2 tablespoons water and salt. Beat till stiff but not dry. Beat yolks till very thick and lemon-colored. Fold yolks into white (see picture 1 on page 582). Heat butter in 10-inch oven-going skillet till a drop of water sizzles. Pour in egg mixture and spread evenly with spatula, leaving higher at sides. Reduce heat. Cook slowly 8 to 10 minutes, or till puffed and

Surprise your family and guests with this Fluffy Omelet. It has that melt-in-the-mouth goodness they'll love. See pictures below to assume perfect results each time.

set. Lift edge with spatula (picture 2)—bottom will be golden.

Cook in slow oven (325°) about 10 minutes, or till knife inserted in center comes out clean. Loosen sides of omelet with spatula. Make shallow cut across omelet slightly above and parallel to skillet handle (picture 3). Tilt pan. Fold upper (smaller) half over lower half. Using spatula, slip omelet onto hot platter (picture 4). Spoon Cheese Sauce over omelet. Makes 3 or 4 servings.

## HAM AND EGG DIVAN

OVEN 350°

Arrange two 10-ounce packages frozen broccoli, cooked and drained, in 10x6x1$\frac{1}{2}$-inch baking dish. Cut 6 hard-cooked eggs in half lengthwise. Remove yolks and mash; mix with 3 tablespoons mayonnaise, 1 tablespoon finely chopped onion, 1 teaspoon prepared mustard, $\frac{1}{2}$ teaspoon Worcestershire sauce, and *half* of one 4$\frac{1}{2}$-ounce can deviled ham. Place *small amount* of remaining ham in egg whites; fill with yolk mixture and top with remaining ham. Arrange eggs on broccoli.

Melt 2 tablespoons butter in saucepan; blend in 2 tablespoons all-purpose flour and $\frac{1}{2}$ teaspoon salt. Add 1$\frac{1}{4}$ cups milk all at once. Cook and stir quickly till mixture thickens and bubbles. Remove from heat. Add 4 ounces sharp process American cheese, diced (1 cup); stir till melted. *Cover* eggs with sauce. Bake at 350° for 20 minutes. Makes 6 servings.

## FRENCH OMELET

*Same ingredients as for scrambled eggs; the difference is in the cooking—*

With a fork, beat 3 eggs, 1 tablespoon water, $\frac{1}{4}$ teaspoon salt, and dash pepper till mixture is blended, but not frothy.

Heat an 8-inch skillet with flared sides. Add 1 tablespoon butter; let sizzle and brown *lightly*. Tilt pan to grease sides.

Pour in omelet mixture, leaving heat moderately high. With fork tines up and parallel to skillet, rapidly stir through top of uncooked egg. Keep omelet an even depth. As you stir uncooked egg zigzag fashion out to edges, cooked bits will come to center. Shake pan constantly to keep egg mixture moving. Cook 2 to 3 minutes.

When egg is set but still shiny, remove pan from heat. If desired, spoon mushrooms, cooked in butter, or other filling across center; fold sides of omelet over, envelope-style, to hold in filling. Tilt pan and roll omelet onto hot plate. Serves 2.

*Easy method:* Heat 1 tablespoon butter in skillet; add egg mixture and cook slowly. Run spatula around edge, lifting to allow uncooked portion to flow underneath. Fold and serve as above.

## HASHED-BROWN OMELET

| | |
|---|---|
| 4 slices bacon | 4 beaten eggs |
| 3 cups shredded cooked potatoes* | 1/4 cup milk |
| 1/4 cup chopped onion | 1 cup shredded sharp process American cheese |
| 1/4 cup chopped green pepper | |

In 10-inch skillet, cook bacon till crisp. Leave 2 tablespoons drippings in skillet; drain bacon and crumble. Mix potatoes, onion, green pepper, and 1/2 teaspoon salt; pat into skillet. Cook over low heat about 20 minutes, or till underside is crisp and brown. Blend eggs, milk, 1/4 teaspoon salt, and dash pepper; stir in bacon and cheese; pour over potatoes. Cover; cook over low heat 8 to 10 minutes. Loosen edges; serve in wedges. Serves 4.

* Or, substitute packaged hash-brown potatoes, cooked.

## SHRIMP EGG FOO YONG

In skillet, cook 1/2 cup chopped onion and 1 clove garlic, minced, in 1 tablespoon hot shortening till tender, but not brown. Combine 6 slightly beaten eggs, one 4 1/2-ounce can (1 cup) shrimp, drained, 1/4 teaspoon salt, dash pepper, and onion.

In skillet, cook egg mixture slowly in 2 tablespoons hot shortening. Run spatula under edge, lifting so uncooked portion flows underneath. When egg is almost cooked but still shiny, loosen edge; roll or fold one half over. Serve on warm platter with Chinese Brown Sauce. Serves 4.

*Chinese Brown Sauce:* Melt 1 tablespoon butter. Combine 2 teaspoons cornstarch and 1 teaspoon sugar; blend into butter. Add 1/2 cup water and 1 1/2 tablespoons soy sauce. Cook, stirring constantly, till mixture is thick and bubbly.

Drain one 5-ounce can water chestnuts; slice water chestnuts and add to sauce; heat through. Makes 3/4 cup sauce.

## TURKEY SOUFFLE

OVEN 325°

In saucepan, melt 3 tablespoons butter; blend in 3 tablespoons all-purpose flour, 1 teaspoon salt, dash pepper, and 1/4 teaspoon paprika. Add 1 cup milk all at once. Cook quickly, stirring constantly, till mixture thickens and bubbles. Remove from heat. Stir in 1 teaspoon grated onion, 1 cup finely chopped cooked turkey or chicken, and 1 tablespoon snipped parsley.

Beat 3 egg yolks till thick and lemon-colored. *Slowly* add turkey mixture to egg yolks, stirring constantly. Cool slightly. Add gradually to 3 stiffly beaten egg whites, folding together thoroughly. Turn into *ungreased* 1-quart souffle dish. Bake at 325° about 50 minutes, or till knife inserted comes out clean. Serve immediately with Dilled Mushroom Sauce. Serves 4.

*Dilled Mushroom Sauce:* Cook 2 tablespoons chopped onion in 2 tablespoons butter till tender, but not brown. Stir in 2 tablespoons all-purpose flour, 1/4 teaspoon dried dillweed, crushed, 1/4 teaspoon salt, dash pepper, and one 3-ounce can chopped mushrooms, drained. Add 1 1/4 cups milk all at once. Cook and stir till mixture thickens and bubbles. Makes 1 1/2 cups.

## CHEESE SOUFFLE

| | |
|---|---|
| ¹/₄ cup butter or margarine | 1 cup milk |
| ¹/₄ cup all-purpose flour | 8 ounces sharp process American cheese, thinly sliced |
| ¹/₂ teaspoon salt | |
| Dash cayenne | 4 eggs, separated |

OVEN 300°

Melt butter; blend in flour, salt, and cayenne. Add milk all at once; cook over medium heat, stirring, till mixture thickens and bubbles. Remove from heat. Add cheese; stir till cheese melts.

Beat egg yolks till very thick and lemon-colored. *Slowly* add cheese mixture, stirring constantly; cool slightly. Beat egg whites to stiff peaks. Gradually pour yolk mixture over; fold together well. Pour into *ungreased* 2-quart souffle dish or casserole. For a top hat that puffs in the oven, trace a circle through mixture 1 inch from edge and 1 inch deep. Bake at 300° for 1¹/₄ hours, or till knife inserted off-center comes out clean. Immediately break apart into servings with 2 forks. Serves 4.

## BROCCOLI SOUFFLE

OVEN 350°

Cook one 10-ounce package frozen chopped broccoli according to package directions. Drain *very thoroughly*. (Chop any large pieces.) Add 2 tablespoons butter or margarine to broccoli; cook and stir over high heat till butter is melted and any excess moisture has evaporated.

Blend in 2 tablespoons all-purpose flour and ¹/₂ teaspoon salt. Add ¹/₂ cup milk all at once. Cook and stir over medium heat till mixture thickens and bubbles. Remove from heat; stir in ¹/₄ cup grated Parmesan cheese. Beat 4 egg yolks till thick and lemon-colored. Slowly add broccoli to egg yolks, stirring constantly; gradually pour over 4 stiffly beaten egg whites, folding together thoroughly. Pour into *ungreased* 1-quart souffle dish.

Bake in moderate oven (350°) for 35 minutes, or till knife inserted halfway between center and edge comes out clean. Serve immediately with Mushroom Sauce (page 642). Makes 4 to 6 servings.

# 13

# SALADS AND DRESSINGS

# VEGETABLE SALADS

To mix great green salads, remember to handle greens with care:
- Be sure greens are dry and chilled. Wash them well when you bring them from market. Then drain thoroughly, wrap in paper toweling and refrigerate about 8 hours. If crisper is full, wrap greens well, and store on shelf in the refrigerator.
- To core lettuce: Smack head, stem end down, on counter top. You can twist core right out. For lettuce cups, run water through core. Leaves peel off. Drain.
- Tear greens into bite-size pieces—don't use a knife or you'll bruise them. (They even taste better when torn.)
- Roll-toss salads in a large bowl. Gently stroke downward to bottom with tool in one hand and up and over with tool in other hand. Add the tomatoes last. This prevents dressing from becoming diluted.
- Watercress and parsley: Wash, then pat dry with paper towels or clean kitchen towel. Store in covered jars in refrigerator.
- A word about your salad bowl: Never soak it. Rinse with lukewarm water—no soap—promptly wipe it dry. Or, if you want your bowl to become seasoned, don't wash. Simply wipe it with paper towels.

## GREEN GODDESS SALAD

| | |
|---|---|
| 6 cups torn romaine, chilled | ½ cup pitted ripe olives, sliced |
| 3 cups torn curly endive, chilled | 1 2-ounce can rolled anchovy fillets |
| 1 9-ounce package frozen artichoke hearts, cooked, drained, and chilled | 2 medium tomatoes, cut in wedges (optional) |

In large salad bowl, combine torn romaine, torn curly endive, cooked and chilled artichoke hearts, sliced ripe olives, anchovy fillets, and tomato wedges. Top salad mixture with desired amount of Green Goddess Dressing. Roll-toss until greens are all well coated. Makes 6 servings.

**Green Goddess Dressing:** In blender container place $3/4$ cup coarsely chopped parsley; $1/2$ cup mayonnaise; $1/2$ cup dairy sour cream; 3 green onion tops; 2 tablespoons tarragon vinegar; 1 tablespoon anchovy paste; $1/2$ teaspoon dried basil, crushed; and $1/4$ teaspoon sugar. Cover and blend till combined. Chill.

## BLUE CHEESE SALAD BOWL

| | |
|---|---|
| 1 small head cauliflower | $1/2$ cup crumbled blue cheese |
| $1/2$ cup onion rings | |
| $1/4$ cup sliced pimiento-stuffed green olives | 1 head lettuce, torn in pieces |
| $2/3$ cup clear French salad dressing with herbs and spices | |

Separate cauliflower into flowerets; slice; add to onion rings and olives. Marinate in dressing $1/2$ hour in refrigerator. Add blue cheese and lettuce. Toss. Serves 8.

## ITALIAN SALAD BOWL

| | |
|---|---|
| $1/2$ medium head lettuce, torn in bite-size pieces | $1/2$ cup sliced fresh mushrooms (optional) |
| $1/2$ medium head romaine, torn in bite-size pieces | 3 green onions, sliced<br>Salt<br>Pepper |
| 2 cups thinly sliced raw zucchini | Italian salad dressing |
| $1/2$ cup sliced radishes | $1/2$ cup crumbled blue cheese |

In large salad bowl, combine lettuce, romaine, zucchini, radishes, mushrooms, and green onions. Season with salt and pepper. Toss lightly with dressing; sprinkle blue cheese over top. Makes 6 servings.

## FRENCH GREEN SALAD

1 clove garlic, cut
½ teaspoon salt
¼ teaspoon dry mustard
¼ teaspoon paprika
¼ cup salad oil

4 cups greens (any combination)
2 tablespoons vinegar
2 tablespoons lemon juice

Rub salad bowl with garlic. Measure in salt, mustard, and paprika. Grind pepper over; blend. Beat in salad oil with fork.

Add greens. Toss till leaves glisten. Sprinkle with vinegar and lemon juice. Toss again. Makes 6 servings.

## TAOS SALAD TOSS

2 cups shredded lettuce
1 15-ounce can (2 cups) dark red kidney beans, drained
2 medium tomatoes, chopped and drained
1 tablespoon chopped canned green chilies
½ cup sliced ripe olives
1 large avocado, mashed
½ cup dairy sour cream

2 tablespoons Italian salad dressing
1 teaspoon instant minced onion
¾ teaspoon chili powder
¼ teaspoon salt
½ cup shredded sharp natural Cheddar cheese
½ cup coarsely crushed corn chips

Combine lettuce, beans, tomatoes, chilies, and olives in salad bowl; chill. For dressing, blend avocado and sour cream. Add Italian dressing, onion, chili powder, salt, and dash pepper; mix well; chill.

Season salad with salt and pepper to taste. Toss with avocado dressing. Top with cheese and corn chips. Garnish with ripe olives, if desired. Makes 4 to 6 servings.

## TOSSED EGG SALAD

| | |
|---|---|
| 1 head lettuce | 1/2 cup salad oil |
| 6 hard-cooked eggs, sliced | 1/4 cup vinegar |
| 1 small onion, thinly sliced and separated in rings | 2 teaspoons Worcestershire sauce |
| 1/2 teaspoon salt | 2 tablespoons snipped parsley |
| 1/4 teaspoon pepper | 1/4 cup grated sharp natural Cheddar cheese |
| Dash paprika | |

Break lettuce in bite-size pieces (about 8 cups) into salad bowl. Alternate layers of egg and onion rings. Combine next 7 ingredients for dressing. Add to lettuce with cheese; toss lightly. Makes 6 servings.

## ORIGINAL CAESAR SALAD

| | |
|---|---|
| Garlic Olive Oil | 1 or 2 1-minute coddled eggs |
| Caesar Croutons | Dash Worcestershire sauce |
| 3 medium heads romaine, chilled | Whole black pepper |
| 2 to 3 tablespoons wine vinegar | 6 tablespoons grated Parmesan cheese |
| 1 lemon, halved | |

One or more days before serving, prepare Garlic Olive Oil. Several hours before serving, prepare Caesar Croutons. At serving time, break romaine in 2- or 3-inch widths into *chilled* salad bowl. Drizzle with about 1/3 cup Garlic Olive Oil, then vinegar. Squeeze lemon over; break in eggs. Season with Worcestershire and salt. Grind pepper over; sprinkle with cheese. Toss lightly till dressing is well combined and romaine is coated. Add 1 cup Caesar Croutons; toss once or twice. Serve *at once* on chilled plates. Garnish with rolled anchovy fillets, if desired. Serves 6 to 8.

*Garlic Olive Oil:* Slice 6 cloves garlic lengthwise in quarters; let stand in 1 cup olive oil or salad oil (or half of each).

*Caesar Croutons:* Cut 3 slices bread into 3/4-inch cubes. Spread out on baking sheet; pour a little Garlic Olive Oil over bread. Heat at 225° about 2 hours. Sprinkle with grated Parmesan cheese. Store croutons, covered, in jar in refrigerator.

## WILTED LEAF LETTUCE

| | |
|---|---|
| 6 slices bacon | 8 cups leaf lettuce torn |
| 1/2 cup sliced green onion | in bite-size pieces |
| 1/4 cup vinegar | 6 radishes, thinly sliced |
| 4 teaspoons sugar | 1 hard-cooked egg, |
| | chopped |

Cook bacon till crisp; drain and crumble, reserving drippings. Add onion to drippings; cook till tender. Add vinegar, 1/4 cup water, sugar, 1/2 teaspoon salt, and bacon; cook and stir till boiling. Place lettuce in bowl; pour hot dressing over; toss to coat. Garnish with radishes and egg. Serves 6.

## WILTED SPINACH SALAD

| | |
|---|---|
| 1 pound fresh spinach | 1 tablespoon lemon |
| 1/2 cup sliced green onion | juice |
| Dash freshly ground | 1 teaspoon sugar |
| pepper | 1/2 teaspoon salt |
| 5 slices bacon, diced | 1 hard-cooked egg, |
| 2 tablespoons wine | coarsely chopped |
| vinegar | |

Wash spinach, discarding stems. Pat dry on paper towels; tear into bowl. Add onion and sprinkle with pepper. Chill.

At serving time, slowly fry bacon in deep chafing dish or electric skillet till crisp-cooked. Add vinegar, lemon juice, sugar, and salt. Gradually add spinach, tossing just till leaves are coated and wilted slightly. Sprinkle with egg. Serves 4 to 6.

## COLESLAW

Shred 3 cups cabbage extra fine using chef's knife or grater. To avoid last-minute fuss, toss cabbage with ice cubes; hold in refrigerator 1 hour. Remove ice; drain. If desired, add 1/4 cup chopped green pepper or minced onion, or 1 cup grated carrot and 1/2 cup raisins.

Toss with one of these slaw dressings:
- Cooked Dressing or mayonnaise.
- Mix 2 to 3 tablespoons sugar, 3 tablespoons vinegar, 2 tablespoons salad oil, and 1 teaspoon salt; stir till sugar dissolves.
- Combine 1/3 cup mayonnaise or salad dressing, 1 tablespoon vinegar, 2 teaspoons sugar, 1/2 teaspoon salt, and 1/2 teaspoon celery seed; stir till sugar dissolves.
- Blend 1/2 cup mayonnaise or salad dressing, 2 tablespoons vinegar, and 1 teaspoon prepared mustard.

## SOUR CREAM CUCUMBERS

Thinly slice 1 cucumber; sprinkle with 1 teaspoon salt, let stand 30 minutes. Drain.

Combine 1/2 cup dairy sour cream, 4 teaspoons vinegar, 1 to 2 drops bottled hot pepper sauce, 2 tablespoons snipped chives, 1/2 teaspoon dried dillweed, and dash pepper; pour over cucumbers. Chill about 30 minutes. Makes 4 or 5 servings.

## CALICO VEGETABLE BOWL

| | |
|---|---|
| 1 cup diced cooked potatoes | 2 tablespoons chopped onion |
| 1 cup diced cooked carrots | 2 tablespoons snipped parsley |
| 1 cup cooked peas | 1/4 cup French salad dressing |
| 1 canned pimiento, chopped | 1/2 head lettuce |

Combine potatoes, carrots, peas, pimiento, onion, and parsley with French dressing. Chill 1 hour. Add lettuce in bite-size pieces; toss. Pass mayonnaise. Serves 6.

## POTLUCK POTATO SALAD

| | |
|---|---|
| 1/4 cup clear French salad dressing with spices and herbs | 1 cup chopped celery |
| | 1/4 cup chopped onion |
| 4 to 5 medium potatoes, cooked in jackets, peeled, and cubed (4 cups) | 4 hard-cooked eggs, sliced |
| | 1 teaspoon salt |
| | 1/2 cup mayonnaise |

Pour French dressing over warm potatoes; chill 2 hours. Add celery, onion, eggs, and salt. Add mayonnaise and mix carefully. Add 1 teaspoon celery seed, if desired. Chill 4 hours. Makes 8 servings.

## SOUR CREAM-POTATO SALAD

1/3 cup Italian salad
   dressing
 7 medium potatoes,
   cooked in jackets,
   peeled, sliced (6 cups)
3/4 cup sliced celery
1/3 cup sliced green onion

 4 hard-cooked eggs
 1 cup mayonnaise or
   salad dressing
1/2 cup dairy sour cream
1 1/2 teaspoons prepared
   horseradish mustard

Pour Italian dressing over warm potatoes; chill 2 hours. Add celery and onion. Chop egg whites; add. Sieve yolks; mix with mayonnaise, sour cream, and mustard; fold into salad. Add salt and celery seed to taste. Chill 2 hours. Makes 8 servings.

## STUFFED TOMATOES

Cut tomatoes in Cups, Fantans, or Daisies. At serving time, salt cut surfaces. Fill with seafood salad, meat salad, egg salad, or a poultry salad.

**Cup:** Peel, if desired. Cut thin slice from top; scoop out center. Invert and chill.

**Fantan:** Turn tomato stem end down. Cut down, *not quite through*, making 5 slices.

**Daisy:** Turn tomato stem end down. Cut down, *not quite through*, in 5 or 6 wedges. Scoop out some of center. Invert; chill.

## HOT FIVE-BEAN SALAD

In large skillet, cook 8 slices bacon till crisp; drain, reserving 1/4 cup drippings. Return reserved drippings to skillet.

Combine 2/3 cup sugar, 2 tablespoons cornstarch, 1 1/2 teaspoons salt, and dash pepper; blend into drippings in skillet. Stir in 3/4 cup vinegar and 1/2 cup water; cook and stir till boiling.

Drain one 15-ounce can dark red kidney beans, one 1-pound can cut green beans, one 1-pound can lima beans, one 1-pound can cut wax beans, and one 15-ounce can garbanzo beans. Stir drained beans into mixture in skillet. Cover and simmer 15 to 20 minutes, stirring occasionally. Turn bean mixture into a serving dish. Crumble the crisp-cooked bacon. Sprinkle over top of beans. Makes 10 to 12 servings.

## THREE-BEAN SALAD

1 1-pound can cut green beans
1 1-pound can cut wax beans
1 15-ounce can dark red kidney beans

½ cup chopped green pepper

* * *

½ cup sugar
⅔ cup vinegar
⅓ cup salad oil
1 teaspoon salt
¼ teaspoon pepper

Drain green beans, wax beans, and kidney beans. Combine; add green pepper. Combine sugar, vinegar, and salad oil; pour over vegetables. Add salt and pepper; toss. Chill overnight. Before serving, toss to coat beans; drain. Makes 6 to 8 servings.

## GERMAN POTATO SALAD

6 slices bacon
½ cup chopped onion
2 tablespoons all-purpose flour
2 tablespoons sugar
1½ teaspoons salt

1 teaspoon celery seed
Dash pepper
1 cup water
½ cup vinegar
6 cups sliced cooked potatoes

Cook bacon till crisp; drain and crumble, reserving ¼ cup drippings. Cook onion in reserved drippings till tender. Blend in flour, sugar, salt, celery seed, and pepper. Add water and vinegar; cook and stir till thickened and bubbly. Add bacon and potatoes, tossing lightly; heat thoroughly, about 10 minutes. Trim with parsley and pimiento, if desired. Makes 8 to 10 servings.

## PERFECTION SALAD

2 envelopes (2
  tablespoons)
  unflavored gelatin
1/2 cup sugar
1/2 cup vinegar
2 tablespoons lemon
  juice

2 cups finely shredded
  cabbage
1 cup chopped celery
1/2 cup chopped green
  pepper
1/4 cup chopped canned
  pimiento

Mix gelatin, sugar, and 1 teaspoon salt. Add 1 1/2 cups boiling water and stir till gelatin dissolves. Add 1 1/2 cups cold water, vinegar, and lemon juice; chill till partially set. Add vegetables; pour into 6 1/2-cup ring mold. Chill till firm. Unmold on crisp greens. Makes 8 to 10 servings.

## SUNSHINE SALAD

Dissolve one 3-ounce package lemon-flavored gelatin in 1 cup boiling water. Drain one 8 3/4-ounce can (1 cup) crushed pineapple; reserve syrup. Add water to syrup to make 1 cup; add to gelatin with 1 tablespoon vinegar and 1/4 teaspoon salt. Chill till partially set. Fold pineapple, 1 cup shredded carrot, and 1/4 cup chopped pecans (optional) into gelatin. Turn into 9x5x3-inch loaf pan. Chill firm. Serves 6.

## CUCUMBER-CHEESE RING

*Refreshing as a cool summer breeze—*

1 3-ounce package
  lime-flavored gelatin
1 cup boiling water
1 3-ounce package
  cream cheese, softened
1 cup mayonnaise or
  salad dressing
1 teaspoon prepared
  horseradish

1/4 teaspoon salt
2 tablespoons lemon
  juice
3/4 cup drained shredded
  *or* ground unpared
  cucumber
1/4 cup finely sliced green
  onion

Dissolve gelatin in boiling water. Add cream cheese, mayonnaise or salad dressing, horseradish, salt, and lemon juice. Beat smooth with electric or rotary beater.

Chill till partially set. Stir in cucumber and sliced green onion. Chill in 3½-cup mold till firm. Makes 5 or 6 servings.

## SPARKLING BEET CUPS

Dissolve one 3-ounce package lemon-flavored gelatin in 1 cup boiling water. Drain one 1-pound can diced beets, reserving ¾ cup liquid. Add reserved liquid, 2 tablespoons vinegar, ½ teaspoon Worcestershire sauce, ½ teaspoon prepared horseradish, 1 teaspoon grated onion, and ½ teaspoon salt to gelatin.

Chill till partially set. Fold in beets and ½ cup chopped celery. Chill in 6 individual molds till firm.

## TOMATO ASPIC

Combine 2 cups tomato juice with ⅓ cup chopped onion, ¼ cup chopped celery, 2 tablespoons brown sugar, 1 teaspoon salt, 2 bay leaves, and 4 cloves; simmer, uncovered, 5 minutes. Strain.

Meanwhile, soften 2 envelopes (2 tablespoons) unflavored gelatin in 1 cup cold tomato juice; dissolve in hot juice mixture. Add 1 cup tomato juice and 3 tablespoons lemon juice. Chill till partially set.

Add 1 cup finely chopped celery. Pour into 5-cup ring mold. Chill till firm. Unmold on lettuce leaves. Serves 8 to 10.

# MAIN-DISH SALADS

## CHICKEN SALAD

3 cups cubed cooked
   chicken
1½ cups diced celery
3 hard-cooked eggs,
   quartered

3 sweet pickles, chopped
1 teaspoon salt
   Mayonnaise or salad
   dressing

Mix chicken, celery, eggs, pickles, and salt. Moisten with mayonnaise. Serves 8.

## JELLIED CHICKEN SALAD

Drain one 8¾-ounce can crushed pineapple, reserving syrup. Soften 2 envelopes (2 tablespoons) unflavored gelatin in ½ cup cold water; dissolve in 3 cups boiling chicken broth. Add ¼ cup lemon juice, ½ teaspoon salt, and reserved syrup.

Chill till partially set. Stir in pineapple, 2 cups diced cooked chicken, ½ cup chopped celery, ¼ cup chopped green pepper, and 1 tablespoon chopped canned pimiento. Pour into 6½-cup ring mold; chill firm; unmold. Serves 8 to 12.

## TURKEY-GRAPE SALAD

1½ cups diced cooked
   turkey
1 cup thinly sliced
   celery

½ cup seedless green
   grapes
½ cup mayonnaise
   Salad greens

Combine turkey, celery, grapes, and mayonnaise. Season with salt and pepper. Toss lightly. Serve on salad greens; trim with additional grapes, if desired. Serves 6.

## CHEF'S SALAD BOWL

Rub salad bowl with cut clove of garlic. Separate leaves of 1 head romaine or 1 bunch leaf lettuce. Arrange in bowl, lining sides. Group atop lettuce: 2 cups cooked ham strips, 8 ounces sharp natural Cheddar cheese, cut in strips, and 3 hard-cooked eggs, sliced. Sprinkle with salt and freshly ground pepper. Pass Italian dressing. Makes 6 servings.

## RICE AND HAM SALAD

1⅓ cups long-grain rice
¼ cup French salad dressing
¾ cup mayonnaise
1 tablespoon finely chopped green onion
½ to 1 teaspoon curry powder
½ teaspoon salt
½ teaspoon dry mustard

8 ounces fully cooked ham, cut in julienne strips (1½ cups)
1 cup sliced raw cauliflower
½ 10-ounce package (1 cup) frozen peas, cooked and chilled
½ cup chopped celery
½ cup thinly sliced radishes
1 casaba melon, chilled

Cook rice according to package directions. Toss with French dressing; chill several hours. Combine mayonnaise, onion, curry, salt, mustard, and dash pepper. Toss with rice. Add ham and vegetables; toss. Cut melon in rings; remove seeds and rind. Mound salad atop melon. Serves 6.

## TACO SALAD

1 pound ground beef
½ envelope (¼ cup) *dry* onion soup mix
¾ cup water
1 medium head lettuce, torn in bite-size pieces (4 cups)
1 large tomato, cut in wedges

1 small onion, thinly sliced and separated in rings
¼ cup chopped green pepper
½ cup sliced ripe olives
4 ounces sharp natural Cheddar cheese, shredded (1 cup)
1 6-ounce package corn chips

In skillet, brown beef. Sprinkle soup mix over meat; stir in water. Simmer, uncovered, 10 minutes. In salad bowl, combine lettuce, tomato, onion, green pepper, olives, and cheese; toss well. Place lettuce mixture on individual salad plates. Spoon on meat; top with corn chips. Serves 4 to 6.

## APPLE-TUNA TOSS

1 medium head lettuce, torn in bite-size pieces (4 cups)

2 cups diced unpared apple

1 11-ounce can mandarin oranges, drained

1 6½- or 7-ounce can tuna, drained and broken in chunks

⅓ cup coarsely chopped walnuts

½ cup mayonnaise or salad dressing

2 teaspoons soy sauce

1 teaspoon lemon juice

In large salad bowl, combine lettuce, apple, oranges, tuna, and nuts; toss together. Combine mayonnaise, soy, and lemon juice; mix well; toss dressing gently with salad. Makes 4 to 6 servings.

## SUMMER TUNA MOLD

Soften 1 envelope (1 tablespoon) unflavored gelatin in ½ cup cold water. Bring one 10¾-ounce can tomato soup to boil; add gelatin; stir to dissolve. Add one 8-ounce package cream cheese, in chunks; beat with rotary beater till smooth. Add 1 cup mayonnaise. Chill till partially set.

Fold in ⅓ cup diced green pepper, ½ cup diced celery, ⅓ cup chopped onion, ¼ cup drained pickle relish, and one 6½- or 7-ounce can tuna, drained and flaked. Chill firm in 8x8x2-inch pan. Serves 6 to 9.

## SHRIMP REMOULADE

In small bowl, combine ¼ cup tarragon vinegar, 2 tablespoons horseradish mustard, 1 tablespoon catsup, ½ teaspoon salt, 1½ teaspoons paprika, and ¼ teaspoon cayenne. Slowly add ½ cup salad oil, beating constantly. Stir in ¼ cup finely chopped celery and ¼ cup snipped green onion. Pour sauce over 2 pounds shrimp, cooked and cleaned. Marinate in the refrigerator for 4 to 5 hours.

Halve and peel 4 medium avocados. Brush with lemon juice. Lift shrimp out of sauce and arrange on avocado halves. Serve with cooked chilled asparagus spears, carrot strips, sliced cooked beets, and sliced hard-cooked eggs. Pass marinade or French dressing. Makes 8 servings.

## FROSTED CHEESE MOLD

In saucepan, soften 2 envelopes (2 tablespoons) unflavored gelatin in 1 cup milk. Stir over low heat till gelatin is dissolved. Remove from heat. With electric mixer, beat two 12-ounce cartons cream-style cottage cheese and 1/2 cup crumbled blue cheese together till well blended. Stir in gelatin mixture. Stir in one 6-ounce can frozen limeade concentrate, thawed, 1/2 cup broken pecans, and 6 drops green food coloring. Chill till mixture mounds when dropped from a spoon.

Whip 1 cup whipping cream. Fold into gelatin mixture. Turn into a 6 1/2-cup ring mold; chill till firm. Unmold onto serving plate. Fill center with melon balls and orange sections. Garnish with Frosted Grapes (page 604) and mint sprigs. Pass lime wedges. Makes 12 to 16 servings.

## MACARONI-CHEESE SALAD

In bowl, combine 1 cup elbow macaroni, cooked, drained, and cooled; one 12-ounce can chopped ham, cut in strips; 1 cup cubed sharp natural Cheddar cheese; 1/2 cup bias-cut celery slices; 1/3 cup chopped green pepper; 1/4 cup sliced green onion; 2 tablespoons chopped canned pimiento; and 1/4 cup drained pickle relish. Blend together 1/2 cup mayonnaise, 1 tablespoon prepared mustard, and 1/4 teaspoon salt. Add to macaroni; toss. Chill. Serves 6.

## CRAB LOUIS

Line 4 large plates with lettuce leaves from large head. Shred remainder of lettuce atop. Use 2 to 3 cups cooked crab meat (or two 7 1/2-ounce cans). Remove bony bits. Reserve claw meat. Place remaining meat in chunks on lettuce.

Cut 2 large tomatoes and 2 hard-cooked eggs in wedges. Circle atop salads. Salt. Pour $1/4$ cup Louis Dressing over each salad. Dash with paprika. Top with claw meat. Pass dressing. Makes 4 servings.

**Louis Dressing:** To 1 cup mayonnaise, add $1/4$ cup whipping cream, whipped, and $1/4$ cup *each* chili sauce, chopped green pepper, and chopped green onion. Add 1 teaspoon lemon juice; salt to taste; chill. Makes 2 cups dressing.

# FRUIT SALADS

### SPICY APRICOT MOLD

Drain one 1-pound can apricot halves and one 8³/₄-ounce can pineapple tidbits, reserving syrups. Combine syrups with 2 tablespoons vinegar, 1 teaspoon whole cloves, and 4 inches stick cinnamon; bring to boil. Simmer 10 minutes; strain; add hot water to make 2 cups. Pour over one 3-ounce package orange-flavored gelatin; stir to dissolve. Chill till partially set. Fold in *well-drained* apricot halves, halved, and pineapple. Pour into 6-cup ring mold. Chill till *almost* firm. Dissolve one 3-ounce package orange-flavored gelatin in ³/₄ cup boiling water; stir in ³/₄ cup apricot nectar. Chill till partially set; whip till fluffy. Swirl in ¹/₂ cup dairy sour cream. Pour over first layer. Chill at least 8 hours. Trim with Frosted Grapes. Serves 8.

*Frosted Grapes:* Brush grapes with slightly beaten egg white; sprinkle with sugar; dry on rack.

### JUBILEE SALAD MOLD

1 10-ounce package
  frozen raspberries,
  thawed
¹/₂ cup currant jelly
2 cups water
2 3-ounce packages red
  raspberry-flavored
  gelatin

¹/₂ cup sherry
¹/₄ cup lemon juice
1 1-pound can (2 cups)
  pitted dark sweet
  cherries, drained

Drain raspberries, reserving syrup. Combine jelly and ¹/₂ *cup of the water;* heat and stir till jelly melts. Add remaining 1¹/₂ cups water and the gelatin; heat and stir till gelatin dissolves.

Remove from heat; add sherry, lemon juice, and reserved raspberry syrup. Chill till partially set. Fold raspberries and cherries into gelatin. Pour into 6-cup mold. Chill till firm. Makes 8 servings.

# CRAN-RASPBERRY RING

1 3-ounce package
    raspberry-flavored
    gelatin
1 3-ounce package
    lemon-flavored gelatin
1½ cups boiling water
1 10-ounce package
    frozen raspberries

1 14-ounce jar (1⅓
    cups) cranberry-
    orange relish
1 7-ounce bottle (about
    1 cup) lemon-lime
    carbonated beverage

Dissolve raspberry- and lemon-flavored gelatin in 1½ cups boiling water. Stir in frozen raspberries, breaking up large pieces with fork. Add cranberry-orange relish. Chill till cold but not set.

Carefully pour in lemon-lime carbonated beverage; stir gently. Chill till partially set. Turn into a 6- or 6½-cup ring mold. Chill till firm. Unmold on crisp greens. Makes 8 to 10 servings.

# CINNAMON-APPLE SALAD

Dissolve two 3-ounce packages lemon-flavored gelatin and ½ cup red cinnamon candies in 3 cups boiling water. Stir in 2 cups unsweetened applesauce, 1 tablespoon lemon juice, and dash salt.

Chill till partially set. Add ½ cup broken walnuts. Pour into 8x8x2-inch pan. Blend two 3-ounce packages cream cheese, softened, ¼ cup milk, and 2 tablespoons mayonnaise; spoon atop. Swirl through salad to marble. Chill firm. Serves 9.

# GREENGAGE PLUM SQUARES

Drain one 1-pound 14-ounce can greengage plums, reserving syrup; sieve plums. Add water to syrup to make 3½ cups; bring to boil; remove from heat. Add one 3-ounce package each lemon-flavored and lime-flavored gelatin; stir to dissolve. Add plums. Chill till partially set. Stir in 1 cup finely chopped celery.

Turn into 8x8x2-inch pan. Blend one 3-ounce package cream cheese, softened, 3 tablespoons light cream, and 1 tablespoon mayonnaise. Spoon atop salad; swirl to marble. Chill firm. Serves 9 to 12.

## ROSY STRAWBERRY RING

2 3-ounce packages
strawberry-flavored
gelatin
2 cups boiling water
2 10-ounce packages
frozen sliced
strawberries

1 13½-ounce can (1⅔
cups) crushed
pineapple
2 large, ripe bananas,
peeled and finely
diced
2 tablespoons lemon
juice

Dissolve gelatin in boiling water. Add berries, stirring occasionally until thawed. Stir in pineapple, bananas, and lemon juice. Pour into 6½-cup mold. Chill till firm, about 5 to 6 hours. Serve with Sour Cream Dressing. Makes 8 servings.

*Sour Cream Dressing:* In small bowl, combine 1 cup dairy sour cream, 1 teaspoon sugar, ¼ teaspoon ground ginger, and dash salt. Chill mixture thoroughly.

## HARVEST FRUIT MOLD

1 11-ounce package
mixed dried fruits
⅓ cup sugar

2 3-ounce packages
orange-flavored
gelatin

Combine fruit and enough water to cover in saucepan; simmer gently, covered, 25 to 30 minutes, adding sugar for last 5 minutes of cooking. Drain fruit, reserving syrup. Add water to syrup to make 2 cups. Dissolve gelatin in 2 cups boiling water; stir in syrup mixture. Chill till partially set.

Pit prunes; cut up all fruit; fold into gelatin. Pour into 6-cup ring mold; chill till firm. Makes 8 servings.

## DOUBLE APPLE SALAD

Pour 1 cup boiling cider or apple juice over one 3-ounce package orange-flavored gelatin and ½ teaspoon salt; stir till gelatin is dissolved. Add 1 cup cider or apple juice; chill till partially set.

Add 1 cup small strips of apple, ¼ cup diced celery, and ¼ cup coarsely broken walnuts. Spoon into a 3-cup ring mold. Chill salad several hours or overnight till firm. Makes 4 to 6 servings.

## • UNMOLD GELATIN LIKE AN EXPERT •

Loosen edge (and around center of ring mold) with spatula. Dip mold to rim in warm water for *few seconds;* tilt slightly; ease gelatin away from one side to let air in.

Tilt and rotate mold so air can loosen gelatin all the way around. Place plate upside down over mold; hold plate and mold together; invert; lift off mold.

## FROSTED CRANBERRY SALAD

1 13½-ounce can crushed pineapple

2 3-ounce packages lemon-flavored gelatin

1 7-ounce bottle ginger ale

1 1-pound can (2 cups) jellied cranberry sauce

1 2-ounce package dessert topping mix

1 8-ounce package cream cheese, softened

½ cup chopped pecans

Drain pineapple, reserving syrup; add water to make 1 cup; heat to boil. Dissolve gelatin in hot liquid; cool. Gently stir in ginger ale; chill till partially set. Blend pineapple and cranberry sauce; fold into gelatin. Turn into 9x9x2-inch dish; chill firm. Prepare topping according to package. Blend in cheese; spread over gelatin. Toast nuts in 1 tablespoon butter at 350° for 10 minutes; sprinkle atop; chill. Serves 9.

## 24-HOUR SALAD

1 1-pound 4$^1$/$_2$-ounce can (2$^1$/$_2$ cups) pineapple tidbits

3 slightly beaten egg yolks

2 tablespoons sugar

2 tablespoons vinegar

1 tablespoon butter

1 1-pound can (2 cups) pitted light sweet cherries, drained

2 pared oranges, cut up, drained

2 cups miniature marshmallows

1 cup whipping cream, whipped

Drain pineapple; reserve 2 tablespoons syrup. In top of double boiler, mix yolks, reserved syrup, sugar, vinegar, butter, and dash salt. Place over, *not touching*, boiling water. Cook and stir till mixture thickens *slightly* and *barely* coats a spoon (about 12 minutes). Cool to room temperature. Combine *well-drained* fruits and marshmallows. Pour custard over; mix gently. Fold in whipped cream. Pour into serving bowl. Cover; chill 24 hours. Serves 6 to 8.

## ORANGE-APRICOT FREEZE

2 8-ounce cartons (2 cups) orange-flavored yogurt

1 1-pound 1-ounce can apricot halves

$^1$/$_2$ cup sugar

$^1$/$_3$ cup coarsely chopped pecans

Stir yogurt in carton to blend. Drain apricots; cut up fruit. Combine yogurt, apricots, sugar, and nuts. Line muffin pan with 12 paper bake cups. Spoon in yogurt mixture; freeze firm. Remove cups from salads; let stand at room temperature a few minutes before serving. Serves 12.

## GINGER FRUIT FREEZE

Mix one 3-ounce package cream cheese, softened, 3 tablespoons mayonnaise, 1 tablespoon lemon juice, and $^1$/$_4$ teaspoon salt.

Stir in $^1$/$_2$ cup chopped preserved kumquats, $^1$/$_2$ cup dates, cut up, $^1$/$_4$ cup quartered maraschino cherries, one

8³/₄-ounce can crushed pineapple, drained, and 2 table-spoons finely chopped candied ginger.

Fold in 1 cup whipping cream, whipped. Pour into 1-quart refrigerator tray. Sprinkle ¹/₄ cup toasted slivered almonds over top. Freeze firm. Makes 6 to 8 servings.

## FROZEN FRUIT SLICES

| | |
|---|---|
| 2 3-ounce packages cream cheese, softened | ¹/₂ cup drained maraschino cherries, quartered |
| 1 cup mayonnaise or salad dressing | 2¹/₂ cups miniature marshmallows |
| 1 1-pound 14-ounce can (3¹/₂ cups) fruit cocktail, well drained | 1 cup whipping cream, whipped |

Blend cheese and mayonnaise. Stir in fruits and marsh-mallows. Fold in whipped cream. Tint with few drops red food coloring or maraschino-cherry juice, if desired.

Pour into two 1-quart round ice-cream containers or refrigerator trays. Freeze firm, about 6 hours or overnight. To serve, let stand out a few minutes, then remove from containers; slice. Serves 10 to 12.

## CLASSIC WALDORF SALAD

*A cool and crunchy favorite—*

Combine 2 cups diced apple, 1 cup 1-inch julienne celery sticks, and ¹/₂ cup broken walnuts. Blend ¹/₄ cup mayon-naise, 1 tablespoon sugar, ¹/₂ teaspoon lemon juice, and dash salt. Fold in ¹/₂ cup whipping cream, whipped; fold dressing into apple mixture; chill. Makes 6 servings.

## WINTER ORANGE BOWL

Lightly toss 7 cups torn lettuce (about 1 head), 2 cups orange sections, and ¹/₂ mild white onion, sliced and separated in rings with ¹/₃ cup Italian salad dressing. Top with Walnut Croutons. Serves 6 to 8.

*Walnut Croutons:* Melt 1 tablespoon butter over medium heat. Add ¹/₄ teaspoon salt and ¹/₂ cup walnut pieces. Stir till crisp.

## FRUIT SALAD SPECIALS

- **Pineapple-carrot Toss:** Drain one 8¾-ounce can pineapple tidbits well. Mix with 2 cups shredded carrots and ½ cup plumped raisins; chill. Just before serving, add mayonnaise to moisten. Serves 6.
- **Banana-nut Salad:** Cut 2 bananas in half crosswise; arrange each half on greens. Combine ¼ cup mayonnaise, 1 tablespoon peanut butter, and 1 tablespoon honey; spoon over bananas. Sprinkle with ¼ cup chopped nuts. Makes 4 servings.
- **Avocado Bowl:** Tear 1 small head lettuce and ½ head curly endive in bite-size pieces into salad bowl. Peel 2 avocados and slice into bowl; add 1 cup each grapefruit and orange sections. Add pomegranate seeds, if desired. Toss with enough French salad dressing to coat. Serves 8.
- **Pineapple Boat:** Cut pineapple in half, keeping leafy top intact. Leaving shells ½ inch thick, hollow out. Cut out core and discard. Dice remaining pineapple; mix with orange sections and strawberries; refill shells. Chill, Trim with mint. Pass Fruit French Dressing (page 615).
- **Stuffed Prune Salad:** For each serving, arrange 2 orange slices on greens. Stuff 2 cooked, pitted prunes with drained cream-style cottage cheese; top with walnut halves; place atop orange slices.

# RELISHES

## PICKLED BEETS

Combine 1/3 cup vinegar, 1/4 cup sugar, 1/4 cup water, 1/2 teaspoon ground cinnamon, 1/4 teaspoon *each* salt and ground cloves. Heat to boiling; add 2 cups sliced, cooked beets. Cover; simmer 5 minutes; chill.

## CHEESE-MARINATED ONIONS

3 ounces blue cheese, crumbled (about 3/4 cup)
1/2 cup salad oil
2 tablespoons lemon juice
1 teaspoon salt
1/2 teaspoon sugar
Dash pepper
Dash paprika
4 medium onions, thinly sliced and separated in rings (about 4 cups)

Mix all ingredients except onions. Pour mixture over onion rings and refrigerate 3 to 4 hours. Good with barbecued meats or in green salad. Makes about 1 quart.

## SVENGALI TOMATOES

In a saucepan, combine one 1-pound can tomatoes, cut up, 1/4 cup canned or frozen cranberry-orange relish, 2 tablespoons light raisins, 1 tablespoon sugar, 1/2 teaspoon *each* salt and ground ginger, and 1/4 teaspoon cayenne; simmer 8 to 10 minutes. Serve warm or chilled.

## PIMIENTO-ONION RELISH

1/3 cup vinegar
1/2 teaspoon *fines herbes*
2 tablespoons sugar
2/3 cup water
1 4-ounce can or jar whole pimientos, quartered
1 medium onion, thinly sliced (about 1 cup)

Combine vinegar, fines herbes, sugar, and water. Add pimientos and onion; marinate overnight. Drain; serve with meat.

## SPEEDY RELISHES

• **Hot Chop-chop:** Combine ½ cup each chopped green pepper, chopped onion, and chili sauce. Chill. Makes 1¼ cups.

• **Pickled Onions:** Cut onions in ¼-inch slices. Separate rings. Chill 2 or 3 days in dill or sweet pickle juice to cover.

## CINNAMON APPLE RINGS

| | |
|---|---|
| ¼ cup sugar | 4 apples (1 pound) |
| ½ cup red cinnamon candies | |

In skillet, combine sugar, candies, and 2 cups water. Stir over medium heat till sugar and candies dissolve. Core the apples, cut crosswise in ½-inch rings, and add to syrup. Simmer gently till transparent but not soft. Cool in syrup.

## CURRIED APPLE RELISH

Melt 2 tablespoons butter in skillet. Stir in 1 teaspoon sugar and ½ teaspoon curry powder. Add one 1-pound 4-ounce can (2½ cups) drained pie-sliced apples; toss to coat. Cook over low heat, stirring occasionally, about 5 minutes, or till apples are heated through. Serve with meat or poultry. Makes 6 to 8 servings.

## HOT CURRIED FRUIT

OVEN 325°

Drain one 1-pound can (2 cups) peach halves and one 1-pound can (2 cups) pear halves. Cut peach and pear halves in half. In 2-quart casserole, mix peaches and pears with one 1-pound 1-ounce can apricot halves, drained, and one 13½-ounce can pineapple chunks, drained.

Blend 2 tablespoons melted butter with ¼ cup brown

sugar and 1 to 1½ teaspoons curry powder. Spoon over fruit. Bake at 325° for 15 minutes. Carefully mix in one 1-pound 1-ounce can (2 cups) dark sweet cherries, drained. Return to oven and bake 15 minutes longer. Serve warm as a meat accompaniment. Serves 8 to 10.

# SALAD DRESSINGS

## FRENCH DRESSING

| | |
|---|---|
| 1/2 cup salad oil | 3/4 teaspoon dry mustard |
| 2 tablespoons vinegar | 1/2 teaspoon salt |
| 2 tablespoons lemon juice | 1/8 teaspoon paprika |
| 1 teaspoon sugar | Dash cayenne |

Combine ingredients in jar; cover and shake well before using. Makes 3/4 cup.

**Blue-cheese French Dressing:** Add 2 ounces blue cheese, crumbled (1/2 cup).

**Vinaigrette Dressing:** Add 2 tablespoons chopped pimiento-stuffed green olives, 1 tablespoon *each* chopped canned pimiento and chives, and 1 hard-cooked egg, chopped, to French Dressing.

**Garlic French Dressing:** Add 1/4 teaspoon garlic powder to French Dressing.

## CREAMY FRENCH DRESSING

| | |
|---|---|
| 1 tablespoon paprika | 1/3 cup vinegar |
| 2 teaspoons sugar | 1 egg |
| 1 teaspoon salt | 1 cup salad oil |
| Dash cayenne | |

Combine dry ingredients. Add vinegar and egg; beat well. Add oil in slow stream, beating constantly with electric or rotary beater till thick. Makes 1 2/3 cups.

## CREAM GODDESS DRESSING

| | |
|---|---|
| 1 cup mayonnaise | 3 tablespoons tarragon vinegar |
| 1/2 cup dairy sour cream | 1 tablespoon lemon juice |
| 1/3 cup snipped parsley | Dash freshly ground pepper |
| 3 tablespoons snipped chives | |
| 3 tablespoons anchovy paste | |

Combine all ingredients. Chill thoroughly. Makes 2 cups dressing.

## ITALIAN DRESSING

| | |
|---|---|
| 1 cup salad oil | 1/4 teaspoon dry mustard |
| 1/3 cup vinegar | 1/4 teaspoon cayenne |
| 1 teaspoon sugar | 1 clove garlic, minced |
| 1/2 teaspoon salt | Dash bottled hot |
| 1/2 teaspoon celery salt | pepper sauce |

Combine ingredients in jar; cover and shake. Makes 1 1/3 cups.

## FRUIT FRENCH DRESSING

Mix 1 cup salad oil, 1/4 cup orange juice, 3 tablespoons lemon juice, 1 tablespoon vinegar, 1/3 cup sugar, and 1 teaspoon each salt, paprika, and grated onion in a jar; cover and shake vigorously. Chill. Shake before serving. Makes about 1 2/3 cups.

## CELERY SEED DRESSING

| | |
|---|---|
| 2/3 cup sugar | 1/3 cup vinegar |
| 1 teaspoon dry mustard | 1 tablespoon lemon |
| 1 teaspoon paprika | juice |
| 1 teaspoon celery seed | 1/2 teaspoon grated onion |
| 1/4 teaspoon salt | 1 cup salad oil |
| 1/3 cup honey | |

Mix dry ingredients; blend in honey, vinegar, lemon juice, and onion. Add oil in slow stream, beating constantly with electric mixer, till thick. Makes 2 cups.

## FLUFFY CITRUS DRESSING

In saucepan, beat 1 egg; add 1/2 cup sugar, 1 tablespoon grated orange peel, 2 teaspoons grated lemon peel, and 2 tablespoons lemon juice. Cook and stir over *low* heat till thick, 5 minutes. Cool well. Fold in 1 cup whipping cream, whipped. Chill. Makes 2 1/3 cups dressing.

## HONEY-LIME DRESSING

| | |
|---|---|
| 1 beaten egg | Dash salt |
| 1/2 cup honey | Dash ground mace |
| 1/4 cup lime juice | 1 cup dairy sour cream |

In saucepan, combine egg, honey, and lime juice; cook and stir over low heat till mixture thickens. Blend in salt and mace; cool. Fold in dairy sour cream. Chill. Makes 1 1/2 cups dressing.

## COOKED DRESSING

Mix together 2 tablespoons all-purpose flour, 2 table-spoons sugar, 1 teaspoon salt, 1 teaspoon dry mustard, and dash cayenne in a small saucepan; add 2 slightly beaten egg yolks and 3/4 cup milk; cook and stir over low heat till thick. Add 1/4 cup vinegar and 1 1/2 teaspoons butter; mix. Cool. Makes 1 cup.

## PINEAPPLE DRESSING

| | |
|---|---|
| 1/3 cup sugar | 3 tablespoons lemon |
| 4 teaspoons cornstarch | juice |
| 1/4 teaspoon salt | 2 beaten eggs |
| 1 cup pineapple juice | 2 3-ounce packages |
| 1/4 cup orange juice | cream cheese, softened |

Blend dry ingredients; add juices. Cook and stir till thickened and bubbly. Cook 2 minutes. Add small amount to eggs. Return to hot mixture. Cook and stir over low heat till slightly thickened, 3 to 5 minutes. Cool 5 minutes. Beat into cream cheese. Chill. Makes 2 1/3 cups dressing.

## SHAWANO DRESSING

Combine 1/2 cup salad oil, 1/3 cup sugar, 1/3 cup catsup, 1/4 cup vinegar, 1 teaspoon each salt and paprika; 1/2 tea-spoon dry mustard, 2 teaspoons grated onion, 1 1/2 tea-spoons bottled steak sauce, and 1 clove garlic, minced. Blend thoroughly with beater. Serve with fruit. Makes 1 1/3 cups.

## RUSSIAN DRESSING

<sup></sup>1/4 cup sugar
3 tablespoons water
1<sup></sup>1/2 teaspoons celery seed
1/2 teaspoon salt
1/2 teaspoon paprika
2<sup></sup>1/2 tablespoons lemon
juice

1 tablespoon each
Worcestershire sauce
and vinegar
1 cup salad oil
1/2 cup catsup
1/4 cup grated onion

Cook sugar and water till mixture spins a thread (232°).
Cool. Mix remaining ingredients; beat in syrup. Chill.
Makes 2 cups.

## AVOCADO DRESSING

1/2 cup mashed ripe
avocado
1 tablespoon lemon
juice
2 teaspoons sugar

1/4 teaspoon salt
1/2 cup whipping cream,
whipped
1/2 teaspoon grated
lemon peel

Blend first 4 ingredients. Fold in whipped cream. Sprinkle
with peel. Chill. Serve within a few hours. Makes about
1<sup></sup>1/2 cups.

## MAYONNAISE

1 teaspoon salt
1/2 teaspoon dry mustard
1/4 teaspoon paprika
Dash cayenne
* * *

2 egg yolks
2 tablespoons vinegar
2 cups salad oil
2 tablespoons lemon
juice

Mix dry ingredients; blend in egg yolks. Add vinegar and
mix well. Add salad oil, 1 teaspoon at a time, beating
with rotary or electric beater, till 1/4 cup has been added.
Add remaining oil in increasing amounts, alternating last
1/2 cup with the lemon juice. Makes 2 cups.

## LOW-CALORIE DRESSINGS

• **Tomato Dressing:** Combine one 8-ounce can tomato
sauce, 2 tablespoons tarragon vinegar, 1 teaspoon onion
juice, 1 teaspoon Worcestershire sauce, 1/2 teaspoon each

salt, dillweed, and dried basil, crushed, in a jar. Cover and shake well. Chill. Shake before serving. Makes 1 cup.

• **Slim-trim Dressing:** Mix 1 tablespoon cornstarch and 1/2 teaspoon dry mustard in a small saucepan. Gradually stir in 1 cup cold water. Cook over medium heat, stirring constantly, till mixture thickens; cool. Add 1/4 cup vinegar, 1/4 cup catsup, 1/2 teaspoon paprika, 1/2 teaspoon prepared horseradish, 1/2 teaspoon Worcestershire sauce, dash noncaloric liquid sweetener, and dash salt. Beat till smooth. Add 1 clove garlic, halved; cover and store in refrigerator. Shake well before using. Makes 1 1/3 cups dressing.

## TOMATO SOUP DRESSING

In a jar, combine 1/2 cup salad oil, 1 cup vinegar, one 10 3/4-ounce can condensed tomato soup, 2 tablespoons sugar, 1 1/2 teaspoons salt, 2 teaspoons dry mustard, 1/2 teaspoon paprika, 1/4 teaspoon garlic powder, 1 1/2 teaspoons Worcestershire sauce, 1 tablespoon grated onion, dash cayenne, and dash pepper. Cover; shake to blend ingredients. Store in refrigerator. Shake before serving. Makes 2 1/4 cups dressing.

## MAYONNAISE VARIATIONS

• **Thousand Island Dressing:** Mix 1 cup mayonnaise, 1/4 cup chili sauce, 2 hard-cooked eggs, chopped, 2 tablespoons each chopped green pepper and chopped celery, 1 1/2 tablespoons finely chopped onion, 1 teaspoon paprika, and 1/2 teaspoon salt. Makes 2 cups.

• **Creamy Mayonnaise:** Whip 1/2 cup whipping cream; fold into 1 cup mayonnaise or salad dressing.

• **Pink Fruit Mayonnaise:** Stir 1/3 cup cranberry-juice cocktail and dash salt into 1 cup mayonnaise. Chill. Add 2 tablespoons toasted chopped almonds.

• **Chili Mayonnaise:** Stir 1/2 cup chili sauce into 1 cup mayonnaise.

• **Herb Dressing:** Mix 1 cup mayonnaise, 1/3 cup finely chopped onion, 1/2 teaspoon grated lemon peel, 2 tablespoons lemon juice, 2 cloves garlic, minced, 1 tablespoon sherry, 2 teaspoons Worcestershire sauce, and 1/2 teaspoon dried mixed salad herbs. Chill. Makes 1 1/2 cups.

• **Chive Mayonnaise:** Mix 1 cup mayonnaise, 1/4 cup

snipped chives, 1 tablespoon lemon juice, 2 teaspoons tarragon vinegar, and dash salt.

- **Curry Dressing:** Mix 1$\frac{1}{2}$ teaspoons beef-flavored gravy base, 3 tablespoons hot water, 1 cup mayonnaise, and $\frac{1}{2}$ teaspoon curry. Chill.
- **Marshmallow Dressing:** To $\frac{1}{2}$ of 7- or 9-ounce jar marshmallow creme, gradually add 1 tablespoon *each* orange and lemon juice. Beat at high speed on electric mixer till fluffy. Fold in $\frac{1}{4}$ cup mayonnaise. Makes 1$\frac{1}{4}$ cups.
- **Creamy Dressing:** Mix $\frac{1}{2}$ cup mayonnaise, $\frac{1}{2}$ cup dairy sour cream, 1 tablespoon lemon juice, 1 tablespoon orange juice, and 2 teaspoons sugar.
- **Blue Cheese Dressing:** Mix 1 cup crumbled blue cheese, 2 cups mayonnaise, $\frac{1}{4}$ cup vinegar, 2 tablespoons sugar, $\frac{1}{2}$ cup dairy sour cream, and 1 clove garlic, minced. Beat till fluffy. Chill.
- **Yogurt Dressing:** Mix 1 cup yogurt, 2 tablespoons mayonnaise, 1 teaspoon sugar, dash lemon juice, and dash salt.
- **Poppy Seed Dressing:** Combine $\frac{1}{2}$ cup mayonnaise, 2 tablespoons sugar, 1 tablespoon poppy seed, and 1 tablespoon lemon juice. Mix till well blended.

# 14

# SOUPS AND SAUCES

## Meat, Vegetable, Fruit, and Dessert Sauces

## SOUPS

# SOUPS

## BROWN STOCK

6 pounds beef soup
  bones (cut in pieces)
1 cup sliced onion
½ cup chopped celery
1 large bay leaf

4 sprigs parsley
8 whole black
  peppercorns
2 teaspoons salt

Place meat bones and 2½ quarts cold water in large kettle. Simmer (*don't boil*), uncovered, 3 hours. Remove bones; cut off meat and chop. Return meat to stock; add remaining ingredients. Simmer, uncovered, 2 hours longer. Strain. (Use meat in soup or hash.) Clarify stock, if desired. Skim off fat, *or* chill and lift off fat. Makes 6 cups.

*To clarify stock:* Crush 1 egg shell; mix with white of 1 egg and ¼ cup water. Stir into hot stock. Bring to boiling. Let stand 5 minutes; strain.

## QUICK MEAT BROTH

Make quick and easy broth soup bases with one of the many beef or chicken products available. Follow package directions for canned condensed broth, bouillon cubes, or meat concentrates.

## RUSSIAN BORSCH

2 cups shredded fresh
  beets
1 cup chopped carrots
1 cup chopped onion
2½ cups Brown Stock or
  1 10½-ounce can
  condensed beef broth
  plus 1 soup can water

1 cup coarsely chopped
  cabbage
1 tablespoon butter
1 tablespoon lemon
  juice
  Dairy sour cream

Cook beets, carrots, and chopped onion, covered, in 2⅔ cups boiling salted water for 20 minutes. Add Brown

Stock, cabbage, and butter; cook, uncovered, 15 minutes. Stir in lemon juice. Serve hot or chilled. Top with sour cream. Serves 6 to 8.

## FRENCH ONION SOUP

1½ pounds (3 large)
    onions, thinly sliced
    (6 cups)
¼ cup butter or
    margarine
3 10½-ounce cans
    condensed beef broth

1 teaspoon
    Worcestershire sauce
¼ teaspoon salt
    Dash pepper
2 French or hard rolls,
    sliced and toasted
    Grated Parmesan
    cheese

Cook onions in butter till lightly browned, about 20 minutes. Add broth and Worcestershire. Bring to boiling. Season with salt and pepper. Sprinkle toast with cheese; place under broiler till cheese is lightly browned. Pour soup in bowls and float toast slices atop. Makes 6 to 8 servings.

## CREAM OF MUSHROOM SOUP

1 cup (about ¼ pound)
    mushrooms
2 tablespoons chopped
    onion
2 tablespoons butter
2 tablespoons all-
    purpose flour

2 cups chicken broth,
    Brown Stock, or
    beef broth
½ cup light cream
¼ teaspoon salt
¼ teaspoon ground
    nutmeg
⅛ teaspoon white pepper

Slice mushrooms through cap and stem; cook with onion in butter 5 minutes. Blend in flour; add broth. Cook and stir till slightly thickened. Cool slightly; add cream and seasonings. Heat through. Serve at once. Makes 4 to 6 servings.

## WHITE STOCK

Combine one 3- to 4-pound veal knuckle, cut in several pieces, 3 quarts cold water, 2 stalks celery, 1 onion, quartered, 1 carrot, sliced, 2 sprigs parsley, 2 cloves garlic,

$^1/_2$ bay leaf, 8 whole black peppercorns, and 1 tablespoon salt in soup kettle.

Simmer (*don't boil*), uncovered, 5 hours. Strain. Clarify, if desired (see recipe for Brown Stock). Use in cream soups for part or all of the milk. Makes 2 quarts.

## CREAM OF TOMATO SOUP

| | |
|---|---|
| 1  1-pound 12-ounce can tomatoes | $^1/_4$ teaspoon pepper |
| 2  slices onion | 2  tablespoons butter |
| 1  bay leaf | 2  tablespoons all-purpose flour |
| 1  teaspoon sugar | $1^1/_2$ cups milk |
| 1  teaspoon salt | |

Combine first 6 ingredients in a 2-quart saucepan. Simmer 10 minutes; sieve. Melt butter; blend in flour. Stir in milk. Cook and stir till thickened. Slowly add hot tomato mixture stirring constantly. Serves 6.

## CREAM OF CELERY SOUP

Cook $1^1/_2$ cups chopped celery, $^1/_3$ cup chopped onion, and $^1/_2$ teaspoon salt in 1 cup water, covered, about 15 minutes or till tender. *Do not drain.* Add $2^1/_2$ cups milk. Blend $^1/_2$ cup milk, 3 tablespoons all-purpose flour, $^1/_2$ teaspoon salt, and $^1/_8$ teaspoon white pepper; add to celery mixture. Cook and stir till bubbly. Stir in 2 tablespoons butter. Season. Serves 6.

## CREAM OF POTATO SOUP

Add 2 cups diced, cooked potatoes and 1 tablespoon chopped canned pimiento to 3 cups Thin White Sauce (page 645). Heat through. Season to taste. Serves 6.

## CHICKEN VELVET SOUP

| | |
|---|---|
| 6  tablespoons butter | 3  cups chicken broth |
| $^1/_3$ cup all-purpose flour | 1  cup finely chopped cooked chicken |
| $^1/_2$ cup milk | |
| $^1/_2$ cup light cream | |

Melt butter in saucepan. Blend in flour; add milk, cream, and broth. Cook and stir till mixture thickens and comes to a boil; reduce heat. Stir in chicken and dash pepper. Heat again just to boiling; serve immediately. Garnish with snipped parsley and pimiento, if desired. Serves 4.

## CREAM OF ONION SOUP

Melt $1/4$ cup butter in skillet. Add 4 cups coarsely chopped onion and $1/4$ teaspoon salt. Cover; cook 15 to 20 minutes, or till tender. Stir in 3 cups Thin White Sauce (page 645), 1 cup milk, and salt and pepper to taste. Heat through. Serves 6.

## VEGETABLE-BEEF SOUP

| | |
|---|---|
| 3 pounds beef shank | 1 1-pound can (2 cups) tomatoes |
| 1 1-pint 2-ounce can tomato juice | 1 cup diced celery |
| $1/3$ cup chopped onion | 1 $8^3/4$-ounce can whole kernel corn |
| 4 teaspoons salt | 1 cup sliced carrots |
| 2 teaspoons Worcestershire sauce | 1 cup diced potatoes |
| $1/4$ teaspoon chili powder | 1 10-ounce package frozen limas |
| 2 bay leaves | |

Combine meat, tomato juice, onion, seasonings, and 6 cups water in soup kettle. Cover and simmer 2 hours. Cut meat from bones in large cubes; strain broth and skim off excess fat. Add meat and vegetables; cover and simmer 1 hour. Serves 8.

## SPLIT PEA SOUP

| | |
|---|---|
| 1 pound ($2^1/4$ cups) green split peas | $1/2$ teaspoon pepper |
| 1 meaty ham bone ($1^1/2$ pounds) | $1/4$ teaspoon dried marjoram, crushed |
| $1^1/2$ cups sliced onion | 1 cup diced celery |
| 1 teaspoon salt | 1 cup diced carrots |

Rinse peas; combine with 2 quarts water, ham bone, onion, salt, pepper, and marjoram. Bring to boiling; cover, reduce heat, and simmer (don't boil) $1^1/2$ hours. Stir occasionally. Remove bone; cut off meat and dice. Return meat to soup; add celery and carrots. Cook slowly, uncovered, 30 to 40 minutes. Serves 6 to 8.

## LENTIL-VEGETABLE SOUP

| | |
|---|---|
| 2 cups lentils | 2 1/2 teaspoons salt |
| 2 slices bacon, diced | 1/4 teaspoon pepper |
| 1/2 cup chopped onion | 1/2 teaspoon dried |
| 1/2 cup chopped celery | oregano, crushed |
| 1/4 cup chopped carrots | 1 1-pound can (2 cups) |
| 3 tablespoons snipped | tomatoes |
| parsley | 2 tablespoons wine |
| 1 clove garlic, minced | vinegar |

Rinse lentils; drain and place in soup kettle. Add 8 cups water and remaining ingredients, except tomatoes and vinegar. Cover and simmer 1 1/2 hours. Add tomatoes (break up any large pieces) and vinegar. Simmer, covered, 30 minutes longer. Season to taste. Makes 8 to 10 servings.

## CHEESE CHOWDER

| | |
|---|---|
| 1/4 cup finely chopped onion | 1/4 cup finely diced carrot |
| 2 tablespoons butter or margarine | 1/4 cup finely diced celery |
| | Dash each salt and paprika |
| 1/4 cup all-purpose flour | 1/2 cup cubed sharp |
| 2 cups milk | process American |
| 1 13 3/4-ounce can (1 3/4 cups) chicken broth (not condensed) | cheese |

Cook onion in butter till tender. Blend in flour; add remaining ingredients except cheese. Cook and stir till thick and bubbly. Reduce heat; add cheese; stir to melt. Simmer 15 minutes. Serves 4.

## ONION-CHEESE SOUP

Cook 1 cup chopped onion (1 large) in 3 tablespoons butter till tender but not brown. Blend in 3 tablespoons all-purpose flour, 1/2 teaspoon salt, and dash pepper. Add 4 cups milk all at once. Heat and stir till boiling. Remove from heat. Add 2 cups shredded sharp process American cheese, stirring to melt cheese. Serves 4 to 6.

## NEW ENGLAND CLAM CHOWDER

| | |
|---|---|
| 2 dozen medium-size quahog clams | 1/2 cup chopped onion |
| | 2 cups milk |
| 1/4 pound salt pork, minced | 1 cup light cream |
| | 3 tablespoons all-purpose flour |
| 4 cups diced potatoes | |

Scrub clams. Cover with salt water (1/3 cup salt to 1 gallon water); let stand 15 minutes; rinse. Repeat twice. Remove clams and dice, reserving 1/2 cup liquor.* Fry pork till crisp; remove bits of pork; reserve. Add 1/2 cup liquor, 1 1/2 cups water, potatoes, and onion to fat. Cook, covered, 15 to 20 minutes. Add clams, 1 3/4 *cups* milk, and cream. Blend 1/4 cup milk and flour; stir into chowder. Heat to boil; stir occasionally. Add 1 1/2 teaspoons salt and dash pepper. Top with pork. Serves 10.

## MANHATTAN CLAM CHOWDER

| | |
|---|---|
| 2 dozen medium-size quahog clams | 2 cups diced potatoes |
| | 1 cup finely diced carrots |
| 3 slices bacon, finely diced | 1 1/2 teaspoons salt |
| 1 cup finely diced celery | 1/4 teaspoon dried thyme, crushed |
| 1 cup chopped onion | |
| 1 1-pound can tomatoes, cut up | |

Thoroughly wash clams. Cover with salt water (1/3 cup salt to 1 gallon water); let stand 15 minutes; rinse. Repeat twice. Place clams in large kettle; add 1 cup water. Cover and steam just till shells open, 5 to 10 minutes. Remove clams from shells; dice finely.* Strain liquor; reserve 1/2 cup.

Partially cook bacon. Add celery and onion; cook till tender. Add 3 cups water and clam liquor. Add remaining ingredients and dash pepper. Cover; simmer about 35 minutes. Blend 2 tablespoons all-purpose flour with 2 tablespoons cold water. Stir into chowder; cook and stir to boiling. Add clams; heat. Serves 6 to 8.

*If desired, substitute two 7½-ounce cans clams *or* 1 pint fresh shucked clams.

## OYSTER STEW

2 tablespoons all-purpose flour
1½ teaspoons salt
1 teaspoon Worcestershire sauce
Dash bottled hot pepper sauce

1 pint shucked oysters, *undrained*
¼ cup butter or margarine
1 quart milk, scalded

Blend flour, seasonings, and 2 tablespoons water in a 3-quart soup kettle. Add undrained oysters and butter. Simmer over very low heat 3 to 4 minutes till edges of oysters curl, stirring gently. Add hot milk; remove from heat and cover. Let stand 15 minutes. Reheat briefly. Top servings with pats of butter. Serves 4 or 5.

## CORN-POTATO CHOWDER

2 medium diced, pared potatoes
1 medium onion, thinly sliced and separated into rings
½ cup chopped celery
1 teaspoon salt

2 cups cooked or canned whole kernel corn
1½ cups milk
¼ teaspoon dried marjoram, crushed
5 slices bacon, crisp-cooked and crumbled

In saucepan, combine potatoes, onion, celery, salt, and ½ cup water. Cover; cook 15 minutes, or till tender. Stir in corn, milk, marjoram, and dash pepper. Heat. Serve topped with bacon. Serves 6.

## BEAN SOUP

Rinse 1 pound dry navy beans; add 2 quarts cold water. Bring to boiling; simmer 2 minutes. Remove from heat. Cover; let stand 1 hour. (Or, add beans to water; soak overnight.) *Do not drain.* Add 1 meaty ham bone, 1 bay leaf, ½ teaspoon salt, and 6 whole black peppercorns. Cover; simmer 3 to 3½ hours, adding 1 medium onion, sliced, the last half hour. Remove ham bone. Mash beans slightly, using potato masher. Cut ham off bone; add ham to soup. Season. Serves 6.

## CRAB BISQUE

| | |
|---|---|
| 1 10½-ounce can condensed cream of mushroom soup | 1½ soup cans milk |
| | 1 cup light cream |
| 1 10½-ounce can condensed cream of asparagus soup | 1 7½-ounce can (1 cup) crab meat, flaked and cartilage removed |
| | ¼ cup dry white wine |

Blend soups; stir in milk and cream. Heat just to boiling. Add crab; heat through. Stir in wine just before serving. Float butter atop. Serves 6 to 8.

## PACIFIC CHOWDER

| | |
|---|---|
| 4 slices bacon | 2 cups milk |
| ¼ cup chopped onion | Dash salt |
| 2 tablespoons chopped green pepper | 1 6½- or 7-ounce can tuna |
| 1 10½-ounce can condensed cream of potato soup | |

Cook bacon; drain, reserving drippings. Crumble and set aside. Cook onion and green pepper in 2 tablespoons of the bacon drippings just till tender. Add cream of potato soup, milk, and salt; heat to boiling. Drain tuna and break in chunks; stir into soup mixture with *half* the crumbled bacon. Heat through. Dash with paprika or ground mace, if desired. Garnish with remaining bacon. Makes 4 servings.

## SOUP GARNISHES

- **For clear soups:** Lemon slices, snipped parsley or chives, tiny meat balls or dumplings, avocado slices.
- **For cream soups:** Sour cream, slivered toasted almonds, croutons (see page 157), shredded cheese, snipped parsley or chives.
- **For chowders, meat soups:** Lemon slices on fish chow-

der, frankfurter slices on pea or bean soup; parsley, crisp-cooked bacon, corn chips, popcorn, or croutons.
• **For chilled soups:** Sour cream, lemon wedges, snipped parsley or chives.

## HOMEMADE CHICKEN SOUP

| | |
|---|---|
| 1 5- to 6-pound ready-to-cook stewing chicken, cut up | 6 medium ears corn* |
| | 1½ cups uncooked Homemade Noodles (pages 368-369) |
| 6 cups water | 1 cup chopped celery |
| ⅓ cup chopped onion | 2 tablespoons snipped parsley |
| 2 teaspoons salt | |
| ¼ teaspoon pepper | |
| 1 bay leaf | |

In large kettle, combine chicken, water, onion, salt, pepper, and bay leaf. Bring to boiling; simmer, covered, about 2 hours, or till chicken is tender. Meanwhile, with sharp knife, makes cuts *through center of corn kernels* in each row of the ears. Cut corn off cobs; scrape cobs. (Should equal 2 cups corn.) Remove chicken from broth; cool and remove meat from bones. Cut chicken into bite-size pieces; set aside. Skim excess fat from broth. Discard bay leaf. Bring broth to boiling. Add corn, Homemade Noodles, celery, and parsley. Simmer, covered, about 8 minutes, or till corn and noodles are barely done. Add chicken and heat through, about 5 minutes. Season with salt and pepper. Makes 8 servings.

*Note:* One 1-pound can cream-style corn may be substituted for fresh corn.

## JULIENNE VEGETABLE SOUP

| | |
|---|---|
| 6 cups beef broth | 1 small onion, cut in thin wedges |
| 2 carrots, cut in julienne strips | ½ teaspoon dried marjoram, crushed |
| 1 medium potato, pared and cut in julienne strips | ¼ teaspoon salt |
| 1 small turnip, pared and cut in julienne strips | |

In saucepan, bring broth, carrots, potato, turnip, onion, marjoram, and salt to boiling. Cover; simmer for 15 to 20 minutes, or till vegetables are tender. Top with seasoned croutons, if desired. Serves 8.

## FISH CHOWDER

| | |
|---|---|
| 1 pound fresh or frozen fish fillets | 3 slices bacon |
| 2 cups cubed, pared potatoes | 1/2 cup chopped onion |
| 2 teaspoons salt | 2 cups milk |
| 1/8 teaspoon pepper | 3 tablespoons all-purpose flour |

Thaw frozen fish. Cut fish into 2-inch pieces. Cook potatoes in 2 cups water for 5 minutes. Add fish, salt, and pepper. Simmer, covered, for 10 to 12 minutes. Cook bacon till crisp. Drain and crumble; reserve drippings. Cook onion in drippings. Add crumbled bacon and onion to fish mixture. Slowly blend milk into flour; add to chowder. Cook, stirring constantly, till mixture thickens. Makes 6 servings.

## MINESTRONE

| | |
|---|---|
| 1/2 pound (1 cup) dry navy beans | 2 teaspoons salt |
| 10 cups water | 1 teaspoon dried basil, crushed |
| 1 cup chopped carrots | 1/4 cup light cream |
| 2 cups finely shredded cabbage | 3 tablespoons grated Parmesan cheese |
| 1 8 1/2-ounce can peas, drained | 3 tablespoons butter |
| 1 8-ounce can cut green beans, drained | 3 tablespoons salad oil |
| 1 8-ounce can tomatoes | 2 tablespoons snipped parsley |
| 4 ounces fine noodles | 1 clove garlic, minced |

Rinse beans; add the 10 cups water. Bring to boiling; simmer 2 minutes. Remove from heat. Cover and let stand 1 hour. (Or, add beans to water; soak overnight.) *Do not drain.* Add carrots; simmer, covered, for 2 1/2 to 3 hours. Add cabbage, peas, green beans, tomatoes, noodles, salt, and basil. Simmer for 20 to 25 minutes, or till noodles are done. Blend in cream, cheese, butter, oil, parsley, and garlic. Serves 10.

## CREOLE GUMBO

3 tablespoons butter
3 tablespoons all-purpose flour
1/2 cup chopped onion
1 clove garlic, minced
1 1-pound can tomatoes, cut up
1/2 cup chopped green pepper
2 bay leaves
1 teaspoon dried oregano, crushed
1 teaspoon dried thyme, crushed
1/2 teaspoon salt
1/4 teaspoon bottled hot pepper sauce
2 4 1/2-ounce cans shrimp, drained and cut up
1 7 1/2-ounce can crab meat, drained and cartilage removed
1 tablespoon filé powder
Hot cooked rice

In large saucepan, melt butter; blend in flour. Cook and stir 7 to 8 minutes, or till golden brown. Stir in onion and garlic; cook till onion is tender. Stir in undrained tomatoes, green pepper, bay leaves, oregano, thyme, salt, pepper sauce, and 1 1/2 cups water. Bring to boiling. Simmer, covered, about 20 minutes. Remove bay leaves. Stir in shrimp and crab; heat through. Remove from heat. Blend a moderate amount hot liquid into filé powder. Return to saucepan; stir till combined. Serve over rice in soup bowls. Pass additional hot pepper sauce, if desired. Serves 5 or 6.

## CORNED BEEF CHOWDER

3 cups milk
1 10 1/2-ounce can condensed cream of potato soup
1 10-ounce package frozen Brussels sprouts, thawed
1 12-ounce can corned beef, broken into pieces

In large saucepan, blend 1 1/3 *cups* of the milk, soup, and dash pepper. Cut up Brussels sprouts; stir into soup. Bring to boiling; stir occasionally. Reduce heat; simmer about

15 minutes, or till Brussels sprouts are tender. Add remaining milk and beef. Heat through. Serves 4 or 5.

## FRESH CORN CHOWDER

| | |
|---|---|
| 6 medium ears corn | ¼ teaspoon white pepper |
| ¼ cup chopped onion | 3 tablespoons all- |
| ½ teaspoon salt | purpose flour |
| 4 cups milk | 1 beaten egg |
| 2 tablespoons butter | |

With sharp knife, make cuts *through center* of kernels. Cut corn off cobs; scrape cobs. In saucepan, combine corn, onion, salt, and ⅓ cup water. Bring to boiling. Simmer, covered, about 15 minutes, or till corn is barely done; stir occasionally. Stir in *3½ cups* of the milk, butter, pepper, and 1 teaspoon salt. Blend remaining ½ cup milk into flour; stir into corn mixture. Cook and stir till thickened and bubbly. Gradually stir a moderate amount of hot mixture into egg; return to hot mixture in saucepan. Cook and stir over low heat for 2 minutes. Garnish with snipped chives and paprika, if desired. Makes 6 servings.

## SAVORY TOMATO SOUP

| | |
|---|---|
| 1 pound beef stew meat, cut in 1-inch cubes | ½ teaspoon dried marjoram, crushed |
| 1 small beef soup bone | ½ teaspoon dried basil, crushed |
| 2 tablespoons shortening | |
| 1 1-pound 12-ounce can tomatoes, cut up *or* 2½ pounds fresh tomatoes, peeled and cubed | ¼ teaspoon dried savory, crushed |
| | ¼ teaspoon dried thyme, crushed |
| 1 cup sliced carrots | ⅛ teaspoon ground mace |
| 1 cup chopped celery | ⅛ teaspoon bottled hot pepper sauce |
| ¼ cup snipped celery leaves | |

In 4½-quart Dutch oven, brown meat and soup bone in hot shortening. Stir in undrained tomatoes, carrots, celery, celery leaves, seasonings, and 1 tablespoon salt. Add 4 cups water. Cover; simmer 4 to 5 hours. Skim off fat. Remove bone. Serves 8.

## CHICKEN SOUPS

*Use broth from Stewed Chicken, canned chicken broth, or chicken bouillon cubes—*

• **Chicken-noodle Soup:** Cook 1 cup noodles in 3 cups chicken broth till noodles are tender. Makes 4 servings.
• **Chicken-rice Soup:** Cook ½ cup rice in 3 cups chicken broth till rice is tender. Makes 4 servings.
• **Tomato-rice Soup:** Cook ½ cup rice and ¼ cup diced celery in 4 cups chicken broth till rice is tender. Add one 10¾-ounce can condensed tomato soup, 1 dried whole red chili, and salt to taste. Heat through. Remove chili. Serves 6.

## CANNED SOUP COMBOS

• **Tomato-chili Stew:** Mix one 11½-ounce can condensed bean with bacon soup, one 10¾-ounce can condensed tomato soup, one 10½-ounce can chili concarne without beans, and 1 can water. Simmer 10 minutes. Serves 5 or 6.
• **Chicken-curry Soup:** Mix one 10½-ounce can condensed cream of chicken soup, 1¼ cups milk, and ½ teaspoon curry powder; chill. Add 2 tablespoons snipped parsley. Serves 3 or 4.
• **Chicken-mushroom Soup:** Combine one 10½-ounce can condensed cream of mushroom soup and one 10½-ounce can condensed cream of chicken soup. Add 1 can water; heat to boiling. Serves 4 or 5.
• **Creole Clam Bisque:** Combine one 10¾-ounce can condensed clam chowder (Manhattan style), one 10½-ounce can condensed chicken gumbo, and 1 can light cream. Heat. Makes 4 or 5 servings.
• **Pea Soup Royale:** Combine one 11¼-ounce can condensed green pea soup, one 10½-ounce can condensed consomme, and ½ soup can milk; heat to boiling. Serves 4.

## SOUP ACCOMPANIMENTS

• **For clear soups:** Crisp crackers, cheese pastry, cheese-spread toast strips.
• **For cream soups:** Seeded crackers, pretzels, cheese popcorn, pickles, olives.

• **For chowders and meat soups:** Oyster crackers, Melba toast, sour pickles, toasted garlic bread, breadsticks, relishes.

## JELLIED CONSOMME

Chill canned condensed consomme in refrigerator 3 hours (or 1 hour in freezer). Spoon into chilled sherbets. Garnish with lemon and parsley. *Or,* serve in half a honeydew melon with lime slices.

## FRENCH VICHYSSOISE

| | |
|---|---|
| 4 leeks (white part), thinly sliced (2½ cups) | 5 medium potatoes, thinly sliced (about 4 cups) |
| 1 medium onion, thinly sliced | 4 cups chicken broth |
| ¼ cup butter or margarine | 2 teaspoons salt |
| | 2 cups milk |
| | 2 cups light cream |
| | 1 cup whipping cream |
| | Snipped chives |

Cook leeks and onion in butter till tender but not brown; add potatoes, broth, and salt. Cook, covered, 35 to 40 minutes.

Rub through fine sieve; return to heat; add milk and light cream. Season to taste. Bring to boiling. Cool; rub through very fine sieve. When cold, add whipping cream. Chill before serving. Garnish with snipped chives. Makes 10 servings.

## QUICK VICHYSSOISE

| | |
|---|---|
| 1½ cups water | 1 4-ounce package whipped cream cheese with onion |
| 2 tablespoons snipped parsley | Snipped chives |
| 2 chicken bouillon cubes | |
| 1 cup light cream | |
| Packaged instant mashed potatoes (enough for 4 servings) | |

Combine water, parsley, and bouillon in saucepan. Cover and bring to boiling, stirring till bouillon cubes dissolve. Remove from heat; add cream; stir in potatoes. Cool at room temperature 15 minutes. Transfer mixture to blender container. Add cream cheese; blend till smooth; chill well. Serve in chilled bowls or cups. Garnish with chives. Serves 4 to 6.

## CUCUMBER SOUP

2 medium cucumbers
1 quart buttermilk
1 tablespoon snipped green onion
1 teaspoon salt
1/4 cup snipped parsley

Pare cucumbers, remove seeds, and grate to make 1 to 1 1/2 cups. Add remaining ingredients; mix well. Cover and chill about 4 hours. Mix again just before serving. Trim with parsley sprigs. Serves 8 to 10.

## GAZPACHO

1 10 1/2-ounce can condensed beef broth
2 1/2 cups tomato juice
3 tablespoons lemon juice
2 tablespoons chopped onion
1 clove garlic, sliced lengthwise
1/4 teaspoon bottled hot pepper sauce
1/2 teaspoon salt
Dash freshly ground pepper
1 cup finely chopped green pepper
1 cup finely chopped cucumber
1 cup finely chopped tomato

In jar, combine first 8 ingredients (spear garlic on wooden pick). Cover; shake well. Chill 4 hours. Remove garlic. Place mixture in freezer about 1 hour, but *do not freeze*. Meanwhile, chill green pepper, cucumber, and tomato. Divide chilled vegetables among soup dishes. Pour soup over. Makes 8 to 10 servings.

## SPARKLING BORSCH

1 1-pound can (2 cups) beets

2 10½-ounce cans condensed consomme

2 tablespoons lemon juice

Dairy sour cream

Drain beets, reserving liquid. Finely chop enough beets to make ⅔ cup. Combine beets, beet liquid, consomme, and lemon juice; chill. Stir just before serving; serve in chilled cups or bowls. Top with sour cream and snipped parsley. Serves 6.

## BLENDER BROCCOLI SOUP

1 10-ounce package frozen chopped broccoli

1½ cups milk

1 cup light cream

1 teaspoon instant minced onion

2 beef bouillon cubes

¼ teaspoon salt

Dash pepper

Dash ground nutmeg

Dairy sour cream

Snipped parsley or chives

Partially thaw broccoli; break in small chunks. Place in blender container with ½ cup of the milk. Blend till broccoli is very fine. Add remaining milk, cream, instant minced onion, bouillon cubes, salt, pepper, and nutmeg. Blend till smooth, 45 to 60 seconds. Chill thoroughly. Serve topped with dollops of dairy sour cream and snipped parsley or chives. Serves 4 or 5.

## CHILLED ASPARAGUS SOUP

1 8-ounce package frozen cut asparagus

1 thin slice onion

½ cup boiling water

1 cup milk

½ cup light cream

½ teaspoon salt

Dash pepper

Cook frozen asparagus and onion slice in the ½ cup boiling water according to package directions; *do not drain.* Cool slightly. In blender container, combine undrained asparagus and onion, milk, light cream, salt, and pepper. Cover and blend till mixture is smooth, 15 to 20 seconds. Chill for 3 to 4 hours. Stir before serving. Makes 4 to 6 servings.

# TOMATO SOUPSHAKE

Combine one $10^3/_4$-ounce can condensed tomato soup, 1 cup light cream, $1/_2$ teaspoon ground nutmeg, $1/_4$ teaspoon salt, and 1 egg (optional) in blender container or shaker. Blend or shake till smooth. Chill. (Add a little milk to thin, if desired.) Serve in chilled cups or mugs. Sprinkle with ground nutmeg. Makes 4 or 5 servings.

# SAUCES

## SAUCE PROVENCALE

4 tomatoes, peeled, cut
in 6 wedges each, and
seeded
1/2 teaspoon sugar
2 tablespoons butter
1/4 cup chopped green
onion

1/2 cup dry white wine
1/2 cup butter
3 cloves garlic, minced
2 tablespoons snipped
parsley

Sprinkle tomatoes with sugar; set aside. Melt 2 tablespoons butter. Add onion and heat through. Add wine;
cook and stir till liquid is slightly reduced. Add tomatoes;
heat through. Add remaining ingredients. Heat, stirring
gently, just till butter melts. Season to taste. Makes 2 1/2
cups.

## CLASSIC HOLLANDAISE

4 egg yolks
1/2 cup butter, cut in
thirds

2 to 3 teaspoons lemon
juice

Place egg yolks and 1/3 of the butter in top of double
boiler. Cook over boiling water till butter melts, stirring
rapidly. (Water in bottom of double boiler should not
touch top pan.) Add 1/3 more of the butter and continue
stirring. As mixture thickens and butter melts, add remaining butter, stirring constantly.

When butter is melted, remove pan from water; stir
rapidly 2 minutes longer. Stir in lemon juice, 1 teaspoon
at a time; season with dash salt and dash white pepper.
Heat again over boiling water, stirring constantly, till
thickened, 2 to 3 minutes. Remove from heat at once. If
sauce curdles, immediately beat in 1 or 2 tablespoons
boiling water. Makes 1 cup.

## SAUCE MOUSSELINE

Fold 1/2 cup whipping cream, whipped, into 1 cup cooled Classic Hollandaise. Spoon over hot fish fillets. Broil 2 inches from heat a few seconds, or till light brown and bubbly. Serve immediately.

## JIFFY HOLLANDAISE

Combine 1/4 cup dairy sour cream, 1/4 cup mayonnaise, 1/2 teaspoon prepared mustard, and 1 teaspoon lemon juice. Cook and stir over low heat till heated through. Makes 1/2 cup sauce.

## BLENDER HOLLANDAISE

3 egg yolks
2 tablespoons lemon juice

Dash cayenne
1/2 cup butter or margarine

Place egg yolks, lemon juice, and cayenne in blender container. Cover; quickly turn blender on and off. Heat butter till melted and almost boiling. Turn blender on high speed; slowly pour in butter, blending till thick and fluffy, about 30 seconds. Heat over warm, not hot, water till ready to serve. Makes 1 cup sauce.

## BEARNAISE SAUCE

In small saucepan, combine 3 tablespoons wine vinegar, 1 teaspoon finely chopped shallots or green onion, 4 peppercorns, crushed, and a Bouquet Garni of a few tarragon and chervil leaves; simmer till liquid is reduced to half. Strain; add 1 tablespoon cold water to herb liquid.

Beat 4 egg yolks in top of double boiler (not over the water). Slowly add herb liquid. Have 1/2 cup butter at room temperature. Add a few tablespoons butter to egg yolks; place over, not touching, boiling water. Cook and stir till butter melts and sauce starts to thicken. Continue adding butter and stirring till all has been used and sauce is smooth as thick cream. Remove from heat. Salt to taste and add 1 teaspoon minced fresh tarragon or 1/4 teaspoon dried tarragon, crushed. Makes 1 cup.

## MUSHROOM SAUCES

• **Wine-mushroom Sauce:** Cook 1 cup sliced fresh mushrooms and 1/4 cup finely chopped green onion in 1/4 cup butter just till tender. Blend in 4 teaspoons cornstarch. Add 3/4 cup Burgundy, 3/4 cup water, 2 tablespoons snipped parsley, 3/4 teaspoon salt, and dash pepper. Cook and stir till bubbly. Serve with steak. Makes 1 1/2 cups.

• **Creamy Mushroom Topper:** Cook 1/4 cup chopped onion in 2 tablespoons butter till just tender. Stir in 1 tablespoon all-purpose flour. Add 1/2 cup light cream, one 3-ounce can sliced mushrooms, drained, 1/2 teaspoon salt, and 1/4 teaspoon pepper. Heat to boiling, stirring constantly. Stir in 1/2 cup dairy sour cream; heat through. Serve with chicken. Makes 1 1/2 cups.

• **Quick Mushroom Sauce:** Stir 1 cup dairy sour cream into one 10 1/2-ounce can condensed cream of mushroom soup; heat.

## CREOLE SAUCE

Cook 1/4 cup finely chopped onion and 3 tablespoons finely chopped green pepper in 1 tablespoon butter till tender. Add one 8-ounce can tomato sauce, one 3-ounce can chopped mushrooms, drained, 1/4 cup water, dash pepper, and dash garlic salt. Cover and simmer 15 minutes. Serve with fish. Makes 1 1/2 cups.

## FLAVORED BUTTERS

• **Lemon Butter:** Melt 1/4 cup butter. Add 1 tablespoon lemon juice, 1 tablespoon snipped parsley, and dash pepper. Serve with cooked asparagus, artichokes, broccoli, or fish. Makes 1/3 cup.

• **Caper Butter:** Place 1/2 cup softened butter or margarine and 3 tablespoons capers *with liquid* in small mixing bowl. Beat till light and fluffy. Serve with fish.

• **Parsley Butter:** Cream 1/2 cup softened butter. Blend in 1 tablespoon snipped parsley, 1 teaspoon lemon juice, 1/8 teaspoon savory, 1/8 teaspoon salt, and dash pepper. Serve on potatoes. Makes 1/2 cup.

• **Garlic Butter:** Combine 1/4 cup softened butter and 1 or 2 cloves garlic, minced. Spread on French bread slices before heating, or melt atop broiled steaks.

## SAUCE MOOREA

3 tablespoons tarragon vinegar
1 teaspoon finely chopped onion
15 peppercorns, crushed
3 beaten egg yolks
$^1/_2$ cup butter, melted

2 tablespoons tomato puree
1 tablespoon lemon juice
$^1/_4$ teaspoon dried tarragon, crushed
Dash salt
Dash cayenne

Combine vinegar, onion, and peppercorns in a saucepan. Boil gently till most of the vinegar has boiled away. Cool; stir in 1 tablespoon water and strain. Place egg yolks in top of double boiler; add vinegar mixture. Place over, *not touching*, boiling water. Cook and stir till thick and creamy. Remove from water; stir till slightly cooled. Gradually stir in melted butter; blend in tomato puree, lemon juice, tarragon, salt, and cayenne. Makes 1 cup.

## CAPER MAYONNAISE

Combine 1 cup mayonnaise, $^1/_4$ cup drained capers, coarsely chopped, 3 tablespoons chopped onion, and 2 tablespoons chopped toasted almonds. Serve warm or chilled over fish or cooked vegetables.

## BROWN SAUCE

$1^1/_2$ tablespoons butter
$1^1/_2$ tablespoons all-purpose flour

2 cups Brown Stock (p. 623) *or* 1 $10^1/_2$-ounce can condensed beef broth plus water to make 2 cups

Melt butter; blend in flour. Cook and stir over low heat till browned. Stir in stock. Bring to boiling and cook 3 to 5 minutes. Reduce heat and simmer 30 minutes, stirring occasionally. Makes about $1^1/_3$ cups.

**Sauce Diable:** Combine $^1/_4$ cup snipped green onion, 3 tablespoons dry white wine, and 8 to 10 peppercorns, crushed. Reduce mixture to $^1/_2$ its volume by boiling. Add $^1/_2$ cup Brown Sauce and $^1/_2$ teaspoon *each* Worcestershire sauce and snipped parsley. Heat through. Serve with broiled chicken or steak. Makes about $^2/_3$ cup.

**Gourmet Sauce:** Reduce 2 cups Brown Sauce to ½ its volume by boiling. Add ⅓ cup dry white wine. Bring just to boiling. Serve hot with roast beef or veal, baked ham, or chicken. Makes 1⅓ cups.

## BORDELAISE SAUCE

| | |
|---|---|
| ½ cup fresh mushrooms, chopped | 2 teaspoons dried tarragon, crushed |
| 1 tablespoon butter | 2 tablespoons lemon juice |
| 3 tablespoons cornstarch | |
| 2 cups beef stock | 3 tablespoons red wine |

Cook mushrooms in butter till tender. Mix cornstarch and cool stock. Stir into mushrooms. Cook and stir to boiling. Add remaining ingredients and dash pepper; simmer 5 to 10 minutes. Makes 2¼ cups.

## MINT SAUCES FOR LAMB

• Combine ½ cup vinegar, ¼ cup each sugar and water, and dash salt. Bring to boiling; reduce heat and simmer, uncovered, 5 minutes. Pour over ½ cup finely snipped mint leaves; steep 30 minutes. Strain; serve hot or cold. Makes ½ cup.
• Heat ½ cup mint jelly slowly till melted, stirring occasionally.

## MUSTARD SAUCES

• Add 1½ to 2 tablespoons prepared mustard to 1 cup hot Medium White Sauce (page 645).
• Combine 2 beaten egg yolks, 1 tablespoon sugar, 3 tablespoons prepared mustard, 2 tablespoons vinegar, 1 tablespoon water, 1 tablespoon butter, 1 tablespoon prepared horseradish, and ½ teaspoon salt in top of double boiler; mix well. Place over, *not touching*, boiling water; cook and stir till thickened, about 2 minutes. Remove from heat. Stir vigorously, if necessary, till sauce is smooth. Cool. Fold in ½ cup whipping cream, whipped; refrigerate. To serve with warm ham, let set at room temperature ½ hour. Makes 1 cup.
• Combine ¼ cup milk and 3 tablespoons *dry* onion

soup mix; let stand 5 minutes. Stir in 1 cup dairy sour cream and 2 tablespoons prepared mustard. Heat, stirring occasionally. Makes 1¼ cups.

## HORSERADISH SAUCES

• Fold 3 tablespoons drained prepared horseradish into ½ cup whipping cream, whipped. Add ½ teaspoon salt.
• Combine 1 cup dairy sour cream, 3 tablespoons drained prepared horseradish, ¼ teaspoon salt, and dash paprika. Chill.
• Whip one 8-ounce package softened cream cheese and 2 to 3 tablespoons prepared horseradish till fluffy. Chill.
• Melt 3 tablespoons butter; blend in 1 teaspoon all-purpose flour. Add ¼ cup vinegar, ¼ cup beef broth, ¼ cup prepared horseradish mustard, and 3 tablespoons brown sugar. Cook slowly, stirring constantly, till thick. Gradually add a little hot mixture to 1 slightly beaten egg yolk. Return to hot mixture. Bring sauce to boiling, stirring constantly. Serve hot with corned beef or ham. Makes 1 cup.

## SAUTERNE SAUCE

In saucepan, combine ¼ cup sauterne and 1 tablespoon instant minced onion; let stand 10 minutes. Add ¾ cup mayonnaise or salad dressing, 2 tablespoons snipped parsley, and 1 tablespoon lemon juice. Heat, stirring constantly, over low heat. Makes 1 cup sauce.

## WHITE SAUCE

Medium: (Makes 1 cup)
  2 tablespoons butter or margarine
  2 tablespoons all-purpose flour
  ¼ teaspoon salt
  1 cup milk
Thick: (Makes 1 cup)
  3 tablespoons butter or margarine

  4 tablespoons all-purpose flour
  ¼ teaspoon salt
  1 cup milk
Thin: (Makes 1 cup)
  1 tablespoon butter or margarine
  1 tablespoon all-purpose flour
  ¼ teaspoon salt
  1 cup milk

Follow picture directions on page 646.

To prepare White Sauce: Melt butter in saucepan over low heat. Blend in flour, salt, and dash white pepper.

Make *Medium* White Sauce for sauces, scalloped and creamed dishes.

Add milk all at once. Cook quickly, stirring constantly, till mixture thickens and bubbles. Remove sauce from heat when it bubbles. Add cheeses or other flavorings at this point, stirring till smooth.

Prepare *Thin* White Sauce for soups and creamed vegetables. Make *Thick* White Sauce for croquettes and souffles.

If sauce cooks too long, it becomes too thick and butter separates out. To repair, stir in a little more milk. Cook quickly, stirring constantly, till sauce bubbles. A wooden spoon or rubber spatula is handy for preparing sauces. Use a heavy saucepan.

## CHEESE SAUCES

• To 1 cup hot Medium White Sauce, add 1 cup shredded sharp natural Cheddar cheese. Stir to melt. Makes 1½ cups sauce.
• Prepare Medium White Sauce *using* 1¼ *cups* milk. Add ½ cup shredded Cheddar cheese and ½ cup shredded Swiss cheese; stir to melt. Makes 1½ cups.
• Prepare Medium White Sauce using 1 chicken bouillon cube instead of salt. Stir in ¼ cup dairy sour cream and ¼ cup crumbled blue cheese. Heat through, *but do not boil.* Makes 1¼ cups.
• Combine one 10½-ounce can condensed cream of mushroom soup and ⅓ cup milk; heat. Add 1 cup shredded sharp process American cheese; stir to melt.

## RAVIGOTE SAUCE

Cook ¼ cup snipped green onion in 1 tablespoon butter till tender. Add 3 tablespoons dry white wine and 1 tablespoon vinegar. Simmer, reducing liquid by half. Melt 1 tablespoon butter; blend in 1 tablespoon all-purpose flour. Add 1 cup light cream. Cook and stir till mixture bubbles. Remove from heat; stir in ¼ teaspoon *each* salt and dried tarragon, crushed. Return to low heat; *gradually* stir in onion mixture. Do not boil. Makes 1 cup.

## TARTARE SAUCE

Combine 1 cup mayonnaise, 3 tablespoons finely chopped dill pickle, 1 tablespoon snipped parsley, 2 teaspoons chopped canned pimiento, and 1 teaspoon grated onion. Chill thoroughly. Makes 1 cup sauce.

## CUCUMBER SAUCE

Cut 1 medium unpared cucumber in half lengthwise; scoop out seeds. Shred enough cucumber to make 1 cup; do not drain. Combine with ½ cup dairy sour cream, ¼ cup mayonnaise, 1 tablespoon snipped parsley, 2 teaspoons grated onion, 2 teaspoons vinegar, ¼ teaspoon salt, and dash pepper; blend. Chill. Serve with fish. Makes 1½ cups.

## SHRIMP SAUCE

Cook ¼ cup chopped green pepper and ¼ cup finely chopped onion in 2 tablespoons butter till tender. Stir in one 10½-ounce can condensed cream of mushroom soup, ½ cup milk, and few drops yellow food coloring. Heat and stir to boiling. Add two 4½- or 5-ounce cans shrimp, drained and split lengthwise. Heat through.

## PLUM SAUCE

In small saucepan, mix one 12-ounce jar plum preserves, 2 tablespoons vinegar, 1 tablespoon brown sugar, 1 tablespoon finely chopped onion, 1 teaspoon crushed red pepper, ½ teaspoon ground ginger, and 1 clove garlic, minced. Bring to boil; stir constantly. Remove from heat; cool slightly. Chill in covered container overnight to blend seasonings. Makes 1¼ cups.

## CUMBERLAND SAUCE

Combine ½ teaspoon shredded orange peel, ¾ cup orange juice, ½ cup currant jelly, 2 tablespoons claret, and ¼ teaspoon ground ginger in a saucepan. Heat till jelly melts, stirring occasionally. Blend 4 teaspoons cornstarch and 1 tablespoon lemon juice till smooth; stir into jelly mixture. Cook and stir till mixture is thick and bubbly; cook 1 to 2 minutes longer. Serve hot or cold with ham. Makes 1½ cups.

## SWEET-SOUR SAUCE

In saucepan, mix 1 cup sugar, ½ cup each white vinegar and water, 1 tablespoon each chopped green pepper and chopped canned pimiento, and ½ teaspoon salt. Simmer 5 minutes. Combine 2 teaspoons cornstarch and 1 tablespoon cold water; add to hot mixture. Cook and stir till sauce thickens and bubbles. Cool. Add 1 teaspoon paprika. Serve with shrimp. Makes about 1½ cups.

## SPICY CHERRY SAUCE

$3/4$ cup sugar
    Dash salt
2 tablespoons cornstarch
$3/4$ cup orange juice
1 tablespoon lemon
    juice

1 1-pound can (2 cups)
    pitted tart red cherries
    (water pack)
1 inch stick cinnamon
$1/2$ teaspoon whole cloves
$1/4$ teaspoon red food
    coloring

Combine sugar, salt, and cornstarch. Stir in orange and lemon juice. Add undrained cherries, spices, and food coloring. Cook, stirring constantly, over medium heat till mixture thickens and comes to boiling. Boil 2 minutes. Before serving, remove cinnamon and cloves. Serve warm with ham. Makes 3 cups sauce.

## RAISIN SAUCE

Combine $1/3$ cup raisins, $1/2$ cup water, $1/3$ cup currant jelly, $1/2$ teaspoon grated orange peel, and $1/2$ cup orange juice in saucepan; bring to boil. Combine 2 tablespoons brown sugar, 1 tablespoon cornstarch, dash each ground allspice and salt; stir into orange mixture. Cook and stir till thick and bubbly. Serve warm with cooked ham. Makes about $1\frac{1}{2}$ cups.

## TANGY CRANBERRY SAUCE

Mix one 1-pound can jellied cranberry sauce, $1/3$ cup bottled steak sauce, 1 tablespoon each brown sugar and salad oil, and 2 teaspoons prepared mustard. Beat with electric or rotary beater. Serve warm or as is with ham or pork. Makes 2 cups.

## APPLESAUCE

**Chunky:** Pare, core, and slice 4 medium apples. Combine 1 cup water, $1/4$ cup sugar, and dash mace; bring to boil. Add apples; cover and simmer 8 minutes, or till tender.

**Smooth:** Pare, quarter, and core 4 medium apples. Combine apples, $1/4$ to $1/2$ cup water, and 2 inches stick cinnamon. Cover and simmer 10 minutes, or till very

tender. Remove cinnamon. Mash apples till smooth. Stir in
1/4 cup sugar. (For larger quantity, don't pare apples; put
cooked sauce through food mill or sieve.)

## RHUBARB SAUCE

    3 cups rhubarb cut in          1/2 to 3/4 cup sugar
      1-inch pieces                1/4 cup water

Bring rhubarb, sugar, and water to boiling; reduce heat.
Cover and cook slowly about 5 minutes, or till tender.
Makes 2 cups.

## CRANBERRY SAUCE

Combine 2 cups sugar and 2 cups water in large saucepan;
stir to dissolve sugar. Heat to boiling; boil 5 minutes. Add
1 pound (4 cups) fresh cranberries; cook about 5 minutes,
or till skins pop. Remove from heat. Serve warm or chilled.
(To mold, cook 10 minutes longer, or till a drop jells on
cold plate. Pour into 4-cup mold. Chill firm.) Makes 4
cups.

## SPRING FRUIT SAUCE

    2 tablespoons sugar            1 tablespoon lemon
    1 tablespoon cornstarch          juice
  1/4 cup light corn syrup         1 cup sliced banana
    1 16-ounce package             Ice cream
      frozen sliced
      strawberries, thawed

In saucepan, combine sugar and cornstarch; stir in light
corn syrup. Add thawed strawberries. Cook, stirring constantly, till slightly thickened. Stir in lemon juice; cool.
Just before serving, stir in banana. Serve over ice cream.
Makes 2 1/2 cups.

## GINGER SUNDAE SAUCE

In small saucepan, mix 1/3 cup light corn syrup, 1/4 cup
*finely* chopped candied ginger, dash salt, and 1/4 cup light
cream. Simmer 5 minutes. Gradually stir in 1/4 cup light
cream. Heat through, but *do not boil*. Remove from heat;

stir in $1/4$ cup butter and $1/2$ teaspoon vanilla. Serve warm over vanilla ice cream. Makes $3/4$ cup.

## BLUEBERRY SAUCE

In saucepan, combine 1 cup sugar, 2 tablespoons cornstarch, $1/4$ teaspoon nutmeg, and dash salt; gradually stir in 1 cup boiling water. Cook and stir till mixture thickens and boils; cook 2 minutes more. Add 2 cups fresh blueberries*; return to boiling. Remove from heat; stir in 3 tablespoons lemon juice; cool. Makes 3 cups.

*Or, use one 10-ounce package frozen unsweetened blueberries, thawed and drained. Increase cornstarch to 3 tablespoons. Stir in blueberries with lemon juice. Do not heat after adding berries.

## MINCEMEAT SUNDAE SAUCE

In saucepan, combine $1/2$ cup sugar, $1/2$ cup orange juice, $1/2$ cup diced pared apple, 1 cup prepared mincemeat, $1/4$ cup chopped walnuts, and $1/4$ cup chopped maraschino cherries. Bring to boil; simmer, uncovered, 10 minutes. Serve warm over ice cream. Makes $1 3/4$ cups sauce.

## QUICK JUBILEE SAUCE

In small bowl, thoroughly combine one 16-ounce jar ($1 1/3$ cups) dark cherry preserves with $1/4$ cup port wine and $1/4$ teaspoon almond extract; chill. Serve over vanilla ice cream. Makes $1 2/3$ cups sauce.

## CUSTARD SAUCE

In heavy saucepan, mix 4 beaten egg yolks, dash salt, and $1/4$ cup sugar. Gradually stir in 2 cups milk, scalded and slightly cooled. Cook over low heat, stirring constantly, till mixture coats metal spoon.

Remove from heat; cool pan at once in cold water; stir a minute or two. Add 1 teaspoon vanilla. Chill. Makes 2 cups.

## REGAL CHOCOLATE SAUCE

1 cup sugar
1 cup water
1/2 cup light corn syrup

3 1-ounce squares
   unsweetened
   chocolate, broken up
1 teaspoon vanilla
1/2 cup evaporated milk

Combine sugar, water, and corn syrup; cook to soft ball stage (236°). Remove from heat. Add chocolate; stir till melted. Add vanilla. Slowly add evaporated milk; mix thoroughly. Cool. Makes 1³/₄ cups.

## HARD SAUCE

Thoroughly cream 1/2 cup butter with 2 cups sifted confectioners' sugar. Add 1 teaspoon vanilla. Spread in 8x8x2-inch pan; chill to harden. Cut in squares.

**Fluffy Hard Sauce:** Stir 1 beaten egg yolk into creamed mixture above. Then, fold in 1 stiffly beaten egg white. Chill.

## BRANDY HARD SAUCE

Place 2 tablespoons brandy *or* rum and 1/3 cup very soft butter in blender container; blend to combine. Add 1 cup sifted confectioners' sugar; blend till smooth. Spoon mixture into mold or small bowl. Chill. At serving time, unmold and sprinkle surface lightly with ground nutmeg.

## TANGY BUTTER SAUCE

Cream 1/2 cup butter or margarine; gradually add 1 cup sifted confectioners' sugar, creaming till light and fluffy. Stir 1 cup cold water into 1 tablespoon cornstarch; cook and stir till thick and bubbly; stir into creamed mixture. Add 1 teaspoon lemon juice and 1¹/₂ teaspoons vanilla. Serve warm over plum pudding or cake. Makes 1²/₃ cups sauce.

## FOAMY SAUCE

Beat together 3 egg yolks, ³/₄ cup sifted confectioners' sugar, 1/2 teaspoon vanilla, rum flavoring to taste (optional), and dash salt. Fold in 1 cup whipping cream, whipped. Chill. Stir. Makes 3 cups.

## BUTTERSCOTCH SAUCE

In heavy saucepan, mix 1 slightly beaten egg yolk, ¼ cup butter, ¼ cup water, ⅔ cup brown sugar, and ⅓ cup light corn syrup. Cook and stir over low heat till thick. Stir before using. Makes 1 cup.

## PINEAPPLE FLUFF

| | |
|---|---|
| ¼ cup sugar | ¾ cup pineapple juice |
| 1 tablespoon all-purpose flour | ½ cup orange juice |
| 1 slightly beaten egg | 1 cup whipping cream |
| | 2 tablespoons sugar |

Mix ¼ cup sugar and flour. Combine egg and 3 tablespoons cold water; add to sugar-flour mixture. Heat juices; slowly stir small amount into egg mixture; return to hot mixture. Cook over low heat till thick. Chill. Whip cream with 2 tablespoons sugar. Fold into juice mixture. Makes 3 cups.

## DAFFODIL LEMON SAUCE

Mix ½ cup sugar, 4 teaspoons cornstarch, dash salt, and dash nutmeg. Gradually stir in 1 cup water. Cook and stir over low heat till thick and bubbly. Stir a little hot mixture into 2 beaten egg yolks; return to hot mixture. Cook and stir 1 minute. Remove from heat; add 2 tablespoons butter, ½ teaspoon grated lemon peel, and 2 tablespoons lemon juice; blend.

## CHERRY SAUCE

Combine ¾ cup sugar, 2 tablespoons cornstarch, and dash salt. Stir in one 1-pound 4-ounce can pitted tart red cherries with juice. Cook quickly, stirring constantly, till thick and bubbly. Reduce heat; cook 1 minute. Add 10 drops red food coloring. Serve warm. Makes 2¾ cups.

## CRIMSON RASPBERRY SAUCE

Thaw and crush one 10-ounce package frozen raspberries. Combine with 1 tablespoon cornstarch. Add $1/2$ cup currant jelly. Cook and stir till bubbly; cook 1 minute. Strain; cool. Makes $1\frac{1}{4}$ cups.

# 15

# VEGETABLES

• **Cooking fresh vegetables:** Add fresh vegetables (prepared according to chart, pages 662–669) to small amount boiling, salted water. Bring water back to boil and begin timing. Cook at gentle boil till tender for time indicated in the chart. (After adding green vegetables to boiling water, don't cover till water returns to boil; cover for remainder of cooking time.)

• **Heating canned vegetables:** Pour liquid from vegetables into saucepan. Simmer down to one-third. Add vegetables to liquid. Season with salt and pepper; add butter. Heat till hot through.

• **Cooking frozen vegetables:** Follow directions on package. Do not thaw before cooking. Exception: Corn on the cob and spinach *should* be partially thawed.

• **Butter-cooked frozen vegetables:** Place 2 tablespoons water, 1 tablespoon butter, and ¼ teaspoon salt in bottom of saucepan. Add frozen block of corn, peas, or French-style green beans; break up with fork. Bring to boil; cook till crisp-tender.

## OVEN-COOKED FROZEN VEGETABLES

*Handy way to fix vegetables for an oven meal—*

Place frozen block of vegetables in greased casserole. Top with 1 to 2 tablespoons butter or margarine; season with salt and pepper. Cover tightly. Bake for time given in chart below. Stir vegetables 15 minutes before cooking time is up; stir again just before serving.

| Vegetable | at 325° (minutes) | at 350° (minutes) |
|---|---|---|
| Cut asparagus | 65 | 55 |
| Cut green beans | 55 | 45 |
| Baby lima beans* | 50 | 40 |
| Broccoli | 55 | 45 |
| Whole kernel corn | 55 | 45 |
| Green peas | 50 | 40 |
| Spinach | 65 | 55 |
| Succotash | 55 | 45 |

*Add 2 tablespoons water before baking.

## VEGETABLES AU GRATIN

1 cup Medium White
  Sauce (page 645)
4 ounces sharp process
  American cheese,
  shredded (1 cup)

4 cups hot cooked or
  canned vegetables,
  drained
1/2 cup fine soft bread
  crumbs
1 tablespoon butter,
  melted

OVEN 350°

Blend white sauce and cheese; combine with vegetables.
Pour into 1-quart casserole. Toss crumbs with butter;
sprinkle atop. Bake at 350° for 20 to 25 minutes or till
browned. Makes 6 to 8 servings.

**Scalloped Vegetables:** Prepare as above except omit
cheese from sauce and increase Medium White Sauce to
1 1/2 cups.

## CREAMED VEGETABLES

1 tablespoon butter
1 tablespoon all-
  purpose flour
3/4 cup milk

2 cups hot cooked or
  canned vegetables,
  drained

Melt butter; blend in flour and dash salt. Add milk all at
once. Cook quickly, stirring constantly, till thickened and
bubbly; pour over vegetables. Serves 4.

# TEMPURA VEGETABLES

Wash fresh asparagus, parsley, spinach, mushrooms, green beans, or cauliflower; cut in bite-size pieces; *dry thoroughly.*

Just before using, make batter: Beat together 1 cup sifted all-purpose flour, 1 cup ice water, 1 slightly beaten egg, 2 tablespoons salad oil, 1/2 teaspoon sugar, and 1/2 teaspoon salt till all ingredients are just well moistened (a few lumps should remain). Keep batter cool with a few ice cubes in the batter.

Dip vegetables in batter; cook in deep hot fat (360° to 365°) till tender and browned. Drain thoroughly. Skim off any batter on surface of fat.

Serve with condiments: Grated fresh gingerroot; equal parts grated turnip and radish; 1 1/2 tablespoons soy sauce mixed with 1/4 cup prepared mustard.

# COOKING VEGETABLES

| Vegetable | How to Prepare | How to Cook | Time |
|---|---|---|---|
| Artichokes, French or globe | Wash. Cut off 1 inch of top, the stem, and tips of leaves. Pull off any loose leaves. Brush cut edges with lemon juice. | Place in boiling salted water to cover with 1 tablespoon lemon juice, 2 cloves garlic, and 1 tablespoon salad oil. Cover; simmer till leaf pulls out easily. Drain. | 20-30 min. |
| Jerusalem | Wash, pare; leave whole or slice. | Cook covered in a small amount of boiling salted water. | 15-35 min. |
| Asparagus | Wash; scrub gently with vegetable brush. If sandy, scrape off the scales. Break stalks—they will snap where tender part starts. | Cut up; cook covered in a small amount of boiling salted water. Or cook whole spears covered in small amount boiling salted water. | 8-10 min.<br>10-15 min. |
| Beans, Green or wax | Wash; remove ends and strings. Cook whole or in 1-inch pieces. Or slit lengthwise. | Cook covered in a small amount of boiling salted water. | 20-30 min. |
| Lima, fresh | Shell and wash. | | 10-12 min. |
| | | Cook covered in a small amount of boiling salted water. | 20-30 min. |
| Lima, dried | Rinse; add 2½ times as much water as beans. Soak overnight. Or bring to boil; simmer 2 minutes; let stand at least 1 hour. | Add salt, cover, and simmer in water used for soaking. | 1 hour |

| Vegetable | Preparation | Cooking Method | Time |
|---|---|---|---|
| Navy, dried | Rinse; add 3 times as much water as beans. Soak overnight. Or bring to boil; simmer 2 minutes; let stand at least 1 hour. | Add salt, cover, and simmer in water used for soaking. | 1½ hours |
| Beets | Cut off all but 1 inch of stems and root. Wash and scrub thoroughly. Do not pare. | Cook covered in boiling salted water. Peel when done. | 35-60 min. |
| | Or pare and slice or cube. Or pare and shred. | Cook covered in a small amount of boiling salted water. | 15-20 min. 10 min. |
| Beet greens | Wash thoroughly. Don't cut off tiny beets. | Salt lightly; cook covered without water except drops that cling to leaves. Reduce heat when steam forms. Turn with fork frequently. | 5-15 min. |
| Broccoli | Remove outer leaves and tough part of stalks. Split rest of stalk almost to flowerets. | Tie stalks in bundle, using folded strip of foil. Stand up in 1 inch boiling salted water. Cover; cook. | 15-20 min. |
| | Or cut in 1-inch pieces. | Cook stalk pieces covered in boiling salted water to cover 5 to 8 minutes; add flowerets. | 10-15 min. total |
| Brussels sprouts | Cut off any wilted leaves. Wash thoroughly. Cut large Brussels sprouts in half lengthwise. | Cook covered in a small amount of boiling salted water. | 10-15 min. |

| Vegetable | How to Prepare | How to Cook | Time |
|---|---|---|---|
| Cabbage, Green | Remove wilted outer leaves. Cut in 6 to 8 wedges. Or shred. | Cook covered in a small amount of boiling salted water. Or cook wedges uncovered in cooking liquid from corned beef. | 10-12 min. 5-7 min. 12-15 min. |
| Carrots | Wash and pare or scrape. Leave whole, slice, or cut in quarters or strips. | Cook covered in small amount boiling salted water, or in consomme. | Whole, 20-25 min. Cut up, 15-20 min. |
| Cauliflower | Remove leaves and some of the woody stem. Leave whole or separate into flowerets. | Cook covered in a small amount of boiling salted water. | Whole, 20-25 min. Flowerets, 10-15 min. |
| Celeriac (celery root) | Cut off leaves and root fibers. Scrape or pare; dice. | Cook covered in a small amount of boiling salted water. | 20-25 min. |
| Celery | Cut off leaves; trim roots. Scrub thoroughly. Slice outer branches into desired lengths. Cut celery hearts lengthwise. | Cook covered in a small amount of boiling salted water, or in consomme. | 10-15 min. |

| Vegetable | Preparation | Cooking | Time |
|---|---|---|---|
| Chard, Swiss | Wash thoroughly; if not young, cut midribs from leaves. | Cook covered in very small amount boiling salted water. If not young, cook midribs 10-15 minutes; then add leaves. | 10-20 min. / 15-25 min. total |
| Corn | Remove husks from fresh corn. Remove silks with stiff brush. Rinse. Cook whole. | Cook covered in small amount boiling salted water. Or cook uncovered in enough boiling salted water to cover ears. | 6-8 min. |
| | Or using a sharp knife, cut off just the tips of the kernels. Carefully scrape cobs with dull edge of knife. | Cook covered in small amount boiling salted water or in milk or butter. | 12-15 min. |
| Dandelion greens | Discard greens with blossom or bud as they will be bitter. Cut off roots; wash thoroughly. | Cook covered in very small amount boiling salted water. Turn with fork frequently. | 10-20 min. |
| Eggplant | Wash; pare if skin is tough. Cut in 1/2-inch slices. | Dip in beaten egg, then in fine dry bread crumbs. Brown slowly on both sides in a small amount of hot fat. Season. | About 4 min. total |
| Kohlrabi | Cut off leaves; wash, pare, and dice or slice. | Cook covered in a small amount of boiling salted water. | 25-30 min. |

| Vegetable | How to Prepare | How to Cook | Time |
|---|---|---|---|
| Leeks | Cut off the green tops to within about 2 inches of white part. Wash thoroughly. | Cook covered in a small amount of boiling salted water. | 15-20 min. |
| Lentils, dried | Wash. Add 2½ times as much water as lentils. | Simmer covered till tender. | About 35 min. |
| Mushrooms | Wash. Cut off tips of stems. Leave whole or slice. | Add to melted butter in skillet; sprinkle with flour; mix. Cover, cook slowly; turn occasionally. | 8-10 min. |
| Okra | Wash pods. Cut off stems. Cut large pods in ½-inch slices. | Cook covered in a small amount of boiling salted water. | 8-15 min. |
| | | Or slice and dip in beaten egg, then in fine dry bread crumbs. Brown slowly on both sides in a small amount of hot fat. | About 4 min. total |
| Onions | Peel onions under water. Slice, cut in quarters, or leave small onions whole. | Cook covered in a small amount of boiling salted water. | 25-35 min. |

| | Preparation | Cooking | Time |
|---|---|---|---|
| Parsnips | Wash thoroughly; pare or scrape. Slice crosswise or lengthwise, as desired. | Cook covered in a small amount of boiling salted water. | 15-20 min. |
| Peas, Green | Shell and wash. | Cook covered in a small amount of boiling salted water. | 8-15 min. |
| Black-eyed | Rinse; add 2½ times as much water as peas. Soak overnight. Or bring to boil; simmer 2 minutes; let stand at least 1 hour. | Add salt, cover, and simmer in water used for soaking. | 35-45 min. |
| Potatoes, | Scrub thoroughly. Cook with skins on. Or wash and pare thinly. Cook whole, quarter, or cube. | Whole—Cook covered in boiling salted water to cover; drain. Cut up—Cook tightly covered in small amount boiling salted water; drain at once. | Whole 25-40 min. Quartered 20-25 min. Cubed 10-15 min. |
| New | Scrub thoroughly; pare narrow strip of peel from center of each potato. Or scrape. | Cook in boiling, salted water. Drain. Peel if desired. | Tiny 15-20 min. |
| Sweet | Scrub thoroughly; cut off woody portions. Cook sweet potatoes in jackets. | Cook covered in boiling salted water to cover. Drain; peel if desired. | 30-40 min. |

| Vegetable | How to Prepare | How to Cook | Time |
|---|---|---|---|
| Rutabagas | Wash, pare thinly. Slice or cube. | Cook covered in small amount boiling salted water. Mash if desired. | 25-40 min. |
| Spinach | Cut off roots; wash several times in lukewarm water, lifting out of water each time. | Cook covered without water except drops that cling to leaves. Reduce heat when steam forms. Turn with fork frequently. | 3-5 min. |
| Squash, Acorn | Wash. Cut in half; remove seeds. Or pare and cube. | Bake cut side down at 350° 35 to 40 min.; turn cut side up; bake till done. Cook cubed squash covered in small amount boiling salted water. | 50-60 min. total About 15 min. |
| Hubbard | Wash; cut in serving pieces; do not pare. Or pare and cube. | Place on baking sheet; season and dot with butter. Cover with foil. Bake at 350° Cook covered in a small amount of boiling salted water. | 1¼ hours About 15 min. |
| Summer | Wash. Slice or cube. | Cook covered in a small amount of boiling salted water. | 15-20 min. |

| | | |
|---|---|---|
| Zucchini | Wash; do not pare. Slice thin. | Season and cook covered in butter in skillet 5 minutes; uncover and cook, turning slices, till tender. | About 10 min. total |
| Tomatoes | Wash ripe tomatoes. Plunge in boiling water, then cool under cold water. Peel; cut out stems. Cut up. (Or cook whole.) | Cook slowly, covered without adding water. Season with salt, pepper, sugar, and a little minced onion. | 10-15 min. |
| Turnips | Wash; pare thinly. Slice or cube. | Cook covered in small amount boiling salted water; mash if desired. | 15-20 min. |

## VEGETABLE TOPPERS

*Concoct clever toppers for vegetables and you'll be the cook-of-the-day—*

• Add toasted walnuts, sauteed mushrooms or onions, or toasted sesame seed.
• Top with grated cheese, snipped chives, or crumbled crisp-cooked bacon.
• Trim with pimiento strips, olive slices, or sprigs of fresh mint.
• Make a quick sauce from canned soup: Thin cream of mushroom, Cheddar cheese, or cream of celery soup with milk; heat.
• Top sauced vegetables with pretty slices or wedges of hard-cooked egg.
• Cook in chicken broth or water plus a chicken bouillon cube.
• Pass a bowl of Hollandaise, cheese sauce (blue, Cheddar, Parmesan, Swiss), or Lemon Butter Sauce.
• Dash with a pinch of dried, crushed herbs while cooking.
• Mix lightly with sliced water chestnuts, canned French-fried onions, or croutons.
• Spoon on dollops of sour cream.

## ARTICHOKE VELVET

| | |
|---|---|
| 2 9-ounce packages frozen artichoke hearts | Dash dried thyme |
| | Dash dried marjoram |
| 1 pint fresh mushrooms, sliced | 4 ounces Swiss cheese, diced (1 cup) |
| 2 tablespoons butter or margarine | 1 tablespoon dry white wine |
| 1 envelope chicken gravy mix | |

OVEN 350°

Cook artichokes according to package directions; drain. Cook mushrooms in butter till tender. Combine artichokes and mushrooms in 1-quart casserole. Prepare gravy mix using package directions. Remove from heat; add herbs and cheese; stir till melted. Add wine; pour over. Bake covered at 350° for 30 minutes. Serves 6 to 8.

*To clean artichokes:* Shower with cold running water. Cut off 1 inch from top. Chop off stem even with base. Pull off loose leaves from bottom. Snip off sharp leaf tips; brush cut edges with lemon.

## ASPARAGUS DRESS-UPS

• Pass Hollandaise or Bearnaise Sauce for spooning over hot asparagus spears; garnish with hard-cooked egg slices.
• Toss hot cooked asparagus with toasted almonds or toasted croutons.
• Heat Italian dressing and pour over hot cooked asparagus, toss lightly.
• **Oriental-style:** Heat large skillet; add 1 tablespoon salad oil. When salad oil is hot, add 3 cups fresh asparagus in bias-cut pieces 1$1/2$ inches long. Sprinkle with $1/2$ teaspoon salt and dash pepper. Cover. Lift skillet slightly above *high* heat and shake constantly while cooking. Cook 4 to 5 minutes or till asparagus is crisp-tender. Reduce heat the last minute of cooking, if necessary. Makes 6 servings.

## BEAN FIX-UPS

• **Green Beans Almond:** Cook 2 tablespoons slivered almonds in 2 tablespoons butter over low heat till golden, stirring occasionally. Remove from heat; add 1 teaspoon lemon juice. Pour over 2 cups hot cooked, drained French-style green beans. Makes 4 servings.
• **Snappy Green Beans:** Cook 4 slices bacon till crisp; drain, reserving 2 tablespoons drippings. Cook $1/4$ cup chopped onion in reserved fat till tender. Add 1 to 2 tablespoons tarragon vinegar, $1/2$ teaspoon salt, and dash pepper. Pour over 2 cups hot cooked drained green beans. Crumble bacon atop. Serves 3 or 4.
• **Herbed Green Beans:** Cook 1 pound fresh green beans, cut in 1-inch lengths (4 cups), covered in small amount boiling salted water 10 minutes; drain. Stir in 2 to 3 tablespoons butter or margarine, $1/2$ cup chopped onion, $1/4$ cup chopped celery, 1 clove garlic, minced, $1/4$ teaspoon dried rosemary, crushed, and $1/4$ teaspoon dried basil, crushed. Cover: cook 10 minutes over low heat till tender. Season to taste with salt. Serves 6 to 8.
• **Succotash:** Combine one 1-pound can (2 cups) limas,

drained, one 12-ounce can (1$\frac{1}{2}$ cups) whole kernel corn, drained, 2 tablespoons butter or margarine, and $\frac{1}{2}$ cup light cream. Heat and season to taste with salt and pepper. Serves 6.

## GREEN BEANS DELUXE

| | |
|---|---|
| 1 9-ounce package frozen *or* 1 1-pound can (2 cups) French-style green beans | 1 small clove garlic, minced |
| | $\frac{1}{2}$ teaspoon salt |
| | Dash pepper |
| 1 tablespoon butter or margarine | 1 medium tomato, cut in wedges |
| $\frac{1}{2}$ cup finely diced cooked ham | |

Cook frozen green beans in small amount of boiling water till just tender; drain. Or heat canned beans and drain. Melt butter in saucepan; add ham and garlic; cook till garlic is softened. Stir in beans, salt, and pepper. Top with tomato wedges; cover and heat through. Makes 4 servings.

## LIMA-CHEESE BAKE

OVEN 350°

Pour boiling water over one 10-ounce package frozen limas; break apart; drain. Blend one 11-ounce can condensed Cheddar cheese soup and $\frac{1}{2}$ cup milk; add limas, $\frac{3}{4}$ cup sliced celery, and $\frac{1}{4}$ cup snipped parsley. Stir in *half* of one 3$\frac{1}{2}$-ounce can French-fried onions. Bake at 350° for 35 minutes. Trim with remaining onions; bake 10 minutes. Makes 6 servings.

## BAKED BEANS

| | |
|---|---|
| 1 pound (2 cups) dry navy beans | $\frac{1}{4}$ cup molasses |
| $\frac{2}{3}$ cup brown sugar | $\frac{1}{4}$ pound salt pork, quartered |
| 1 teaspoon dry mustard | $\frac{1}{2}$ cup chopped onion |

OVEN 300°

Rinse beans; add to 2 quarts cold water. Bring to boiling; simmer 2 minutes. Remove from heat; cover. Let stand 1 hour. (Or, add beans to water; soak overnight.)

Add $\frac{1}{2}$ teaspoon salt to beans and soaking water. Bring to boiling. Reduce heat; simmer, covered, till beans are tender, about 1 hour. Drain, reserving liquid. Combine sugar, mustard, molasses, $\frac{1}{2}$ teaspoon salt, and $\frac{1}{8}$ teaspoon pepper. Stir in 2 cups reserved cooking liquid. Add mixture to beans, salt pork, and onion in 2-quart bean pot or casserole; stir to blend. Cover; bake at 300° for $3\frac{1}{2}$ to 4 hours. Stir occasionally. Add more bean liquid or water, if needed. Serves 6 to 8.

**New England Baked Beans:** Prepare Baked Beans decreasing brown sugar to $\frac{1}{3}$ cup and increasing molasses to $\frac{1}{2}$ cup.

## EASY BAKED BEANS

OVEN 325°

Cook 4 slices bacon till crisp; drain, reserving 2 tablespoons drippings. Crumble bacon. Cook $\frac{1}{2}$ cup chopped onion in drippings till tender; add with bacon to two 1-pound cans pork and beans in tomato sauce, 2 tablespoons brown sugar, 1 tablespoon Worcestershire sauce, and 1 teaspoon prepared mustard; mix well. Bake uncovered in $1\frac{1}{2}$-quart casserole at 325° for $1\frac{1}{2}$ to $1\frac{3}{4}$ hours. Makes 6 servings.

## BEET FAVORITES

• **Harvard Beets:** Drain one 1-pound can diced beets, reserving $\frac{1}{3}$ cup liquid. In saucepan, combine 2 tablespoons sugar, 1 tablespoon cornstarch, and $\frac{1}{4}$ teaspoon salt. Stir in reserved liquid, $\frac{1}{4}$ cup vinegar, and 2 tablespoons butter. Cook and stir till mixture thickens and bubbles. Add beets; heat through. Serves 4 or 5.

• **Orange-glazed Beets:** Melt 3 tablespoons butter in skillet; stir in $\frac{1}{4}$ cup orange marmalade and 1 tablespoon orange juice. Add 2 cups cooked or canned drained beets. Cook and stir over low heat till beets are hot and glazed, about 6 to 8 minutes. Makes 4 servings.

• **Beets in Cream:** Combine $\frac{1}{2}$ cup dairy sour cream, 2 tablespoons milk, 1 tablespoon sliced green onion, 1 tablespoon vinegar, 1 teaspoon sugar, ¼ teaspoon salt, and dash cayenne. Heat through over low heat (do not boil). Spoon over 3 cups sliced and halved beets, cooked and drained. Stir, if desired. Makes 4 servings.

• **Cranberry-sauced Beets:** Combine 1 tablespoon cornstarch, 1 tablespoon sugar, and dash salt in saucepan. Gradually stir in 1 cup cranberry-juice cocktail. Cook and stir over medium heat till mixture thickens and bubbles. Add two 1-pound cans sliced beets, drained, and ¼ teaspoon grated orange peel. Simmer, uncovered, 10 minutes. Makes 8 servings.

## BEETS WITH PINEAPPLE

| | |
|---|---|
| 2 tablespoons brown sugar | 1 tablespoon butter or margarine |
| 1 tablespoon cornstarch | 1 tablespoon lemon juice |
| ¼ teaspoon salt | |
| * * * | 1 1-pound can (2 cups) sliced beets, drained |
| 1 8¾-ounce can (1 cup) pineapple tidbits | |

Combine sugar, cornstarch, and salt in saucepan. Stir in pineapple (with syrup). Cook, stirring constantly, till mixture thickens and bubbles. Add butter, lemon juice, and beets. Cook over medium heat about 5 minutes or till hot. Serves 4.

## BROCCOLI SPECIALS

• Dot cooked broccoli with butter, then sprinkle with lemon juice.
• Try Hollandaise, cheese, or mustard sauce with cooked broccoli.
• Top cooked broccoli with pimiento strips and shredded Swiss cheese.

## BROCCOLI CASSEROLE

OVEN 350°

Cook two 10-ounce packages frozen cut broccoli following package directions; drain. Cook 2 cups frozen whole small onions or 3 medium onions, quartered, in boiling, salted water till tender. Drain.

In saucepan, melt 2 tablespoons butter; blend in 2 tablespoons all-purpose flour, $1/4$ teaspoon salt, and dash pepper. Add 1 cup milk; cook and stir till bubbly. Reduce heat; blend in one 3-ounce package cream cheese till smooth. Place vegetables in $1^1/2$-quart casserole. Pour sauce over; mix lightly. Top with $1/2$ cup shredded sharp process American cheese. Melt 2 tablespoons butter; toss with 1 cup soft bread crumbs. Sprinkle atop casserole. Bake at 350° for 40 to 45 minutes. Serves 6.

## BRUSSELS SPROUTS FIX-UPS

• Sprinkle cooked sprouts lightly with ground nutmeg, crushed sage, or caraway.
• Toss cooked sprouts with butter and warm croutons.
• Add sliced canned water chestnuts to sprouts for added crispness.

## BRUSSELS SPROUTS POLONAISE

| | |
|---|---|
| 1 pound Brussels sprouts | 1 hard-cooked egg, |
| 2 tablespoons butter | finely chopped |
| $1/4$ cup fine dry bread | 2 tablespoons snipped |
| crumbs | parsley |

Cut large sprouts in half. Cook, covered, in boiling, salted water 10 to 15 minutes or till just tender; drain. Heat butter till lightly browned; blend in crumbs, egg, and parsley. Spoon over sprouts; toss lightly. Serves 6 to 8.

## COMPANY CABBAGE

| | |
|---|---|
| 2 tablespoons butter or | $1/2$ cup dairy sour cream |
| margarine | 1 tablespoon sugar |
| 8 cups finely shredded | 2 tablespoons vinegar |
| cabbage | 1 teaspoon salt |
| 1 clove garlic, minced | $1/4$ teaspoon caraway seed |

Heat butter in large skillet. Add cabbage, garlic, and $1/4$ cup water. Cover tightly and steam over low heat 10 to 12 minutes. Blend next 4 ingredients; stir into cabbage.

Heat through but do not boil. Sprinkle with caraway. Serves 6.

## PENNSYLVANIA RED CABBAGE

2 tablespoons bacon drippings
4 cups shredded red cabbage
2 cups cubed unpared apple
1/4 cup brown sugar
1/4 cup vinegar
1 1/4 teaspoons salt
Dash pepper
1/2 teaspoon caraway seed

Heat drippings in skillet; add remaining ingredients and 1/4 cup water. Cook covered over low heat; stir occasionally. For crisp cabbage, cook 15 minutes; for tender, 25 to 30 minutes. Serves 4 or 5.

## SUNSHINE CARROTS

5 medium carrots
1 tablespoon sugar
1 teaspoon cornstarch
1/4 teaspoon ground ginger
1/4 teaspoon salt
1/4 cup orange juice
2 tablespoons butter or margarine

Cut carrots on the bias in 1-inch chunks. Cook, covered, in boiling salted water till just tender, about 20 minutes; drain. In saucepan, mix sugar, cornstarch, ginger, and salt. Add juice; cook and stir till thick and bubbly. Boil 1 minute. Stir in butter. Toss with carrots. Serves 4.

## CARROT WINNERS

• **Skillet Carrots:** Melt 3 tablespoons butter or margarine in a skillet. Add 8 medium carrots, coarsely shredded. Sprinkle with 1/2 teaspoon salt. Cover and cook just till tender, about 5 to 8 minutes. Top with snipped parsley.
• **Glazed Carrots:** Heat together 1/3 cup brown sugar and 2 tablespoons butter till sugar dissolves. Add 8 cooked carrots (whole or halved lengthwise); cook over medium heat, turning carrots till well glazed and tender, about 12 minutes.
• **Basil Carrots:** In medium skillet, melt 2 tablespoons butter. Add 6 medium carrots, thinly sliced on bias.

Sprinkle with ¼ teaspoon salt and ¼ teaspoon dried basil, crushed. Cover; simmer 10 to 12 minutes or till tender. Makes 6 servings.

• **Minted Carrots:** Combine 2 tablespoons butter, 1 tablespoon honey, and 2 teaspoons chopped fresh mint; heat to melt butter. Add 5 or 6 carrots, cut in strips, cooked and drained. Simmer till glazed, about 8 minutes. Makes 4 or 5 servings.

## CHEESED CAULIFLOWER

OVEN 375°

Remove leaves and trim base from 1 medium head cauliflower. Wash. Cook whole in boiling salted water 15 to 20 minutes, or till tender. Drain. Place on ungreased shallow baking pan. Sprinkle with salt. Mix ½ cup mayonnaise and 2 teaspoons prepared mustard; spread over cauliflower. Top with ¾ cup shredded sharp process cheese. Bake at 375° about 10 minutes or till cheese is melted. Serves 4 or 5.

## CAULIFLOWER MEDLEY

| | |
|---|---|
| 2 tablespoons salad oil | ½ teaspoon salt |
| 2 cups small fresh cauliflowerets | 2 tablespoons chopped canned pimiento |
| 2 10-ounce packages frozen peas | |

Heat oil in skillet. Add cauliflowerets and cook covered over low heat 10 to 12 minutes; stir occasionally. Add peas, salt, and dash pepper; cover. Cook 10 minutes; stir in pimiento. Serves 8.

## CELERY ORIENTAL

Slice 6 to 8 large, outside celery branches on the bias. Cook in small amount boiling salted water till just crisp-tender; drain.

Cook 1 cup sliced fresh mushrooms in 3 tablespoons butter or margarine till tender; add celery and ¼ cup toasted blanched almond halves. Toss lightly till hot. Makes 4 to 6 servings.

## CORN ON THE COB IDEAS

- Remove husks from corn. Remove silk with stiff brush. Cook. Serve with flavored butter, if desired.
- **Kettle-cooked Corn:** Cook covered in small amount boiling salted water (or cook in enough boiling salted water to cover) about 6 to 8 minutes. Don't overcook.
- **Foil-baked Corn:** Spread corn with butter or margarine or any of the flavored butters listed below. Sprinkle with salt and pepper. Wrap securely in foil. Bake in a very hot oven (450°) for 25 minutes, or till done. Turn several times.
- **Zippy Butter:** To 1/2 cup softened butter add 1 tablespoon prepared mustard, 1 teaspoon prepared horseradish, 1/2 teaspoon salt, and dash freshly ground pepper. Blend with spoon till fluffy.
- **Herb Butter:** To 1/2 cup softened butter add 1/2 teaspoon dried rosemary, crushed, and 1/2 teaspoon dried marjoram, crushed. Blend till light and fluffy.

## SCALLOPED CORN SUPREME

1 beaten egg
1 cup milk
1 cup cracker crumbs
1 1-pound 1-ounce can (2 cups) cream-style corn

1/4 cup finely chopped onion
3 tablespoons chopped canned pimiento
1 tablespoon butter or margarine, melted

OVEN 350°

Mix egg, milk, 2/3 *cup* crumbs, 3/4 teaspoon salt, and dash pepper. Stir in corn, onion, and pimiento. Turn into 1-quart casserole. Toss melted butter with remaining crumbs; sprinkle atop corn mixture. Bake at 350° for 65 to 70 minutes. Serves 6.

## CORN PUDDING

3 slightly beaten eggs
2 cups drained cooked or canned whole kernel corn
2 cups milk, scalded

1/3 cup finely chopped onion
1 tablespoon butter, melted
1 teaspoon sugar
1 teaspoon salt

OVEN 350°

Combine ingredients; pour into greased 1 1/2-quart casserole. Set in shallow pan; fill pan to 1 inch with hot water. Bake at 350° for 40 to 45 minutes, or till knife inserted off center comes out clean. Let stand 10 minutes at room temperature. Serves 6.

## SWISS CORN BAKE

OVEN 350°

Cook 3 cups fresh-cut corn in 1 cup boiling salted water for 2 to 3 minutes, or till just tender; *or* cook two 9-ounce packages frozen corn according to package directions; drain well.

Combine corn, one 6-ounce can evaporated milk, 1 beaten egg, 2 tablespoons finely chopped onion, 1/2 teaspoon salt, dash pepper, and 3/4 cup shredded process Swiss cheese. Turn into 10x6x1 1/2-inch baking dish. Toss 1/2 cup soft bread crumbs with 1 tablespoon melted butter and 1/4 cup shredded Swiss cheese. Sprinkle over top. Bake at 350° for 25 minutes. Serves 6.

## PANFRIED EGGPLANT

1 medium eggplant
1 slightly beaten egg
1 tablespoon cold water

1/2 cup fine dry bread crumbs
1/2 teaspoon salt
Dash pepper

Pare eggplant. Cut in half lengthwise, then cut crosswise making 1/2-inch-thick slices. Combine egg and water. Dip eggplant in egg mixture, then in mixture of bread crumbs, salt, and pepper. Cook eggplant in hot oil for 2 to 3 minutes on each side, or till tender and brown. Drain on paper towels. Sprinkle with additional salt. Keep warm in slow oven while cooking remaining eggplant. Makes 4 to 6 servings.

## MUSHROOM FEATURES

• **Fresh Mushroom Saute:** Wash 5 ounces (2 cups) mushrooms. Slice through cap and stem. Sprinkle with 1 teaspoon all-purpose flour. Melt 1 tablespoon butter in medium skillet. Add mushrooms; cover and cook over low heat 8 to 10 minutes, or till tender, stirring occasionally. Season with salt and pepper. Serves 2 as a vegetable or 4 as a meat accompaniment.

• **Creamed Mushrooms:** Prepare and cook mushrooms as for Fresh Mushroom Saute but increase flour to 1 tablespoon. Before seasoning, add 1 teaspoon soy sauce. Slowly stir in ³/₄ cup light cream. Cook and stir till mixture thickens. Season. Serve with steak or over toast points. Makes 4 servings.

## ONION FIX-UPS

• To creamed onions add shredded cheese and chopped peanuts.

• **Dutch Glazed Onions:** Drain one 1-pound can small whole onions, reserving ¹/₄ cup liquid. In skillet, combine 2 tablespoons butter, 1 tablespoon sugar, and reserved liquid. Cook and stir till blended. Add onions; cook about 10 minutes, or till mixture browns lightly; stir often. Makes 4 servings.

• **Gourmet Onions:** Melt 3 tablespoons butter. Stir in ¹/₂ teaspoon sugar, ¹/₄ teaspoon salt, ¹/₄ teaspoon pepper, and ¹/₄ cup sherry. Add 10 to 12 small cooked onions; heat quickly, about 5 minutes, stirring occasionally. Turn into serving dish; top with ¹/₄ cup shredded Parmesan cheese. Serves 6.

## GOLDEN ONION RINGS

Cut 6 medium Bermuda or mild white onions into slices ¹/₄ inch thick. Separate into rings. Combine 1 cup plus 2 tablespoons sifted all-purpose flour, ¹/₂ teaspoon salt, 1 slightly beaten egg, 1 cup milk, and 2 tablespoons salad oil. Beat together just till dry ingredients are well moistened. Coat onion rings with batter. Fry, a few at a time, in deep hot fat (375°), stirring once to separate rings. When onions are golden, drain on paper towels. Just before serving, sprinkle with salt.

## PARSNIPS

• Add butter or cream to cooked 1-inch cubes of parsnips; season to taste.
• Cut parsnips in half lengthwise; cook and drain. Brown lightly in butter; season. Sprinkle with a little sugar, if desired.

## DRESS-UPS FOR PEAS

• **Minted Peas:** Drain liquid from one 1-pound can (2 cups) peas into a saucepan. Cook till ¼ cup liquid remains. Add peas, ½ teaspoon salt, dash pepper, 1 tablespoon butter, and ¼ cup mint-flavored jelly. Heat through. Serves 4.
• **Peas in Cream:** Heat 3 tablespoons butter and ½ cup water to boiling in saucepan. Add 1 to 1½ cups fresh shelled peas (1 to 1½ pounds in shell), 2 cups finely torn leaf lettuce, 2 tablespoons finely chopped onion, 1 tablespoon snipped parsley, 1 teaspoon sugar, ½ teaspoon salt, and dash pepper. Cover; simmer 8 to 15 minutes. Don't drain. Add ⅓ cup cream. Makes 4 servings.
• **Peas and Onions:** Combine cooked drained peas and tiny onions. Toss with butter and canned mushrooms; heat through. Dash with dried thyme, crushed.
• **Quick Creamed Peas:** Combine one 4-ounce carton chive whipped cream cheese, ¼ cup milk, and ¼ teaspoon salt. Heat and stir over low heat just till warm. Pour over cooked peas *or* a combination of cooked peas and tiny new potatoes. Stir gently to coat.

## SPRINGTIME PEAS

| | |
|---|---|
| 2 pounds fresh peas, unshelled | Dash pepper |
| | Dash dried thyme, |
| 3 to 6 lettuce leaves | crushed |
| ⅓ cup sliced green onion | 3 tablespoons butter or |
| 1 teaspoon sugar | margarine |
| ½ teaspoon salt | |

Shell peas. Cover bottom of skillet with lettuce; top with peas and onion. Sprinkle on sugar and seasonings; add butter. Cover tightly and cook over *low heat* 10 to 15 minutes, or till peas are done. Serves 4.

## PEA PODS ORIENTAL

| | |
|---|---|
| 1/2 pound fresh *or* 1 7-ounce package frozen Chinese pea pods, thawed | 1 5-ounce can (²/₃ cup) bamboo shoots, drained |
| 1 tablespoon salad oil | 1 5-ounce can (²/₃ cup) water chestnuts, drained and sliced |
| 1 teaspoon soy sauce | 1 chicken bouillon cube |
| 1 medium clove garlic, minced | 1 teaspoon cornstarch |

If fresh peas are used, wash and remove tips and strings. In a preheated medium-size skillet, place oil, soy sauce, and garlic. Cook over low heat till garlic has browned; add fresh or frozen peas, bamboo shoots, and water chestnuts. Toss and cook over high heat for 1 minute. Dissolve bouillon cube in 1/4 cup boiling water; add to peas. Cover and cook over medium heat for 2 minutes. Combine cornstarch and 1 teaspoon cold water. Stir into peas. Cook, uncovered, over high heat till thickened, about 1 minute. Makes 4 servings.

## SKILLET-FRIED POTATOES

• **Hash-browns:** Boil 3 medium potatoes in jackets; chill. Peel and shred to make 3 cups. Add 1 to 2 tablespoons grated onion, 1 teaspoon salt, and dash pepper. Melt 1/4 cup butter in a 10-inch skillet. Pat potatoes into pan, leaving 1/2-inch space around edge. Brown about 9 minutes. Reduce heat if necessary. Cut with spatula to make 4 wedges; turn. Brown 7 minutes longer, till golden. Serves 4.

• **Fresh-fries:** Pare 3 medium potatoes; slice thin. Season; fry, covered, in 3 tablespoons bacon drippings or other fat 10 minutes. Uncover and brown other side, about 10 minutes, loosening occasionally.

## FRENCH FRIES

Cut pared potatoes lengthwise in strips. Fry small amount at a time in deep, hot fat (360°) for 6 to 7 minutes, or till crisp and golden. Drain on paper towels. Sprinkle with salt and serve at once.

*Note:* Do not French-fry new potatoes.

## POTATOES MANY WAYS

• **Boiled Potatoes:** Cook potatoes according to basic directions (page 667). For dry mealy potatoes, drain and shake gently over low heat when done. Season with salt and pepper; add butter.

• **Parsleyed New Potatoes:** Scrub or scrape 1½ pounds tiny new potatoes. Cook in boiling salted water 15 to 20 minutes; drain. Pare, if desired. Meanwhile, melt ¼ cup butter in saucepan; stir in ¼ cup snipped parsley and 1 tablespoon lemon juice. Pour over hot potatoes. Serves 4 to 6.

• **Mashed Potatoes:** Pare potatoes. Cook in boiling salted water till tender. Drain and shake over low heat to dry. Remove pan from heat. Mash with potato masher or electric mixer using lowest speed. Gradually add hot milk as needed and continue beating till light and fluffy. Add salt, pepper, and butter as desired.

• **Oven-browned Potatoes:** Pare medium potatoes; cook in boiling salted water 15 minutes; drain. About 45 minutes before meat roast is done (oven temperature 325°), place hot potatoes in drippings around roast, turning potatoes to coat.

• **Potato Patties:** Combine 2 cups cold mashed potatoes, 1 slightly beaten egg, ¼ cup chopped onion, and salt and pepper to taste. Mix well. Shape in 6 patties. Dip in flour, then brown slowly in butter, about 5 minutes on each side. Makes 6 servings.

## CREAMED PEAS AND NEW POTATOES

1½ pounds (about 15) tiny
   new potatoes
1 to 1½ cups fresh peas
   (1 to 1½ pounds in
   shell)
3 tablespoons sliced
   green onion

4 teaspoons butter or
   margarine
4 teaspoons all-purpose
   flour
1 cup milk

Scrub potatoes; pare off narrow strip of peel around center of each. Cook in boiling salted water 15 to 20 minutes; drain. Meanwhile, cook peas and onion in small amount of boiling salted water 8 to 15 minutes; drain. Make a white sauce of butter, flour, dash salt, and milk. Combine vegetables and sauce. Serves 4 to 6.

## BAKED POTATOES

OVEN 425°

Select uniform baking potatoes. (Don't use new potatoes.) Scrub with brush. For soft skins, rub with shortening. Prick with fork. Bake at 425° for 40 to 60 minutes. *Or,* if potatoes share oven, bake at 350° to 375° for 70 to 80 minutes. When done, roll gently under hand to make mealy. Cut crisscross in top with fork; press ends, push up fluff. Top with butter.

**Foil-baked:** Scrub, dry, prick, and wrap potatoes in foil. Bake at 350° 1½ hours.

## BAKED POTATO TOPPERS

• Whip 1 cup shredded sharp process cheese and ¼ cup soft butter till fluffy. Add ½ cup dairy sour cream and 2 tablespoons snipped green onion; whip.

• Soften one 8-ounce package cream cheese. Add ⅓ cup light cream; beat fluffy. Add 1 tablespoon snipped chives, 1½ teaspoons lemon juice, and ½ teaspoon garlic salt; blend well.

## STUFFED BAKED POTATOES

OVEN 375°

Bake 4 medium potatoes in 375° oven. Cut slice from top of each. Scoop out inside; mash. Add butter, salt, pepper, and hot milk to moisten. Beat fluffy. Fill shells 1/2 *full* with mashed potatoes. Combine 1 cup drained, seasoned cooked or canned peas and 2 tablespoons snipped green onion; divide among potato shells. Pile remaining mashed potatoes atop. Return to oven (375°) 12 to 15 minutes. Serves 4.

## VOLCANO POTATOES

OVEN 350°

Pare 4 or 5 medium potatoes. Cook, drain, and mash. Season with salt and pepper. Whip potatoes with enough hot milk (about 3/4 cup) to make light and fluffy. Pile into greased 8-inch round baking dish, mounding into volcano shape. Make a crater in center. Fold 1/2 cup shredded sharp process cheese into 1/2 cup whipping cream, whipped. Pour over top. Bake at 350° about 20 minutes, or till lightly browned. Makes 6 servings.

## SCALLOPED POTATOES

| | |
|---|---|
| 6 to 8 medium potatoes, pared and thinly sliced (6 cups) | 1/3 cup all-purpose flour |
| | 1 1/2 teaspoons salt |
| | 1/8 teaspoon pepper |
| 1/4 cup finely chopped onion | * * * |
| | 2 cups milk |

OVEN 350°

Place *half* the potatoes in greased 2-quart casserole. Add *half* the onion. *Sift half* the flour over; sprinkle with *half* the seasonings. Repeat layers. Pour milk over all. If desired, sprinkle top with 3 tablespoons buttered fine dry bread crumbs. Cover and bake at 350° for 1 1/4 to 1 1/2 hours. Uncover; bake 15 minutes. Serves 6.

## DUCHESS POTATOES

| | |
|---|---|
| 3 tablespoons butter | 4 cups hot mashed |
| 1 beaten egg | potatoes |

Beat 1 *tablespoon* of the butter, egg, and salt and pepper to taste into potatoes. Using pastry bag with large star tip, pipe hot potatoes around steak (see pages 439–441) on wooden plank.* Melt remaining butter and drizzle over potatoes. Broil 4 inches from heat 7 minutes. Serves 6 to 8.

*Or pipe 2-inch rosettes on greased baking sheet. Drizzle with melted butter. Bake at 500° for 10 to 12 minutes.

## SWEET POTATO TREATS

• **Candied Sweets:** Cut 6 medium sweet potatoes, cooked and peeled, in ½-inch slices. Layer potatoes in buttered 1½-quart casserole with ¾ cup brown sugar, 1 teaspoon salt, and ¼ cup butter, ending with sugar and butter. Bake uncovered at 375° about 30 minutes or till glazed. Add ½ cup miniature marshmallows last 5 minutes; brown lightly. Serves 6.

• **Baked Sweet Potatoes:** Scrub sweet potatoes. Bake at 375° to 400° for 40 to 45 minutes. Pass butter, salt, and pepper.

• **Mashed Sweet Potatoes:** Peel hot cooked sweet potatoes. Mash. Beat till fluffy gradually adding hot milk as needed. Beat in salt, pepper, and butter to taste.

## RICE TIPS

• Rice forms a part of many main dishes, salads, and even desserts. But served simply with butter or seasonings, it plays the role of a vegetable in meal plans.

• Test rice for doneness by pinching a grain between thumb and forefinger. When no hard core remains, it's done.

• **Plain Rice:** For 3 to 4 cups of cooked rice, combine 1 cup uncooked long-grain rice, 2 cups cold water, and ½ to 1 teaspoon salt in a 2-quart saucepan; cover with tight-fitting lid. Bring to a vigorous boil, then turn heat low. Continue cooking 14 minutes (do not lift cover). Remove from heat; let stand, covered, 10 minutes.

• **Browned Rice:** Toast 1 cup long-grain rice in ungreased skillet over medium heat, shaking often, about 20 minutes or till golden brown. Turn into 1-quart casserole; add 1/4 teaspoon salt and 2 1/2 cups hot water, stirring to separate rice. Cover and bake at 350° about 1 hour or till rice is tender and all water is absorbed. Fluff with a fork. Trim with chopped canned pimiento if desired. Makes 6 servings.

## BUTTER-BAKED RICE

2 teaspoons salt
2 cups water
1 cup long-grain rice
1/3 cup butter or margarine
Dash garlic salt

1 13 3/4-ounce can chicken broth or 2 chicken bouillon cubes dissolved in 1 3/4 cups boiling water
Finely snipped parsley
1/4 cup toasted slivered almonds

OVEN 325°

Combine salt and 2 cups water; bring to boiling and pour over rice. Let stand 30 minutes. Rinse rice with cold water; drain well. Melt butter in skillet. Add rice and cook over medium heat, stirring frequently, till butter is almost absorbed, about 5 minutes. Turn into 1-quart casserole; sprinkle with garlic salt. Pour broth over. Bake, covered, at 325° for 45 minutes. Add parsley; fluff with fork. Sprinkle with almonds. Bake, uncovered, 10 minutes longer. Makes 6 or 7 servings.

## WILD RICE AND MUSHROOMS

1 3-ounce can (2/3 cup) broiled sliced mushrooms
1 10 1/2-ounce can condensed beef broth
2 medium onions, finely chopped

1/2 cup wild rice
1 cup long-grain rice
2 tablespoons butter
2 tablespoons snipped parsley

Drain mushrooms, reserving liquid. Mix beef broth, liquid, and enough water to make 2 cups. Add onions and bring to boil. Add rinsed wild rice; reduce heat; cover and simmer 20 minutes. Add long-grain rice; return to boil; reduce heat; cover and simmer 20 minutes longer. Add mushrooms and butter; heat briefly; add parsley. Serves 6 to 8.

## RUTABAGA AND APPLE

3 cups cubed pared rutabaga

1 medium apple, pared, cored, and sliced

6 tablespoons brown sugar

2 tablespoons butter

OVEN 350°

Cook rutabaga in boiling salted water 20 to 25 minutes, or till just tender; drain. Place *half* rutabaga and *half* apple in 1-quart casserole. Sprinkle with *half* brown sugar; dot with *half* butter; sprinkle with salt. Repeat layers. Bake, covered, at 350° for 30 minutes. Serves 4 to 6.

## SAUERKRAUT PROVENCALE

1/3 cup chopped onion

2 tablespoons butter, melted

1/3 cup canned condensed beef broth

1 14-ounce can sauerkraut, drained

2 tablespoons chopped pimiento

1/2 cup dairy sour cream
   Poppy seed

Cook onion in butter till tender but not brown. Add broth, sauerkraut, and pimiento; mix lightly. Simmer covered 10 minutes. Serve topped with sour cream and dashed with poppy seed. Serves 4.

## SPINACH IDEAS

• Serve cooked spinach with lemon wedges or vinegar, and hard-cooked egg slices.
• **Spinach Surprise:** Cook 1 pound fresh spinach; drain and chop. Add 2 tablespoons butter, 1/4 cup light cream, and 1/2 tablespoon prepared horseradish. Heat and season to taste. Garnish with hard-cooked egg slices. Serves 3 or 4.
• **Chinese Spinach:** Wash and pat dry 1 pound fresh

spinach. Remove stems and cut into 1-inch pieces. Tear leaves into bite-size pieces. Heat 2 tablespoons salad oil and 1 tablespoon soy sauce in skillet; add spinach stems and leaves. Cover and cook 1 minute or till just wilted. Uncover; cook and toss till spinach is tender-crisp and well coated, about 2 minutes. Serves 4.

## SPINACH ELEGANTE

2 10-ounce packages
   frozen chopped
   spinach
3 slices bacon, cooked
   and crumbled
1 6-ounce can sliced
   mushrooms, drained (1
   cup)

1/4 teaspoon dried
   marjoram, crushed
1 cup dairy sour cream
1/2 cup shredded sharp
   process American
   cheese

OVEN 325°

Cook spinach according to package directions. Drain well; spread on bottom of 10x6x1½-inch baking dish. Arrange bacon and mushrooms over spinach. Sprinkle with dash pepper and marjoram. Bake at 325° for 15 minutes. Cover with sour cream and cheese. Return to oven 5 minutes or till cheese melts. Serves 6.

## SQUASH SQUARES IN SOUR CREAM

Cook and drain 4 cups cubed, pared butternut or Hubbard squash. Meanwhile, cook 1 medium onion, sliced, in 2 tablespoons butter till tender but not brown. Remove from heat; add 1 cup dairy sour cream and ½ teaspoon salt; stir well. Place hot cooked squash on platter; sprinkle with pepper; pour sauce over. Sprinkle with ½ teaspoon dillweed. Serves 4 to 6.

## BAKED ACORN SQUASH

• Halve and seed squash; bake cut side down in shallow pan at 350° for 35 to 40 minutes. Turn cut side up; salt. Fill if desired. Bake about 20 minutes longer.
• **Squash and Sausage:** After turning, brush each half with

butter, drizzle with 1 tablespoon honey, and fill with 3 browned sausage links. Bake 25 minutes.

• **Squash and Applesauce:** After turning squash, brush with butter; sprinkle with brown sugar. Fill each with 1/2 cup hot applesauce. Finish baking.

• **Squash with Onions:** For 6 halves, after turning, sprinkle with salt; fill with 2 cups drained cooked tiny onions and 1/2 cup broken walnuts. Mix 1/2 cup melted butter, 1/2 cup dark corn syrup, and 1/4 teaspoon *each* salt and ground cinnamon; spoon over. Finish baking.

## CANDIED SQUASH RINGS

OVEN 350°

Cut 2 acorn squash crosswise in 1-inch slices; discard seeds and ends; season. Arrange in single layer in shallow baking dish; cover and bake at 350° for 30 to 35 minutes. Combine 2/3 cup brown sugar and 1/4 cup soft butter; spread over squash. Bake, uncovered, 15 to 20 minutes, basting occasionally. Serves 6.

## CHEDDAR SQUASH BAKE

6 cups thinly sliced unpared zucchini, cooked and drained

2 slightly beaten egg yolks

1 cup dairy sour cream

2 tablespoons all-purpose flour

2 stiffly beaten egg whites

1 1/2 cups shredded Cheddar cheese

6 slices bacon, cooked

1 tablespoon butter, melted

1/4 cup fine dry bread crumbs

OVEN 350°

Salt cooked squash. Mix next 3 ingredients; fold in whites. Layer *half* the squash, egg mixture, and cheese in 12x7 1/2x 2-inch baking dish; crumble bacon; sprinkle atop. Repeat layers. Mix butter and crumbs; sprinkle over. Bake at 350° for 20 to 25 minutes. Serves 8 to 10.

## SUMMER SQUASH IDEAS

- **Dilly Squash:** Slice 1 pound yellow summer squash crosswise ¼ inch thick. Melt 2 tablespoons butter in skillet; add squash, 1 tablespoon snipped parsley, ¼ teaspoon dried dillweed, ¼ teaspoon salt, and dash onion powder. Cover; cook over low heat 8 to 10 minutes or till tender, stirring occasionally. Serves 4 to 6.
- **Confetti Squash:** Steam tiny yellow summer squash (less than 3 inches long) till tender. Split lengthwise and brush cut surfaces with melted butter. Season with salt and pepper. Sprinkle with snipped parsley and chopped canned pimiento. Place in shallow pan; heat in 350° oven.
- **Zucchini Parmesan:** Place 3 cups thinly sliced zucchini, 2 tablespoons butter, ½ teaspoon salt, and dash pepper in skillet. Cover and cook slowly 5 minutes. Uncover and cook, turning slices, 5 minutes more. Sprinkle with 2 tablespoons grated Parmesan cheese. Serves 4.
- **Zucchini Half Shells:** Trim ends of 6 small zucchini; cut in half lengthwise. Melt ¼ cup butter in large skillet; add 1 tablespoon grated onion and 1 beef bouillon cube, crushed. Add zucchini, cut side down, and cook till golden. Turn; add 2 tablespoons water; cover and cook over low heat about 10 minutes. Serves 5 or 6.

## TOMATO DRESS-UPS

- **Fried Tomatoes:** Cut unpared *green* tomatoes in ½-inch slices. Dip in seasoned flour. Brown *slowly* in hot fat on both sides. *Or,* dip ½-inch *ripe* tomato slices into beaten egg mixed with water, then into crumbs; fry *quickly* in hot fat; season.
- **Broiled Tomatoes:** Broil tomato halves, cut side up, 3 inches from heat about 5 minutes or till hot through (don't turn). If desired, dot with butter, season, and sprinkle with crushed herbs before broiling. *Or,* combine ½ cup dairy sour cream, ¼ cup mayonnaise, 2 tablespoons finely chopped onion, ¼ teaspoon dried dillweed, and ¼ teaspoon salt. Spoon over hot broiled tomatoes.
- **Baked Tomatoes:** Place tomato halves in shallow baking pan. Sprinkle with seasoned salt and buttered cracker crumbs if desired. Bake at 375° about 20 minutes.

## SCALLOPED TOMATOES

| | |
|---|---|
| 1 cup chopped celery | 1 1-pound 12-ounce can tomatoes |
| 1/2 cup finely chopped onion | 1 tablespoon sugar |
| 2 tablespoons butter or margarine | 1 teaspoon salt |
| 2 tablespoons all-purpose flour | Dash pepper |
| 3 slices bread, toasted | 2 teaspoons prepared mustard |

OVEN 350°

Cook celery and onion in butter until just tender; blend in flour. Butter toast; cut in 1/2-inch cubes. Break up tomatoes; add to celery mixture with *half* the toast cubes and remaining ingredients. Pour into 1 1/2-quart casserole; top with remaining toast. Bake at 350° for 50 minutes. Serves 8.

## TOMATOES AND OKRA

Cook 1 1/2 cups fresh okra cut in 1/2-inch slices, covered, in small amount boiling salted water 10 minutes; drain. (*Or*, cook one 10-ounce package frozen okra according to package directions; drain.) Cook 1/2 cup chopped onion and 1/2 cup chopped green pepper in 2 tablespoons salad oil till tender but not brown; blend in 1 tablespoon sugar, 1 teaspoon all-purpose flour, 3/4 teaspoon salt, and 1/4 teaspoon pepper. Add 3 tomatoes, peeled and quartered, and okra; heat through. Serves 4.

## TURNIPS

• Drain cooked turnips; mash. Add butter, salt, and pepper to taste.
• Cook sliced turnips in beef broth. Season with salt and pepper; add butter.
• **Lemon Parsleyed Turnips:** Cook 2 cups turnip sticks in boiling salted water till tender, 20 minutes; drain. Add 1 tablespoon butter, 2 teaspoons snipped parsley, 1 teaspoon finely chopped onion, and 1 teaspoon lemon juice; toss. Serves 4.

Look for additional seasonings for vegetables on pages 770–771.

# 16

pages **693** through **718**

# MEAL PLANNING AND NUTRITION

# DAILY FOOD GUIDE

For a well-balanced diet, select foods recommended from the Basic 4 Food Groups—milk, meat, vegetable-fruit, and bread-cereal. Add foods such as butter and sugar, and increase servings, if desired.

## MILK GROUP

Milk is the main source of calcium needed for strong teeth and bones. It also provides protein, riboflavin, phosphorus, and vitamin A.

This group includes milk—fluid, whole, evaporated, skim, and dry—buttermilk, cheese, and ice cream.

The daily recommended allowances for the Milk Group are given in amounts of whole fluid milk (8 ounces per cup).

| | |
|---|---|
| Children under 9 | 2 to 3 cups |
| Children 9 to 12 | 3 or more cups |
| Teen-agers | 4 or more cups |
| Adults | 2 or more cups |

Cheese and ice cream may replace part of the daily requirement of milk. The equivalents are as follows:

1-inch cube Cheddar cheese = $\frac{1}{2}$ cup milk
$\frac{1}{2}$ cup cottage cheese = $\frac{1}{3}$ cup milk
2 tablespoons cream cheese = 1 tablespoon milk
$\frac{1}{2}$ cup ice cream = $\frac{1}{4}$ cup milk

## MEAT GROUP

Meat provides protein used by the body for growth and repair of body tissues. It also provides iron, thiamine, niacin, riboflavin, and other nutrients.

The Meat Group includes beef, veal, pork, lamb, poultry, fish, and eggs. Dry beans, dry peas, nuts, and peanut butter are alternate sources of protein.

Two or more servings should be eaten each day. Consider the following amounts as one serving:

2 or 3 ounces lean cooked meat, fish, or poultry
2 eggs
1 cup cooked dry beans, dry peas, or lentils
4 tablespoons peanut butter

## VEGETABLE-FRUIT GROUP

Vegetables and fruits are valuable sources of vitamin C, vitamin A, and other nutrients. The group is divided into 3 sections: good and fair sources of vitamin C, good sources of vitamin A, and other fruits and vegetables including potatoes.

Grapefruit, oranges, and their juices are excellent sources of vitamin C. Other good sources are broccoli, cantaloupe, mango, peppers, and fresh strawberries.

The fair sources of vitamin C are asparagus tips, Brussels sprouts, raw cabbage, honeydew melon, potatoes, sweet potatoes cooked in the jacket, spinach, tangerine and tangerine juice, tomatoes and tomato juice, and watermelon.

Fruits and vegetables which are good sources of vitamin A are apricots, broccoli, cantaloupe, carrots, dark green leaves, pumpkin, spinach, sweet potatoes, and winter squash.

Four or more servings of the Vegetable-fruit Group should be eaten each day. This should include 1 serving of a good source of vitamin C or 2 servings of a fair source. Every other day include 1 serving of a good source of vitamin A. Count the following amounts as 1 serving:
$1/2$ cup of fruit or vegetable
1 medium apple, banana, or potato
$1/2$ grapefruit or cantaloupe

## BREAD-CEREAL GROUP

Rich sources of thiamine, niacin, riboflavin, and other nutrients are whole grain, enriched, or restored breads and cereals. Check the labels to be sure your purchase has been enriched.

This group includes breads, cereals, cornmeal, crackers, flour, grits, macaroni, spaghetti, noodles, rice, quick breads, and other baked products.

Four or more servings should be eaten each day. Count as 1 serving:

1 slice of bread
1 ounce ready-to-eat cereal
1/2 cup cooked cereal or pasta

# MEAL PLANNING

Compliments galore are in store for you when you serve a nutritious, attractive, and delicious meal.

The Daily Food Guide on pages 695–697 is your assurance of a nutritious meal. The following six menu planning steps have included selections from the 4 food groups. Begin your meal planning by following these steps:

1. Select a main dish which will provide each family member with one serving from the Meat Group.

2. Add a bread or cereal product which will complement the main dish. It will provide one serving from the Bread-cereal Group. (Remember, potatoes count as a Vegetable-fruit Group serving.)

3. Select a vegetable to serve hot or cold. Include a good source of vitamin A at least every other day.

4. Decide upon a fruit or vegetable salad which will complement the meal. This will provide another serving from the Vegetable-fruit Group.

5. Top off the meal with a dessert. For those who dislike milk, desserts can provide an excellent disguise.

6. Choose a beverage to be served with the meal or dessert. A selection from the Milk Group should be made if it hasn't already been included in the meal.

A selection from each of the above steps may not be desired or needed for every meal. Just be sure that the daily meals provide the correct number of selections from each of the 4 food groups.

Mealtime can relieve worry and tension, especially when you sit down to an attractive meal. Consider yourself an artist painting a picture. The table setting is the background and the meal is the center of focus. Together they create an atmosphere which influences the appetite of your guests. Create a pleasing picture each time you serve a meal. It doesn't have to be a masterpiece.

To make the meal attractive, consider the color of the

food. A variety of colors which complement each other is pleasing to the eye and more appetizing.

The shapes of foods should also harmonize—some whole, some chopped, some mashed. Fruits and vegetables can add this variety by the ways they are cut or served. For example, potatoes can be served mashed, sliced, cubed, or whole.

Limit the number of mixtures served in a meal. For example, when serving a casserole, complement it with sliced tomatoes or lettuce wedge rather than a tossed vegetable salad.

A garnish is an eye-catcher and the fun of meal preparation. Keep it simple and it will add sparkle to the meal.

Create a pleasing table setting for family and for guests. For interesting ideas, see Table Settings, Chapter 17.

The true reward for meal planning is to serve mouth-watering food. When flavors and textures complement each other, food is delicious. Keep in mind the following tips when planning a meal.

• Serve a crisp food with a soft food.

• Accent a bland flavor with a zippy or tart food. Imagine the flavor of each food to determine which accent will blend.

• Season carefully to complement, not hide, the flavor of the food. Usually one highly seasoned food per meal is enough.

• Serve only one starchy food at each meal—potatoes, rice, macaroni, spaghetti, noodles, and sometimes squash or corn. The exception is bread or rolls which can be served with almost any meal.

• Plan a dessert that fits with the meal—a light dessert with a hearty meal, a rich dessert with a light meal.

• Accent hot foods with a cold food served with the main course. Serve hot foods hot, cold foods, cold.

• Add variety to your meals by trying a new food, a new seasoning, or a new way of preparing an old favorite. This keeps meal preparation interesting and rewarding. Your family will also enjoy a variety of foods. Caution: Try only one new food per meal, especially with young children.

• Let your imagination run and plan menus with an inquisitive spirit. Use the following menus for meal planning ideas.

| Beef Main Dish | Starchy Complement | Vegetable |
|---|---|---|
| Beef Pot Roast* | Pot Roasted Potatoes<br>Baked Potato | Pot Roasted Carrots and Onions<br>Broccoli Casserole* |
| Roast Peppered Rib Eye* | Rice with Gravy<br>Boiled New Potatoes | Asparagus Tips<br>Creamed Green Peas |
| Stuffed Tenderloin* | Stuffing*<br>Butter-baked Rice* | Cheesed Cauliflower*<br>Glazed Carrots* |
| Deviled Swiss Steak* | Scalloped Potatoes*<br>Mashed Potatoes | Buttered Green Beans<br>Diced Beets |
| Twin Meat Loaves* | Volcano Potatoes*<br>Baked Potato | Broccoli Spears<br>Leaf Spinach |
| Broiled Beef Steak* | Duchess Potatoes* | Green Peas in Potato Cups<br>Creamed Mushrooms* |
| Outdoor Burgers* | Hamburger Bun<br>Foiled Potatoes* | Roasted Corn*<br>Grilled Tomatoes* |
| Lasagne* | Buttered French Bread<br>Butterhorns* | Italian Green Beans<br>Relishes |
| Hamburger-cheese Bake* | Hard Roll | Wax Beans<br>Raw Cauliflowerets marinated in Italian Salad Dressing |

* All starred recipes appear in this cook book.

| Salad | Dessert | Accent |
|---|---|---|
| Classic Waldorf Salad* Lettuce Wedge with Italian Salad Dressing | Pineapple Chiffon Cake* Sherbet | Pickles Sour Cream Potato Topper |
| Cherry Gelatin Salad Jubilee Salad Mold* | Ice Cream and Oatmeal Cookies* Coffee-mallow Towers* | Chicken Velvet Soup* (appetizer) Relishes |
| Carrot-raisin Salad 24-hour Salad* | Coconut Cream Pie* Black Forest Cake* | Crab Apple (garnish) Pimiento Daisy (on meat) |
| Spicy Apricot Mold* Frozen Fruit Slices* | Chocolate Cake Coffee and Sandies* | Almonds (on beans) Oysters on Half Shell (appetizer) |
| Perfection Salad* Sour Cream Cucumbers* | Ice Cream with Blueberry Sauce* Fruit Compote | Spiced Peach (garnish) Zippy Butter* (for potatoes) |
| Citrus Salad Tossed Salad with French Salad Dressing | Ice Cream with Brownies Concord Grape Pie* | Broiled Tomatoes Cinnamon Apple Rings* |
| Coleslaw* Honeydew Balls | Strawberry Glaze Pie* Mocha Cupcakes* | Condiments Relishes |
| Original Caesar Salad* Tossed Green Salad | Hot Fruit Compote* Peach Pie* | Lime Icebergs* (appetizer) |
| Pickled Beets and Onion Rings Orange-apricot Freeze* | Pineapple Sherbet* Chocolate Roll* | Herb Butter* (for roll) Dessert Mints |

* All starred recipes appear in this cook book.

| Veal Main Dish | Starchy Complement | Vegetable |
|---|---|---|
| Stuffed Breast of Veal* | Sausage-apple Stuffing* Browned Rice* | Cream-style Corn Zucchini Half Shells* |
| Veal Chops* | Noodles Romano* Potato Patties* | Buttered Green Beans with Almonds Sauerkraut |
| Veal Parmigiano* | Noodles Wild Rice | Brussels Sprouts Fried Okra |
| Chopstick Veal Bake* | Spicy Fruit Puffs* | Asparagus Spears Summer Squash Slices |

| Pork Main Dish | Starchy Complement | Vegetable |
|---|---|---|
| Crown Roast of Pork* | Corn Stuffing* Parsleyed New Potatoes* (served in crown) | Beets Green Beans |
| Fruit Stuffed Pork* | Baked Potatoes Baked Sweet Potatoes* | Buttered Brussels Sprouts Corn on the cob |
| Oven Barbecued Ribs* | Buttered French Bread Mashed Potatoes | Confetti Squash* Sauerkraut |
| Baked Ham | Baked Potatoes Creamed Potatoes | Company Cabbage* Asparagus with Croutons |
| Ham Loaf* | Scalloped Potatoes* Mashed Sweet Potatoes* | Broccoli Spears Buttered Green Peas |
| Broiled Ham Slice* | Lemon Parsleyed Turnips* Potato Patties* | Buttered Green Beans Cooked Carrots |

* All starred recipes appear in this cook book.

| Salad | Dessert | Accent |
|---|---|---|
| Lettuce Wedge with Salad Dressing<br>Ginger Fruit Freeze* | Cherries Jubilee*<br>Brownie Torte* | Vinaigrette Dressing* (for salad) |
| Sliced Tomatoes<br>Cheese Stuffed Celery Sticks | Apple Pie<br>Two-berry Parfaits* | Cheddar Cheese Wedge (on pie)<br>Vanilla Wafer (with dessert) |
| Banana-nut Salad*<br>Winter Orange Bowl* | Cream Puffs*<br>Marble Chiffon Cake* | Poppy Seed (add to noodles) |
| Pineapple Boat* | Nutmeg Feather Cake*<br>Cherry Puff* | Fruit French Dressing*<br>Ice Cream (with dessert) |

| Salad | Dessert | Accent |
|---|---|---|
| Tossed Green Salad<br>Applesauce | Cheesecake Supreme*<br>Spice Nut Cake* | Russian Salad Dressing*<br>Water Chestnuts (on beans) |
| Italian Salad Bowl*<br>Wilted Leaf Lettuce* | Kona Coffee Torte*<br>Raspberry Sherbet | Pineapple juice (appetizer)<br>Sugar Cookies* |
| Citrus Salad<br>Tossed Vegetable Salad | Banana-apricot Pie*<br>Berry Floating Island* | Small Mints (after dinner) |
| Apple Pinwheel Salad<br>Lemon Gelatin with Apricots | Sherbet with Spritz*<br>Peanut Brittle Pie* | Tangy Mustard Glaze* (for ham) |
| Green Goddess Salad*<br>Pineapple Rings with Stewed Prune Centers | Swedish Fruit Soup*<br>Butterscotch Sundae (Butterscotch Sauce*) | Pimiento Strips (for broccoli spears)<br>Horseradish Sauce* (for ham) |
| Frozen Fruit Slices*<br>Avocado-grapefruit Sections | Marble Chiffon Cake*<br>Fluffy Tapioca Pudding* | Raisin Sauce* (for ham) |

* All starred recipes appear in this cook book.

| Lamb Main Dish | Starchy Complement | Vegetable |
|---|---|---|
| Roast Leg of Lamb* | Baked Potato<br>Butter-baked Rice* | Zucchini Parmesan*<br>Creamed Peas |
| Lamb Chops Supreme* | Buttered Rice<br>Parsleyed New Potatoes* | Pea Pods Oriental*<br>Buttered Spinach |
| Lamb Stew* | Bread Sticks<br>Cheese Swirls* | Relishes |

| Variety Meats Main Dish | Starchy Complement | Vegetable |
|---|---|---|
| Creamed Sweetbreads* | Pastry Shells<br>Toast Points | Fresh Mushroom Saute*<br>Broiled Tomatoes* |
| Beef and Kidney Pie* | Boiled Potatoes | Buttered Asparagus<br>Beets |
| Panfried Liver* | Hash-brown Potatoes* | Baked Squash<br>Scalloped Corn Supreme* |

| Poultry Main Dish | Starchy Complement | Vegetable |
|---|---|---|
| Perfect Fried Chicken* | French Fries*<br>Mashed Potatoes | Carrots<br>Brussels Sprouts Polonaise* |
| Barbecued Chicken* | Boiled New Potatoes<br>Potluck Potato Salad* | Peas in Cream*<br>Summer Squash |
| Chicken Livers and Rice* | Hard Sesame Seed Roll | Italian Green Beans<br>Squash Rings |

* All starred recipes appear in this cook book.

| Salad | Dessert | Accent |
|---|---|---|
| Jubilee Salad Mold* <br> Fresh Fruit Salad | Lemon Chiffon Pie* <br> Regal Plum <br> Pudding* | Mint Sauce* <br> Honey-lime <br> Dressing* |
| Sparkling Beet <br> Cups* <br> Sliced Tomatoes | Hot Fruit Compote* <br> Fudge Ribbon Pie* | Lemon Wedge (for <br> spinach) |
| Individual Gelatin <br> Salads <br> Orange-apricot <br> Freeze* | Chocolate Mint <br> Dessert* <br> Carrot-pineapple <br> Cake* | Salad Dressing |

| Salad | Dessert | Accent |
|---|---|---|
| Strawberry- <br> pineapple Salad <br> Apple-raisin Salad | Ice Cream <br> Prize Chocolate <br> Cake* | Butterscotch Bars* |
| Pear Half filled <br> with Raspberries <br> French Green Salad* | Angel Cake* <br> Chocolate <br> Charlotte Russe* | Whipped Cream <br> (on dessert) <br> Jellied Consomme* <br> in Honeydew <br> melon (appetizer) |
| Fresh Fruit Toss <br> Cucumber-cheese <br> Ring* | Ice Cream with <br> Chocolate Wafer <br> Fresh Fruit Plate | Melted Marsh- <br> mallows (atop <br> squash) <br> Vanilla Wafer |

| Salad | Dessert | Accent |
|---|---|---|
| Three-bean Salad* <br> Orange Gelatin <br> Salad | Stirred Custard* <br> with Raspberries <br> Parfait and Cookie | Cream Gravy* |
| Harvest Fruit Mold* <br> Peach with Cottage <br> Cheese Salad | Toffee Bars* <br> Strawberry <br> Shortcake* | Creamy Dressing* <br> (for salad) <br> Relishes |
| Golden Peach Plate* <br> Pear and <br> Strawberry Salad | Gingerbread* <br> Custard Pie* | Pineapple Fluff* <br> (for gingerbread) <br> Spiced Tea* |

* All starred recipes appear in this cook book.

| Poultry Main Dish | Starchy Complement | Vegetable |
|---|---|---|
| Chicken Curry* | Rice<br>East Indian Rice Ring* | Buttered Carrots<br>Chinese Pea Pods |
| Roast Turkey | Chestnut Stuffing*<br>Mashed Potatoes | Succotash*<br>Creamed Onions |
| Oven Fried Turkey* | Parsleyed New Potatoes* | Swiss Corn Bake*<br>Tomatoes and Okra* |
| Turkey Noodle Bake* | Sourdough Bread* | Green Peas<br>Harvard Beets* |
| Roast Domestic Duck* | Orange Stuffing*<br>Fluffy Rice | Buttered Asparagus Spears<br>Glazed Carrots* |
| Broiled Cornish Hen* | Wild Rice and Mushrooms*<br>Mashed Sweet Potatoes | Buttered Broccoli Spears<br>Cut Green Beans |

| Fish, Seafood Main Dish | Starchy Complement | Vegetable |
|---|---|---|
| Fried Fish* | Potatoes Au Gratin<br>French Bread | Asparagus<br>Corn on the Cob |
| Halibut Royale* | Creamed Peas and New Potatoes*<br>Mashed Potatoes | Brussels Sprouts with Water Chestnuts |
| Boiled Lobster* | Poppy Seed Rolls<br>Breadsticks | Celery Oriental*<br>Artichoke Velvet* |
| Tuna Salad Bake* | Cloverleaf Rolls*<br>Double Corn Sticks* | Carrots |

* All starred recipes appear in this cook book.

| Salad | Dessert | Accent |
| --- | --- | --- |
| Lime Gelatin Squares<br>Mixed Greens Salad | Sherbet with Cookie<br>Fruit Pie | Condiments<br>Marinated Artichokes* |
| Ginger Fruit Freeze*<br>Cran-raspberry Ring* | Daisy Marble Cake*<br>Lemon Angel Torte* | Cranberry Sauce*<br>(relish) |
| Winter Orange Bowl*<br>Tossed Salad | Regal Plum Pudding*<br>Fresh Fruit Tarts* | Relishes |
| Sunshine Salad*<br>Fresh Fruit Salad | Chocolate Fudge Cake*<br>Ice Cream | Gazpacho*<br>(appetizer)<br>Honey-lime Dressing*<br>(for salad) |
| French Green Salad*<br>Cherry, Marshmallow, and Banana Salad | Pots de Creme*<br>Strawberry Glaze Pie* | Sugar Cookie<br>Nut trim on salad |
| Golden Peach Plate*<br>Lettuce Slice with Salad Dressing | Assorted Cookies<br>Baked Alaska* | Demitasse*<br>Russian Dressing*<br>(for salad) |

| Salad | Dessert | Accent |
| --- | --- | --- |
| Pineapple and Melon Balls<br>Calico Vegetable Bowl* | Pumpkin Pie*<br>Baked Apples* | Whipped Cream Dollop (for pie)<br>Hard Sauce*<br>(for apple) |
| Peach Half filled with Blueberries<br>Rosy Strawberry Ring* | Golden Chiffon Cake*<br>Applesauce Cake* | Pimiento-onion Relish*<br>Shredded Cheese<br>(for potatoes) |
| Tossed Green Salad<br>Wilted Spinach Salad* | Raspberry Bombe*<br>Meringue Shells* filled with Fresh Fruit | Drawn Butter<br>Sparkling Borsch*<br>(appetizer) |
| Tomato Slices<br>Grapefruit Sections | Cherry Burgundy Pie*<br>Chocolate Souffle* | Spiced Peaches<br>(relish)<br>Relishes |

* All starred recipes appear in this cook book.

| Fish, Seafood Main Dish | Starchy Complement | Vegetable |
|---|---|---|
| Fried Fish* | Potatoes Au Gratin French Bread | Asparagus Corn on the Cob |
| Halibut Royale* | Creamed Peas and New Potatoes* Mashed Potatoes | Brussels Sprouts with Water Chestnuts |
| Boiled Lobster* | Poppy Seed Rolls Breadsticks | Celery Oriental* Artichoke Velvet* |
| Tuna Salad Bake* | Cloverleaf Rolls* Double Corn Sticks* | Carrots |

| Salad | Dessert | Accent |
|---|---|---|
| Pineapple and Melon Balls Calico Vegetable Bowl* | Pumpkin Pie* Baked Apples* | Whipped Cream Dollop (for pie) Hard Sauce* (for apple) |
| Peach Half filled with Blueberries Rosy Strawberry Ring* | Golden Chiffon Cake* Applesauce Cake* | Pimiento-onion Relish* Shredded Cheese (for potatoes) |
| Tossed Green Salad Wilted Spinach Salad* | Raspberry Bombe* Meringue Shells* filled with Fresh Fruit | Drawn Butter Sparkling Borsch* (appetizer) |
| Tomato Slices Grapefruit Sections | Cherry Burgundy Pie* Chocolate Souffle* | Spiced Peaches (relish) Relishes |

* All starred recipes appear in this cook book.

# LUNCHES ON THE GO

When filling a lunch box, whether it's for travel or picnics, business or school, keep in mind the following tips:
• For convenience, make a week's supply of sandwiches at once. Wrap individually, placing all of one kind in a box; label with contents and date; freeze. Take wrapped sandwiches from freezer in the morning. They'll be just right for eating at lunch.
• Freeze a can of vegetable or fruit juice overnight. It will be thawed by lunchtime and in the meantime, keeps the rest of the food cool.
• Use a variety of breads: white, rye, whole wheat, French, or nut breads.
• Fixing roast beef or ham sandwiches? Four or five paper-thin slices "bite" easier than one thick slice.
• Keep poultry, eggs, and mayonnaise mixtures, such as ham and potato salads, cool at all times. Keep creamed mixtures at serving temperature—soups hot, puddings and custards cold.
• When packing lettuce and tomato slices, wrap each in foil or clear plastic wrap so they will stay fresh longer. Just before eating, put them into the sandwich.
• Pack salad dressing in a container and pour over salad just before eating.
• An orange partially peeled, then wrapped makes peeling at lunchtime a snap.
• Purchase individual packages of pickles and potato chips to make packing easy.
• Cupcakes baked in paper bake cups and frosted with butter-type frosting travel well.
• The menus on pages 710–711 can be stowed in a lunch box or served to the family at home for a noon meal.

| Main Dish or Sandwich | Salad or Vegetable | Dessert | Beverage |
|---|---|---|---|
| Chili Con Carne* Crackers | Tossed Vegetable Salad with French Dressing | Scotch Short-bread* | Milk |
| Vegetable Beef Soup* Crackers | Mixed Fruit Salad | Cake Brownie* | Orange Drink |
| Cheese Chowder* Melba Toast | Whole Apple | Everyday Cupcakes* | Tomato Juice |
| Chilled Asparagus Soup* Sesame Seed Crackers | Nectarine | Fruitcake | Spiced Tea* |
| Old Time Beef Stew* Hard Roll | Celery Sticks Olives | Red Cherry Pie* | Lemonade* |
| Wiener-bean Bake* Boston Brown Bread | Pineapple-carrot Toss* | Peanut Butter Cupcakes* | Coffee |
| Club Sandwich* | Orange Olives and Pickles | Jelly Roll* Slice | Breakfast Cocoa* |
| Corned Beef on Rye with Dill Pickles | Coleslaw* | Peach Pie* | Raspberry Cooler* |
| Sliced Ham on Whole Wheat Hard Cooked Egg | Tomato Slices | Chocolate Pudding* | Iced Tea |

* All starred recipes appear in this cook book.

| Main Dish or Sandwich | Salad or Vegetable | Dessert | Beverage |
| --- | --- | --- | --- |
| Roast Beef Sandwich Potato Chips | Three Bean Salad* | Ripe Plum | Eggnog* |
| Submarine Sandwich* | Applesauce | Lemon Pudding Cake* | Carbonated Beverage |
| Swiss Cheese on English Muffin | Raw Cauli- flowerets Pickles | Ginger- bread* | Grape Juice |
| Bacon-peanut butter Sandwich | Carrot Sticks Radishes | Apricot Foldovers* | Hot Mulled Cider* |
| Chef's Salad Bowl* Raisin- cinnamon Rolls* | | Pecan Crispies* | Chocolate Malted Milk |
| Cottage Cheese Best Nut Loaf* | Mixed Fruit Salad Shawano Dressing* | Gumdrop Gems* | Hot Tea |

* All starred recipes appear in this cook book.

# ENTERTAINING MENUS

## • HEARTY AND LIGHT COMBINATIONS TO SPARK MORNING OR MIDDAY •

### Pancake Breakfast

Sliced Bananas in
Orange Juice
Canadian-style Bacon*
Feather Pancakes*
Lingonberry Sauce*
Coffee

### Hearty Breakfast

Apple Juice
Broiled Bacon*
Scrambled Eggs*
Cornmeal Waffles*
Butter          Honey Butter*
Coffee

### Brunch

Wine Eggs Mornay*
Asparagus Spears
Green Goddess Salad*
Ruby Fruit Compote*
Demitasse

### Weekend Brunch

Grapefruit Juice
Sausage*                    Bacon*
Cheese Scrambled Eggs*
Herbed Tomatoes*
Cinnamon Crescents*
Hot Fruit Compote*
Coffee

### Indoor-outdoor Brunch

Limeade*
Ham and Fruit Kabobs*
Cheddar Bran Muffins*
Whipped Butter
Tossed Green Salad
Strawberry-rhubarb Pie*
Iced Tea

### Children's Lunch

Nutty Pups*
Pineapple-carrot Toss*
Potato Chips      Pickle Relish
Popcorn Pops*
Milk

### Ladies Only

Crab-artichoke Bake*
Assorted Relishes
Hard Rolls          Butter Roses
Orange Souffle*
Coffee                    Tea

### Club Women's Lunch

Club Chicken Casserole*
Tomato Slices      Carrot Sticks
Cran-raspberry Ring*
Fudge Ribbon Pie*

* All starred recipes appear in this cook book.

### Easter Breakfast

Fruit Cup*
Crisp Bacon
Goldenrod Eggs*
Golden Bubble Ring*
Coffee

### Tea or Reception

Jigsaw Sandwiches*
Watercress Pinwheels*
Chicken Puffs*
Pecan Tassies*
Small Mints*

Tea        Punch        Coffee

## • FESTIVE DINNERS, BUFFETS FOR ENTERTAINING TWO TO TWENTY •

### Dinner for Two

Hot Sherried Consomme*
Roast Pheasant*
Riced Potatoes
Green Beans Almond*
Fresh Orange Salad
Creme de Menthe Parfait
Coffee

_____

### Dinner for Four

Green Pepper Strips
Cauliflowerets
Carrot Sticks
Vegetable Dip
Beef Fondue*
Creamy Onion Dip*
Cocktail Sauce*
Butter-browned Mushrooms
Mustard Sauce*
Tossed Green Salad
Oil and Vinegar Dressing
French Bread        Butter
Pineapple Sherbet*        Wafers
Coffee

### Duck Dinner

Two-tone Cocktail*
Roast Domestic Duck*
Orange Stuffing*
Wild Rice and Mushrooms*
Frenched Green Beans
Bibb Lettuce Salad
Curry Dressing*
Spiced Crab Apples
Hard Rolls        Butter
Raspberry Sherbet
Coffee

_____

### Potluck Buffet

*An informal get-together
for several families—*
Swedish Meatballs*
Noodle Ring
Peas with Mushrooms
Spiced Peach Halves
Carrot and Celery Sticks
Olives
Buttered Rolls
Chocolate Cake*
Coffee        Milk

_____

* *All starred recipes appear in this cook book.*

### Dinner for Six

Madrilene
Flounder Provencale*
Buttered Peas
French Green Salad*
Popovers*
Currant Jelly        Butter
Pots de Creme*
Coffee

### Late Evening Buffet

Guacamole*
Olive Cheese Ball*
Corn Chips
Assorted Crackers
Ham and Rye Rounds*
Coconut Macaroons*
Raspberry Foldovers*
Cafe au Lait*

### Saint and Sinner Dinner

Cheese Board
Assorted Crackers
Broiled Beef Steak*
Boiled Lobster*
Buttered Asparagus
Grapefruit-avocado Salad
Brioche*        Butter
Cherries Jubilee*
Coffee

### Men Only

Cheese Stuffed Apples*
Assorted Crackers
Shrimp Cocktail
Hasenpfeffer*
Mashed Potatoes        Gravy
Peas and Carrots
Men's Favorite Salad*
Dinner Rolls        Butter
Red Cherry Pie*
Coffee

## • FOOD FOR SPECIAL OCCASIONS— HOLIDAYS, PICNICS, AND PARTIES •

### Thanksgiving Buffet

Swedish Pickled Shrimp*
Cold Sliced Smoked Turkey
Frosted Cranberry Salad*
Buttered Dinner Rolls
Pumpkin Pie*
Coffee        Tea

### Christmas Dinner

Oysters Rockefeller*
Roast Domestic Goose*
Baked Potatoes        Butter
Broccoli Casserole*
Classic Waldorf Salad*
Tutti-frutti Tortoni*
Coffee        Tea

### Outdoor Barbecue

Barbecued Short Ribs*
Roasted Corn*
Grilled Garlic Slices*
Italian Salad Bowl*
Cantaloupe and Ice Cream
Beverage

### Supper Party

Classic Cheese Fondue*
French Bread
Apple Wedges
Spiced Tea*

---

* All starred recipes appear in this cook book.

# NUTRITIONAL LABELING

At first glance, labels on many packaged foods may seem confusing. But, take a longer look and you'll discover information that can make you a wiser shopper.

As required by the Food and Drug Administration, the type of label shown must be on all foods to which vitamins or minerals have been added and that are advertised as having special nutritional qualities.

Ingredients are listed in descending order of amounts except on packaged foods considered to be standards, such as mayonnaise and ice cream, which are covered by separate regulations.

The U.S. Recommended Daily Allowances are based on the levels of protein, vitamins, and minerals needed by most people to maintain good health.

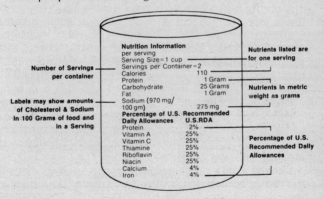

| | | |
|---|---|---|
| Number of Servings per container | **Nutrition Information** per serving Serving Size = 1 cup Servings per Container = 2 | Nutrients listed are for one serving |
| | Calories 110 | |
| | Protein 1 Gram | |
| | Carbohydrate 25 Grams | Nutrients in metric weight as grams |
| | Fat 1 Gram | |
| Labels may show amounts of Cholesterol & Sodium in 100 Grams of food and in a Serving | Sodium (970 mg/ 100 gm) 275 mg | |
| | **Percentage of U.S. Recommended Daily Allowances U.S.RDA** | |
| | Protein 2% | |
| | Vitamin A 25% | |
| | Vitamin C 25% | |
| | Thiamine 25% | Percentage of U.S. Recommended Daily Allowances |
| | Riboflavin 25% | |
| | Niacin 25% | |
| | Calcium 4% | |
| | Iron 4% | |

# FOOD STORAGE GUIDE

**Fresh Fruit:** Sort to remove injured fruit before storing. Refrigerate ripe tomatoes, apples, oranges, lemons, grapefruit, limes, kumquats, tangerines, peaches, apricots, cherries, grapes, pears, plums, and rhubarb in a loosely covered container or perforated moisture-vaporproof bag to reduce wilting and drying. Store bananas, melons, avocados, and pineapple at cool room temperature. Store berries dry in the refrigerator; wash before serving.

To ripen fruit, place in well-ventilated area at room temperature; avoid direct sunlight. Tomatoes, peaches, bananas, avocados, pears, and plums can be ripened. Refrigerate ripened fruit, except bananas, till ready to use.

**Fresh Vegetables:** White potatoes, sweet potatoes, onions, and winter squash should be stored unwashed in a cool, dry dark place with good ventilation. Wash and thoroughly drain salad greens, celery, green onions, asparagus, and cabbage. Refrigerate in individual moisture-vaporproof bags. Remove tops of carrots, beets, and radishes; refrigerate in individual moisture-vaporproof bags. Husked sweet corn may be refrigerated in moisture-vaporproof bag for a short period of time. Leave peas in the pod and refrigerate.

**Dried fruit, nuts:** Store dried fruit in tightly closed container at room temperature. Nuts will keep longer if refrigerated in tightly covered containers. Unshelled and unsalted nuts stay fresher.

**Canned Fruit:** Store in cool dry place. Open canned foods may be stored in original can, covered, in refrigerator.

**Flour, cereals:** Store at room temperature in tight containers.

**Dairy products, eggs:** Cottage cheese, hard cheese, milk, and butter should be tightly covered and stored in refrigerator. Store strong-flavored cheeses, such as Limburger, refrigerated in a tightly covered jar. Eggs are stored in a covered container or original carton in refrigerator.

Egg yolks can be refrigerated in tightly covered container for 2 to 3 days. Egg whites keep for a week to 10 days refrigerated in a tightly covered container.

**Meat, poultry, fish:** Fresh meat and poultry should be loosely wrapped and stored in the refrigerator. Fresh meat prepackaged in moisture-vaporproof wrap can be refrigerated as is for 1 to 2 days. For longer storage it should be loosened at both ends. Fresh meat, paper wrapped from the butcher, should be rewrapped loosely in waxed paper. Cool and refrigerate cooked meat promptly, then cover to prevent drying. Cured meat and luncheon meat should be refrigerated in original wrap. Most canned hams should be refrigerated (see label).

Giblets should be removed from poultry, wrapped loosely, and stored separately. Remove stuffing and meat from bones of cooked poultry as soon as possible; chill; cover or wrap separately. Do not chop fresh poultry until ready to use. Fish should be stored in moisture-vaporproof bags or tightly covered container in refrigerator. For maximum quality of refrigerated meat stored at 36° to 40°, see chart below.

| MEAT | TIME |
|------|------|
| **BEEF** | |
| Roasts | 3 to 5 days |
| Steaks | 3 to 5 days |
| Ground beef, stew meat | 2 days |
| **PORK** | |
| Roasts | 3 to 5 days |
| Hams, picnics, whole | 7 days |
| Bacon | 7 to 14 days |
| Chops, spareribs | 2 to 3 days |
| Pork sausage | 1 to 2 days |
| **VEAL** | |
| Roasts | 3 to 5 days |
| Chops | 4 days |
| **LAMB** | |
| Roasts | 3 to 5 days |
| Chops | 3 to 5 days |
| Ground lamb | 2 days |
| **POULTRY** | |
| Chickens, whole | 1 to 2 days |
| Chickens, cut up | 2 days |
| Turkeys, whole | 1 to 2 days |
| **COOKED MEATS** | |
| Leftover cooked meats | 4 days |
| Cooked poultry | 2 days |
| Hams, picnics | 7 days |
| Frankfurters | 4 to 5 days |
| Sliced luncheon meats | 3 days |
| Unsliced Bologna | 4 to 6 days |

# 17

# SPECIAL HELPS

Partially set gelatin is like egg white.

Snip and measure fresh herbs in one step.

Peel citrus fruit. Cut down side of one section membrane—slide fruit section off.

Snip fresh herbs; crush dried.
Arrange containers alphabetically for quick use.

Use decorating equipment for pretty stuffed eggs
and celery, or planked potatoes.

# MOVING TO METRIC

One day soon, the United States will change from the inch-pound system of measurement to the metric system. The change will come gradually, but come it will. Legislation is now pending in the United States Congress; Canada already has started to convert. Adapting to the metric system will be easy if we begin now to think metric.

Why change? The United States is changing mainly for economic reasons. Most of the countries of the world—almost 95 percent of the world's population—already use metric units or are converting to the metric system. Establishing business agreements based on this efficient, nearly universal system will greatly increase our world trade.

Already the metric system is making inroads into some aspects of our daily living—metric sizes are given on prescription drugs, camera film, and skis, for example. Most of the major changes will be in manufacturing and industry, but as a consumer, you and your family will notice changes in food packaging, clothing sizes, speed limits, and weather reports.

## LEARNING THE METRIC LANGUAGE

The key to learning the metric system is relating to concepts in metric terms and avoiding, wherever possible, converting measurements from metric to inch-pound units. You'll find it helpful to associate the new metric measurements with a familiar object or activity (see chart at top of page 725).

Fortunately, the metric system is simpler than our present one. All relationships between the various units work in powers of ten, just as pennies and dimes do in our money system.

It is only necessary to learn four basic metric units for everyday use—meter, liter, gram, and degree Celsius.

**Meter** becomes the unit for measuring length, replacing inch, foot, yard, and mile.

**Liter** will be the metric unit for volume, eliminating the pint, quart, gallon, fluid ounce, teaspoon, tablespoon, and cup.

**Gram** becomes the metric measure of weight, replacing the ounce and pound.

**Degree Celsius** is the metric measurement of temperature.

When these basic units are inconvenient in size for a particular measurement, multiples are used for large measures and submultiples for small measures. Because all multiples and submultiples are factors of ten, changing from one multiple of a unit to another is done simply by moving the decimal point. The larger and smaller units are obtained by combining prefixes with the basic unit.

## PREFIXES USED IN COOKING

| Prefix | Symbol | Means Multiply By |
|--------|--------|-------------------|
| kilo   | k      | 1000              |
| centi  | c      | 0.01              |
| milli  | m      | 0.001             |

Thus, the term kilogram means 1000 grams, a centigram is 1/100 of a gram; and a milligram is 1/1000 of a gram. Prefixes always remain the same whether they are combined with a gram, meter, or liter.

When writing metrics, don't use periods after the symbols, and always leave a space between the number and the metric symbol. Also, never use an "s" after a plural measurement, as the number itself indicates plurality. And finally, don't capitalize symbols unless otherwise designated.

## SHOPPING WITH METRIC

The new metric units will make shopping easier. The numerous sizes of packaged, canned, and frozen foods will, in most cases, be replaced by fewer and simpler metric sizes. These changes in units will make calculations uncomplicated, which, in turn, will make price comparisons and unit pricing easier. For foods sold by number, such as fruits and vegetables, the method of purchase will not

## PUTTING METRIC UNITS IN PERSPECTIVE

| Quantity | Unit | Symbol | Example |
| --- | --- | --- | --- |
| Length | millimeter | mm | About the thickness of a dime |
| | centimeter | cm | The width of your fingernail |
| | meter | m | About 3 inches longer than a yard |
| | kilometer | km | About two-thirds of a mile |
| Weight (mass) | gram | g | The weight of a paper clip |
| | kilogram | kg | Slightly more than 2 pounds |
| Volume | milliliter | ml | A pinch of salt |
| | liter | l | About 1/4 cup larger than a quart |

change. But, foods sold by weight, such as meat or potatoes, will be sold by the kilogram, and foods sold by volume, such as milk, will be sold by the liter.

When the transition period begins, packages will give both the metric and the conventional unit of measure. Eventually, only the metric unit will appear on the package label.

## METRIC IN THE KITCHEN

Cooking with metric measures will be as easy as cooking with our present measures. Techniques won't change—we will measure out ingredients just as we always have. The difference will be in the measuring utensils. Most recipe ingredients will be listed in milliliters or grams rather than in cups, tablespoons, teaspoons, pounds, or ounces.

For metric recipes, new metric measures are being developed. These will be similar in appearance and use to our present measures, but based on metric units. There still will be three types of measures—liquid measures, dry measures, and a set of small "spoon" measures.

**Liquid measures** will be available in three sizes—a 250 ml measure graduated in 25 ml (slightly larger than our

8-ounce liquid measuring cup), a 500 ml measure graduated in 25 ml, and a 1000 ml or 1-liter measure graduated in 50 ml.

**Dry measure set** will include 250 ml (slightly larger than our present 1-cup measure), 125 ml, and 50 ml measures.

**Small liquid and dry measure set** will include five measures marked as 1 ml, 2 ml, 5 ml (size of a teaspoon), 15 ml (size of a tablespoon), and 25 ml (size of a coffee measure). The different number of measures in the metric sets—three instead of four in dry measures and five instead of four in small measures—will help distinguish the metric measures from our present measuring utensils.

Cookware volumes will be marked in liters, and bakeware dimensions will be described in centimeters. Measurement of temperature will change from degrees Fahrenheit to degrees Celsius. (For the range of temperatures used in cooking, the number of degrees Celsius is about half the number of degrees Fahrenheit.)

If you're concerned about what will happen to your old recipes and cook books, there's no need to be. You may continue to use your existing measuring utensils when preparing your old recipes, and use your set of metric measures for your new collection of metric recipes.

## OVEN TEMPERATURES

|  | Degrees Fahrenheit | Degrees Celsius |
|---|---|---|
| Very slow oven | 250-275 | 120-135 |
| Slow oven | 300-325 | 150-165 |
| Moderate oven | 350-375 | 175-190 |
| Hot oven | 400-425 | 205-220 |
| Very hot oven | 450-475 | 230-245 |

# TO MEASURE CORRECTLY

Measuring equipment may be made of metal, glass, or plastic. Choose the material and design that suits you best.

Individual cups are for measuring dry ingredients. Glass cups with pour spouts are marked for liquid levels. The standard measuring cup has the capacity of $1/2$ pint or 8 ounces. It may save time to have large glass measures on hand, too. The standard individual measuring spoons are in sets of 1 tablespoon, 1 teaspoon, $1/2$ teaspoon, $1/4$ teaspoon, and sometimes $1/8$ teaspoon. Warped measuring spoons and dented cups result in inaccurate measurements.

Measuring tools are a must in any kitchen for consistent results in cooking. Learn to use these tools for accurate measuring.

For dry ingredients, use fractional individual measuring cups, in sets of 1 cup, $1/2$ cup, $1/3$ cup, and $1/4$ cup sizes. For less than a $1/4$-cup measure, use standard measuring spoons. Use glass cups for liquids.

Measuring spoons are used for small amounts of liquid or dry foods. Dip spoon into dry ingredients and level off with straightedge. Do not pour or level ingredients over a bowl of another ingredient.

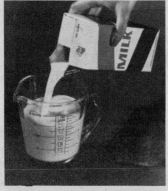

Liquids—place standard glass measuring cup on flat surface. Bend down to read the desired mark at eye level. The cup has a rim above the last cup level to prevent spilling and a spout for pouring.

Dry ingredients—pile lightly into measuring cup with spoon. Do not shake cup. Level off with straight edge of spatula. Pack brown sugar so firmly in cup that it will keep the cup shape when turned out.

If the volume is not marked on bottom of pan or dish, fill a cup or quart measure with water; pour into pan or dish. Repeat till full. Determine surface area by measuring from the inside edges of pan or dish.

# BEFORE-AND-AFTER MEASUREMENTS IN FOOD PREPARATION

Foods change measure when you crumble, cook, shred, or chop them. Questions pop up every day: How many crackers in a cup of crumbs? How many fresh cherries will fill a pie when pitted? How much sauce can be made from a pound of cranberries? In this chart, you'll find the answers to these and similar questions.

| | Food | Amount before Preparation | Approximate Measure after Preparation |
|---|---|---|---|
| Cereals | Cornmeal | 1 cup (5 ounces) | 5$\frac{1}{2}$ cups cooked |
| | Macaroni | 4 ounces (1 cup) | 2 cups cooked |
| | Noodles | 4 ounces (3 cups) | 3 cups cooked |
| | Quick-cooking oats | 1 cup (3 ounces) | 1$\frac{3}{4}$ cups cooked |
| | Rice, long-grain | 1 cup (7 ounces) | 3 cups cooked |
| | packaged precooked | 1 cup (3 ounces) | 2 cups cooked |
| | Spaghetti | 8 ounces | 4 cups cooked |
| Crumbs | Bread | 1$\frac{1}{2}$ slices | 1 cup soft crumbs |

| | Food | Amount before Preparation | Approximate Measure after Preparation |
|---|---|---|---|
| | | 1 slice | ¼ cup fine dry crumbs |
| | Chocolate wafers | 19 wafers | 1 cup crumbs |
| | Graham crackers | 14 square crackers | 1 cup fine crumbs |
| | Potato chips | 4 ounces | 2 cups coarsely crushed |
| | Saltine crackers | 28 crackers | 1 cup finely crushed |
| | Vanilla wafers | 22 wafers | 1 cup finely crushed |
| | Zwieback | 6 ounces | 2 cups finely crushed |
| | Rich round crackers | 24 crackers | 1 cup finely crushed |
| | Gingersnap cookies | 15 cookies | 1 cup finely crushed |
| Dairy products | Blue cheese | 4 ounces | 1 cup crumbled |
| | Cheese, American or Cheddar | 4 ounces | 1 cup shredded or cubed |
| | Cream, whipping | 1 cup | 2 cups whipped |
| Dried fruit | Apples | 4 cups (12 ounces) | 5 cups cooked |
| | Apricots | 3 cups (11 ounces) | 4 cups cooked |
| | Figs | 3 cups (16 ounces) | 3 cups cooked |

| | Food | Amount before Preparation | Approximate Measure after Preparation |
|---|---|---|---|
| | Mixed fruit | 3 cups (12 ounces) | $3^1/_2$ cups cooked |
| | Peaches | 3 cups (11 ounces) | 5 cups cooked |
| | Pears | 3 cups (14 ounces) | 5 cups cooked |
| | Prunes, with pits | 3 cups (16 ounces) | 5 cups cooked |
| Dried vegetables | Kidney beans | 1 cup | $2^1/_4$ cups cooked |
| | Lima beans | 1 cup | $2^1/_4$ cups cooked |
| | Navy beans | 1 cup | $2^1/_4$ cups cooked |
| | Peas, green | 1 cup | $2^1/_4$ cups cooked |
| Fresh fruit | Apples, whole | 1 pound (3 medium) | $2^3/_4$ cups pared and diced or sliced |
| | Apricots, whole | 1 pound (8 to 12) | $2^1/_2$ cups halved or sliced |
| | Avocado | 1 pound (2 medium) | $2^1/_2$ cups sliced |
| | Bananas, whole | 1 pound (3 to 4) | 2 cups sliced or $1^1/_3$ cups mashed |
| | Cherries, red | 1 pound | 2 cups pitted |
| | Cranberries | 1 pound (4 cups) | 4 cups sauce |
| | Grapes | 1 pound | $2^1/_2$ cups seeded |

|  | Food | Amount before Preparation | Approximate Measure after Preparation |
|---|---|---|---|
|  | Lemon | 1 medium | 3 tablespoons juice<br>2 teaspoons grated peel |
|  | Orange | 1 medium | 1/4 to 1/3 cup juice<br>1/2 cup diced or sectioned |
|  | Peaches | 1 medium | 1/2 cup sliced |
|  | Pears | 1 medium | 1/2 cup sliced |
|  | Rhubarb, cut | 1 pound (4 to 8 pieces) | 2 cups cooked |
|  | Strawberries | 1 quart | 4 cups sliced |
| Fresh vegetables | Beans, green | 1 pound (3 cups) | 2 1/2 cups cooked |
|  | Beets, without tops | 1 pound (4 medium) | 2 cups cooked and diced |
|  | Brussels sprouts | 1 pound (4 cups) | 2 1/2 cups cooked |
|  | Cabbage | 1 pound (1 small head) | 5 cups shredded or 2 cups cooked |
|  | Carrots, without tops | 1 pound (6 to 8 medium) | 3 cups shredded or 2 1/2 cups diced or 2 to 2 1/2 cups cooked |
|  | Celery | 1 medium bunch | 4 1/2 cups diced or chopped |

| | Food | Amount before Preparation | Approximate Measure after Preparation |
|---|---|---|---|
| | Corn, ears | 12 medium | 2½ cups cooked |
| | Green onions with tops | 1 bunch (7 medium onions) | ½ cup sliced |
| | Green pepper | 1 large (6 ounces) | 1 cup diced |
| | Mushrooms, crowns | ¼ pound (1¼ cups) | ½ cup cooked |
| | sliced | ¼ pound (1¼ cups) | ⅜ cup cooked |
| | chopped | ¼ pound (1¼ cups) | ⅜ cup cooked |
| | Olives, stuffed | 4 ounces (48 small) | 1 cup sliced |
| | Onions | 1 medium | ½ cup chopped |
| | Potatoes | 1 pound (3 medium) | 2 cups pared and thinly sliced or 2 cups cubed and cooked or 1¾ cups mashed |
| | Radishes | 1 bunch | about 1 cup sliced |
| | Spinach | 1 pound (4 cups) | 1½ cups cooked |
| | Tomatoes | 1 pound (4 small) | 1½ cups cooked |
| Nuts | Almonds in shell | 1 pound | 1¼ cups shelled |

| Food | Amount before Preparation | Approximate Measure after Preparation |
|------|---------------------------|----------------------------------------|
| Pecans in shell | 1 pound | 2 cups halved or chopped |
| Walnuts in shell | 1 pound | 1½ to 1¾ cups halved or chopped |

# Ingredients—
# how to use them

## FLOUR

**All-purpose flour** is the "backbone" ingredient in most baked goods. It's usually a blend of hard and soft wheats to give best all-around results. The terms white, wheat, or plain flours are synonymous.

**Self-rising flour** contains leavening and salt. When used in quick breads, omit baking powder, soda, and salt. It cannot be used for baking yeast breads.

**Cake flour,** for delicate cakes, is softer and whiter than all-purpose flour.

Sift all white or wheat flour once; pile lightly into measuring cup with spoon. Do not shake cup; level with spatula.

Whole wheat (also referred to as graham flour), rye and buckwheat flours, bran, cornmeal, and oatmeal are available for special uses. These flours are usually used in combination with all-purpose flour. Whole-grain flours and meals are not sifted. Stir them, then spoon lightly into measuring cup and level.

## FATS AND OILS

**Fats** are solid at room temperature and are made from vegetable or animal products, or a combination of both. Solid fats include hydrogenated vegetable fats, lard, butter, and margarine. Hydrogenated fats are the most common shortening used in baked goods. Butter or margarine is used for flavor and to modify textures. Its creaming quality is not as good as hydrogenated fats. Lard and vegetable oils do not cream well.

**Oils** are fats that are liquid at room temperature and are usually of vegetable origin. Salad oil has been processed to stay clear when refrigerated; cooking oils become cloudy. The frequently used oils are corn, cottonseed, olive, peanut, soybean, and safflower. Vegetable oils are used for salad dressings, cooking fat, and in some baked products (with the exception of olive oil).

**Drippings** are fats usually obtained by cooking fat meats (bacon, pork, beef, etc.).

## LEAVENINGS

**Leavenings** are substances that form bubbles of gas (carbon dioxide) or physical leavenings such as steam and air. The gas, air, or steam expands when a batter or dough is heated, making baked product light and affecting grain and texture.

Leavening agents include yeast, baking powder, and soda (plus a food acid).

**Yeast** is a tiny plant that produces carbon dioxide from sugar when temperature and moisture are favorable for its growth. Yeast comes in two forms—active dry and compressed. Before active dry yeast is used, soften it in warm water (110°) for 5 to 10 minutes. Soften compressed yeast in lukewarm water or other liquid (85°) for the same time.

**Baking powder** can be SAS-phosphate (double-acting), phosphate, or tartrate type. The double-acting type frees a small amount of gas when combined with liquid, the major part when heated.

Phosphate type gives off part of its gas when mixed with liquid and the remaining when heated. Tartrate type reacts almost entirely when combined with the liquid. The gas formed expands when batter is heated. *Recipes in this book are based on double-acting baking powder.*

**Baking soda** gives off gas when mixed with a food acid such as buttermilk, sour milk, molasses, vinegar, or lemon juice. One-fourth teaspoon baking soda plus ½ cup sour milk is equivalent to 1 teaspoon baking powder (double-acting) and ½ cup liquid.

## EGGS

**Slightly beaten eggs** are whole eggs beaten with fork only long enough to break up the yolks and have streaks of white and yellow. Used to thicken custards and to coat foods with egg and crumbs.

**Beaten eggs** are whipped till whites and yolks are blended. Used to give light texture to batters and doughs and as a binder in baked products, salad dressings.

**Well-beaten eggs** are whole eggs beaten until light in color and texture.

**Well-beaten egg yolks** are beaten till fine, thick, and literally lemon-colored foam is formed. Used in sponge cakes.

**Stiffly beaten egg whites** are beaten till peaks stand up straight, but are still moist and glossy. Often egg whites are beaten to *soft peaks*—the peaks droop over slightly. Sugar is then added gradually while beating to stiff peaks. This increases the air-holding property of the egg whites. Angel cake is leavened by expansion of air held in egg whites and by steam during baking. Macaroons, souffles, and chiffon pies all rely on stiffly beaten egg whites for lightness.

## SUGAR

**Sugar**—this term refers to beet or cane granulated white sugar.

**Confectioners'** or powdered sugar is granulated sugar crushed and screened to desired fineness. Often used in frostings.

**Brown sugar** is refined less than granulated sugar. The darker the color the more molasses remaining on the sugar crystals and the stronger the flavor.

**Granulated brown sugar** is measured like white sugar. Adjust recipes when substituting for moist brown sugar.

## THICKENING AGENTS

**Flour** may be thoroughly blended with fat before liquid is added. Or, it may be blended with cold liquid or with sugar before combining with hot mixture. Cook and stir till thickened and bubbly.

**Cornstarch** may be blended with cold liquid or sugar before adding to hot mixture. Cook and stir till thick and bubbly.

**Tapioca**—Quick-cooking tapioca is used in recipes in this book. It is added to the liquid mixture. No soaking is necessary. Heat just to boiling; don't overcook. Cool without stirring. If using pearl tapioca, use about double the amount and soak several hours. Cook till transparent.

**Eggs** are slightly beaten when used for thickening. To add them to a hot mixture, stir small amount of hot mixture into eggs; then stir egg mixture into remaining hot mixture. Cook and stir over low heat.

## GELATIN

**Gelatin**—This term used without further description means granulated unflavored gelatin. To use, soften 1 envelope (1 tablespoon) in $1/2$ cup cold liquid; allow to stand a few minutes. Stir over direct heat till dissolved, about 2 or 3 minutes, or dissolve over boiling water. Or, blend 1 tablespoon or more sugar with gelatin (don't soften); dissolve directly in hot liquid. One envelope unflavored gelatin will set 2 cups liquid. Remember to count the liquid used for softening as part of the total liquid.

**Flavored gelatin** is a mixture of gelatin, sugar, fruit acids, flavors, and coloring. Dissolve in boiling liquid. One 3-ounce package of flavored gelatin will set 2 cups of liquid and 2 cups well-drained fruit.

## MILK

**Skim milk** has a milk fat content of less than 0.5 percent.

**Low fat milk** has a milk fat content between that of skim milk and whole milk.

**Homogenized whole milk** (about 3.25 percent milk fat) is pasteurized milk that has been treated so the cream will not rise to the top.

**Evaporated milk** is whole milk with 60 percent of the water removed. When mixed with an equal volume of water, its nutritive value is similar to that of whole milk. Undiluted, it can be used in place of cream, or when chilled until fine ice crystals form, it can be whipped.

**Sweetened condensed milk** is concentrated whole milk mixed with sugar.

**Nonfat dry milk** is skim milk with the water removed. Reconstitute with water according to package directions.

# CREAM

**Light cream or half-and-half** is used in coffee or for table use. It is used in our recipes where richness is desired.

**Whipping cream** contains 30 to 40 percent fat. Chill well before beating. Chill bowl and beaters, too.

**Dairy sour cream** is commercially cultured light cream. It has a pleasant tang and a smooth, thick texture. It's used to give richness and zesty flavor.

# TABLE SETTINGS

Half the fun of preparing a delicious meal lies in planning a pretty table setting as a background for serving. Gone are the days when only guests were treated to the best linen, china, flatware, and crystal, while the family faced the same table setting day in and day out.

Taking the time to set an attractive table makes every meal more enjoyable, since the setting is as much a part of the meal as the food which is served. An imaginative setting seems to make food taste better.

Where to begin? Your table settings should reflect your own interests and life-style. A brightly colored set of place mats or a basket filled with garden flowers could be your inspiration. Notice store displays and advertisements; don't be afraid to experiment with different combinations.

Basically, table settings include the table covering and centerpiece as well as the dinnerware and glassware. Coordinating the colors, designs, and styles is the secret to making the table setting an attractive background for the food.

## TABLE COVERINGS

The traditional table "linens" have been expanded to include nearly every fabric on the market plus plastics, woven straw fibers, and paper products. A collection of cloths, mats, runners, and napkins in a variety of colors and materials lets you choose and change table settings to match your mood or to create a special theme.

A good basic collection includes easy-care place mats for everyday use, plus several tablecloths that you can use for both formal and informal settings. If you entertain frequently, you'll probably want a wide selection of colors, patterns, and materials in cloths, mats, runners, and napkins to use interchangeably.

When buying table coverings, look for the fiber content listed on the "hangtags." This determines the amount of care they'll need and the amount of wear they'll give. Disposable paper table coverings also are available in many colors and designs.

**Tablecloths:** The first consideration in buying tablecloths is the size of your table, so measure before you go shopping. For a formal tablecloth, allow an overhang of 16 to 24 inches on each side. An informal cloth needs less drop; allow 10 to 14 inches. Banquet cloths are the only ones that should touch the floor. Tablecloth hems should be narrow, with even, straight stitches. Hand-sewn hems are more elegant than machine-stitched hems.

Tablecloths often are placed over a table pad that fits the table exactly, or over a heavy white material called a silence cloth, which extends 3 to 5 inches over the edge. Cloths with delicate embroidery or lace show off best when placed over a bare table.

A tablecloth may have a fold down the center of the table, with the fold in the cloth tentwise to the surface of the table. Be sure to press out all other folds.

Remove any spots before laundering and do any mending that's needed, as the washing may accentuate frayed areas. To save last-minute ironing, carefully roll pressed tablecloth on cylinder of paper before storing, or hang on clothes hanger.

For an easy table covering when you want something different, consider using a permanent-press bed sheet. They're available in various colors and patterns.

**Place Mats:** Because they come in such a wide range of colors, designs, materials, sizes, and shapes, place mats are the most versatile of all table covers. They are acceptable for every occasion except the afternoon tea or the most formal dinner.

Each mat should be large enough to hold an entire place setting but not so large that it overlaps other mats on the table. Mats generally are available in sizes that range from 12 to 14 inches deep and 16 to 18 inches wide.

When the shape of the place mat allows, lay the edge of the mat even with the edge of the table. The center of the table may be left bare or covered by a matching or coordinating table runner. Cloth napkins are most appropriate with cloth place mats. Paper napkins may be used with others.

**Table Runners:** A comparative newcomer to the tabletop scene is the table runner. These narrow lengths of fabric are placed on either side of the table to hold numerous place settings. Or, two runners may be crisscrossed to accommodate four places. Fabric for table runners is sold by the yard, so it's easy to get the exact length needed for your table.

**Napkins:** Tablecloths and place mats often are sold with a set of coordinating napkins. For mixing and matching, single napkins also are available in a variety of colors, designs, and fabrics. Paper napkins are used widely for everyday meals and for brunches and informal luncheons.

Sizes of napkins vary. Dinner napkins are 18, 20, 22, or 24 inches square. "Lapkins," which measure 12 by 16 inches, are a favorite of men at buffet dinners. Luncheon and breakfast napkins are 17 inches square. Tea napkins are 12 inches square, and cocktail napkins are either 4 by 7 inches or 6 by 8 inches.

Folded napkins, generally rectangular or square, are placed so that the open corner is at lower right. Cloth napkins may also be rolled inside napkin rings.

At one time, it was customary for each family member to have a personal napkin ring. Today, they're available in many colors, styles, and materials from engraved silver to brightly woven straw and clear plastic. Whether used with mats, runners, or cloths, carefully chosen napkins and rings can brighten any place setting.

## TABLEWARE

The size of your family, the type of entertaining you do, the decor of your home, your budget, and your personal taste—all are factors to consider when choosing your dinnerware, flatware, and glassware.

**Dinnerware** is the single word that encompasses that wide world of china, stoneware, pottery, and plastic. Colors, patterns, and styles of dinnerware range from bold to traditional.

Start with a set of dishes that harmonizes with the color and formality of your home. A set of one-color dishes makes a smart, basic investment. Or, choose a simple pattern of dinnerware that you can use with several color schemes. Many dinnerware patterns have the advantage of being sold by the individual piece as well as in single or group place settings.

When selecting dinnerware, you know you want it to be beautiful, in good taste, long-lasting, and functional. But shape and care requirements also are important.

Cups should be shaped so they do not tip easily and should fit firmly in the saucer. Handles should be large enough to be easy to grasp and comfortable to hold.

Plates that are round are easier to stack than square or free-form ones. Heavily embossed patterns collect dust and food in the grooves and may need to be cleaned frequently with a brush.

Types of dinnerware range from plastics to earthenware, including ironstone and ovenware, to fine china and bone china. Their differences in composition give them a formal or informal feeling.

**Glassware** adds the dimension of height to your table setting. Base your choice on the pattern of dinnerware and the occasion or style of service.

For buffet service, sturdy tumblers or low goblets are best, since they're informal in character and easy to carry. Dinner glassware usually means a footed tumbler of medium height. Very tall goblets are appropriate only on formal tables. Stemmed goblets tip easily, so check the base for proportionate breadth and weight.

When choosing crystal glassware, look for clarity and luster. Listen for a bell-like tone when you tap the rim of the goblet with your fingernail while holding the base.

**Flatware** is available in a variety of patterns and should be chosen to harmonize with the table setting. Whether you select sterling silver, silverplate, gold electroplate, or stainless, consider the following questions:

Is the pattern of flatware one you will be happy to use for many years, or will it "go out of style?"

Is the pattern still appealing when arranged in four or more place settings? (One that you like individually may become quite monotonous when it is repeated.)

Do the pieces remain flat on the table when arranged in a place setting?

Is the structural design such that each piece is suited to its job? Is there proportion, harmony, and balance?

Is the greatest weight and thickness in the handle and

points that will receive the most pressure? (The knife should not be heavy. The fork should taper from each end toward a point of maximum depth at the narrowest part of the handle.)

Is the bowl of the spoon in proportion to the handle? Test by balancing.

Is the knife easy to hold? (The handle should provide ample room for the hand. The blade should be thick and balanced to provide comfort for the index finger.)

**Special care** is what all your tableware deserves. Check the manufacturer's instructions for specific requirements.

You can wash all dinnerware and flatware by hand and most by machine. In either case, rinse them as soon as possible. If a dishwasher is used, be sure to load the plates properly so they don't rub against each other and cause scratching. Use a mild soap or detergent.

Dishes may be air-dried, but flatware is best dried quickly to retain its luster.

Wash glassware in warm, sudsy water; rinse in cool water; drain; and dry with a lint-free towel. Ammonia or bluing in the dishwasher will add luster, but don't use either with metallic-banded glassware.

Never use abrasive cleaning powders or pads. Use borax on a soft cloth to remove coffee or tea stains in cups.

Store fine china with separating pads between the plates and preferably inside zippered cases or plastic bags. Store glassware right side up on shelves to avoid chipping the drinking edge.

## CENTERPIECES

For a centerpiece, let your mood and resources be your guide. There's no end to the list of materials that lend themselves to creative, imaginative centerpieces—flowers, plants, fruits, vegetables, branches of trees and shrubbery, candles, driftwood. Special containers are not necessary. Take a fresh look at your miscellaneous possessions. You might use cream pitchers, low dishes, wicker baskets, or even bottles.

As the focal point, the centerpiece should be in harmony with the rest of the table. It can echo the lines of your flatware and glassware or pick up the colors of your china. A centerpiece coordinated with table linen colors gives a unifying effect.

For variety, place decorations at the end or on one side of the table. This also gives the table a more balanced look when serving an odd number of guests.

Candles, especially the highly decorated ones, often are used more for decorations than for light. Candles used after dusk should be lit.

Flowers are a natural favorite for table decorations. Always place formal arrangements for sit-down meals in the center so they will look good from all directions. Keep height below 14 inches. Taller ones may be used on buffet tables. Set potted plants in saucers or leakproof containers.

Make sure containers and contents are in keeping with each other. For example, pottery, tinware, or lined baskets are more appropriate for an informal arrangement than for a formal one.

To help prolong the life of flower arrangements, make sure the containers are clean. Before arranging florist's flowers, clip the stem ends, then place in a deep container of water. Remove foliage from the part of the stem that will be under water. Leaves that remain under water decay quickly and cause the water in the container to become murky.

Before putting dahlias, poppies, and other flowers with hollow stems in an arrangement, sear stem ends over an open flame to prevent sap escaping.

For shrubs and mums, pound the bottom 2 inches of stem before putting into water. Paring the outer bark from stem base also helps ensure water intake by shrubs.

## SETTING THE TABLE

Making your dinner table an enjoyable place to eat involves not only having the right combination of table appointments, but knowing how to set the table correctly.

Depending on the style of service, the dinner plates are set in the center of each place setting, or in a stack in front of the person who will be serving. Allow 20 to 30 inches for each place setting.

Arrange forks, knives, and spoons in the order they will be used, first items to the outside. This makes it easy for guests to choose the proper implement. Place the china, silverware, and napkin in a line about one inch from the edge of the table.

Forks are placed to the left of the plate. The salad fork, if used, may be placed on either side of the dinner fork, depending on when the salad is to be served. If the salad is served before the main course, the salad fork goes to the left of the dinner fork. If it is served with or after the main course, the salad fork usually is placed to the right of the dinner fork. A salad fork is not essential if the salad accompanies the main course.

Knives and spoons are placed to the right of the plate, with the knife closest to the plate and the blade facing the plate.

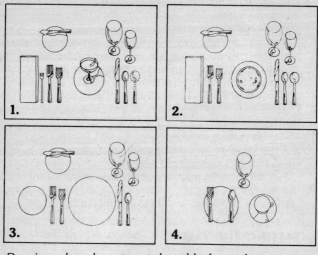

Drawings show how to set the table for each course. (1) Appetizer course: Provide seafood fork, if needed, napkin, and silverware and glassware for the rest of the meal. Serve the appetizer on an underliner plate. (2) Soup course: Provide a soup spoon. Place soup bowl on an underliner plate. This course is often omitted, especially if an appetizer is served. (3) Main course: Provide dinner plate, salad plate (optional), bread-and-butter plate and knife (optional), dinner fork, salad fork (optional), knife and spoon. Provide a glass for each beverage. Include a napkin if no previous courses have been served. (4) Dessert course: Serve dessert from the kitchen with the necessary silverware. Serve coffee with the dessert at the table or later in the living room.

If a bread-and-butter plate is used, place it above the forks, with the bread-and-butter knife straight across the top of the plate. (This plate may be omitted if table space is limited.)

The salad plate may take several placements. If a bread-and-butter plate is used, place the salad plate to the left and below the bread-and-butter plate. When no bread-and-butter plate is used, place the salad plate at the tip of the forks.

Place napkins to the left of the forks with the open corners at the lower right. The napkin is placed on the dinner plate or in the center of the place setting when both salad and bread-and-butter plates are on the table.

The water glass or goblet belongs at the tip of the knife. If wine is served, set the wine glass above the spoons, below and to the right of the water glass.

## STYLES OF SERVICE

You may use several styles of food service when entertaining.

Continental service, also referred to as formal or Russian service, requires servants to serve the food. With today's informal life-style, this service is rarely used.

When English service is used, dinner plates are stacked in front of the host, who serves the meat. The hostess serves the vegetables, then the plates are passed to guests. A variation of this style is family-style service. All food for the entrée is served by one person, then the filled plates are passed to the guests.

Other popular styles include country-style service and blue-plate service. For country-style service, filled serving dishes are placed on the table at the beginning of the meal. The person closest to the dish helps himself and passes the dish to the person on his right. For blue-plate service, plates are filled in the kitchen, then placed on the table just before guests sit down at the table.

Buffet-style is another service style. Containers of food are placed on a table, counter, or side buffet. Guests help themselves to the food, then sit down at set tables or small tray tables placed around the room, or balance plates or trays on their laps.

## • TABLE SET FOR FAMILY-STYLE SERVICE •

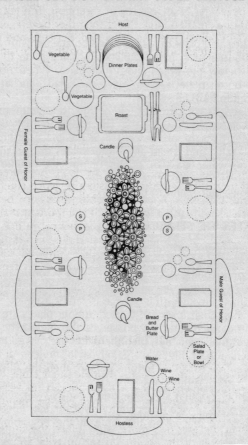

## TEAS AND RECEPTIONS

One of the most delightful traditions in entertaining is the afternoon tea or reception. When the tea is small, the beverage and simple foods may be placed on a tray or small table. Arrange a teapot, hot water pot, sugar, and creamer to the right of the hostess for easy serving. Cups and saucers, stacked plates, silverware, and napkins are placed to her left.

A formal tea or reception usually is given in honor of a person or a special occasion. It is customary to serve two beverages at a large tea or reception. The tea service sits at one end of a large table. The other beverage, coffee or a light punch, is at the other end. Set cups and saucers on the left, teaspoons and napkins on the right, and food platters in easy reach along the length of the table.

## BUFFET TABLES

A successful buffet always look delightfully easy to the guests—but, as every hostess knows, it does require special planning. If space allows, place the buffet table in the middle of the room so guests can circulate around it. Or, you may choose to place the table just far enough away from the wall for the hostess to work comfortably behind it. Use a cart or small table nearby for beverage.

When setting the buffet table, it is important that guests can serve themselves in a logical sequence. At one end of the table, place the dinner plates and the main dish. Other foods, such as the salad, vegetable, buttered rolls, and relishes, along with serving pieces, are placed near the edge of the table within easy reach of guests. Leave enough space near serving dishes for guests to set their places.

### • ONE-LINE BUFFET •

Set the table attractively. If the table is crowded, serve the beverage from a nearby cart or small table. Arrange silver and napkins so they can be picked up last on the table. Carefully go over every item on the menu to see that everything is in order.

When the group is quite large, place the buffet table in the center of the room and set up twin arrangements of plates, food, silver, and napkins on each side of the table. Suggest that guests form two lines to help themselves to the food. The beverage may be placed on a separate serving table or cart.

If a sit-down buffet is possible, arrange small tables in another room with silver, napkins, and water glasses. Provide beverage cups, cream, and sugar at each table. Place beverage containers on the tables or have the beverage served, if desired.

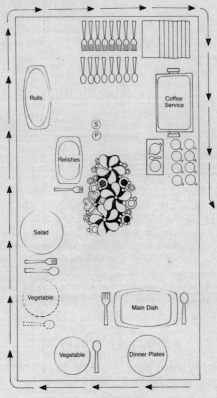

# • BUFFET WITH BEVERAGE CART •

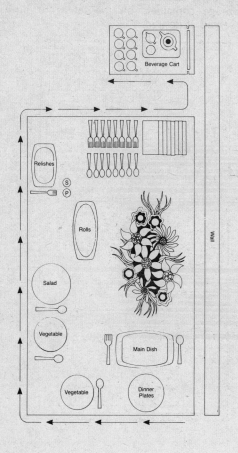

Beverage Cart

Wall

Relishes

S
P

Rolls

Salad

Vegetable

Main Dish

Vegetable

Dinner Plates

# 18

# INDEX

# CREATIVE USES FOR LEFTOVERS

# CALORIE TALLY

Whether it's maintaining weight, gaining weight, or losing weight, calories can make the difference. What are calories? The food we eat is burned (oxidized) by basic body functions and activity, or stored by the body. When food is burned it forms heat energy which is measured in units called calories; when stored, it forms fat body tissue and causes a gain in weight.

The daily balance of calories eaten and burned by the body can be figured by following these steps:

1. Estimate your desirable weight for height by consulting a weight chart.

2. Multiply your desirable weight by the number 15.6 if you are a woman and 17.5 if you are a man. (These numbers are based on light amounts of physical activity. Additional calories will be needed by those who regularly engage in strenuous activities. Since many people tend to overestimate their energy requirements, the above is a satisfactory guide for most of today's occupations.)

3. Subtract 10 calories for each year of age over 22. (Desired weight at age 22 should be maintained throughout life. As you grow older, fewer calories are required to maintain this weight.)

## A

Calories

**Apple**
Baked, sweetened,
  1 medium . . . . . . . . . .188
Fresh, 1 medium (2½-
  inch diameter) . . . . . . 70
Juice, canned, 1 cup . . .120
**Apple brown betty,**
  1 cup . . . . . . . . . . . . . . . .345
**Applesauce, canned**
  sweetened, 1 cup . . . . . .230
  Unsweetened, 1 cup . . .100

**Apricots**
Canned, ½ cup in
  syrup . . . . . . . . . . . . . .110
Dried, cooked,
  unsweetened, ½ cup
  in juice . . . . . . . . . . . .120
Fresh, 3 . . . . . . . . . . . . . . 55
Nectar, ½ cup . . . . . . . . 70
**Asparagus**
Canned spears, green,
  medium, 6 spears . . . . 20
Cooked, 1 cup cut
  spears . . . . . . . . . . . . . 35
Frozen, 6 spears . . . . . . . 23
**Avocado, peeled, ½**
  (3⅓x4¼ inches) . . . . . .185

## B

Calories

Bacon, 2 crisp strips ......100
Bacon, Canadian,
  3 slices ...............195
Banana, 1 medium
  (6x1½ inches) ........ 85
Beans
  Baked with tomato
    sauce and pork,
    ½ cup .............160
  Green, snap, cooked,
    1 cup .............. 30
  Lima, baby, cooked,
    1 cup .............180
  Yellow or wax, cooked,
    1 cup ............. 22
Beef cuts, cooked
  Corned, canned, 3
    slices (3x2x¼ inch) ..185
  Hamburger, 1 patty
    (4 ounces uncooked) .245
  Pot roast, lean and fat,
    3 ounces ...........245
  Rib roast, 3 ounces ....375
  Round steak, 3 ounces .220
  Sirloin steak, broiled,
    3 ounces ...........330
Beef liver, fried, 2 ounces .130
Beef tongue, braised,
  3 ounces ...........210
Beets, cooked, diced,
  1 cup ............... 50
Biscuit, baking powder, 1
  (2½-inch diameter) ....140
Blueberries, raw, 1 cup ... 85
Bread
  Boston brown, 1 slice
    (3x¾ inch) .........100
  Raisin, 1 slice ......... 60
  Rye, 1 slice ........... 55
  White, 1 slice ......... 60
  Whole wheat, 1 slice .. 55
Broccoli, spears, cooked,
  1 cup ............... 40
Brussels sprouts, cooked,
  1 cup ............... 45

Butter or margarine,
  1 tablespoon ..........100

## C

Calories

Cabbage, cooked, 1 cup .. 35
Cake
  Angel, 2-inch wedge ...110
  Chocolate, 2 layers,
    chocolate icing,
    2-inch wedge .......445
  Cupcake, plain,
    chocolate icing, 1
    (2¾-inch diameter) ..185
  Gingerbread, 2x2x2
    inches ............175
  Plain, 2 layers,
    chocolate icing,
    2-inch wedge .......370
  Pound, 1 slice
    (2¾x3x⅝-inch) .....140
  Sponge, 2-inch wedge ...120
Candy
  Caramel, 1 ounce ......115
  Chocolate creams, 1 ... 51
  Chocolate, milk,
    1 ounce ...........150
  Chocolate, mints,
    1 medium
    (20 per pound) ...... 87
  Gumdrops, 8 small .... 33
  Jelly beans, 5 ......... 33
  Peanut brittle, 1 piece
    (2½x2½x⅜-inch) ...110
Cantaloupe, ½ (5-inch
  diameter) ............ 60
Carrots, cooked, diced,
  1 cup ............... 45
Catsup, 1 tablespoon ..... 15
Cauliflower, cooked
  flowerets, 1 cup ....... 25
Celery, raw, 2 stalks
  (8 inches long) ........ 10
Cereals, cooked
  Oatmeal, 1 cup .......130
  Wheat, rolled, 1 cup ...175

## N-O

Calories

## P

Calories

## T-Y

# COOKING TERMS

**Antipasto**—A first course of assorted relishes, smoked, or pickled meats or fish.

**Au gratin**—Topped with bread crumbs or shredded cheese and browned.

**Au jus**—Served in natural meat juices from roasting.

**Bake**—To cook covered or uncovered in an oven or oven-type appliance. For meats cooked uncovered, it's called roasting.

**Baste**—To moisten foods during cooking with pan drippings or special sauce to add flavor and prevent drying.

**Beat**—To make mixture smooth by adding air with a brisk whipping or stirring motion using spoon or electric mixer.

**Bechamel**—Rich, white cream sauce.

**Bisque**—A thick cream soup containing fish or game; or pureed vegetables.

**Blanch**—To precook in boiling water or steam to prepare foods for canning or freezing, or to loosen skin.

**Blend**—To thoroughly mix two or more ingredients until smooth and uniform.

**Boil**—To cook in liquid at boiling temperature (212° at sea level) where bubbles rise to the surface and break. For a full rolling boil, bubbles form rapidly throughout the mixture.

**Braise**—To cook slowly with a small amount of liquid in tightly covered pan on top of range or in oven.

**Bread**—To coat with bread crumbs before cooking.

**Broil**—To cook by direct heat, usually in broiler, or over coals.

**Candied**—To cook in sugar or syrup when applied to sweet potatoes and carrots. For fruit or fruit peel, to cook in heavy syrup till translucent and well coated.

**Caramelize**—To melt sugar slowly over low heat until it becomes brown in color.

**Chill**—To place in refrigerator to reduce temperature.

**Chop**—To cut in pieces about the size of peas with knife, chopper, or blender.

**Cool**—To remove from heat and let stand at room temperature.

**Coq au vin**—Chicken in red wine sauce.

**Court bouillon**—A broth flavored with meat, fish, and various vegetables. Used for poaching and for sauce.

**Cream**—To beat with spoon or electric mixer till mixture is soft and smooth. When applied to blending shortening and sugar, mixture is beaten till light and fluffy.

**Crepe Suzette**—A thin sweet pancake usually served rolled with hot orange sauce flavored with curaçao or other liqueurs. Usually set aflame before serving.

**Croissant**—Flaky, crescent-shaped roll.

**Crouton**—A small cube of dry toasted bread served atop soup or salad.

**Cut in**—To mix shortening with dry ingredients using pastry blender or knives.

**Dice**—To cut food in small cubes of uniform size and shape.

**Dissolve**—To disperse a dry substance in a liquid to form a solution.

**Dredge**—To sprinkle or coat with flour or other fine substance.

**Fillet**—A strip of lean meat or of fish without bone.

**Flake**—To break lightly into small pieces.

**Fold**—To add ingredients gently to a mixture. Using a spatula, cut down through mixture; go across bottom of bowl and up and over, close to surface. Turn bowl frequently for even distribution.

**Fricassee**—A stew of meat or poultry in gravy.

**Fry**—To cook in hot shortening. Pan-frying is to cook in a small amount of shortening. Deep-fat frying is to cook immersed in large amount of shortening.

**Garnish**—To trim with small pieces of colorful foods (pepper, pimiento, lemon).

**Gazpacho**—A cold soup made of raw chopped vegetables; Spanish.

**Glaze**—A mixture applied to food which hardens or becomes firm and/or adds flavor and a glossy appearance.

**Grate**—To rub on a grater that separates the food into very fine particles.

**Julienne**—Match-like strips of vegetables, fruits, or meats.

**Knead**—To work the dough with the heel of the hand with a pressing, folding motion.

**Lyonnaise**—A dish, usually potatoes, cooked with onions.

**Marinate**—To allow a food to stand in a liquid to tenderize or to add flavor.

**Mince**—To chop food in very small pieces.

**Minestrone**—A thick vegetable soup.

**Mix**—To combine ingredients, usually by stirring, till evenly distributed.

**Mocha**—Chocolate-coffee flavor.

**Mornay**—A cheese-flavored white sauce.

**Mousse**—Sweetened, flavored whipped cream, sometimes with gelatin, frozen without stirring and served as a dessert.

**Paella**—Classic saffron rice dish made with chicken, seafood, and vegetables.

**Panbroil**—To cook uncovered on hot surface, removing fat as it accumulates.

**Panfry**—To cook in small amount of hot shortening.

**Partially set**—To chill gelatin until the consistency of egg white.

**Petit four**—Small tea cake, frosted and often decorated with frosting flowers.

**Pilaf**—A rice dish with meat or poultry and vegetables, or raisins and spices. Fried in oil, then steamed and seasoned.

**Pit**—To remove pits from fruits.

**Poach**—To cook in hot liquid, being careful that food holds its shape while cooking.

**Polenta**—Thick cornmeal mush, often served with sauce, gravy, or stew. May be cooked firm and sliced; or cooked just till consistency of mashed potatoes.

**Pots de creme**—Delicate chilled dessert pudding, often chocolate, served in cups.

**Poulet**—Chicken; French.

**Praline**—Flat sugar candy with nuts.

**Precook**—To cook food partially or completely before final cooking or reheating.

**Puree**—A paste or thick liquid suspension of food.

**Quiche Lorraine**—Savory hot custard tart containing bacon, onions, and cheese.

**Ragout**—A highly seasoned stew of meat and vegetables.

**Ratatouille**—A stew of eggplant, green pepper, tomatoes, and squash, seasoned with garlic and other condiments. Sometimes meat is added. Serve hot or cold.

**Roast**—To cook uncovered without water added, usually in an oven.

**Roulade**—A thin slice of meat rolled up with or without stuffing, then cooked.

**Roux**—A mixture of flour and fat that is cooked, sometimes till the flour browns, and is used to thicken soups and sauces.

**Sauerbraten**—Pot roast of beef marinated in vinegar-spice mixture, then braised.

**Saute**—To brown or cook in a small amount of hot shortening.

**Scald**—To bring to a temperature just below the boiling point where tiny bubbles form at the edge of the pan.

**Scallop**—To bake food, usually in a casserole, with sauce or other liquid. Crumbs are often sprinkled atop.

**Score**—To cut narrow grooves or slits partway through the outer surface of food.

**Sear**—To brown the surface of meat very quickly by intense heat.

**Shred**—To rub on a shredder to form small, long narrow pieces.

**Sift**—To put one or more dry ingredients through a sieve or sifter.

**Simmer**—To cook in liquid over low heat at a temperature of 185° to 210° where bubbles form at a slow rate and burst before reaching the surface.

**Soft peaks**—To beat egg whites or whipping cream till peaks are formed when beaters are lifted, but tips curl over.

**Souffle**—A puffy egg dish with a white sauce base having seasonings and added ingredients, such as cheese, tuna, or chocolate.

**Steam**—To cook in steam with or without pressure. A small amount of boiling water is used, more water being added during steaming process if necessary.

**Steep**—To extract color, flavor, or other qualities from a substance by leaving it in liquid just below the boiling point.

**Sterilize**—To destroy microorganisms by boiling, dry heat, or steam.

**Stew**—To simmer slowly in a small amount of liquid.

**Stiff peaks**—To beat egg whites till peaks stand up straight when beaters are lifted, but are still moist and glossy.

**Stir**—To mix ingredients with a circular motion until well blended.

**Stroganoff**—Usually beef sliced thin and cooked with sauce of broth, sour cream, and seasonings.

**Toss**—To mix ingredients lightly.

**Truss**—To secure fowl or other meat with skewers to hold its shape during cooking.

**Welsh rarebit**—Melted cheese, usually mixed with milk, ale, or beer, and served over toast or crackers.

**Whip**—To beat rapidly to incorporate air and produce expansion, as in heavy cream or egg whites.

**Wiener schnitzel**—Thin breaded veal cutlet.

# SEASONING GUIDE

Get acquainted with spices and herbs. Add in small amounts, $1/4$ teaspoon for each 4 servings. Taste before adding more. Crush dried herbs or snip fresh herbs before using. If substituting fresh for dried, use 3 times more fresh herbs.

Freeze fresh herbs and enjoy them all winter long. Wash, then blanch the herbs in boiling water for 10 seconds. Chill in ice water 1 minute; pat dry. Package in small moisture-vaporproof bags or foil; seal; label. Freeze. Use while frosty.

## Appetizers, Soups

CRANBERRY JUICE: Add cinnamon, allspice, and/or cloves. Serve hot or chilled.

FRUIT COCKTAIL: Try adding mint or rosemary.

STUFFED CELERY: Mix caraway seed with cream cheese; fill celery. Dash with paprika.

TOMATO COCKTAIL: Add $1/4$ teaspoon dried basil, per cup.

CHICKEN SOUP: Add a dash of rosemary, tarragon, or nutmeg. Sprinkle paprika atop for color.

CLAM CHOWDER: Add a dash of caraway seed, sage, or thyme.

CONSOMME: Dash in basil, marjoram, savory, or tarragon.

FISH CHOWDER: Add bay leaves, curry powder, or dill.

MUSHROOM SOUP: Season with curry, oregano, or marjoram.

ONION SOUP: Add marjoram.

OYSTER STEW: Lightly add cayenne, mace, or marjoram.

POTATO SOUP: Dash with mustard or basil. Top with snipped chives or parsley.

SPLIT-PEA SOUP: Add dash basil, chili powder, or rosemary.

TOMATO SOUP: Dash in basil, dill, oregano, sage, or tarragon.

VEGETABLE SOUP: Try all-spice, oregano, sage, or thyme.

## Breads, Pasta

BISCUITS: Add caraway seed, thyme, or savory to flour. Serve with meat.

BREAD: Make each loaf a surprise by adding caraway seed, cardamom, or poppy seed.

COFFEE CAKE: Mix crushed aniseed in batter. For variety, sprinkle cinnamon-sugar mixture atop or add poppy seed-filling.

CORN BREAD: Add poultry seasoning or caraway seed to dry ingredients. Be adventuresome; add ½ teaspoon rosemary to batter.

CROUTONS: Toss toast cubes in melted butter seasoned with basil, marjoram, or onion salt.

DOUGHNUTS: Add mace or nutmeg to dry ingredients. After frying, roll in cinnamon sugar.

DUMPLINGS: Add thyme or parsley (fresh or flakes) to batter.

MUFFINS: Blueberry—add dash of nutmeg to dry ingredients. Season plain muffins with caraway seed or cinnamon.

NOODLES: Butter, then sprinkle with poppy seed.

ROLLS: Add caraway seed. Or, sprinkle with sesame seed.

SPAGHETTI: Toss with butter, Parmesan, and snipped chives.

WAFFLES: Add poultry seasoning to batter; serve with creamed chicken. Or, add cardamom to honey; pour over waffles.

## Eggs, Cheese

BAKED EGGS: Sprinkle dash of thyme or paprika over the top.

CREAMED EGGS: Add mace.

DEVILED EGGS: Add celery seed, cumin, mustard, savory, chili powder, or curry powder.

OMELET: Try with dash of marjoram or rosemary (go easy!).

SCRAMBLED EGGS: Sprinkle lightly with basil, thyme, rosemary, or marjoram. Add seasonings near the end of cooking.

SOUFFLE: Add ¼ teaspoon marjoram to 4-egg souffle. To cheese souffle, add basil or savory.

CHEESE CASSEROLES: Spark with dash sage or marjoram.

CHEESE FONDUE: Try adding a dash of basil or nutmeg.

CHEESE RAREBIT: Try with mace or mustard.

CHEESE SAUCE: Add mustard or a dash of marjoram or thyme.

CHEESE SPREAD: Blend sage, caraway seed, thyme, or celery seed into melted process cheese.

COTTAGE CHEESE: Blend in chives or a dash of sage, caraway seed, dill, anise, or cumin. Prepare several hours ahead of time.

CREAM CHEESE: Blend in curry powder, marjoram, caraway seed, or dill. Sprinkle paprika or cayenne atop. Use as celery filling or appetizer spread.

## Meats, Poultry, Fish

BEEF STEW: Add subtle flavor with allspice, basil, celery seed, or oregano. Or, add bouquet garni of chives, savory, and thyme; remove before serving.

BEEF POT ROAST: Season 3-pound pot roast with 1/4 teaspoon each dry mustard, marjoram, rosemary, and thyme.

HAM LOAF: Add ground cloves or ginger.

LAMB CHOPS: Dash with marjoram; broil. Or, sprinkle with dill near end of broiling.

LAMB STEW: Add bouquet garni of rosemary, parsley, and celery, or parsley, thyme, and basil. Remove before serving.

MEAT LOAF: Add dash of oregano and basil.

PORK CHOPS: Sprinkle lightly with sage, thyme, or cloves.

PORK ROAST: Combine rosemary and parsley; sprinkle over.

VEAL CUTLETS: Pound in mixture of basil and marjoram.

VEAL ROAST: Combine bay leaf, parsley, and thyme; sprinkle atop.

CHICKEN, BROILED: Sprinkle lightly with marjoram, rosemary, or savory; broil.

CHICKEN PIE: Add poultry seasoning or sage to crust; or, season filling with dill or ginger.

CHICKEN, STEWED: Add dash of basil, bay leaf, or cumin.

CHICKEN STUFFING: For variety, add basil, celery seed, marjoram, oregano, poppy seed, or thyme.

DUCK: Add celery seed, rosemary, or oregano to stuffing.

FISH FILLETS: Sprinkle with marjoram, savory, tarragon, or thyme; or paprika for color.

SALMON OR TUNA CASSEROLE: Add dash dill or parsley.

## Vegetables

ASPARAGUS: Add caraway seed, dill, mustard, nutmeg, sesame seed, or tarragon.

BEETS: Sprinkle with allspice, bay leaves, celery seed, cloves, dill, or ginger before cooking.

BROCCOLI: Flavor with mustard, oregano, or tarragon butter.

CABBAGE: Cook with basil, dill, mustard, savory, or tarragon.

CARROTS: Dash with chili powder, ginger, mace, marjoram, or poppy seed for a variation.

CAULIFLOWER: Season with curry powder, dill, mustard, nutmeg, savory, or tarragon.

CORN: Add celery seed, chili powder, chives, or curry powder.

EGGPLANT: Add allspice, basil, chili powder, or thyme.

GREEN BEANS: Perk up with basil, bay leaves, dill, marjoram, mustard, oregano, or sesame seed.

ONIONS: Season with ginger, mustard, nutmeg, oregano, poppy seed, sage, or thyme.

PEAS: Add chili powder, dill, marjoram, mint, mustard, oregano, poppy seed, or savory.

POTATOES, SWEET: Season with allspice, cardamom, cinnamon, ginger, or nutmeg.

POTATOES, WHITE: Sprinkle in caraway seed, chives, dill, mace, mint, poppy seed, or thyme.

RICE: Season with cumin, curry powder, parsley, or saffron.

SQUASH, SUMMER: Season with basil, mace, marjoram, or mustard.

SQUASH, WINTER: While it cooks add a dash of allspice, basil, cinnamon, cloves, or ginger.

TOMATOES: Sprinkle fresh with basil, celery seed, dill, or thyme. Season stewed tomatoes with parsley, chives, oregano, or some herb-seasoned croutons.

## Desserts

APPLE PIE: Add cinnamon to the crust. To the filling add aniseed, cardamom, or nutmeg.

BANANAS: Slice; pour cream over. Sprinkle with nutmeg.

CHERRY PIE: Add dash mace.

CHOCOLATE CAKE: Add a dash of ground cinnamon.

CHOCOLATE PUDDING: Add a dash of allspice, cloves, or mace.

CUSTARDS: Sprinkle with nutmeg, cinnamon, or cardamom.

DESSERT COFFEE: Place 1 crushed cardamom seed in each demitasse cup. Fill with demitasse coffee. Or, place cinnamon stick in coffee grounds; perk.

MELON OR FRUIT CUP: Chill; sprinkle with cardamom seed.

PEACH COBBLER: Add nutmeg to the biscuit topper.

PEACH PIE: Add generous shake of cinnamon or nutmeg.

PEARS: Dot fresh or canned pear halves with butter; sprinkle with sugar and cinnamon. Broil.

PUMPKIN PIE: Add allspice, cardamom, ginger, or nutmeg.

RHUBARB SAUCE: Add dash of ground nutmeg.

RICE PUDDING: Season with cloves, ginger, or nutmeg.

SPICY ICE CREAM: Blend 1 teaspoon cinnamon into 1 quart softened ice cream. Freeze. Spoon over sliced peaches or apple crisp.

SPRITZ COOKIES. Add 1/2 teaspoon cardamom to dough.

STEWED PRUNES: Add a stick of cinnamon while cooking.

SUGAR COOKIES: Stir aniseed into dry ingredients.

YELLOW CAKE: To favorite recipe, add mace or $1/2$ teaspoon nutmeg and $1/4$ teaspoon allspice.

# INDEX

**Bold face numbers indicate chapter.**

## I

## J

## K

## W

## Y

## Z

# OVEN CHARTS

## OVEN CHART

| | |
|---|---|
| Very slow oven | 250°–275° |
| Slow oven | 300°–325° |
| Moderate oven | 350°–375° |
| Hot oven | 400°–425° |
| Very hot oven | 450°–475° |
| Extremely hot oven | 500°–525° |

## BROILING*

| | Total time in minutes |
|---|---|
| Beef steaks | |
| 1-inch | |
| Rare | 8–10 |
| Medium | 12–14 |
| Well-done | 18–20 |
| 1½-inch | |
| Rare | 14–16 |
| Medium | 18–20 |
| Well-done | 25–30 |
| 2-inch | |
| Rare | 20–25 |
| Medium | 30–35 |
| Well-done | 40–45 |
| Hamburgers | |
| ¾-inch | 10 |
| Lamb chops, steaks | |
| 1-inch | |
| Medium | 12–14 |
| 1½-inch | |
| Medium | 18 |
| Ham slice | |
| Fully cooked, bone-in | |
| ½-inch | 10–12 |
| 1-inch | 16–20 |

| | |
|---|---|
| Chicken halves | 40 |
| (5 to 7 inches from heat) | |
| Fish fillets | 10–15 |

(*Broil 1 to 1½-inch steaks and chops so surface is 3 inches from heat, thicker cuts 4 to 5 inches from heat.)

## THERMOMETER READINGS FOR MEATS

| | Temp. of meat |
|---|---|
| Beef | |
| Rare | 140° |
| Medium | 160° |
| Well-done | 170° |
| Veal | 170° |
| Lamb | |
| Rare | 140° |
| Medium | 160° |
| Well-done | 170°–180° |
| Fresh pork | 170° |
| Smoked pork | |
| Fully cooked | 140° |
| Cook-before-eating | 160° |

## CANDY AND FROSTING

| | Temp. of syrup |
|---|---|
| Thread | 230°–234° |
| Soft ball | 234°–240° |
| Firm ball | 244°–248° |
| Hard ball | 250°–266° |
| Soft crack | 270°–290° |
| Hard crack | 300°–310° |

# WEIGHTS
AND MEASURES

## WEIGHTS AND MEASURES

3 teaspoons=1 tablespoon
4 tablespoons=¼ cup
5⅓ tablespoons=⅓ cup
8 tablespoons=½ cup
10⅔ tablespoons=⅔ cup
12 tablespoons=¾ cup
16 tablespoons=1 cup
1 ounce=28.35 grams
1 gram=0.035 ounces

1 cup=8 fluid ounces
1 cup=½ pint
2 cups=1 pint
4 cups=1 quart
4 quarts=1 gallon
8 quarts=1 peck
4 pecks=1 bushel
1 quart=946.4 milliliters
1 liter=1.06 quarts

## EMERGENCY SUBSTITUTIONS

1 cup cake flour=1 cup
minus 2 tablespoons all-
purpose flour

1 tablespoon cornstarch
(for thickening)=2 table-
spoons flour or 4 tea-
spoons quick-cooking
tapioca

1 teaspoon baking powder
=¼ teaspoon baking
soda plus ½ cup butter-
milk or sour milk (to
replace ½ cup of liquid
called for in recipe)

1 cake compressed yeast=
1 package or 2 teaspoons
active dry yeast

1 cup whole milk=½ cup
evaporated milk plus ½
cup water or 1 cup re-

constituted nonfat dry
milk plus 2½ teaspoons
butter or margarine

1 cup sour milk or butter-
milk=1 tablespoon
lemon juice or vinegar
plus sweet milk to make
1 cup (let stand 5 min.)

1 whole egg=2 egg yolks
(in custards)

1 square (1 ounce) un-
sweetened chocolate=3
tablespoons cocoa
(regular-type, dry) plus
1 tablespoon butter or
margarine

1 tablespoon fresh snipped
herbs=1 teaspoon dried
herbs

1 small fresh onion=1

tablespoon instant minced onion, rehydrated
1 teaspoon dry mustard= 1 tablespoon prepared mustard
1 clove garlic=⅛ teaspoon garlic powder
1 cup tomato juice=½ cup tomato sauce plus ½ cup water
1 cup catsup or chili sauce =1 cup tomato sauce plus ½ cup sugar and 2 tablespoons vinegar (for use in cooked mixtures)

## HOW MUCH AND HOW MANY

### Butter, chocolate

2 tablespoons butter=1 ounce
1 stick or ¼ pound butter =½ cup
1 square chocolate=1 ounce

### Crumbs

28 saltine crackers=1 cup fine crumbs
14 square graham crackers =1 cup fine crumbs
22 vanilla wafers=1 cup fine crumbs
1½ slices bread=1 cup soft crumbs
1 slice bread=¼ cup fine dry crumbs

### Cereals

4 ounces macaroni (1–1¼ cups)=2¼ cups cooked
4 ounces noodles (3 cups) =3 cups cooked
7 ounces spaghetti=4 cups cooked
1 cup packaged precooked rice=2 cups cooked

### Fruits, vegetables

Juice of 1 lemon=3 tablespoons
Grated peel of 1 lemon=1 teaspoon
Juice of 1 orange=about ⅓ cup
Grated peel of 1 orange= about 2 teaspoons
1 medium apple, chopped =about 1 cup
1 medium onion, chopped =½ cup

### Cream, cheese, eggs

1 cup whipping cream= 2 cups whipped
1 pound American cheese, shredded=4 cups
¼ pound blue cheese, crumbled=1 cup
8 egg whites=1 cup
8 egg yolks=¾ cup

### Nuts

1 pound walnuts in shell= 1½ to 1¾ cups shelled
1 pound almonds in shell= 1¼ cups shelled

## CAN SIZES

8 ounce=1 cup

Picnic=1¼ cups or 10½ to 12 ounces

12-ounce vacuum=1½ cups

No. 300=1¾ cups or 14 to 16 ounces

No. 303=2 cups or 16 to 17 ounces

No. 2=2½ cups or 20 ounces

No. 2½=3½ cups or 29 ounces

No. 3 cylinder=5¾ cups or 46 fluid ounces

No. 10=12 to 13 cups or 6 pounds 8 ounces to 7 pounds 5 ounces (equal to 7 No. 303 cans or 5 No. 2 cans)

## WHITE SAUCE

Medium (1 cup)
  2 tablespoons butter
  2 tablespoons all-purpose flour
  ¼ teaspoon salt
  1 cup milk
Thick (1 cup)
  3 tablespoons butter
  4 tablespoons all-purpose flour
  ¼ teaspoon salt
  1 cup milk

Thin (1 cup)
  1 tablespoon butter
  1 tablespoon all-purpose flour
  ¼ teaspoon salt
  1 cup milk

Melt butter in saucepan over low heat. Blend in flour, salt, and dash white pepper. Add milk all at once. Cook quickly, stirring constantly, till mixture thickens and bubbles.

## PLAIN PASTRY

Single crust
  1½ cups sifted all-purpose flour
  ½ teaspoon salt
  ½ cup shortening
  4 to 5 tablespoons cold water
Double crust or lattice-top
  2 cups sifted all-purpose flour
  1 teaspoon salt
  ⅔ cup shortening
  5 to 7 tablespoons cold water

Sift flour and salt. Cut in shortening till pieces are size of small peas. Sprinkle water over, 1 tablespoon at a time, tossing mixture after each addition. Form into ball; flatten on lightly floured surface. Roll ⅛ inch thick from center to edge.